THE HISTORIES OF HERODOTUS

HERODOTUS

Volumes I & II

HERODOTUS

Translated by
G. C. MACAULAY

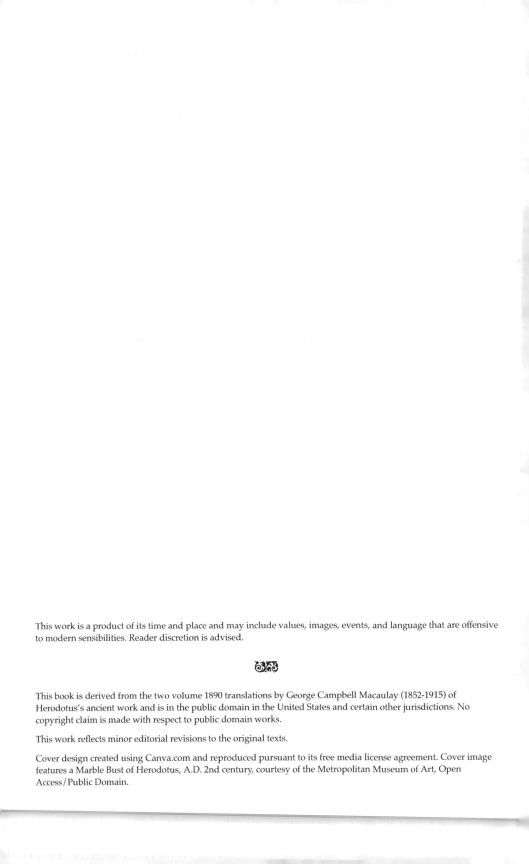

This book is derived from the two volume 1890 translations by George Campbell Macaulay (1852-1915) of Herodotus's ancient work and is in the public domain in the United States and certain other jurisdictions. No copyright claim is made with respect to public domain works.

This work reflects minor editorial revisions to the original texts.

Cover design created using Canva.com and reproduced pursuant to its free media license agreement. Cover image features a Marble Bust of Herodotus, A.D. 2nd century, courtesy of the Metropolitan Museum of Art, Open Access/Public Domain.

CONTENTS

THE FIRST BOOK OF THE HISTORIES, CALLED CLIO

This is the Showing forth of the Inquiry of Herodotus of Halicarnassos, to the end that neither the deeds of men may be forgotten by lapse of time, nor the works great and marvelous, which have been produced some by Hellenes and some by Barbarians, may lose their renown; and especially that the causes may be remembered for which these waged war with one another.

1. Those of the Persians who have knowledge of history declare that the Phoenicians first began the quarrel. These, they say, came from that which is called the Erythraian Sea to this of ours; and having settled in the land where they continue even now to dwell, set themselves forthwith to make long voyages by sea. And conveying merchandise of Egypt and of Assyria they arrived at other places and also at Argos; now Argos was at that time in all points the first of the States within that land which is now called Hellas;—the Phoenicians arrived then at this land of Argos, and began to dispose of their ship's cargo: and on the fifth or sixth day after they had arrived, when their goods had been almost all sold, there came down to the sea a great company of women, and among them the daughter of the king; and her name, as the Hellenes also agree, was Io the daughter of Inachos. These standing near to the stern of the ship were buying of the wares such as pleased them most, when of a sudden the Phoenicians, passing the word from one to another, made a rush upon them; and the greater part of the women escaped by flight, but Io and certain others were carried off. So they put them on board their ship, and forthwith departed, sailing away to Egypt.

2. In this manner the Persians report that Io came to Egypt, not agreeing therein with the Hellenes, and this they say was the first beginning of wrongs. Then after this, they say, certain Hellenes (but the name of the people they are not able to report) put in to the city of Tyre in Phenicia and carried off the king's daughter Europa;—these would doubtless be Cretans;—and so they were quits for the former injury. After this however the Hellenes, they say, were the authors of the second wrong; for they sailed in to Aia of Colchis and to the river Phasis with a ship of war, and from thence, after they had done the other busi-

ness for which they came, they carried off the king's daughter Medea: and the king of Colchis sent a herald to the land of Hellas and demanded satisfaction for the rape and to have his daughter back; but they answered that, as the Barbarians had given them no satisfaction for the rape of Io the Argive, so neither would they give satisfaction to the Barbarians for this.

3. In the next generation after this, they say, Alexander the son of Priam, having heard of these things, desired to get a wife for himself by violence from Hellas, being fully assured that he would not be compelled to give any satisfaction for this wrong, inasmuch as the Hellenes gave none for theirs. So he carried off Helen, and the Hellenes resolved to send messengers first and to demand her back with satisfaction for the rape; and when they put forth this demand, the others alleged to them the rape of Medea, saying that the Hellenes were now desiring satisfaction to be given to them by others, though they had given none themselves nor had surrendered the person when demand was made.

4. Up to this point, they say, nothing more happened than the carrying away of women on both sides; but after this the Hellenes were very greatly to blame; for they set the first example of war, making an expedition into Asia before the Barbarians made any into Europe. Now they say that in their judgment, though it is an act of wrong to carry away women by force, it is a folly to set one's heart on taking vengeance for their rape, and the wise course is to pay no regard when they have been carried away; for it is evident that they would never be carried away if they were not themselves willing to go. And the Persians say that they, namely the people of Asia, when their women were carried away by force, had made it a matter of no account, but the Hellenes on account of a woman of Lacedaemon gathered together a great armament, and then came to Asia and destroyed the dominion of Priam; and that from this time forward they had always considered the Hellenic race to be their enemy: for Asia and the Barbarian races which dwell there the Persians claim as belonging to them; but Europe and the Hellenic race they consider to be parted off from them.

5. The Persians for their part say that things happened thus; and they conclude that the beginning of their quarrel with the Hellenes was on account of the taking of Ilion: but as regards Io the Phoenicians do not agree with the Persians in telling the tale thus; for they deny that they carried her off to Egypt by violent means, and they say on the other hand that when they were in Argos she was intimate with the master of their ship, and perceiving that she was with child, she was ashamed to confess it to her parents, and therefore sailed away with the Phoenicians of her own will, for fear of being found out. These are the tales told by the Persians and the Phoenicians severally: and concerning these things I am not going to say that they happened thus or thus, but when I have pointed to the man who first within my own knowledge began to commit wrong against the Hellenes, I shall go forward further with the story, giving an account of the cities of men, small as well as great: for those which in old times were great have for the most part become small, while those that were in my own time great used in former times to be small: so then, since I know that human prosperity never continues steadfast, I shall make mention of both indifferently.

6. Croesus was Lydian by race, the son of Alyattes and ruler of the nations which dwell on this side of the river Halys; which river, flowing from the South between the Syrians and the Paphlagonians, runs out towards the North Wind into that Sea which is called the Euxine. This Croesus, first of all the Barbarians of whom we have knowledge, subdued

certain of the Hellenes and forced them to pay tribute, while others he gained over and made them his friends. Those whom he subdued were the Ionians, the Aiolians, and the Dorians who dwell in Asia; and those whom he made his friends were the Lacedemonians. But before the reign of Croesus all the Hellenes were free; for the expedition of the Kimmerians, which came upon Ionia before the time of Croesus, was not a conquest of the cities but a plundering incursion only.

7. Now the supremacy which had belonged to the Heracleidai came to the family of Croesus, called Mermnadai, in the following manner:—Candaules, whom the Hellenes call Myrsilos, was ruler of Sardis and a descendant of Alcaios, son of Heracles: for Agron, the son of Ninos, the son of Belos, the son of Alcaios, was the first of the Heracleidai who became king of Sardis, and Candaules the son of Myrsos was the last; but those who were kings over this land before Agrond, were descendants of Lydos the son of Atys, whence this whole nation was called Lydian, having been before called Meonian. From these the Heracleidai, descended from Heracles and the slave-girl of Iardanos, obtained the government, being charged with it by reason of an oracle; and they reigned for two-and-twenty generations of men, five hundred and five years, handing on the power from father to son, till the time of Clandaules the son of Myrsos.

8. This Candaules then of whom I speak had become passionately in love with his own wife; and having become so, he deemed that his wife was fairer by far than all other women; and thus deeming, to Gyges the son of Daskylos (for he of all his spearmen was the most pleasing to him), to this Gyges, I say, he used to impart as well the more weighty of his affairs as also the beauty of his wife, praising it above measure: and after no long time, since it was destined that evil should happen to Candaules, he said to Gyges as follows: "Gyges, I think that thou dost not believe me when I tell thee of the beauty of my wife, for it happens that men's ears are less apt of belief than their eyes: contrive therefore means by which thou mayest look upon her naked." But he cried aloud and said: "Master, what word of unwisdom is this which thou dost utter, bidding me look upon my mistress naked? When a woman puts off her tunic she puts off her modesty also. Moreover of old time those fair sayings have been found out by men, from which we ought to learn wisdom; and of these one is this,—that each man should look on his own: but I believe indeed that she is of all women the fairest and I entreat thee not to ask of me that which it is not lawful for me to do."

9. With such words as these he resisted, fearing lest some evil might come to him from this; but the king answered him thus: "Be of good courage, Gyges, and have no fear, either of me, that I am saying these words to try thee, or of my wife, lest any harm may happen to thee from her. For I will contrive it so from the first that she shall not even perceive that she has been seen by thee. I will place thee in the room where we sleep, behind the open door; and after I have gone in, my wife also will come to lie down. Now there is a seat near the entrance of the room, and upon this she will lay her garments as she takes them off one by one; and so thou wilt be able to gaze upon her at full leisure. And when she goes from the chair to the bed and thou shalt be behind her back, then let it be thy part to take care that she sees thee not as thou goest through the door."

10. He then, since he might not avoid it, gave consent: and Candaules, when he considered that it was time to rest, led Gyges to the chamber; and straightway after this the woman also appeared: and Gyges looked upon her after she came in and as she laid down her garments; and when she had her back turned towards him, as she went to the bed,

then he slipped away from his hiding-place and was going forth. And as he went out, the woman caught sight of him, and perceiving that which had been done by her husband she did not cry out, though struck with shame, but she made as though she had not perceived the matter, meaning to avenge herself upon Candaules: for among the Lydians as also among most other Barbarians it is a shame even for a man to be seen naked.

11. At the time then she kept silence, as I say, and made no outward sign; but as soon as day had dawned, and she made ready those of the servants whom she perceived to be the most attached to herself, and after that she sent to summon Gyges. He then, not supposing that anything of that which had been done was known to her, came upon her summons; for he had been accustomed before to go whenever the queen summoned him. And when Gyges was come, the woman said to him these words: "There are now two ways open to thee, Gyges, and I give thee the choice which of the two thou wilt prefer to take. Either thou must slay Candaules and possess both me and the kingdom of Lydia, or thou must thyself here on the spot be slain, so that thou mayest not in future, by obeying Candaules in all things, see that which thou shouldest not. Either he must die who formed this design, or thou who hast looked upon me naked and done that which is not accounted lawful." For a time then Gyges was amazed at these words, and afterwards he began to entreat her that she would not bind him by necessity to make such a choice: then however, as he could not prevail with her, but saw that necessity was in truth set before him either to slay his master or to be himself slain by others, he made the choice to live himself; and he inquired further as follows: "Since thou dost compel me to take my master's life against my own will, let me hear from thee also what is the manner in which we shall lay hands upon him." And she answering said: "From that same place shall the attempt be, where he displayed me naked; and we will lay hands upon him as he sleeps."

12. So after they had prepared the plot, when night came on, (for Gyges was not let go nor was there any way of escape for him, but he must either be slain himself or slay Candaules), he followed the woman to the bedchamber; and she gave him a dagger and concealed him behind that very same door. Then afterwards, while Candaules was sleeping, Gyges came privily up to him and slew him, and he obtained both his wife and his kingdom: of him moreover Archilochos the Parian, who lived about that time, made mention in a trimeter iambic verse.

13. He obtained the kingdom however and was strengthened in it by means of the Oracle at Delphi; for when the Lydians were angry because of the fate of Candaules, and had risen in arms, a treaty was made between the followers of Gyges and the other Lydians to this effect, that if the Oracle should give answer that he was to be king of the Lydians, he should be king, and if not, he should give back the power to the sons of Heracles. So the Oracle gave answer, and Gyges accordingly became king: yet the Pythian prophetess said this also, that vengeance for the Heracleidai should come upon the descendants of Gyges in the fifth generation. Of this oracle the Lydians and their kings made no account until it was in fact fulfilled.

14. Thus the Mermnadai obtained the government having driven out from it the Heracleidai: and Gyges when he became ruler sent votive offerings to Delphi not a few, for of all the silver offerings at Delphi his are more in number than those of any other man; and besides the silver he offered a vast quantity of gold, and especially one offering which is more worthy of mention than the rest, namely six golden mixing-bowls, which are dedicated there as his gift: of these the weight is thirty talents, and they stand in the treasury of

the Corinthians, (though in truth this treasury does not belong to the State of the Corinthians, but is that of Kypselos the son of Aëtion). This Gyges was the first of the Barbarians within our knowledge who dedicated votive offerings at Delphi, except only Midas the son of Gordias king of Phrygia, who dedicated for an offering the royal throne on which he sat before all to decide causes; and this throne, a sight worth seeing, stands in the same place with the bowls of Gyges. This gold and silver which Gyges dedicated is called Gygian by the people of Delphi, after the name of him who offered it.

Now Gyges also, as soon as he became king, led an army against Miletos and Smyrna, and he took the lower town of Colophon: but no other great deed did he do in his reign, which lasted eight-and-thirty years, therefore we will pass him by with no more mention than has already been made,

15. and I will speak now of Ardys the son of Gyges, who became king after Gyges. He took Priene and made an invasion against Miletos; and while he was ruling over Sardis, the Kimmerians driven from their abodes by the nomad Scythians came to Asia and took Sardis except the citadel.

16. Now when Ardys had been king for nine-and-forty years, Sadyattes his son succeeded to his kingdom, and reigned twelve years; and after him Alyattes. This last made war against Kyaxares the descendant of Deïokes and against the Medes, and he drove the Kimmerians forth out of Asia, and he took Smyrna which had been founded from Colophon, and made an invasion against Clazomenai. From this he returned not as he desired, but with great loss: during his reign however he performed other deeds very worthy of mention as follows:—

17. He made war with those of Miletos, having received this war as an inheritance from his father: for he used to invade their land and besiege Miletos in the following manner:—whenever there were ripe crops upon the land, then he led an army into their confines, making his march to the sound of pipes and harps and flutes both of male and female tone: and when he came to the Milesian land, he neither pulled down the houses that were in the fields, nor set fire to them nor tore off their doors, but let them stand as they were; the trees however and the crops that were upon the land he destroyed, and then departed by the way he came: for the men of Miletos had command of the sea, so that it was of no use for his army to blockade them: and he abstained from pulling down the houses to the end that the Milesians might have places to dwell in while they sowed and tilled the land, and by the means of their labor he might have somewhat to destroy when he made his invasion.

18. Thus he continued to war with them for eleven years; and in the course of these years the Milesians suffered two great defeats, once when they fought a battle in the district of Limenion in their own land, and again in the plain of Maiander. Now for six of the eleven years Sadyattes the son of Ardys was still ruler of the Lydians, the same who was wont to invade the land of Miletos at the times mentioned; for this Sadyattes was he who first began the war: but for the five years which followed these first six the war was carried on by Alyattes the son of Sadyattes, who received it as an inheritance from his father (as I have already said) and applied himself to it earnestly. And none of the Ionians helped those of Miletos bear the burden of this war except only the men of Chios. These came to their aid to pay back like with like, for the Milesians had formerly assisted the Chians throughout their war with the people of Erythrai.

19. Then in the twelfth year of the war, when standing corn was being burnt by the

army of the Lydians, it happened as follows:—as soon as the corn was kindled, it was driven by a violent wind and set fire to the temple of Athene surnamed of Assessos; and the temple being set on fire was burnt down to the ground. Of this no account was made then; but afterwards when the army had returned to Sardis, Alyattes fell sick, and as his sickness lasted long, he sent messengers to inquire of the Oracle at Delphi, either being advised to do so by some one, or because he himself thought it best to send and inquire of the god concerning his sickness. But when these arrived at Delphi, the Pythian prophetess said that she would give them no answer, until they should have built up again the temple of Athene which they had burnt at Assessos in the land of Miletos.

20. Thus much I know by the report of the people of Delphi; but the Milesians add to this that Periander the son of Kypselos, being a special guest-friend of Thrasybulos the then despot of Miletos, heard of the oracle which had been given to Alyattes, and sending a messenger told Thrasybulos, in order that he might have knowledge of it beforehand and take such counsel as the case required. This is the story told by the Milesians.

21. And Alyattes, when this answer was reported to him, sent a herald forthwith to Miletos, desiring to make a truce with Thrasybulos and the Milesians for so long a time as he should be building the temple. He then was being sent as envoy to Miletos; and Thrasybulos in the meantime being informed beforehand of the whole matter and knowing what Alyattes was meaning to do, contrived this device:—he gathered together in the market-place all the store of provisions which was found in the city, both his own and that which belonged to private persons; and he proclaimed to the Milesians that on a signal given by him they should all begin to drink and make merry with one another.

22. This Thrasybulos did and thus proclaimed to the end that the herald from Sardis, seeing a vast quantity of provisions carelessly piled up, and the people feasting, might report this to Alyattes: and so on fact it happened; for when the herald returned to Sardis after seeing this and delivering to Thrasybulos the charge which was given to him by the king of Lydia, the peace which was made, came about, as I am informed, merely because of this. For Alyattes, who thought that there was a great famine in Miletos and that the people had been worn down to the extreme of misery, heard from the herald, when he returned from Miletos, the opposite to that which he himself supposed. And after this the peace was made between them on condition of being guest-friends and allies to one another, and Alyattes built two temples to Athene at Assessos in place of one, and himself recovered from his sickness. With regard then to the war waged by Alyattes with the Milesians and Thrasybulos things went thus.

23. As for Periander, the man who gave information about the oracle to Thrasybulos, he was the son of Kypselos, and despot of Corinth. In his life, say the Corinthians, (and with them agree the Lesbians), there happened to him a very great marvel, namely that Arion of Methymna was carried ashore at Tainaron upon a dolphin's back. This man was a harper second to none of those who then lived, and the first, so far as we know, who composed a dithyramb, naming it so and teaching it to a chorus at Corinth.

24. This Arion, they say, who for the most part of his time stayed with Periander, conceived a desire to sail to Italy and Sicily; and after he had there acquired large sums of money, he wished to return again to Corinth. He set forth therefore from Taras, and as he had faith in Corinthians more than in other men, he hired a ship with a crew of Corinthians. These, the story says, when out in open sea, formed a plot to cast Arion overboard and so possess his wealth; and he having obtained knowledge of this made entreaties to

them, offering them his wealth and asking them to grant him his life. With this however he did not prevail upon them, but the men who were conveying him bade him either slay himself there, that he might receive burial on the land, or leap straightway into the sea. So Arion being driven to a strait entreated them that, since they were so minded, they would allow him to take his stand in full minstrel's garb upon the deck of the ship and sing; and he promised to put himself to death after he had sung. They then, well pleased to think that they should hear the best of all minstrels upon earth, drew back from the stern towards the middle of the ship; and he put on the full minstrel's garb and took his lyre, and standing on the deck performed the Orthian measure. Then as the measure ended, he threw himself into the sea just as he was, in his full minstrel's garb; and they went on sailing away to Corinth, but him, they say, a dolphin supported on its back and brought him to shore at Tainaron: and when he had come to land he proceeded to Corinth with his minstrel's garb. Thither having arrived he related all that had been done; and Periander doubting of his story kept Arion in guard and would let him go nowhere, while he kept careful watch for those who had conveyed him. When these came, he called them and inquired of them if they had any report to make of Arion; and when they said that he was safe in Italy and that they had left him at Taras faring well, Arion suddenly appeared before them in the same guise as when he made his leap from the ship; and they being struck with amazement were no longer able to deny when they were questioned. This is the tale told by the Corinthians and Lesbians alike, and there is at Tainaron a votive offering of Arion of no great size, namely a bronze figure of a man upon a dolphin's back.

25. Alyattes the Lydian, when he had thus waged war against the Milesians, afterwards died, having reigned seven-and-fifty years. This king, when he recovered from his sickness, dedicated a votive offering at Delphi (being the second of his house who had so done), namely a great mixing-bowl of silver with a stand for it of iron welded together, which last is a sight worth seeing above all the offerings at Delphi and the work of Glaucos the Chian, who of all men first found out the art of welding iron.

26. After Alyattes was dead Croesus the son of Alyattes received the kingdom in succession, being five-and-thirty years of age. He (as I said) fought against the Hellenes and of them he attacked the Ephesians first. The Ephesians then, being besieged by him, dedicated their city to Artemis and tied a rope from the temple to the wall of the city: now the distance between the ancient city, which was then being besieged, and the temple is seven furlongs. These, I say, where the first upon whom Croesus laid hands, but afterwards he did the same to the other Ionian and Aiolian cities one by one, alleging against them various causes of complaint, and making serious charges against those in whose cases he could find serious grounds, while against others of them he charged merely trifling offences.

27. Then when the Hellenes in Asia had been conquered and forced to pay tribute, he designed next to build for himself ships and to lay hands upon those who dwelt in the islands; and when all was prepared for his building of ships, they say that Bias of Priene (or, according to another account, Pittacos of Mytilene) came to Sardis, and being asked by Croesus whether there was any new thing doing in Hellas, brought to an end his building of ships by this saying: "O king," said he, "the men of the islands are hiring a troop of ten thousand horse, and with this they mean to march to Sardis and fight against thee." And Croesus, supposing that what he reported was true, said: "May the gods put it into the minds of the dwellers of the islands to come with horses against the sons of the Lydians!"

And he answered and said: "O king, I perceive that thou dost earnestly desire to catch the men of the islands on the mainland riding upon horses; and it is not unreasonable that thou shouldest wish for this: what else however thinkest thou the men of the islands desire and have been praying for ever since the time they heard that thou wert about to build ships against them, than that they might catch the Lydians upon the sea, so as to take vengeance upon thee for the Hellenes who dwell upon the mainland, whom thou dost hold enslaved?" Croesus, they say, was greatly pleased with this conclusion, and obeying his suggestion, for he judged him to speak suitably, he stopped his building of ships; and upon that he formed a friendship with the Ionians dwelling in the islands.

28. As time went on, when nearly all those dwelling on this side the river Halys had been subdued, (for except the Kilikians and Lykians Croesus subdued and kept under his rule all the nations, that is to say Lydians, Phrygians, Mysians, Mariandynoi, Chalybians, Paphlagonians, Thracians both Thynian and Bithynian, Carians, Ionians, Dorians, Aiolians, and Pamphylians),

29, when these, I say, had been subdued, and while he was still adding to his Lydian dominions, there came to Sardis, then at the height of its wealth, all the wise men of the Hellas who chanced to be alive at that time, brought thither severally by various occasions; and of them one was Solon the Athenian, who after he had made laws for the Athenians at their bidding, left his native country for ten years and sailed away saying that he desired to visit various lands, in order that he might not be compelled to repeal any of the laws which he had proposed. For of themselves the Athenians were not competent to do this, having bound themselves by solemn oaths to submit for ten years to the laws which Solon should propose for them.

30. So Solon, having left his native country for this reason and for the sake of seeing various lands, came to Amasis in Egypt, and also to Croesus at Sardis. Having there arrived he was entertained as a guest by Croesus in the king's palace; and afterwards, on the third or fourth day, at the bidding of Croesus his servants led Solon round to see his treasuries; and they showed him all things, how great and magnificent they were: and after he had looked upon them all and examined them as he had occasion, Croesus asked him as follows: "Athenian guest, much report of thee has come to us, both in regard to thy wisdom and thy wanderings, how that in thy search for wisdom thou hast traversed many lands to see them; now therefore a desire has come upon me to ask thee whether thou hast seen any whom thou deemest to be of all men the most happy." This he asked supposing that he himself was the happiest of men; but Solon, using no flattery but the truth only, said: "Yes, O king, Tellos the Athenian." And Croesus, marveling at that which he said, asked him earnestly: "In what respect dost thou judge Tellos to be the most happy?" And he said: "Tellos, in the first place, living while his native State was prosperous, had sons fair and good and saw from all of them children begotten and living to grow up; and secondly he had what with us is accounted wealth, and after his life a most glorious end: for when a battle was fought by the Athenians at Eleusis against the neighboring people, he brought up supports and routed the foe and there died by a most fair death; and the Athenians buried him publicly where he fell, and honored him greatly."

31. So when Solon had moved Croesus to inquire further by the story of Tellos, recounting how many points of happiness he had, the king asked again whom he had seen proper to be placed next after this man, supposing that he himself would certainly obtain at least the second place; but he replied: "Cleobis and Biton: for these, who were of

Argos by race, possessed a sufficiency of wealth and, in addition to this, strength of body such as I shall tell. Both equally had won prizes in the games, and moreover the following tale is told of them:—There was a feast of Hera among the Argives and it was by all means necessary that their mother should be borne in a car to the temple. But since their oxen were not brought up in time from the field, the young men, barred from all else by lack of time, submitted themselves to the yoke and drew the wain, their mother being borne by them upon it; and so they brought it on for five-and-forty furlongs, and came to the temple. Then after they had done this and had been seen by the assembled crowd, there came to their life a most excellent ending; and in this the deity declared that it was better for man to die than to continue to live. For the Argive men were standing round and extolling the strength of the young men, while the Argive women were extolling the mother to whose lot it had fallen to have such sons; and the mother being exceedingly rejoiced both by the deed itself and by the report made of it, took her stand in front of the image of the goddess and prayed that she would give to Cleobis and Biton her sons, who had honored her greatly, that gift which is best for man to receive: and after this prayer, when they had sacrificed and feasted, the young men lay down to sleep within the temple itself, and never rose again, but were held bound in this last end. And the Argives made statues in the likeness of them and dedicated them as offerings at Delphi, thinking that they had proved themselves most excellent."

32. Thus Solon assigned the second place in respect of happiness to these: and Croesus was moved to anger and said: "Athenian guest, hast thou then so cast aside our prosperous state as worth nothing, that thou dost prefer to us even men of private station?" And he said: "Croesus, thou art inquiring about human fortunes of one who well knows that the Deity is altogether envious and apt to disturb our lot. For in the course of long time a man may see many things which he would not desire to see, and suffer also many things which he would not desire to suffer. The limit of life for a man I lay down at seventy years: and these seventy years give twenty-five thousand and two hundred days, not reckoning for any intercalated month. Then if every other one of these years shall be made longer by one month, that the seasons may be caused to come round at the due time of the year, the intercalated months will be in number five-and-thirty besides the seventy years; and of these months the days will be one thousand and fifty. Of all these days, being in number twenty-six thousand two hundred and fifty, which go to the seventy years, one day produces nothing at all which resembles what another brings with it. Thus then, O Croesus, man is altogether a creature of accident. As for thee, I perceive that thou art both great in wealth and king of many men, but that of which thou didst ask me I cannot call thee yet, until I learn that thou hast brought thy life to a fair ending: for the very rich man is not at all to be accounted more happy than he who has but his subsistence from day to day, unless also the fortune go with him of ending his life well in possession of all things fair. For many very wealthy men are not happy, while many who have but a moderate living are fortunate; and in truth the very rich man who is not happy has two advantages only as compared with the poor man who is fortunate, whereas this latter has many as compared with the rich man who is not happy. The rich man is able better to fulfil his desire, and also to endure a great calamity if it fall upon him; whereas the other has advantage over him in these things which follow:—he is not indeed able equally with the rich man to endure a calamity or to fulfil his desire, but these his good fortune keeps away from him, while he is sound of limb, free from disease, untouched by

suffering, the father of fair children and himself of comely form; and if in addition to this he shall end his life well, he is worthy to be called that which thou seekest, namely a happy man; but before he comes to his end it is well to hold back and not to call him yet happy but only fortunate. Now to possess all these things together is impossible for one who is mere man, just as no single land suffices to supply all things for itself, but one thing it has and another it lacks, and the land that has the greatest number of things is the best: so also in the case of a man, no single person is complete in himself, for one thing he has and another he lacks; but whosoever of men continues to the end in possession of the greatest number of these things and then has a gracious ending of his life, he is by me accounted worthy, O king, to receive this name. But we must of everything examine the end and how it will turn out at the last, for to many God shows but a glimpse of happiness and then plucks them up by the roots and overturns them."

33. Thus saying he refused to gratify Croesus, who sent him away from his presence holding him in no esteem, and thinking him utterly senseless in that he passed over present good things and bade men look to the end of every matter.

34. After Solon had departed, a great retribution from God came upon Croesus, probably because he judged himself to be the happiest of all men. First there came and stood by him a dream, which showed to him the truth of the evils that were about to come to pass in respect of his son. Now Croesus had two sons, of whom one was deficient, seeing that he was deaf and dumb, while the other far surpassed his companions of the same age in all things: and the name of this last was Atys. As regards this Atys then, the dream signified to Croesus that he should lose him by the blow of an iron spear-point: and when he rose up from sleep and considered the matter with himself, he was struck with fear on account of the dream; and first he took for his son a wife; and whereas his son had been wont to lead the armies of the Lydians, he now no longer sent him forth anywhere on any such business; and the javelins and lances and all such things which men use for fighting he conveyed out of the men's apartments and piled them up in the inner bed-chambers, for fear lest something hanging up might fall down upon his son.

35. Then while he was engaged about the marriage of his son, there came to Sardis a man under a misfortune and with hands not clean, a Phrygian by birth and of the royal house. This man came to the house of Croesus, and according to the customs which prevail in that land made request that he might have cleansing; and Croesus gave him cleansing: now the manner of cleansing among the Lydians is the same almost as that which the Hellenes use. So when Croesus had done that which was customary, he asked of him whence he came and who he was, saying as follows: "Man, who art thou, and from what region of Phrygia didst thou come to sit upon my hearth? And whom of men or women didst thou slay?" And he replied: "O king, I am the son of Gordias, the son of Midas, and I am called Adrastos; and I slew my own brother against my will, and therefore am I here, having been driven forth by my father and deprived of all that I had." And Croesus answered thus: "Thou art, as it chances, the offshoot of men who are our friends and thou hast come to friends, among whom thou shalt want of nothing so long as thou shalt remain in our land: and thou wilt find it most for thy profit to bear this misfortune as lightly as may be." So he had his abode with Croesus.

36. During this time there was produced in the Mysian Olympos a boar of monstrous size. This, coming down from the mountain aforesaid, ravaged the fields of the Mysians, and although the Mysians went out against it often, yet they could do it no hurt, but

rather received hurt themselves from it; so at length messengers came from the Mysians to Croesus and said: "O king, there has appeared in our land a boar of monstrous size, which lays waste our fields; and we, desiring eagerly to take it, are not able: now therefore we ask of thee to send with us thy son and also a chosen band of young men with dogs, that we may destroy it out of our land." Thus they made request, and Croesus calling to mind the words of the dream spoke to them as follows: "As touching my son, make no further mention of him in this matter; for I will not send him with you, seeing that he is newly married and is concerned now with the affairs of his marriage: but I will send with you chosen men of the Lydians and the whole number of my hunting dogs, and I will give command to those who go, to be as zealous as may be in helping you to destroy the wild beast out of your land."

37. Thus he made reply, and while the Mysians were being contented with this answer, there came in also the son of Croesus, having heard of the request made by the Mysians: and when Croesus said that he would not send his son with them, the young man spoke as follows: "My father, in times past the fairest and most noble part was allotted to us, to go out continually to wars and to the chase and so have good repute; but now thou hast debarred me from both of these, although thou hast not observed in me any cowardly or faint-hearted spirit. And now with what face must I appear when I go to and from the market-place of the city? What kind of a man shall I be esteemed by the citizens, and what kind of a man shall I be esteemed by my newly-married wife? With what kind of a husband will she think that she is mated? Therefore either let me go to the hunt, or persuade me by reason that these things are better for me done as now they are."

38. And Croesus made answer thus: "My son, not because I have observed in thee any spirit of cowardice or any other ungracious thing, do I act thus; but a vision of a dream came and stood by me in my sleep and told me that thou shouldest be short-lived, and that thou shouldest perish by a spear-point of iron. With thought of this vision therefore I both urged on this marriage for thee, and I refuse now to send thee upon the matter which is being taken in hand, having a care of thee that I may steal thee from thy fate at least for the period of my own life, if by any means possible for me to do so. For thou art, as it chances, my only son: the other I do not reckon as one, seeing that he is deficient in hearing."

39. The young man made answer thus: "It may well be forgiven in thee, O my father, that thou shouldest have a care of me after having seen such a vision; but that which thou dost not understand, and in which the meaning of the dream has escaped thee, it is right that I should expound to thee. Thou sayest the dream declared that I should end my life by means of a spear-point of iron: but what hands has a boar, or what spear-point of iron, of which thou art afraid? If the dream had told thee that I should end my life by a tusk, or any other thing which resembles that, it would be right for thee doubtless to do as thou art doing; but it said 'by a spear-point.' Since therefore our fight will not be with men, let me now go."

40. Croesus made answer: "My son, thou dost partly prevail with me by declaring thy judgment about the dream; therefore, having been prevailed upon by thee, I change my resolution and allow thee to go to the chase."

41. Having thus said Croesus went to summon Adrastos the Phrygian; and when he came, he addressed him thus: "Adrastos, when thou wast struck with a grievous misfortune (with which I reproach thee not), I cleansed thee, and I have received thee into my

house supplying all thy costs. Now therefore, since having first received kindness from me thou art bound to requite me with kindness, I ask of thee to be the protector of my son who goes forth to the chase, lest any evil robbers come upon you by the way to do you harm; and besides this thou too oughtest to go where thou mayest become famous by thy deeds, for it belongs to thee as an inheritance from thy fathers so to do, and moreover thou hast strength for it."

42. Adrastos made answer: "O king, but for this I should not have been going to any such contest of valor; for first it is not fitting that one who is suffering such a great misfortune as mine should seek the company of his fellows who are in prosperity, and secondly I have no desire for it; and for many reasons I should have kept myself away. But now, since thou art urgent with me, and I ought to gratify thee (for I am bound to requite thee with kindness), I am ready to do this: expect therefore that thy son, whom thou commandest me to protect, will return home to thee unhurt, so far as his protector may avail to keep him safe."

43. When he had made answer to Croesus in words like these, they afterwards set forth provided with chosen young men and with dogs. And when they were come to Mount Olympos, they tracked the animal; and having found it and taken their stand round in a circle, they were hurling against it their spears. Then the guest, he who had been cleansed of manslaughter, whose name was Adrastos, hurling a spear at it missed the boar and struck the son of Croesus. So he being struck by the spear-point fulfilled the saying of the dream. And one ran to report to Croesus that which had come to pass, and having come to Sardis he signified to him of the combat and of the fate of his son. And Croesus was very greatly disturbed by the death of his son, and was much the more moved to complaining by this, namely that his son was slain by the man whom he had himself cleansed of manslaughter. And being grievously troubled by the misfortune he called upon Zeus the Cleanser, protesting to him that which he had suffered from his guest, and he called moreover upon the Protector of Suppliants and the Guardian of Friendship, naming still the same god, and calling upon him as the Protector of Suppliants because when he received the guest into his house he had been fostering ignorantly the slayer of his son, and as the Guardian of Friendship because having sent him as a protector he had found him the worst of foes.

45. After this the Lydians came bearing the corpse, and behind it followed the slayer: and he taking his stand before the corpse delivered himself up to Croesus, holding forth his hands and bidding the king slay him over the corpse, speaking of his former misfortune and saying that in addition to this he had now been the destroyer of the man who had cleansed him of it; and that life for him was no more worth living. But Croesus hearing this pitied Adrastos, although he was himself suffering so great an evil of his own, and said to him: "Guest, I have already received from thee all the satisfaction that is due, seeing that thou dost condemn thyself to suffer death; and not thou alone art the cause of this evil, except in so far as thou wert the instrument of it against thine own will, but someone, as I suppose, of the gods, who also long ago signified to me that which was about to be." So Croesus buried his son as was fitting: but Adrastos the son of Gordias, the son of Midas, he who had been the slayer of his own brother and the slayer also of the man who had cleansed him, when silence came of all men round about the tomb, recognizing that he was more grievously burdened by misfortune than all men of whom he knew, slew himself upon the grave.

46. For two years then Croesus remained quiet in his mourning, because he was deprived of his son: but after this period of time the overthrowing of the rule of Astyages the son of Kyaxares by Cyrus the son of Cambyses, and the growing greatness of the Persians caused Croesus to cease from his mourning, and led him to a care of cutting short the power of the Persians, if by any means he might, while yet it was in growth and before they should have become great.

So having formed this design he began forthwith to make trial of the Oracles, both those of the Hellenes and that in Libya, sending messengers some to one place and some to another, some to go to Delphi, others to Abai of the Phokians, and others to Dodona; and some were sent to the shrine of Amphiaraos and to that of Trophonios, others to Branchidai in the land of Miletos: these are the Oracles of the Hellenes to which Croesus sent messengers to seek divination; and others he sent to the shrine of Ammon in Libya to inquire there. Now he was sending the messengers abroad to the end that he might try the Oracles and find out what knowledge they had, so that if they should be found to have knowledge of the truth, he might send and ask them secondly whether he should attempt to march against the Persians.

47. And to the Lydians whom he sent to make trial of the Oracles he gave charge as follows,—that from the day on which they set out from Sardis they should reckon up the number of the days following and on the hundredth day they should consult the Oracles, asking what Croesus the son of Alyattes king of the Lydians chanced then to be doing: and whatever the Oracles severally should prophesy, this they should cause to be written down and bear it back to him. Now what the other Oracles prophesied is not by any reported, but at Delphi, so soon as the Lydians entered the sanctuary of the temple to consult the god and asked that which they were commanded to ask, the Pythian prophetess spoke thus in hexameter measure:

"But the number of sand I know, and the measure of drops in the ocean;
The dumb man I understand, and I hear the speech of the speechless:
And there hath come to my soul the smell of a strong-shelled tortoise
Boiling in caldron of bronze, and the flesh of a lamb mingled with it;
Under it bronze is laid, it hath bronze as a clothing upon it."

48. When the Pythian prophetess had uttered this oracle, the Lydians caused the prophecy to be written down, and went away at once to Sardis. And when the rest also who had been sent round were there arrived with the answers of the Oracles, then Croesus unfolded the writings one by one and looked upon them: and at first none of them pleased him, but when he heard that from Delphi, forthwith he did worship to the god and accepted the answer, judging that the Oracle at Delphi was the only true one, because it had found out what he himself had done. For when he had sent to the several Oracles his messengers to consult the gods, keeping well in mind the appointed day he contrived the following device,—he thought of something which it would be impossible to discover or to conceive of, and cutting up a tortoise and a lamb he boiled them together himself in a cauldron of bronze, laying a cover of bronze over them.

49. This then was the answer given to Croesus from Delphi; and as regards the answer of Amphiaraos, I cannot tell what he replied to the Lydians after they had done the things

customary in his temple, for there is no record of this any more than of the others, except only that Croesus thought that he also possessed a true Oracle.

50. After this with great sacrifices he endeavored to win the favor of the god at Delphi: for of all the animals that are fit for sacrifice he offered three thousand of each kind, and he heaped up couches overlaid with gold and overlaid with silver, and cups of gold, and robes of purple, and tunics, making of them a great pyre, and this he burnt up, hoping by these means the more to win over the god to the side of the Lydians: and he proclaimed to all the Lydians that every one of them should make sacrifice with that which each man had. And when he had finished the sacrifice, he melted down a vast quantity of gold, and of it he wrought half-plinths making them six palms in length and three in breadth, and in height one palm; and their number was one hundred and seventeen. Of these four were of pure gold weighing two talents and a half each, and others of gold alloyed with silver weighing two talents. And he caused to be made also an image of a lion of pure gold weighing ten talents; which lion, when the temple of Delphi was being burnt down, fell from off the half-plinths, for upon these it was set, and is placed now in the treasury of the Corinthians, weighing six talents and a half, for three talents and a half were melted away from it.

51. So Croesus having finished all these things sent them to Delphi, and with them these besides:—two mixing bowls of great size, one of gold and the other of silver, of which the golden bowl was placed on the right hand as one enters the temple, and the silver on the left, but the places of these also were changed after the temple was burnt down, and the golden bowl is now placed in the treasury of the people of Clazomenai, weighing eight and a half talents and twelve pounds over, while the silver one is placed in the corner of the vestibule and holds six hundred amphors (being filled with wine by the Delphians on the feast of the Theophania): this the people of Delphi say is the work of Theodoros the Samian, and, as I think, rightly, for it is evident to me that the workmanship is of no common kind: moreover Croesus sent four silver wine-jars, which stand in the treasury of the Corinthians, and two vessels for lustral water, one of gold and the other of silver, of which the gold one is inscribed "from the Lacedemonians," who say that it is their offering: therein however they do not speak rightly; for this also is from Croesus, but one of the Delphians wrote the inscription upon it, desiring to gratify the Lacedemonians; and his name I know but will not make mention of it. The boy through whose hand the water flows is from the Lacedemonians, but neither of the vessels for lustral water. And many other votive offerings Croesus sent with these, not specially distinguished, among which are certain castings of silver of a round shape, and also a golden figure of a woman three cubits high, which the Delphians say is a statue of the baker of Croesus. Moreover Croesus dedicated the ornaments from his wife's neck and her girdles.

52. These are the things which he sent to Delphi; and to Amphiaraos, having heard of his valor and of his evil fate, he dedicated a shield made altogether of gold throughout, and a spear all of solid gold, the shaft being of gold also as well as the two points, which offerings were both remaining even to my time at Thebes in the temple of Ismenian Apollo.

53. To the Lydians who were to carry these gifts to the temples Croesus gave charge that they should ask the Oracles this question also,—whether Croesus should march against the Persians, and if so, whether he should join with himself any army of men as his friends. And when the Lydians had arrived at the places to which they had been sent

and had dedicated the votive offerings, they inquired of the Oracles and said: "Croesus, king of the Lydians and of other nations, considering that these are the only true Oracles among men, presents to you gifts such as your revelations deserve, and asks you again now whether he shall march against the Persians, and if so, whether he shall join with himself any army of men as allies." They inquired thus, and the answers of both the Oracles agreed in one, declaring to Croesus that if he should march against the Persians he should destroy a great empire: and they counselled him to find out the most powerful of the Hellenes and join these with himself as friends.

54. So when the answers were brought back and Croesus heard them, he was delighted with the oracles, and expecting that he would certainly destroy the kingdom of Cyrus, he sent again to Pytho, and presented to the men of Delphi, having ascertained the number of them, two staters of gold for each man: and in return for this the Delphians gave to Croesus and to the Lydians precedence in consulting the Oracle and freedom from all payments, and the right to front seats at the games, with this privilege also for all time, that any one of them who wished should be allowed to become a citizen of Delphi.

55. And having made presents to the men of Delphi, Croesus consulted the Oracle the third time; for from the time when he learnt the truth of the Oracle, he made abundant use of it. And consulting the Oracle he inquired whether his monarchy would endure for a long time. And the Pythian prophetess answered him thus:

"But when it cometh to pass that a mule of the Medes shall be monarch
Then by the pebbly Hermos, O Lydian delicate-footed,
Flee and stay not, and be not ashamed to be callèd a coward."

56. By these lines when they came to him Croesus was pleased more than by all the rest, for he supposed that a mule would never be ruler of the Medes instead of a man, and accordingly that he himself and his heirs would never cease from their rule. Then after this he gave thought to inquire which people of the Hellenes he should esteem the most powerful and gain over to himself as friends. And inquiring he found that the Lacedemonians and the Athenians had the pre-eminence, the first of the Dorian and the others of the Ionian race. For these were the most eminent races in ancient time, the second being a Pelasgian and the first a Hellenic race: and the one never migrated from its place in any direction, while the other was very exceedingly given to wanderings; for in the reign of Deucalion this race dwelt in Pthiotis, and in the time of Doros the son of Hellen in the land lying below Ossa and Olympos, which is called Histiaiotis; and when it was driven from Histiaiotis by the sons of Cadmos, it dwelt in Pindos and was called Makednian; and thence it moved afterwards to Dryopis, and from Dryopis it came finally to Peloponnesus, and began to be called Dorian.

57. What language however the Pelasgians used to speak I am not able with certainty to say. But if one must pronounce judging by those that still remain of the Pelasgians who dwelt in the city of Creston above the Tyrsenians, and who were once neighbors of the race now called Dorian, dwelling then in the land which is now called Thessaliotis, and also by those that remain of the Pelasgians who settled at Plakia and Skylake in the region of the Hellespont, who before that had been settlers with the Athenians, and of the natives of the various other towns which are really Pelasgian, though they have lost the name,—if one must pronounce judging by these, the Pelasgians used to speak a Barbarian language.

If therefore all the Pelasgian race was such as these, then the Attic race, being Pelasgian, at the same time when it changed and became Hellenic, unlearnt also its language. For the people of Creston do not speak the same language with any of those who dwell about them, nor yet do the people of Phakia, but they speak the same language one as the other: and by this it is proved that they still keep unchanged the form of language which they brought with them when they migrated to these places.

58. As for the Hellenic race, it has used ever the same language, as I clearly perceive, since it first took its rise; but since the time when it parted off feeble at first from the Pelasgian race, setting forth from a small beginning it has increased to that great number of races which we see, and chiefly because many Barbarian races have been added to it besides. Moreover it is true, as I think, of the Pelasgian race also, that so far as it remained Barbarian it never made any great increase.

59. Of these races then Croesus was informed that the Athenian was held subject and torn with faction by Peisistratos the son of Hippocrates, who then was despot of the Athenians. For to Hippocrates, when as a private citizen he went to view the Olympic games, a great marvel had occurred. After he had offered the sacrifice, the caldrons which were standing upon the hearth, full of pieces of flesh and of water, boiled without fire under them and ran over. And Chilon the Lacedemonian, who chanced to have been present and to have seen the marvel, advised Hippocrates first not to bring into his house a wife to bear him children, and secondly, if he happened to have one already, to dismiss her, and if he chanced to have a son, to disown him. When Chilon had thus recommended, Hippocrates, they say, was not willing to be persuaded, and so there was born to him afterwards this Peisistratos; who, when the Athenians of the shore were at feud with those of the plain, Megacles the son of Alcmaion being leader of the first faction, and Lycurgos the son of Aristolaïdes of that of the plain, aimed at the despotism for himself and gathered a third party. So then, after having collected supporters and called himself leader of the men of the mountain-lands, he contrived a device as follows:—he inflicted wounds upon himself and upon his mules, and then drove his car into the market-place, as if he had just escaped from his opponents, who, as he alleged, had desired to kill him when he was driving into the country: and he asked the commons that he might obtain some protection from them, for before this he had gained reputation in his command against the Megarians, during which he took Nisaia and performed other signal service. And the commons of the Athenians being deceived gave him those men chosen from the dwellers in the city who became not indeed the spear-men of Peisistratos but his club-men; for they followed behind him bearing wooden clubs. And these made insurrection with Peisistratos and obtained possession of the Acropolis. Then Peisistratos was ruler of the Athenians, not having disturbed the existing magistrates nor changed the ancient laws; but he administered the State under that constitution of things which was already established, ordering it fairly and well.

60. However, no long time after this the followers of Megacles and those of Lycurgos joined together and drove him forth. Thus Peisistratos had obtained possession of Athens for the first time, and thus he lost the power before he had it firmly rooted. But those who had driven out Peisistratos became afterwards at feud with one another again. And Megacles, harassed by the party strife, sent a message to Peisistratos asking whether he was willing to have his daughter to wife on condition of becoming despot. And Peisistratos having accepted the proposal and made an agreement on these terms, they contrived with

a view to his return a device the most simple by far, as I think, that ever was practiced, considering at least that it was devised at a time when the Hellenic race had been long marked off from the Barbarian as more skillful and further removed from foolish simplicity, and among the Athenians who are accounted the first of the Hellenes in ability. In the deme of Paiania there was a woman whose name was Phya, in height four cubits all but three fingers, and also fair of form. This woman they dressed in full armor and caused her to ascend a chariot and showed her the bearing in which she might best beseem her part, and so they drove to the city, having sent on heralds to run before them, who, when they arrived at the city, spoke that which had been commanded them, saying as follows: "O Athenians, receive with favor Peisistratos, whom Athene herself, honoring him most of all men, brings back to her Acropolis." So the heralds went about hither and thither saying this, and straightway there came to the demes in the country round a report that Athene was bringing Peisistratos back, while at the same time the men of the city, persuaded that the woman was the very goddess herself, were paying worship to the human creature and receiving Peisistratos.

61. So having received back the despotism in the manner which has been said, Peisistratos according to the agreement made with Megacles married the daughter of Megacles; but as he had already sons who were young men, and as the descendants of Alcmaion were said to be under a curse, therefore not desiring that children should be born to him from his newly-married wife, he had commerce with her not in the accustomed manner. And at first the woman kept this secret, but afterwards she told her mother, whether in answer to her inquiry or not I cannot tell; and the mother told her husband Megacles. He then was very indignant that he should be dishonored by Peisistratos; and in his anger straightway he proceeded to compose his quarrel with the men of his faction. And when Peisistratos heard of that which was being done against himself, he departed wholly from the land and came to Eretria, where he took counsel together with his sons: and the advice of Hippias having prevailed, that they should endeavor to win back the despotism, they began to gather gifts of money from those States which owed them obligations for favors received: and many contributed great sums, but the Thebans surpassed the rest in the giving of money. Then, not to make the story long, time elapsed and at last everything was prepared for their return. For certain Argives came as mercenaries from the Peloponnesus, and a man of Naxos had come to them of his own motion, whose name was Lygdamis, and showed very great zeal in providing both money and men.

62. So starting from Eretria after the lapse of ten years they returned back; and in Attica the first place of which they took possession was Marathon. While they were encamping here, their partisans from the city came to them, and also others flowed in from the various demes, to whom despotic rule was more welcome than freedom. So these were gathering themselves together; but the Athenians in the city, so long as Peisistratos was collecting the money, and afterwards when he took possession of Marathon, made no account of it; but when they heard that he was marching from Marathon towards the city, then they went to the rescue against him. These then were going in full force to fight against the returning exiles, and the forces of Peisistratos, as they went towards the city starting from Marathon, met them just when they came to the temple of Athene Pallenis, and there encamped opposite to them. Then moved by divine guidance there came into the presence of Peisistratos Amphilytos the Arcarnanian, a soothsayer, who approaching him uttered an oracle in hexameter verse, saying thus:

"But now the cast hath been made and the net hath been widely extended,
And in the night the tunnies will dart through the moon-lighted waters."

63. This oracle he uttered to him being divinely inspired, and Peisistratos, having understood the oracle and having said that he accepted the prophecy which was uttered, led his army against the enemy. Now the Athenians from the city were just at that time occupied with the morning meal, and some of them after their meal with games of dice or with sleep; and the forces of Peisistratos fell upon the Athenians and put them to flight. Then as they fled, Peisistratos devised a very skillful counsel, to the end that the Athenians might not gather again into one body but might remain scattered abroad. He mounted his sons on horseback and sent them before him; and overtaking the fugitives they said that which was commanded them by Peisistratos, bidding them be of good cheer and that each man should depart to his own home.

64. Thus then the Athenians did, and so Peisistratos for the third time obtained possession of Athens, and he firmly rooted his despotism by many foreign mercenaries and by much revenue of money, coming partly from the land itself and partly from about the river Strymon, and also by taking as hostages the sons of those Athenians who had remained in the land and had not at once fled, and placing them in the hands of Naxos; for this also Peisistratos conquered by war and delivered into the charge of Lygdamis. Moreover besides this he cleansed the island of Delos in obedience to the oracles; and his cleansing was of the following kind:—so far as the view from the temple extended he dug up all the dead bodies which were buried in this part and removed them to another part of Delos. So Peisistratos was despot of the Athenians; but of the Athenians some had fallen in the battle, and others of them with the sons of Alcmaion were exiles from their native land.

65. Such was the condition of things which Croesus heard was prevailing among the Athenians during this time; but as to the Lacedemonians he heard that they had escaped from great evils and had now got the better of the Tegeans in the war. For when Leon and Hegesicles were kings of Sparta, the Lacedemonians, who had good success in all their other wars, suffered disaster in that alone which they waged against the men of Tegea. Moreover in the times before this they had the worst laws of almost all the Hellenes, both in matters which concerned themselves alone and also in that they had no dealings with strangers. And they made their change to a good constitution of laws thus:—Lycurgos, a man of the Spartans who was held in high repute, came to the Oracle at Delphi, and as he entered the sanctuary of the temple, straightway the Pythian prophetess said as follows:

"Lo, thou art come, O Lycurgos, to this rich shrine of my temple,
Loved thou by Zeus and by all who possess the abodes of Olympos.
Whether to call thee a god, I doubt, in my voices prophetic,
God or a man, but rather a god I think, O Lycurgos."

66. Some say in addition to this that the Pythian prophetess also set forth to him the order of things which is now established for the Spartans; but the Lacedemonians themselves say that Lycurgos having become guardian of Leobotes his brother's son, who was king of the Spartans, brought in these things from Crete. For as soon as he became guardian, he changed all the prevailing laws, and took measures that they should not

transgress his institutions: and after this Lycurgos established that which appertained to war, namely *Enomoties* and *Triecads* and Common Meals, and in addition to this the Ephors and the Senate. Having changed thus, the Spartans had good laws; and to Lycurgos after he was dead they erected a temple, and they pay him great worship. So then, as might be supposed, with a fertile land and with no small number of men dwelling in it, they straightway shot up and became prosperous: and it was no longer sufficient for them to keep still; but presuming that they were superior in strength to the Arcadians, they consulted the Oracle at Delphi respecting conquest of the whole of Arcadia; and the Pythian prophetess gave answer thus:

> *"The land of Arcadia thou askest; thou askest me much; I refuse it;*
> *Many there are in Arcadian land, stout men, eating acorns;*
> *These will prevent thee from this: but I am not grudging towards thee;*
> *Tegea beaten with sounding feet I will give thee to dance in,*
> *And a fair plain I will give thee to measure with line and divide it."*

When the Lacedemonians heard report of this, they held off from the other Arcadians, and marched against the Tegeans with fetters in their hands, trusting to a deceitful oracle and expecting that they would make slaves of the men of Tegea. But having been worsted in the encounter, those of them who were taken alive worked wearing the fetters which they themselves brought with them and having "measured with line and divided" the plain of the Tegeans. And these fetters with which they had been bound were preserved even to my own time at Tegea, hanging about the temple of Athene Alea.

67. In the former war then I say they struggled against the Tegeans continually with ill success; but in the time of Croesus and in the reign of Anaxandrides and Ariston at Lacedaemon the Spartans had at length become victors in the war; and they became so in the following manner:—As they continued to be always worsted in the war by the men of Tegea, they sent messengers to consult the Oracle at Delphi and inquired what god they should propitiate in order to get the better of the men of Tegea in the war: and the Pythian prophetess made answer to them that they should bring into their land the bones of Orestes the son of Agamemnon. Then as they were not able to find the grave of Orestes, they sent men again to go to the god and to inquire about the spot where Orestes was laid: and when the messengers who were sent asked this, the prophetess said as follows:

> *"Tegea there is, in Arcadian land, in a smooth place founded;*
> *Where there do blow two blasts by strong compulsion together;*
> *Stroke too there is and stroke in return, and trouble on trouble.*
> *There Agamemnon's son in the life-giving earth is reposing;*
> *Him if thou bring with thee home, of Tegea thou shalt be master."*

When the Lacedemonians had heard this they were none the less far from finding it out, though they searched all places; until the time that Lichas, one of those Spartans who are called "Well-doers," discovered it. Now the "Well-doers" are of the citizens the eldest who are passing from the ranks of the "Horsemen," in each year five; and these are bound during that year in which they pass out from the "Horsemen," to allow themselves to be sent without ceasing to various places by the Spartan State.

68. Lichas then, being one of these, discovered it in Tegea by means both of fortune and ability. For as there were at that time dealings under truce with the men of Tegea, he had come to a forge there and was looking at iron being wrought; and he was in wonder as he saw that which was being done. The smith therefore, perceiving that he marveled at it, ceased from his work and said: "Surely, thou stranger of Lacedaemon, if thou hadst seen that which I once saw, thou wouldst have marveled much, since now it falls out that thou dost marvel so greatly at the working of this iron; for I, desiring in this enclosure to make a well, lighted in my digging upon a coffin of seven cubits in length; and not believing that ever there had been men larger than those of the present day, I opened it, and I saw that the dead body was equal in length to the coffin: then after I had measured it, I filled in the earth over it again." He then thus told him of that which he had seen; and the other, having thought upon that which was told, conjectured that this was Orestes according to the saying of the Oracle, forming his conjecture in the following manner:—whereas he saw that the smith had two pairs of bellows, he concluded that these were the winds spoken of, and that the anvil and the hammer were the stroke and the stroke in return, and that the iron which was being wrought was the trouble laid upon trouble, making comparison by the thought that iron has been discovered for the evil of mankind. Having thus conjectured he came back to Sparta and declared the whole matter to the Lacedemonians; and they brought a charge against him on a fictitious pretext and drove him out into exile. So having come to Tegea, he told the smith of his evil fortune and endeavored to hire from him the enclosure, but at first he would not allow him to have it: at length however Lichas persuaded him and he took up his abode there; and he dug up the grave and gathered together the bones and went with them away to Sparta. From that time, whenever they made trial of one another, the Lacedemonians had much the advantage in the war; and by now they had subdued to themselves the greater part of Peloponnesus besides.

69. Croesus accordingly being informed of all these things was sending messengers to Sparta with gifts in their hands to ask for an alliance, having commanded them what they ought to say: and they when they came said: "Croesus king of the Lydians and also of other nations sent us hither and saith as follows: O Lacedemonians, whereas the god by an oracle bade me join with myself the Hellene as a friend, therefore, since I am informed that ye are the chiefs of Hellas, I invite you according to the oracle, desiring to be your friend and your ally apart from all guile and deceit." Thus did Croesus announce to the Lacedemonians through his messengers; and the Lacedemonians, who themselves also had heard of the oracle given to Croesus, were pleased at the coming of the Lydians and exchanged oaths of friendship and alliance: for they were bound to Croesus also by some services rendered to them even before this time; since the Lacedemonians had sent to Sardis and were buying gold there with purpose of using it for the image of Apollo which is now set up on Mount Thornax in the Lacedemonian land; and Croesus, when they desired to buy it, gave it them as a gift.

70. For this reason therefore the Lacedemonians accepted the alliance, and also because he chose them as his friends, preferring them to all the other Hellenes. And not only were they ready themselves when he made his offer, but they caused a mixing-bowl to be made of bronze, covered outside with figures round the rim and of such a size as to hold three hundred amphors, and this they conveyed, desiring to give it as a gift in return to Croesus. This bowl never came to Sardis for reasons of which two accounts are given as

follows:—The Lacedemonians say that when the bowl was on its way to Sardis and came opposite the land of Samos, the men of Samos having heard of it sailed out with ships of war and took it away; but the Samians themselves say that the Lacedemonians who were conveying the bowl, finding that they were too late and hearing that Sardis had been taken and Croesus was a prisoner, sold the bowl in Samos, and certain private persons bought it and dedicated it as a votive offering in the temple of Hera; and probably those who had sold it would say when they returned to Sparta that it had been taken from them by the Samians.

71. Thus then it happened about the mixing-bowl: but meanwhile Croesus, mistaking the meaning of the oracle, was making a march into Cappadokia, expecting to overthrow Cyrus and the power of the Persians: and while Croesus was preparing to march against the Persians, one of the Lydians, who even before this time was thought to be a wise man but in consequence of this opinion got a very great name for wisdom among the Lydians, had advised Croesus as follows (the name of the man was Sandanis):—"O king, thou art preparing to march against men who wear breeches of leather, and the rest of their clothing is of leather also; and they eat food not such as they desire but such as they can obtain, dwelling in a land which is rugged; and moreover they make no use of wine but drink water; and no figs have they for dessert, nor any other good thing. On the one hand, if thou shalt overcome them, what wilt thou take away from them, seeing they have nothing? and on the other hand, if thou shalt be overcome, consider how many good things thou wilt lose; for once having tasted our good things, they will cling to them fast and it will not be possible to drive them away. I for my own part feel gratitude to the gods that they do not put it into the minds of the Persians to march against the Lydians." Thus he spoke not persuading Croesus: for it is true indeed that the Persians before they subdued the Lydians had no luxury nor any good thing.

72. Now the Cappadokians are called by the Hellenes Syrians; and these Syrians, before the Persians had rule, were subjects of the Medes, but at this time they were subjects of Cyrus. For the boundary between the Median empire and the Lydian was the river Halys; and this flows from the mountain-land of Armenia through the Kilikians, and afterwards, as it flows, it has the Matienians on the right hand and the Phrygians on the other side; then passing by these and flowing up towards the North Wind, it bounds on the one side the Cappadokian Syrians and on the left hand the Paphlagonians. Thus the river Halys cuts off from the rest almost all the lower parts of Asia by a line extending from the sea that is opposite Cyprus to the Euxine. And this tract is the neck of the whole peninsula, the distance of the journey being such that five days are spent on the way by a man without encumbrance.

73. Now for the following reasons Croesus was marching into Cappadokia:—first because he desired to acquire the land in addition to his own possessions, and then especially because he had confidence in the oracle and wished to take vengeance on Cyrus for Astyages. For Cyrus the son of Cambyses had conquered Astyages and was keeping him in captivity, who was brother by marriage to Croesus and king of the Medes: and he had become the brother by marriage of Croesus in this manner:—A horde of the nomad Scythians at feud with the rest withdrew and sought refuge in the land of the Medes: and at this time the ruler of the Medes was Kyaxares the son of Phraortes, the son of Deïokes, who at first dealt well with these Scythians, being suppliants for his protection; and esteeming them very highly he delivered boys to them to learn their speech and the art of

shooting with the bow. Then time went by, and the Scythians used to go out continually to the chase and always brought back something; till once it happened that they took nothing, and when they returned with empty hands Kyaxares (being, as he showed on this occasion, not of an eminently good disposition) dealt with them very harshly and used insult towards them. And they, when they had received this treatment from Kyaxares, considering that they had suffered indignity, planned to kill and to cut up one of the boys who were being instructed among them, and having dressed his flesh as they had been wont to dress the wild animals, to bear it to Kyaxares and give it to him, pretending that it was game taken in hunting; and when they had given it, their design was to make their way as quickly as possible to Alyattes the son of Sadyattes at Sardis. This then was done; and Kyaxares with the guests who ate at his table tasted of that meat, and the Scythians having so done became suppliants for the protection of Alyattes.

74. After this, seeing that Alyattes would not give up the Scythians when Kyaxares demanded them, there had arisen war between the Lydians and the Medes lasting five years; in which years the Medes often discomfited the Lydians and the Lydians often discomfited the Medes (and among others they fought also a battle by night): and as they still carried on the war with equally balanced fortune, in the sixth year a battle took place in which it happened, when the fight had begun, that suddenly the day became night. And this change of the day Thales the Milesian had foretold to the Ionians laying down as a limit this very year in which the change took place. The Lydians however and the Medes, when they saw that it had become night instead of day, ceased from their fighting and were much more eager both of them that peace should be made between them. And they who brought about the peace between them were Syennesis the Kilikian and Labynetos the Babylonian: these were they who urged also the taking of the oath by them, and they brought about an interchange of marriages; for they decided that Alyattes should give his daughter Aryenis to Astyages the son of Kyaxares, seeing that without the compulsion of a strong tie agreements are apt not to hold strongly together. Now these nations observe the same ceremonies in taking oaths as the Hellenes, and in addition to them they make incision into the skin of their arms, and then lick up the blood each of the other.

75. This Astyages then, being his mother's father, Cyrus had conquered and made prisoner for a reason which I shall declare in the history which comes after. This then was the complaint which Croesus had against Cyrus when he sent to the Oracles to ask if he should march against the Persians; and when a deceitful answer had come back to him, he marched into the dominion of the Persians, supposing that the answer was favorable to himself. And when Croesus came to the river Halys, then, according to my account, he passed his army across by the bridges which there were; but, according to the account which prevails among the Hellenes, Thales the Milesian enabled him to pass his army across. For, say they, when Croesus was at a loss how his army should pass over the river (since, they add, there were not yet at that time the bridges which now there are), Thales being present in the army caused the river, which flowed then on the left hand of the army, to flow partly also on the right; and he did it thus:—beginning above the camp he proceeded to dig a deep channel, directing it in the form of a crescent moon, so that the river might take the camp there pitched in the rear, being turned aside from its ancient course by this way along the channel, and afterwards passing by the camp might fall again into its ancient course; so that as soon as the river was thus parted in two it became

fordable by both branches: and some say even that the ancient course of the river was altogether dried up. But this tale I do not admit as true, for how then did they pass over the
river as they went back?

76. And Croesus, when he had passed over with his army, came to that place in
Cappadokia which is called Pteria (now Pteria is the strongest place in this country, and is
situated somewhere about in a line with the city of Sinope on the Euxine). Here he
encamped and ravaged the fields of the Syrians. Moreover he took the city of the Pterians,
and sold the people into slavery, and he took also all the towns that lay about it; and the
Syrians, who were not guilty of any wrong, he forced to remove from their homes. Meanwhile Cyrus, having gathered his own forces and having taken up in addition to them all
who dwelt in the region between, was coming to meet Croesus. Before he began however
to lead forth his army, he had sent heralds to the Ionians and tried to induce them to revolt
from Croesus; but the Ionians would not do as he said. Then when Cyrus was come and
had encamped over against Croesus, they made trial of one another by force of arms in the
land of Pteria: and after hard fighting, when many had fallen on both sides, at length,
night having come on, they parted from one the other with no victory on either side.

77. Thus the two armies contended with one another: and Croesus being ill satisfied
with his own army in respect of number (for the army which he had when he fought was
far smaller than that of Cyrus), being dissatisfied with it I say on this account, as Cyrus
did not attempt to advance against him on the following day, marched back to Sardis,
having it in his mind to call the Egyptians to his help according to the oath which they
had taken (for he had made an alliance with Amasis king of Egypt before he made the
alliance with the Lacedemonians), and to summon the Babylonians as well (for with these
also an alliance had been concluded by him, Labynetos being at that time ruler of the
Babylonians), and moreover to send a message to the Lacedemonians bidding them
appear at a fixed time: and then after he had got all these together and had gathered his
own army, his design was to let the winter go by and at the coming of spring to march
against the Persians. So with these thoughts in his mind, as soon as he came to Sardis he
proceeded to send heralds to his several allies to give them notice that by the fifth month
from that time they should assemble at Sardis: but the army which he had with him and
which had fought with the Persians, an army which consisted of mercenary troops, he let
go and disbanded altogether, never expecting that Cyrus, after having contended against
him with such even fortune, would after all march upon Sardis.

78. When Croesus had these plans in his mind, the suburb of the city became of a
sudden all full of serpents; and when these had appeared, the horses leaving off to feed in
their pastures came constantly thither and devoured them. When Croesus saw this he
deemed it to be a portent, as indeed it was: and forthwith he dispatched messengers to the
dwelling of the Telmessians, who interpret omens: and the messengers who were sent to
consult arrived there and learnt from the Telmessians what the portent meant to signify,
but they did not succeed in reporting the answer to Croesus, for before they sailed back to
Sardis Croesus had been taken prisoner. The Telmessians however gave decision thus: that
an army speaking a foreign tongue was to be looked for by Croesus to invade his land,
and that this when it came would subdue the native inhabitants; for they said that the
serpent was born of the soil, while the horse was an enemy and a stranger. The men of
Telmessos thus made answer to Croesus after he was already taken prisoner, not knowing
as yet anything of the things which had happened to Sardis and to Croesus himself.

79. Cyrus, however, so soon as Croesus marched away after the battle which had been fought in Pteria, having learnt that Croesus meant after he had marched away to disband his army, took counsel with himself and concluded that it was good for him to march as quickly as possible to Sardis, before the power of the Lydians should be again gathered together. So when he had resolved upon this, he did it without delay: for he marched his army into Lydia with such speed that he was himself the first to announce his coming to Croesus. Then Croesus, although he had come to a great strait, since his affairs had fallen out altogether contrary to his own expectation, yet proceeded to lead forth the Lydians into battle. Now there was at this time no nation in Asia more courageous or more stout in battle than the Lydian; and they fought on horseback carrying long spears, the men being excellent in horsemanship.

80. So when the armies had met in that plain which is in front of the city of Sardis,—a plain wide and open, through which flow rivers (and especially the river Hyllos) all rushing down to join the largest called Hermos, which flows from the mountain sacred to the Mother surnamed "of Dindymos" and runs out into the sea by the city of Phocaia,— then Cyrus, when he saw the Lydians being arrayed for battle, fearing their horsemen, did on the suggestion of Harpagos a Mede as follows:—all the camels which were in the train of his army carrying provisions and baggage he gathered together, and he took off their burdens and set men upon them provided with the equipment of cavalry: and having thus furnished them forth he appointed them to go in front of the rest of the army towards the horsemen of Croesus; and after the camel-troop he ordered the infantry to follow; and behind the infantry he placed his whole force of cavalry. Then when all his men had been placed in their several positions, he charged them to spare none of the other Lydians, slaying all who might come in their way, but Croesus himself they were not to slay, not even if he should make resistance when he was captured. Such was his charge: and he set the camels opposite the horsemen for this reason,—because the horse has a fear of the camel and cannot endure either to see his form or to scent his smell: for this reason then the trick had been devised, in order that the cavalry of Croesus might be useless, that very force wherewith the Lydian king was expecting most to shine. And as they were coming together to the battle, so soon as the horses scented the camels and saw them they turned away back, and the hopes of Croesus were at once brought to naught. The Lydians however for their part did not upon that act as cowards, but when they perceived what was coming to pass they leapt from their horses and fought with the Persians on foot. At length, however, when many had fallen on either side, the Lydians turned to flight; and having been driven within the wall of their fortress they were besieged by the Persians.

81. By these then a siege had been established: but Croesus, supposing that the siege would last a long time, proceeded to send from the fortress other messengers to his allies. For the former messengers were sent round to give notice that they should assemble at Sardis by the fifth month, but these he was sending out to ask them to come to his assistance as quickly as possible, because Croesus was being besieged.

82. So then in sending to his other allies he sent also to Lacedaemon. But these too, the Spartans I mean, had themselves at this very time (for so it had fallen out) a quarrel in hand with the Argives about the district called Thyrea. For this Thyrea, being part of the Argive possessions, the Lacedemonians had cut off and taken for themselves. Now the whole region towards the west extending as far down as Malea was then possessed by the Argives, both the parts situated on the mainland and also the island of Kythera with the

other islands. And when the Argives had come to the rescue to save their territory from being cut off from them, then the two sides came to a parley together and agreed that three hundred should fight of each side, and whichever side had the better in the fight that nation should possess the disputed land: they agreed moreover that the main body of each army should withdraw to their own country, and not stand by while the contest was fought, for fear lest, if the armies were present, one side seeing their countrymen suffering defeat should come up to their support. Having made this agreement they withdrew; and chosen men of both sides were left behind and engaged in fight with one another. So they fought and proved themselves to be equally matched; and there were left at last of six hundred men three, on the side of the Argives Alkenor and Chromios, and on the side of the Lacedemonians Othryades: these were left alive when night came on. So then the two men of the Argives, supposing that they were the victors, set off to run to Argos, but the Lacedemonian Othryades, after having stripped the corpses of the Argives and carried their arms to his own camp, remained in his place. On the next day both the two sides came thither to inquire about the result; and for some time both claimed the victory for themselves, the one side saying that of them more had remained alive, and the others declaring that these had fled away, whereas their own man had stood his ground and had stripped the corpses of the other party: and at length by reason of this dispute they fell upon one another and began to fight; and after many had fallen on both sides, the Lacedemonians were the victors. The Argives then cut their hair short, whereas formerly they were compelled by law to wear it long, and they made a law with a curse attached to it, that from that time forth no man of the Argives should grow the hair long nor their women wear ornaments of gold, until they should have won back Thyrea. The Lacedemonians however laid down for themselves the opposite law to this, namely that they should wear long hair from that time forward, whereas before that time they had not their hair long. And they say that the one man who was left alive of the three hundred, namely Othryades, being ashamed to return to Sparta when all his comrades had been slain, slew himself there in Thyrea.

83. Such was the condition of things at Sparta when the herald from Sardis arrived asking them to come to the assistance of Croesus, who was being besieged. And they notwithstanding their own difficulties, as soon as they heard the news from the herald, were eager to go to his assistance; but when they had completed their preparations and their ships were ready, there came another message reporting that the fortress of the Lydians had been taken and that Croesus had been made prisoner. Then (and not before) they ceased from their efforts, being grieved at the event as at a great calamity.

84. Now the taking of Sardis came about as follows:—When the fourteenth day came after Croesus began to be besieged, Cyrus made proclamation to his army, sending horsemen round to the several parts of it, that he would give gifts to the man who should first scale the wall. After this the army made an attempt; and when it failed, then after all the rest had ceased from the attack, a certain Mardian whose name was Hyroiades made an attempt to approach on that side of the citadel where no guard had been set; for they had no fear that it would ever be taken from that side, seeing that here the citadel is precipitous and unassailable. To this part of the wall alone Meles also, who formerly was king of Sardis, did not carry round the lion which his concubine bore to him, the Telmessians having given decision that if the lion should be carried round the wall, Sardis should be safe from capture: and Meles having carried it round the rest of the wall, that is to say

those parts of the citadel where the fortress was open to attack, passed over this part as being unassailable and precipitous: now this is a part of the city which is turned towards Tmolos. So then this Mardian Hyroiades, having seen on the day before how one of the Lydians had descended on that side of the citadel to recover his helmet which had rolled down from above, and had picked it up, took thought and cast the matter about in his own mind. Then he himself ascended first, and after him came up others of the Persians, and many having thus made approach, Sardis was finally taken and the whole city was given up to plunder.

85. Meanwhile to Croesus himself it happened thus:—He had a son, of whom I made mention before, who was of good disposition enough but deprived of speech. Now in his former time of prosperity Croesus had done everything that was possible for him, and besides other things which he devised he had also sent messengers to Delphi to inquire concerning him. And the Pythian prophetess spoke to him thus:

"Lydian, master of many, much blind to destiny, Croesus,
Do not desire to hear in thy halls that voice which is prayed for,
Voice of thy son; much better if this from thee were removèd,
Since he shall first utter speech in an evil day of misfortune."

Now when the fortress was being taken, one of the Persians was about to slay Croesus taking him for another; and Croesus for his part, seeing him coming on, cared nothing for it because of the misfortune which was upon him, and to him it was indifferent that he should be slain by the stroke; but this voiceless son, when he saw the Persian coming on, by reason of terror and affliction burst the bonds of his utterance and said: "Man, slay not Croesus." This son, I say, uttered voice then first of all, but after this he continued to use speech for the whole time of his life.

86. The Persians then had obtained possession of Sardis and had taken Croesus himself prisoner, after he had reigned fourteen years and had been besieged fourteen days, having fulfilled the oracle in that he had brought to an end his own great empire. So the Persians having taken him brought him into the presence of Cyrus: and he piled up a great pyre and caused Croesus to go up upon it bound in fetters, and along with him twice seven sons of Lydians, whether it was that he meant to dedicate this offering as first-fruits of his victory to some god, or whether he desired to fulfil a vow, or else had heard that Croesus was a god-fearing man and so caused him to go up on the pyre because he wished to know if any one of the divine powers would save him, so that he should not be burnt alive. He, they say, did this; but to Croesus as he stood upon the pyre there came, although he was in such evil case, a memory of the saying of Solon, how he had said with divine inspiration that no one of the living might be called happy. And when this thought came into his mind, they say that he sighed deeply and groaned aloud, having been for long silent, and three times he uttered the name of Solon. Hearing this, Cyrus bade the interpreters ask Croesus who was this person on whom he called; and they came near and asked. And Croesus for a time, it is said, kept silence when he was asked this, but afterwards being pressed he said: "One whom more than much wealth I should have desired to have speech with all monarchs." Then, since his words were of doubtful import, they asked again of that which he said; and as they were urgent with him and gave him no peace, he told how once Solon an Athenian had come, and having inspected all his wealth

had made light of it, with such and such words; and how all had turned out for him according as Solon had said, not speaking at all especially with a view to Croesus himself, but with a view to the whole human race and especially those who seem to themselves to be happy men. And while Croesus related these things, already the pyre was lighted and the edges of it roundabout were burning. Then they say that Cyrus, hearing from the interpreters what Croesus had said, changed his purpose and considered that he himself also was but a man, and that he was delivering another man, who had been not inferior to himself in felicity, alive to the fire; and moreover he feared the requital, and reflected that there was nothing of that which men possessed which was secure; therefore, they say, he ordered them to extinguish as quickly as possible the fire that was burning, and to bring down Croesus and those who were with him from the pyre; and they using endeavors were not able now to get the mastery of the flames.

87. Then it is related by the Lydians that Croesus, having learned how Cyrus had changed his mind, and seeing that everyone was trying to put out the fire but that they were no longer able to check it, cried aloud entreating Apollo that if any gift had ever been given by him which had been acceptable to the god, he would come to his aid and rescue him from the evil which was now upon him. So he with tears entreated the god, and suddenly, they say, after clear sky and calm weather clouds gathered and a storm burst, and it rained with a very violent shower, and the pyre was extinguished. Then Cyrus, having perceived that Croesus was a lover of the gods and a good man, caused him to be brought down from the pyre and asked him as follows: "Croesus, tell me who of all men was it who persuaded thee to march upon my land and so to become an enemy to me instead of a friend?" and he said: "O king, I did this to thy felicity and to my own misfortune, and the causer of this was the god of the Hellenes, who incited me to march with my army. For no one is so senseless as to choose of his own will war rather peace, since in peace the sons bury their fathers, but in war the fathers bury their sons. But it was pleasing, I suppose, to the divine powers that these things should come to pass thus."

88. So he spoke, and Cyrus loosed his bonds and caused him to sit near himself and paid to him much regard, and he marveled both himself and all who were about him at the sight of Croesus. And Croesus wrapped in thought was silent; but after a time, turning round and seeing the Persians plundering the city of the Lydians, he said: "O king, must I say to thee that which I chance to have in my thought, or must I keep silent in this my present fortune?" Then Cyrus bade him say boldly whatsoever he desired; and he asked him saying: "What is the business that this great multitude of men is doing with so much eagerness?" and he said: "They are plundering thy city and carrying away thy wealth." And Croesus answered: "Neither is it my city that they are plundering nor my wealth which they are carrying away; for I have no longer any property in these things: but it is thy wealth that they are carrying and driving away."

89. And Cyrus was concerned by that which Croesus had said, and he caused all the rest to withdraw and asked Croesus what he discerned for his advantage as regards that which was being done; and he said: "Since the gods gave me to thee as a slave, I think it right if I discern anything more than others to signify it to thee. The Persians, who are by nature unruly, are without wealth: if therefore thou shalt suffer them to carry off in plunder great wealth and to take possession of it, then it is to be looked for that thou wilt experience this result, thou must expect namely that whosoever gets possession of the largest share will make insurrection against thee. Now therefore, if that which I say is

pleasing to thee, do this:—set spearmen of thy guard to watch at all the gates, and let these take away the things, and say to the men who were bearing them out of the city that they must first be tithed for Zeus: and thus thou on the one hand wilt not be hated by them for taking away the things by force, and they on the other will willingly let the things go, acknowledging within themselves that thou art doing that which is just."

90. Hearing this, Cyrus was above measure pleased, because he thought that Croesus advised well; and he commended him much and enjoined the spearmen of his guard to perform that which Croesus had advised: and after that he spoke to Croesus thus: "Croesus, since thou art prepared, like a king as thou art, to do good deeds and speak good words, therefore ask me for a gift, whatsoever thou desirest to be given thee forthwith." And he said: "Master, thou wilt most do me a pleasure if thou wilt permit me to send to the god of the Hellenes, whom I honored most of all gods, these fetters, and to ask him whether it is accounted by him right to deceive those who do well to him." Then Cyrus asked him what accusation he made against the god, that he thus requested; and Croesus repeated to him all that had been in his mind, and the answers of the Oracles, and especially the votive offerings, and how he had been incited by the prophecy to march upon the Persians: and thus speaking he came back again to the request that it might be permitted to him to make this reproach against the god. And Cyrus laughed and said: "Not this only shalt thou obtain from me, Croesus, but also whatsoever thou mayst desire of me at any time." Hearing this Croesus sent certain of the Lydians to Delphi, enjoining them to lay the fetters upon the threshold of the temple and to ask the god whether he felt no shame that he had incited Croesus by his prophecies to march upon the Persians, persuading him that he should bring to an end the empire of Cyrus, seeing that these were the first-fruits of spoil which he had won from it,—at the same time displaying the fetters. This they were to ask, and moreover also whether it was thought right by the gods of the Hellenes to practice ingratitude.

91. When the Lydians came and repeated that which they were enjoined to say, it is related that the Pythian prophetess spoke as follows: "The fated destiny it is impossible even for a god to escape. And Croesus paid the debt due for the sin of his fifth ancestor, who being one of the spearmen of the Heracleidai followed the treacherous device of a woman, and having slain his master took possession of his royal dignity, which belonged not to him of right. And although Loxias eagerly desired that the calamity of Sardis might come upon the sons of Croesus and not upon Croesus himself, it was not possible for him to draw the Destinies aside from their course; but so much as these granted he brought to pass, and gave it as a gift to Croesus: for he put off the taking of Sardis by three years; and let Croesus be assured that he was taken prisoner later by these years than the fated time: moreover secondly, he assisted him when he was about to be burnt. And as to the oracle which was given, Croesus finds fault with good ground: for Loxias told him beforehand that if he should march upon the Persians he should destroy a great empire: and he upon hearing this, if he wished to take counsel well, ought to have sent and asked further whether the god meant his own empire or that of Cyrus: but as he did not comprehend that which was uttered and did not ask again, let him pronounce himself to be the cause of that which followed. To him also when he consulted the Oracle for the last time Loxias said that which he said concerning a mule; but this also he failed to comprehend: for Cyrus was in fact this mule, seeing that he was born of parents who were of two different races, his mother being of nobler descent and his father of less noble: for she was a

Median woman, daughter of Astyages and king of the Medes, but he was a Persian, one of a race subject to the Medes, and being inferior in all respects he was the husband of one who was his royal mistress." Thus the Pythian prophetess replied to the Lydians, and they brought the answer back to Sardis and repeated it to Croesus; and he, when he heard it, acknowledged that the fault was his own and not that of the god. With regard then to the empire of Croesus and the first conquest of Ionia, it happened thus.

92. Now there are in Hellas many other votive offerings made by Croesus and not only those which have been mentioned: for first at Thebes of the Boeotians there is a tripod of gold, which he dedicated to the Ismenian Apollo; then at Ephesos there are the golden cows and the greater number of the pillars of the temple; and in the temple of Athene Pronaia at Delphi a large golden shield. These were still remaining down to my own time, but others of his votive offerings have perished: and the votive offerings of Croesus at Branchidai of the Milesians were, as I am told, equal in weight and similar to those at Delphi. Now those which he sent to Delphi and to the temple of Amphiaraos he dedicated of his own goods and as first-fruits of the wealth inherited from his father; but the other offerings were made of the substance of a man who was his foe, who before Croesus became king had been factious against him and had joined in endeavoring to make Pantaleon ruler of the Lydians. Now Pantaleon was a son of Alyattes and a brother of Croesus, but not by the same mother, for Croesus was born to Alyattes of a Carian woman, but Pantaleon of an Ionian. And when Croesus had gained possession of the kingdom by the gift of his father, he put to death the man who opposed him, drawing him upon the carding-comb; and his property, which even before that time he had vowed to dedicate, he then offered in the manner mentioned to those shrines which have been named. About his votive offerings let it suffice to have said so much.

93. Of marvels to be recorded the land of Lydia has no great store as compared with other lands, excepting the gold-dust which is carried down from Tmolos; but one work it has to show which is larger far than any other except only those in Egypt and Babylon: for there is there the sepulchral monument of Alyattes the father of Croesus, of which the base is made of larger stones and the rest of the monument is of earth piled up. And this was built by contributions of those who practiced trade and of the artisans and the girls who plied their traffic there; and still there existed to my own time boundary-stones five in number erected upon the monument above, on which were carved inscriptions telling how much of the work was done by each class; and upon measurement it was found that the work of the girls was the greatest in amount. For the daughters of the common people in Lydia practice prostitution one and all, to gather for themselves dowries, continuing this until the time when they marry; and the girls give themselves away in marriage. Now the circuit of the monument is six furlongs and two hundred feet, and the breadth is thirteen hundred feet. And adjoining the monument is a great lake, which the Lydians say has a never-failing supply of water, and it is called the lake of Gyges. Such is the nature of this monument.

94. Now the Lydians have very nearly the same customs as the Hellenes, with the exception that they prostitute their female children; and they were the first of men, so far as we know, who struck and used coin of gold or silver; and also they were the first retail-traders. And the Lydians themselves say that the games which are now in use among them and among the Hellenes were also their invention. These they say were invented among them at the same time as they colonized Tyrsenia, and this is the

account they give of them:—In the reign of Atys the son of Manes their king there came to be a grievous dearth over the whole of Lydia; and the Lydians for a time continued to endure it, but afterwards, as it did not cease, they sought for remedies; and one devised one thing and another of them devised another thing. And then were discovered, they say, the ways of playing with the dice and the knucklebones and the ball, and all the other games excepting draughts (for the discovery of this last is not claimed by the Lydians). These games they invented as a resource against the famine, and thus they used to do:—on one of the days they would play games all the time in order that they might not feel the want of food, and on the next they ceased from their games and had food: and thus they went on for eighteen years. As however the evil did not slacken but pressed upon them ever more and more, therefore their king divided the whole Lydian people into two parts, and he appointed by lot one part to remain and the other to go forth from the land; and the king appointed himself to be over that one of the parts which had the lot to stay in the land, and his son to be over that which was departing; and the name of his son was Tyrsenos. So the one party of them, having obtained the lot to go forth from the land, went down to the sea at Smyrna and built ships for themselves, wherein they placed all the movable goods which they had and sailed away to seek for means of living and a land to dwell in; until after passing by many nations they came at last to the land of the Ombricans, and there they founded cities and dwell up to the present time: and changing their name they were called after the king's son who led them out from home, not Lydians but Tyrsenians, taking the name from him.

The Lydians then had been made subject to the Persians as I say:

95, and after this our history proceeds to inquire about Cyrus, who he was that destroyed the empire of Croesus, and about the Persians, in what manner they obtained the lead of Asia. Following then the report of some of the Persians,—those I mean who do not desire to glorify the history of Cyrus but to speak that which is in fact true,—according to their report, I say, I shall write; but I could set forth also the other forms of the story in three several ways.

The Assyrians ruled Upper Asia for five hundred and twenty years, and from them the Medes were the first who made revolt. These having fought for their freedom with the Assyrians proved themselves good men, and thus they pushed off the yoke of slavery from themselves and were set free; and after them the other nations also did the same as the Medes: and when all on the continent were thus independent, they returned again to despotic rule as follows:—

96. There appeared among the Medes a man of great ability whose name was Deïokes, and this man was the son of Phraortes. This Deïokes, having formed a desire for despotic power, did thus:—whereas the Medes dwelt in separate villages, he, being even before that time of great repute in his own village, set himself to practice just dealing much more and with greater zeal than before; and this he did although there was much lawlessness throughout the whole of Media, and although he knew that injustice is ever at feud with justice. And the Medes of the same village, seeing his manners, chose him for their judge. So he, since he was aiming at power, was upright and just, and doing thus he had no little praise from his fellow-citizens, insomuch that those of the other villages learning that Deïokes was a man who more than all others gave decision rightly, whereas before this they had been wont to suffer from unjust judgments, themselves also when they heard it

came gladly to Deïokes to have their causes determined, and at last they trusted the business to no one else.

97. Then, as more and more continually kept coming to him, because men learnt that his decisions proved to be according to the truth, Deïokes perceiving that everything was referred to himself would no longer sit in the place where he used formerly to sit in public to determine causes, and said that he would determine causes no more, for it was not profitable for him to neglect his own affairs and to determine causes for his neighbors all through the day. So then, since robbery and lawlessness prevailed even much more in the villages than they did before, the Medes having assembled together in one place considered with one another and spoke about the state in which they were: and I suppose the friends of Deïokes spoke much to this effect: "Seeing that we are not able to dwell in the land under the present order of things, let us set up a king from among ourselves, and thus the land will be well governed and we ourselves shall turn to labor, and shall not be ruined by lawlessness." By some such words as these they persuaded themselves to have a king.

98. And when they straightway proposed the question whom they should set up to be king, Deïokes was much put forward and commended by everyone, until at last they agreed that he should be their king. And he bade them build for him a palace worthy of the royal dignity and strengthen him with a guard of spearmen. And the Medes did so: for they built him a large and strong palace in that part of the land which he told them, and they allowed him to select spearmen from all the Medes. And when he had obtained the rule over them, he compelled the Medes to make one fortified city and pay chief attention to this, having less regard to the other cities. And as the Medes obeyed him in this also, he built large and strong walls, those which are now called Agbatana, standing in circles one within the other. And this wall is so contrived that one circle is higher than the next by the height of the battlements alone. And to some extent, I suppose, the nature of the ground, seeing that it is on a hill, assists towards this end; but much more was it produced by art, since the circles are in all seven in number. And within the last circle are the royal palace and the treasure-houses. The largest of these walls is in size about equal to the circuit of the wall round Athens; and of the first circle the battlements are white, of the second black, of the third crimson, of the fourth blue, of the fifth red: thus are the battlements of all the circles colored with various tints, and the two last have their battlements one of them overlaid with silver and the other with gold.

99. These walls then Deïokes built for himself and round his own palace, and the people he commanded to dwell round about the wall. And after all was built, Deïokes established the rule, which he was the first to establish, ordaining that none should enter into the presence of the king, but that they deal with him always through messengers; and that the king should be seen by no one; and moreover that to laugh or to spit in presence is unseemly, and this last for every one without exception. Now he surrounded himself with this state to the end that his fellows, who had been brought up with him and were of no meaner family nor behind him in manly virtue, might not be grieved by seeing him and make plots against him, but that being unseen by them he might be thought to be of different mould.

100. Having set these things in order and strengthened himself in his despotism, he was severe in preserving justice; and the people used to write down their causes and send them in to his presence, and he determined the questions which were brought in to him

and sent them out again. Thus he used to do about the judgment of causes; and he also took order for this, that is to say, if he heard that any one was behaving in an unruly manner, he sent for him and punished him according as each act of wrong deserved, and he had watchers and listeners about all the land over which he ruled.

101. Deïokes then united the Median race alone, and was ruler of this: and of the Medes there are the tribes which here follow, namely, Busai, Paretakenians, Struchates, Arizantians, Budians, Magians: the tribes of the Medes are so many in number.

102. Now the son of Deïokes was Phraortes, who when Deïokes was dead, having been king for three-and-fifty years, received the power in succession; and having received it he was not satisfied to be ruler of the Medes alone, but marched upon the Persians; and attacking them first before others, he made these first subject to the Medes. After this, being ruler of these two nations and both of them strong, he proceeded to subdue Asia going from one nation to another, until at last he marched against the Assyrians, those Assyrians I mean who dwelt at Nineveh, and who formerly had been rulers of the whole, but at that time they were left without support their allies having revolted from them, though at home they were prosperous enough. Phraortes marched, I say, against these, and was both himself slain, after he had reigned two-and-twenty years, and the greater part of his army was destroyed.

103. When Phraortes had brought his life to an end, Kyaxares the son of Phraortes, the son of Deïokes, received the power. This king is said to have been yet much more warlike than his forefathers; and he first banded the men of Asia into separate divisions, that is to say, he first arrayed apart from one another the spearmen and the archers and the horse-men, for before that time they were all mingled together without distinction. This was he who fought with the Lydians when the day became night as they fought, and who also united under his rule the whole of Asia above the river Halys. And having gathered together all his subjects he marched upon Nineveh to avenge his father, and also because he desired to conquer that city. And when he had fought a battle with the Assyrians and had defeated them, while he was sitting down before Nineveh there came upon him a great army of Scythians, and the leader of them was Madyas the son of Protohyas, king of the Scythians. These had invaded Asia after driving the Kimmerians out of Europe, and in pursuit of them as they fled they had come to the land of Media.

104. Now from the Maiotian lake to the river Phasis and to the land of the Colchians is a journey of thirty days for one without encumbrance; and from Colchis it is not far to pass over to Media, for there is only one nation between them, the Saspeirians, and passing by this nation you are in Media. However the Scythians did not make their inva-sion by this way, but turned aside from it to go by the upper road which is much longer, keeping Mount Caucasus on their right hand. Then the Medes fought with the Scythians, and having been worsted in the battle they lost their power, and the Scythians obtained rule over all Asia.

105. Thence they went on to invade Egypt; and when they were in Syria which is called Palestine, Psammetichos king of Egypt met them; and by gifts and entreaties he turned them from their purpose, so that they should not advance any further: and as they retreated, when they came to the city of Ascalon in Syria, most of the Scythians passed through without doing any damage, but a few of them who had stayed behind plundered the temple of Aphrodite Urania. Now this temple, as I find by inquiry, is the most ancient of all the temples which belong to this goddess; for the temple in Cyprus was founded

from this, as the people of Cyprus themselves report, and it was the Phoenicians who founded the temple in Kythera, coming from this land of Syria. So these Scythians who had plundered the temple at Ascalon, and their descendants forever, were smitten by the divinity with a disease which made them women instead of men: and the Scythians say that it was for this reason that they were diseased, and that for this reason travelers who visit Scythia now, see among them the affection of those who by the Scythians are called *Enareës*.

106. For eight-and-twenty years then the Scythians were rulers of Asia, and by their unruliness and reckless behavior everything was ruined; for on the one hand they exacted that in tribute from each people which they laid upon them, and apart from the tribute they rode about and carried off by force the possessions of each tribe. Then Kyaxares with the Medes, having invited the greater number of them to a banquet, made them drunk and slew them; and thus the Medes recovered their power, and had rule over the same nations as before; and they also took Nineveh,—the manner how it was taken I shall set forth in another history, —and made the Assyrians subject to them excepting only the land of Babylon.

107. After this Kyaxares died, having reigned forty years including those years during which the Scythians had rule, and Astyages son of Kyaxares received from him the kingdom. To him was born a daughter whom he named Mandane; and in his sleep it seemed to him that there passed from her so much water as to fill his city and also to flood the whole of Asia. This dream he delivered over to the Magian interpreters of dreams, and when he heard from them the truth at each point he became afraid. And afterwards when this Mandane was of an age to have a husband, he did not give her in marriage to any one of the Medes who were his peers, because he feared the vision; but he gave her to a Persian named Cambyses, whom he found to be of a good descent and of a quiet disposition, counting him to be in station much below a Mede of middle rank.

108. And when Mandane was married to Cambyses, in the first year Astyages saw another vision. It seemed to him that from the womb of this daughter a vine grew, and this vine overspread the whole of Asia. Having seen this vision and delivered it to the interpreters of dreams, he sent for his daughter, being then with child, to come from the land of the Persians. And when she had come he kept watch over her, desiring to destroy that which should be born of her; for the Magian interpreters of dreams signified to him that the offspring of his daughter should be king in his room. Astyages then desiring to guard against this, when Cyrus was born, called Harpagos, a man who was of kin near him and whom he trusted above all the other Medes, and had made him manager of all his affairs; and to him he said as follows: "Neglect not by any means, Harpagos, the matter which I shall lay upon thee to do, and beware lest thou set me aside, and choosing the advantage of others instead, bring thyself afterwards to destruction. Take the child which Mandane bore, and carry it to thy house and slay it; and afterwards bury it in whatsoever manner thou thyself desirest." To this he made answer: "O king, never yet in any past time didst thou discern in me an offence against thee, and I keep watch over myself also with a view to the time that comes after, that I may not commit any error towards thee. If it is indeed thy pleasure that this should so be done, my service at least must be fitly rendered."

109. Thus he made answer, and when the child had been delivered to him adorned as for death, Harpagos went weeping to his wife all the words which had been spoken by

Astyages. And she said to him: "Now, therefore, what is it in thy mind to do?" and he made answer: "Not according as Astyages enjoined: for not even if he shall come to be yet more out of his senses and more mad than he now is, will I agree to his will or serve him in such a murder as this. And for many reasons I will not slay the child; first because he is a kin to me, and then because Astyages is old and without male issue, and if after he is dead the power shall come through me, does not the greatest of dangers then await me? To secure me, this child must die; but one of the servants of Astyages must be the slayer of it, and not one of mine."

110. Thus he spoke, and straightway sent a messenger to that one of the herdsmen of Astyages who he knew fed his herds on the pastures which were most suitable for his purpose, and on the mountains most haunted by wild beasts. The name of this man was Mitradates, and he was married to one who was his fellow-slave; and the name of the woman to whom he was married was Kyno in the tongue of the Hellenes and in the Median tongue Spaco, for what the Hellenes call *kyna* (bitch) the Medes call *spaca*. Now, it was on the skirts of the mountains that this herdsman had his cattle-pastures, from Agbatana towards the North Wind and towards the Euxine Sea. For here in the direction of the Saspeirians the Median land is very mountainous and lofty and thickly covered with forests; but the rest of the land of Media is all level plain. So when this herdsman came, being summoned with much urgency, Harpagos said these words: "Astyages bids thee take this child and place it on the most desolate part of the mountains, so that it may perish as quickly as possible. And he bade me to say that if thou do not kill it, but in any way shalt preserve it from death, he will slay thee by the most evil kind of destruction: and I have been appointed to see that the child is laid forth."

111. Having heard this and having taken up the child, the herdsman went back by the way he came, and arrived at his dwelling. And his wife also, as it seems, having been every day on the point of bearing a child, by a providential chance brought her child to birth just at that time, when the herdsman was gone to the city. And both were in anxiety, each for the other, the man having fear about the child-bearing of his wife, and the woman about the cause why Harpagos had sent to summon her husband, not having been wont to do so aforetime. So as soon as he returned and stood before her, the woman seeing him again beyond her hopes was the first to speak, and asked him for what purpose Harpagos had sent for him so urgently. And he said: "Wife, when I came to the city I saw and heard that which I would I had not seen, and which I should wish had never chanced to those whom we serve. For the house of Harpagos was all full of mourning, and I being astonished thereat went within: and as soon as I entered I saw laid out to view an infant child gasping for breath and screaming, which was adorned with gold ornaments and embroidered clothing: and when Harpagos saw me he bade me forthwith to take up the child and carry it away and lay it on that part of the mountains which is most haunted by wild beasts, saying that it was Astyages who laid this task upon me, and using to me many threats, if I should fail to do this. And I took it up and bore it away, supposing that it was the child of some one of the servants of the house, for never could I have supposed whence it really was; but I marveled to see it adorned with gold and raiment, and I marveled also because mourning was made for it openly in the house of Harpagos. And straightway as we went by the road, I learnt the whole of the matter from the servant who went with me out of the city and placed in my hands the babe, namely that it was in truth the son of Mandane the daughter of

Astyages, and of Cambyses the son of Cyrus, and that Astyages bade slay it. And now here it is."

112. And as he said this the herdsman uncovered it and showed it to her. And she, seeing that the child was large and of fair form, wept and clung to the knees of her husband, beseeching him by no means to lay it forth. But he said that he could not do otherwise than so, for watchers would come backwards and forwards sent by Harpagos to see that this was done, and he would perish by a miserable death if he should fail to do this. And as she could not after all persuade her husband, the wife next said as follows: "Since then I am unable to persuade thee not to lay it forth, do thou this which I shall tell thee, if indeed it needs must be seen laid forth. I also have borne a child, but I have borne it dead. Take this and expose it, and let us rear the child of the daughter of Astyages as if it were our own. Thus thou wilt not be found out doing a wrong to those whom we serve, nor shall we have taken ill counsel for ourselves; for the dead child will obtain a royal burial and the surviving one will not lose his life."

113. To the herdsman it seemed that, the case standing thus, his wife spoke well, and forthwith he did so. The child which he was bearing to put to death, this he delivered to his wife, and his own, which was dead, he took and placed in the chest in which he had been bearing the other; and having adorned it with all the adornment of the other child, he bore it to the most desolate part of the mountains and placed it there. And when the third day came after the child had been laid forth, the herdsman went to the city, leaving one of his under-herdsmen to watch there, and when he came to the house of Harpagos he said that he was ready to display the dead body of the child; and Harpagos sent the most trusted of his spearmen, and through them he saw and buried the herdsman's child. This then had had burial, but him who was afterwards called Cyrus the wife of the herdsman had received, and was bringing him up, giving him no doubt some other name, not Cyrus.

114. And when the boy was ten years old, it happened with regard to him as follows, and this made him known. He was playing in the village in which were stalls for oxen, he was playing there, I say, with other boys of his age in the road. And the boys in their play chose as their king this one who was called the son of the herdsman: and he set some of them to build palaces and others to be spearmen of his guard, and one of them no doubt he appointed to be the eye of the king, and to one he gave the office of bearing the messages, appointing a work for each one severally. Now one of these boys who was playing with the rest, the son of Artembares a man of repute among the Medes, did not do that which Cyrus appointed him to do; therefore Cyrus bade the other boys seize him hand and foot, and when they obeyed his command he dealt with the boy very roughly, scourging him. But he, so soon as he was let go, being made much more angry because he considered that he had been treated with indignity, went down to the city and complained to his father of the treatment which he had met with from Cyrus, calling him not Cyrus, for this was not yet his name, but the son of the herdsman of Astyages. And Artembares in the anger of the moment went at once to Astyages, taking the boy with him, and he declared that he had suffered things that were unfitting and said: "O king, by thy slave, the son of a herdsman, we have been thus outraged," showing him the shoulders of his son.

115. And Astyages having heard and seen this, wishing to punish the boy to avenge the honor of Artembares, sent for both the herdsman and his son. And when both were present, Astyages looked at Cyrus and said: "Didst thou dare, being the son of so mean a

father as this, to treat with such unseemly insult the son of this man who is first in my favor?" And he replied thus: "Master, I did so to him with right. For the boys of the village, of whom he also was one, in their play set me up as king over them, for I appeared to them most fitted for this place. Now the other boys did what I commanded them, but this one disobeyed and paid no regard, until at last he received the punishment due. If therefore for this I am worthy to suffer any evil, here I stand before thee."

116. While the boy thus spoke, there came upon Astyages a sense of recognition of him and the lineaments of his face seemed to him to resemble his own, and his answer appeared to be somewhat over free for his station, while the time of the laying forth seemed to agree with the age of the boy. Being struck with amazement by these things, for a time he was speechless; and having at length with difficulty recovered himself, he said, desiring to dismiss Artembares, in order that he might get the herdsman by himself alone and examine him: "Artembares, I will so order these things that thou and thy son shall have no cause to find fault"; and so he dismissed Artembares, and the servants upon the command of Astyages led Cyrus within. And when the herdsman was left alone with the king, Astyages being alone with him asked whence he had received the boy, and who it was who had delivered the boy to him. And the herdsman said that he was his own son, and that the mother was living with him still as his wife. But Astyages said that he was not well advised in desiring to be brought to extreme necessity, and as he said this he made a sign to the spearmen of his guard to seize him. So he, as he was being led away to the torture, then declared the story as it really was; and beginning from the beginning he went through the whole, telling the truth about it, and finally ended with entreaties, asking that he would grant him pardon.

117. So when the herdsman had made known the truth, Astyages now cared less about him, but with Harpagos he was very greatly displeased and bade his spearmen summon him. And when Harpagos came, Astyages asked him thus: "By what death, Harpagos, didst thou destroy the child whom I delivered to thee, born of my daughter?" and Harpagos, seeing that the herdsman was in the king's palace, turned not to any false way of speech, lest he should be convicted and found out, but said as follows: "O king, so soon as I received the child, I took counsel and considered how I should do according to thy mind, and how without offence to thy command I might not be guilty of murder against thy daughter and against thyself. I did therefore thus:—I called this herdsman and delivered the child to him, saying first that thou wert he who bade him slay it—and in this at least I did not lie, for thou didst so command. I delivered it, I say, to this man commanding him to place it upon a desolate mountain, and to stay by it and watch it until it should die, threatening him with all kinds of punishment if he should fail to accomplish this. And when he had done that which was ordered and the child was dead, I sent the most trusted of my eunuchs and through them I saw and buried the child. Thus, O king, it happened about this matter, and the child had this death which I say."

118. So Harpagos declared the truth, and Astyages concealed the anger which he kept against him for that which had come to pass, and first he related the matter over again to Harpagos according as he had been told it by the herdsman, and afterwards, when it had been thus repeated by him, he ended by saying that the child was alive and that that which had come to pass was well, "for," continued he, "I was greatly troubled by that which had been done to this child, and I thought it no light thing that I had been made at variance with my daughter. Therefore consider that this is a happy change of fortune, and

first send thy son to be with the boy who is newly come, and then, seeing that I intend to make a sacrifice of thanksgiving for the preservation of the boy to those gods to whom that honor belongs, be here thyself to dine with me."

119. When Harpagos heard this, he did reverence and thought it a great matter that his offence had turned out for his profit and moreover that he had been invited to dinner with happy augury; and so he went to his house. And having entered it straightway, he sent forth his son, for he had one only son of about thirteen years old, bidding him go to the palace of Astyages and do whatsoever the king should command; and he himself being overjoyed told his wife that which had befallen him. But Astyages, when the son of Harpagos arrived, cut his throat and divided him limb from limb, and having roasted some pieces of the flesh and boiled others he caused them to be dressed for eating and kept them ready. And when the time arrived for dinner and the other guests were present and also Harpagos, then before the other guests and before Astyages himself were placed tables covered with flesh of sheep; but before Harpagos was placed the flesh of his own son, all but the head and the hands and the feet, and these were laid aside covered up in a basket. Then when it seemed that Harpagos was satisfied with food, Astyages asked him whether he had been pleased with the banquet; and when Harpagos said that he had been very greatly pleased, they who had been commanded to do this brought to him the head of his son covered up, together with the hands and the feet; and standing near they bade Harpagos uncover and take of them that which he desired. So when Harpagos obeyed and uncovered, he saw the remains of his son; and seeing them he was not overcome with amazement but contained himself: and Astyages asked him whether he perceived of what animal he had been eating the flesh: and he said that he perceived, and that whatsoever the king might do was well pleasing to him. Thus having made answer and taking up the parts of the flesh which still remained he went to his house; and after that, I suppose, he would gather all the parts together and bury them.

120. On Harpagos Astyages laid this penalty; and about Cyrus he took thought, and summoned the same men of the Magians who had given judgment about his dream in the manner which has been said: and when they came, Astyages asked how they had given judgment about his vision; and they spoke according to the same manner, saying that the child must have become king if he had lived on and had not died before. He made answer to them thus: "The child is alive and not dead: and while he was dwelling in the country, the boys of the village appointed him king; and he performed completely all those things which they do who are really kings; for he exercised rule, appointed to their places spearmen of the guard and doorkeepers and bearers of messages and all else. Now therefore, to what does it seem to you that these things tend?" The Magians said: "If the child is still alive and became king without any arrangement, be thou confident concerning him and have good courage, for he shall not be ruler again the second time; since some even of our oracles have had but small results, and that at least which has to do with dreams comes often in the end to a feeble accomplishment." Astyages made answer in these words: "I myself also, O Magians, am most disposed to believe that this is so, namely that since the boy was named king the dream has had its fulfilment and that this boy is no longer a source of danger to me. Nevertheless give counsel to me, having well considered what is likely to be most safe both for my house and for you." Replying to this the Magians said: "To us also, O king, it is of great consequence that thy rule should stand firm; for in the other case it is transferred to strangers, coming round to this boy who is a

Persian, and we being Medes are made slaves and become of no account in the eyes of the Persians, seeing that we are of different race; but while thou art established as our king, who art one of our own nation, we both have our share of rule and receive great honors from thee. Thus then we must by all means have a care of thee and of thy rule. And now, if we saw in this anything to cause fear, we would declare all to thee beforehand: but as the dream has had its issue in a trifling manner, both we ourselves are of good cheer and we exhort thee to be so likewise: and as for this boy, send him away from before thine eyes to the Persians and to his parents."

121. When he heard this Astyages rejoiced, and calling Cyrus spoke to him thus: "My son, I did thee wrong by reason of a vision of a dream which has not come to pass, but thou art yet alive by thine own destiny; now therefore go in peace to the land of the Persians, and I will send with thee men to conduct thee: and when thou art come thither, thou shalt find a father and a mother not after the fashion of Mitradates the herdsman and his wife."

122. Thus having spoken Astyages sent Cyrus away; and when he had returned and come to the house of Cambyses, his parents received him; and after that, when they learnt who he was, they welcomed him not a little, for they had supposed without doubt that their son had perished straightway after his birth; and they inquired in what manner he had survived. And he told them, saying that before this he had not known but had been utterly in error; on the way, however, he had learnt all his own fortunes: for he had supposed without doubt that he was the son of the herdsman of Astyages, but since his journey from the city began he had learnt the whole story from those who conducted him. And he said that he had been brought up by the wife of the herdsman, and continued to praise her throughout, so that Kyno was the chief person in his tale. And his parents took up this name from him, and in order that their son might be thought by the Persians to have been preserved in a more supernatural manner, they set on foot a report that Cyrus when he was exposed had been reared by a bitch: and from that source has come this report.

123. Then as Cyrus grew to be a man, being of all those of his age the most courageous and the best beloved, Harpagos sought to become his friend and sent him gifts, because he desired to take vengeance on Astyages. For he saw not how from himself, who was in a private station, punishment should come upon Astyages; but when he saw Cyrus growing up, he endeavored to make him an ally, finding a likeness between the fortunes of Cyrus and his own. And even before that time he had effected something: for Astyages being harsh towards the Medes, Harpagos communicated severally with the chief men of the Medes, and persuaded them that they must make Cyrus their leader and cause Astyages to cease from being king. When he had effected this and when all was ready, then Harpagos wishing to make known his design to Cyrus, who lived among the Persians, could do it no other way, seeing that the roads were watched, but devised a scheme as follows:—he made ready a hare, and having cut open its belly but without pulling off any of the fur, he put into it, just as it was, a piece of paper, having written upon it that which he thought good; and then he sewed up again the belly of the hare, and giving nets as if he were a hunter to that one of his servants whom he trusted most, he sent him away to the land of the Persians, enjoining him by word of mouth to give the hare to Cyrus, and to tell him at the same time to open it with his own hands and let no one else be present when he did so.

124. This then was accomplished, and Cyrus having received from him the hare, cut it open; and having found within it the paper he took and read it over. And the writing said this: "Son of Cambyses, over thee the gods keep guard, for otherwise thou wouldst never have come to so much good fortune. Do thou therefore take vengeance on Astyages who is thy murderer, for so far as his will is concerned thou art dead, but by the care of the gods and of me thou art still alive; and this I think thou hast long ago learnt from first to last, both how it happened about thyself, and also what things I have suffered from Astyages, because I did not slay thee but gave thee to the herdsman. If therefore thou wilt be guided by me, thou shalt be ruler of all that land over which now Astyages is ruler. Persuade the Persians to revolt, and march any army against the Medes: and whether I shall be appointed leader of the army against thee, or any other of the Medes who are in repute, thou hast what thou desirest; for these will be the first to attempt to destroy Astyages, revolting from him and coming over to thy party. Consider then that here at least all is ready, and therefore do this and do it with speed."

125. Cyrus having heard this began to consider in what manner he might most skillfully persuade the Persians to revolt, and on consideration he found that this was the most convenient way, and so in fact he did:—He wrote first on a paper that which he desired to write, and he made an assembly of the Persians. Then he unfolded the paper and reading from it said that Astyages appointed him commander of the Persians; "and now, O Persians," he continued, "I give you command to come to me each one with a reaping-hook." Cyrus then proclaimed this command. (Now there are of the Persians many tribes, and some of them Cyrus gathered together and persuaded to revolt from the Medes, namely those, upon which all the other Persians depend, the Pasargadai, the Maraphians and the Maspians, and of these the Pasargadai are the most noble, of whom also the Achaimenidai are a clan, whence are sprung the Perseïd kings. But other Persian tribes there are, as follows:—the Panthaliaians, the Derusiaians and the Germanians, these are all tillers of the soil; and the rest are nomad tribes, namely the Daoi, Mardians, Dropicans and Sagartians.)

126. Now there was a certain region of the Persian land which was overgrown with thorns, extending some eighteen or twenty furlongs in each direction; and when all had come with that which they had been before commanded to bring, Cyrus bade them clear this region for cultivation within one day: and when the Persians had achieved the task proposed, then he bade them come to him on the next day bathed and clean. Meanwhile Cyrus, having gathered together in one place all the flocks of goats and sheep and the herds of cattle belonging to his father, slaughtered them and prepared with them to entertain the host of the Persians, and moreover with wine and other provisions of the most agreeable kind. So when the Persians came on the next day, he made them recline in a meadow and feasted them. And when they had finished dinner, Cyrus asked them whether that which they had on the former day or that which they had now seemed to them preferable. They said that the difference between them was great, for the former day had for them nothing but evil, and the present day nothing but good. Taking up this saying Cyrus proceeded to lay bare his whole design, saying: "Men of the Persians, thus it is with you. If ye will do as I say, ye have these and ten thousand other good things, with no servile labor; but if ye will not do as I say, ye have labors like that of yesterday innumerable. Now therefore do as I say and make yourselves free: for I seem to myself to have been born by providential fortune to take these matters in hand; and I think that ye are not

worse men than the Medes, either in other matters or in those which have to do with war. Consider then that this is so, and make revolt from Astyages forthwith."

127. So the Persians having obtained a leader willingly attempted to set themselves free, since they had already for a long time been indignant to be ruled by the Medes: but when Astyages heard that Cyrus was acting thus, he sent a messenger and summoned him; and Cyrus bade the messenger report to Astyages that he would be with him sooner than he would himself desire. So Astyages hearing this armed all the Medes, and blinded by divine providence he appointed Harpagos to be the leader of the army, forgetting what he had done to him. Then when the Medes had marched out and began to fight with the Persians, some of them continued the battle, namely those who had not been made partakers in the design, while others went over to the Persians; but the greater number were willfully slack and fled.

128. So when the Median army had been shamefully dispersed, so soon as Astyages heard of it he said, threatening Cyrus: "But not even so shall Cyrus at least escape punishment." Thus having spoken he first impaled the Magian interpreters of dreams who had persuaded him to let Cyrus go, and then he armed those of the Medes, youths and old men, who had been left behind in the city. These he led out and having engaged battle with the Persians he was worsted, and Astyages himself was taken alive, and he lost also those of the Medes whom he had led forth.

129. Then when Astyages was a prisoner, Harpagos came and stood near him and rejoiced over him and insulted him; and besides other things which he said to grieve him, he asked him especially how it pleased him to be a slave instead of a king, making reference to that dinner at which Astyages had feasted him with the flesh of his own son. He looking at him asked him in return whether he claimed the work of Cyrus as his own deed: and Harpagos said that since he had written the letter, the deed was justly his. Then Astyages declared him to be at the same time the most unskillful and the most unjust of men; the most unskillful because, when it was in his power to become king (as it was, if that which had now been done was really brought about by him), he had conferred the chief power on another, and the most unjust, because on account of that dinner he had reduced the Medes to slavery. For if he must needs confer the kingdom on some other and not keep it himself, it was more just to give this good thing to one of the Medes rather than to one of the Persians; whereas now the Medes, who were guiltless of this, had become slaves instead of masters, and the Persians who formerly were slaves of the Medes had now become their masters.

130. Astyages then, having been king for five-and-thirty years, was thus caused to cease from being king; and the Medes stooped under the yoke of the Persians because of his cruelty, after they had ruled Asia above the river Halys for one hundred and twenty-eight years, except during that period for which the Scythians had rule. Afterwards however it repented them that they had done this, and they revolted from Dareios, and having revolted they were subdued again, being conquered in a battle. At this time then, I say, in the reign of Astyages, the Persians with Cyrus rose up against the Medes and from that time forth were rulers of Asia: but as for Astyages, Cyrus did no harm to him besides, but kept him with himself until he died. Thus born and bred Cyrus became king; and after this he subdued Croesus, who was the first to begin the quarrel, as I have before said; and having subdued him he then became ruler of all Asia.

131. These are the customs, so far as I know, which the Persians practice:—Images and

temples and altars they do not account it lawful to erect, nay they even charge with folly those who do these things; and this, as it seems to me, because they do not account the gods to be in the likeness of men, as do the Hellenes. But it is their wont to perform sacrifices to Zeus going up to the most lofty of the mountains, and the whole circle of the heavens they call Zeus: and they sacrifice to the Sun and the Moon and the Earth, to Fire and to Water and to the Winds: these are the only gods to whom they have sacrificed ever from the first; but they have learnt also to sacrifice to Aphrodite Urania, having learnt it both from the Assyrians and the Arabians; and the Assyrians call Aphrodite Mylitta, the Arabians Alitta, and the Persians Mitra.

132. Now this is the manner of sacrifice for the gods aforesaid which is established among the Persians:—they make no altars neither do they kindle fire; and when they mean to sacrifice they use no libation nor music of the pipe nor chaplets nor meal for sprinkling; but when a man wishes to sacrifice to any one of the gods, he leads the animal for sacrifice to an unpolluted place and calls upon the god, having his *tiara* wreathed round generally with a branch of myrtle. For himself alone separately the man who sacrifices may not request good things in his prayer, but he prays that it may be well with all the Persians and with the king; for he himself also is included of course in the whole body of Persians. And when he has cut up the victim into pieces and boiled the flesh, he spreads a layer of the freshest grass and especially clover, upon which he places forthwith all the pieces of flesh; and when he has placed them in order, a Magian man stands by them and chants over them a theogony (for of this nature they say that their incantation is), seeing that without a Magian it is not lawful for them to make sacrifices. Then after waiting a short time the sacrificer carries away the flesh and uses it for whatever purpose he pleases.

133. And of all days their wont is to honor most that on which they were born, each one: on this they think it right to set out a feast more liberal than on other days; and in this feast the wealthier of them set upon the table an ox or a horse or a camel or an ass, roasted whole in an oven, and the poor among them set out small animals in the same way. They have few solid dishes, but many served up after as dessert, and these not in a single course; and for this reason the Persians say that the Hellenes leave off dinner hungry, because after dinner they have nothing worth mentioning served up as dessert, whereas if any good dessert were served up they would not stop eating so soon. To wine-drinking they are very much given, and it is not permitted for a man to vomit or to make water in presence of another. Thus do they provide against these things; and they are wont to deliberate when drinking hard about the most important of their affairs, and whatsoever conclusion has pleased them in their deliberation, this on the next day, when they are sober, the master of the house in which they happen to be when they deliberate lays before them for discussion: and if it pleases them when they are sober also, they adopt it, but if it does not please them, they let it go: and that on which they have had the first deliberation when they are sober, they consider again when they are drinking.

134. When they meet one another in the roads, by this you may discern whether those who meet are of equal rank,—for instead of greeting by words they kiss one another on the mouth; but if one of them is a little inferior to the other, they kiss one another on the cheeks, and if one is of much less noble rank than the other, he falls down before him and does worship to him. And they honor of all most after themselves those nations which dwell nearest to them, and next those which dwell next nearest, and so they go on giving honor in proportion to distance; and they hold least in honor those who dwell furthest off

from themselves, esteeming themselves to be by far the best of all the human race on every point, and thinking that others possess merit according to the proportion which is here stated, and that those who dwell furthest from themselves are the worst. And under the supremacy of the Medes the various nations used also to govern one another according to the same rule as the Persians observe in giving honor, the Medes governing the whole and in particular those who dwelt nearest to themselves, and these having rule over those who bordered upon them, and those again over the nations that were next to them: for the race went forward thus ever from government by themselves to government through others.

135. The Persians more than any other men admit foreign usages; for they both wear the Median dress judging it to be more comely than their own, and also for fighting the Egyptian corslet: moreover they adopt all kinds of luxuries when they hear of them, and in particular they have learnt from the Hellenes to have commerce with boys. They marry each one several lawful wives, and they get also a much larger number of concubines.

136. It is established as a sign of manly excellence next after excellence in fight, to be able to show many sons; and to those who have most the king sends gifts every year: for they consider number to be a source of strength. And they educate their children, beginning at five years old and going on till twenty, in three things only, in riding, in shooting, and in speaking the truth: but before the boy is five years old he does not come into the presence of his father, but lives with the women; and it is so done for this reason, that if the child should die while he is being bred up, he may not be the cause of any grief to his father.

137. I commend this custom of theirs, and also the one which is next to be mentioned, namely that neither the king himself shall put any to death for one cause alone, nor any of the other Persians for one cause alone shall do hurt that is irremediable to any of his own servants; but if after reckoning he finds that the wrongs done are more in number and greater than the services rendered, then only he gives vent to his anger. Moreover they say that no one ever killed his own father or mother, but whatever deeds have been done which seemed to be of this nature, if examined must necessarily, they say, be found to be due either to changelings or to children of adulterous birth; for, say they, it is not reasonable to suppose that the true parent would be killed by his own son.

138. Whatever things it is not lawful for them to do, these it is not lawful for them even to speak of: and the most disgraceful thing in their estimation is to tell an lie, and next to this to owe money, this last for many other reasons, but especially because it is necessary, they say, for him who owes money, also sometimes to tell lies: and whosoever of the men of the city has leprosy or whiteness of skin, he does not come into a city nor mingle with the other Persians; and they say that he has these diseases because he has offended in some way against the Sun: but a stranger who is taken by these diseases, in many regions they drive out of the country altogether, and also white doves, alleging against them the same cause. And into a river they neither make water nor spit, neither do they wash their hands in it, nor allow any other to do these things, but they reverence rivers very greatly.

139. This moreover also has chanced to them, which the Persians have themselves failed to notice but I have not failed to do so:—their names, which are formed to correspond with their bodily shapes or their magnificence of station, end all with the same letter, that letter which the Dorians call *san* and the Ionians *sigma*; with this you will find,

if you examine the matter, that all the Persian names end, not some with this and others with other letters, but all alike.

140. So much I am able to say for certain from my own knowledge about them: but what follows is reported about their dead as a secret mystery and not with clearness, namely that the body of a Persian man is not buried until it has been torn by a bird or a dog. (The Magians I know for a certainty have this practice, for they do it openly.) However that may be, the Persians cover the body with wax and then bury it in the earth. Now the Magians are distinguished in many ways from other men, as also from the priests in Egypt: for these last esteem it a matter of purity to kill no living creature except the animals which they sacrifice; but the Magians kill with their own hands all creatures except dogs and men, and they even make this a great end to aim at, killing both ants and serpents and all other creeping and flying things. About this custom then be it as it was from the first established; and I return now to the former narrative.

141. The Ionians and Aiolians, as soon as the Lydians had been subdued by the Persians, sent messengers to Cyrus at Sardis, desiring to be his subjects on the same terms as they had been subjects of Croesus. And when he heard that which they proposed to him, he spoke to them a fable, saying that a certain player on the pipe saw fishes in the sea and played on his pipe, supposing that they would come out to land; but being deceived in his expectation, he took a casting-net and enclosed a great multitude of the fishes and drew them forth from the water: and when he saw them leaping about, he said to the fishes: "Stop dancing I pray you now, seeing that ye would not come out and dance before when I piped." Cyrus spoke this fable to the Ionians and Aiolians for this reason, because the Ionians had refused to comply before, when Cyrus himself by a messenger requested them to revolt from Croesus, while now when the conquest had been made they were ready to submit to Cyrus. Thus he said to them in anger, and the Ionians, when they heard this answer brought back to their cities, put walls round about them severally, and gathered together to the Panionion, all except the men of Miletos, for with these alone Cyrus had sworn an agreement on the same terms as the Lydians had granted. The rest of the Ionians resolved by common consent to send messengers to Sparta, to ask the Spartans to help the Ionians.

142. These Ionians to whom belongs the Panionion had the fortune to build their cities in the most favorable position for climate and seasons of any men whom we know: for neither the regions above Ionia nor those below, neither those towards the East nor those towards the West, produce the same results as Ionia itself, the regions in the one direction being oppressed by cold and moisture, and those in the other by heat and drought. And these do not use all the same speech, but have four different variations of language. First of their cities on the side of the South lies Miletos, and next to it Myus and Priene. These are settlements made in Caria, and speak the same language with one another; and the following are in Lydia,—Ephesos, Colophon, Lebedos, Teos, Clazomenai, Phocaia: these cities resemble not at all those mentioned before in the speech which they use, but they agree one with another. There remain besides three Ionian cities, of which two are established in the islands of Samos and Chios, and one is built upon the mainland, namely Erythrai: now the men of Chios and of Erythrai use the same form of language, but the Samians have one for themselves alone. Thus there result four separate forms of language.

143. Of these Ionians then those of Miletos were sheltered from danger, since they had sworn an agreement; and those of them who lived in islands had no cause for fear, for the

Phoenicians were not yet subjects of the Persians and the Persians themselves were not sea-men. Now these were parted off from the other Ionians for no other reason than this: —The whole Hellenic nation was at that time weak, but of all its races the Ionian was much the weakest and of least account: except Athens, indeed, it had no considerable city. Now the other Ionians, and among them the Athenians, avoided the name, not wishing to be called Ionians, nay even now I perceive that the greater number of them are ashamed of the name: but these twelve cities not only prided themselves on the name but established a temple of their own, to which they gave the name of Panionion, and they made resolution not to grant a share in it to any other Ionians (nor indeed did any ask to share it except those of Smyrna);

144, just as the Dorians of that district which is now called the Five Cities but was formerly called the Six Cities, take care not to admit any of the neighboring Dorians to the temple of Triopion, and even exclude from sharing in it those of their own body who commit any offence as regards the temple. For example, in the games of the Triopian Apollo they used formerly to set bronze tripods as prizes for the victors, and the rule was that those who received them should not carry them out of the temple but dedicate them then and there to the god. There was a man then of Halicarnassos, whose name was Agasicles, who being a victor paid no regard to this rule, but carried away the tripod to his own house and hung it up there upon a nail. On this ground the other five cities, Lindos, Ialysos and Cameiros, Cos and Cnidos, excluded the sixth city Halicarnassos from sharing in the temple.

145. Upon these they laid this penalty: but as for the Ionians, I think that the reason why they made of themselves twelve cities and would not receive any more into their body, was because when they dwelt in Peloponnesus there were of them twelve divisions, just as now there are twelve divisions of the Achaians who drove the Ionians out: for first, (beginning from the side of Sikyon) comes Pellene, then Aigeira and Aigai, in which last is the river Crathis with a perpetual flow (whence the river of the same name in Italy received its name), and Bura and Helike, to which the Ionians fled for refuge when they were worsted by the Achaians in fight, and Aigion and Rhypes and Patreis and Phareis and Olenos, where is the great river Peiros, and Dyme and Tritaieis, of which the last alone has an inland position. These form now twelve divisions of the Achaians, and in former times they were divisions of the Ionians.

146. For this reason then the Ionians also made for themselves twelve cities; for at any rate to say that these are any more Ionians than the other Ionians, or have at all a nobler descent, is mere folly, considering that a large part of them are Abantians from Euboea, who have no share even in the name of Ionia, and Minyai of Orchomenos have been mingled with them, and Cadmeians and Dryopians and Phokians who seceded from their native State and Molossians and Pelasgians of Arcadia and Dorians of Epidauros and many other races have been mingled with them; and those of them who set forth to their settlements from the City Hall of Athens and who esteem themselves the most noble by descent of the Ionians, these, I say, brought no women with them to their settlement, but took Carian women, whose parents they slew: and on account of this slaughter these women laid down for themselves a rule, imposing oaths on one another, and handed it on to their daughters, that they should never eat with their husbands, nor should a wife call her own husband by name, for this reason, because the Ionians had slain their fathers and

husbands and children and then having done this had them to wife. This happened at Miletos.

147. Moreover some of them set Lykian kings over them, descendants of Glaucos and Hippolochos, while others were ruled by Cauconians of Pylos, descendants of Codros the son of Melanthos, and others again by princes of the two races combined. Since however these hold on to the name more than the other Ionians, let them be called, if they will, the Ionians of truly pure descent; but in fact all are Ionians who have their descent from Athens and who keep the feast of Apaturia; and this all keep except the men of Ephesos and Colophon: for these alone of all the Ionians do not keep the Apaturia, and that on the ground of some murder committed.

148. Now the Panionion is a sacred place on the north side of Mycale, set apart by common agreement of the Ionians for Poseidon of Helike; and this Mycale is a promontory of the mainland running out Westwards towards Samos, where the Ionians gathering together from their cities used to hold a festival which they called the Panionia. (And not only the feasts of the Ionians but also those of all the Hellenes equally are subject to this rule, that their names all end in the same letter, just like the names of the Persians.)

These then are the Ionian cities:

149, and those of Aiolia are as follows:—Kyme, which is called Phriconis, Larisai, Neon-teichos, Temnos, Killa, Notion, Aigiroëssa, Pitane, Aigaiai, Myrina, Gryneia; these are the ancient cities of the Aiolians, eleven in number, since one, Smyrna, was severed from them by the Ionians; for these cities, that is those on the mainland, used also formerly to be twelve in number. And these Aiolians had the fortune to settle in a land which is more fertile than that of the Ionians but in respect of climate less favored.

150. Now the Aiolians lost Smyrna in the following manner:—certain men of Colophon, who had been worsted in party strife and had been driven from their native city, were received there for refuge: and after this the Colophonian exiles watched for a time when the men of Smyrna were celebrating a festival to Dionysos outside the walls, and then they closed the gates against them and got possession of the city. After this, when the whole body of Aiolians came to the rescue, they made an agreement that the Ionians should give up the movable goods, and that on this condition the Aiolians should abandon Smyrna. When the men of Smyrna had done this, the remaining eleven cities divided them amongst themselves and made them their own citizens.

151. These then are the Aiolian cities upon the mainland, with the exception of those situated on Mount Ida, for these are separate from the rest. And of those which are in the islands, there are five in Lesbos, for the sixth which was situated in Lesbos, namely Arisba, was enslaved by the men of Methymna, though its citizens were of the same race as they; and in Tenedos there is one city, and another in what are called the "Hundred Isles." Now the Lesbians and the men of Tenedos, like those Ionians who dwelt in the islands, had no cause for fear; but the remaining cities came to a common agreement to follow the Ionians whithersoever they should lead.

152. Now when the messengers from the Ionians and Aiolians came to Sparta (for this business was carried out with speed), they chose before all others to speak for them the Phocaian, whose name was Pythermos. He then put upon him a purple cloak, in order that as many as possible of the Spartans might hear of it and come together, and having been introduced before the assembly he spoke at length, asking the Spartans to help them. The

Lacedemonians however would not listen to him, but resolved on the contrary not to help the Ionians. So they departed, and the Lacedemonians, having dismissed the messengers of the Ionians, sent men notwithstanding in a ship of fifty oars, to find out, as I imagine, about the affairs of Cyrus and about Ionia. These when they came to Phocaia sent to Sardis the man of most repute among them, whose name was Lacrines, to report to Cyrus the saying of the Lacedemonians, bidding him do hurt to no city of the Hellas, since they would not permit it.

153. When the herald had spoken thus, Cyrus is said to have asked those of the Hellenes whom he had with him, what men the Lacedemonians were and how many in number, that they made this proclamation to him; and hearing their answer he said to the Spartan herald: "Never yet did I fear men such as these, who have a place appointed in the midst of their city where they gather together and deceive one another by false oaths: and if I continue in good health, not the misfortunes of the Ionians will be for them a subject of talk, but rather their own." These words Cyrus threw out scornfully with reference to the Hellenes in general, because they have got for themselves markets and practice buying and selling there; for the Persians themselves are not wont to use markets nor have they any market-place at all. After this he entrusted Sardis to Tabalos a Persian, and the gold both of Croesus and of the other Lydians he gave to Pactyas a Lydian to take charge of, and himself marched away to Agbatana, taking with him Croesus and making for the present no account of the Ionians. For Babylon stood in his way still, as also the Bactrian nation and the Sacans and the Egyptians; and against these he meant to make expeditions himself, while sending some other commander about the Ionians.

154. But when Cyrus had marched away from Sardis, Pactyas caused the Lydians to revolt from Tabalos and from Cyrus. This man went down to the sea, and having in his possession all the gold that there had been in Sardis, he hired for himself mercenaries and persuaded the men of the sea-coast to join his expedition. So he marched on Sardis and besieged Tabalos, having shut himself up in the citadel.

155. Hearing this on his way, Cyrus said to Croesus as follows: "Croesus, what end shall I find of these things which are coming to pass? The Lydians will not cease as it seems, from giving trouble to me and from having it themselves. I doubt me if it were not best to sell them all as slaves; for as it is, I see that I have done in like manner as if one should slay the father and then spare his sons: just so I took prisoner and am carrying away thee, who wert much more than the father of the Lydians, while to the Lydians themselves I delivered up their city; and can I feel surprise after this that they have revolted from me?" Thus he said what was in his mind, but Croesus answered him as follows, fearing lest he should destroy Sardis: "O king, that which thou hast said is not without reason; but do not thou altogether give vent to thy wrath, nor destroy an ancient city which is guiltless both of the former things and also of those which have come to pass now: for as to the former things it was I who did them and I bear the consequences heaped upon my head; and as for what is now being done, since the wrongdoer is Pactyas to whom thou didst entrust the charge of Sardis, let him pay the penalty. But the Lydians I pray thee pardon, and lay upon them commands as follows, in order that they may not revolt nor be a cause of danger to thee:—send to them and forbid them to possess weapons of war, but bid them on the other hand put on tunics under their outer garments and be shod with buskins, and proclaim to them that they train their sons to play the lyre and the harp and to be retail-dealers; and soon thou shalt see, O king, that they have

become women instead of men, so that there will be no fear that they will revolt from thee."

156. Croesus, I say, suggested to him this, perceiving that this was better for the Lydians than to be reduced to slavery and sold; for he knew that if he did not offer a sufficient reason, he would not persuade Cyrus to change his mind, and he feared lest at some future time, if they should escape the present danger, the Lydians might revolt from the Persians and be destroyed. And Cyrus was greatly pleased with the suggestion made and slackened from his wrath, saying that he agreed with his advice. Then he called Mazares a Mede, and laid charge upon him to proclaim to the Lydians that which Croesus suggested, and moreover to sell into slavery all the rest who had joined with the Lydians in the expedition to Sardis, and finally by all means to bring Pactyas himself alive to Cyrus.

157. Having given this charge upon the road, he continued his march to the native land of the Persians; but Pactyas hearing that an army was approaching to fight against him was struck with fear and fled away forthwith to Kyme. Then Mazares the Mede marched upon Sardis with a certain portion of the army of Cyrus, and as he did not find Pactyas or his followers any longer at Sardis, he first compelled the Lydians to perform the commands of Cyrus, and by his commands the Lydians changed the whole manner of their life. After this Mazares proceeded to send messengers to Kyme bidding them give up Pactyas: and the men of Kyme resolved to refer to the god at Branchidai the question what counsel they should follow. For there was there an Oracle established of old time, which all the Ionians and Aiolians were wont to consult; and this place is in the territory of Miletos above the port of Panormos.

158. So the men of Kyme sent messengers to the Branchidai to inquire of the god, and they asked what course they should take about Pactyas so as to do that which was pleasing to the gods. When they thus inquired, the answer was given them that they should deliver up Pactyas to the Persians: and the men of Kyme, having heard this answer reported, were disposed to give him up. Then when the mass of the people were thus disposed, Aristodicos the son of Heracleides, a man of repute among the citizens, stopped the men of Kyme from doing so, having distrust of the answer and thinking that those sent to inquire were not speaking the truth; until at last other messengers were sent to the Oracle to ask a second time about Pactyas, and of them Aristodicos was one.

159. When these came to Branchidai, Aristodicos stood forth from the rest and consulted the Oracle, asking as follows: Lord, there came to us a suppliant for protection Pactyas the Lydian, flying from a violent death at the hands of the Persians, and they demand him from us, bidding the men of Kyme give him up. But we, though we fear the power of the Persians, yet have not ventured up to this time to deliver to them the suppliant, until thy counsel shall be clearly manifested to us, saying which of the two things we ought to do." He thus inquired, but the god again declared to them the same answer, bidding them deliver up Pactyas to the Persians. Upon this Aristodicos with deliberate purpose did as follows:—he went all round the temple destroying the nests of the sparrows and of all the other kinds of birds which had been hatched on the temple: and while he was doing this, it is said that a voice came from the inner shrine directed to Aristodicos and speaking thus: "Thou most impious of men, why dost thou dare to do this? Dost thou carry away by force from my temple the suppliants for my protection?" And Aristodicos, it is said, not being at all at a loss replied to this: "Lord, dost thou thus come to the assistance of thy suppliants, and yet biddest the men of Kyme deliver up theirs?" and the

god answered him again thus: "Yea, I bid you do so, that ye may perish the more quickly for your impiety; so that ye may not at any future time come to the Oracle to ask about delivering up of suppliants."

160. When the men of Kyme heard this saying reported, not wishing either to be destroyed by giving him up or to be besieged by keeping him with them, they sent him away to Mytilene. Those of Mytilene however, when Mazares sent messages to them, were preparing to deliver up Pactyas for a price, but what the price was I cannot say for certain, since the bargain was never completed; for the men of Kyme, when they learnt that this was being done by the Mytilenians, sent a vessel to Lesbos and conveyed away Pactyas to Chios. After this he was dragged forcibly from the temple of Athene Poliuchos by the Chians and delivered up: and the Chians delivered him up receiving Atarneus in return, (now this Atarneus is a region of Mysia opposition Lesbos). So the Persians having received Pactyas kept him under guard, meaning to produce him before Cyrus. And a long time elapsed during which none of the Chians either used barley-meal grown in this region of Atarneus, for pouring out in sacrifice to any god, or baked cakes for offering of the corn which grew there, but all the produce of this land was excluded from every kind of sacred service.

161. The men of Chios had then delivered up Pactyas; and after this Mazares made expedition against those who had joined in besieging Tabalos: and first he reduced to slavery those of Priene, then he overran the whole plain of the Maiander making spoil of it for his army, and Magnesia in the same manner: and straightway after this he fell sick and died.

162. After he was dead, Harpagos came down to take his place in command, being also a Mede by race (this was the man whom the king of the Medes Astyages feasted with the unlawful banquet, and who helped to give the kingdom to Cyrus). This man, being appointed commander then by Cyrus, came to Ionia and proceeded to take the cities by throwing up mounds against them: for when he had enclosed any people within their walls, then he threw up mounds against the walls and took their city by storm; and the first city of Ionia upon which he made an attempt was Phocaia.

163. Now these Phocaians were the first of the Hellenes who made long voyages, and these are they who discovered the Adriatic and Tyrsenia and Iberia and Tartessos: and they made voyages not in round ships, but in vessels of fifty oars. These came to Tartessos and became friends with the king of the Tartessians whose name was Arganthonios: he was ruler of the Tartessians for eighty years and lived in all one hundred and twenty. With this man, I say, the Phocaians became so exceedingly friendly, that first he bade them leave Ionia and dwell wherever they desired in his own land; and as he did not prevail upon the Phocaians to do this, afterwards, hearing from them of the Mede how his power was increasing, he gave them money to build a wall about their city: and he did this without sparing, for the circuit of the wall is many furlongs in extent, and it is built all of large stones closely fitted together.

164. The wall of the Phocaians was made in this manner: and Harpagos having marched his army against them began to besiege them, at the same time holding forth to them proposals and saying that it was enough to satisfy him if the Phocaians were willing to throw down one battlement of their wall and dedicate one single house. But the Phocaians, being very greatly grieved at the thought of subjection, said that they wished to deliberate about the matter for one day and after that they would give their answer; and

they asked him to withdraw his army from the wall while they were deliberating. Harpagos said that he knew very well what they were meaning to do, nevertheless he was willing to allow them to deliberate. So in the time that followed, when Harpagos had withdrawn his army from the wall, the Phocaians drew down their fifty-oared galleys to the sea, put into them their children and women and all their movable goods, and besides them the images out of the temples and the other votive offerings except such as were made of bronze or stone or consisted of paintings, all the rest, I say, they put into the ships, and having embarked themselves they sailed towards Chios; and the Persians obtained possession of Phocaia, the city being deserted of the inhabitants.

165. But as for the Phocaians, since the men of Chios would not sell them at their request the islands called Oinussai, from the fear lest these islands might be made a seat of trade and their island might be shut out, therefore they set out for Kyrnos: for in Kyrnos twenty years before this they had established a city named Alalia, in accordance with an oracle, (now Arganthonios by that time was dead). And when they were setting out for Kyrnos they first sailed to Phocaia and slaughtered the Persian garrison, to whose charge Harpagos had delivered the city; then after they had achieved this they made solemn imprecations on any one of them who should be left behind from their voyage, and moreover they sank a mass of iron in the sea and swore that not until that mass should appear again on the surface would they return to Phocaia. However as they were setting forth to Kyrnos, more than half of the citizens were seized with yearning and regret for their city and for their native land, and they proved false to their oath and sailed back to Phocaia. But those of them who kept the oath still, weighed anchor from the islands of Oinussai and sailed.

166. When these came to Kyrnos, for five years they dwelt together with those who had come thither before, and they founded temples there. Then, since they plundered the property of all their neighbors, the Tyrsenians and Carthaginians made expedition against them by agreement with one another, each with sixty ships. And the Phocaians also manned their vessels, sixty in number, and came to meet the enemy in that which is called the Sardinian sea: and when they encountered one another in the sea-fight the Phocaians won a kind of Cadmean victory, for forty of their ships were destroyed and the remaining twenty were disabled, having had their prows bent aside. So they sailed in to Alalia and took up their children and their women and their other possessions as much as their ships proved capable of carrying, and then they left Kyrnos behind them and sailed to Rhegion.

167. But as for the crews of the ships that were destroyed, the Carthaginians and Tyrsenians obtained much the greater number of them, and these they brought to land and killed by stoning. After this the men of Agylla found that everything which passed by the spot where the Phocaians were laid after being stoned, became either distorted, or crippled, or paralyzed, both small cattle and beasts of burden and human creatures: so the men of Agylla sent to Delphi desiring to purge themselves of the offence; and the Pythian prophetess bade them do that which the men of Agylla still continue to perform, that is to say, they make great sacrifices in honor of the dead, and hold at the place a contest of athletics and horse-racing. These then of the Phocaians had the fate which I have said; but those of them who took refuge at Rhegion started from thence and took possession of that city in the land of Oinotria which now is called Hyele. This they founded having learnt from a man of Poseidonia that the Pythian prophetess by her answer meant them to found a temple to Kyrnos, who was a hero, and not to found a settlement in the island of Kyrnos.

168. About Phocaia in Ionia it happened thus, and nearly the same thing also was done by the men of Teos: for as soon as Harpagos took their wall with a mound, they embarked in their ships and sailed straightway for Thrace; and there they founded the city of Abdera, which before them Timesios of Clazomenai founded and had no profit therefrom, but was driven out by the Thracians; and now he is honored as a hero by the Teïans in Abdera.

169. These alone of all the Ionians left their native cities because they would not endure subjection: but the other Ionians except the Milesians did indeed contend in arms with Harpagos like those who left their homes, and proved themselves brave men, fighting each for his own native city; but when they were defeated and captured they remained all in their own place and performed that which was laid upon them: but the Milesians, as I have also said before, had made a sworn agreement with Cyrus himself and kept still. Thus for the second time Ionia had been reduced to subjection. And when Harpagos had conquered the Ionians on the mainland, then the Ionians who dwelt in the islands, being struck with fear by these things, gave themselves over to Cyrus.

170. When the Ionians had been thus evilly entreated but were continuing still to hold their gatherings as before at the Panionion, Bias a man of Priene set forth to the Ionians, as I am informed, a most profitable counsel, by following which they might have been the most prosperous of all the Hellenes. He urged that the Ionians should set forth in one common expedition and sail to Sardinia, and after that found a single city for all the Ionians: and thus they would escape subjection and would be prosperous, inhabiting the largest of all islands and being rulers over others; whereas, if they remained in Ionia, he did not perceive, he said, that freedom would any longer exist for them. This was the counsel given by Bias of Priene after the Ionians had been ruined; but a good counsel too was given before the ruin of Ionia by Thales a man of Miletos, who was by descent of Phoenician race. He advised the Ionians to have one single seat of government, and that this should be at Teos (for Teos, he said, was in the center of Ionia), and that the other cities should be inhabited as before, but accounted just as if they were demes.

These men set forth to them counsels of the kind which I have said:

171. but Harpagos, after subduing Ionia, proceeded to march against the Carians and Caunians and Lykians, taking also Ionians and Aiolians to help him. Of these the Carians came to the mainland from the islands; for being of old time subjects of Minos and being called Leleges, they used to dwell in the islands, paying no tribute, so far back as I am able to arrive by hearsay, but whenever Minos required it, they used to supply his ships with seamen: and as Minos subdued much land and was fortunate in his fighting, the Carian nation was of all nations by much the most famous at that time together with him. And they produced three inventions of which the Hellenes adopted the use; that is to say, the Carians were those who first set the fashion of fastening crests on helmets, and of making the devices which are put onto shields, and these also were the first who made handles for their shields, whereas up to that time all who were wont to use shields carried them without handles and with leathern straps to guide them, having them hung about their necks and their left shoulders. Then after the lapse of a long time the Dorians and Ionians drove the Carians out of the islands, and so they came to the mainland. With respect to the Carians the Cretans relate that it happened thus; the Carians themselves however do not agree with this account, but suppose that they are dwellers on the mainland from the beginning, and that they went always by the same name which they have now: and they

point as evidence of this to an ancient temple of Carian Zeus at Mylasa, in which the Mysians and Lydians share as being brother races of the Carians, for they say that Lydos and Mysos were brothers of Car; these share in it, but those who being of another race have come to speak the same language as the Carians, these have no share in it.

172. It seems to me however that the Caunians are dwellers there from the beginning, though they say themselves that they came from Crete: but they have been assimilated to the Carian race in language, or else the Carians to the Caunian race, I cannot with certainty determine which. They have customs however in which they differ very much from all other men as well as from the Carians; for example the fairest thing in their estimation is to meet together in numbers for drinking, according to equality of age or friendship, both men, women, and children; and again when they had founded temples for foreign deities, afterwards they changed their purpose and resolved to worship only their own native gods, and the whole body of Caunian young men put on their armor and made pursuit as far as the borders of the Calyndians, beating the air with their spears; and they said that they were casting the foreign gods out of the land. Such are the customs which these have.

173. The Lykians however have sprung originally from Crete (for in old time the whole of Crete was possessed by Barbarians): and when the sons of Europa, Sarpedon and Minos, came to be at variance in Crete about the kingdom, Minos having got the better in the strife of parties drove out both Sarpedon himself and those of his party: and they having been expelled came to the land of Milyas in Asia, for the land which now the Lykians inhabit was anciently called Milyas, and the Milyans were then called Solymoi. Now while Sarpedon reigned over them, they were called by the name which they had when they came thither, and by which the Lykians are even now called by the neighboring tribes, namely Termilai; but when from Athens Lycos the son of Pandion came to the land of the Termilai and to Sarpedon, he too having been driven out by his brother namely Aigeus, then by the name taken from Lycos they were called after a time Lykians. The customs which these have are partly Cretan and partly Carian; but one custom they have which is peculiar to them, and in which they agree with no other people, that is they call themselves by their mothers and not by their fathers; and if one asks his neighbor who he is, he will state his parentage on the mother's side and enumerate his mother's female ascendants: and if a woman who is a citizen marry a slave, the children are accounted to be of gentle birth; but if a man who is a citizen, though he were the first man among them, have a slave for wife or concubine, the children are without civil rights.

174. Now the Carians were reduced to subjection by Harpagos without any brilliant deed displayed either by the Carians themselves or by those of the Hellenes who dwell in this land. Of these last there are besides others the men of Cnidos, settlers from Lacedaemon, whose land runs out into the sea, being in fact the region which is called Triopion, beginning from the peninsula of Bybassos: and since all the land of Cnidos except a small part is washed by the sea (for the part of it which looks towards the North is bounded by the Gulf of Keramos, and that which looks to the South by the sea off Syme and Rhodes), therefore the men of Cnidos began to dig through this small part, which is about five furlongs across, while Harpagos was subduing Ionia, desiring to make their land an island: and within the isthmus all was theirs, for where the territory of Cnidos ends in the direction of the mainland, here is the isthmus which they were digging across. And while the Cnidians were working at it with a great number of men, it was perceived that the

men who worked suffered injury much more than might have been expected and in a more supernatural manner, both in other parts of their bodies and especially in their eyes, when the rock was being broken up; so they sent men to ask the Oracle at Delphi what the cause of the difficulty was. And the Pythian prophetess, as the men of Cnidos themselves report, gave them this reply in trimeter verse:—

"Fence not the place with towers, nor dig the isthmus through;
Zeus would have made your land an island, had he willed."

When the Pythian prophetess had given this oracle, the men of Cnidos not only ceased from their digging but delivered themselves to Harpagos without resistance, when he came against them with his army.

175. There were also the Pedasians, who dwelt in the inland country above Halicarnas-sos; and among these, whenever anything hurtful is about to happen either to themselves or to their neighbors, the priestess of Athene has a great beard: this befell them three times. These of all about Caria were the only men who held out for any time against Harpagos, and they gave him trouble more than any other people, having fortified a mountain called Lide.

176. After a time the Pedasians were conquered; and the Lykians, when Harpagos marched his army into the plain of Xanthos, came out against him and fought, few against many, and displayed proofs of valor; but being defeated and confined within their city, they gathered together into the citadel their wives and their children, their property and their servants, and after that they set fire to this citadel, so that it was all in flames, and having done so and sworn terrible oaths with one another, they went forth against the enemy and were slain in fight, that is to say all the men of Xanthos: and of the Xanthians who now claim to be Lykians the greater number have come in from abroad, except only eighty households; but these eighty households happened at that time to be away from their native place, and so they escaped destruction. Thus Harpagos obtained possession of Caunos, for the men of Caunos imitated in most respects the behavior of the Lykians.

177. So Harpagos was conquering the coast regions of Asia; and Cyrus himself mean-while was doing the same in the upper parts of it, subduing every nation and passing over none. Now most of these actions I shall pass over in silence, but the undertakings which gave him trouble more than the rest and which are the most worthy of note, of these I shall make mention.

178. Cyrus, so soon as he had made subject to himself all other parts of the mainland, proceeded to attack the Assyrians. Now Assyria has doubtless many other great cities, but the most famous and the strongest, and the place where the seat of their monarchy had been established after Nineveh was destroyed, was Babylon; which was a city such as I shall say.—It lies in a great plain, and in size it is such that each face measures one hundred and twenty furlongs, the shape of the whole being square; thus the furlongs of the circuit of the city amount in all to four hundred and eighty. Such is the size of the city of Babylon, and it had a magnificence greater than all other cities of which we have knowledge. First there runs round it a trench deep and broad and full of water; then a wall fifty royal cubits in thickness and two hundred cubits in height: now the royal cubit is larger by three fingers than the common cubit.

179. I must also tell in addition to this for what purpose the earth was used, which was

taken out of the trench, and in what manner the wall was made. As they dug the trench they made the earth which was carried out of the excavation into bricks, and having moulded enough bricks they baked them in kilns; and then afterwards, using hot asphalt for mortar and inserting reed mats at every thirty courses of brickwork, they built up first the edges of the trench and then the wall itself in the same manner: and at the top of the wall along the edges they built chambers of one story facing one another; and between the rows of chambers they left space to drive a four-horse chariot. In the circuit of the wall there are set a hundred gates made of bronze throughout, and the gate-posts and lintels likewise. Now there is another city distant from Babylon a space of eight days' journey, of which the name is Is; and there is a river there of no great size, and the name of the river is also Is, and it sends its stream into the river Euphrates. This river Is throws up together with its water lumps of asphalt in great abundance, and thence was brought the asphalt for the wall of Babylon.

180. Babylon then was walled in this manner; and there are two divisions of the city; for a river whose name is Euphrates parts it in the middle. This flows from the land of the Armenians and is large and deep and swift, and it flows out into the Erythraian sea. The wall then on each side has its bends carried down to the river, and from this point the return walls stretch along each bank of the stream in the form of a rampart of baked bricks: and the city itself is full of houses of three and four stories, and the roads by which it is cut up run in straight lines, including the cross roads which lead to the river; and opposite to each road there were set gates in the rampart which ran along the river, in many in number as the ways, and these also were of bronze and led like the ways to the river itself.

181. This wall then which I have mentioned is as it were a cuirass for the town, and another wall runs round within it, not much weaker for defense than the first but enclosing a smaller space. And in each division of the city was a building in the midst, in the one the king's palace of great extent and strongly fortified round, and in the other the temple of Zeus Belos with bronze gates, and this exists still up to my time and measures two furlongs each way, being of a square shape: and in the midst of the temple is built a solid tower measuring a furlong both in length and in breadth, and on this tower another tower has been erected, and another again upon this, and so on up to the number of eight towers. An ascent to these has been built running outside round about all the towers; and when one reaches about the middle of the ascent one finds a stopping-place and seats to rest upon, on which those who ascend sit down and rest: and on the top of the last tower there is a large cell, and in the cell a large couch is laid, well covered, and by it is placed a golden table: and there is no image there set up nor does any human being spend the night there except only one woman of the natives of the place, whomsoever the god shall choose from all the woman, as say the Chaldeans who are the priests of this god.

182. These same men say also, but I do not believe them, that the god himself comes often to the cell and rests upon the couch, as happens likewise in the Egyptian Thebes according to the report of the Egyptians, for there also a woman sleeps in the temple of the Theban Zeus (and both these women are said to abstain from commerce with men), and as happens also with the prophetess of the god in Patara of Lykia, whenever there is one, for there is not always an Oracle there, but whenever there is one, then she is shut up during the nights in the temple within the cell.

183. There is moreover in the temple at Babylon another cell below, wherein is a great

image of Zeus sitting, made of gold, and by it is placed a large table of gold, and his foot-stool and seat are of gold also; and, as the Chaldeans reported, the weight of the gold of which these things are made is eight hundred talents. Outside this cell is an altar of gold; and there is also another altar of great size, where full-grown animals are sacrificed, whereas on the golden altar it is not lawful to sacrifice any but young sucklings only: and also on the larger altar the Chaldeans offer one thousand talents of frankincense every year at the time when they celebrate the feast in honor of this god. There was moreover in these precincts still remaining at the time of Cyrus, a statue twelve cubits high, of gold and solid. This I did not myself see, but that which is related by the Chaldeans I relate. Against this statue Dareios the son of Hystaspes formed a design, but he did not venture to take it: it was taken however by Xerxes the son of Dareios, who also killed the priest when he forbade him to meddle with the statue. This temple, then, is thus adorned with magnificence, and there are also many private votive-offerings.

184. Of this Babylon, besides many other rulers, of whom I shall make mention in the Assyrian history, and who added improvement to the walls and temples, there were also two who were women. Of these, the one who ruled first, named Semiramis, who lived five generations before the other, produced banks of earth in the plain which are a sight worth seeing; and before this the river used to flood like a sea over the whole plain.

185. The queen who lived after her time, named Nitocris, was wiser than she who had reigned before; and in the first place she left behind her monuments which I shall tell of; then secondly, seeing that the monarchy of the Medes was great and not apt to remain still, but that besides other cities even Nineveh had been captured by it, she made provision against it in so far as she was able. First, as regards the river Euphrates which flows through the midst of their city, whereas before this it flowed straight, she by digging channels above made it so winding that it actually comes three times in its course to one of the villages in Assyria; and the name of the village to which the Euphrates comes is Ardericca; and at this day those who travel from this Sea of ours to Babylon, in their voyage down the river Euphrates arrive three times at this same village and on three separate days. This she did thus; and she also piled up a mound along each bank of the river, which is worthy to cause wonder for its size and height: and at a great distance above Babylon, she dug a basin for a lake, which she caused to extend along at a very small distance from the river, excavating it everywhere of such depth as to come to water, and making the extent such that the circuit of it measured four hundred and twenty furlongs: and the earth which was dug out of this excavation she used up by piling it in mounds along the banks of the river: and when this had been dug by her she brought stones and set them all round it as a facing wall. Both these two things she did, that is she made the river to have a winding course, and she made the place which was dug out all into a swamp, in order that the river might run more slowly, having its force broken by going round many bends, and that the voyages might be winding to Babylon, and after the voyages there might succeed a long circuit of the pool. These works she carried out in that part where the entrance to the country was, and the shortest way to it from Media, so that the Medes might not have dealings with her kingdom and learn of her affairs.

186. These defenses she cast round her city from the depth; and she made the following addition which was dependent upon them:—The city was in two divisions, and the river occupied the space between; and in the time of the former rulers, when any one wished to pass over from the one division to the other, he had to pass over in a boat, and

that, as I imagine, was troublesome: she however made provision also for this; for when she was digging the basin for the lake she left this other monument of herself derived from the same work, that is, she caused stones to be cut of very great length, and when the stones were prepared for her and the place had been dug out, she turned aside the whole stream of the river into the place which she had been digging; and while this was being filled with water, the ancient bed of the river being dried up in the meantime, she both built up with baked bricks after the same fashion as the wall the edges of the river, where it flows through the city, and the places of descent leading from the small gateways to the river; and also about the middle of the city, as I judge, with the stones which she had caused to be dug out she proceeded to build a bridge, binding together the stones with iron and lead: and upon the top she laid squared timbers across, to remain there while it was daytime, over which the people of Babylon made the passage across; but at night they used to take away these timbers for this reason, namely that they might not go backwards and forwards by night and steal from one another: and when the place dug out had been made into a lake full of water by the river, and at the same time the bridge had been completed, then she conducted the Euphrates back into its ancient channel from the lake, and so the place dug out being made into a swamp was thought to have served a good purpose, and there had been a bridge set up for the men of the city.

187. This same queen also contrived a snare of the following kind:—Over that gate of the city through which the greatest number of people passed she set up for herself a tomb above the very gate itself. And on the tomb she engraved writing which said thus: "If any of the kings of Babylon who come after me shall be in want of wealth, let him open my tomb and take as much as he desires; but let him not open it for any other cause, if he be not in want; for that will not be well." This tomb was undisturbed until the kingdom came to Dareios; but to Dareios it seemed that it was a monstrous thing not to make any use of this gate, and also, when there was money lying there, not to take it, considering that the money itself invited him to do so. Now the reason why he would not make any use of this gate was because the corpse would have been above his head as he drove through. He then, I say, opened the tomb and found not indeed money but the corpse, with writing which said thus: "If thou hadst not been insatiable of wealth and basely covetous, thou wouldest not have opened the resting-places of the dead."

188. This queen then is reported to have been such as I have described: and it was the son of this woman, bearing the same name as his father, Labynetos, and being ruler over the Assyrians, against whom Cyrus was marching. Now the great king makes his marches not only well furnished from home with provisions for his table and with cattle, but also taking with him water from the river Choaspes, which flows by Susa, of which alone and of no other river the king drinks: and of this water of the Choaspes boiled, a very great number of wagons, four-wheeled and drawn by mules, carry a supply in silver vessels, and go with him wherever he may march at any time.

189. Now when Cyrus on his way towards Babylon arrived at the river Gyndes,—of which river the springs are in the mountains of the Matienians, and it flows through the Dardanians and runs into another river, the Tigris, which flowing by the city of Opis runs out into the Erythraian Sea,—when Cyrus, I say, was endeavoring to cross this river Gyndes, which is a navigable stream, then one of his sacred white horses in high spirit and wantonness went into the river and endeavored to cross, but the stream swept it under water and carried it off forthwith. And Cyrus was greatly moved with anger

against the river for having done thus insolently, and he threatened to make it so feeble that for the future even women could cross it easily without wetting the knee. So after this threat he ceased from his march against Babylon and divided his army into two parts; and having divided it he stretched lines and marked out straight channels, one hundred and eighty on each bank of the Gyndes, directed every way, and having disposed his army along them he commanded them to dig: so, as a great multitude was working, the work was completed indeed, but they spent the whole summer season at this spot working.

190. When Cyrus had taken vengeance on the river Gyndes by dividing it into three hundred and sixty channels, and when the next spring was just beginning, then at length he continued his advance upon Babylon: and the men of Babylon had marched forth out of their city and were awaiting him. So when in his advance he came near to the city, the Babylonians joined battle with him, and having been worsted in the fight they were shut up close within their city. But knowing well even before this that Cyrus was not apt to remain still, and seeing him lay hands on every nation equally, they had brought in provisions beforehand for very many years. So while these made no account of the siege, Cyrus was in straits what to do, for much time went by and his affairs made no progress onwards.

191. Therefore, whether it was some other man who suggested it to him when he was in a strait what to do, or whether he of himself perceived what he ought to do, he did as follows:—The main body of his army he posted at the place where the river runs into the city, and then again behind the city he set others, where the river issues forth from the city; and he proclaimed to his army that so soon as they should see that the stream had become passable, they should enter by this way into the city. Having thus set them in their places and in this manner exhorted them he marched away himself with that part of his army which was not fit for fighting: and when he came to the lake, Cyrus also did the same things which the queen of the Babylonians had done as regards the river and the lake; that is to say, he conducted the river by a channel into the lake, which was at that time a swamp, and so made the former course of the river passable by the sinking of the stream. When this had been done in such a manner, the Persians who had been posted for this very purpose entered by the bed of the river Euphrates into Babylon, the stream having sunk so far that it reached about to the middle of a man's thigh. Now if the Babylonians had had knowledge of it beforehand or had perceived that which was being done by Cyrus, they would have allowed the Persians to enter the city and then destroyed them miserably; for if they had closed all the gates that led to the river and mounted themselves upon the ramparts which were carried along the banks of the stream, they would have caught them as it were in a fish-wheal: but as it was, the Persians came upon them unexpectedly; and owing to the size of the city (so it is said by those who dwell there) after those about the extremities of the city had suffered capture, those Babylonians who dwelt in the middle did not know that they had been captured; but as they chanced to be holding a festival, they went on dancing and rejoicing during this time until they learnt the truth only too well.

Babylon then had thus been taken for the first time:

192, and as to the resources of the Babylonians how great they are, I shall show by many other proofs and among them also by this:—For the support of the great king and his army, apart from the regular tribute the whole land of which he is ruler has been distributed into portions. Now whereas twelve months go to make up the year, for four of these he has his support from the territory of Babylon, and for the remaining eight months from the whole of the rest of Asia; thus the Assyrian land is in regard to resources the third part of all Asia: and the government, or satrapy as it is called by the Persians, of this territory is of all the governments by far the best; seeing that when Tritantaichmes son of Artabazos had this province from the king, there came in to him every day an *artab* full of silver coin (now the *artab* is a Persian measure and holds more than the *medimnos* of Attica by three Attic *choinikes*); and of horses he had in this province as his private property, apart from the horses for use in war, eight hundred stallions and sixteen thousand mares, for each of these stallions served twenty mares: of Indian hounds moreover such a vast number were kept that four large villages in the plain, being free from other contributions, had been appointed to provide food for the hounds.

193. Such was the wealth which belonged to the ruler of Babylon. Now the land of the Assyrians has but little rain; and this little gives nourishment to the root of the corn, but the crop is ripened and the ear comes on by the help of watering from the river, not as in Egypt by the coming up of the river itself over the fields, but the crop is watered by hand or with swing-buckets. For the whole Babylonian territory like the Egyptian is cut up into channels, and the largest of the channels is navigable for ships and runs in the direction of the sunrising in winter from the Euphrates to another river, namely the Tigris, along the bank of which lay the city of Nineveh. This territory is of all that we know the best by far for producing corn: as to trees, it does not even attempt to bear them, either fig or vine or olive, but for producing corn it is so good that it returns as much as two-hundred-fold for the average, and when it bears at its best it produces three-hundred-fold. The leaves of the wheat and barley there grow to be full four fingers broad; and from millet and sesame seed how large a tree grows, I know myself but shall not record, being well aware that even what has already been said relating to the crops produced has been enough to cause disbelief in those who have not visited the Babylonian land. They use no oil of olives, but only that which they make of sesame seed; and they have date-palms growing over all the plain, most of them fruit-bearing, of which they make both solid food and wine and honey; and to these they attend in the same manner as to fig-trees, and in particular they take the fruit of those palms which the Hellenes call male-palms, and tie them upon the date-bearing palms, so that their gall-fly may enter into the date and ripen it and that the fruit of the palm may not fall off: for the male-palm produces gall-flies in its fruit just as the wild-fig does.

194. But the greatest marvel of all the things in the land after the city itself, to my mind is this which I am about to tell: Their boats, those I mean which go down the river to Babylon, are round and all of leather: for they make ribs for them of willow which they cut in the land of the Armenians who dwell above the Assyrians, and round these they stretch hides which serve as a covering outside by way of hull, not making broad the stern nor gathering in the prow to a point, but making the boats round like a shield: and after that they stow the whole boat with straw and suffer it to be carried down the stream full of cargo; and for the most part these boats bring down casks of palm-wood filled with wine. The boat is kept straight by two steering-oars and two men standing upright, and the man inside pulls his oar while the man outside pushes. These vessels are made both of very large size and also smaller, the largest of them having a burden of as much as five thousand talents' weight; and in each one there is a live ass, and in those of larger size several. So when they have arrived at Babylon in their voyage and have disposed of their

cargo, they sell by auction the ribs of the boat and all the straw, but they pack the hides upon their asses and drive them off to Armenia: for up the stream of the river it is not possible by any means to sail, owing to the swiftness of the current; and for this reason they make their boats not of timber but of hides. Then when they have come back to the land of the Armenians, driving their asses with them, they make other boats in the same manner.

195. Such are their boats; and the following is the manner of dress which they use, namely a linen tunic reaching to the feet, and over this they put on another of wool, and then a white mantle thrown round, while they have shoes of a native fashion rather like the Boeotian slippers. They wear their hair long and bind their heads round with fillets, and they are anointed over the whole of their body with perfumes. Each man has a seal and a staff carved by hand, and on each staff is carved either an apple or a rose or a lily or an eagle or some other device, for it is not their custom to have a staff without a device upon it.

196. Such is the equipment of their bodies: and the customs which are established among them are as follows, the wisest in our opinion being this, which I am informed that the Enetoi in Illyria also have. In every village once in each year it was done as follows:— When the maidens grew to the age for marriage, they gathered these all together and brought them in a body to one place, and round them stood a company of men: and the crier caused each one severally to stand up, and proceeded to sell them, first the most comely of all, and afterwards, when she had been sold and had fetched a large sum of money, he would put up another who was the most comely after her: and they were sold for marriage. Now all the wealthy men of the Babylonians who were ready to marry vied with one another in bidding for the most beautiful maidens; those however of the common sort who were ready to marry did not require a fine form, but they would accept money together with less comely maidens. For when the crier had made an end of selling the most comely of the maidens, then he would cause to stand up that one who was least shapely, or any one of them who might be crippled in any way, and he would make proclamation of her, asking who was willing for least gold to have her in marriage, until she was assigned to him who was willing to accept least: and the gold would be got from the sale of the comely maidens, and so those of beautiful form provided dowries for those which were unshapely or crippled; but to give in marriage one's own daughter to whomsoever each man would, was not allowed, nor to carry off the maiden after buying her without a surety; for it was necessary for the man to provide sureties that he would marry her, before he took her away; and if they did not agree well together, the law was laid down that he should pay back the money. It was allowed also for anyone who wished it to come from another village and buy. This then was their most honorable custom; it does not however still exist at the present time, but they have found out of late another way, in order that the men may not ill-treat them or take them to another city: for since the time when being conquered they were oppressed and ruined, each one of the common people when he is in want of livelihood prostitutes his female children.

197. Next in wisdom to that, is this other custom which was established among them: —they bear out the sick into the market-place; for of physicians they make no use. So people come up to the sick man and give advice about his disease, if any one himself has ever suffered anything like that which the sick man has, or saw any other who had suffered it; and coming near they advise and recommend those means by which they

themselves got rid of a like disease or seen some other get rid of it: and to pass by the sick man in silence is not permitted to them, nor until one has asked what disease he has.

198. They bury their dead in honey, and their modes of lamentation are similar to those used in Egypt. And whenever a Babylonian man has intercourse with his wife, he sits by incense offered, and his wife does the same on the other side, and when it is morning they wash themselves, both of them, for they will touch no vessel until they have washed themselves: and the Arabians do likewise in this matter.

199. Now the most shameful of the customs of the Babylonians is as follows: every woman of the country must sit down in the precincts of Aphrodite once in her life and have commerce with a man who is a stranger: and many women who do not deign to mingle with the rest, because they are made arrogant by wealth, drive to the temple with pairs of horses in covered carriages, and so take their place, and a large number of attendants follow after them; but the greater number do thus,—in the sacred enclosure of Aphrodite sit great numbers of women with a wreath of cord about their heads; some come and others go; and there are passages in straight lines going between the women in every direction, through which the strangers pass by and make their choice. Here when a woman takes her seat she does not depart again to her house until one of the strangers has thrown a silver coin into her lap and has had commerce with her outside the temple, and after throwing it he must say these words only: "I demand thee in the name of the goddess Mylitta": now Mylitta is the name given by the Assyrians to Aphrodite: and the silver coin may be of any value; whatever it is she will not refuse it, for that is not lawful for her, seeing that this coin is made sacred by the act: and she follows the man who has first thrown and does not reject any: and after that she departs to her house, having acquitted herself of her duty to the goddess, nor will you be able thenceforth to give any gift so great as to win her. So then as many as have attained to beauty and stature are speedily released, but those of them who are unshapely remain there much time, not being able to fulfil the law; for some of them remain even as much as three or four years: and in some parts of Cyprus too there is a custom similar to this.

200. These customs then are established among the Babylonians: and there are of them three tribes which eat nothing but fish only: and when they have caught them and dried them in the sun they do thus,—they throw them into brine, and then pound them with pestles and strain them through muslin; and they have them for food either kneaded into a soft cake, or baked like bread, according to their liking.

201. When this nation also had been subdued by Cyrus, he had a desire to bring the Massagetai into subjection to himself. This nation is reputed to be both great and warlike, and to dwell towards the East and the sunrising, beyond the river Araxes and over against the Issedonians: and some also say that this nation is of Scythian race.

202. Now the Araxes is said by some to be larger and by others to be smaller than the Ister: and they say that there are many islands in it about equal in size to Lesbos, and in them people dwelling who feed in the summer upon roots of all kinds which they dig up and certain fruits from trees, which have been discovered by them for food, they store up, it is said, in the season when they are ripe and feed upon them in the winter. Moreover it is said that other trees have been discovered by them which yield fruit of such a kind that when they have assembled together in companies in the same place and lighted a fire, they sit round in a circle and throw some of it into the fire, and they smell the fruit which is thrown on, as it burns, and are intoxicated by the scent as the Hellenes are with wine,

and when more of the fruit is thrown on they become more intoxicated, until at last they rise up to dance and begin to sing. This is said to be their manner of living: and as to the river Araxes, it flows from the land of the Matienians, whence flows the Gyndes which Cyrus divided into the three hundred and sixty channels, and it discharges itself by forty branches, of which all except one end in swamps and shallow pools; and among them they say that men dwell who feed on fish eaten raw, and who are wont to use as clothing the skins of seals: but the one remaining branch of the Araxes flows with unimpeded course into the Caspian Sea.

203. Now the Caspian Sea is apart by itself, not having connection with the other Sea: for all that Sea which the Hellenes navigate, and the Sea beyond the Pillars, which is called Atlantis, and the Erythraian Sea are in fact all one, but the Caspian is separate and lies apart by itself. In length it is a voyage of fifteen days if one uses oars, and in breadth, where it is broadest, a voyage of eight days. On the side towards the West of this Sea the Caucasus runs along by it, which is of all mountain-ranges both the greatest in extent and the loftiest: and the Caucasus has many various races of men dwelling in it, living for the most part on the wild produce of the forests; and among them there are said to be trees which produce leaves of such a kind that by pounding them and mixing water with them they paint figures upon their garments, and the figures do not wash out, but grow old with the woolen stuff as if they had been woven into it at the first: and men say that the sexual intercourse of these people is open like that of cattle.

204. On the West then of this Sea which is called Caspian the Caucasus is the boundary, while towards the East and the rising sun a plain succeeds which is of limitless extent to the view. Of this great plain then the Massagetai occupy a large part, against whom Cyrus had become eager to march; for there were many strong reasons which incited him to it and urged him onwards,—first the manner of his birth, that is to say the opinion held of him that he was more than a mere mortal man, and next the success which he had met with in his wars, for whithersoever Cyrus directed his march, it was impossible for that nation to escape.

205. Now the ruler of the Massagetai was a woman, who was queen after the death of her husband, and her name was Tomyris. To her Cyrus sent and wooed her, pretending that he desired to have her for his wife: but Tomyris understanding that he was wooing not herself but rather the kingdom of the Massagetai, rejected his approaches: and Cyrus after this, as he made no progress by craft, marched to the Araxes, and proceeded to make an expedition openly against the Massagetai, forming bridges of boats over the river for his army to cross, and building towers upon the vessels which gave them passage across the river.

206. While he was busied about this labor, Tomyris sent a herald and said thus: "O king of the Medes, cease to press forward the work which thou art now pressing forward; for thou canst not tell whether these things will be in the end for thy advantage or no; cease to do so, I say, and be king over thine own people, and endure to see us ruling those whom we rule. Since however I know that thou wilt not be willing to receive this counsel, but dost choose anything rather than to be at rest, therefore if thou art greatly anxious to make trial of the Massagetai in fight, come now, leave that labor which thou hast in yoking together the banks of the river, and cross over into our land, when we have first withdrawn three days' journey from the river: or if thou desirest rather to receive us into your land, do thou this same thing thyself." Having heard this Cyrus called together the

first men among the Persians, and having gathered these together he laid the matter before them for discussion, asking their advice as to which of the two things he should do: and their opinions all agreed in one, bidding him receive Tomyris and her army into his country.

207. But Croesus the Lydian, being present and finding fault with this opinion, declared an opinion opposite to that which had been set forth, saying as follows: "O king, I told thee in former time also, that since Zeus had given me over to thee, I would avert according to my power whatever occasion of falling I might see coming near thy house: and now my sufferings, which have been bitter, have proved to be lessons of wisdom to me. If thou dost suppose that thou art immortal and that thou dost command an army which is also immortal, it will be of no use for me to declare to thee my judgment; but if thou hast perceived that thou art a mortal man thyself and dost command others who are so likewise, then learn this first, that for the affairs of men there is a revolving wheel, and that this in its revolution suffers not the same persons always to have good fortune. I therefore now have an opinion about the matter laid before us, which is opposite to that of these men: for if we shall consent to receive the enemy into our land, there is for thee this danger in so doing:—if thou shalt be worsted thou wilt lose in addition all thy realm, for it is evident that if the Massagetai are victors they will not turn back and fly, but will march upon the provinces of thy realm; and on the other hand if thou shalt be the victor, thou wilt not be victor so fully as if thou shouldest overcome the Massagetai after crossing over into their land and shouldest pursue them when they fled. For against that which I said before I will set the same again here, and say that thou, when thou hast conquered, wilt march straight against the realm of Tomyris. Moreover besides that which has been said, it is a disgrace and not to be endured that Cyrus the son of Cambyses should yield to a woman and so withdraw from her land. Now therefore it seems good to me that we should cross over and go forward from the crossing as far as they go in their retreat, and endeavor to get the better of them by doing as follows:—The Massagetai, as I am informed, are without experience of Persian good things, and have never enjoyed any great luxuries. Cut up therefore cattle without stint and dress the meat and set out for these men a banquet in our camp: moreover also provide without stint bowls of unmixed wine and provisions of every kind; and having so done, leave behind the most worthless part of thy army and let the rest begin to retreat from the camp towards the river: for if I am not mistaken in my judgment, they when they see a quantity of good things will fall to the feast, and after that it remains for us to display great deeds."

208. These were the conflicting opinions; and Cyrus, letting go the former opinion and choosing that of Croesus, gave notice to Tomyris to retire, as he was intending to cross over to her. She then proceeded to retire, as she had at first engaged to do, but Cyrus delivered Croesus into the hands of his son Cambyses, to whom he meant to give the kingdom, and gave him charge earnestly to honor him and to treat him well, if the crossing over to go against the Massagetai should not be prosperous. Having thus charged him and sent these away to the land of the Persians, he crossed over the river both himself and his army.

209. And when he had passed over the Araxes, night having come on he saw a vision in his sleep in the land of the Massagetai, as follows:—in his sleep it seemed to Cyrus that he saw the eldest of the sons of Hystaspes having upon his shoulders wings, and that with the one of these he overshadowed Asia and with the other Europe. Now of Hystaspes the

son of Arsames, who was a man of the Achaimenid clan, the eldest son was Dareios, who was then, I suppose, a youth of about twenty years of age, and he had been left behind in the land of the Persians, for he was not yet of full age to go out to the wars. So then when Cyrus awoke he considered with himself concerning the vision: and as the vision seemed to him to be of great import, he called Hystaspes, and having taken him apart by himself he said: "Hystaspes, thy son has been found plotting against me and against my throne: and how I know this for certain I will declare to thee:—The gods have a care of me and show me beforehand all the evils that threaten me. So in the night that is past while sleeping I saw the eldest of thy sons having upon his shoulders wings, and with the one of these he overshadowed Asia and with the other Europe. To judge by this vision then, it cannot be but that he is plotting against me. Do thou therefore go by the quickest way back to Persia and take care that, when I return thither after having subdued these regions, thou set thy son before me to be examined."

210. Cyrus said thus supposing that Dareios was plotting against him; but in fact the divine powers were showing him beforehand that he was destined to find his end there and that his kingdom was coming about to Dareios. To this then Hystaspes replied as follows: "O king, heaven forbid that there should be any man of Persian race who would plot against thee, and if there be any, I pray that he perish as quickly as may be; seeing that thou didst make the Persians to be free instead of slaves, and to rule all nations instead of being ruled by others. And if any vision announces to thee that my son is planning rebellion against thee, I deliver him over to thee to do with him whatsoever thou wilt."

211. Hystaspes then, having made answer with these words and having crossed over the Araxes, was going his way to the Persian land to keep watch over his son Dareios for Cyrus; and Cyrus meanwhile went forward and made a march of one day from the Araxes according to the suggestion of Croesus. After this when Cyrus and the best part of the army of the Persians had marched back to the Araxes, and those who were unfit for fighting had been left behind, then a third part of the army of the Massagetai came to the attack and proceeded to slay, not without resistance, those who were left behind of the army of Cyrus; and seeing the feast that was set forth, when they had overcome their enemies they lay down and feasted, and being satiated with food and wine they went to sleep. Then the Persians came upon them and slew many of them, and took alive many more even than they slew, and among these the son of the queen Tomyris, who was leading the army of the Massagetai; and his name was Spargapises.

212. She then, when she heard that which had come to pass concerning the army and also the things concerning her son, sent a herald to Cyrus and said as follows: "Cyrus, insatiable of blood, be not elated with pride by this which has come to pass, namely because with that fruit of the vine, with which ye fill yourselves and become so mad that as the wine descends into your bodies, evil words float up upon its stream,—because setting a snare, I say, with such a drug as this thou didst overcome my son, and not by valor in fight. Now therefore receive the word which I utter, giving thee good advice:— Restore to me my son and depart from this land without penalty, triumphant over a third part of the army of the Massagetai: but if thou shalt not do so, I swear to thee by the Sun, who is lord of the Massagetai, that surely I will give thee thy fill of blood, insatiable as thou art."

213. When these words were reported to him Cyrus made no account of them; and the

son of the queen Tomyris, Spargapises, when the wine left him and he learnt in what evil case he was, entreated Cyrus that he might be loosed from his chains and gained his request, and then so soon as he was loosed and had got power over his hands he put himself to death.

214. He then ended his life in this manner; but Tomyris, as Cyrus did not listen to her, gathered together all her power and joined battle with Cyrus. This battle of all the battles fought by Barbarians I judge to have been the fiercest, and I am informed that it happened thus:—first, it is said, they stood apart and shot at one another, and afterwards when their arrows were all shot away, they fell upon one another and engaged in close combat with their spears and daggers; and so they continued to be in conflict with one another for a long time, and neither side would flee; but at last the Massagetai got the better in the fight: and the greater part of the Persian army was destroyed there on the spot, and Cyrus himself brought his life to an end there, after he had reigned in all thirty years wanting one. Then Tomyris filled a skin with human blood and had search made among the Persian dead for the corpse of Cyrus: and when she found it, she let his head down into the skin and doing outrage to the corpse she said at the same time this: "Though I yet live and have overcome thee in fight, nevertheless thou didst undo me by taking my son with craft: but I according to my threat will give thee thy fill of blood." Now as regards the end of the life of Cyrus there are many tales told, but this which I have related is to my mind the most worthy of belief.

215. As to the Massagetai, they wear a dress which is similar to that of the Scythians, and they have a manner of life which is also like theirs; and there are of them horsemen and also men who do not ride on horses (for they have both fashions), and moreover there are both archers and spearmen, and their custom it is to carry battle-axes; and for everything they use either gold or bronze, for in all that has to do with spear-points or arrowheads or battle-axes they use bronze, but for head-dresses and girdles and belts round the arm-pits they employ gold as ornament: and in like manner as regards their horses, they put breast-plates of bronze about their chests, but on their bridles and bits and cheek-pieces they employ gold. Iron however and silver they use not at all, for they have them not in their land, but gold and bronze in abundance.

216. These are the customs which they have:—Each marries a wife, but they have their wives in common; for that which the Hellenes say that the Scythians do, is not in fact done by the Scythians but by the Massagetai, that is to say, whatever woman a man of the Massagetai may desire he hangs up his quiver in front of the wagon and has commerce with her freely. They have no precise limit of age laid down for their life, but when a man becomes very old, his nearest of kin come together and slaughter him solemnly and cattle also with him; and then after that they boil the flesh and banquet upon it. This is considered by them the happiest lot; but him who has ended his life by disease they do not eat, but cover him up in the earth, counting it a misfortune that he did not attain to being slaughtered. They sow no crops but live on cattle and on fish, which last they get in abundance from the river Araxes; moreover they are drinkers of milk. Of gods they reverence the Sun alone, and to him they sacrifice horses: and the rule of the sacrifice is this:—to the swiftest of the gods they assign the swiftest of all mortal things.

THE SECOND BOOK OF THE
HISTORIES, CALLED EUTERPE

1. When Cyrus had brought his life to an end, Cambyses received the royal power in succession, being the son of Cyrus and of Cassandane the daughter of Pharnaspes, for whose death, which came about before his own, Cyrus had made great mourning himself and also had proclaimed to all those over whom he bore rule that they should make mourning for her: Cambyses, I say, being the son of this woman and of Cyrus, regarded the Ionians and Aiolians as slaves inherited from his father; and he proceeded to march an army against Egypt, taking with him as helpers not only the other nations of which he was the ruler, but also those of the Hellenes over whom he had power besides.

2. Now the Egyptians, before the time when Psammetichos became king over them, were wont to suppose that they had come into being first of all men; but since the time when Psammetichos having become king desired to know what men had come into being first, they suppose that the Phrygians came into being before themselves, but they themselves before all other men. Now Psammetichos, when he was not able by inquiry to find out any means of knowing who had come into being first of all men, contrived a device of the following kind:—Taking two new-born children belonging to persons of the common sort he gave them to a shepherd to bring up at the place where his flocks were, with a manner of bringing up such as I shall say, charging him namely that no man should utter any word in their presence, and that they should be placed by themselves in a room where none might come, and at the proper time he should bring to them she-goats, and when he had satisfied them with milk he should do for them whatever else was needed. These things Psammetichos did and gave him this charge wishing to hear what word the children would let break forth first, after they had ceased from wailings without sense. And accordingly so it came to pass; for after a space of two years had gone by, during which the shepherd went on acting so, at length, when he opened the door and entered, both the children fell before him in entreaty and uttered the word *bekos*, stretching forth their hands. At first when he heard this the shepherd kept silence; but since this word was often repeated, as he visited them constantly and attended to them, at last he declared the

matter to his master, and at his command he brought the children before his face. Then Psammetichos having himself also heard it, began to inquire about what nation of men named anything *bekos*, and inquiring he found that the Phrygians had this name for bread. In this manner and guided by an indication such as this, the Egyptians were brought to allow that the Phrygians were a more ancient people than themselves.

3. That so it came to pass I heard from the priests of that Hephaistos who dwells at Memphis; but the Hellenes relate, besides many other idle tales, that Psammetichos cut out the tongues of certain women, and then caused the children to live with these women.

With regard then to the rearing of the children they related so much as I have said: and I heard also other things at Memphis when I had speech with the priests of Hephaistos. Moreover I visited both Thebes and Heliopolis for this very cause, namely because I wished to know whether the priests at these places would agree in their accounts with those at Memphis; for the men of Heliopolis are said to be the most learned in records of the Egyptians. Those of their narrations which I heard with regard to the gods I am not earnest to relate in full, but I shall name them only, because I consider that all men are equally ignorant of these matters: and whatever things of them I may record, I shall record only because I am compelled by the course of the story.

4. But as to those matters which concern men, the priests agreed with one another in saying that the Egyptians were the first of all men on earth to find out the course of the year, having divided the seasons into twelve parts to make up the whole; and this they said they found out from the stars: and they reckon to this extent more wisely than the Hellenes, as it seems to me, inasmuch as the Hellenes throw in an intercalated month every other year, to make the seasons right, whereas the Egyptians, reckoning the twelve months at thirty days each, bring in also every year five days beyond the number, and thus the circle of their seasons is completed and comes round to the same point whence it set out. They said moreover that the Egyptians were the first who brought into use appellations for the twelve gods and the Hellenes took up the use from them; and that they were the first who assigned altars and images and temples to the gods, and who engraved figures on stones; and with regard to the greater number of these things they showed me by actual facts that they had happened so. They said also that the first man who became king of Egypt was Min; and that in his time all Egypt except the district of Thebes was a swamp, and none of the regions were then above water which now lie below the lake of Moiris, to which lake it is a voyage of seven days up the river from the sea:

5, and I thought that they said well about the land; for it is manifest in truth even to a person who has not heard it beforehand but has only seen, at least if he have understanding, that the Egypt to which the Hellenes come in ships is a land which has been won by the Egyptians as an addition, and that it is a gift of the river: moreover the regions which lie above this lake also for a distance of three days' sail, about which they did not go on to say anything of this kind, are nevertheless another instance of the same thing: for the nature of the land of Egypt is as follows:—First when you are still approaching it in a ship and are distant a day's run from the land, if you let down a sounding-line you will bring up mud and will find yourself in eleven fathoms. This then so far shows that there is a silting forward of the land.

6. Then secondly, as to Egypt itself, the extent of it along the sea is sixty *schoines*, according to our definition of Egypt as extending from the Gulf of Plinthine to the Serbonian lake, along which stretches Mount Casion; from this lake then the sixty *schoines*

are reckoned: for those of men who are poor in land have their country measured by fathoms, those who are less poor by furlongs, those who have much land by parasangs, and those who have land in very great abundance by *schoines*: now the parasang is equal to thirty furlongs, and each *schoine*, which is an Egyptian measure, is equal to sixty furlongs. So there would be an extent of three thousand six hundred furlongs for the coast-land of Egypt.

7. From thence and as far as Heliopolis inland Egypt is broad, and the land is all flat and without springs of water and formed of mud: and the road as one goes inland from the sea to Heliopolis is about the same in length as that which leads from the altar of the twelve gods at Athens to Pisa and the temple of Olympian Zeus: reckoning up you would find the difference very small by which these roads fail of being equal in length, not more indeed than fifteen furlongs; for the road from Athens to Pisa wants fifteen furlongs of being fifteen hundred, while the road to Heliopolis from the sea reaches that number completely.

8. From Heliopolis however, as you go up, Egypt is narrow; for on the one side a mountain-range belonging to Arabia stretches along by the side of it, going in a direction from North towards the midday and the South Wind, tending upwards without a break to that which is called the Erythraian Sea, in which range are the stone-quarries which were used in cutting stone for the pyramids at Memphis. On this side then the mountain ends where I have said, and then takes a turn back; and where it is widest, as I was informed, it is a journey of two months across from East to West; and the borders of it which turn towards the East are said to produce frankincense. Such then is the nature of this mountain-range; and on the side of Egypt towards Libya another range extends, rocky and enveloped in sand: in this are the pyramids, and it runs in the same direction as those parts of the Arabian mountains which go towards the midday. So then, I say, from Heliopolis the land has no longer a great extent so far as it belongs to Egypt, and for about four days' sail up the river Egypt properly so called is narrow: and the space between the mountain-ranges which have been mentioned is plain-land, but where it is narrowest it did not seem to me to exceed two hundred furlongs from the Arabian mountains to those which are called the Libyan. After this again Egypt is broad.

9. Such is the nature of this land: and from Heliopolis to Thebes is a voyage up the river of nine days, and the distance of the journey in furlongs is four thousand eight hundred and sixty, the number of the *schoines* being eighty-one. If these measures of Egypt in furlongs be put together the result is as follows:—I have already before this shown that the distance along the sea amounts to three thousand six hundred furlongs, and I will now declare what the distance is inland from the sea to Thebes, namely six thousand one hundred and twenty furlongs: and again the distance from Thebes to the city called Elephantine is one thousand eight hundred furlongs.

10. Of this land then, concerning which I have spoken, it seemed to myself also, according as the priests said, that the greater part had been won as an addition by the Egyptians; for it was evident to me that the space between the aforesaid mountain-ranges, which lie above the city of Memphis, once was a gulf of the sea, like the regions about Ilion and Teuthrania and Ephesos and the plain of the Maiander, if it be permitted to compare small things with great; and small these are in comparison, for of the rivers which heaped up the soil in those regions none is worthy to be compared in volume with a single one of the mouths of the Nile, which has five mouths. Moreover there are other

rivers also, not in size at all equal to the Nile, which have performed great feats; of which I can mention the names of several, and especially the Acheloös, which flowing through Acarnania and so issuing out into the sea has already made half of the Echinades from islands into mainland.

11. Now there is in the land of Arabia, not far from Egypt, a gulf of the sea running in from that which is called the Erythraian Sea, very long and narrow, as I am about to tell. With respect to the length of the voyage along it, one who set out from the innermost point to sail out through it into the open sea, would spend forty days upon the voyage, using oars; and with respect to breadth, where the gulf is broadest it is half a day's sail across: and there is in it an ebb and flow of tide every day. Just such another gulf I suppose that Egypt was, and that the one ran in towards Ethiopia from the Northern Sea, and the other, the Arabian, of which I am about to speak, tended from the South towards Syria, the gulfs boring in so as almost to meet at their extreme points, and passing by one another with but a small space left between. If then the stream of the Nile should turn aside into this Arabian gulf, what would hinder that gulf from being filled up with silt as the river continued to flow, at all events within a period of twenty thousand years? indeed for my part I am of opinion that it would be filled up even within ten thousand years. How, then, in all the time that has elapsed before I came into being should not a gulf be filled up even of much greater size than this by a river so great and so active?

12. As regards Egypt then, I both believe those who say that things are so, and for myself also I am strongly of opinion that they are so; because I have observed that Egypt runs out into the sea further than the adjoining land, and that shells are found upon the mountains of it, and an efflorescence of salt forms upon the surface, so that even the pyramids are being eaten away by it, and moreover that of all the mountains of Egypt, the range which lies above Memphis is the only one which has sand: besides which I notice that Egypt resembles neither the land of Arabia, which borders upon it, nor Libya, nor yet Syria (for they are Syrians who dwell in the parts of Arabia lying along the sea), but that it has soil which is black and easily breaks up, seeing that it is in truth mud and silt brought down from Ethiopia by the river: but the soil of Libya, we know, is reddish in color and rather sandy, while that of Arabia and Syria is somewhat clayey and rocky.

13. The priests also gave me a strong proof concerning this land as follows, namely that in the reign of king Moiris, whenever the river reached a height of at least eight cubits it watered Egypt below Memphis; and not yet nine hundred years had gone by since the death of Moiris, when I heard these things from the priests: now however, unless the river rises to sixteen cubits, or fifteen at the least, it does not go over the land. I think too that those Egyptians who dwell below the lake of Moiris and especially in that region which is called the Delta, if that land continues to grow in height according to this proportion and to increase similarly in extent, will suffer for all remaining time, from the Nile not overflowing their land, that same thing which they themselves said that the Hellenes would at some time suffer: for hearing that the whole land of the Hellenes has rain and is not watered by rivers as theirs is, they said that the Hellenes would at some time be disappointed of a great hope and would suffer the ills of famine. This saying means that if the god shall not send them rain, but shall allow drought to prevail for a long time, the Hellenes will be destroyed by hunger; for they have in fact no other supply of water to save them except from Zeus alone.

14. This has been rightly said by the Egyptians with reference to the Hellenes: but now

let me tell how matters are with the Egyptians themselves in their turn. If, in accordance with what I before said, their land below Memphis (for this is that which is increasing) shall continue to increase in height according to the same proportion as in past time, assuredly those Egyptians who dwell here will suffer famine, if their land shall not have rain nor the river be able to go over their fields. It is certain however that now they gather in fruit from the earth with less labor than any other men and also with less than the other Egyptians; for they have no labor in breaking up furrows with a plough nor in hoeing nor in any other of those labors which other men have about a crop; but when the river has come up of itself and watered their fields and after watering has left them again, then each man sows his own field and turns into it swine, and when he has trodden the seed into the ground by means of the swine, after that he waits for the harvest; and when he has threshed the corn by means of the swine, then he gathers it in.

15. If we desire to follow the opinions of the Ionians as regards Egypt, who say that the Delta alone is Egypt, reckoning its sea-coast to be from the watch-tower called of Perseus to the fish-curing houses of Pelusion, a distance of forty *schoines*, and counting it to extend inland as far as the city of Kercasoros, where the Nile divides and runs to Pelusion and Canobos, while as for the rest of Egypt, they assign it partly to Libya and partly to Arabia, —if, I say, we should follow this account, we should thereby declare that in former times the Egyptians had no land to live in; for, as we have seen, their Delta at any rate is alluvial, and has appeared (so to speak) lately, as the Egyptians themselves say and as my opinion is. If then at the first there was no land for them to live in, why did they waste their labor to prove that they had come into being before all other men? They needed not to have made trial of the children to see what language they would first utter. However I am not of opinion that the Egyptians came into being at the same time as that which is called by the Ionians the Delta, but that they existed always ever since the human race came into being, and that as their land advanced forwards, many of them were left in their first abodes and many came down gradually to the lower parts. At least it is certain that in old times Thebes had the name of Egypt, and of this the circumference measures six thousand one hundred and twenty furlongs.

16. If then we judge aright of these matters, the opinion of the Ionians about Egypt is not sound: but if the judgment of the Ionians is right, I declare that neither the Hellenes nor the Ionians themselves know how to reckon since they say that the whole earth is made up of three divisions, Europe, Asia, and Libya: for they ought to count in addition to these the Delta of Egypt, since it belongs neither to Asia nor to Libya; for at least it cannot be the river Nile by this reckoning which divides Asia from Libya, but the Nile is cleft at the point of this Delta so as to flow round it, and the result is that this land would come between Asia and Libya.

17. We dismiss then the opinion of the Ionians, and express a judgment of our own in this matter also, that Egypt is all that land which is inhabited by Egyptians, just as Kilikia is that which is inhabited by Kilikians and Assyria that which is inhabited by Assyrians, and we know of no boundary properly speaking between Asia and Libya except the borders of Egypt. If however we shall adopt the opinion which is commonly held by the Hellenes, we shall suppose that the whole of Egypt, beginning from the Cataract and the city of Elephantine, is divided into two parts and that it thus partakes of both the names, since one side will thus belong to Libya and the other to Asia; for the Nile from the Cataract onwards flows to the sea cutting Egypt through the midst; and as far as the city

of Kercasoros the Nile flows in one single stream, but from this city onwards it is parted into three ways; and one, which is called the Pelusian mouth, turns towards the East; the second of the ways goes towards the West, and this is called the Canobic mouth; but that one of the ways which is straight runs thus,—when the river in its course downwards comes to the point of the Delta, then it cuts the Delta through the midst and so issues out to the sea. In this we have a portion of the water of the river which is not the smallest nor the least famous, and it is called the Sebennytic mouth. There are also two other mouths which part off from the Sebennytic and go to the sea, and these are called, one the Saïtic, the other the Mendesian mouth. The Bolbitinitic and Bucolic mouths, on the other hand, are not natural but made by digging.

18. Moreover also the answer given by the Oracle of Ammon bears witness in support of my opinion that Egypt is of the extent which I declare it to be in my account; and of this answer I heard after I had formed my own opinion about Egypt. For those of the city of Marea and of Apis, dwelling in the parts of Egypt which border on Libya, being of opinion themselves that they were Libyans and not Egyptians, and also being burdened by the rules of religious service, because they desired not to be debarred from the use of cows' flesh, sent to Ammon saying that they had naught in common with the Egyptians, for they dwelt outside the Delta and agreed with them in nothing; and they said they desired that it might be lawful for them to eat everything without distinction. The god however did not permit them to do so, but said that that land which was Egypt which the Nile came over and watered, and that those were Egyptians who dwelling below the city of Elephantine drank of that river. Thus it was answered to them by the Oracle about this:

19, and the Nile, when it is in flood, goes over not only the Delta but also of the land which is called Libyan and of that which is called Arabian sometimes as much as two days' journey on each side, and at times even more than this or at times less.

As regards the nature of the river, neither from the priests nor yet from any other man was I able to obtain any knowledge: and I was desirous especially to learn from them about these matters, namely why the Nile comes down increasing in volume from the summer solstice onwards for a hundred days, and then, when it has reached the number of these days, turns and goes back, failing in its stream, so that through the whole winter season it continues to be low, and until the summer solstice returns. Of none of these things was I able to receive any account from the Egyptians, when I inquired of them what power the Nile has whereby it is of a nature opposite to that of other rivers. And I made inquiry, desiring to know both this which I say and also why, unlike all other rivers, it does not give rise to any breezes blowing from it.

20. However some of the Hellenes who desired to gain distinction for cleverness have given an account of this water in three different ways: two of these I do not think it worthwhile even to speak of except only to indicate their nature; of which the one says that the Etesian Winds are the cause that makes the river rise, by preventing the Nile from flowing out into the sea. But often the Etesian Winds fail and yet the Nile does the same work as it is wont to do; and moreover, if these were the cause, all the other rivers also which flow in a direction opposed to the Etesian Winds ought to have been affected in the same way as the Nile, and even more, in as much as they are smaller and present to them a feebler flow of stream: but there are many of these rivers in Syria and many also in Libya, and they are affected in no such manner as the Nile.

21. The second way shows more ignorance than that which has been mentioned, and it

is more marvelous to tell; for it says that the river produces these effects because it flows from the Ocean, and that the Ocean flows round the whole earth.

22. The third of the ways is much the most specious, but nevertheless it is the most mistaken of all: for indeed this way has no more truth in it than the rest, alleging as it does that the Nile flows from melting snow; whereas it flows out of Libya through the midst of the Ethiopians, and so comes out into Egypt. How then should it flow from snow, when it flows from the hottest parts to those which are cooler? And indeed most of the facts are such as to convince a man (one at least who is capable of reasoning about such matters), that it is not at all likely that it flows from snow. The first and greatest evidence is afforded by the winds, which blow hot from these regions; the second is that the land is rainless always and without frost, whereas after snow has fallen rain must necessarily come within five days, so that if it snowed in those parts rain would fall there; the third evidence is afforded by the people dwelling there, who are of a black color by reason of the burning heat. Moreover kites and swallows remain there through the year and do not leave the land; and cranes flying from the cold weather which comes on in the region of Scythia come regularly to these parts for wintering: if then it snowed ever so little in that land through which the Nile flows and in which it has its rise, none of these things would take place, as necessity compels us to admit.

23. As for him who talked about the Ocean, he carried his tale into the region of the unknown, and so he need not be refuted; since I for my part know of no river Ocean existing, but I think that Homer or one of the poets who were before him invented the name and introduced it into his verse.

24. If however after I have found fault with the opinions proposed, I am bound to declare an opinion of my own about the matters which are in doubt, I will tell what to my mind is the reason why the Nile increases in the summer. In the winter season the Sun, being driven away from his former path through the heaven by the stormy winds, comes to the upper parts of Libya. If one would set forth the matter in the shortest way, all has now been said; for whatever region this god approaches most and stands directly above, this it may reasonably be supposed is most in want of water, and its native streams of rivers are dried up most.

25. However, to set it forth at greater length, thus it is:—the Sun passing in his course by the upper parts of Libya, does thus, that is to say, since at all times the air in those parts is clear and the country is warm, because there are no cold winds, in passing through it the Sun does just as he was wont to do in the summer, when going through the midst of the heaven, that is he draws to himself the water, and having drawn it he drives it away to the upper parts of the country, and the winds take it up and scattering it abroad melt it into rain; so it is natural that the winds which blow from this region, namely the South and South-west Winds, should be much the most rainy of all the winds. I think however that the Sun does not send away from himself all the water of the Nile of each year, but that he also lets some remain behind with himself. Then when the winter becomes milder, the Sun returns back again to the midst of the heaven, and from that time onwards he draws equally from all rivers; but in the meanwhile they flow in large volume, since water of rain mingles with them in great quantity, because their country receives rain then and is filled with torrent streams. In summer however they are weak, since not only the showers of rain fail then, but also they are drawn by the Sun. The Nile however, alone of all rivers, not having rain and being drawn by the Sun, naturally flows during this time of winter in

this you will disembark and make a journey by land of forty days; for in the Nile
.p rocks stand forth out of the water, and there are many reefs, by which it is not
ossible for a vessel to pass. Then after having passed through this country in the forty
days which I have said, you will embark again in another vessel and sail for twelve days;
and after this you will come to a great city called Meroe. This city is said to be the mother-
city of all the other Ethiopians: and they who dwell in it reverence of the gods Zeus and
Dionysos alone, and these they greatly honor; and they have an Oracle of Zeus established, and make warlike marches whensoever this god commands them by prophesyings
and to whatsoever place he commands.

30. Sailing from this city you will come to the "Deserters" in another period of time
equal to that in which you came from Elephantine to the mother-city of the Ethiopians.
Now the name of these "Deserters" is *Asmach*, and this word signifies, when translated
into the tongue of the Hellenes, "those who stand on the left hand of the king." These
were two hundred and forty thousand Egyptians of the warrior class, who revolted and
went over to the Ethiopians for the following cause:—In the reign of Psammetichos
garrisons were set, one towards the Ethiopians at the city of Elephantine, another towards
the Arabians and Assyrians at Daphnai of Pelusion, and another towards Libya at Marea:
and even in my own time the garrisons of the Persians too are ordered in the same manner
as these were in the reign of Psammetichos, for both at Elephantine and at Daphnai the
Persians have outposts. The Egyptians then of whom I speak had served as outposts for
three years and no one relieved them from their guard; accordingly they took counsel
together, and adopting a common plan they all in a body revolted from Psammetichos and
set out for Ethiopia. Hearing this Psammetichos set forth in pursuit, and when he came up
with them he entreated them much and endeavored to persuade them not to desert the
gods of their country and their children and wives: upon which it is said that one of them
pointed to his privy member and said that wherever this was, there would they have both
children and wives. When these came to Ethiopia they gave themselves over to the king of
the Ethiopians; and he rewarded them as follows:—there were certain of the Ethiopians
who had come to be at variance with him; and he bade them drive these out and dwell in
their land. So since these men settled in the land of the Ethiopians, the Ethiopians have
come to be of milder manners, from having learnt the customs of the Egyptians.

31. The Nile then, besides that part of its course which is in Egypt, is known as far as a
four months' journey by river and land: for that is the number of months which are found
by reckoning to be spent in going from Elephantine to these "Deserters": and the river
runs from the West and the setting of the sun. But what comes after that no one can clearly
say; for this land is desert by reason of the burning heat.

32. Thus much however I heard from men of Kyrene, who told me that they had
been to the Oracle of Ammon, and had come to speech with Etearchos king of the
Ammonians: and it happened that after speaking of other matters they fell to discourse
about the Nile and how no one knew the sources of it; and Etearchos said that once
there had come to him men of the Nasamonians (this is a Libyan race which dwells in
the Syrtis, and also in the land to the East of the Syrtis reaching to no great distance),
and when the Nasamonians came and were asked by him whether they were able to tell
him anything more than he knew about the desert parts of Libya, they said that there
had been among them certain sons of chief men, who were of unruly disposition; and
these when they grew up to be men had devised various other extravagant things and

also they had told off by lot five of themselves to go to see the desert parts of Libya and to try whether they could discover more than those who had previously explored furthest: for in those parts of Libya which are by the Northern Sea, beginning from Egypt and going as far as the headland of Soloeis, which is the extreme point of Libya, Libyans (and of them many races) extend along the whole coast, except so much as the Hellenes and Phoenicians hold; but in the upper parts, which lie above the sea-coast and above those people whose land comes down to the sea, Libya is full of wild beasts; and in the parts above the land of wild beasts it is full of sand, terribly waterless and utterly desert. These young men then (said they), being sent out by their companions well furnished with supplies of water and provisions, went first through the inhabited country, and after they had passed through this they came to the country of wild beasts, and after this they passed through the desert, making their journey towards the West Wind; and having passed through a great tract of sand in many days, they saw at last trees growing in a level place; and having come up to them, they were beginning to pluck the fruit which was upon the trees: but as they began to pluck it, there came upon them small men, of less stature than men of the common size, and these seized them and carried them away; and neither could the Nasamonians understand anything of their speech nor could those who were carrying them off understand anything of the speech of the Nasamonians: and they led them (so it was said) through very great swamps, and after passing through these they came to a city in which all the men were in size like those who carried them off and in color of skin black; and by the city ran a great river, which ran from the West towards the sunrising, and in it were seen crocodiles.

33. Of the account given by Etearchos the Ammonian let so much suffice as is here said, except that, as the men of Kyrene told me, he alleged that the Nasamonians returned safe home, and that the people to whom they had come were all wizards. Now this river which ran by the city, Etearchos conjectured to be the Nile, and moreover reason compels us to think so; for the Nile flows from Libya and cuts Libya through in the midst, and as I conjecture, judging of what is not known by that which is evident to the view, it starts at a distance from its mouth equal to that of the Ister: for the river Ister begins from the Keltoi and the city of Pyrene and so runs that it divides Europe in the midst (now the Keltoi are outside the Pillars of Heracles and border upon the Kynesians, who dwell furthest towards the sunset of all those who have their dwelling in Europe); and the Ister ends, having its course through the whole of Europe, by flowing into the Euxine Sea at the place where the Milesians have their settlement of Istria.

34. Now the Ister, since it flows through land which is inhabited, is known by the reports of many; but of the sources of the Nile no one can give an account, for the part of Libya through which it flows is uninhabited and desert. About its course however so much as it was possible to learn by the most diligent inquiry has been told; and it runs out into Egypt. Now Egypt lies nearly opposite to the mountain districts of Kilikia; and from thence to Sinope, which lies upon the Euxine Sea, is a journey in the same straight line of five days for a man without encumbrance; and Sinope lies opposite to the place where the Ister runs out into the sea: thus I think that the Nile passes through the whole of Libya and is of equal measure with the Ister.

Of the Nile then let so much suffice as has been said.

35. Of Egypt however I shall make my report at length, because it has wonders more in

number than any other land, and works too it has to show as much as any land, which are beyond expression great: for this reason then more shall be said concerning it.

The Egyptians in agreement with their climate, which is unlike any other, and with the river, which shows a nature different from all other rivers, established for themselves manners and customs in a way opposite to other men in almost all matters: for among them the women frequent the market and carry on trade, while the men remain at home and weave; and whereas others weave pushing the woof upwards, the Egyptians push it downwards: the men carry their burdens upon their heads and the women upon their shoulders: the women make water standing up and the men crouching down: they ease themselves in their houses and they eat without in the streets, alleging as reason for this that it is right to do secretly the things that are unseemly though necessary, but those which are not unseemly, in public: no woman is a minister either of male or female divinity, but men of all, both male and female: to support their parents the sons are in no way compelled, if they do not desire to do so, but the daughters are forced to do so, be they never so unwilling.

36. The priests of the gods in other lands wear long hair, but in Egypt they shave their heads: among other men the custom is that in mourning those whom the matter concerns most nearly have their hair cut short, but the Egyptians, when deaths occur, let their hair grow long, both that on the head and that on the chin, having before been close shaven: other men have their daily living separated from beasts, but the Egyptians have theirs together with beasts: other men live on wheat and barley, but to any one of the Egyptians who makes his living on these it is a great reproach; they make their bread of maize, which some call spelt; they knead dough with their feet and clay with their hands, with which also they gather up dung: and whereas other men, except such as have learnt otherwise from the Egyptians, have their members as nature made them, the Egyptians practice circumcision: as to garments, the men wear two each and the women but one: and whereas others make fast the rings and ropes of the sails outside the ship, the Egyptians do this inside: finally in the writing of characters and reckoning with pebbles, while the Hellenes carry the hand from the left to the right, the Egyptians do this from the right to the left; and doing so they say that they do it themselves rightwise and the Hellenes leftwise: and they use two kinds of characters for writing, of which the one kind is called sacred and the other common.

37. They are religious excessively beyond all other men, and with regard to this they have customs as follows:—they drink from cups of bronze and rinse them out every day, and not some only do this but all: they wear garments of linen always newly washed, and this they make a special point of practice: they circumcise themselves for the sake of cleanliness, preferring to be clean rather than comely. The priests shave themselves all over their body every other day, so that no lice or any other foul thing may come to be upon them when they minister to the gods; and the priests wear garments of linen only and sandals of papyrus, and any other garment they may not take nor other sandals; these wash themselves in cold water twice in the day and twice again in the night; and other religious services they perform (one may almost say) of infinite number. They enjoy also good things not a few, for they do not consume or spend anything of their own substance, but there is sacred bread baked for them and they have each great quantity of flesh of oxen and geese coming in to them each day, and also wine of grapes is given to them; but it is not permitted to them to taste of fish: beans moreover the Egyptians do not at all sow

in their land, and those which grow they neither eat raw nor boil for food; nay the priests do not endure even to look upon them, thinking this to be an unclean kind of pulse: and there is not one priest only for each of the gods but many, and of them one is chief-priest, and whenever a priest dies his son is appointed to his place.

38. The males of the ox kind they consider to belong to Epaphos, and on account of him they test them in the following manner:—If the priest sees one single black hair upon the beast he counts it not clean for sacrifice; and one of the priests who is appointed for the purpose makes investigation of these matters, both when the beast is standing upright and when it is lying on its back, drawing out its tongue moreover, to see if it is clean in respect of the appointed signs, which I shall tell of in another part of the history: he looks also at the hairs of the tail to see if it has them growing in the natural manner: and if it be clean in respect of all these things, he marks it with a piece of papyrus, rolling this round the horns, and then when he has plastered sealing-earth over it he sets upon it the seal of his signet-ring, and after that they take the animal away. But for one who sacrifices a beast not sealed the penalty appointed is death.

39. In this way then the beast is tested; and their appointed manner of sacrifice is as follows:—they lead the sealed beast to the altar where they happen to be sacrificing and then kindle a fire: after that, having poured libations of wine over the altar so that it runs down upon the victim and having called upon the god, they cut its throat, and having cut its throat they sever the head from the body. The body then of the beast they flay, but upon the head they make many imprecations first, and then they who have a market and Hellenes sojourning among them for trade, these carry it to the market-place and sell it, while they who have no Hellenes among them cast it away into the river: and this is the form of imprecation which they utter upon the heads, praying that if any evil be about to befall either themselves who are offering sacrifice or the land of Egypt in general, it may come rather upon this head. Now as regards the heads of the beasts which are sacrificed and the pouring over them of the wine, all the Egyptians have the same customs equally for all their sacrifices; and by reason of this custom none of the Egyptians eat of the head either of this or of any other kind of animal:

40, but the manner of disemboweling the victims and of burning them is appointed among them differently for different sacrifices; I shall speak however of the sacrifices to that goddess whom they regard as the greatest of all, and to whom they celebrate the greatest feast.—When they have flayed the bullock and made imprecation, they take out the whole of its lower entrails but leave in the body the upper entrails and the fat; and they sever from it the legs and the end of the loin and the shoulders and the neck: and this done, they fill the rest of the body of the animal with consecrated loaves and honey and raisins and figs and frankincense and myrrh and every other kind of spices, and having filled it with these they offer it, pouring over it great abundance of oil. They make their sacrifice after fasting, and while the offerings are being burnt, they all beat themselves for mourning, and when they have finished beating themselves they set forth as a feast that which they left unburnt of the sacrifice.

41. The clean males then of the ox kind, both full-grown animals and calves, are sacrificed by all the Egyptians; the females however they may not sacrifice, but these are sacred to Isis; for the figure of Isis is in the form of a woman with cow's horns, just as the Hellenes present Io in pictures, and all the Egyptians without distinction reverence cows far more than any other kind of cattle; for which reason neither man nor woman of

Egyptian race would kiss a man who is a Hellene on the mouth, nor will they use a knife or roasting-spits or a caldron belonging to a Hellene, nor taste of the flesh even of a clean animal if it has been cut with the knife of a Hellene. And the cattle of this kind which die they bury in the following manner:—the females they cast into the river, but the males they bury, each people in the suburb of their town, with one of the horns, or sometimes both, protruding to mark the place; and when the bodies have rotted away and the appointed time comes on, then to each city comes a boat from that which is called the island of Prosopitis (this is in the Delta, and the extent of its circuit is nine *schoines*). In this island of Prosopitis is situated, besides many other cities, that one from which the boats come to take up the bones of the oxen, and the name of the city is Atarbechis, and in it there is set up a holy temple of Aphrodite. From this city many go abroad in various directions, some to one city and others to another, and when they have dug up the bones of the oxen they carry them off, and coming together they bury them in one single place. In the same manner as they bury the oxen they bury also their other cattle when they die; for about them also they have the same law laid down, and these also they abstain from killing.

42. Now all who have a temple set up to the Theban Zeus or who are of the district of Thebes, these, I say, all sacrifice goats and abstain from sheep: for not all the Egyptians equally reverence the same gods, except only Isis and Osiris (who they say is Dionysos), these they all reverence alike: but they who have a temple of Mendes or belong to the Mendesian district, these abstain from goats and sacrifice sheep. Now the men of Thebes and those who after their example abstain from sheep, say that this custom was established among them for the cause which follows:—Heracles (they say) had an earnest desire to see Zeus, and Zeus did not desire to be seen of him; and at last when Heracles was urgent in entreaty Zeus contrived this device, that is to say, he flayed a ram and held in front of him the head of the ram which he had cut off, and he put on over him the fleece and then showed himself to him. Hence the Egyptians make the image of Zeus into the face of a ram; and the Ammonians do so also after their example, being settlers both from the Egyptians and from the Ethiopians, and using a language which is a medley of both tongues: and in my opinion it is from this god that the Ammonians took the name which they have, for the Egyptians call Zeus *Amun*. The Thebans then do not sacrifice rams but hold them sacred for this reason; on one day however in the year, on the feast of Zeus, they cut up in the same manner and flay one single ram and cover with its skin the image of Zeus, and then they bring up to it another image of Heracles. This done, all who are in the temple beat themselves in lamentation for the ram, and then they bury it in a sacred tomb.

43. About Heracles I heard the account given that he was of the number of the twelve gods; but of the other Heracles whom the Hellenes know I was not able to hear in any part of Egypt: and moreover to prove that the Egyptians did not take the name of Heracles from the Hellenes, but rather the Hellenes from the Egyptians,—that is to say those of the Hellenes who gave the name Heracles to the son of Amphitryon,—of that, I say, besides many other evidences there is chiefly this, namely that the parents of this Heracles, Amphitryon and Alcmene, were both of Egypt by descent, and also that the Egyptians say that they do not know the names either of Poseidon or of the Dioscuroi, nor have these been accepted by them as gods among the other gods; whereas if they had received from the Hellenes the name of any divinity, they would naturally have preserved the memory

of these most of all, assuming that in those times as now some of the Hellenes were wont to make voyages and were sea-faring folk, as I suppose and as my judgment compels me to think; so that the Egyptians would have learnt the names of these gods even more than that of Heracles. In fact however Heracles is a very ancient Egyptian god; and (as they say themselves) it is seventeen thousand years to the beginning of the reign of Amasis from the time when the twelve gods, of whom they count that Heracles is one, were begotten of the eight gods.

44. I moreover, desiring to know something certain of these matters so far as might be, made a voyage also to Tyre of Phenicia, hearing that in that place there was a holy temple of Heracles; and I saw that it was richly furnished with many votive offerings besides, and especially there were in it two pillars, the one of pure gold and the other of an emerald stone of such size as to shine by night: and having come to speech with the priests of the god, I asked them how long time it was since their temple had been set up: and these also I found to be at variance with the Hellenes, for they said that at the same time when Tyre was founded, the temple of the god also had been set up, and that it was a period of two thousand three hundred years since their people began to dwell at Tyre. I saw also at Tyre another temple of Heracles, with the surname Thasian; and I came to Thasos also and there I found a temple of Heracles set up by the Phoenicians, who had sailed out to seek for Europa and had colonized Thasos; and these things happened full five generations of men before Heracles the son of Amphitryon was born in Hellas. So then my inquiries show clearly that Heracles is an ancient god, and those of the Hellenes seem to me to act most rightly who have two temples of Heracles set up, and who sacrifice to the one as an immortal god and with the title Olympian, and make offerings of the dead to the other as a hero.

45. Moreover, besides many other stories which the Hellenes tell without due consideration, this tale is especially foolish which they tell about Heracles, namely that when he came to Egypt, the Egyptians put on him wreaths and led him forth in procession to sacrifice him to Zeus; and he for some time kept quiet, but when they were beginning the sacrifice of him at the altar, he betook himself to prowess and slew them all. I for my part am of opinion that the Hellenes when they tell this tale are altogether without knowledge of the nature and customs of the Egyptians; for how should they for whom it is not lawful to sacrifice even beasts, except swine and the males of oxen and calves (such of them as are clean) and geese, how should these sacrifice human beings? Besides this, how is it in nature possible that Heracles, being one person only and moreover a man (as they assert), should slay many myriads? Having said so much of these matters, we pray that we may have grace from both the gods and the heroes for our speech.

46. Now the reason why those of the Egyptians whom I have mentioned do not sacrifice goats, female or male, is this:—the Mendesians count Pan to be one of the eight gods (now these eight gods they say came into being before the twelve gods), and the painters and image-makers represent in painting and in sculpture the figure of Pan, just as the Hellenes do, with goat's face and legs, not supposing him to be really like this but to resemble the other gods; the cause however why they represent him in this form I prefer not to say. The Mendesians then reverence all goats and the males more than the females (and the goatherds too have greater honor than other herdsmen), but of the goats one especially is reverenced, and when he dies there is great mourning in all the Mendesian district: and both the goat and Pan are called in the Egyptian tongue *Mendes*. Moreover in

my lifetime there happened in that district this marvel, that is to say a he-goat had inter-course with a woman publicly, and this was so done that all men might have evidence of it.

47. The pig is accounted by the Egyptians an abominable animal; and first, if any of them in passing by touch a pig, he goes into the river and dips himself forthwith in the water together with his garments; and then too swineherds, though they be native Egyptians, unlike all others do not enter any of the temples in Egypt, nor is anyone willing to give his daughter in marriage to one of them or to take a wife from among them; but the swineherds both give in marriage to one another and take from one another. Now to the other gods the Egyptians do not think it right to sacrifice swine; but to the Moon and to Dionysos alone at the same time and on the same full-moon they sacrifice swine, and then eat their flesh: and as to the reason why, when they abominate swine at all their other feasts, they sacrifice them at this, there is a story told by the Egyptians; and this story I know, but it is not a seemly one for me to tell. Now the sacrifice of the swine to the Moon is performed as follows:—when the priest has slain the victim, he puts together the end of the tail and the spleen and the caul, and covers them up with the whole of the fat of the animal which is about the paunch, and then he offers them with fire; and the rest of the flesh they eat on that day of full moon upon which they have held the sacrifice, but on any day after this they will not taste of it: the poor however among them by reason of the scantiness of their means shape pigs of dough and having baked them they offer these as a sacrifice.

48. Then for Dionysos on the eve of the festival each one kills a pig by cutting its throat before his own doors, and after that he gives the pig to the swineherd who sold it to him, to carry away again; and the rest of the feast of Dionysos is celebrated by the Egyptians in the same way as by the Hellenes in almost all things except choral dances, but instead of the *phallos* they have invented another contrivance, namely figures of about a cubit in height worked by strings, which women carry about the villages, with the privy member made to move and not much less in size than the rest of the body: and a flute goes before and they follow singing the praises of Dionysos. As to the reason why the figure has this member larger than is natural and moves it, though it moves no other part of the body, about this there is a sacred story told.

49. Now I think that Melampus the son of Amytheon was not without knowledge of these rites of sacrifice, but was acquainted with them: for Melampus is he who first set forth to the Hellenes the name of Dionysos and the manner of sacrifice and the procession of the *phallos*. Strictly speaking indeed, he when he made it known did not take in the whole, but those wise men who came after him made it known more at large. Melampus then is he who taught of the *phallos* which is carried in procession for Dionysos, and from him the Hellenes learnt to do that which they do. I say then that Melampus being a man of ability contrived for himself an art of divination, and having learnt from Egypt he taught the Hellenes many things, and among them those that concern Dionysos, making changes in some few points of them: for I shall not say that that which is done in worship of the god in Egypt came accidentally to be the same with that which is done among the Hellenes, for then these rites would have been in character with the Hellenic worship and not lately brought in; nor certainly shall I say that the Egyptians took from the Hellenes either this or any other customary observance: but I think it most probable that Melampus learnt the matters concerning Dionysos from

Cadmos the Tyrian and from those who came with him from Phenicia to the land which we now call Boeotia.

50. Moreover the naming of almost all the gods has come to Hellas from Egypt: for that it has come from the Barbarians I find by inquiry is true, and I am of opinion that most probably it has come from Egypt, because, except in the case of Poseidon and the Dioscuroi (in accordance with that which I have said before), and also of Hera and Hestia and Themis and the Charites and Nereïds, the Egyptians have had the names of all the other gods in their country for all time. What I say here is that which the Egyptians think themselves: but as for the gods whose names they profess that they do not know, these I think received their naming from the Pelasgians, except Poseidon; but about this god the Hellenes learnt from the Libyans, for no people except the Libyans have had the name of Poseidon from the first and have paid honor to this god always. Nor, it may be added, have the Egyptians any custom of worshipping heroes.

51. These observances then, and others besides these which I shall mention, the Hellenes have adopted from the Egyptians; but to make, as they do, the images of Hermes with the *phallos* they have learnt not from the Egyptians but from the Pelasgians, the custom having been received by the Athenians first of all the Hellenes and from these by the rest; for just at the time when the Athenians were beginning to rank among the Hellenes, the Pelasgians became dwellers with them in their land, and from this very cause it was that they began to be counted as Hellenes. Whosoever has been initiated in the mysteries of the Cabeiroi, which the Samothrakians perform having received them from the Pelasgians, that man knows the meaning of my speech; for these very Pelasgians who became dwellers with the Athenians used to dwell before that time in Samothrake, and from them the Samothrakians received their mysteries. So then the Athenians were the first of the Hellenes who made the images of Hermes with the *phallos*, having learnt from the Pelasgians; and the Pelasgians told a sacred story about it, which is set forth in the mysteries in Samothrake.

52. Now the Pelasgians formerly were wont to make all their sacrifices calling upon the gods in prayer, as I know from that which I heard at Dodona, but they gave no title or name to any of them, for they had not yet heard any, but they called them gods ({theous}) from some such notion as this, that they had set ({thentes}) in order all things and so had the distribution of everything. Afterwards, when much time had elapsed, they learnt from Egypt the names of the gods, all except Dionysos, for his name they learnt long afterwards; and after a time the Pelasgians consulted the Oracle at Dodona about the names, for this prophetic seat is accounted to be the most ancient of the Oracles which are among the Hellenes, and at that time it was the only one. So when the Pelasgians asked the Oracle at Dodona whether they should adopt the names which had come from the Barbarians, the Oracle in reply bade them make use of the names. From this time they sacrificed using the names of the gods, and from the Pelasgians the Hellenes afterwards received them:

53, but whence the several gods had their birth, or whether they all were from the beginning, and of what form they are, they did not learn till yesterday, as it were, or the day before: for Hesiod and Homer I suppose were four hundred years before my time and not more, and these are they who made a theogony for the Hellenes and gave the titles to the gods and distributed to them honors and arts, and set forth their forms: but the poets who are said to have been before these men were really in my opinion after them. Of these things the first are said by the priestesses of Dodona, and the latter things, those namely which have regard to Hesiod and Homer, by myself.

54. As regards the Oracles both that among the Hellenes and that in Libya, the Egyptians tell the following tale. The priests of the Theban Zeus told me that two women in the service of the temple had been carried away from Thebes by Phoenicians, and that they had heard that one of them had been sold to go into Libya and the other to the Hellenes; and these women, they said, were they who first founded the prophetic seats among the nations which have been named: and when I inquired whence they knew so perfectly of this tale which they told, they said in reply that a great search had been made by the priests after these women, and that they had not been able to find them, but they had heard afterwards this tale about them which they were telling.

55. This I heard from the priests at Thebes, and what follows is said by the prophetesses of Dodona. They say that two black doves flew from Thebes to Egypt, and came one of them to Libya and the other to their land. And this latter settled upon an oak-tree and spoke with human voice, saying that it was necessary that a prophetic seat of Zeus should be established in that place; and they supposed that that was of the gods which was announced to them, and made one accordingly: and the dove which went away to the Libyans, they say, bade the Libyans to make an Oracle of Ammon; and this also is of Zeus. The priestesses of Dodona told me these things, of whom the eldest was named Promeneia, the next after her Timarete, and the youngest Nicandra; and the other people of Dodona who were engaged about the temple gave accounts agreeing with theirs.

56. I however have an opinion about the matter as follows:—If the Phoenicians did in truth carry away the consecrated women and sold one of them into Libya and the other into Hellas, I suppose that in the country now called Hellas, which was formerly called Pelasgia, this woman was sold into the land of the Thesprotians; and then being a slave there she set up a sanctuary of Zeus under a real oak-tree; as indeed it was natural that being an attendant of the sanctuary of Zeus at Thebes, she should there, in the place to which she had come, have a memory of him; and after this, when she got understanding of the Hellenic tongue, she established an Oracle, and she reported, I suppose, that her sister had been sold in Libya by the same Phoenicians by whom she herself had been sold.

57. Moreover, I think that the women were called doves by the people of Dodona for the reason that they were Barbarians and because it seemed to them that they uttered voice like birds; but after a time (they say) the dove spoke with human voice, that is when the woman began to speak so that they could understand; but so long as she spoke a Barbarian tongue she seemed to them to be uttering voice like a bird: for had it been really a dove, how could it speak with human voice? And in saying that the dove was black, they indicate that the woman was Egyptian. The ways of delivering oracles too at Thebes in Egypt and at Dodona closely resemble one another, as it happens, and also the method of divination by victims has come from Egypt.

58. Moreover, it is true also that the Egyptians were the first of men who made solemn assemblies and processions and approaches to the temples, and from them the Hellenes have learnt them, and my evidence for this is that the Egyptian celebrations of these have been held from a very ancient time, whereas the Hellenic were introduced but lately.

59. The Egyptians hold their solemn assemblies not once in the year but often, especially and with the greatest zeal and devotion at the city of Bubastis for Artemis, and next at Busiris for Isis; for in this last-named city there is a very great temple of Isis, and this

city stands in the middle of the Delta of Egypt; now Isis is in the tongue of the Hellenes Demeter: thirdly, they have a solemn assembly at the city of Saïs for Athene, fourthly at Heliopolis for the Sun (Helios), fifthly at the city of Buto in honor of Leto, and sixthly at the city of Papremis for Ares.

60. Now, when they are coming to the city of Bubastis they do as follows:—they sail men and women together, and a great multitude of each sex in every boat; and some of the women have rattles and rattle with them, while some of the men play the flute during the whole time of the voyage, and the rest, both women and men, sing and clap their hands; and when as they sail they come opposite to any city on the way they bring the boat to land, and some of the women continue to do as I have said, others cry aloud and jeer at the women in that city, some dance, and some stand up and pull up their garments. This they do by every city along the river-bank; and when they come to Bubastis they hold festival celebrating great sacrifices, and more wine of grapes is consumed upon that festival than during the whole of the rest of the year. To this place (so say the natives) they come together year by year even to the number of seventy myriads of men and women, besides children.

61. Thus it is done here; and how they celebrate the festival in honor of Isis at the city of Busiris has been told by me before: for, as I said, they beat themselves in mourning after the sacrifice, all of them both men and women, very many myriads of people; but for whom they beat themselves it is not permitted to me by religion to say: and so many as there are of the Carians dwelling in Egypt do this even more than the Egyptians them-selves, inasmuch as they cut their foreheads also with knives; and by this it is manifested that they are strangers and not Egyptians.

62. At the times when they gather together at the city of Saïs for their sacrifices, on a certain night they all kindle lamps many in number in the open air round about the houses; now the lamps are saucers full of salt and oil mixed, and the wick floats by itself on the surface, and this burns during the whole night; and to the festival is given the name *Lychnocaia* (the lighting of the lamps). Moreover those of the Egyptians who have not come to this solemn assembly observe the night of the festival and themselves also light lamps all of them, and thus not in Saïs alone are they lighted, but overall Egypt: and as to the reason why light and honor are allotted to this night, about this there is a sacred story told.

63. To Heliopolis and Buto they go year by year and do sacrifice only: but at Papremis they do sacrifice and worship as elsewhere, and besides that, when the sun begins to go down, while some few of the priests are occupied with the image of the god, the greater number of them stand in the entrance of the temple with wooden clubs, and other persons to the number of more than a thousand men with purpose to perform a vow, these also having all of them staves of wood, stand in a body opposite to those: and the image, which is in a small shrine of wood covered over with gold, they take out on the day before to another sacred building. The few then who have been left about the image, draw a wain with four wheels, which bears the shrine and the image that is within the shrine, and the other priests standing in the gateway try to prevent it from entering, and the men who are under a vow come to the assistance of the god and strike them, while the others defend themselves. Then there comes to be a hard fight with staves, and they break one another's heads, and I am of opinion that many even die of the wounds they receive; the Egyptians however told me that no one died. This solemn

assembly the people of the place say that they established for the following reason:—the mother of Ares, they say, used to dwell in this temple, and Ares, having been brought up away from her, when he grew up came thither desiring to visit his mother, and the attendants of his mother's temple, not having seen him before, did not permit him to pass in, but kept him away; and he brought men to help him from another city and handled roughly the attendants of the temple, and entered to visit his mother. Hence, they say, this exchange of blows has become the custom in honor of Ares upon his festival.

64. The Egyptians were the first who made it a point of religion not to lie with women in temples, nor to enter into temples after going away from women without first bathing: for almost all other men except the Egyptians and the Hellenes lie with women in temples and enter into a temple after going away from women without bathing, since they hold that there is no difference in this respect between men and beasts: for they say that they see beasts and the various kinds of birds coupling together both in the temples and in the sacred enclosures of the gods; if then this were not pleasing to the god, the beasts would not do so.

65. Thus do these defend that which they do, which by me is disallowed: but the Egyptians are excessively careful in their observances, both in other matters which concern the sacred rites and also in those which follow:—Egypt, though it borders upon Libya, does not very much abound in wild animals, but such as they have are one and all accounted by them sacred, some of them living with men and others not. But if I should say for what reasons the sacred animals have been thus dedicated, I should fall into discourse of matters pertaining to the gods, of which I most desire not to speak; and what I have actually said touching slightly upon them, I said because I was constrained by necessity. About these animals there is a custom of this kind:—persons have been appointed of the Egyptians, both men and women, to provide the food for each kind of beast separately, and their office goes down from father to son; and those who dwell in the various cities perform vows to them thus, that is, when they make a vow to the god to whom the animal belongs, they shave the head of their children either the whole or the half or the third part of it, and then set the hair in the balance against silver, and whatever it weighs, this the man gives to the person who provides for the animals, and she cuts up fish of equal value and gives it for food to the animals. Thus food for their support has been appointed: and if any one kill any of these animals, the penalty, if he do it with his own will, is death, and if against his will, such penalty as the priests may appoint: but whosoever shall kill an ibis or a hawk, whether it be with his will or against his will, must die.

66. Of the animals that live with men there are great numbers, and would be many more but for the accidents which befall the cats. For when the females have produced young they are no longer in the habit of going to the males, and these seeking to be united with them are not able. To this end then they contrive as follows,—they either take away by force or remove secretly the young from the females and kill them (but after killing they do not eat them), and the females being deprived of their young and desiring more, therefore come to the males, for it is a creature that is fond of its young. Moreover when a fire occurs, the cats seem to be divinely possessed; for while the Egyptians stand at intervals and look after the cats, not taking any care to extinguish the fire, the cats slipping through or leaping over the men, jump into the fire; and when this happens, great mourning comes upon the Egyptians. And in whatever houses a cat has died by a natural

death, all those who dwell in this house shave their eyebrows only, but those in whose houses a dog has died shave their whole body and also their head.

67. The cats when they are dead are carried away to sacred buildings in the city of Bubastis, where after being embalmed they are buried; but the dogs they bury each people in their own city in sacred tombs; and the ichneumons are buried just in the same way as the dogs. The shrew-mice however and the hawks they carry away to the city of Buto, and the ibises to Hermopolis; the bears (which are not commonly seen) and the wolves, not much larger in size than foxes, they bury on the spot where they are found lying.

68. Of the crocodile the nature is as follows:—during the four most wintry months this creature eats nothing: she has four feet and is an animal belonging to the land and the water both; for she produces and hatches eggs on the land, and the most part of the day she remains upon dry land, but the whole of the night in the river, for the water in truth is warmer than the unclouded open air and the dew. Of all the mortal creatures of which we have knowledge this grows to the greatest bulk from the smallest beginning; for the eggs which she produces are not much larger than those of geese and the newly-hatched young one is in proportion to the egg, but as he grows he becomes as much as seventeen cubits long and sometimes yet larger. He has eyes like those of a pig and teeth large and tusky, in proportion to the size of his body; but unlike all other beasts he grows no tongue, neither does he move his lower jaw, but brings the upper jaw towards the lower, being in this too unlike all other beasts. He has moreover strong claws and a scaly hide upon his back which cannot be pierced; and he is blind in the water, but in the air he is of very keen sight. Since he has his living in the water he keeps his mouth all full within of leeches; and whereas all other birds and beasts fly from him, the trochilus is a creature which is at peace with him, seeing that from her he receives benefit; for the crocodile having come out of the water to the land and then having opened his mouth (this he is wont to do generally towards the West Wind), the trochilus upon that enters into his mouth and swallows down the leeches, and he being benefited is pleased and does no harm to the trochilus.

69. Now for some of the Egyptians the crocodiles are sacred animals, and for others not so, but they treat them on the contrary as enemies: those however who dwell about Thebes and about the lake of Moiris hold them to be most sacred, and each of these two peoples keeps one crocodile selected from the whole number, which has been trained to tameness, and they put hanging ornaments of molten stone and of gold into the ears of these and anklets round the front feet, and they give them food appointed and victims of sacrifices and treat them as well as possible while they live, and after they are dead they bury them in sacred tombs, embalming them: but those who dwell about the city of Elephantine even eat them, not holding them to be sacred. They are called not crocodiles but *champsai*, and the Ionians gave them the name of crocodile, comparing their form to that of the crocodiles (lizards) which appear in their country in the stone walls.

70. There are many ways in use of catching them and of various kinds: I shall describe that which to me seems the most worthy of being told. A man puts the back of a pig upon a hook as bait, and lets it go into the middle of the river, while he himself upon the bank of the river has a young live pig, which he beats; and the crocodile hearing its cries makes for the direction of the sound, and when he finds the pig's back he swallows it down: then they pull, and when he is drawn out to land, first of all the hunter forthwith plasters up his eyes with mud, and having so done he very easily gets the mastery of him, but if he does not do so he has much trouble.

71. The river-horse is sacred in the district of Papremis, but for the other Egyptians he is not sacred; and this is the appearance which he presents: he is four-footed, cloven-hoofed like an ox, flat-nosed, with a mane like a horse and showing teeth like tusks, with a tail and voice like a horse, and in size as large as the largest ox; and his hide is so exceedingly thick that when it has been dried shafts of javelins are made of it.

72. There are moreover otters in the river, which they consider to be sacred; and of fish also they esteem that which is called the *lepidotos* to be sacred, and also the eel; and these they say are sacred to the Nile: and of birds the fox-goose.

73. There is also another sacred bird called the phoenix which I did not myself see except in painting, for in truth he comes to them very rarely, at intervals, as the people of Heliopolis say, of five hundred years; and these say that he comes regularly when his father dies; and if he be like the painting, he is of this size and nature, that is to say, some of his feathers are of gold color and others red, and in outline and size he is as nearly as possible like an eagle. This bird they say (but I cannot believe the story) contrives as follows:—setting forth from Arabia he conveys his father, they say, to the temple of the Sun (Helios) plastered up in myrrh, and buries him in the temple of the Sun; and he conveys him thus:—he forms first an egg of myrrh as large as he is able to carry, and then he makes trial of carrying it, and when he has made trial sufficiently, then he hollows out the egg and places his father within it and plasters over with other myrrh that part of the egg where he hollowed it out to put his father in, and when his father is laid in it, it proves (they say) to be of the same weight as it was; and after he has plastered it up, he conveys the whole to Egypt to the temple of the Sun. Thus they say that this bird does.

74. There are also about Thebes sacred serpents, not at all harmful to men, which are small in size and have two horns growing from the top of the head: these they bury when they die in the temple of Zeus, for to this god they say that they are sacred.

75. There is a region moreover in Arabia, situated nearly over against the city of Buto, to which place I came to inquire about the winged serpents: and when I came thither I saw bones of serpents and spines in quantity so great that it is impossible to make report of the number, and there were heaps of spines, some heaps large and others less large and others smaller still than these, and these heaps were many in number. This region in which the spines are scattered upon the ground is of the nature of an entrance from a narrow mountain pass to a great plain, which plain adjoins the plain of Egypt; and the story goes that at the beginning of spring winged serpents from Arabia fly towards Egypt, and the birds called ibises meet them at the entrance to this country and do not suffer the serpents to go by but kill them. On account of this deed it is (say the Arabians) that the ibis has come to be greatly honored by the Egyptians, and the Egyptians also agree that it is for this reason that they honor these birds.

76. The outward form of the ibis is this:—it is a deep black all over, and has legs like those of a crane and a very curved beak, and in size it is about equal to a rail: this is the appearance of the black kind which fight with the serpents, but of those which most crowd round men's feet (for there are two several kinds of ibises) the head is bare and also the whole of the throat, and it is white in feathering except the head and neck and the extremities of the wings and the rump (in all these parts of which I have spoken it is a deep black), while in legs and in the form of the head it resembles the other. As for the serpent its form is like that of the watersnake; and it has wings not feathered but most

nearly resembling the wings of the bat. Let so much suffice as has been said now concerning sacred animals.

77. Of the Egyptians themselves, those who dwell in the part of Egypt which is sown for crops practice memory more than any other men and are the most learned in history by far of all those of whom I have had experience: and their manner of life is as follows:— For three successive days in each month they purge, hunting after health with emetics and clysters, and they think that all the diseases which exist are produced in men by the food on which they live; for the Egyptians are from other causes also the most healthy of all men next after the Libyans (in my opinion on account of the seasons, because the seasons do not change, for by the changes of things generally, and especially of the seasons, diseases are most apt to be produced in men), and as to their diet, it is as follows:—they eat bread, making loaves of maize, which they call *kyllestis*, and they use habitually a wine made out of barley, for vines they have not in their land. Of their fish some they dry in the sun and then eat them without cooking, others they eat cured in brine. Of birds they eat quails and ducks and small birds without cooking, after first curing them; and everything else which they have belonging to the class of birds or fishes, except such as have been set apart by them as sacred, they eat roasted or boiled.

78. In the entertainments of the rich among them, when they have finished eating, a man bears round a wooden figure of a dead body in a coffin, made as like the reality as may be both by painting and carving, and measuring about a cubit or two cubits each way; and this he shows to each of those who are drinking together, saying: "When thou lookest upon this, drink and be merry, for thou shalt be such as this when thou art dead." Thus they do at their carousals.

79. The customs which they practice are derived from their fathers and they do not acquire others in addition; but besides other customary things among them which are worthy of mention, they have one song, that of Linos, the same who is sung of both in Phenicia and in Cyprus and elsewhere, having however a name different according to the various nations. This song agrees exactly with that which the Hellenes sing calling on the name of Linos, so that besides many other things about which I wonder among those matters which concern Egypt, I wonder especially about this, namely whence they got the song of Linos. It is evident however that they have sung this song from immemorial time, and in the Egyptian tongue Linos is called Maneros. The Egyptians told me that he was the only son of him who first became king of Egypt, and that he died before his time and was honored with these lamentations by the Egyptians, and that this was their first and only song.

80. In another respect the Egyptians are in agreement with some of the Hellenes, namely with the Lacedemonians, but not with the rest, that is to say, the younger of them when they meet the elder give way and move out of the path, and when their elders approach they rise out of their seat. In this which follows however they are not in agreement with any of the Hellenes,—instead of addressing one another in the roads they do reverence, lowering their hand down to their knee.

81. They wear tunics of linen about their legs with fringes, which they call *calasiris*; above these they have garments of white wool thrown over: woolen garments however are not taken into the temples, nor are they buried with them, for this is not permitted by religion. In these points they are in agreement with the observances called Orphic and Bacchic (which are really Egyptian), and also with those of the Pythagoreans, for one who

takes part in these mysteries is also forbidden by religious rule to be buried in woolen garments; and about this there is a sacred story told.

82. Besides these things the Egyptians have found out also to what god each month and each day belongs, and what fortunes a man will meet with who is born on any particular day, and how he will die, and what kind of a man he will be: and these inventions were taken up by those of the Hellenes who occupied themselves about poesy. Portents too have been found out by them more than by all other men besides; for when a portent has happened, they observe and write down the event which comes of it, and if ever afterwards anything resembling this happens, they believe that the event which comes of it will be similar.

83. Their divination is ordered thus:—the art is assigned not to any man, but to certain of the gods, for there are in their land Oracles of Heracles, of Apollo, of Athene, of Artemis, of Ares, and of Zeus, and moreover that which they hold most in honor of all, namely the Oracle of Leto which is in the city of Buto. The manner of divination however is not yet established among them according to the same fashion everywhere, but is different in different places.

84. The art of medicine among them is distributed thus:—each physician is a physician of one disease and of no more; and the whole country is full of physicians, for some profess themselves to be physicians of the eyes, others of the head, others of the teeth, others of the affections of the stomach, and others of the more obscure ailments.

85. Their fashions of mourning and of burial are these:—Whenever any household has lost a man who is of any regard amongst them, the whole number of women of that house forthwith plaster over their heads or even their faces with mud. Then leaving the corpse within the house they go themselves to and fro about the city and beat themselves, with their garments bound up by a girdle and their breasts exposed, and with them go all the women who are related to the dead man, and on the other side the men beat themselves, they too having their garments bound up by a girdle; and when they have done this, they then convey the body to the embalming.

86. In this occupation certain persons employ themselves regularly and inherit this as a craft. These, whenever a corpse is conveyed to them, show to those who brought it wooden models of corpses made like reality by painting, and the best of the ways of embalming they say is that of him whose name I think it impiety to mention when speaking of a matter of such a kind; the second which they show is less good than this and also less expensive; and the third is the least expensive of all. Having told them about this, they inquire of them in which way they desire the corpse of their friend to be prepared. Then they after they have agreed for a certain price depart out of the way, and the others being left behind in the buildings embalm according to the best of these ways thus:—First with a crooked iron tool they draw out the brain through the nostrils, extracting it partly thus and partly by pouring in drugs; and after this with a sharp stone of Ethiopia they make a cut along the side and take out the whole contents of the belly, and when they have cleared out the cavity and cleansed it with palm-wine they cleanse it again with spices pounded up: then they fill the belly with pure myrrh pounded up and with cassia and other spices except frankincense, and sew it together again. Having so done they keep it for embalming covered up in natron for seventy days, but for a longer time than this it is not permitted to embalm it; and when the seventy days are past, they wash the corpse and roll its whole body up in fine linen cut into bands, smearing these beneath with gum,

which the Egyptians use generally instead of glue. Then the kinsfolk receive it from them and have a wooden figure made in the shape of a man, and when they have had this made they enclose the corpse, and having shut it up within, they store it then in a sepulchral chamber, setting it to stand upright against the wall.

87. Thus they deal with the corpses which are prepared in the most costly way; but for those who desire the middle way and wish to avoid great cost they prepare the corpse as follows:—having filled their syringes with the oil which is got from cedar-wood, with this they forthwith fill the belly of the corpse, and this they do without having either cut it open or taken out the bowels, but they inject the oil by the breech, and having stopped the drench from returning back they keep it then the appointed number of days for embalming, and on the last of the days they let the cedar oil come out from the belly, which they before put in; and it has such power that it brings out with it the bowels and interior organs of the body dissolved; and the natron dissolves the flesh, so that there is left of the corpse only the skin and the bones. When they have done this they give back the corpse at once in that condition without working upon it any more.

88. The third kind of embalming, by which are prepared the bodies of those who have less means, is as follows:—they cleanse out the belly with a purge and then keep the body for embalming during the seventy days, and at once after that they give it back to the bringers to carry away.

89. The wives of men of rank when they die are not given at once to be embalmed, nor such women as are very beautiful or of greater regard than others, but on the third or fourth day after their death (and not before) they are delivered to the embalmers. They do so about this matter in order that the embalmers may not abuse their women, for they say that one of them was taken once doing so to the corpse of a woman lately dead, and his fellow-craftsman gave information.

90. Whenever anyone, either of the Egyptians themselves or of strangers, is found to have been carried off by a crocodile or brought to his death by the river itself, the people of any city by which he may have been cast up on land must embalm him and lay him out in the fairest way they can and bury him in a sacred burial-place, nor may any of his relations or friends besides touch him, but the priests of the Nile themselves handle the corpse and bury it as that of one who was something more than man.

91. Hellenic usages they will by no means follow, and to speak generally they follow those of no other men whatever. This rule is observed by most of the Egyptians; but there is a large city named Chemmis in the Theban district near Neapolis, and in this city there is a temple of Perseus the son of Danae which is of a square shape, and round it grow date-palms: the gateway of the temple is built of stone and of very great size, and at the entrance of it stand two great statues of stone. Within this enclosure is a temple-house and in it stands an image of Perseus. These people of Chemmis say that Perseus is wont often to appear in their land and often within the temple, and that a sandal which has been worn by him is found sometimes, being in length two cubits, and whenever this appears all Egypt prospers. This they say, and they do in honor of Perseus after Hellenic fashion thus,—they hold an athletic contest, which includes the whole list of games, and they offer in prizes cattle and cloaks and skins: and when I inquired why to them alone Perseus was wont to appear, and wherefore they were separated from all the other Egyptians in that they held an athletic contest, they said that Perseus had been born of their city, for Danaos and Lynkeus were men of Chemmis and had sailed to Hellas, and from them they traced a

descent and came down to Perseus: and they told me that he had come to Egypt for the reason which the Hellenes also say, namely to bring from Libya the Gorgon's head, and had then visited them also and recognized all his kinsfolk, and they said that he had well learnt the name of Chemmis before he came to Egypt, since he had heard it from his mother, and that they celebrated an athletic contest for him by his own command.

92. All these are customs practiced by the Egyptians who dwell above the fens: and those who are settled in the fen-land have the same customs for the most part as the other Egyptians, both in other matters and also in that they live each with one wife only, as do the Hellenes; but for economy in respect of food they have invented these things besides: —when the river has become full and the plains have been flooded, there grow in the water great numbers of lilies, which the Egyptians call *lotos*; these they cut with a sickle and dry in the sun, and then they pound that which grows in the middle of the lotos and which is like the head of a poppy, and they make of it loaves baked with fire. The root also of this lotos is edible and has a rather sweet taste: it is round in shape and about the size of an apple. There are other lilies too, in flower resembling roses, which also grow in the river, and from them the fruit is produced in a separate vessel springing from the root by the side of the plant itself, and very nearly resembles a wasp's comb: in this there grow edible seeds in great numbers of the size of an olive-stone, and they are eaten either fresh or dried. Besides this they pull up from the fens the papyrus which grows every year, and the upper parts of it they cut off and turn to other uses, but that which is left below for about a cubit in length they eat or sell: and those who desire to have the papyrus at its very best bake it in an oven heated red-hot, and then eat it. Some too of these people live on fish alone, which they dry in the sun after having caught them and taken out the entrails, and then when they are dry, they use them for food.

93. Fish which swim in shoals are not much produced in the rivers, but are bred in the lakes, and they do as follows:—When there comes upon them the desire to breed, they swim out in shoals towards the sea; and the males lead the way shedding forth their milt as they go, while the females, coming after and swallowing it up, from it become impregnated: and when they have become full of young in the sea they swim up back again, each shoal to its own haunts. The same however no longer lead the way as before, but the lead comes now to the females, and they leading the way in shoals do just as the males did, that is to say they shed forth their eggs by a few grains at a time, and the males coming after swallow them up. Now these grains are fish, and from the grains which survive and are not swallowed, the fish grow which afterwards are bred up. Now those of the fish which are caught as they swim out to sea are found to be rubbed on the left side of the head, but those which are caught as they swim up again are rubbed on the right side. This happens to them because as they swim down to the sea they keep close to the land on the left side of the river, and again as they swim up they keep to the same side, approaching and touching the bank as much as they can, for fear doubtless of straying from their course by reason of the stream. When the Nile begins to swell, the hollow places of the land and the depressions by the side of the river first begin to fill, as the water soaks through from the river, and so soon as they become full of water, at once they are all filled with little fishes; and whence these are in all likelihood produced, I think that I perceive. In the preceding year, when the Nile goes down, the fish first lay eggs in the mud and then retire with the last of the retreating waters; and when the time comes round again, and the water once more

comes over the land, from these eggs forthwith are produced the fishes of which I speak.

94. Thus it is as regards the fish. And for anointing those of the Egyptians who dwell in the fens use oil from the castor-berry, which oil the Egyptians call *kiki*, and thus they do:— they sow along the banks of the rivers and pools these plants, which in a wild form grow of themselves in the land of the Hellenes; these are sown in Egypt and produce berries in great quantity but of an evil smell; and when they have gathered these, some cut them up and press the oil from them, others again roast them first and then boil them down and collect that which runs away from them. The oil is fat and not less suitable for burning than olive-oil, but it gives forth a disagreeable smell.

95. Against the gnats, which are very abundant, they have contrived as follows:—those who dwell above the fen-land are helped by the towers, to which they ascend when they go to rest; for the gnats by reason of the winds are not able to fly up high: but those who dwell in the fen-land have contrived another way instead of the towers, and this is it:— every man of them has got a casting net, with which by day he catches fish, but in the night he uses it for this purpose, that is to say he puts the casting-net round about the bed in which he sleeps, and then creeps in under it and goes to sleep: and the gnats, if he sleeps rolled up in a garment or a linen sheet, bite through these, but through the net they do not even attempt to bite.

96. Their boats with which they carry cargoes are made of the thorny acacia, of which the form is very like that of the Kyrenian lotos, and that which exudes from it is gum. From this tree they cut pieces of wood about two cubits in length and arrange them like bricks, fastening the boat together by running a great number of long bolts through the two-cubit pieces; and when they have thus fastened the boat together, they lay cross-pieces over the top, using no ribs for the sides; and within they caulk the seams with papyrus. They make one steering-oar for it, which is passed through the bottom of the boat; and they have a mast of acacia and sails of papyrus. These boats cannot sail up the river unless there be a very fresh wind blowing, but are towed from the shore: down-stream however they travel as follows:—they have a door-shaped crate made of tamarisk wood and reed mats sewn together, and also a stone of about two talents weight bored with a hole; and of these the boatman lets the crate float on in front of the boat, fastened with a rope, and the stone drag behind by another rope. The crate then, as the force of the stream presses upon it, goes on swiftly and draws on the *baris*(for so these boats are called), while the stone dragging after it behind and sunk deep in the water keeps its course straight. These boats they have in great numbers and some of them carry many thousands of talents' burden.

97. When the Nile comes over the land, the cities alone are seen rising above the water, resembling more nearly than anything else the islands in the Egean sea; for the rest of Egypt becomes a sea and the cities alone rise above water. Accordingly, whenever this happens, they pass by water not now by the channels of the river but over the midst of the plain: for example, as one sails up from Naucratis to Memphis the passage is then close by the pyramids, whereas the usual passage is not the same even here, but goes by the point of the Delta and the city of Kercasoros; while if you sail over the plain to Naucratis from the sea and from Canobos, you will go by Anthylla and the city called after Archander.

98. Of these Anthylla is a city of note and is especially assigned to the wife of him who reigns over Egypt, to supply her with sandals, (this is the case since the time when Egypt

came to be under the Persians): the other city seems to me to have its name from Archander the son-in-law of Danaos, who was the son of Phthios, the son of Achaios; for it is called the City of Archander. There might indeed be another Archander, but in any case the name is not Egyptian.

99. Hitherto my own observation and judgment and inquiry are the vouchers for that which I have said; but from this point onwards I am about to tell the history of Egypt according to that which I heard, to which will be added also something of that which I have myself seen.

Of Min, who first became king of Egypt, the priests said that on the one hand he banked off the site of Memphis from the river: for the whole stream of the river used to flow along by the sandy mountain-range on the side of Libya, but Min formed by embankments that bend of the river which lies to the South about a hundred furlongs above Memphis, and thus he dried up the old stream and conducted the river so that it flowed in the middle between the mountains: and even now this bend of the Nile is by the Persians kept under very careful watch, that it may flow in the channel to which it is confined, and the bank is repaired every year; for if the river should break through and overflow in this direction, Memphis would be in danger of being overwhelmed by flood. When this Min, who first became king, had made into dry land the part which was dammed off, on the one hand, I say, he founded in it that city which is now called Memphis; for Memphis too is in the narrow part of Egypt; and outside the city he dug round it on the North and West a lake communicating with the river, for the side towards the East is barred by the Nile itself. Then secondly he established in the city the temple of Hephaistos a great work and most worthy of mention.

100. After this man the priests enumerated to me from a papyrus roll the names of other kings, three hundred and thirty in number; and in all these generations of men eighteen were Ethiopians, one was a woman, a native Egyptian, and the rest were men and of Egyptian race: and the name of the woman who reigned was the same as that of the Babylonian queen, namely Nitocris. Of her they said that desiring to take vengeance for her brother, whom the Egyptians had slain when he was their king and then, after having slain him, had given his kingdom to her,—desiring, I say, to take vengeance for him, she destroyed by craft many of the Egyptians. For she caused to be constructed a very large chamber underground, and making as though she would handsel it but in her mind devising other things, she invited those of the Egyptians whom she knew to have had most part in the murder, and gave a great banquet. Then while they were feasting, she let in the river upon them by a secret conduit of large size. Of her they told no more than this, except that, when this had been accomplished, she threw herself into a room full of embers, in order that she might escape vengeance.

101. As for the other kings, they could tell me of no great works which had been produced by them, and they said that they had no renown except only the last of them, Moris: he (they said) produced as a memorial of himself the gateway of the temple of Hephaistos which is turned towards the North Wind, and dug a lake, about which I shall set forth afterwards how many furlongs of circuit it has, and in it built pyramids of the size which I shall mention at the same time when I speak of the lake itself. He, they said, produced these works, but of the rest none produced any.

102. Therefore passing these by I shall make mention of the king who came after these, whose name was Sesostris. He (the priests said) first of all set out with ships of war from

the Arabian gulf and subdued those who dwelt by the shores of the Erythraian Sea, until as he sailed he came to a sea which could no further be navigated by reason of shoals: then secondly, after he had returned to Egypt, according to the report of the priests he took a great army and marched over the continent, subduing every nation which stood in his way: and those of them whom he found valiant and fighting desperately for their freedom, in their lands he set up pillars which told by inscriptions his own name and the name of his country, and how he had subdued them by his power; but as to those of whose cities he obtained possession without fighting or with ease, on their pillars he inscribed words after the same tenor as he did for the nations which had shown themselves courageous, and in addition he drew upon them the hidden parts of a woman, desiring to signify by this that the people were cowards and effeminate.

103. Thus doing he traversed the continent, until at last he passed over to Europe from Asia and subdued the Scythians and also the Thracians. These, I am of opinion, were the furthest people to which the Egyptian army came, for in their country the pillars are found to have been set up, but in the land beyond this they are no longer found. From this point he turned and began to go back; and when he came to the river Phasis, what happened then I cannot say for certain, whether the king Sesostris himself divided off a certain portion of his army and left the men there as settlers in the land, or whether some of his soldiers were wearied by his distant marches and remained by the river Phasis.

104. For the people of Colchis are evidently Egyptian, and this I perceived for myself before I heard it from others. So when I had come to consider the matter I asked them both; and the Colchians had remembrance of the Egyptians more than the Egyptians of the Colchians; but the Egyptians said they believed that the Colchians were a portion of the army of Sesostris. That this was so I conjectured myself not only because they are dark-skinned and have curly hair (this of itself amounts to nothing, for there are other races which are so), but also still more because the Colchians, Egyptians, and Ethiopians alone of all the races of men have practiced circumcision from the first. The Phoenicians and the Syrians who dwell in Palestine confess themselves that they have learnt it from the Egyptians, and the Syrians about the river Thermodon and the river Parthenios, and the Macronians, who are their neighbors, say that they have learnt it lately from the Colchians. These are the only races of men who practice circumcision, and these evidently practice it in the same manner as the Egyptians. Of the Egyptians themselves however and the Ethiopians, I am not able to say which learnt from the other, for undoubtedly it is a most ancient custom; but that the other nations learnt it by intercourse with the Egyptians, this among others is to me a strong proof, namely that those of the Phoenicians who have intercourse with Hellas cease to follow the example of the Egyptians in this matter, and do not circumcise their children.

105. Now let me tell another thing about the Colchians to show how they resemble the Egyptians:—they alone work flax in the same fashion as the Egyptians, and the two nations are like one another in their whole manner of living and also in their language: now the linen of Colchis is called by the Hellenes Sardonic, whereas that from Egypt is called Egyptian.

106. The pillars which Sesostris of Egypt set up in the various countries are for the most part no longer to be seen extant; but in Syria Palestine I myself saw them existing with the inscription upon them which I have mentioned and the emblem. Moreover in Ionia there are two figures of this man carved upon rocks, one on the road by which one

goes from the land of Ephesos to Phocaia, and the other on the road from Sardis to Smyrna. In each place there is a figure of a man cut in the rock, of four cubits and a span in height, holding in his right hand a spear and in his left a bow and arrows, and the other equipment which he has is similar to this, for it is both Egyptian and Ethiopian: and from the one shoulder to the other across the breast runs an inscription carved in sacred Egyptian characters, saying thus, "This land with my shoulders I won for myself." But who he is and from whence, he does not declare in these places, though in other places he has declared this. Some of those who have seen these carvings conjecture that the figure is that of Memnon, but herein they are very far from the truth.

107. As this Egyptian Sesostris was returning and bringing back many men of the nations whose lands he had subdued, when he came (said the priests) to Daphnai in the district of Pelusion on his journey home, his brother to whom Sesostris had entrusted the charge of Egypt invited him and with him his sons to a feast; and then he piled the house round with brushwood and set it on fire: and Sesostris when he discovered this forthwith took counsel with his wife, for he was bringing with him (they said) his wife also; and she counselled him to lay out upon the pyre two of his sons, which were six in number, and so to make a bridge over the burning mass, and that they passing over their bodies should thus escape. This, they said, Sesostris did, and two of his sons were burnt to death in this manner, but the rest got away safe with their father.

108. Then Sesostris, having returned to Egypt and having taken vengeance on his brother, employed the multitude which he had brought in of those whose lands he had subdued, as follows:—these were they who drew the stones which in the reign of this king were brought to the temple of Hephaistos, being of very great size; and also these were compelled to dig all the channels which now are in Egypt; and thus (having no such purpose) they caused Egypt, which before was all fit for riding and driving, to be no longer fit for this from thenceforth: for from that time forward Egypt, though it is plain land, has become all unfit for riding and driving, and the cause has been these channels, which are many and run in all directions. But the reason why the king cut up the land was this, namely because those of the Egyptians who had their cities not on the river but in the middle of the country, being in want of water when the river went down from them, found their drink brackish because they had it from wells.

109. For this reason Egypt was cut up; and they said that this king distributed the land to all the Egyptians, giving an equal square portion to each man, and from this he made his revenue, having appointed them to pay a certain rent every year: and if the river should take away anything from any man's portion, he would come to the king and declare that which had happened, and the king used to send men to examine and to find out by measurement how much less the piece of land had become, in order that for the future the man might pay less, in proportion to the rent appointed: and I think that thus the art of geometry was found out and afterwards came into Hellas also. For as touching the sun-dial and the gnomon and the twelve divisions of the day, they were learnt by the Hellenes from the Babylonians.

110. He moreover alone of all the Egyptian kings had rule over Ethiopia; and he left as memorials of himself in front of the temple of Hephaistos two stone statues of thirty cubits each, representing himself and his wife, and others of twenty cubits each representing his four sons: and long afterwards the priest of Hephaistos refused to permit Dareios the Persian to set up a statue of himself in front of them, saying that deeds had not been done

by him equal to those which were done by Sesostris the Egyptian; for Sesostris had subdued other nations besides, not fewer than he, and also the Scythians; but Dareios had not been able to conquer the Scythians: wherefore it was not just that he should set up a statue in front of those which Sesostris had dedicated, if he did not surpass him in his deeds. Which speech, they say, Dareios took in good part.

111. Now after Sesostris had brought his life to an end, his son Pheros, they told me, received in succession the kingdom, and he made no warlike expedition, and moreover it chanced to him to become blind by reason of the following accident:—when the river had come down in flood rising to a height of eighteen cubits, higher than ever before that time, and had gone over the fields, a wind fell upon it and the river became agitated by waves: and this king (they say) moved by presumptuous folly took a spear and cast it into the midst of the eddies of the stream; and immediately upon this he had a disease of the eyes and was by it made blind. For ten years then he was blind, and in the eleventh year there came to him an oracle from the city of Buto saying that the time of his punishment had expired, and that he should see again if he washed his eyes with the water of a woman who had accompanied with her own husband only and had no knowledge of other men: and first he made trial of his own wife, and then, as he continued blind, he went on to try all the women in turn; and when he had at last regained his sight he gathered together all the women of whom he had made trial, excepting her by whose means he had regained his sight, to one city which now is named Erythrabolos, and having gathered them to this he consumed them all by fire, as well as the city itself; but as for her by whose means he had regained his sight, he had her himself to wife. Then after he had escaped the malady of his eyes he dedicated offerings at each one of the temples which were of renown, and especially (to mention only that which is most worthy of mention) he dedicated at the temple of the Sun works which are worth seeing, namely two obelisks of stone, each of a single block, measuring in length a hundred cubits each one and in breadth eight cubits.

112. After him, they said, there succeeded to the throne a man of Memphis, whose name in the tongue of the Hellenes was Proteus; for whom there is now a sacred enclosure at Memphis, very fair and well ordered, lying on that side of the temple of Hephaistos which faces the North Wind. Round about this enclosure dwell Phoenicians of Tyre, and this whole region is called the Camp of the Tyrians. Within the enclosure of Proteus there is a temple called the temple of the "foreign Aphrodite," which temple I conjecture to be one of Helen the daughter of Tyndareus, not only because I have heard the tale how Helen dwelt with Proteus, but also especially because it is called by the name of the "foreign Aphrodite," for the other temples of Aphrodite which there are have none of them the addition of the word "foreign" to the name.

113. And the priests told me, when I inquired, that the things concerning Helen happened thus:—Alexander having carried off Helen was sailing away from Sparta to his own land, and when he had come to the Egean Sea contrary winds drove him from his course to the Sea of Egypt; and after that, since the blasts did not cease to blow, he came to Egypt itself, and in Egypt to that which is now named the Canobic mouth of the Nile and to Taricheiai. Now there was upon the shore, as still there is now, a temple of Heracles, in which if any man's slave take refuge and have the sacred marks set upon him, giving himself over to the god, it is not lawful to lay hands upon him; and this custom has continued still unchanged from the beginning down to my own time. Accordingly the attendants of Alexander, having heard of the custom which existed about the temple, ran

away from him, and sitting down as suppliants of the god, accused Alexander, because they desired to do him hurt, telling the whole tale how things were about Helen and about the wrong done to Menelaos; and this accusation they made not only to the priests but also to the warden of this river-mouth, whose name was Thonis.

114. Thonis then having heard their tale sent forthwith a message to Proteus at Memphis, which said as follows: "There hath come a stranger, a Teucrian by race, who hath done in Hellas an unholy deed; for he hath deceived the wife of his own host, and is come hither bringing with him this woman herself and very much wealth, having been carried out of his way by winds to thy land. Shall we then allow him to sail out unharmed, or shall we first take away from him that which he brought with him?" In reply to this Proteus sent back a messenger who said thus: "Seize this man, whosoever he may be, who has done impiety to his own host, and bring him away into my presence, that I may know what he will find to say."

115. Hearing this, Thonis seized Alexander and detained his ships, and after that he brought the man himself up to Memphis and with him Helen and the wealth he had, and also in addition to them the suppliants. So when all had been conveyed up thither, Proteus began to ask Alexander who he was and from whence he was voyaging; and he both recounted to him his descent and told him the name of his native land, and moreover related of his voyage, from whence he was sailing. After this Proteus asked him whence he had taken Helen; and when Alexander went astray in his account and did not speak the truth, those who had become suppliants convicted him of falsehood, relating in full the whole tale of the wrong done. At length Proteus declared to them this sentence, saying, "Were it not that I count it a matter of great moment not to slay any of those strangers who being driven from their course by winds have come to my land hitherto, I should have taken vengeance on thee on behalf of the man of Hellas, seeing that thou, most base of men, having received from him hospitality, didst work against him a most impious deed. For thou didst go in to the wife of thine own host; and even this was not enough for thee, but thou didst stir her up with desire and hast gone away with her like a thief. Moreover not even this by itself was enough for thee, but thou art come hither with plunder taken from the house of thy host. Now therefore depart, seeing that I have counted it of great moment not to be a slayer of strangers. This woman indeed and the wealth which thou hast I will not allow thee to carry away, but I shall keep them safe for the Hellene who was thy host, until he come himself and desire to carry them off to his home; to thyself however and thy fellow-voyagers I proclaim that ye depart from your anchoring within three days and go from my land to some other; and if not, that ye will be dealt with as enemies."

116. This the priests said was the manner of Helen's coming to Proteus; and I suppose that Homer also had heard this story, but since it was not so suitable to the composition of his poem as the other which he followed, he dismissed it finally, making it clear at the same time that he was acquainted with that story also: and according to the manner in which he described the wanderings of Alexander in the Iliad (nor did he elsewhere retract that which he had said) it is clear that when he brought Helen he was carried out of his course, wandering to various lands, and that he came among other places to Sidon in Phenicia. Of this the poet has made mention in the "prowess of Diomede," and the verses run this:

"There she had robes many-colored, the works of women of Sidon,
Those whom her son himself the god-like of form Alexander
Carried from Sidon, what time the broad sea-path he sailed over
Bringing back Helene home, of a noble father begotten."

And in the Odyssey also he has made mention of it in these verses:

"Such had the daughter of Zeus, such drugs of exquisite cunning,
Good, which to her the wife of Thon, Polydamna, had given,
Dwelling in Egypt, the land where the bountiful meadow produces
Drugs more than all lands else, many good being mixed, many evil."

And thus too Menelaos says to Telemachos:

"Still the gods stayed me in Egypt, to come back hither desiring,
Stayed me from voyaging home, since sacrifice was due I performed not."

In these lines he makes it clear that he knew of the wandering of Alexander to Egypt, for Syria borders upon Egypt and the Phoenicians, of whom is Sidon, dwell in Syria.

117. By these lines and by this passage it is also most clearly shown that the "Cyprian Epic" was not written by Homer but by some other man: for in this it is said that on the third day after leaving Sparta Alexander came to Ilion bringing with him Helen, having had a "gently-blowing wind and a smooth sea," whereas in the Iliad it says that he wandered from his course when he brought her.

118. Let us now leave Homer and the "Cyprian" Epic; but this I will say, namely that I asked the priests whether it is but an idle tale which the Hellenes tell of that which they say happened about Ilion; and they answered me thus, saying that they had their knowledge by inquiries from Menelaos himself. After the rape of Helen there came indeed, they said, to the Teucrian land a large army of Hellenes to help Menelaos; and when the army had come out of the ships to land and had pitched its camp there, they sent messengers to Ilion, with whom went also Menelaos himself; and when these entered within the wall they demanded back Helen and the wealth which Alexander had stolen from Menelaos and had taken away; and moreover they demanded satisfaction for the wrongs done: and the Teucrians told the same tale then and afterwards, both with oath and without oath, namely that in deed and in truth they had not Helen nor the wealth for which demand was made, but that both were in Egypt; and that they could not justly be compelled to give satisfaction for that which Proteus the king of Egypt had. The Hellenes however thought that they were being mocked by them and besieged the city, until at last they took it; and when they had taken the wall and did not find Helen, but heard the same tale as before, then they believed the former tale and sent Menelaos himself to Proteus.

119. And Menelaos having come to Egypt and having sailed up to Memphis, told the truth of these matters, and not only found great entertainment, but also received Helen unhurt, and all his own wealth besides. Then however, after he had been thus dealt with, Menelaos showed himself ungrateful to the Egyptians; for when he set forth to sail away, contrary winds detained him, and as this condition of things lasted long, he devised an impious deed; for he took two children of natives and made sacrifice of them. After this,

when it was known that he had done so, he became abhorred, and being pursued he escaped and got away in his ships to Libya; but whither he went besides after this, the Egyptians were not able to tell. Of these things they said that they found out part by inquiries, and the rest, namely that which happened in their own land, they related from sure and certain knowledge.

120. Thus the priests of the Egyptians told me; and I myself also agree with the story which was told of Helen, adding this consideration, namely that if Helen had been in Ilion she would have been given up to the Hellenes, whether Alexander consented or no; for Priam assuredly was not so mad, nor yet the others of his house, that they were desirous to run risk of ruin for themselves and their children and their city, in order that Alexander might have Helen as his wife: and even supposing that during the first part of the time they had been so inclined, yet when many others of the Trojans besides were losing their lives as often as they fought with the Hellenes, and of the sons of Priam himself always two or three or even more were slain when a battle took place (if one may trust at all to the Epic poets),—when, I say, things were coming thus to pass, I consider that even if Priam himself had had Helen as his wife, he would have given her back to the Achaians, if at least by so doing he might be freed from the evils which oppressed him. Nor even was the kingdom coming to Alexander next, so that when Priam was old the government was in his hands; but Hector, who was both older and more of a man than he, would have received it after the death of Priam; and him it behooved not to allow his brother to go on with his wrong-doing, considering that great evils were coming to pass on his account both to himself privately and in general to the other Trojans. In truth however they lacked the power to give Helen back; and the Hellenes did not believe them, though they spoke the truth; because, as I declare my opinion, the divine power was purposing to cause them utterly to perish, and so make it evident to men that for great wrongs great also are the chastisements which come from the gods. And thus have I delivered my opinion concerning these matters.

121. After Proteus, they told me, Rhampsinitos received in succession the kingdom, who left as a memorial of himself that gateway to the temple of Hephaistos which is turned towards the West, and in front of the gateway he set up two statues, in height five-and-twenty cubits, of which the one which stands on the North side is called by the Egyptians Summer and the one on the South side Winter; and to that one which they call Summer they do reverence and make offerings, while to the other which is called Winter they do the opposite of these things. (a) This king, they said, got great wealth of silver, which none of the kings born after him could surpass or even come near to; and wishing to store his wealth in safety he caused to be built a chamber of stone, one of the walls whereof was towards the outside of his palace: and the builder of this, having a design against it, contrived as follows, that is, he disposed one of the stones in such a manner that it could be taken out easily from the wall either by two men or even by one. So when the chamber was finished, the king stored his money in it, and after some time the builder, being near the end of his life, called to him his sons (for he had two) and to them he related how he had contrived in building the treasury of the king, and all in forethought for them, that they might have ample means of living. And when he had clearly set forth to them everything concerning the taking out of the stone, he gave them the measurements, saying that if they paid heed to this matter they would be stewards of the king's treasury. So he ended his life, and his sons made no long delay in setting to work, but

went to the palace by night, and having found the stone in the wall of the chamber they dealt with it easily and carried forth for themselves great quantity of the wealth within. (b) And the king happening to open the chamber, he marveled when he saw the vessels falling short of the full amount, and he did not know on whom he should lay the blame, since the seals were unbroken and the chamber had been close shut; but when upon his opening the chamber a second and a third time the money was each time seen to be diminished, for the thieves did not slacken in their assaults upon it, he did as follows:— having ordered traps to be made he set these round about the vessels in which the money was; and when the thieves had come as at former times and one of them had entered, then so soon as he came near to one of the vessels he was straightway caught in the trap: and when he perceived in what evil case he was, straightway calling his brother he showed him what the matter was, and bade him enter as quickly as possible and cut off his head, for fear lest being seen and known he might bring about the destruction of his brother also. And to the other it seemed that he spoke well, and he was persuaded and did so; and fitting the stone into its place he departed home bearing with him the head of his brother. (c) Now when it became day, the king entered into the chamber and was very greatly amazed, seeing the body of the thief held in the trap without his head, and the chamber unbroken, with no way to come in or go out: and being at a loss he hung up the dead body of the thief upon the wall and set guards there, with charge if they saw any one weeping or bewailing himself to seize him and bring him before the king. And when the dead body had been hung up, the mother was greatly grieved, and speaking with the son who survived she enjoined him, in whatever way he could, to contrive means by which he might take down and bring home the body of his dead brother; and if he should neglect to do this, she earnestly threatened that she would go and give information to the king that he had the money. (d) So as the mother dealt hardly with the surviving son, and he though saying many things to her did not persuade her, he contrived for his purpose a device as follows:—Providing himself with asses he filled some skins with wine and laid them upon the asses, and after that he drove them along: and when he came opposite to those who were guarding the corpse hung up, he drew towards him two or three of the necks of the skins and loosened the cords with which they were tied. Then when the wine was running out, he began to beat his head and cry out loudly, as if he did not know to which of the asses he should first turn; and when the guards saw the wine flowing out in streams, they ran together to the road with drinking vessels in their hands and collected the wine that was poured out, counting it so much gain; and he abused them all violently, making as if he were angry, but when the guards tried to appease him, after a time he feigned to be pacified and to abate his anger, and at length he drove his asses out of the road and began to set their loads right. Then more talk arose among them, and one or two of them made jests at him and brought him to laugh with them; and in the end he made them a present of one of the skins in addition to what they had. Upon that they lay down there without more ado, being minded to drink, and they took him into their company and invited him to remain with them and join them in their drinking: so he (as may be supposed) was persuaded and stayed. Then as they in their drinking bade him welcome in a friendly manner, he made a present to them also of another of the skins; and so at length having drunk liberally the guards became completely intoxicated; and being over-come by sleep they went to bed on the spot where they had been drinking. He then, as it was now far on in the night, first took down the body of his brother, and then in mockery shaved the right cheeks of all the guards; and after that he put the dead body upon the asses and drove them away home, having accomplished that which was enjoined him by his mother. (e) Upon this the king, when it was reported to him that the dead body of the thief had been stolen away, displayed great anger; and desiring by all means that it should be found out who it might be who devised these things, did this (so at least they said, but I do not believe the account),—he caused his own daughter to sit in the stews, and enjoined her to receive all equally, and before having commerce with anyone to compel him to tell her what was the most cunning and what the most unholy deed which had been done by him in all his life-time; and whosoever should relate that which had happened about the thief, him she must seize and not let him go out. Then as she was doing that which was enjoined by her father, the thief, hearing for what purpose this was done and having a desire to get the better of the king in resource, did thus:—from the body of one lately dead he cut off the arm at the shoulder and went with it under his mantle: and having gone in to the daughter of the king, and being asked that which the others also were asked, he related that he had done the most unholy deed when he cut off the head of his brother, who had been caught in a trap in the king's treasure-chamber, and the most cunning deed in that he made drunk the guards and took down the dead body of his brother hanging up; and she when she heard it tried to take hold of him, but the thief held out to her in the darkness the arm of the corpse, which she grasped and held, thinking that she was holding the arm of the man himself; but the thief left it in her hands and departed, escaping through the door. (f) Now when this also was reported to the king, he was at first amazed at the ready invention and daring of the fellow, and then afterwards he sent round to all the cities and made proclamation granting a free pardon to the thief, and also promising a great reward if he would come into his presence. The thief accordingly trusting to the proclamation came to the king, and Rhampsinitos greatly marveled at him, and gave him this daughter of his to wife, counting him to be the most knowing of all men; for as the Egyptians were distinguished from all other men, so was he from the other Egyptians.

122. After these things they said this king went down alive to that place which by the Hellenes is called Hades, and there played at dice with Demeter, and in some throws he overcame her and in others he was overcome by her; and he came back again having as a gift from her a handkerchief of gold: and they told me that because of the going down of Rhampsinitos the Egyptians after he came back celebrated a feast, which I know of my own knowledge also that they still observe even to my time; but whether it is for this cause that they keep the feast or for some other, I am not able to say. However, the priests weave a robe completely on the very day of the feast, and forthwith they bind up the eyes of one of them with a fillet, and having led him with the robe to the way by which one goes to the temple of Demeter, they depart back again themselves. This priest, they say, with his eyes bound up is led by two wolves to the temple of Demeter, which is distant from the city twenty furlongs, and then afterwards the wolves lead him back again from the temple to the same spot.

123. Now as to the tales told by the Egyptians, any man may accept them to whom such things appear credible; as for me, it is to be understood throughout the whole of the history that I write by hearsay that which is reported by the people in each place. The Egyptians say that Demeter and Dionysos are rulers of the world below; and the Egyptians are also the first who reported the doctrine that the soul of man is immortal, and that

when the body dies, the soul enters into another creature which chances then to be coming to the birth, and when it has gone the round of all the creatures of land and sea and of the air, it enters again into a human body as it comes to the birth; and that it makes this round in a period of three thousand years. This doctrine certain Hellenes adopted, some earlier and some later, as if it were of their own invention, and of these men I know the names but I abstain from recording them.

124. Down to the time when Rhampsinitos was king, they told me there was in Egypt nothing but orderly rule, and Egypt prospered greatly; but after him Cheops became king over them and brought them to every kind of evil: for he shut up all the temples, and having first kept them from sacrificing there, he then bade all the Egyptians work for him. So some were appointed to draw stones from the stone-quarries in the Arabian mountains to the Nile, and others he ordered to receive the stones after they had been carried over the river in boats, and to draw them to those which are called the Libyan mountains; and they worked by a hundred thousand men at a time, for each three months continually. Of this oppression there passed ten years while the causeway was made by which they drew the stones, which causeway they built, and it is a work not much less, as it appears to me, than the pyramid; for the length of it is five furlongs and the breadth ten fathoms and the height, where it is highest, eight fathoms, and it is made of stone smoothed and with figures carved upon it. For this, they said, the ten years were spent, and for the underground chambers on the hill upon which the pyramids stand, which he caused to be made as sepulchral chambers for himself in an island, having conducted thither a channel from the Nile. For the making of the pyramid itself there passed a period of twenty years; and the pyramid is square, each side measuring eight hundred feet, and the height of it is the same. It is built of stone smoothed and fitted together in the most perfect manner, not one of the stones being less than thirty feet in length.

125. This pyramid was made after the manner of steps, which some call "rows" and others "bases": and when they had first made it thus, they raised the remaining stones with machines made of short pieces of timber, raising them first from the ground to the first stage of the steps, and when the stone got up to this it was placed upon another machine standing on the first stage, and so from this it was drawn to the second upon another machine; for as many as were the courses of the steps, so many machines there were also, or perhaps they transferred one and the same machine, made so as easily to be carried, to each stage successively, in order that they might take up the stones; for let it be told in both ways, according as it is reported. However that may be, the highest parts of it were finished first, and afterwards they proceeded to finish that which came next to them, and lastly they finished the parts of it near the ground and the lowest ranges. On the pyramid it is declared in Egyptian writing how much was spent on radishes and onions and leeks for the workmen, and if I rightly remember that which the interpreter said in reading to me this inscription, a sum of one thousand six hundred talents of silver was spent; and if this is so, how much besides is likely to have been expended upon the iron with which they worked, and upon bread and clothing for the workmen, seeing that they were building the works for the time which has been mentioned and were occupied for no small time besides, as I suppose, in the cutting and bringing of the stones and in working at the excavation under the ground?

126. Cheops moreover came, they said, to such a pitch of wickedness, that being in want of money he caused his own daughter to sit in the stews, and ordered her to obtain

from those who came a certain amount of money (how much it was they did not tell me); but she not only obtained the sum appointed by her father, but also she formed a design for herself privately to leave behind her a memorial, and she requested each man who came in to her to give her one stone upon her building: and of these stones, they told me, the pyramid was built which stands in front of the great pyramid in the middle of the three, each side being one hundred and fifty feet in length.

127. This Cheops, the Egyptians said, reigned fifty years; and after he was dead his brother Chephren succeeded to the kingdom. This king followed the same manner as the other, both in all the rest and also in that he made a pyramid, not indeed attaining to the measurements of that which was built by the former (this I know, having myself also measured it), and moreover there are no underground chambers beneath nor does a channel come from the Nile flowing to this one as to the other, in which the water coming through a conduit built for it flows round an island within, where they say that Cheops himself is laid: but for a basement he built the first course of Ethiopian stone of divers colors; and this pyramid he made forty feet lower than the other as regards size, building it close to the great pyramid. These stand both upon the same hill, which is about a hundred feet high. And Chephren they said reigned fifty and six years.

128. Here then they reckon one hundred and six years, during which they say that there was nothing but evil for the Egyptians, and the temples were kept closed and not opened during all that time. These kings the Egyptians by reason of their hatred of them are not very willing to name; nay, they even call the pyramids after the name of Philitis the shepherd, who at that time pastured flocks in those regions.

129. After him, they said, Mykerinos became king over Egypt, who was the son of Cheops; and to him his father's deeds were displeasing, and he both opened the temples and gave liberty to the people, who were ground down to the last extremity of evil, to return to their own business and to their sacrifices;: also he gave decisions of their causes juster than those of all the other kings besides. In regard to this then they commend this king more than all the other kings who had arisen in Egypt before him; for he not only gave good decisions, but also when a man complained of the decision, he gave him recompense from his own goods and thus satisfied his desire. But while Mykerinos was acting mercifully to his subjects and practicing this conduct which has been said, calamities befell him, of which the first was this, namely that his daughter died, the only child whom he had in his house: and being above measure grieved by that which had befallen him, and desiring to bury his daughter in a manner more remarkable than others, he made a cow of wood, which he covered over with gold, and then within it he buried this daughter who, as I said, had died.

130. This cow was not covered up in the ground, but it might be seen even down to my own time in the city of Saïs, placed within the royal palace in a chamber which was greatly adorned; and they offer incense of all kinds before it every day, and each night a lamp burns beside it all through the night. Near this cow in another chamber stand images of the concubines of Mykerinos, as the priests at Saïs told me; for there are in fact colossal wooden statues, in number about twenty, made with naked bodies; but who they are I am not able to say, except only that which is reported.

131. Some however tell about this cow and the colossal statues the following tale, namely that Mykerinos was enamored of his own daughter and afterwards ravished her; and upon this they say that the girl strangled herself for grief, and he buried her in this

cow; and her mother cut off the hands of the maids who had betrayed the daughter to her father; wherefore now the images of them have suffered that which the maids suffered in their life. In thus saying they speak idly, as it seems to me, especially in what they say about the hands of the statues; for as to this, even we ourselves saw that their hands had dropped off from lapse of time, and they were to be seen still lying at their feet even down to my time.

132. The cow is covered up with a crimson robe, except only the head and the neck, which are seen, overlaid with gold very thickly; and between the horns there is the disc of the sun figured in gold. The cow is not standing up but kneeling, and in size it is equal to a large living cow. Every year it is carried forth from the chamber, at those times, I say, the Egyptians beat themselves for that god whom I will not name upon occasion of such a matter; at these times, I say, they also carry forth the cow to the light of day, for they say that she asked of her father Mykerinos, when she was dying, that she might look upon the sun once in the year.

133. After the misfortune of his daughter it happened, they said, secondly to this king as follows:—An oracle came to him from the city of Buto, saying that he was destined to live but six years more, in the seventh year to end his life: and he being indignant at it sent to the Oracle a reproach against the god, making complaint in reply that whereas his father and uncle, who had shut up the temples and had not only not remembered the gods, but also had been destroyers of men, had lived for a long time, he himself, who practiced piety, was destined to end his life so soon: and from the Oracle there came a second message, which said that it was for this very cause that he was bringing his life to a swift close; for he had not done that which it was appointed for him to do, since it was destined that Egypt should suffer evils for a hundred and fifty years, and the two kings who had risen before him had perceived this, but he had not. Mykerinos having heard this, and considering that this sentence had been passed upon him beyond recall, procured many lamps, and whenever night came on he lighted these and began to drink and take his pleasure, ceasing neither by day nor by night; and he went about to the fen-country and to the woods and wherever he heard there were the most suitable places for enjoyment. This he devised (having a mind to prove that the Oracle spoke falsely) in order that he might have twelve years of life instead of six, the nights being turned into days.

134. This king also left behind him a pyramid, much smaller than that of his father, of a square shape and measuring on each side three hundred feet lacking twenty, built moreover of Ethiopian stone up to half the height. This pyramid some of the Hellenes say was built by the courtesan Rhodopis, not therein speaking rightly: and besides this it is evident to me that they who speak thus do not even know who Rhodopis was, for otherwise they would not have attributed to her the building of a pyramid like this, on which have been spent (so to speak) innumerable thousands of talents: moreover they do not know that Rhodopis flourished in the reign of Amasis, and not in this king's reign; for Rhodopis lived very many years later than the kings who left behind the pyramids. By descent she was of Thrace, and she was a slave of Iadmon the son of Hephaistopolis a Samian, and a fellow-slave of Esop the maker of fables; for he too was once the slave of Iadmon, as was proved especially in this fact, namely that when the people of Delphi repeatedly made proclamation in accordance with an oracle, to find someone who would take up the blood-money for the death of Esop, no one else appeared, but at length the grandson of Iadmon, called Iadmon also, took it up; and thus it is shown that Esop too was the slave of Iadmon.

135. As for Rhodopis, she came to Egypt brought by Xanthes the Samian, and having come thither to exercise her calling she was redeemed from slavery for a great sum by a man of Mytilene, Charaxos son of Scamandronymos and brother of Sappho the lyric poet. Thus was Rhodopis set free, and she remained in Egypt and by her beauty won so much liking that she made great gain of money for one like Rhodopis, though not enough to suffice for the cost of such a pyramid as this. In truth there is no need to ascribe to her very great riches, considering that the tithe of her wealth may still be seen even to this time by anyone who desires it: for Rhodopis wished to leave behind her a memorial of herself in Hellas, namely to cause a thing to be made such as happens not to have been thought of or dedicated in a temple by any besides, and to dedicate this at Delphi as a memorial of herself. Accordingly with the tithe of her wealth she caused to be made spits of iron of size large enough to pierce a whole ox, and many in number, going as far therein as her tithe allowed her, and she sent them to Delphi: these are even at the present time lying there, heaped all together behind the altar which the Chians dedicated, and just opposite to the cell of the temple. Now at Naucratis, as it happens, the courtesans are rather apt to win credit; for this woman first, about whom the story to which I refer is told, became so famous that all the Hellenes without exception come to know the name of Rhodopis, and then after her one whose name was Archidiche became a subject of song over all Hellas, though she was less talked of than the other. As for Charaxos, when after redeeming Rhodopis he returned back to Mytilene, Sappho in an ode violently abused him. Of Rhodopis then I shall say no more.

136. After Mykerinos the priests said Asychis became king of Egypt, and he made for Hephaistos the temple gateway which is towards the sunrising, by far the most beautiful and the largest of the gateways; for while they all have figures carved upon them and innumerable ornaments of building besides, this has them very much more than the rest. In this king's reign they told me that, as the circulation of money was very slow, a law was made for the Egyptians that a man might have that money lent to him which he needed, by offering as security the dead body of his father; and there was added moreover to this law another, namely that he who lent the money should have a claim also to the whole sepulchral chamber belonging to him who received it, and that the man who offered that security should be subject to this penalty, if he refused to pay back the debt, namely that neither the man himself should be allowed to have burial when he died, either in that family burial-place or in any other, nor should he be allowed to bury any one of his kinsmen whom he lost by death. This king desiring to surpass the kings of Egypt who had arisen before him left as a memorial of himself a pyramid which he made of bricks, and on it there is an inscription carved in stone and saying thus: "Despise not me in comparison with the pyramids of stone, seeing that I excel them as much as Zeus excels the other gods; for with a pole they struck into the lake, and whatever of the mud attached itself to the pole, this they gathered up and made bricks, and in such manner they finished me."

Such were the deeds which this king performed;

137, and after him reigned a blind man of the city of Anysis, whose name was Anysis. In his reign the Ethiopians and Sabacos the king of the Ethiopians marched upon Egypt with a great host of men; so this blind man departed, flying to the fen-country, and the Ethiopian was king over Egypt for fifty years, during which he performed deeds as follows:—whenever any man of the Egyptians committed any transgression, he would never put him to death, but he gave sentence upon each man according to the greatness of the wrong-doing, appointing them work at throwing up an embankment before that city from whence each man came of those who committed wrong. Thus the cities were made higher still than before; for they were embanked first by those who dug the channels in the reign of Sesostris, and then secondly in the reign of the Ethiopian, and thus they were made very high: and while other cities in Egypt also stood high, I think in the town at Bubastis especially the earth was piled up. In this city there is a temple very well worthy of mention, for though there are other temples which are larger and built with more cost, none more than this is a pleasure to the eyes. Now Bubastis in the Hellenic tongue is Artemis,

138, and her temple is ordered thus:—Except the entrance it is completely surrounded by water; for channels come in from the Nile, not joining one another, but each extending as far as the entrance of the temple, one flowing round on the one side and the other on the other side, each a hundred feet broad and shaded over with trees; and the gateway has a height of ten fathoms, and it is adorned with figures six cubits high, very noteworthy. This temple is in the middle of the city and is looked down upon from all sides as one goes round, for since the city has been banked up to a height, while the temple has not been moved from the place where it was at the first built, it is possible to look down into it: and round it runs a stone wall with figures carved upon it, while within it there is a grove of very large trees planted round a large temple-house, within which is the image of the goddess: and the breadth and length of the temple is a furlong every way. Opposite the entrance there is a road paved with stone for about three furlongs, which leads through the market-place towards the East, with a breadth of about four hundred feet; and on this side and on that grow trees of height reaching to heaven: and the road leads to the temple of Hermes. This temple then is thus ordered.

139. The final deliverance from the Ethiopian came about (they said) as follows:—he fled away because he had seen in his sleep a vision, in which it seemed to him that a man came and stood by him and counselled him to gather together all the priests of Egypt and cut them asunder in the midst. Having seen this dream, he said that it seemed to him that the gods were foreshowing him this to furnish an occasion against him, in order that he might do an impious deed with respect to religion, and so receive some evil either from the gods or from men: he would not however do so, but in truth (he said) the time had expired, during which it had been prophesied to him that he should rule Egypt before he departed thence. For when he was in Ethiopia the Oracles which the Ethiopians consult had told him that it was fated for him to rule Egypt fifty years: since then this time was now expiring, and the vision of the dream also disturbed him, Sabacos departed out of Egypt of his own free will.

140. Then when the Ethiopian had gone away out of Egypt, the blind man came back from the fen-country and began to rule again, having lived there during fifty years upon an island which he had made by heaping up ashes and earth: for whenever any of the Egyptians visited him bringing food, according as it had been appointed to them severally to do without the knowledge of the Ethiopian, he bade them bring also some ashes for their gift. This island none was able to find before Amyrtaios; that is, for more than seven hundred years the kings who arose before Amyrtaios were not able to find it. Now the name of this island is Elbo, and its size is ten furlongs each way.

141. After him there came to the throne the priest of Hephaistos, whose name was Sethos. This man, they said, neglected and held in no regard the warrior class of the Egyp-

tians, considering that he would have no need of them; and besides other slights which he put upon them, he also took from them the yokes of corn-land which had been given to them as a special gift in the reigns of the former kings, twelve yokes to each man. After this, Sanacharib king of the Arabians and of the Assyrians marched a great host against Egypt. Then the warriors of the Egyptians refused to come to the rescue, and the priest, being driven into a strait, entered into the sanctuary of the temple and bewailed to the image of the god the danger which was impending over him; and as he was thus lamenting, sleep came upon him, and it seemed to him in his vision that the god came and stood by him and encouraged him, saying that he should suffer no evil if he went forth to meet the army of the Arabians; for he himself would send him helpers. Trusting in these things seen in sleep, he took with him, they said, those of the Egyptians who were willing to follow him, and encamped in Pelusion, for by this way the invasion came: and not one of the warrior class followed him, but shop-keepers and artisans and men of the market. Then after they came, there swarmed by night upon their enemies mice of the fields, and ate up their quivers and their bows, and moreover the handles of their shields, so that on the next day they fled, and being without defense of arms great numbers fell. And at the present time this king stands in the temple of Hephaistos in stone, holding upon his hand a mouse, and by letters inscribed he says these words: "Let him who looks upon me learn to fear the gods."

142. So far in the story the Egyptians and the priests were they who made the report, declaring that from the first king down to this priest of Hephaistos who reigned last, there had been three hundred and forty-one generations of men, and that in them there had been the same number of chief-priests and of kings: but three hundred generations of men are equal to ten thousand years, for a hundred years is three generations of men; and in the one-and-forty generations which remain, those I mean which were added to the three hundred, there are one thousand three hundred and forty years. Thus in the period of eleven thousand three hundred and forty years they said that there had arisen no god in human form; nor even before that time or afterwards among the remaining kings who arose in Egypt, did they report that anything of that kind had come to pass. In this time they said that the sun had moved four times from his accustomed place of rising, and where he now sets he had thence twice had his rising, and in the place from whence he now rises he had twice had his setting; and in the meantime nothing in Egypt had been changed from its usual state, neither that which comes from the earth nor that which comes to them from the river nor that which concerns diseases or deaths.

143. And formerly when Hecataios the historian was in Thebes, and had traced his descent and connected his family with a god in the sixteenth generation before, the priests of Zeus did for him much the same as they did for me (though I had not traced my descent). They led me into the sanctuary of the temple, which is of great size, and they counted up the number, showing colossal wooden statues in number the same as they said; for each chief-priest there sets up in his lifetime an image of himself: accordingly the priests, counting and showing me these, declared to me that each one of them was a son succeeding his own father, and they went up through the series of images from the image of the one who had died last, until they had declared this of the whole number. And when Hecataios had traced his descent and connected his family with a god in the sixteenth generation, they traced a descent in opposition to this, besides their numbering, not accepting it from him that a man had been born from a god; and they traced their counter-

descent thus, saying that each one of the statues had been *piromis* son of *piromis*, until they had declared this of the whole three hundred and forty-five statues, each one being surnamed *piromis*; and neither with a god nor a hero did they connect their descent. Now *piromis* means in the tongue of Hellas "honorable and good man."

144. From their declaration then it followed, that they of whom the images were had been of form like this, and far removed from being gods: but in the time before these men they said that gods were the rulers in Egypt, not mingling with men, and that of these always one had power at a time; and the last of them who was king over Egypt was Oros the son of Osiris, whom the Hellenes call Apollo: he was king over Egypt last, having deposed Typhon. Now Osiris in the tongue of Hellas is Dionysos.

145. Among the Hellenes Heracles and Dionysos and Pan are accounted the latest-born of the gods; but with the Egyptians Pan is a very ancient god, and he is one of those which are called the eight gods, while Heracles is of the second rank, who are called the twelve gods, and Dionysos is of the third rank, namely of those who were born of the twelve gods. Now as to Heracles I have shown already how many years old he is according to the Egyptians themselves, reckoning down to the reign of Amasis, and Pan is said to have existed for yet more years than these, and Dionysos for the smallest number of years as compared with the others; and even for this last they reckon down to the reign of Amasis fifteen thousand years. This the Egyptians say that they know for a certainty, since they always kept a reckoning and wrote down the years as they came. Now the Dionysos who is said to have been born of Semele the daughter of Cadmos, was born about sixteen hundred years before my time, and Heracles who was the son of Alcmene, about nine hundred years, and that Pan who was born of Penelope, for of her and of Hermes Pan is said by the Hellenes to have been born, came into being later than the wars of Troy, about eight hundred years before my time.

146. Of these two accounts every man may adopt that one which he shall find the more credible when he hears it. I however, for my part, have already declared my opinion about them. For if these also, like Heracles the son of Amphitryon, had appeared before all men's eyes and had lived their lives to old age in Hellas, I mean Dionysos the son of Semele and Pan the son of Penelope, then one would have said that these also had been born mere men, having the names of those gods who had come into being long before: but as it is, with regard to Dionysos the Hellenes say that as soon as he was born Zeus sewed him up in his thigh and carried him to Nysa, which is above Egypt in the land of Ethiopia; and as to Pan, they cannot say whither he went after he was born. Hence it has become clear to me that the Hellenes learnt the names of these gods later than those of the other gods, and trace their descent as if their birth occurred at the time when they first learnt their names.

Thus far then the history is told by the Egyptians themselves;

147, but I will now recount that which other nations also tell, and the Egyptians in agreement with the others, of that which happened in this land: and there will be added to this also something of that which I have myself seen.

Being set free after the reign of the priest of Hephaistos, the Egyptians, since they could not live any time without a king, set up over them twelve kings, having divided all Egypt into twelve parts. These made intermarriages with one another and reigned, making agreement that they would not put down one another by force, nor seek to get an advantage over one another, but would live in perfect friendship: and the reason why they made these agreements, guarding them very strongly from violation, was this, namely that an oracle had been given to them at first when they began to exercise their rule, that he of them who should pour a libation with a bronze cup in the temple of Hephaistos, should be king of all Egypt (for they used to assemble together in all the temples).

148. Moreover they resolved to join all together and leave a memorial of themselves; and having so resolved they caused to be made a labyrinth, situated a little above the lake of Moiris and nearly opposite to that which is called the City of Crocodiles. This I saw myself, and I found it greater than words can say. For if one should put together and reckon up all the buildings and all the great works produced by the Hellenes, they would prove to be inferior in labor and expense to this labyrinth, though it is true that both the temple at Ephesos and that at Samos are works worthy of note. The pyramids also were greater than words can say, and each one of them is equal to many works of the Hellenes, great as they may be; but the labyrinth surpasses even the pyramids. It has twelve courts covered in, with gates facing one another, six upon the North side and six upon the South, joining on one to another, and the same wall surrounds them all outside; and there are in it two kinds of chambers, the one kind below the ground and the other above upon these, three thousand in number, of each kind fifteen hundred. The upper set of chambers we ourselves saw, going through them, and we tell of them having looked upon them with our own eyes; but the chambers underground we heard about only; for the Egyptians who had charge of them were not willing on any account to show them, saying that here were the sepulchres of the kings who had first built this labyrinth and of the sacred crocodiles. Accordingly we speak of the chambers below by what we received from hearsay, while those above we saw ourselves and found them to be works of more than human greatness. For the passages through the chambers, and the goings this way and that way through the courts, which were admirably adorned, afforded endless matter for marvel, as we went through from a court to the chambers beyond it, and from the chambers to colonnades, and from the colonnades to other rooms, and then from the chambers again to other courts. Over the whole of these is a roof made of stone like the walls; and the walls are covered with figures carved upon them, each court being surrounded with pillars of white stone fitted together most perfectly; and at the end of the labyrinth, by the corner of it, there is a pyramid of forty fathoms, upon which large figures are carved, and to this there is a way made under ground.

149. Such is this labyrinth; but a cause for marvel even greater than this is afforded by the lake, which is called the lake of Moiris, along the side of which this labyrinth is built. The measure of its circuit is three thousand six hundred furlongs (being sixty *schoines*), and this is the same number of furlongs as the extent of Egypt itself along the sea. The lake lies extended lengthwise from North to South, and in depth where it is deepest it is fifty fathoms. That this lake is artificial and formed by digging is self-evident, for about in the middle of the lake stand two pyramids, each rising above the water to a height of fifty fathoms, the part which is built below the water being of just the same height; and upon each is placed a colossal statue of stone sitting upon a chair. Thus the pyramids are a hundred fathoms high; and these hundred fathoms are equal to a furlong of six hundred feet, the fathom being measured as six feet or four cubits, the feet being four palms each, and the cubits six. The water in the lake does not come from the place where it is, for the country there is very deficient in water, but it has been brought thither from the Nile by a canal: and for six months the water flows into the lake, and for six months out into the

Nile again; and whenever it flows out, then for the six months it brings into the royal treasury a talent of silver a day from the fish which are caught, and twenty pounds when the
water comes in.

150. The natives of the place moreover said that this lake had an outlet underground to
the Syrtis which is in Libya, turning towards the interior of the continent upon the
Western side and running along by the mountain which is above Memphis. Now since I
did not see anywhere existing the earth dug out of this excavation (for that was a matter
which drew my attention), I asked those who dwelt nearest to the lake where the earth
was which had been dug out. These told me to what place it had been carried away; and I
readily believed them, for I knew by report that a similar thing had been done at Nineveh,
the city of the Assyrians. There certain thieves formed a design once to carry away the
wealth of Sardanapallos son of Ninos, the king, which wealth was very great and was
kept in treasure-houses under the earth. Accordingly they began from their own dwelling,
and making estimate of their direction they dug underground towards the king's palace;
and the earth which was brought out of the excavation they used to carry away, when
night came on, to the river Tigris which flows by the city of Nineveh, until at last they
accomplished that which they desired. Similarly, as I heard, the digging of the lake in
Egypt was effected, except that it was done not by night but during the day; for as they
dug the Egyptians carried to the Nile the earth which was dug out; and the river, when it
received it, would naturally bear it away and disperse it. Thus is this lake said to have
been dug out.

151. Now the twelve kings continued to rule justly, but in course of time it happened
thus:—After sacrifice in the temple of Hephaistos they were about to make libation on the
last day of the feast, and the chief-priest, in bringing out for them the golden cups with
which they had been wont to pour libations, missed his reckoning and brought eleven
only for the twelve kings. Then that one of them who was standing last in order, namely
Psammetichos, since he had no cup took off from his head his helmet, which was of
bronze, and having held it out to receive the wine he proceeded to make libation: likewise
all the other kings were wont to wear helmets and they happened to have them then. Now
Psammetichos held out his helmet with no treacherous meaning; but they taking note of
that which had been done by Psammetichos and of the oracle, namely how it had been
declared to them that whosoever of them should make libation with a bronze cup should
be sole king of Egypt, recollecting, I say, the saying of the Oracle, they did not indeed
deem it right to slay Psammetichos, since they found by examination that he had not done
it with any forethought, but they determined to strip him of almost all his power and to
drive him away into the fen-country, and that from the fen-country he should not hold
any dealings with the rest of Egypt.

152. This Psammetichos had formerly been a fugitive from the Ethiopian Sabacos who
had killed his father Necos, from him, I say, he had then been a fugitive in Syria; and
when the Ethiopian had departed in consequence of the vision of the dream, the Egyptians who were of the district of Saïs brought him back to his own country. Then afterwards, when he was king, it was his fate to be a fugitive a second time on account of the
helmet, being driven by the eleven kings into the fen-country. So then holding that he had
been grievously wronged by them, he thought how he might take vengeance on those
who had driven him out: and when he had sent to the Oracle of Leto in the city of Buto,
where the Egyptians have their most truthful Oracle, there was given to him the reply that

vengeance would come when men of bronze appeared from the sea. And he was strongly disposed not to believe that bronze men would come to help him; but after no long time had passed, certain Ionians and Carians who had sailed forth for plunder were compelled to come to shore in Egypt, and they having landed and being clad in bronze armor, one of the Egyptians, not having before seen men clad in bronze armor, came to the fen-land and brought a report to Psammetichos that bronze men had come from the sea and were plundering the plain. So he, perceiving that the saying of the Oracle was coming to pass, dealt in a friendly manner with the Ionians and Carians, and with large promises he persuaded them to take his part. Then when he had persuaded them, with the help of those Egyptians who favored his cause and of these foreign mercenaries he overthrew the kings.

153. Having thus got power over all Egypt, Psammetichos made for Hephaistos that gateway of the temple at Memphis which is turned towards the South Wind; and he built a court for Apis, in which Apis is kept when he appears, opposite to the gateway of the temple, surrounded all with pillars and covered with figures; and instead of columns there stand to support the roof of the court colossal statues twelve cubits high. Now Apis is in the tongue of the Hellenes Epaphos.

154. To the Ionians and to the Carians who had helped him Psammetichos granted portions of land to dwell in, opposite to one another with the river Nile between, and these were called "Encampments": these portions of land he gave them, and he paid them besides all that he had promised: moreover he placed with them Egyptian boys to have them taught the Hellenic tongue; and from these, who learnt the language thoroughly, are descended the present class of interpreters in Egypt. Now the Ionians and Carians occupied these portions of land for a long time, and they are towards the sea a little below the city of Bubastis, on that which is called the Pelusian mouth of the Nile. These men king Amasis afterwards removed from thence and established them at Memphis, making them into a guard for himself against the Egyptians: and they being settled in Egypt, we who are Hellenes know by intercourse with them the certainty of all that which happened in Egypt beginning from king Psammetichos and afterwards; for these were the first men of foreign tongue who settled in Egypt: and in the land from which they were removed there still remained down to my time the sheds where their ships were drawn up and the ruins of their houses.

Thus then Psammetichos obtained Egypt:

155, and of the Oracle which is in Egypt I have made mention often before this, and now I will give an account of it, seeing that it is worthy to be described. This Oracle which is in Egypt is sacred to Leto, and it is established in a great city near that mouth of the Nile which is called Sebennytic, as one sails up the river from the sea; and the name of this city where the Oracle is found is Buto, as I have said before in mentioning it. In this Buto there is a temple of Apollo and Artemis; and the temple-house of Leto, in which the Oracle is, is both great in itself and has a gateway of the height of ten fathoms: but that which caused me most to marvel of the things to be seen there, I will now tell. There is in this sacred enclosure a house of Leto made of one single stone as regards both height and length, and of which all the walls are in these two directions equal, each being forty cubits; and for the covering in of the roof there lies another stone upon the top, the cornice measuring four cubits.

156. This house then of all the things that were to be seen by me in that temple is the most marvelous, and among those which come next is the island called Chemmis. This is

situated in a deep and broad lake by the side of the temple at Buto, and it is said by the Egyptians that this island is a floating island. I myself did not see it either floating about or moved from its place, and I feel surprise at hearing of it, wondering if it be indeed a floating island. In this island of which I speak there is a great temple-house of Apollo, and three several altars are set up within, and there are planted in the island many palm-trees and other trees, both bearing fruit and not bearing fruit. And the Egyptians, when they say that it is floating, add this story, namely that in this island, which formerly was not floating, Leto, being one of the eight gods who came into existence first, and dwelling in the city of Buto where she has this Oracle, received Apollo from Isis as a charge and preserved him, concealing him in the island which is said now to be a floating island, at that time when Typhon came after him seeking everywhere and desiring to find the son of Osiris. Now they say that Apollo and Artemis are children of Dionysos and of Isis, and that Leto became their nurse and preserver; and in the Egyptian tongue Apollo is Oros, Demeter is Isis, and Artemis is Bubastis. From this story and from no other Æschylus the son of Euphorion took this which I shall say, wherein he differs from all the preceding poets; he represented namely that Artemis was the daughter of Demeter. For this reason then, they say, it became a floating island.

Such is the story which they tell;

157, but as for Psammetichos, he was king over Egypt for four-and-fifty years, of which for thirty years save one he was sitting before Azotos, a great city of Syria, besieging it, until at last he took it: and this Azotos of all cities about which we have knowledge held out for the longest time under a siege.

158. The son of Psammetichos was Necos, and he became king of Egypt. This man was the first who attempted the channel leading to the Erythraian Sea, which Dareios the Persian afterwards completed: the length of this is a voyage of four days, and in breadth it was so dug that two triremes could go side by side driven by oars; and the water is brought into it from the Nile. The channel is conducted a little above the city of Bubastis by Patumos the Arabian city, and runs into the Erythraian Sea: and it is dug first along those parts of the plain of Egypt which lie towards Arabia, just above which run the mountains which extend opposite Memphis, where are the stone-quarries,—along the base of these mountains the channel is conducted from West to East for a great way; and after that it is directed towards a break in the hills and tends from these mountains towards the noon-day and the South Wind to the Arabian gulf. Now in the place where the journey is least and shortest from the Northern to the Southern Sea (which is also called Erythraian), that is from Mount Casion, which is the boundary between Egypt and Syria, the distance is exactly a thousand furlongs to the Arabian gulf; but the channel is much longer, since it is more winding; and in the reign of Necos there perished while digging it twelve myriads of the Egyptians. Now Necos ceased in the midst of his digging, because the utterance of an Oracle impeded him, which was to the effect that he was working for the Barbarian: and the Egyptians call all men Barbarians who do not agree with them in speech.

159. Thus having ceased from the work of the channel, Necos betook himself to waging wars, and triremes were built by him, some for the Northern Sea and others in the Arabian gulf for the Erythraian Sea; and of these the sheds are still to be seen. These ships he used when he needed them; and also on land Necos engaged battle at Magdolos with the Syrians, and conquered them; and after this he took Cadytis, which is a great city of

Syria: and the dress which he wore when he made these conquests he dedicated to Apollo, sending it to Branchidai of the Milesians. After this, having reigned in all sixteen years, he brought his life to an end, and handed on the kingdom to Psammis his son.

160. While this Psammis was king of Egypt, there came to him men sent by the Eleians, who boasted that they ordered the contest at Olympia in the most just and honorable manner possible and thought that not even the Egyptians, the wisest of men, could find out anything besides, to be added to their rules. Now when the Eleians came to Egypt and said that for which they had come, then this king called together those of the Egyptians who were reputed the wisest, and when the Egyptians had come together they heard the Eleians tell of all that which it was their part to do in regard to the contest; and when they had related everything, they said that they had come to learn in addition anything which the Egyptians might be able to find out besides, which was juster than this. They then having consulted together asked the Eleians whether their own citizens took part in the contest; and they said that it was permitted to anyone who desired it, both of their own people and of the other Hellenes equally, to take part in the contest: upon which the Egyptians said that in so ordering the games they had wholly missed the mark of justice; for it could not be but that they would take part with the man of their own State, if he was contending, and so act unfairly to the stranger: but if they really desired, as they said, to order the games justly, and if this was the cause for which they had come to Egypt, they advised them to order the contest so as to be for strangers alone to contend in, and that no Eleian should be permitted to contend. Such was the suggestion made by the Egyptians to the Eleians.

161. When Psammis had been king of Egypt for only six years and had made an expedition to Ethiopia and immediately afterwards had ended his life, Apries the son of Psammis received the kingdom in succession. This man came to be the most prosperous of all the kings up to that time except only his forefather Psammetichos; and he reigned five-and-twenty years, during which he led an army against Sidon and fought a sea-fight with the king of Tyre. Since however it was fated that evil should come upon him, it came by occasion of a matter which I shall relate at greater length in the Libyan history, and at present but shortly. Apries having sent a great expedition against the Kyrenians, met with correspondingly great disaster; and the Egyptians considering him to blame for this revolted from him, supposing that Apries had with forethought sent them out to evident calamity, in order (as they said) that there might be a slaughter of them, and he might the more securely rule over the other Egyptians. Being indignant at this, both these men who had returned from the expedition and also the friends of those who had perished made revolt openly.

162. Hearing this Apries sent to them Amasis, to cause them to cease by persuasion; and when he had come and was seeking to restrain the Egyptians, as he was speaking and telling them not to do so, one of the Egyptians stood up behind him and put a helmet upon his head, saying as he did so that he put it on to crown him king. And to him this that was done was in some degree not unwelcome, as he proved by his behavior; for as soon as the revolted Egyptians had set him up as king, he prepared to march against Apries: and Apries hearing this sent to Amasis one of the Egyptians who were about his own person, a man of reputation, whose name was Patarbemis, enjoining him to bring Amasis alive into his presence. When this Patarbemis came and summoned Amasis, the latter, who happened to be sitting on horseback, lifted up his leg and behaved in an

unseemly manner, bidding him take that back to Apries. Nevertheless, they say, Patarbemis made demand of him that he should go to the king, seeing that the king had sent to summon him; and he answered him that he had for some time past been preparing to do so, and that Apries would have no occasion to find fault with him. Then Patarbemis both perceiving his intention from that which he said, and also seeing his preparations, departed in haste, desiring to make known as quickly as possible to the king the things which were being done: and when he came back to Apries not bringing Amasis, the king paying no regard to that which he said, but being moved by violent anger, ordered his ears and his nose to be cut off. And the rest of the Egyptians who still remained on his side, when they saw the man of most repute among them thus suffering shameful outrage, waited no longer but joined the others in revolt, and delivered themselves over to Amasis.

163. Then Apries having heard this also, armed his foreign mercenaries and marched against the Egyptians: now he had about him Carian and Ionian mercenaries to the number of thirty thousand; and his royal palace was in the city of Saïs, of great size and worthy to be seen. So Apries and his army were going against the Egyptians, and Amasis and those with him were going against the mercenaries; and both sides came to the city of Momemphis and were about to make trial of one another in fight.

164. Now of the Egyptians there are seven classes, and of these one class is called that of the priests, and another that of the warriors, while the others are the cowherds, swine-herds, shopkeepers, interpreters, and boatmen. This is the number of the classes of the Egyptians, and their names are given them from the occupations which they follow. Of them the warriors are called Calasirians and Hermotybians, and they are of the following districts, —for all Egypt is divided into districts.

165. The districts of the Hermotybians are those of Busiris, Saïs, Chemmis, Papremis, the island called Prosopitis, and the half of Natho,—of these districts are the Hermoty-bians, who reached when most numerous the number of sixteen myriads. Of these not one has learnt anything of handicraft, but they are given up to war entirely.

166. Again the districts of the Calasirians are those of Thebes, Bubastis, Aphthis, Tanis, Mendes, Sebennytos, Athribis, Pharbaithos, Thmuïs Onuphis, Anytis, Myecphoris,—this last is on an island opposite to the city of Bubastis. These are the districts of the Calasiri-ans; and they reached, when most numerous, to the number of five-and-twenty myriads of men; nor is it lawful for these, any more than for the others, to practice any craft; but they practice that which has to do with war only, handing down the tradition from father to son.

167. Now whether the Hellenes have learnt this also from the Egyptians, I am not able to say for certain, since I see that the Thracians also and Scythians and Persians and Lydians and almost all the Barbarians esteem those of their citizens who learn the arts, and the descendants of them, as less honorable than the rest; while those who have got free from all practice of manual arts are accounted noble, and especially those who are devoted to war: however that may be, the Hellenes have all learnt this, and especially the Lacedemonians; but the Corinthians least of all cast slight upon those who practice hand-icrafts.

168. The following privilege was specially granted to this class and to none others of the Egyptians except the priests, that is to say, each man had twelve yokes of land specially granted to him free from imposts: now the yoke of land measures a hundred

Egyptian cubits every way, and the Egyptian cubit is, as it happens, equal to that of Samos. This, I say, was a special privilege granted to all, and they also had certain advantages in turn and not the same men twice; that is to say, a thousand of the Calasirians and a thousand of the Hermotybians acted as body-guard to the king during each year; and these had besides their yokes of land an allowance given them for each day of five pounds weight of bread to each man, and two pounds of beef, and four half-pints of wine. This was the allowance given to those who were serving as the king's bodyguard for the time being.

169. So when Apries leading his foreign mercenaries, and Amasis at the head of the whole body of the Egyptians, in their approach to one another had come to the city of Momemphis, they engaged battle: and although the foreign troops fought well, yet being much inferior in number they were worsted by reason of this. But Apries is said to have supposed that not even a god would be able to cause him to cease from his rule, so firmly did he think that it was established. In that battle then, I say, he was worsted, and being taken alive was brought away to the city of Saïs, to that which had formerly been his own dwelling but from thenceforth was the palace of Amasis. There for some time he was kept in the palace, and Amasis dealt well with him; but at last, since the Egyptians blamed him, saying that he acted not rightly in keeping alive him who was the greatest foe both to themselves and to him, therefore he delivered Apries over to the Egyptians; and they strangled him, and after that buried him in the burial-place of his fathers: this is in the temple of Athene, close to the sanctuary, on the left hand as you enter. Now the men of Saïs buried all those of this district who had been kings, within the temple; for the tomb of Amasis also, though it is further from the sanctuary than that of Apries and his forefathers, yet this too is within the court of the temple, and it consists of a colonnade of stone of great size, with pillars carved to imitate date-palms, and otherwise sumptuously adorned; and within the colonnade are double-doors, and inside the doors a sepulchral chamber.

170. Also at Saïs there is the burial-place of him whom I account it not pious to name in connexion with such a matter, which is in the temple of Athene behind the house of the goddess, stretching along the whole wall of it; and in the sacred enclosure stand great obelisks of stone, and near them is a lake adorned with an edging of stone and fairly made in a circle, being in size, as it seemed to me, equal to that which is called the "Round Pool" in Delos.

171. On this lake they perform by night the show of his sufferings, and this the Egyptians call Mysteries. Of these things I know more fully in detail how they take place, but I shall leave this unspoken; and of the mystic rites of Demeter, which the Hellenes call *thesmophoria*, of these also, although I know, I shall leave unspoken all except so much as piety permits me to tell. The daughters of Danaos were they who brought this rite out of Egypt and taught it to the women of the Pelasgians; then afterwards when all the inhabitants of Peloponnese were driven out by the Dorians, the rite was lost, and only those who were left behind of the Peloponnesians and not driven out, that is to say the Arcadians, preserved it.

172. Apries having thus been overthrown, Amasis became king, being of the district of Saïs, and the name of the city whence he was is Siuph. Now at the first the Egyptians despised Amasis and held him in no great regard, because he had been a man of the people and was of no distinguished family; but afterwards Amasis won them over to

himself by wisdom and not willfulness. Among innumerable other things of price which he had, there was a foot-basin of gold in which both Amasis himself and all his guests were wont always to wash their feet. This he broke up, and of it he caused to be made the image of a god, and set it up in the city, where it was most convenient; and the Egyptians went continually to visit the image and did great reverence to it. Then Amasis, having learnt that which was done by the men of the city, called together the Egyptians and made known to them the matter, saying that the image had been produced from the foot-basin, into which formerly the Egyptians used to vomit and make water, and in which they washed their feet, whereas now they did to it great reverence; and just so, he continued, had he himself now fared, as the foot-basin; for though formerly he was a man of the people, yet now he was their king, and he bade them accordingly honor him and have regard for him.

173. In such manner he won the Egyptians to himself, so that they consented to be his subjects; and his ordering of affairs was thus:—In the early morning, and until the time of the filling of the market he did with a good will the business which was brought before him; but after this he passed the time in drinking and in jesting at his boon-companions, and was frivolous and playful. And his friends being troubled at it admonished him in some such words as these: "O king, thou dost not rightly govern thyself in thus letting thyself descend to behavior so trifling; for thou oughtest rather to have been sitting throughout the day stately upon a stately throne and administering thy business; and so the Egyptians would have been assured that they were ruled by a great man, and thou wouldest have had a better report: but as it is, thou art acting by no means in a kingly fashion." And he answered them thus: "They who have bows stretch them at such time as they wish to use them, and when they have finished using them they loose them again; for if they were stretched tight always they would break, so that the men would not be able to use them when they needed them. So also is the state of man: if he should always be in earnest and not relax himself for sport at the due time, he would either go mad or be struck with stupor before he was aware; and knowing this well, I distribute a portion of the time to each of the two ways of living." Thus he replied to his friends.

174. It is said however that Amasis, even when he was in a private station, was a lover of drinking and of jesting, and not at all seriously disposed; and whenever his means of livelihood failed him through his drinking and luxurious living, he would go about and steal; and they from whom he stole would charge him with having their property, and when he denied it would bring him before the judgment of an Oracle, whenever there was one in their place; and many times he was convicted by the Oracles and many times he was absolved: and then when finally he became king he did as follows:—as many of the gods as had absolved him and pronounced him not to be a thief, to their temples he paid no regard, nor gave anything for the further adornment of them, nor even visited them to offer sacrifice, considering them to be worth nothing and to possess lying Oracles; but as many as had convicted him of being a thief, to these he paid very great regard, considering them to be truly gods, and to present Oracles which did not lie.

175. First in Saïs he built and completed for Athene a temple-gateway which is a great marvel, and he far surpassed herein all who had done the like before, both in regard to height and greatness, so large are the stones and of such quality. Then secondly he dedicated great colossal statues and man-headed sphinxes very large, and for restoration he brought other stones of monstrous size. Some of these he caused to be brought from the

stone-quarries which are opposite Memphis, others of very great size from the city of Elephantine, distant a voyage of not less than twenty days from Saïs: and of them all I marvel most at this, namely a monolith chamber which he brought from the city of Elephantine; and they were three years engaged in bringing this, and two thousand men were appointed to convey it, who all were of the class of boatmen. Of this house the length outside is one-and-twenty cubits, the breadth is fourteen cubits, and the height eight. These are the measures of the monolith house outside; but the length inside is eighteen cubits and five-sixths of a cubit, the breadth twelve cubits, and the height five cubits. This lies by the side of the entrance to the temple; for within the temple they did not draw it, because, as it said, while the house was being drawn along, the chief artificer of it groaned aloud, seeing that much time had been spent and he was wearied by the work; and Amasis took it to heart as a warning and did not allow them to draw it further onwards. Some say on the other hand that a man was killed by it, of those who were heaving it with levers, and that it was not drawn in for that reason.

176. Amasis also dedicated in all the other temples which were of repute, works which are worth seeing for their size, and among them also at Memphis the colossal statue which lies on its back in front of the temple of Hephaistos, whose length is five-and-seventy feet; and on the same base made of the same stone are set two colossal statues, each of twenty feet in length, one on this side and the other on that side of the large statue. There is also another of stone of the same size in Saïs, lying in the same manner as that at Memphis. Moreover Amasis was he who built and finished for Isis her temple at Memphis, which is of great size and very worthy to be seen.

177. In the reign of Amasis it is said that Egypt became more prosperous than at any other time before, both in regard to that which comes to the land from the river and in regard to that which comes from the land to its inhabitants, and that at this time the inhabited towns in it numbered in all twenty thousand. It was Amasis too who established the law that every year each one of the Egyptians should declare to the ruler of his district, from what source he got his livelihood, and if any man did not do this or did not make declaration of an honest way of living, he should be punished with death. Now Solon the Athenian received from Egypt this law and had it enacted for the Athenians, and they have continued to observe it, since it is a law with which none can find fault.

178. Moreover Amasis became a lover of the Hellenes; and besides other proofs of friendship which he gave to several among them, he also granted the city of Naucratis for those of them who came to Egypt to dwell in; and to those who did not desire to stay, but who made voyages thither, he granted portions of land to set up altars and make sacred enclosures for their gods. Their greatest enclosure and that one which has most name and is most frequented is called the Hellenion, and this was established by the following cities in common:—of the Ionians Chios, Teos, Phocaia, Clazomenai, of the Dorians Rhodes, Cnidos, Halicarnassos, Phaselis, and of the Aiolians Mytilene alone. To these belongs this enclosure and these are the cities which appoint superintendents of the port; and all other cities which claim a share in it, are making a claim without any right. Besides this the Eginetans established on their own account a sacred enclosure dedicated to Zeus, the Samians one to Hera, and the Milesians one to Apollo.

179. Now in old times Naucratis alone was an open trading-place, and no other place in Egypt: and if any one came to any other of the Nile mouths, he was compelled to swear that he came not thither of his own will, and when he had thus sworn his innocence he

had to sail with his ship to the Canobic mouth, or if it were not possible to sail by reason of contrary winds, then he had to carry his cargo round the head of the Delta in boats to Naucratis: thus highly was Naucratis privileged.

180. Moreover when the Amphictyons had let out the contract for building the temple which now exists at Delphi, agreeing to pay a sum of three hundred talents, (for the temple which formerly stood there had been burnt down of itself), it fell to the share of the people of Delphi to provide the fourth part of the payment; and accordingly the Delphians went about to various cities and collected contributions. And when they did this they got from Egypt as much as from any place, for Amasis gave them a thousand talents' weight of alum, while the Hellenes who dwelt in Egypt gave them twenty pounds of silver.

181. Also with the people of Kyrene Amasis made an agreement for friendship and alliance; and he resolved too to marry a wife from thence, whether because he desired to have a wife of Hellenic race, or apart from that, on account of friendship for the people of Kyrene: however that may be, he married, some say the daughter of Battos, others of Arkesilaos, and others of Critobulos, a man of repute among the citizens; and her name was Ladike. Now whenever Amasis lay with her he found himself unable to have intercourse, but with his other wives he associated as he was wont; and as this happened repeatedly, Amasis said to his wife, whose name was Ladike: "Woman, thou hast given me drugs, and thou shalt surely perish more miserably than any other woman." Then Ladike, when by her denials Amasis was not at all appeased in his anger against her, made a vow in her soul to Aphrodite, that if Amasis on that night had intercourse with her (seeing that this was the remedy for her danger), she would send an image to be dedicated to her at Kyrene; and after the vow immediately Amasis had intercourse, and from thenceforth whenever Amasis came in to her he had intercourse with her; and after this he became very greatly attached to her. And Ladike paid the vow that she had made to the goddess; for she had an image made and sent it to Kyrene, and it was still preserved even to my own time, standing with its face turned away from the city of the Kyrenians. This Ladike Cambyses, having conquered Egypt and heard from her who she was, sent back unharmed to Kyrene.

182. Amasis also dedicated offerings in Hellas, first at Kyrene an image of Athene covered over with gold and a figure of himself made like by painting; then in the temple of Athene at Lindson two images of stone and a corslet of linen worthy to be seen; and also at Samos two wooden figures of himself dedicated to Hera, which were standing even to my own time in the great temple, behind the doors. Now at Samos he dedicated offerings because of the guest-friendship between himself and Polycrates the son of Aiakes; at Lindos for no guest-friendship but because the temple of Athene at Lindos is said to have been founded by the daughters of Danaos, who had touched land there at the time when they were fleeing from the sons of Aigyptos. These offerings were dedicated by Amasis; and he was the first of men who conquered Cyprus and subdued it so that it paid him tribute.

THE THIRD BOOK OF THE
HISTORIES, CALLED THALEIA

1. Against this Amasis then Cambyses the son of Cyrus was making his march, taking with him not only other nations of which he was ruler, but also Hellenes, both Ionians and Aiolians: and the cause of the expedition was as follows:—Cambyses sent an envoy to Egypt and asked Amasis to give him his daughter; and he made the request by counsel of an Egyptian, who brought this upon Amasis having a quarrel with him for the following reason:—at the time when Cyrus sent to Amasis and asked him for a physician of the eyes, whosoever was the best of those in Egypt, Amasis had selected him from all the physicians in Egypt and had torn him away from his wife and children and delivered him up to Persia. Having, I say, this cause of quarrel, the Egyptian urged Cambyses on by his counsel bidding him ask Amasis for his daughter, in order that he might either be grieved if he gave her, or if he refused to give her, might offend Cambyses. So Amasis, who was vexed by the power of the Persians and afraid of it, knew neither how to give nor how to refuse: for he was well assured that Cambyses did not intend to have her as his wife but as a concubine. So making account of the matter thus, he did as follows:—there was a daughter of Apries the former king, very tall and comely of form and the only person left of his house, and her name was Nitetis. This girl Amasis adorned with raiment and with gold, and sent her away to Persia as his own daughter: but after a time, when Cambyses saluted her calling her by the name of her father, the girl said to him: "O king, thou dost not perceive how thou hast been deceived by Amasis; for he adorned me with ornaments and sent me away giving me to thee as his own daughter, whereas in truth I am the daughter of Apries against whom Amasis rose up with the Egyptians and murdered him, who was his lord and master." These words uttered and this occasion having arisen, led Cambyses the son of Cyrus against Egypt, moved to very great anger.

2. Such is the report made by the Persians; but as for the Egyptians they claim Cambyses as one of themselves, saying that he was born of this very daughter of Apries; for they say that Cyrus was he who sent to Amasis for his daughter, and not Cambyses. In saying this however they say not rightly; nor can they have failed to observe (for the

Egyptians fully as well as any other people are acquainted with the laws and customs of the Persians), first that it is not customary among them for a bastard to become king, when there is a son born of a true marriage, and secondly that Cambyses was the son of Cassandane the daughter of Pharnaspes, a man of the Achaimenid family, and not the son of the Egyptian woman: but they pervert the truth of history, claiming to be kindred with the house of Cyrus. Thus it is with these matters;

3, and the following story is also told, which for my part I do not believe, namely that one of the Persian women came in to the wives of Cyrus, and when she saw standing by the side of Cassandane children comely of form and tall, she was loud in her praises of them, expressing great admiration; and Cassandane, who was the wife of Cyrus, spoke as follows: "Nevertheless, though I am the mother of such children of these, Cyrus treats me with dishonor and holds in honor her whom he has brought in from Egypt." Thus she spoke, they say, being vexed by Nitetis, and upon that Cambyses the elder of her sons said: "For this cause, mother, when I am grown to be a man, I will make that which is above in Egypt to be below, and that which is below above." This he is reported to have said when he was perhaps about ten years old, and the women were astonished by it: and he, they say, kept it ever in mind, and so at last when he had become a man and had obtained the royal power, he made the expedition against Egypt.

4. Another thing also contributed to this expedition, which was as follows:—There was among the foreign mercenaries of Amasis a man who was by race of Halicarnassos, and his name was Phanes, one who was both capable in judgment and valiant in that which pertained to war. This Phanes, having (as we may suppose) some quarrel with Amasis, fled away from Egypt in a ship, desiring to come to speech with Cambyses: and as he was of no small repute among the mercenaries and was very closely acquainted with all the affairs of Egypt, Amasis pursued him and considered it a matter of some moment to capture him: and he pursued by sending after him the most trusted of his eunuchs with a trireme, who captured him in Lykia; but having captured him he did not bring him back to Egypt, since Phanes got the better of him by cunning; for he made his guards drunk and escaped to Persia. So when Cambyses had made his resolve to march upon Egypt, and was in difficulty about the march, as to how he should get safely through the waterless region, this man came to him and besides informing of the other matters of Amasis, he instructed him also as to the march, advising him to send to the king of the Arabians and ask that he would give him safety of passage through this region.

5. Now by this way only is there a known entrance to Egypt: for from Phenicia to the borders of the city of Cadytis belongs to the Syrians who are called of Palestine, and from Cadytis, which is a city I suppose not much less than Sardis, from this city the trading stations on the sea-coast as far as the city of Ienysos belong to the king of Arabia, and then from Ienysos again the country belongs to the Syrians as far as the Serbonian lake, along the side of which Mount Casion extends towards the Sea. After that, from the Serbonian lake, in which the story goes that Typhon is concealed, from this point onwards the land is Egypt. Now the region which lies between the city of Ienysos on the one hand and Mount Casion and the Serbonian lake on the other, which is of no small extent but as much as a three days' journey, is grievously destitute of water.

6. And one thing I shall tell of, which few of those who go in ships to Egypt have observed, and it is this:—into Egypt from all parts of Hellas and also from Phenicia are

brought twice every year earthenware jars full of wine, and yet it may almost be said that you cannot see there one single empty wine-jar.

7. In what manner, then, it will be asked, are they used up? This also I will tell. The head-man of each place must collect all the earthenware jars from his own town and convey them to Memphis, and those at Memphis must fill them with water and convey them to these same waterless regions of Syria: this the jars which come regularly to Egypt and are emptied there, are carried to Syria to be added to that which has come before. It was the Persians who thus prepared this approach to Egypt, furnishing it with water in the manner which has been said, from the time when they first took possession of Egypt: but at the time of which I speak, seeing that water was not yet provided, Cambyses, in accordance with what he was told by his Halicarnassian guest, sent envoys to the Arabian king and from him asked and obtained the safe passage, having given him pledges of friendship and received them from him in return.

8. Now the Arabians have respect for pledges of friendship as much as those men in all the world who regard them most; and they give them in the following manner:—A man different from those who desire to give the pledges to one another, standing in the midst between the two, cuts with a sharp stone the inner parts of the hands, along by the thumbs, of those who are giving the pledges to one another, and then he takes a thread from the cloak of each one and smears with the blood seven stones laid in the midst between them; and as he does this he calls upon Dionysos and Urania. When the man has completed these ceremonies, he who has given the pledges commends to the care of his friends the stranger (or the fellow-tribesman, if he is giving the pledges to one who is a member of his tribe), and the friends think it right that they also should have regard for the pledges given. Of gods they believe in Dionysos and Urania alone: moreover they say that the cutting of their hair is done after the same fashion as that of Dionysos himself; and they cut their hair in a circle round, shaving away the hair of the temples. Now they call Dionysos Orotalt and Urania they call Alilat.

9. So then when the Arabian king had given the pledge of friendship to the men who had come to him from Cambyses, he contrived as follows:—he took skins of camels and filled them with water and loaded them upon the backs of all the living camels that he had; and having so done he drove them to the waterless region and there awaited the army of Cambyses. This which has been related is the more credible of the accounts given, but the less credible must also be related, since it is a current account. There is a great river in Arabia called Corys, and this runs out into the Sea which is called Erythraian. From this river then it is said that the king of the Arabians, having got a conduit pipe made by sewing together raw ox-hides and other skins, of such a length as to reach to the waterless region, conducted the water through these forsooth, and had great cisterns dug in the waterless region, that they might receive the water and preserve it. Now it is a journey of twelve days from the river to this waterless region; and moreover the story says that he conducted the water by three conduit-pipes to three different parts of it.

10. Meanwhile Psammenitos the son of Amasis was encamped at the Pelusian mouth of the Nile waiting for the coming of Cambyses: for Cambyses did not find Amasis yet living when he marched upon Egypt, but Amasis had died after having reigned forty and four years during which no great misfortune had befallen him: and when he had died and had been embalmed he was buried in the burial-place in the temple, which he had built for himself. Now when Psammenitos son of Amasis was reigning as king, there happened

to the Egyptians a prodigy, the greatest that had ever happened: for rain fell at Thebes in Egypt, where never before had rain fallen nor afterwards down to my time, as the Thebans themselves say; for in the upper parts of Egypt no rain falls at all: but at the time of which I speak rain fell at Thebes in a drizzling shower.

11. Now when the Persians had marched quite through the waterless region and were encamped near the Egyptians with design to engage battle, then the foreign mercenaries of the Egyptian king, who were Hellenes and Carians, having a quarrel with Phanes because he had brought against Egypt an army of foreign speech, contrived against him as follows:—Phanes had children whom he had left behind in Egypt: these they brought to their camp and into the sight of their father, and they set up a mixing-bowl between the two camps, and after that they brought up the children one by one and cut their throats so that the blood ran into the bowl. Then when they had gone through the whole number of the children, they brought and poured into the bowl both wine and water, and not until the mercenaries had all drunk of the blood, did they engage battle. Then after a battle had been fought with great stubbornness, and very many had fallen of both the armies, the Egyptians at length turned to flight.

12. I was witness moreover of a great marvel, being informed of it by the natives of the place; for of the bones scattered about of those who fell in this fight, each side separately, since the bones of the Persians were lying apart on one side according as they were divided at first, and those of the Egyptians on the other, the skulls of the Persians are so weak that if you shall hit them only with a pebble you will make a hole in them, while those of the Egyptians are so exceedingly strong that you would hardly break them if you struck them with a large stone. The cause of it, they say, was this, and I for my part readily believe them, namely that the Egyptians beginning from their early childhood shave their heads, and the bone is thickened by exposure to the sun: and this is also the cause of their not becoming bald-headed; for among the Egyptians you see fewer bald-headed men than among any other race. This then is the reason why these have their skulls strong; and the reason why the Persians have theirs weak is that they keep them delicately in the shade from the first by wearing *tiaras*, that is felt caps. So far of this: and I saw also a similar thing to this at Papremis, in the case of those who were slain together with Achaimenes the son of Dareios, by Inaros the Libyan.

13. The Egyptians when they turned to flight from the battle fled in disorder: and they being shut up in Memphis, Cambyses sent a ship of Mytilene up the river bearing a Persian herald, to summon the Egyptians to make terms of surrender; but they, when they saw the ship had entered into Memphis, pouring forth in a body from the fortress both destroyed the ship and also tore the men in it limb from limb, and so bore them into the fortress. After this the Egyptians being besieged, in course of time surrendered themselves; and the Libyans who dwell on the borders of Egypt, being struck with terror by that which had happened to Egypt, delivered themselves up without resistance, and they both laid on themselves a tribute and sent presents: likewise also those of Kyrene and Barca, being struck with terror equally with the Libyans, acted in a similar manner: and Cambyses accepted graciously the gifts which came from the Libyans, but as for those which came from the men of Kyrene, finding fault with them, as I suppose, because they were too small in amount (for the Kyrenians sent in fact five hundred pounds' weight of silver), he took the silver by handfuls and scattered it with his own hand among his soldiers.

14. On the tenth day after that on which he received the surrender of the fortress of Memphis, Cambyses set the king of the Egyptians Psammenitos, who had been king for six months, to sit in the suburb of the city, to do him dishonor,—him I say with other Egyptians he set there, and he proceeded to make trial of his spirit as follows:—having arrayed his daughter in the clothing of a slave, he sent her forth with a pitcher to fetch water, and with her he sent also other maidens chosen from the daughters of the chief men, arrayed as was the daughter of the king: and as the maidens were passing by their fathers with cries and lamentation, the other men all began to cry out and lament aloud, seeing that their children had been evilly entreated, but Psammenitos when he saw it before his eyes and perceived it bent himself down to the earth. Then when the water-bearers had passed by, next Cambyses sent his son with two thousand Egyptians besides who were of the same age, with ropes bound round their necks and bits placed in their mouths; and these were being led away to execution to avenge the death of the Mytilenians who had been destroyed at Memphis with their ship: for the Royal Judges had decided that for each man ten of the noblest Egyptians should lose their lives in retaliation. He then, when he saw them passing out by him and perceived that his son was leading the way to die, did the same as he had done with respect to his daughter, while the other Egyptians who sat round him were lamenting and showing signs of grief. When these also had passed by, it chanced that a man of his table companions, advanced in years, who had been deprived of all his possessions and had nothing except such things as a beggar possesses, and was asking alms from the soldiers, passed by Psammenitos the son of Amasis and the Egyptians who were sitting in the suburb of the city: and when Psammenitos saw him he uttered a great cry of lamentation, and he called his companion by name and beat himself upon the head. Now there was, it seems, men set to watch him, who made known to Cambyses all that he did on the occasion of each going forth: and Cambyses marveled at that which he did, and he sent a messenger and asked him thus: "Psammenitos, thy master Cambyses asks thee for what reason, when thou sawest thy daughter evilly entreated and thy son going to death, thou didst not cry aloud nor lament for them, whereas thou didst honor with these signs of grief the beggar who, as he hears from others, is not in any way related to thee?" Thus he asked, and the other answered as follows: "O son of Cyrus, my own troubles were too great for me to lament them aloud, but the trouble of my companion was such as called for tears, seeing that he has been deprived of great wealth, and has come to beggary upon the threshold of old age." When this saying was reported by the messenger, it seemed to them that it was well spoken; and, as is reported by the Egyptians, Croesus shed tears (for he also, as fortune would have it, had accompanied Cambyses to Egypt) and the Persians who were present shed tears also; and there entered some pity into Cambyses himself, and forthwith he bade them save the life of the son of Psammenitos from among those who were being put to death, and also he bade them raise Psammenitos himself from his place in the suburb of the city and bring him into his own presence.

15. As for the son, those who went for him found that he was no longer alive, but had been cut down first of all, but Psammenitos himself they raised from his place and brought him into the presence of Cambyses, with whom he continued to live for the rest of his time without suffering any violence; and if he had known how to keep himself from meddling with mischief, he would have received Egypt so as to be ruler of it, since the Persians are wont to honor the sons of kings, and even if the kings have revolted from

them, they give back the power into the hands of their sons. Of this, namely that it is their established rule to act so, one may judge by many instances besides and especially by the case of Thannyras the son of Inaros, who received back the power which his father had, and by that of Pausiris the son of Amyrtaios, for he too received back the power of his father: yet it is certain that no men ever up to this time did more evil to the Persians than Inaros and Amyrtaios. As it was, however, Psammenitos devised evil and received the due reward: for he was found to be inciting the Egyptians to revolt; and when this became known to Cambyses, Psammenitos drank bull's blood and died forthwith. Thus he came to his end.

16. From Memphis Cambyses came to the city of Saïs with the purpose of doing that which in fact he did: for when he had entered into the palace of Amasis, he forthwith gave command to bring the corpse of Amasis forth out of his burial-place; and when this had been accomplished, he gave command to scourge it and pluck out the hair and stab it, and to do to it dishonor in every possible way besides: and when they had done this too until they were wearied out, for the corpse being embalmed held out against the violence and did not fall to pieces in any part, Cambyses gave command to consume it with fire, enjoining thereby a thing which was not permitted by religion: for the Persians hold fire to be a god. To consume corpses with fire then is by no means according to the custom of either people, of the Persians for the reason which has been mentioned, since they say that it is not right to give the dead body of a man to a god; while the Egyptians have the belief established that fire is a living wild beast, and that it devours everything which it catches, and when it is satiated with the food it dies itself together with that which it devours: but it is by no means their custom to give the corpse of a man to wild beasts, for which reason they embalm it, that it may not be eaten by worms as it lies in the tomb. Thus then Cambyses was enjoining them to do that which is not permitted by the customs of either people. However, the Egyptians say that it was not Amasis who suffered this outrage, but another of the Egyptians who was of the same stature of body as Amasis; and that to him the Persians did outrage, thinking that they were doing it to Amasis: for they say that Amasis learnt from an Oracle that which was about to happen with regard to himself after his death; and accordingly, to avert the evil which threatened to come upon him, he buried the dead body of this man who was scourged within his own sepulchral chamber near the doors, and enjoined his son to lay his own body as much as possible in the inner recess of the chamber. These injunctions, said to have been given by Amasis with regard to his burial and with regard to the man mentioned, were not in my opinion really given at all, but I think that the Egyptians make pretense of it from pride and with no good ground.

17. After this Cambyses planned three several expeditions, one against the Carthaginians, another against the Ammonians, and a third against the "Long-lived" Ethiopians, who dwell in that part of Libya which is by the Southern Sea: and in forming these designs he resolved to send his naval force against the Carthaginians, and a body chosen from his land-army against the Ammonians; and to the Ethiopians to send spies first, both to see whether the table of the Sun existed really, which is said to exist among these Ethiopians, and in addition to this to spy out all else, but pretending to be bearers of gifts for their king.

18. Now the table of the Sun is said to be as follows:—there is a meadow in the suburb of their city full of flesh-meat boiled of all four-footed creatures; and in this, it is said,

those of the citizens who are in authority at the time place the flesh by night, managing the matter carefully, and by day any man who wishes comes there and feasts himself; and the natives (it is reported) say that the earth of herself produces these things continually.

19. Of such nature is the so-called table of the Sun said to be. So when Cambyses had resolved to send the spies, forthwith he sent for those men of the Ichthyophagoi who understood the Ethiopian tongue, to come from the city of Elephantine: and while they were going to fetch these men, he gave command to the fleet to sail against Carthage: but the Phoenicians said that they would not do so, for they were bound not to do so by solemn vows, and they would not be acting piously if they made expedition against their own sons: and as the Phoenicians were not willing, the rest were rendered unequal to the attempt. Thus then the Carthaginians escaped being enslaved by the Persians; for Cambyses did not think it right to apply force to compel the Phoenicians, both because they had delivered themselves over to the Persians of their own accord and because the whole naval force was dependent upon the Phoenicians. Now the men of Cyprus also had delivered themselves over to the Persians, and were joining in the expedition against Egypt.

20. Then as soon as the Ichthyophagoi came to Cambyses from Elephantine, he sent them to the Ethiopians, enjoining them what they should say and giving them gifts to bear with them, that is to say a purple garment, and a collar of twisted gold with bracelets, and an alabaster box of perfumed ointment, and a jar of palm-wine. Now these Ethiopians to whom Cambyses was sending are said to be the tallest and the most beautiful of all men; and besides other customs which they are reported to have different from other men, there is especially this, it is said, with regard to their regal power,—whomsoever of the men of their nation they judge to be the tallest and to have strength in proportion to his stature, this man they appoint to reign over them.

21. So when the Ichthyophagoi had come to this people they presented their gifts to the king who ruled over them, and at the same time they said as follows: "The king of the Persians Cambyses, desiring to become a friend and guest to thee, sent us with command to come to speech with thee, and he gives thee for gifts these things which he himself most delights to use." The Ethiopian however, perceiving that they had come as spies, spoke to them as follows: "Neither did the king of the Persians send you bearing gifts because he thought it a matter of great moment to become my guest-friend, nor do ye speak true things (for ye have come as spies of my kingdom), nor again is he a righteous man; for if he had been righteous he would not have coveted a land other than his own, nor would he be leading away into slavery men at whose hands he has received no wrong. Now however give him this bow and speak to him these words: The king of the Ethiopians gives this counsel to the king of the Persians, that when the Persians draw their bows (of equal size to mine) as easily as I do this, then he should march against the Long-lived Ethiopians, provided that he be superior in numbers; but until that time he should feel gratitude to the gods that they do not put it into the mind of the sons of the Ethiopians to acquire another land in addition to their own."

22. Having thus said and having unbent the bow, he delivered it to those who had come. Then he took the garment of purple and asked what it was and how it had been made: and when the Ichthyophagoi had told him the truth about the purple-fish and the dyeing of the tissue, he said that the men were deceitful and deceitful also were their garments. Then secondly he asked concerning the twisted gold of the collar and the

bracelets; and when the Ichthyophagoi were setting forth to him the manner in which it was fashioned, the king broke into a laugh and said, supposing them to be fetters, that they had stronger fetters than those in their country. Thirdly he asked about the perfumed ointment, and when they had told him of the manner of its making and of the anointing with it, he said the same as he had said before about the garment. Then when he came to the wine, and had learned about the manner of its making, being exceedingly delighted with the taste of the drink he asked besides what food the king ate, and what was the longest time that a Persian man lived. They told him that he ate bread, explaining to him first the manner of growing the wheat, and they said that eighty years was the longest term of life appointed for a Persian man. In answer to this the Ethiopian said that he did not wonder that they lived but a few years, when they fed upon dung; for indeed they would not be able to live even so many years as this, if they did not renew their vigor with the drink, indicating to the Ichthyophagoi the wine; for in regard to this, he said, his people were much behind the Persians.

23. Then when the Ichthyophagoi asked the king in return about the length of days and the manner of life of his people, he answered that the greater number of them reached the age of a hundred and twenty years, and some surpassed even this; and their food was boiled flesh and their drink was milk. And when the spies marveled at the number of years, he conducted them to a certain spring, in the water of which they washed and became more sleek of skin, as if it were a spring of oil; and from it there came a scent as it were of violets: and the water of this spring, said the spies, was so exceedingly weak that it was not possible for anything to float upon it, either wood or any of those things which are lighter than wood, but they all went to the bottom. If this water which they have be really such as it is said to be, it would doubtless be the cause why the people are long-lived, as making use of it for all the purposes of life. Then when they departed from this spring, he led them to a prison-house for men, and there all were bound in fetters of gold. Now among these Ethiopians bronze is the rarest and most precious of all things. Then when they had seen the prison-house they saw also the so-called table of the Sun:

24, and after this they saw last of all their receptacles of dead bodies, which are said to be made of crystal in the following manner:—when they have dried the corpse, whether it be after the Egyptian fashion or in some other way, they cover it over completely with plaster and then adorn it with painting, making the figure as far as possible like the living man. After this they put about it a block of crystal hollowed out; for this they dig up in great quantity and it is very easy to work: and the dead body being in the middle of the block is visible through it, but produces no unpleasant smell nor any other effect which is unseemly, and it has all its parts visible like the dead body itself. For a year then they who are most nearly related to the man keep the block in their house, giving to the dead man the first share of everything and offering to him sacrifices: and after this period they carry it out and set it up round about the city.

25. After they had seen all, the spies departed to go back; and when they reported these things, forthwith Cambyses was enraged and proceeded to march his army against the Ethiopians, not having ordered any provision of food nor considered with himself that he was intending to march an army to the furthest extremities of the earth; but as one who is mad and not in his right senses, when he heard the report of the Ichthyophagoi he began the march, ordering those of the Hellenes who were present to remain behind in Egypt, and taking with him his whole land force: and when in the course of his march he

had arrived at Thebes, he divided off about fifty thousand of his army, and these he enjoined to make slaves of the Ammonians and to set fire to the seat of the Oracle of Zeus, but he himself with the remainder of his army went on against the Ethiopians. But before the army had passed over the fifth part of the way, all that they had of provisions came to an end completely; and then after the provisions the beasts of burden also were eaten up and came to an end. Now if Cambyses when he perceived this had changed his plan and led his army back, he would have been a wise man in spite of his first mistake; as it was, however, he paid no regard, but went on forward without stopping. The soldiers accordingly, so long as they were able to get anything from the ground, prolonged their lives by eating grass; but when they came to the sand, some did a fearful deed, that is to say, out of each company of ten they selected by lot one of themselves and devoured him: and Cambyses, when he heard it, being alarmed by this eating of one another gave up the expedition against the Ethiopians and set forth to go back again; and he arrived at Thebes having suffered loss of a great number of his army. Then from Thebes he came down to Memphis and allowed the Hellenes to sail away home.

26. Thus fared the expedition against the Ethiopians: and those of the Persians who had been sent to march against the Ammonians set forth from Thebes and went on their way with guides; and it is known that they arrived at the city of Oasis, which is inhabited by Samians said to be of the Aischrionian tribe, and is distant seven days' journey from Thebes over sandy desert: now this place is called in the speech of the Hellenes the "Isle of the Blessed." It is said that the army reached this place, but from that point onwards, except the Ammonians themselves and those who have heard the account from them, no man is able to say anything about them; for they neither reached the Ammonians nor returned back. This however is added to the story by the Ammonians themselves:—they say that as the army was going from this Oasis through the sandy desert to attack them, and had got to a point about mid-way between them and the Oasis, while they were taking their morning meal a violent South Wind blew upon them, and bearing with it heaps of the desert sand it buried them under it, and so they disappeared and were seen no more. Thus the Ammonians say that it came to pass with regard to this army.

27. When Cambyses arrived at Memphis, Apis appeared to the Egyptians, whom the Hellenes call Epaphos: and when he had appeared, forthwith the Egyptians began to wear their fairest garments and to have festivities. Cambyses accordingly seeing the Egyptians doing thus, and supposing that they were certainly acting so by way of rejoicing because he had fared ill, called for the officers who had charge of Memphis; and when they had come into his presence, he asked them why when he was at Memphis on the former occasion, the Egyptians were doing nothing of this kind, but only now, when he came there after losing a large part of his army. They said that a god had appeared to them, who was wont to appear at intervals of long time, and that whenever he appeared, then all the Egyptians rejoiced and kept festival. Hearing this Cambyses said that they were lying, and as liars he condemned them to death.

28. Having put these to death, next he called the priests into his presence; and when the priests answered him after the same manner, he said that it should not be without his knowledge if a tame god had come to the Egyptians; and having so said he bade the priests bring Apis away into his presence: so they went to bring him. Now this Apis-Epaphos is a calf born of a cow who after this is not permitted to conceive any other offspring; and the Egyptians say that a flash of light comes down from heaven upon this

cow, and of this she produces Apis. This calf which is called Apis is black and has the following signs, namely a white square upon the forehead, and on the back the likeness of an eagle, and in the tail the hairs are double, and on the tongue there is a mark like a beetle.

29. When the priests had brought Apis, Cambyses being somewhat affected with madness drew his dagger, and aiming at the belly of Apis, struck his thigh: then he laughed and said to the priests: "O ye wretched creatures, are gods born such as this, with blood and flesh, and sensible of the stroke of iron weapons? Worthy indeed of Egyptians is such a god as this. Ye however at least shall not escape without punishment for making a mock of me." Having thus spoken he ordered those whose duty it was to do such things, to scourge the priests without mercy, and to put to death any one of the other Egyptians whom they should find keeping the festival. Thus the festival of the Egyptians had been brought to an end, and the priests were being chastised, and Apis wounded by the stroke in his thigh lay dying in the temple.

30. Him, when he had brought his life to an end by reason of the wound, the priests buried without the knowledge of Cambyses: but Cambyses, as the Egyptians say, immediately after this evil deed became absolutely mad, not having been really in his right senses even before that time: and the first of his evil deeds was that he put to death his brother Smerdis, who was of the same father and the same mother as himself. This brother he had sent away from Egypt to Persia in envy, because alone of all the Persians he had been able to draw the bow which the Ichthyophagoi brought from the Ethiopian king, to an extent of about two finger-breadths; while of the other Persians not one had proved able to do this. Then when Smerdis had gone away to Persia, Cambyses saw a vision in his sleep of this kind:—it seemed to him that a messenger came from Persia and reported that Smerdis sitting upon the royal throne had touched the heaven with his head. Fearing therefore with regard to this lest his brother might slay him and reign in his stead, he sent Prexaspes to Persia, the man whom of all the Persians he trusted most, with command to slay him. He accordingly went up to Susa and slew Smerdis; and some say that he took him out of the chase and so slew him, others that he brought him to the Erythraian Sea and drowned him.

31. This they say was the first beginning of the evil deeds of Cambyses; and next after this he put to death his sister, who had accompanied him to Egypt, to whom also he was married, she being his sister by both parents. Now he took her to wife in the following manner (for before this the Persians had not been wont at all to marry their sisters):— Cambyses fell in love with one of his sisters, and desired to take her to wife; so since he had it in mind to do that which was not customary, he called the Royal Judges and asked them whether there existed any law which permitted him who desired it to marry his sister. Now the Royal Judges are men chosen out from among the Persians, and hold their office until they die or until some injustice is found in them, so long and no longer. These pronounce decisions for the Persians and are the expounders of the ordinances of their fathers, and all matters are referred to them. So when Cambyses asked them, they gave him an answer which was both upright and safe, saying that they found no law which permitted a brother to marry his sister, but apart from that they had found a law to the effect that the king of the Persians might do whatsoever he desired. Thus on the one hand they did not tamper with the law for fear of Cambyses, and at the same time, that they might not perish themselves in maintaining the law, they found another law beside that

which was asked for, which was in favor of him who wished to marry his sisters. So Cambyses at that time took to wife her with whom he was in love, but after no long time he took another sister. Of these it was the younger whom he put to death, she having accompanied him to Egypt.

32. About her death, as about the death of Smerdis, two different stories are told. The Hellenes say that Cambyses had matched a lion's cub in fight with a dog's whelp, and this wife of his was also a spectator of it; and when the whelp was being overcome, another whelp, its brother, broke its chain and came to help it; and having become two instead of one, the whelps then got the better of the cub: and Cambyses was pleased at the sight, but she sitting by him began to weep; and Cambyses perceived it and asked wherefore she wept; and she said that she had wept when she saw that the whelp had come to the assistance of its brother, because she remembered Smerdis and perceived that there was no one who would come to his assistance. The Hellenes say that it was for this saying that she was killed by Cambyses: but the Egyptians say that as they were sitting round at table, the wife took a lettuce and pulled off the leaves all round, and then asked her husband whether the lettuce was fairer when thus plucked round or when covered with leaves, and he said "when covered with leaves": she then spoke thus: "Nevertheless thou didst once produce the likeness of this lettuce, when thou didst strip bare the house of Cyrus." And he moved to anger leapt upon her, being with child, and she miscarried and died.

33. These were the acts of madness done by Cambyses towards those of his own family, whether the madness was produced really on account of Apis or from some other cause, as many ills are wont to seize upon men; for it is said moreover that Cambyses had from his birth a certain grievous malady, that which is called by some the "sacred" disease: and it was certainly nothing strange that when the body was suffering from a grievous malady, the mind should not be sound either.

34. The following also are acts of madness which he did to the other Persians:—To Prexaspes, the man whom he honored most and who used to bear his messages (his son also was cup-bearer to Cambyses, and this too was no small honor),—to him it is said that he spoke as follows: "Prexaspes, what kind of a man do the Persians esteem me to be, and what speech do they hold concerning me?" and he said: "Master, in all other respects thou art greatly commended, but they say that thou art overmuch given to love of wine." Thus he spoke concerning the Persians; and upon that Cambyses was roused to anger, and answered thus: "It appears then that the Persians say I am given to wine, and that there-fore I am beside myself and not in my right mind; and their former speech then was not sincere." For before this time, it seems, when the Persians and Croesus were sitting with him in council, Cambyses asked what kind of a man they thought he was as compared with his father Cyrus; and they answered that he was better than his father, for he not only possessed all that his father had possessed, but also in addition to this had acquired Egypt and the Sea. Thus the Persians spoke; but Croesus, who was present and was not satisfied with their judgment, spoke thus to Cambyses: "To me, O son of Cyrus, thou dost not appear to be equal to thy father, for not yet hast thou a son such as he left behind him in you." Hearing this Cambyses was pleased, and commended the judgment of Croesus.

35. So calling to mind this, he said in anger to Prexaspes: "Learn then now for thyself whether the Persians speak truly, or whether when they say this they are themselves out of their senses: for if I, shooting at thy son there standing before the entrance of the cham-ber, hit him in the very middle of the heart, the Persians will be proved to be speaking

falsely, but if I miss, then thou mayest say that the Persians are speaking the truth and that I am not in my right mind." Having thus said he drew his bow and hit the boy; and when the boy had fallen down, it is said that he ordered them to cut open his body and examine the place where he was hit; and as the arrow was found to be sticking in the heart, he laughed and was delighted, and said to the father of the boy: "Prexaspes, it has now been made evident, as thou seest, that I am not mad, but that it is the Persians who are out of their senses; and now tell me, whom of all men didst thou ever see before this time hit the mark so well in shooting?" Then Prexaspes, seeing that the man was not in his right senses and fearing for himself, said: "Master, I think that not even God himself could have hit the mark so fairly." Thus he did at that time: and at another time he condemned twelve of the Persians, men equal to the best, on a charge of no moment, and buried them alive with the head downwards.

36. When he was doing these things, Croesus the Lydian judged it right to admonish him in the following words: "O king, do not thou indulge the heat of thy youth and passion in all things, but retain and hold thyself back: it is a good thing to be prudent, and forethought is wise. Thou however are putting to death men who are of thine own people, condemning them on charges of no moment, and thou art putting to death men's sons also. If thou do many such things, beware lest the Persians make revolt from thee. As for me, thy father Cyrus gave me charge, earnestly bidding me to admonish thee, and suggest to thee that which I should find to be good." Thus he counselled him, manifesting good-will towards him; but Cambyses answered: "Dost *thou* venture to counsel me, who excel-lently well didst rule thine own country, and well didst counsel my father, bidding him pass over the river Araxes and go against the Massagetai, when they were willing to pass over into our land, and so didst utterly ruin thyself by ill government of thine own land, and didst utterly ruin Cyrus, who followed thy counsel. However thou shalt not escape punishment now, for know that before this I had very long been desiring to find some occasion against thee." Thus having said he took his bow meaning to shoot him, but Croesus started up and ran out: and so since he could not shoot him, he gave orders to his attendants to take and slay him. The attendants however, knowing his moods, concealed Croesus, with the intention that if Cambyses should change his mind and seek to have Croesus again, they might produce him and receive gifts as the price of saving his life; but if he did not change his mind nor feel desire to have him back, then they might kill him. Not long afterwards Cambyses did in fact desire to have Croesus again, and the atten-dants perceiving this reported to him that he was still alive: and Cambyses said that he rejoiced with Croesus that he was still alive, but that they who had preserved him should not get off free, but he would put them to death: and thus he did.

37. Many such acts of madness did he both to Persians and allies, remaining at Memphis and opening ancient tombs and examining the dead bodies. Likewise also he entered into the temple of Hephaistos and very much derided the image of the god: for the image of Hephaistos very nearly resembles the Phoenician *Pataicoi*, which the Phoeni-cians carry about on the prows of their triremes; and for him who has not seen these, I will indicate its nature,—it is the likeness of a dwarfish man. He entered also into the temple of the Cabeiroi, into which it is not lawful for anyone to enter except the priest only, and the images there he even set on fire, after much mockery of them. Now these also are like the images of Hephaistos, and it is said that they are the children of that god.

38. It is clear to me therefore by every kind of proof that Cambyses was mad exceed-

ingly; for otherwise he would not have attempted to deride religious rites and customary observances. For if one should propose to all men a choice, bidding them select the best customs from all the customs that there are, each race of men, after examining them all, would select those of his own people; thus all think that their own customs are by far the best: and so it is not likely that any but a madman would make a jest of such things. Now of the fact that all men are thus wont to think about their customs, we may judge by many other proofs and more specially by this which follows:—Dareios in the course of his reign summoned those of the Hellenes who were present in his land, and asked them for what price they would consent to eat up their fathers when they died; and they answered that for no price would they do so. After this Dareios summoned those Indians who are called Callatians, who eat their parents, and asked them in presence of the Hellenes, who understood what they said by help of an interpreter, for what payment they would consent to consume with fire the bodies of their fathers when they died; and they cried out aloud and bade him keep silence from such words. Thus then these things are established by usage, and I think that Pindar spoke rightly in his verse, when he said that "of all things law is king."

39. Now while Cambyses was marching upon Egypt, the Lacedemonians also had made an expedition against Samos and against Polycrates the son of Aiakes, who had risen against the government and obtained rule over Samos. At first he had divided the State into three parts and had given a share to his brothers Pantagnotos and Syloson; but afterwards he put to death one of these, and the younger, namely Syloson, he drove out, and so obtained possession of the whole of Samos. Then, being in possession, he made a guest-friendship with Amasis the king of Egypt, sending him gifts and receiving gifts in return from him. After this straightway within a short period of time the power of Polycrates increased rapidly, and there was much fame of it not only in Ionia, but also over the rest of Hellas: for to whatever part he directed his forces, everything went fortunately for him: and he had got for himself a hundred fifty-oared galleys and a thousand archers, and he plundered from all, making no distinction of any; for it was his wont to say that he would win more gratitude from his friend by giving back to him that which he had taken, than by not taking at all. So he had conquered many of the islands and also many cities of the continent, and besides other things he gained the victory in a sea-fight over the Lesbians, as they were coming to help the Milesians with their forces, and conquered them: these men dug the whole trench round the wall of the city of Samos working in chains.

40. Now Amasis, as may be supposed, did not fail to perceive that Polycrates was very greatly fortunate, and it was to him an object of concern; and as much more good fortune yet continued to come to Polycrates, he wrote upon a paper these words and sent them to Samos: "Amasis to Polycrates thus saith:—It is a pleasant thing indeed to hear that one who is a friend and guest is faring well; yet to me thy great good fortune is not pleasing, since I know that the Divinity is jealous; and I think that I desire, both for myself and for those about whom I have care, that in some of our affairs we should be prosperous and in others should fail, and thus go through life alternately faring well and ill, rather than that we should be prosperous in all things: for never yet did I hear tell of any one who was prosperous in all things and did not come to an utterly evil end at the last. Now therefore do thou follow my counsel and act as I shall say with respect to thy prosperous fortunes. Take thought and consider, and that which thou findest to be the most valued by thee, and

for the loss of which thou wilt most be vexed in thy soul, that take and cast away in such a manner that it shall never again come to the sight of men; and if in future from that time forward good fortune does not befall thee in alternation with calamities, apply remedies in the manner by me suggested."

41. Polycrates, having read this and having perceived by reflection that Amasis suggested to him good counsel, sought to find which one of his treasures he would be most afflicted in his soul to lose; and seeking he found this which I shall say:—he had a signet which he used to wear, enchased in gold and made of an emerald stone; and it was the work of Theodoros the son of Telecles of Samos. Seeing then that he thought it good to cast this away, he did thus:—he manned a fifty-oared galley with sailors and went on board of it himself; and then he bade them put out into the deep sea. And when he had got to a distance from the island, he took off the signet-ring, and in the sight of all who were with him in the ship he threw it into the sea. Thus having done he sailed home; and when he came to his house he mourned for his loss.

42. But on the fifth or sixth day after these things it happened to him as follows:—a fisherman having caught a large and beautiful fish, thought it right that this should be given as a gift to Polycrates. He bore it therefore to the door of the palace and said that he desired to come into the presence of Polycrates, and when he had obtained this he gave him the fish, saying: "O king, having taken this fish I did not think fit to bear it to the market, although I am one who lives by the labor of his hands; but it seemed to me that it was worthy of thee and of thy monarchy: therefore I bring it and present it to thee." He then, being pleased at the words spoken, answered thus: "Thou didst exceedingly well, and double thanks are due to thee, for thy words and also for thy gift; and we invite thee to come to dinner." The fisherman then, thinking this a great thing, went away to this house; and the servants as they were cutting up the fish found in its belly the signet-ring of Polycrates. Then as soon as they had seen it and taken it up, they bore it rejoicing to Polycrates, and giving him the signet-ring they told him in what manner it had been found: and he perceiving that the matter was of God, wrote upon paper all that he had done and all that had happened to him, and having written he dispatched it to Egypt.

43. Then Amasis, when he had read the paper which had come from Polycrates, perceived that it was impossible for man to rescue man from the event which was to come to pass, and that Polycrates was destined not to have a good end, being prosperous in all things, seeing that he found again even that which he cast away. Therefore he sent an envoy to him in Samos and said that he broke off the guest-friendship; and this he did lest when a fearful and great mishap befell Polycrates, he might himself be grieved in his soul as for a man who was his guest.

44. It was this Polycrates then, prosperous in all things, against whom the Lacedemonians were making an expedition, being invited by those Samians who afterwards settled at Kydonia in Crete, to come to their assistance. Now Polycrates had sent an envoy to Cambyses the son of Cyrus without the knowledge of the Samians, as he was gathering an army to go against Egypt, and had asked him to send to him in Samos and to ask for an armed force. So Cambyses hearing this very readily sent to Samos to ask Polycrates to send a naval force with him against Egypt: and Polycrates selected of the citizens those whom he most suspected of desiring to rise against him and sent them away in forty triremes, charging Cambyses not to send them back.

45. Now some say that those of the Samians who were sent away by Polycrates never

reached Egypt, but when they arrived on their voyage at Carpathos, they considered with themselves, and resolved not to sail on any further: others say that they reached Egypt and being kept under guard there, they made their escape from thence. Then, as they were sailing in to Samos, Polycrates encountered them with ships and engaged battle with them; and those who were returning home had the better and landed in the island; but having fought a land-battle in the island, they were worsted, and so sailed to Lacedaemon. Some however say that those from Egypt defeated Polycrates in the battle; but this in my opinion is not correct, for there would have been no need for them to invite the assistance of the Lacedemonians if they had been able by themselves to bring Polycrates to terms. Moreover, it is not reasonable either, seeing that he had foreign mercenaries and native archers very many in number, to suppose that he was worsted by the returning Samians, who were but few. Then Polycrates gathered together the children and wives of his subjects and confined them in the ship-sheds, keeping them ready so that, if it should prove that his subjects deserted to the side of the returning exiles, he might burn them with the sheds.

46. When those of the Samians who had been driven out by Polycrates reached Sparta, they were introduced before the magistrates and spoke at length, being urgent in their request. The magistrates however at the first introduction replied that they had forgotten the things which had been spoken at the beginning, and did not understand those which were spoken at the end. After this they were introduced a second time, and bringing with them a bag they said nothing else but this, namely that the bag was in want of meal; to which the others replied that they had overdone it with the bag. However, they resolved to help them.

47. Then the Lacedemonians prepared a force and made expedition to Samos, in repayment of former services, as the Samians say, because the Samians had first helped them with ships against the Messenians; but the Lacedemonians say that they made the expedition not so much from desire to help the Samians at their request, as to take vengeance on their own behalf for the robbery of the mixing-bowl which they had been bearing as a gift to Croesus, and of the corslet which Amasis the king of Egypt had sent as a gift to them; for the Samians had carried off the corslet also in the year before they took the bowl; and it was of linen with many figures woven into it and embroidered with gold and with cotton; and each thread of this corslet is worthy of admiration, for that being itself fine it has in it three hundred and sixty fibers, all plain to view. Such another as this moreover is that which Amasis dedicated as an offering to Athene at Lindos.

48. The Corinthians also took part with zeal in this expedition against Samos, that it might be carried out; for there had been an offence perpetrated against them also by the Samians a generation before the time of this expedition and about the same time as the robbery of the bowl. Periander the son of Kypselos had dispatched three hundred sons of the chief men of Corcyra to Alyattes at Sardis to be made eunuchs; and when the Corinthians who were conducting the boys had put in to Samos, the Samians, being informed of the story and for what purpose they were being conducted to Sardis, first instructed the boys to lay hold of the temple of Artemis, and then they refused to permit the Corinthians to drag the suppliants away from the temple: and as the Corinthians cut the boys off from supplies of food, the Samians made a festival, which they celebrate even to the present time in the same manner: for when night came on, as long as the boys were suppliants they arranged dances of maidens and youths, and in arranging the dances they

made it a rule of the festival that sweet cakes of sesame and honey should be carried, in order that the Corcyrean boys might snatch them and so have support; and this went on so long that at last the Corinthians who had charge of the boys departed and went away; and as for the boys, the Samians carried them back to Corcyra.

49. Now, if after the death of Periander the Corinthians had been on friendly terms with the Corcyreans, they would not have joined in the expedition against Samos for the cause which has been mentioned; but as it is, they have been ever at variance with one another since they first colonized the island. This then was the cause why the Corinthians had a grudge against the Samians.

50. Now Periander had chosen out the sons of the chief men of Corcyra and was sending them to Sardis to be made eunuchs, in order that he might have revenge; since the Corcyreans had first begun the offence and had done to him a deed of reckless wrong. For after Periander had killed his wife Melissa, it chanced to him to experience another misfortune in addition to that which had happened to him already, and this was as follows:—He had by Melissa two sons, the one of seventeen and the other of eighteen years. These sons their mother's father Procles, who was despot of Epidauros, sent for to himself and kindly entertained, as was to be expected seeing that they were the sons of his own daughter; and when he was sending them back, he said in taking leave of them: "Do ye know, boys, who it was that killed your mother?" Of this saying the elder of them took no account, but the younger, whose name was Lycophron, was grieved so greatly at hearing it, that when he reached Corinth again he would neither address his father, nor speak to him when his father would have conversed with him, nor give any reply when he asked questions, regarding him as the murderer of his mother. At length Periander being enraged with his son drove him forth out of his house.

51. And having driven him forth, he asked of the elder son what his mother's father had said to them in his conversation. He then related how Procles had received them in a kindly manner, but of the saying which he had uttered when he parted from them he had no remembrance, since he had taken no note of it. So Periander said that it could not be but that he had suggested to them something, and urged him further with questions; and he after that remembered, and told of this also. Then Periander taking note of it and not desiring to show any indulgence, sent a messenger to those with whom the son who had been driven forth was living at that time, and forbade them to receive him into their houses; and whenever having been driven away from one house he came to another, he was driven away also from this, since Periander threatened those who received him, and commanded them to exclude him; and so being driven away again he would go to another house, where persons lived who were his friends, and they perhaps received him because he was the son of Periander, notwithstanding that they feared.

52. At last Periander made a proclamation that whosoever should either receive him into their houses or converse with him should be bound to pay a fine to Apollo, stating the amount that it should be. Accordingly, by reason of this proclamation no one was willing either to converse with him or to receive him into their house; and moreover even he himself did not think it fit to attempt it, since it had been forbidden, but he lay about in the porticoes enduring exposure: and on the fourth day after this, Periander seeing him fallen into squalid misery and starvation felt pity for him; and abating his anger he approached him and began to say: "Son, which of these two is to be preferred, the fortune which thou dost now experience and possess, or to inherit the power and wealth which I possess now,

by being submissive to thy father's will? Thou however, being my son and the prince of wealthy Corinth, didst choose nevertheless the life of a vagabond by making opposition and displaying anger against him with whom it behooved thee least to deal so; for if any misfortune happened in those matters, for which cause thou hast suspicion against me, this has happened to me first, and I am sharer in the misfortune more than others, inasmuch as I did the deed myself. Do thou however, having learnt by how much to be envied is better than to be pitied, and at the same time what a grievous thing it is to be angry against thy parents and against those who are stronger than thou, come back now to the house." Periander with these words endeavored to restrain him; but he answered nothing else to his father, but said only that he ought to pay a fine to the god for having come to speech with him. Then Periander, perceiving that the malady of his son was hopeless and could not be overcome, dispatched a ship to Corcyra, and so sent him away out of his sight, for he was ruler also of that island; and having sent him away, Periander proceeded to make war against his father-in-law Procles, esteeming him most to blame for the condition in which he was; and he took Epidauros and took also Procles himself and made him a prisoner.

53. When however, as time went on, Periander had passed his prime and perceived within himself that he was no longer able to overlook and manage the government of the State, he sent to Corcyra and summoned Lycophron to come back and take the supreme power; for in the elder of his sons he did not see the required capacity, but perceived clearly that he was of wits too dull. Lycophron however did not deign even to give an answer to the bearer of his message. Then Periander, clinging still in affection to the youth, sent to him next his own daughter, the sister of Lycophron, supposing that he would yield to her persuasion more than to that of others; and she arrived there and spoke to him thus: "Boy, dost thou desire that both the despotism should fall to others, and also the substance of thy father, carried off as plunder, rather than that thou shouldest return back and possess them? Come back to thy home: cease to torment thyself. Pride is a mischievous possession. Heal not evil with evil. Many prefer that which is reasonable to that which is strictly just; and many ere now in seeking the things of their mother have lost the things of their father. Despotism is an insecure thing, and many desire it: moreover he is now an old man and past his prime. Give not thy good things unto others." She thus said to him the most persuasive things, having been before instructed by her father: but he in answer said, that he would never come to Corinth so long as he heard that his father was yet alive. When she had reported this, Periander the third time sent an envoy, and said that he desired himself to come to Corcyra, exhorting Lycophron at the same time to come back to Corinth and to be his successor on the throne. The son having agreed to return on these terms, Periander was preparing to sail to Corcyra and his son to Corinth; but the Corcyreans, having learnt all that had taken place, put the young man to death, in order that Periander might not come to their land. For this cause it was that Periander took vengeance on those of Corcyra.

54. The Lacedemonians then had come with a great armament and were besieging Samos; and having made an attack upon the wall, they occupied the tower which stands by the sea in the suburb of the city, but afterwards when Polycrates came up to the rescue with a large body they were driven away from it. Meanwhile by the upper tower which is upon the ridge of the mountain there had come out to the fight the foreign mercenaries and many of the Samians themselves, and these stood their ground against the Lacedemo-

nians for a short while and then began to fly backwards; and the Lacedemonians followed and were slaying them.

55. Now if the Lacedemonians there present had all been equal on that day to Archias and Lycopas, Samos would have been captured; for Archias and Lycopas alone rushed within the wall together with the flying Samians, and being shut off from retreat were slain within the city of the Samians. I myself moreover had converse in Pitane (for to that deme he belonged) with the third in descent from this Archias, another Archias the son of Samios the son of Archias, who honored the Samians of all strangers most; and not only so, but he said that his own father had been called Samios because *his* father Archias had died by a glorious death in Samos; and he said that he honored Samians because his grandfather had been granted a public funeral by the Samians.

56. The Lacedemonians then, when they had been besieging Samos for forty days and their affairs made no progress, set forth to return to Peloponnesus. But according to the less credible account which has been put abroad of these matters Polycrates struck in lead a quantity of a certain native coin, and having gilded the coins over, gave them to the Lacedemonians, and they received them and upon that set forth to depart. This was the first expedition which the Lacedemonians (being Dorians) made into Asia.

57. Those of the Samians who had made the expedition against Polycrates themselves also sailed away, when the Lacedemonians were about to desert them, and came to Siphnos: for they were in want of money, and the people of Siphnos were then at their greatest height of prosperity and possessed wealth more than all the other islanders, since they had in their island mines of gold and silver, so that there is a treasury dedicated at Delphi with the tithe of the money which came in from these mines, and furnished in a manner equal to the wealthiest of these treasuries: and the people used to divide among themselves the money which came in from the mines every year. So when they were establishing the treasury, they consulted the Oracle as to whether their present prosperity was capable of remaining with them for a long time, and the Pythian prophetess gave them this reply:

> *"But when with white shall be shining the hall of the city*
>   *in Siphnos,*
> *And when the market is white of brow, one wary is needed*
> *Then, to beware of an army of wood and a red-colored herald."*

Now just at that time the market-place and city hall of the Siphnians had been decorated with Parian marble.

58. This oracle they were not able to understand either then at first or when the Samians had arrived: for as soon as the Samians were putting in to Siphnos they sent one of their ships to bear envoys to the city: now in old times all ships were painted with red, and this was that which the Pythian prophetess was declaring beforehand to the Siphnians, bidding them guard against the "army of wood" and the "red-colored herald." The messengers accordingly came and asked the Siphnians to lend them ten talents; and as they refused to lend to them, the Samians began to lay waste their lands: so when they were informed of it, forthwith the Siphnians came to the rescue, and having engaged battle with them were defeated, and many of them were cut off by the Samians and shut

out of the city; and the Samians after this imposed upon them a payment of a hundred talents.

59. Then from the men of Hermion they received by payment of money the island of Hydrea, which is near the coast of Peloponnese, and they gave it in charge to the Troizenians, but they themselves settled at Kydonia which is in Crete, not sailing thither for that purpose but in order to drive the Zakynthians out of the island. Here they remained and were prosperous for five years, so much so that they were the builders of the temples which are now existing in Kydonia, and also of the house of Dictyna. In the sixth year however the Eginetans together with the Cretans conquered them in a sea-fight and brought them to slavery; and they cut off the prows of their ships, which were shaped like boars, and dedicated them in the temple of Athene in Egina. This the Eginetans did because they had a grudge against the Samians; for the Samians had first made expedition against Egina, when Amphicrates was king in Samos, and had done much hurt to the Eginetans and suffered much hurt also from them. Such was the cause of this event:

60, and about the Samians I have spoken at greater length, because they have three works which are greater than any others that have been made by Hellenes: first a passage beginning from below and open at both ends, dug through a mountain not less than a hundred and fifty fathoms in height; the length of the passage is seven furlongs and the height and breadth each eight feet, and throughout the whole of it another passage has been dug twenty cubits in depth and three feet in breadth, through which the water is conducted and comes by the pipes to the city, brought from an abundant spring: and the designer of this work was a Megarian, Eupalinos the son of Naustrophos. This is one of the three; and the second is a mole in the sea about the harbor, going down to a depth of as much as twenty fathoms; and the length of the mole is more than two furlongs. The third work which they have executed is a temple larger than all the other temples of which we know. Of this the first designer was Rhoicos the son of Philes, a native of Samos. For this reason I have spoken at greater length of the Samians.

61. Now while Cambyses the son of Cyrus was spending a long time in Egypt and had gone out of his right mind, there rose up against him two brothers, Magians, of whom the one had been left behind by Cambyses as caretaker of his household. This man, I say, rose up against him perceiving that the occurrence of the death of Smerdis was being kept secret, and that there were but few of the Persians who were aware of it, while the greater number believed without doubt that he was still alive. Therefore he endeavored to obtain the kingdom, and he formed his plan as follows:—he had a brother (that one who, as I said, rose up with him against Cambyses), and this man in form very closely resembled Smerdis the son of Cyrus, whom Cambyses had slain, being his own brother. He was like Smerdis, I say, in form, and not only so but he had the same name, Smerdis. Having persuaded this man that he would manage everything for him, the Magian Patizeithes brought him and seated him upon the royal throne: and having so done he sent heralds about to the various provinces, and among others one to the army in Egypt, to proclaim to them that they must obey Smerdis the son of Cyrus for the future instead of Cambyses.

62. So then the other heralds made this proclamation, and also the one who was appointed to go to Egypt, finding Cambyses and his army at Agbatana in Syria, stood in the midst and began to proclaim that which had been commanded to him by the Magian. Hearing this from the herald, and supposing that the herald was speaking the truth and that he had himself been betrayed by Prexaspes, that is to say, that when Prexaspes was

sent to kill Smerdis he had not done so, Cambyses looked upon Prexaspes and said: "Prex-aspes, was it thus that thou didst perform for me the thing which I gave over to thee to do?" and he said: "Master, the saying is not true that Smerdis thy brother has risen up against thee, nor that thou wilt have any contention arising from him, either great or small: for I myself, having done that which thou didst command me to do, buried him with my own hands. If therefore the dead have risen again to life, then thou mayest expect that Astyages also the Mede will rise up against thee; but if it is as it was before time, there is no fear now that any trouble shall spring up for you, at least from him. Now therefore I think it well that some should pursue after the herald and examine him, asking from whom he has come to proclaim to us that we are to obey Smerdis as king."

63. When Prexaspes had thus spoken, Cambyses was pleased with the advice, and accordingly the herald was pursued forthwith and returned. Then when he had come back, Prexaspes asked him as follows: "Man, thou sayest that thou art come as a messenger from Smerdis the son of Cyrus: now therefore speak the truth and go away in peace. I ask thee whether Smerdis himself appeared before thine eyes and charged thee to say this, or some one of those who serve him." He said: "Smerdis the son of Cyrus I have never yet seen, since the day that king Cambyses marched to Egypt: but the Magian whom Cambyses appointed to be guardian of his household, he, I say, gave me this charge, saying that Smerdis the son of Cyrus was he who laid the command upon me to speak these things to you." Thus he spoke to them, adding no falsehoods to the first, and Cambyses said: "Prexaspes, thou hast done that which was commanded thee like an honest man, and hast escaped censure; but who of the Persians may this be who has risen up against me and usurped the name of Smerdis?" He said: "I seem to myself, O king, to have understanding of this which has come to pass: the Magians have risen against thee, Patizeithes namely, whom thou didst leave as caretaker of thy household, and his brother Smerdis."

64. Then Cambyses, when he heard the name of Smerdis, perceived at once the true meaning of this report and of the dream, for he thought in his sleep that someone had reported to him that Smerdis was sitting upon the royal throne and had touched the heaven with his head: and perceiving that he had slain his brother without need, he began to lament for Smerdis; and having lamented for him and sorrowed greatly for the whole mishap, he was leaping upon his horse, meaning as quickly as possible to march his army to Susa against the Magian; and as he leapt upon his horse, the cap of his sword-sheath fell off, and the sword being left bare struck his thigh. Having been wounded then in the same part where he had formerly struck Apis the god of the Egyptians, and believing that he had been struck with a mortal blow, Cambyses asked what was the name of that town, and they said "Agbatana." Now even before this he had been informed by the Oracle at the city of Buto that in Agbatana he should bring his life to an end: and he supposed that he should die of old age in Agbatana in Media, where was his chief seat of power; but the oracle, it appeared, meant in Agbatana of Syria. So when by questioning now he learnt the name of the town, being struck with fear both by the calamity caused by the Magian and at the same time by the wound, he came to his right mind, and understanding the meaning of the oracle he said: "Here it is fated that Cambyses the son of Cyrus shall end his life."

65. So much only he said at that time; but about twenty days afterwards he sent for the most honorable of the Persians who were with him, and said to them as follows: "Per-

sians, it has become necessary for me to make known to you the thing which I was wont
to keep concealed beyond all other things. Being in Egypt I saw a vision in my sleep,
which I would I had never seen, and it seemed to me that a messenger came from home
and reported to me that Smerdis was sitting upon the royal throne and had touched the
heaven with his head. Fearing then lest I should be deprived of my power by my brother, I
acted quickly rather than wisely; for it seems that it is not possible for man to avert that
which is destined to come to pass. I therefore, fool that I was, sent away Prexaspes to Susa
to kill Smerdis; and when this great evil had been done, I lived in security, never considering the danger that some other man might at some time rise up against me, now that
Smerdis had been removed: and altogether missing the mark of that which was about to
happen, I have both made myself the murderer of my brother, when there was no need,
and I have been deprived none the less of the kingdom; for it was in fact Smerdis the
Magian of whom the divine power declared to me beforehand in the vision that he should
rise up against me. So then, as I say, this deed has been done by me, and ye must imagine
that ye no longer have Smerdis the son of Cyrus alive: but it is in truth the Magians who
are masters of your kingdom, he whom I left as guardian of my household and his brother
Smerdis. The man then who ought above all others to have taken vengeance on my behalf
for the dishonor which I have suffered from the Magians, has ended his life by an unholy
death received from the hands of those who were his nearest of kin; and since he is no
more, it becomes most needful for me, as the thing next best of those which remain, to
charge you, O Persians, with that which dying I desire should be done for me. This then I
lay upon you, calling upon the gods of the royal house to witness it,—upon you and most
of all upon those of the Achaemenidai who are present here,—that ye do not permit the
return of the chief power to the Medes, but that if they have acquired it by craft, by craft
they be deprived of it by you, or if they have conquered it by any kind of force, by force
and by a strong hand ye recover it. And if ye do this, may the earth bring forth her
produce and may your wives and your cattle be fruitful, while ye remain free for ever; but
if ye do not recover the power nor attempt to recover it, I pray that curses the contrary of
these blessings may come upon you, and moreover that each man of the Persians may
have an end to his life like that which has come upon me." Then as soon as he had
finished speaking these things, Cambyses began to bewail and make lamentation for all
his fortunes.

66. And the Persians, when they saw that the king had begun to bewail himself, both
rent the garments which they wore and made lamentation without stint. After this, when
the bone had become diseased and the thigh had mortified, Cambyses the son of Cyrus
was carried off by the wound, having reigned in all seven years and five months, and
being absolutely childless both of male and female offspring. The Persians meanwhile
who were present there were very little disposed to believe that the power was in the
hands of the Magians: on the contrary, they were surely convinced that Cambyses had
said that which he said about the death of Smerdis to deceive them, in order that all the
Persians might be moved to war against him. These then were surely convinced that
Smerdis the son of Cyrus was established to be king; for Prexaspes also very strongly
denied that he had slain Smerdis, since it was not safe, now that Cambyses was dead, for
him to say that he had destroyed with his own hand the son of Cyrus.

67. Thus when Cambyses had brought his life to an end, the Magian became king
without disturbance, usurping the place of his namesake Smerdis the son of Cyrus; and he

reigned during the seven months which were wanting yet to Cambyses for the completion of the eight years: and during them he performed acts of great benefit to all his subjects, so that after his death all those in Asia except the Persians themselves mourned for his loss: for the Magian sent messengers abroad to every nation over which he ruled, and proclaimed freedom from military service and from tribute for three years.

68. This proclamation, I say, he made at once when he established himself upon the throne: but in the eighth month it was discovered who he was in the following manner:— There was one Otanes the son of Pharnaspes, in birth and in wealth not inferior to any of the Persians. This Otanes was the first who had had suspicion of the Magian, that he was not Smerdis the son of Cyrus but the person that he really was, drawing his inference from these facts, namely that he never went abroad out of the fortress, and that he did not summon into his presence any of the honorable men among the Persians: and having formed a suspicion of him, he proceeded to do as follows:—Cambyses had taken to wife his daughter, whose name was Phaidyme; and this same daughter the Magian at that time was keeping as his wife and living with her as with all the rest also of the wives of Cambyses. Otanes therefore sent a message to this daughter and asked her who the man was by whose side she slept, whether Smerdis the son of Cyrus or some other. She sent back word to him saying that she did not know, for she had never seen Smerdis the son of Cyrus, nor did she know otherwise who he was who lived with her. Otanes then sent a second time and said: "If thou dost not thyself know Smerdis the son of Cyrus, then do thou ask of Atossa who this man is, with whom both she and thou live as wives; for assuredly it must be that she knows her own brother."

69. To this the daughter sent back word: "I am not able either to come to speech with Atossa or to see any other of the women who live here with me; for as soon as this man, whosoever he may be, succeeded to the kingdom, he separated us and placed us in different apartments by ourselves." When Otanes heard this, the matter became more and more clear to him, and he sent another message in to her, which said: "Daughter, it is right for thee, nobly born as thou art, to undertake any risk which thy father bids thee take upon thee: for if in truth this is not Smerdis the son of Cyrus but the man whom I suppose, he ought not to escape with impunity either for taking thee to his bed or for holding the dominion of Persians, but he must pay the penalty. Now therefore do as I say. When he sleeps by thee and thou perceivest that he is sound asleep, feel his ears; and if it prove that he has ears, then believe that thou art living with Smerdis the son of Cyrus, but if not, believe that it is with the Magian Smerdis." To this Phaidyme sent an answer saying that, if she should do so, she would run a great risk; for supposing that he should chance not to have his ears, and she were detected feeling for them, she was well assured that he would put her to death; but nevertheless she would do this. So she undertook to do this for her father: but as for this Magian Smerdis, he had had his ears cut off by Cyrus the son of Cambyses when he was king, for some grave offence. This Phaidyme then, the daughter of Otanes, proceeding to perform all that she had undertaken for her father, when her turn came to go to the Magian (for the wives of the Persians go in to them regularly each in her turn), came and lay down beside him: and when the Magian was in deep sleep, she felt his ears; and perceiving not with difficulty but easily that her husband had no ears, so soon as it became day she sent and informed her father of that which had taken place.

70. Then Otanes took to him Aspathines and Gobryas, who were leading men among

the Persians and also his own most trusted friends, and related to them the whole matter: and they, as it then appeared, had suspicions also themselves that it was so; and when Otanes reported this to them, they readily accepted his proposals. Then it was resolved by them that each one should associate with himself that man of the Persians whom he trusted most; so Otanes brought in Intaphrenes, Gobryas brought in Megabyzos, and Aspathines brought in Hydarnes. When they had thus become six, Dareios the son of Hystaspes arrived at Susa, having come from the land of Persia, for of this his father was governor. Accordingly when he came, the six men of the Persians resolved to associate Dareios also with themselves.

71. These then having come together, being seven in number, gave pledges of faith to one another and deliberated together; and when it came to Dareios to declare his opinion, he spoke to them as follows: "I thought that I alone knew this, namely that it was the Magian who was reigning as king and that Smerdis the son of Cyrus had brought his life to an end; and for this very reason I am come with earnest purpose to contrive death for the Magian. Since however it has come to pass that ye also know and not I alone, I think it well to act at once and not to put the matter off, for that is not the better way." To this replied Otanes: "Son of Hystaspes, thou art the scion of a noble stock, and thou art showing thyself, as it seems, in no way inferior to thy father: do not however hasten this enterprise so much without consideration, but take it up more prudently; for we must first become more in numbers, and then undertake the matter." In answer to this Dareios said: "Men who are here present, if ye shall follow the way suggested by Otanes, know that ye will perish miserably; for someone will carry word to the Magian, getting gain thereby privately for himself. Your best way would have been to do this action upon your own risk alone; but since it seemed good to you to refer the matter to a greater number, and ye communicated it to me, either let us do the deed to-day, or be ye assured that if this present day shall pass by, none other shall prevent me as your accuser, but I will myself tell these things to the Magian."

72. To this Otanes, when he saw Dareios in violent haste, replied: "Since thou dost compel us to hasten the matter and dost not permit us to delay, come expound to us thyself in what manner we shall pass into the palace and lay hands upon them: for that there are guards set in various parts, thou knowest probably thyself as well as we, if not from sight at least from hearsay; and in what manner shall we pass through these?" Dareios made reply with these words: "Otanes, there are many things in sooth which it is not possible to set forth in speech, but only in deed; and other things there are which in speech can be set forth, but from them comes no famous deed. Know ye however that the guards which are set are not difficult to pass: for in the first place, we being what we are, there is no one who will not let us go by, partly, as may be supposed, from having respect for us, and partly also perhaps from fear; and secondly I have myself a most specious pretext by means of which we may pass by; for I shall say that I am just now come from the Persian land and desire to declare to the king a certain message from my father: for where it is necessary that a lie be spoken, let it be spoken; seeing that we all aim at the same object, both they who lie and they who always speak the truth; those lie whenever they are likely to gain anything by persuading with their lies, and these tell the truth in order that they may draw to themselves gain by the truth, and that things may be entrusted to them more readily. Thus, while practicing different ways, we aim all at the same thing. If however they were not likely to make any gain by it, the truth-teller would

lie and the liar would speak the truth, with indifference. Whosoever then of the door-keepers shall let us pass by of his own free will, for him it shall be the better afterwards; but whosoever shall endeavor to oppose our passage, let him then and there be marked as our enemy, and after that let us push in and set about our work."

73. Then said Gobryas: "Friends, at what time will there be a fairer opportunity for us either to recover our rule, or, if we are not able to get it again, to die? seeing that we being Persians on the one hand lie under the rule of a Mede, a Magian, and that too a man whose ears have been cut off. Moreover all those of you who stood by the side of Cambyses when he was sick remember assuredly what he laid upon the Persians as he was bringing his life to an end, if they should not attempt to win back the power; and this we did not accept then, but supposed that Cambyses had spoken in order to deceive us. Now therefore I give my vote that we follow the opinion of Dareios, and that we do not depart from this assembly to go anywhither else but straight to attack the Magian." Thus spoke Gobryas, and they all approved of this proposal.

74. Now while these were thus taking counsel together, it was coming to pass by coin-cidence as follows:—The Magians taking counsel together had resolved to join Prexaspes with themselves as a friend, both because he had suffered grievous wrong from Camby-ses, who had killed his son by shooting him, and because he alone knew for a certainty of the death of Smerdis the son of Cyrus, having killed him with his own hands, and finally because Prexaspes was in very great repute among the Persians. For these reasons they summoned him and endeavored to win him to be their friend, engaging him by pledge and with oaths, that he would assuredly keep to himself and not reveal to any man the deception which had been practiced by them upon the Persians, and promising to give him things innumerable in return. After Prexaspes had promised to do this, the Magians, having persuaded him so far, proposed to him a second thing, and said that they would call together all the Persians to come up to the wall of the palace, and bade him go up upon a tower and address them, saying that they were living under the rule of Smerdis the son of Cyrus and no other. This they so enjoined because they supposed that he had the greatest credit among the Persians, and because he had frequently declared the opinion that Smerdis the son of Cyrus was still alive, and had denied that he had slain him.

75. When Prexaspes said that he was ready to do this also, the Magians having called together the Persians caused him to go up upon a tower and bade him address them. Then he chose to forget those things which they asked of him, and beginning with Achaimenes he traced the descent of Cyrus on the father's side, and then, when he came down to Cyrus, he related at last what great benefits he had conferred upon the Persians; and having gone through this recital he proceeded to declare the truth, saying that formerly he kept it secret, since it was not safe for him to tell of that which had been done, but at the present time he was compelled to make it known. He proceeded to say how he had himself slain Smerdis the son of Cyrus, being compelled by Cambyses, and that it was the Magians who were now ruling. Then he made imprecation of many evils on the Persians, if they did not win back again the power and take vengeance upon the Magians, and upon that he let himself fall down from the tower head foremost. Thus Prexaspes ended his life, having been throughout his time a man of repute.

76. Now the seven of the Persians, when they had resolved forthwith to lay hands upon the Magians and not to delay, made prayer to the gods and went, knowing nothing

of that which had been done with regard to Prexaspes: and as they were going and were in the middle of their course, they heard that which had happened about Prexaspes. Upon that they retired out of the way and again considered with themselves, Otanes and his supporters strongly urging that they should delay and not set to the work when things were thus disturbed, while Dareios and those of his party urged that they should go forthwith and do that which had been resolved, and not delay. Then while they were contending, there appeared seven pairs of hawks pursuing two pairs of vultures, plucking out their feathers and tearing them. Seeing this the seven all approved the opinion of Dareios and thereupon they went to the king's palace, encouraged by the sight of the birds.

77. When they appeared at the gates, it happened nearly as Dareios supposed, for the guards, having respect for men who were chief among the Persians, and not suspecting that anything would be done by them of the kind proposed, allowed them to pass in under the guiding of heaven, and none asked them any question. Then when they had passed into the court, they met the eunuchs who bore in the messages to the king; and these inquired of them for what purpose they had come, and at the same time they threatened with punishment the keepers of the gates for having let them pass in, and tried to stop the seven when they attempted to go forward. Then they gave the word to one another and drawing their daggers stabbed these men there upon the spot, who tried to stop them, and themselves went running on towards the chamber of the men.

78. Now the Magians happened both of them to be there within, consulting about that which had been done by Prexaspes. So when they saw that the eunuchs had been attacked and were crying aloud, they ran back both of them, and perceiving that which was being done they turned to self-defense: and one of them got down his bow and arrows before he was attacked, while the other had recourse to his spear. Then they engaged in combat with one another; and that one of them who had taken up his bow and arrows found them of no use, since his enemies were close at hand and pressed hard upon him, but the other defended himself with his spear, and first he struck Aspathines in the thigh, and then Intaphrenes in the eye; and Intaphrenes lost his eye by reason of the wound, but his life he did not lose. These then were wounded by one of the Magians, but the other, when his bow and arrows proved useless to him, fled into a bedchamber which opened into the chamber of the men, intending to close the door; and with him there rushed in two of the seven, Dareios and Gobryas. And when Gobryas was locked together in combat with the Magian, Dareios stood by and was at a loss what to do, because it was dark, and he was afraid lest he should strike Gobryas. Then seeing him standing by idle, Gobryas asked why he did not use his hands, and he said: "Because I am afraid lest I may strike thee": and Gobryas answered: "Thrust with thy sword even though it stab through us both." So Dareios was persuaded, and he thrust with his danger and happened to hit the Magian.

79. So when they had slain the Magians and cut off their heads, they left behind those of their number who were wounded, both because they were unable to go, and also in order that they might take charge of the fortress, and the five others taking with them the heads of the Magians ran with shouting and clashing of arms and called upon the other Persians to join them, telling them of that which had been done and showing the heads, and at the same time they proceeded to slay every one of the Magians who crossed their path. So the Persians when they heard of that which had been brought to pass by the seven and of the deceit of the Magians, thought good themselves also to do the same, and drawing their daggers they killed the Magians wherever they found one; so that if night

had not come on and stopped them, they would not have left a single Magian alive. This day the Persians celebrate in common more than all other days, and upon it they keep a great festival which is called by the Persians the festival of the slaughter of the Magians, on which no Magian is permitted to appear abroad, but the Magians keep themselves within their houses throughout that day.

80. When the tumult had subsided and more than five days had elapsed, those who had risen against the Magians began to take counsel about the general state, and there were spoken speeches which some of the Hellenes do not believe were really uttered, but spoken they were nevertheless. On the one hand Otanes urged that they should resign the government into the hands of the whole body of the Persians, and his words were as follows: "To me it seems best that no single one of us should henceforth be ruler, for that is neither pleasant nor profitable. Ye saw the insolent temper of Cambyses, to what lengths it went, and ye have had experience also of the insolence of the Magian: and how should the rule of one alone be a well-ordered thing, seeing that the monarch may do what he desires without rendering any account of his acts? Even the best of all men, if he were placed in this disposition, would be caused by it to change from his wonted disposition: for insolence is engendered in him by the good things which he possesses, and envy is implanted in man from the beginning; and having these two things, he has all vice: for he does many deeds of reckless wrong, partly moved by insolence proceeding from satiety, and partly by envy. And yet a despot at least ought to have been free from envy, seeing that he has all manner of good things. He is however naturally in just the opposite temper towards his subjects; for he grudges to the nobles that they should survive and live, but delights in the basest of citizens, and he is more ready than any other man to receive calumnies. Then of all things he is the most inconsistent; for if you express admiration of him moderately, he is offended that no very great court is paid to him, whereas if you pay court to him extravagantly, he is offended with you for being a flatterer. And the most important matter of all is that which I am about to say:—he disturbs the customs handed down from our fathers, he is a ravisher of women, and he puts men to death without trial. On the other hand the rule of many has first a name attaching to it which is the fairest of all names, that is to say 'Equality'; next, the multitude does none of those things which the monarch does: offices of state are exercised by lot, and the magistrates are compelled to render account of their action: and finally all matters of deliberation are referred to the public assembly. I therefore give as my opinion that we let monarchy go and increase the power of the multitude; for in the many is contained everything."

81. This was the opinion expressed by Otanes; but Megabyzos urged that they should entrust matters to the rule of a few, saying these words: "That which Otanes said in opposition to a tyranny, let it be counted as said for me also, but in that which he said urging that we should make over the power to the multitude, he has missed the best counsel: for nothing is more senseless or insolent than a worthless crowd; and for men flying from the insolence of a despot to fall into that of unrestrained popular power, is by no means to be endured: for he, if he does anything, does it knowing what he does, but the people cannot even know; for how can that know which has neither been taught anything noble by others nor perceived anything of itself, but pushes on matters with violent impulse and without understanding, like a torrent stream? Rule of the people then let them adopt who are foes to the Persians; but let us choose a company of the best men, and to them attach

the chief power; for in the number of these we shall ourselves also be, and it is likely that the resolutions taken by the best men will be the best."

82. This was the opinion expressed by Megabyzos; and thirdly Dareios proceeded to declare his opinion, saying: "To me it seems that in those things which Megabyzos said with regard to the multitude he spoke rightly, but in those which he said with regard to the rule of a few, not rightly: for whereas there are three things set before us, and each is supposed to be the best in its own kind, that is to say a good popular government, and the rule of a few, and thirdly the rule of one, I say that this last is by far superior to the others; for nothing better can be found than the rule of an individual man of the best kind; seeing that using the best judgment he would be guardian of the multitude without reproach; and resolutions directed against enemies would so best be kept secret. In an oligarchy however it happens often that many, while practicing virtue with regard to the common-wealth, have strong private enmities arising among themselves; for as each man desires to be himself the leader and to prevail in counsels, they come to great enmities with one another, whence arise factions among them, and out of the factions comes murder, and from murder results the rule of one man; and thus it is shown in this instance by how much that is the best. Again, when the people rules, it is impossible that corruption should not arise, and when corruption arises in the commonwealth, there arise among the corrupt men not enmities but strong ties of friendship: for they who are acting corruptly to the injury of the commonwealth put their heads together secretly to do so. And this continues so until at last someone takes the leadership of the people and stops the course of such men. By reason of this the man of whom I speak is admired by the people, and being so admired he suddenly appears as monarch. Thus he too furnishes herein an example to prove that the rule of one is the best thing. Finally, to sum up all in a single word, whence arose the liberty which we possess, and who gave it to us? Was it a gift of the people or of an oligarchy or of a monarch? I therefore am of opinion that we, having been set free by one man, should preserve that form of rule, and in other respects also that we should not annul the customs of our fathers which are ordered well; for that is not the better way."

83. These three opinions then had been proposed, and the other four men of the seven gave their assent to the last. So when Otanes, who was desirous to give equality to the Persians, found his opinion defeated, he spoke to those assembled thus: "Partisans, it is clear that some one of us must become king, selected either by casting lots, or by entrusting the decision to the multitude of the Persians and taking him whom it shall choose, or by some other means. I therefore shall not be a competitor with you, for I do not desire either to rule or to be ruled; and on this condition I withdraw from my claim to rule, namely that I shall not be ruled by any of you, either I myself or my descendants in future time." When he had said this, the six made agreement with him on those terms, and he was no longer a competitor with them, but withdrew from the assembly; and at the present time this house remains free alone of all the Persian houses, and submits to rule only so far as it wills to do so itself, not transgressing the laws of the Persians.

84. The rest however of the seven continued to deliberate how they should establish a king in the most just manner; and it was resolved by them that to Otanes and his descen-dants in succession, if the kingdom should come to any other of the seven, there should be given as special gifts a Median dress every year and all those presents which are esteemed among the Persians to be the most valuable: and the reason why they determined that

these things should be given to him, was because he first suggested to them the matter and combined them together. These were special gifts for Otanes; and this they also determined for all in common, namely that any one of the seven who wished might pass in to the royal palaces without any to bear in a message, unless the king happened to be sleeping with his wife; and that it should not be lawful for the king to marry from any other family, but only from those of the men who had made insurrection with him: and about the kingdom they determined this, namely that the man whose horse should first neigh at sunrise in the suburb of the city when they were mounted upon their horses, he should have the kingdom.

85. Now Dareios had a clever horse-keeper, whose name was Oibares. To this man, when they had left their assembly, Dareios spoke these words: "Oibares, we have resolved to do about the kingdom thus, namely that the man whose horse first neighs at sunrise, when we are mounted upon our horses he shall be king. Now therefore, if thou hast any cleverness, contrive that we may obtain this prize, and not any other man." Oibares replied thus: "If, my master, it depends in truth upon this whether thou be king or no, have confidence so far as concerns this and keep a good heart, for none other shall be king before thee; such charms have I at my command." Then Dareios said: "If then thou hast any such trick, it is time to devise it and not to put things off, for our trial is to-morrow." Oibares therefore hearing this did as follows:—when night was coming on he took one of the mares, namely that one which the horse of Dareios preferred, and this he led into the suburb of the city and tied her up: then he brought to her the horse of Dareios, and having for some time led him round her, making him go so close by so as to touch the mare, at last he let the horse mount.

86. Now at dawn of day the six came to the place as they had agreed, riding upon their horses; and as they rode through by the suburb of the city, when they came near the place where the mare had been tied up on the former night, the horse of Dareios ran up to the place and neighed; and just when the horse had done this, there came lightning and thunder from a clear sky: and the happening of these things to Dareios consummated his claim, for they seemed to have come to pass by some design, and the others leapt down from their horses and did obeisance to Dareios.

87. Some say that the contrivance of Oibares was this, but others say as follows (for the story is told by the Persians in both ways), namely that he touched with his hands the parts of this mare and kept his hand hidden in his trousers; and when at sunrise they were about to let the horses go, this Oibares pulled out his hand and applied it to the nostrils of the horse of Dareios; and the horse, perceiving the smell, snorted and neighed.

88. So Dareios the son of Hystaspes had been declared king; and in Asia all except the Arabians were his subjects, having been subdued by Cyrus and again afterwards by Cambyses. The Arabians however were never obedient to the Persians under conditions of subjection, but had become guest-friends when they let Cambyses pass by to Egypt: for against the will of the Arabians the Persians would not be able to invade Egypt. Moreover Dareios made the most noble marriages possible in the estimation of the Persians; for he married two daughters of Cyrus, Atossa and Artystone, of whom the one, Arossa, had before been the wife of Cambyses her brother and then afterwards of the Magian, while Artystone was a virgin; and besides them he married the daughter of Smerdis the son of Cyrus, whose name was Parmys; and he also took to wife the daughter of Otanes, he who had discovered the Magian; and all things became filled with his power. And first he

caused to be a carving in stone, and set it up; and in it there was the figure of a man on horseback, and he wrote upon it writing to this effect: "Dareios son of Hystaspes by the excellence of his horse," mentioning the name of it, "and of his horse-keeper Oibares obtained the kingdom of the Persians."

89. Having so done in Persia, he established twenty provinces, which the Persians themselves call *satrapies*; and having established the provinces and set over them rulers, he appointed tribute to come to him from them according to races, joining also to the chief races those who dwelt on their borders, or passing beyond the immediate neighbors and assigning to various races those which lay more distant. He divided the provinces and the yearly payment of tribute as follows: and those of them who brought in silver were commanded to pay by the standard of the Babylonian talent, but those who brought in gold by the Euboïc talent; now the Babylonian talent is equal to eight-and-seventy Euboïc pounds. For in the reign of Cyrus, and again of Cambyses, nothing was fixed about tribute, but they used to bring gifts: and on account of this appointing of tribute and other things like this, the Persians say that Dareios was a shopkeeper, Cambyses a master, and Cyrus a father; the one because he dealt with all his affairs like a shopkeeper, the second because he was harsh and had little regard for any one, and the other because he was gentle and contrived for them all things good.

90. From the Ionians and the Magnesians who dwell in Asia and the Aiolians, Carians, Lykians, Milyans and Pamphylians (for one single sum was appointed by him as tribute for all these) there came in four hundred talents of silver. This was appointed by him to be the first division. From the Mysians and Lydians and Lasonians and Cabalians and Hytennians there came in five hundred talents: this is the second division. From the Hellespontians who dwell on the right as one sails in and the Phrygians and the Thracians who dwell in Asia and the Paphlagonians and Mariandynoi and Syrians the tribute was three hundred and sixty talents: this is the third division. From the Kilikians, besides three hundred and sixty white horses, one for every day in the year, there came also five hundred talents of silver; of these one hundred and forty talents were spent upon the horsemen which served as a guard to the Kilikian land, and the remaining three hundred and sixty came in year by year to Dareios: this is the fourth division.

91. From that division which begins with the city of Posideion, founded by Amphilochos the son of Amphiaraos on the borders of the Kilikians and the Syrians, and extends as far as Egypt, not including the territory of the Arabians (for this was free from payment), the amount was three hundred and fifty talents; and in this division are the whole of Phenicia and Syria which is called Palestine and Cyprus: this is the fifth division. From Egypt and the Libyans bordering upon Egypt, and from Kyrene and Barca, for these were so ordered as to belong to the Egyptian division, there came in seven hundred talents, without reckoning the money produced by the lake of Moiris, that is to say from the fish; without reckoning this, I say, or the corn which was contributed in addition by measure, there came in seven hundred talents; for as regards the corn, they contribute by measure one hundred and twenty thousand bushels for the use of those Persians who are established in the "White Fortress" at Memphis, and for their foreign mercenaries: this is the sixth division. The Sattagydai and Gandarians and Dadicans and Aparytai, being joined together, brought in one hundred and seventy talents: this is the seventh division. From Susa and the rest of the land of the Kissians there came in three hundred: this is the eighth division.

92. From Babylon and from the rest of Assyria there came in to him a thousand talents of silver and five hundred boys for eunuchs: this is the ninth division. From Agbatana and from the rest of Media and the Paricanians and Orthocorybantians, four hundred and fifty talents: this is the tenth division. The Caspians and Pausicans and Pantimathoi and Dareitai, contributing together, brought in two hundred talents: this is the eleventh division. From the Bactrians as far as the Aigloi the tribute was three hundred and sixty talents: this is the twelfth division.

93. From Pactyïke and the Armenians and the people bordering upon them as far as the Euxine, four hundred talents: this is the thirteenth division. From the Sagartians and Sarangians and Thamanaians and Utians and Mycans and those who dwell in the islands of the Erythraian Sea, where the king settles those who are called the "Removed," from all these together a tribute was produced of six hundred talents: this is the fourteenth division. The Sacans and the Caspians brought in two hundred and fifty talents: this is the fifteenth division. The Parthians and Chorasmians and Sogdians and Areians three hundred talents: this is the sixteenth division.

94. The Paricanians and Ethiopians in Asia brought in four hundred talents: this is the seventeenth division. To the Matienians and Saspeirians and Alarodians was appointed a tribute of two hundred talents: this is the eighteenth division. To the Moschoi and Tibarenians and Macronians and Mossynoicoi and Mares three hundred talents were ordered: this is the nineteenth division. Of the Indians the number is far greater than that of any other race of men of whom we know; and they brought in a tribute larger than all the rest, that is to say three hundred and sixty talents of gold-dust: this is the twentieth division.

95. Now if we compare Babylonian with Euboïc talents, the silver is found to amount to nine thousand eight hundred and eighty talents; and if we reckon the gold at thirteen times the value of silver, weight for weight, the gold-dust is found to amount to four thousand six hundred and eighty Euboïc talents. These being all added together, the total which was collected as yearly tribute for Dareios amounts to fourteen thousand five hundred and sixty Euboïc talents: the sums which are less than these I pass over and do not mention.

96. This was the tribute which came in to Dareios from Asia and from a small part of Libya: but as time went on, other tribute came in also from the islands and from those who dwell in Europe as far as Thessaly. This tribute the king stores up in his treasury in the following manner:—he melts it down and pours it into jars of earthenware, and when he has filled the jars he takes off the earthenware jar from the metal; and when he wants money he cuts off so much as he needs on each occasion.

97. These were the provinces and the assessments of tribute: and the Persian land alone has not been mentioned by me as paying a contribution, for the Persians have their land to dwell in free from payment. The following moreover had no tribute fixed for them to pay, but brought gifts, namely the Ethiopians who border upon Egypt, whom Cambyses subdued as he marched against the Long-lived Ethiopians, those who dwell about Nysa, which is called "sacred," and who celebrate the festivals in honor of Dionysos: these Ethiopians and those who dwell near them have the same kind of seed as the Callantian Indians, and they have underground dwellings. These both together brought every other year, and continue to bring even to my own time, two quart measures of unmelted gold and two hundred blocks of ebony and five Ethiopian boys and twenty large elephant tusks. The Colchians also had set themselves among those who brought gifts, and with

them those who border upon them extending as far as the range of the Caucasus (for the Persian rule extends as far as these mountains, but those who dwell in the parts beyond Caucasus toward the North Wind regard the Persians no longer),—these, I say, continued to bring the gifts which they had fixed for themselves every four years even down to my own time, that is to say, a hundred boys and a hundred maidens. Finally, the Arabians brought a thousand talents of frankincense every year. Such were the gifts which these brought to the king apart from the tribute.

98. Now this great quantity of gold, out of which the Indians bring in to the king the gold-dust which has been mentioned, is obtained by them in a manner which I shall tell:— That part of the Indian land which is towards the rising sun is sand; for of all the peoples in Asia of which we know or about which any certain report is given, the Indians dwell furthest away towards the East and the sunrising; seeing that the country to the East of the Indians is desert on account of the sand. Now there are many tribes of Indians, and they do not agree with one another in language; and some of them are pastoral and others not so, and some dwell in the swamps of the river and feed upon raw fish, which they catch by fishing from boats made of cane; and each boat is made of one joint of cane. These Indians of which I speak wear clothing made of rushes: they gather and cut the rushes from the river and then weave them together into a kind of mat and put it on like a corslet.

99. Others of the Indians, dwelling to the East of these, are pastoral and eat raw flesh: these are called Padaians, and they practice the following customs:—whenever any of their tribe falls ill, whether it be a woman or a man, if a man then the men who are his nearest associates put him to death, saying that he is wasting away with the disease and his flesh is being spoilt for them: and meanwhile he denies stoutly and says that he is not ill, but they do not agree with him; and after they have killed him they feast upon his flesh: but if it be a woman who falls ill, the women who are her greatest intimates do to her in the same manner as the men do in the other case. For in fact even if a man has come to old age they slay him and feast upon him; but very few of them come to be reckoned as old, for they kill everyone who falls into sickness, before he reaches old age.

100. Other Indians have on the contrary a manner of life as follows:—they neither kill any living thing nor do they sow any crops nor is it their custom to possess houses; but they feed on herbs, and they have a grain of the size of millet, in a sheath, which grows of itself from the ground; this they gather and boil with the sheath, and make it their food: and whenever any of them falls into sickness, he goes to the desert country and lies there, and none of them pay any attention either to one who is dead or to one who is sick.

101. The sexual intercourse of all these Indians of whom I have spoken is open like that of cattle, and they have all one color of skin, resembling that of the Ethiopians: moreover the seed which they emit is not white like that of other races, but black like their skin; and the Ethiopians also are similar in this respect. These tribes of Indians dwell further off than the Persian power extends, and towards the South Wind, and they never became subjects of Dareios.

102. Others however of the Indians are on the borders of the city of Caspatyros and the country of Pactyïke, dwelling towards the North of the other Indians; and they have a manner of living nearly the same as that of the Bactrians: these are the most warlike of the Indians, and these are they who make expeditions for the gold. For in the parts where they live it is desert on account of the sand; and in this desert and sandy tract are produced ants, which are in size smaller than dogs but larger than foxes, for there are some of them

kept at the residence of the king of Persia, which are caught here. These ants then make their dwelling underground and carry up the sand just in the same manner as the ants found in the land of the Hellenes, which they themselves also very much resemble in form; and the sand which is brought up contains gold. To obtain this sand the Indians make expeditions into the desert, each one having yoked together three camels, placing a female in the middle and a male like a trace-horse to draw by each side. On this female he mounts himself, having arranged carefully that she shall be taken to be yoked from young ones, the more lately born the better. For their female camels are not inferior to horses in speed, and moreover they are much more capable of bearing weights.

103. As to the form of the camel, I do not here describe it, since the Hellenes for whom I write are already acquainted with it, but I shall tell that which is not commonly known about it, which is this:—the camel has in the hind legs four thighs and four knees, and its organs of generation are between the hind legs, turned towards the tail.

104. The Indians, I say, ride out to get the gold in the manner and with the kind of yoking which I have described, making calculations so that they may be engaged in carrying it off at the time when the greatest heat prevails; for the heat causes the ants to disappear underground. Now among these nations the sun is hottest in the morning hours, not at midday as with others, but from sunrise to the time of closing the market: and during this time it produces much greater heat than at midday in Hellas, so that it is said that then they drench themselves with water. Midday however has about equal degree of heat with the Indians as with other men, while after midday their sun becomes like the morning sun with other men, and after this, as it goes further away, it produces still greater coolness, until at last at sunset it makes the air very cool indeed.

105. When the Indians have come to the place with bags, they fill them with the sand and ride away back as quickly as they can, for forthwith the ants, perceiving, as the Persians allege, by the smell, begin to pursue them: and this animal, they say, is superior to every other creature in swiftness, so that unless the Indians got a start in their course, while the ants were gathering together, not one of them would escape. So then the male camels, for they are inferior in speed of running to the females, if they drag behind are even let loose from the side of the female, one after the other; the females however, remembering the young which they left behind, do not show any slackness in their course. Thus it is that the Indians get most part of the gold, as the Persians say; there is however other gold also in their land obtained by digging, but in smaller quantities.

106. It seems indeed that the extremities of the inhabited world had allotted to them by nature the fairest things, just as it was the lot of Hellas to have its seasons far more fairly tempered than other lands: for first, India is the most distant of inhabited lands towards the East, as I have said a little above, and in this land not only the animals, birds as well as four-footed beasts, are much larger than in other places (except the horses, which are surpassed by those of Media called Nessaian), but also there is gold in abundance there, some got by digging, some brought down by rivers, and some carried off as I explained just now: and there also the trees which grow wild produce wool which surpasses in beauty and excellence that from sheep, and the Indians wear clothing obtained from these trees.

107. Then again Arabia is the furthest of inhabited lands in the direction of the midday, and in it alone of all lands grow frankincense and myrrh and cassia and cinnamon and gum-mastich. All these except myrrh are got with difficulty by the Arabians. Frankincense

they collect by burning the storax, which is brought thence to the Hellenes by the Phoenicians, by burning this, I say, so as to produce smoke they take it; for these trees which produce frankincense are guarded by winged serpents, small in size and of various colors, which watch in great numbers about each tree, of the same kind as those which attempt to invade Egypt: and they cannot be driven away from the trees by any other thing but only the smoke of storax.

108. The Arabians say also that all the world would have been by this time filled with these serpents, if that did not happen with regard to them which I knew happened with regard to vipers: and it seems that the Divine Providence, as indeed was to be expected, seeing that it is wise, has made all those animals prolific which are of cowardly spirit and good for food, in order that they may not be all eaten up and their race fail, whereas it has made those which are bold and noxious to have small progeny. For example, because the hare is hunted by every beast and bird as well as by man, therefore it is so very prolific as it is: and this is the only one of all beasts which becomes pregnant again before the former young are born, and has in its womb some of its young covered with fur and others bare; and while one is just being shaped in the matrix, another is being conceived. Thus it is in this case; whereas the lioness, which is the strongest and most courageous of creatures, produces one cub once only in her life; for when she produces young she casts out her womb together with her young; and the cause of it is this:—when the cub being within the mother begins to move about, then having claws by far sharper than those of any other beast he tears the womb, and as he grows larger he proceeds much further in his scratching: at last the time of birth approaches and there is now nothing at all left of it in a sound condition.

109. Just so also, if vipers and the winged serpents of the Arabians were produced in the ordinary course of their nature, man would not be able to live upon the earth; but as it is, when they couple with one another and the male is in the act of generation, as he lets go from him the seed, the female seizes hold of his neck, and fastening on to it does not relax her hold till she has eaten it through. The male then dies in the manner which I have said, but the female pays the penalty of retribution for the male in this manner:—the young while they are still in the womb take vengeance for their father by eating through their mother, and having eaten through her belly they thus make their way out for themselves. Other serpents however, which are not hurtful to man, produce eggs and hatch from them a very large number of offspring. Now vipers are distributed over all the earth; but the others, which are winged, are found in great numbers together in Arabia and in no other land: therefore it is that they appear to be numerous.

110. This frankincense then is obtained thus by the Arabians; and cassia is obtained as follows:—they bind up in cows'-hide and other kinds of skins all their body and their face except only the eyes, and then go to get the cassia. This grows in a pool not very deep, and round the pool and in it lodge, it seems, winged beasts nearly resembling bats, and they squeak horribly and are courageous in fight. These they must keep off from their eyes, and so cut the cassia.

111. Cinnamon they collect in a yet more marvelous manner than this: for where it grows and what land produces it they are not able to tell, except only that some say (and it is a probable account) that it grows in those regions where Dionysos was brought up; and they say that large birds carry those dried sticks which we have learnt from the Phoenicians to call cinnamon, carry them, I say, to nests which are made of clay and stuck on to

precipitous sides of mountains, which man can find no means of scaling. With regard to this then the Arabians practice the following contrivance:—they divide up the limbs of the oxen and asses that die and of their other beasts of burden, into pieces as large as convenient, and convey them to these places, and when they have laid them down not far from the nests, they withdraw to a distance from them: and the birds fly down and carry the limbs of the beasts of burden off to their nests; and these are not able to bear them, but break down and fall to the earth; and the men come up to them and collect the cinnamon. Thus cinnamon is collected and comes from this nation to the other countries of the world.

112. Gum-mastich however, which the Arabians call *ladanon*, comes in a still more extraordinary manner; for though it is the most sweet-scented of all things, it comes in the most evil-scented thing, since it is found in the beards of he-goats, produced there like resin from wood: this is of use for the making of many perfumes, and the Arabians use it more than anything else as incense.

113. Let what we have said suffice with regard to spices; and from the land of Arabia there blows a scent of them most marvelously sweet. They have also two kinds of sheep which are worthy of admiration and are not found in any other land: the one kind has the tail long, not less than three cubits in length; and if one should allow these to drag these after them, they would have sores from their tails being worn away against the ground; but as it is, every one of the shepherds knows enough of carpentering to make little cars, which they tie under the tails, fastening the tail of each animal to a separate little car. The other kind of sheep has the tail broad, even as much as a cubit in breadth.

114. As one passes beyond the place of the midday, the Ethiopian land is that which extends furthest of all inhabited lands towards the sunset. This produces both gold in abundance and huge elephants and trees of all kinds growing wild and ebony, and men who are of all men the tallest, the most beautiful and the most long-lived.

115. These are the extremities in Asia and in Libya; but as to the extremities of Europe towards the West, I am not able to speak with certainty: for neither do I accept the tale that there is a river called in Barbarian tongue Eridanos, flowing into the sea which lies towards the North Wind, whence it is said that amber comes; nor do I know of the real existence of "Tin Islands" from which tin comes to us: for first the name Eridanos itself declares that it is Hellenic and that it does not belong to a Barbarian speech, but was invented by some poet; and secondly I am not able to hear from anyone who has been an eye-witness, though I took pains to discover this, that there is a sea on the other side of Europe. However that may be, tin and amber certainly come to us from the extremity of Europe.

116. Then again towards the North of Europe, there is evidently a quantity of gold by far larger than in any other land: as to how it is got, here again I am not able to say for certain, but it is said to be carried off from the griffins by Arimaspians, a one-eyed race of men. But I do not believe this tale either, that nature produces one-eyed men which in all other respects are like other men. However, it would seem that the extremities which bound the rest of the world on every side and enclose it in the midst, possess the things which by us are thought to be the most beautiful and the most rare.

117. Now there is a plain in Asia bounded by mountains on all sides, and through the mountains there are five clefts. This plain belonged once to the Chorasmians, and it lies on the borders of the Chorasmians themselves, the Hyrcanians, Parthians, Sarangians, and Thamanaians; but from the time that the Persians began to bear rule it belongs to the king.

From this enclosing mountain of which I speak there flows a great river, and its name is Akes. This formerly watered the lands of these nations which have been mentioned, being divided into five streams and conducted through a separate cleft in the mountains to each separate nation; but from the time that they have come to be under the Persians they have suffered as follows:—the king built up the clefts in the mountains and set gates at each cleft; and so, since the water has been shut off from its outlet, the plain within the mountains is made into a sea, because the river runs into it and has no way out in any direction. Those therefore who in former times had been wont to make use of the water, not being able now to make use of it are in great trouble: for during the winter they have rain from heaven, as also other men have, but in the summer they desire to use the water when they sow millet and sesame seed. So then, the water not being granted to them, they come to the Persians both themselves and their wives, and standing at the gates of the king's court they cry and howl; and the king orders that for those who need it most, the gates which lead to their land shall be opened; and when their land has become satiated with drinking in the water, these gates are closed, and he orders the gates to be opened for others, that is to say those most needing it of the rest who remain: and, as I have heard, he exacts large sums of money for opening them, besides the regular tribute.

118. Thus it is with these matters: but of the seven men who had risen against the Magian, it happened to one, namely Intaphrenes, to be put to death immediately after their insurrection for an outrage which I shall relate. He desired to enter into the king's palace and confer with the king; for the law was in fact so, that those who had risen up against the Magian were permitted to go in to the king's presence without any one to announce them, unless the king happened to be lying with his wife. Accordingly Intaphrenes did not think it fit that any one should announce his coming; but as he was one of the seven, he desired to enter. The gatekeeper however and the bearer of messages endeavored to prevent him, saying that the king was lying with his wife: but Intaphrenes believing that they were not speaking the truth, drew his sword and cut off their ears and their noses, and stringing these upon his horse's bridle he tied them round their necks and so let them go.

119. Upon this they showed themselves to the king and told the cause for which they had suffered this; and Dareios, fearing that the six might have done this by common design, sent for each one separately and made trial of his inclinations, as to whether he approved of that which had been done: and when he was fully assured that Intaphrenes had not done this in combination with them, he took both Intaphrenes himself and his sons and all his kinsmen, being much disposed to believe that he was plotting insurrection against him with the help of his relations; and having seized them he put them in bonds as for execution. Then the wife of Intaphrenes, coming constantly to the doors of the king's court, wept and bewailed herself; and by doing this continually after the same manner she moved Dareios to pity her. Accordingly he sent a messenger and said to her: "Woman, king Dareios grants to thee to save from death one of thy kinsmen who are lying in bonds, whomsoever thou desirest of them all." She then, having considered with herself, answered thus: "If in truth the king grants me the life of one, I choose of them all my brother." Dareios being informed of this, and marveling at her speech, sent and addressed her thus: "Woman, the king asks thee what was in thy mind, that thou didst leave thy husband and thy children to die, and didst choose thy brother to survive, seeing that he is surely less near to thee in blood than thy children, and less dear to thee than thy

husband." She made answer: "O king, I might, if heaven willed, have another husband and other children, if I should lose these; but another brother I could by no means have, seeing that my father and my mother are no longer alive. This was in my mind when I said those words." To Dareios then it seemed that the woman had spoken well, and he let go not only him for whose life she asked, but also the eldest of her sons because he was pleased with her: but all the others he slew. One therefore of the seven had perished immediately in the manner which has been related.

120. Now about the time of the sickness of Cambyses it had come to pass as follows:— There was one Oroites, a Persian, who had been appointed by Cyrus to be governor of the province of Sardis. This man had set his desire upon an unholy thing; for though from Polycrates the Samian he had never suffered anything nor heard any offensive word nor even seen him before that time, he desired to take him and put him to death for a reason of this kind, as most who report the matter say:—while Oroites and another Persian whose name was Mitrobates, ruler of the province of Daskyleion, were sitting at the door of the king's court, they came from words to strife with one another; and as they debated their several claims to excellence, Mitrobates taunting Oroites said: "Dost *thou* count thyself a man, who didst never yet win for the king the island of Samos, which lies close to thy province, when it is so exceedingly easy of conquest that one of the natives of it rose up against the government with fifteen men-at-arms and got possession of the island, and is now despot of it?" Some say that because he heard this and was stung by the reproach, he formed the desire, not so much to take vengeance on him who said this, as to bring Polycrates to destruction at all costs, since by reason of him he was ill spoken of:

121, the lesser number however of those who tell the tale say that Oroites sent a herald to Samos to ask for something or other, but what it was is not mentioned; and Polycrates happened to be lying down in the men's chamber of his palace, and Anacreon also of Teos was present with him: and somehow, whether it was by intention and because he made no account of the business of Oroites, or whether some chance occurred to bring it about, it happened that the envoy of Oroites came into his presence and spoke with him, and Polycrates, who chanced to be turned away towards the wall, neither turned round at all nor made any answer.

122. The cause then of the death of Polycrates is reported in these two different ways, and we may believe whichever of them we please. Oroites however, having his residence at that Magnesia which is situated upon the river Maiander, sent Myrsos the son of Gyges, a Lydian, to Samos bearing a message, since he had perceived the designs of Polycrates. For Polycrates was the first of the Hellenes of whom we have any knowledge, who set his mind upon having command of the sea, excepting Minos the Cnossian and any other who may have had command of the sea before his time. Of that which we call mortal race Polycrates was the first; and he had great expectation of becoming ruler of Ionia and of the islands. Oroites accordingly, having perceived that he had this design, sent a message to him and said thus: "Oroites to Polycrates saith as follows: I hear that thou art making plans to get great power, and that thou hast not wealth according to thy high thoughts. Now therefore if thou shalt do as I shall say, thou wilt do well for thyself on the one hand, and also save me from destruction: for king Cambyses is planning death for me, and this is reported to me so that I cannot doubt it. Do thou then carry away out of danger both myself and with me my wealth; and of this keep a part for thyself and a part let me keep, and then so far as wealth may bring it about, thou shalt be ruler of all Hellas. And if thou

dost not believe that which I say about the money, send someone, whosoever happens to be most trusted by thee, and to him I will show it."

123. Polycrates having heard this rejoiced, and was disposed to agree; and as he had a great desire, it seems, for wealth, he first sent Maiandrios the son of Maiandrios, a native of Samos who was his secretary, to see it: this man was the same who not long after these events dedicated all the ornaments of the men's chamber in the palace of Polycrates, ornaments well worth seeing, as an offering to the temple of Hera. Oroites accordingly, having heard that the person sent to examine might be expected soon to come, did as follows, that is to say, he filled eight chests with stones except a small depth at the very top of each, and laid gold above upon the stones; then he tied up the chests and kept them in readiness. So Maiandrios came and looked at them and brought back word to Polycrates:

124, and he upon that prepared to set out thither, although the diviners and also his friends strongly dissuaded him from it, and in spite moreover of a vision which his daughter had seen in sleep of this kind,—it seemed to her that her father was raised up on high and was bathed by Zeus and anointed by the Sun. Having seen this vision, she used every kind of endeavor to dissuade Polycrates from leaving his land to go to Oroites, and besides that, as he was going to his fifty-oared galley she accompanied his departure with prophetic words: and he threatened her that if he should return safe, she should remain unmarried for long; but she prayed that this might come to pass, for she desired rather, she said, to be unmarried for long than to be an orphan, having lost her father.

125. Polycrates however neglected every counsel and set sail to go to Oroites, taking with him, besides many others of his friends, Demokedes also the son of Calliphon, a man of Croton, who was a physician and practiced his art better than any other man of his time. Then when he arrived at Magnesia, Polycrates was miserably put to death in a manner unworthy both of himself and of his high ambition: for excepting those who become despots of the Syracusans, not one besides of the Hellenic despots is worthy to be compared with Polycrates in magnificence. And when he had killed him in a manner not fit to be told, Oroites impaled his body: and of those who accompanied him, as many as were Samians he released, bidding them be grateful to him that they were free men; but all those of his company who were either allies or servants, he held in the estimation of slaves and kept them. Polycrates then being hung up accomplished wholly the vision of his daughter, for he was bathed by Zeus whenever it rained, and anointed by the Sun, giving forth moisture himself from his body.

126. To this end came the great prosperity of Polycrates, as Amasis the king of Egypt had foretold to him: but not long afterwards retribution overtook Oroites in his turn for the murder of Polycrates. For after the death of Cambyses and the reign of the Magians Oroites remained at Sardis and did no service to the Persians, when they had been deprived of their empire by the Medes; moreover during this time of disturbance he slew Mitrobates the governor in Daskyleion, who had brought up against him the matter of Polycrates as a reproach; and he slew also Cranaspes the son of Mitrobates, both men of repute among the Persians: and besides other various deeds of insolence, once when a bearer of messages had come to him from Dareios, not being pleased with the message which he brought he slew him as he was returning, having set men to lie in wait for him by the way; and having slain him he made away with the bodies both of the man and of his horse.

127. Dareios accordingly, when he had come to the throne, was desirous of taking

vengeance upon Oroites for all his wrongdoings and especially for the murder of Mitrobates and his son. However he did not think it good to act openly and to send an army against him, since his own affairs were still in a disturbed state and he had only lately come to the throne, while he heard that the strength of Oroites was great, seeing that he had a bodyguard of a thousand Persian spearmen and was in possession of the divisions of Phrygia and Lydia and Ionia. Therefore Dareios contrived as follows:—having called together those of the Persians who were of most repute, he said to them: "Persians, which of you all will undertake to perform this matter for me with wisdom, and not by force or with tumult? for where wisdom is wanted, there is no need of force. Which of you, I say, will either bring Oroites alive to me or slay him? for he never yet did any service to the Persians, and on the other hand he has done to them great evil. First he destroyed two of us, Mitrobates and his son; then he slays the men who go to summon him, sent by me, displaying insolence not to be endured. Before therefore he shall accomplish any other evil against the Persians, we must check his course by death."

128. Thus Dareios asked, and thirty men undertook the matter, each one separately desiring to do it himself; and Dareios stopped their contention and bade them cast lots: so when they cast lots, Bagaios the son of Artontes obtained the lot from among them all. Bagaios accordingly, having obtained the lot, did thus:—he wrote many papers dealing with various matters and on them set the seal of Dareios, and with them he went to Sardis. When he arrived there and came into the presence of Oroites, he took the covers off the papers one after another and gave them to the Royal Secretary to read; for all the governors of provinces have Royal Secretaries. Now Bagaios thus gave the papers in order to make trial of the spearmen of the guard, whether they would accept the motion to revolt from Oroites; and seeing that they paid great reverence to the papers and still more to the words which were recited from them, he gave another paper in which were contained these words: "Persians, king Dareios forbids you to serve as guards to Oroites": and they hearing this lowered to him the points of their spears. Then Bagaios, seeing that in this they were obedient to the paper, took courage upon that and gave the last of the papers to the secretary; and in it was written: "King Dareios commands the Persians who are in Sardis to slay Oroites." So the spearmen of the guard, when they heard this, drew their swords and slew him forthwith. Thus did retribution for the murder of Polycrates the Samian overtake Oroites.

129. When the wealth of Oroites had come or had been carried up to Susa, it happened not long after, that king Dareios while engaged in hunting wild beasts twisted his foot in leaping off his horse, and it was twisted, as it seems, rather violently, for the ball of his ankle-joint was put out of the socket. Now he had been accustomed to keep about him those of the Egyptians who were accounted the first in the art of medicine, and he made use of their assistance then: but these by wrenching and forcing the foot made the evil continually greater. For seven days then and seven nights Dareios was sleepless owing to the pain which he suffered; and at last on the eighth day, when he was in a wretched state, someone who had heard talk before while yet at Sardis of the skill of Demokedes of Croton, reported this to Dareios; and he bade them bring him forthwith into his presence. So having found him somewhere unnoticed among the slaves of Oroites, they brought him forth into the midst dragging fetters after him and clothed in rags.

130. When he had been placed in the midst of them, Dareios asked him whether he understood the art; but he would not admit it, fearing lest, if he declared himself to be

what he was, he might lose forever the hope of returning to Hellas: and it was clear to Dareios that he understood that art but was practicing another, and he commanded those who had brought him thither to produce scourges and pricks. Accordingly upon that he spoke out, saying that he did not understand it precisely, but that he had kept company with a physician and had some poor knowledge of the art. Then after this, when Dareios had committed the case to him, by using Hellenic drugs and applying mild remedies after the former violent means, he caused him to get sleep, and in a short time made him perfectly well, though he had never hoped to be sound of foot again. Upon this Dareios presented him with two pairs of golden fetters; and he asked him whether it was by design that he had given to him a double share of his suffering, because he had made him well. Being pleased by this saying, Dareios sent him to visit his wives, and the eunuchs in bringing him in said to the women that this was he who had restored to the king his life. Then each one of them plunged a cup into the gold-chest and presented Demokedes with so abundant a gift that his servant, whose name was Skiton, following and gathering up the coins which fell from the cups, collected for himself a very large sum of gold.

131. This Demokedes came from Croton, and became the associate of Polycrates in the following manner:—at Croton he lived in strife with his father, who was of a harsh temper, and when he could no longer endure him, he departed and came to Egina. Being established there he surpassed in the first year all the other physicians, although he was without appliances and had none of the instruments which are used in the art. In the next year the Eginetan State engaged him for a payment of one talent, in the third year he was engaged by the Athenians for a hundred pounds weight of silver, and in the fourth by Polycrates for two talents. Thus he arrived in Samos; and it was by reason of this man more than anything else that the physicians of Croton got their reputation: for this event happened at the time when the physicians of Croton began to be spoken of as the first in Hellas, while the Kyrenians were reputed to have the second place. About this same time also the Argives had the reputation of being the first musicians in Hellas.

132. Then Demokedes having healed king Dareios had a very great house in Susa, and had been made a table-companion of the king; and except the one thing of returning to the land of the Hellenes, he had everything. And first as regards the Egyptian physicians who tried to heal the king before him, when they were about to be impaled because they had proved inferior to a physician who was a Hellene, he asked their lives of the king and rescued them from death: then secondly, he rescued an Eleian prophet, who had accompanied Polycrates and had remained unnoticed among the slaves. In short Demokedes was very great in the favor of the king.

133. Not long time after this another thing came to pass which was this:—Atossa the daughter of Cyrus and wife of Dareios had a tumor upon her breast, which afterwards burst and then was spreading further: and so long as it was not large, she concealed it and said nothing to anybody, because she was ashamed; but afterwards when she was in evil case, she sent for Demokedes and showed it to him: and he said that he would make her well, and caused her to swear that she would surely do for him in return that which he should ask of her; and he would ask, he said, none of such things as are shameful.

134. So when after this by his treatment he had made her well, then Atossa instructed by Demokedes uttered to Dareios in his bedchamber some such words as these: "O king, though thou hast such great power, thou dost sit still, and dost not win in addition any nation or power for the Persians: and yet it is reasonable that a man who is both young

and master of much wealth should be seen to perform some great deed, in order that the Persians may know surely that he is a man by whom they are ruled. It is expedient indeed in two ways that thou shouldest do so, both in order that the Persians may know that their ruler is a man, and in order that they may be worn down by war and not have leisure to plot against thee. For now thou mightest display some great deed, while thou art still young; seeing that as the body grows the spirit grows old also with it, and is blunted for every kind of action." Thus she spoke according to instructions received, and he answered thus: "Woman, thou hast said all the things which I myself have in mind to do; for I have made the plan to yoke together a bridge from this continent to the other and to make expedition against the Scythians, and these designs will be by way of being fulfilled within a little time." Then Atossa said: "Look now,—forbear to go first against the Scythians, for these will be in thy power whenever thou desirest: but do thou, I pray thee, make an expedition against Hellas; for I am desirous to have Lacedemonian women and Argive and Athenian and Corinthian, for attendants, because I hear of them by report: and thou hast the man who of all men is most fitted to show thee all things which relate to Hellas and to be thy guide, that man, I mean, who healed thy foot." Dareios made answer: "Woman, since it seems good to thee that we should first make trial of Hellas, I think it better to send first to them men of the Persians together with him of whom thou speakest, to make investigation, that when these have learnt and seen, they may report each several thing to us; and then I shall go to attack them with full knowledge of all."

135. Thus he said, and he proceeded to do the deed as he spoke the word: for as soon as day dawned, he summoned fifteen Persians, men of repute, and bade them pass through the coasts of Hellas in company with Demokedes, and take care not to let Demokedes escape from them, but bring him back at all costs. Having thus commanded them, next he summoned Demokedes himself and asked him to act as a guide for the whole of Hellas and show it to the Persians, and then return back: and he bade him take all his movable goods and carry them as gifts to his father and his brothers, saying that he would give him in their place many times as much; and besides this, he said, he would contribute to the gifts a merchant ship filled with all manner of goods, which should sail with him. Dareios, as it seems to me, promised him these things with no crafty design; but Demokedes was afraid that Dareios was making trial of him, and did not make haste to accept all that was offered, but said that he would leave his own things where they were, so that he might have them when he came back; he said however that he accepted the merchant ship which Dareios promised him for the presents to his brothers. Dareios then, having thus given command to him also, sent them away to the sea.

136. So these, when they had gone down to Phenicia and in Phenicia to the city of Sidon, forthwith manned two triremes, and besides them they also filled a large ship of burden with all manner of goods. Then when they had made all things ready they set sail for Hellas, and touching at various places they saw the coast regions of it and wrote down a description, until at last, when they had seen the greater number of the famous places, they came to Taras in Italy. There from complaisance to Demokedes Aristophilides the king of the Tarentines unfastened and removed the steering-oars of the Median ships, and also confined the Persians in prison, because, as he alleged, they came as spies. While they were being thus dealt with, Demokedes went away and reached Croton; and when he had now reached his own native place, Aristophilides set the Persians free and gave back to them those parts of their ships which he had taken away.

137. The Persians then sailing thence and pursuing Demokedes reached Croton, and finding him in the market-place they laid hands upon him; and some of the men of Croton fearing the Persian power were willing to let him go, but others took hold of him and struck with their staves at the Persians, who pleaded for themselves in these words: "Men of Croton, take care what ye are about: ye are rescuing a man who was a slave of king Dareios and who ran away from him. How, think you, will king Dareios be content to receive such an insult; and how shall this which ye do be well for you, if ye take him away from us? Against what city, think you, shall we make expedition sooner than against this, and what city before this shall we endeavor to reduce to slavery?" Thus saying they did not however persuade the men of Croton, but having had Demokedes rescued from them and the ship of burden which they were bringing with them taken away, they set sail to go back to Asia, and did not endeavor to visit any more parts of Hellas or to find out about them, being now deprived of their guide. This much however Demokedes gave them as a charge when they were putting forth to sea, bidding them say to Dareios that Demokedes was betrothed to the daughter of Milon: for the wrestler Milon had a great name at the king's court; and I suppose that Demokedes was urgent for this marriage, spending much money to further it, in order that Dareios might see that he was held in honor also in his own country.

138. The Persians however, after they had put out from Croton, were cast away with their ships in Iapygia; and as they were remaining there as slaves, Gillos a Tarentine exile rescued them and brought them back to king Dareios. In return for this Dareios offered to give him whatsoever thing he should desire; and Gillos chose that he might have the power of returning to Taras, narrating first the story of his misfortune: and in order that he might not disturb all Hellas, as would be the case if on his account a great armament should sail to invade Italy, he said it was enough for him that the men of Cnidos should be those who brought him back, without any others; because he supposed that by these, who were friends with the Tarentines, his return from exile would most easily be effected. Dareios accordingly having promised proceeded to perform; for he sent a message to Cnidos and bade them being back Gillos to Taras: and the men of Cnidos obeyed Dareios, but nevertheless they did not persuade the Tarentines, and they were not strong enough to apply force. Thus then it happened with regard to these things; and these were the first Persians who came from Asia to Hellas, and for the reason which has been mentioned these were sent as spies.

139. After this king Dareios took Samos before all other cities, whether of Hellenes or Barbarians, and for a cause which was as follows:—When Cambyses the son of Cyrus was marching upon Egypt, many Hellenes arrived in Egypt, some, as might be expected, joining in the campaign to make profit, and some also coming to see the land itself; and among these was Syoloson the son of Aiakes and brother of Polycrates, an exile from Samos. To this Syloson a fortunate chance occurred, which was this:—he had taken and put upon him a flame-colored mantle, and was about the market-place in Memphis; and Dareios, who was then one of the spearmen of Cambyses and not yet held in any great estimation, seeing him had a desire for the mantle, and going up to him offered to buy it. Then Syloson, seeing that Dareios very greatly desired the mantle, by some divine inspiration said: "I will not sell this for any sum, but I will give it thee for nothing, if, as it appears, it must be thine at all costs." To this Dareios agreed and received from him the garment.

140. Now Syloson supposed without any doubt that he had altogether lost this by easy simplicity; but when in course of time Cambyses was dead, and the seven Persians had risen up against the Magian, and of the seven Dareios had obtained the kingdom, Syloson heard that the kingdom had come about to that man to whom once in Egypt he had given the garment at his request: accordingly he went up to Susa and sat down at the entrance of the king's palace, and said that he was a benefactor of Dareios. The keeper of the door hearing this reported it to the king; and he marveled at it and said to him: "Who then of the Hellenes is my benefactor, to whom I am bound by gratitude? seeing that it is now but a short time that I possess the kingdom, and as yet scarcely one of them has come up to our court; and I may almost say that I have no debt owing to a Hellene. Nevertheless bring him in before me, that I may know what he means when he says these things." Then the keeper of the door brought Syloson before him, and when he had been set in the midst, the interpreters asked him who he was and what he had done, that he called himself the benefactor of the king. Syloson accordingly told all that had happened about the mantle, and how he was the man who had given it; to which Dareios made answer: "O most noble of men, thou art he who when as yet I had no power gavest me a gift, small it may be, but nevertheless the kindness is counted with me to be as great as if I should now receive some great thing from some-one. Therefore I will give thee in return gold and silver in abundance, that thou mayest not ever repent that thou didst render a service to Dareios the son of Hystaspes." To this Syloson replied: "To me, O king, give neither gold nor silver, but recover and give to me my fatherland Samos, which now that my brother Polycrates has been slain by Oroites is possessed by our slave. This give to me without bloodshed or selling into slavery."

141. Dareios having heard this prepared to send an expedition with Otanes as commander of it, who had been one of the seven, charging him to accomplish for Syloson all that which he had requested. Otanes then went down to the sea-coast and was preparing the expedition.

142. Now Maiandrios the son of Maiandrios was holding the rule over Samos, having received the government as a trust from Polycrates; and he, though desiring to show himself the most righteous of men, did not succeed in so doing: for when the death of Polycrates was reported to him, he did as follows:—first he founded an altar to Zeus the Liberator and marked out a sacred enclosure round it, namely that which exists still in the suburb of the city: then after he had done this he gathered together an assembly of all the citizens and spoke these words: "To me, as ye know as well as I, has been entrusted the scepter of Polycrates and all his power; and now it is open to me to be your ruler; but that for the doing of which I find fault with my neighbor, I will myself refrain from doing, so far as I may: for as I did not approve of Polycrates acting as master of men who were not inferior to himself, so neither do I approve of any other who does such things. Now Poly-crates for his part fulfilled his own appointed destiny, and I now give the power into the hands of the people, and proclaim to you equality. These privileges however I think it right to have assigned to me, namely that from the wealth of Polycrates six talents should be taken out and given to me as a special gift; and in addition to this I choose for myself and for my descendants in succession the priesthood of Zeus the Liberator, to whom I myself founded a temple, while I bestow liberty upon you." He, as I say, made these offers to the Samians; but one of them rose up and said: "Nay, but unworthy too art *thou* to be

our ruler, seeing that thou art of mean birth and a pestilent fellow besides. Rather take care that thou give an account of the money which thou hadst to deal with."

143. Thus said one who was a man of repute among the citizens, whose name was Telesarchos; and Maiandrios perceiving that if he resigned the power, some other would be set up as despot instead of himself, did not keep the purpose at all of resigning it; but having retired to the fortress he sent for each man separately, pretending that he was going to give an account of the money, and so seized them and put them in bonds. These then had been put in bonds; but Maiandrios after this was overtaken by sickness, and his brother, whose name was Lycaretos, expecting that he would die, put all the prisoners to death, in order that he might himself more easily get possession of the power over Samos: and all this happened because, as it appears, they did not choose to be free.

144. So when the Persians arrived at Samos bringing Syloson home from exile, no one raised a hand against them, and moreover the party of Maiandrios and Maiandrios himself said that they were ready to retire out of the island under a truce. Otanes therefore having agreed on these terms and having made a treaty, the most honorable of the Persians had seats placed for them in front of the fortress and were sitting there.

145. Now the despot Maiandrios had a brother who was somewhat mad, and his name was Charilaos. This man for some offence which he had been committed had been confined in an underground dungeon, and at this time of which I speak, having heard what was being done and having put his head through out of the dungeon, when he saw the Persians peacefully sitting there he began to cry out and said that he desired to come to speech with Maiandrios. So Maiandrios hearing his voice bade them loose him and bring him into his presence; and as soon as he was brought he began to abuse and revile him, trying to persuade him to attack the Persians, and saying thus: "Thou basest of men, didst thou put me in bonds and judge me worthy of the dungeon underground, who am thine own brother and did no wrong worthy of bonds, and when thou seest the Persians casting thee forth from the land and making thee homeless, dost thou not dare to take any revenge, though they are so exceedingly easy to be overcome? Nay, but if in truth thou art afraid of them, give me thy mercenaries and I will take vengeance on them for their coming here; and thyself I am willing to let go out of the island."

146. Thus spoke Charilaos, and Maiandrios accepted that which he said, not, as I think, because he had reached such a height of folly as to suppose that his own power would overcome that of the king, but rather because he grudged Syloson that he should receive from him the State without trouble, and with no injury inflicted upon it. Therefore he desired to provoke the Persians to anger and make the Samian power as feeble as possible before he gave it up to him, being well assured that the Persians, when they had suffered evil, would be likely to be as bitter against the Samians as well as against those who did the wrong, and knowing also that he had a safe way of escape from the island whenever he desired: for he had had a secret passage made under ground, leading from the fortress to the sea. Maiandrios then himself sailed out from Samos; but Charilaos armed all the mercenaries, and opening wide the gates sent them out upon the Persians, who were not expecting any such thing, but supposed that all had been arranged: and the mercenaries falling upon them began to slay those of the Persians who had seats carried for them and were of most account. While these were thus engaged, the rest of the Persian force came to the rescue, and the mercenaries were hard pressed and forced to retire to the fortress.

147. Then Otanes the Persian commander, seeing that the Persians had suffered greatly,

purposely forgot the commands which Dareios gave him when he sent him forth, not to kill any one of the Samians nor to sell any into slavery, but to restore the island to Syloson free from all suffering of calamity,—these commands, I say, he purposely forgot, and gave the word to his army to slay every one whom they should take, man or boy, without distinction. So while some of the army were besieging the fortress, others were slaying everyone who came in their way, in sanctuary or out of sanctuary equally.

148. Meanwhile Maiandrios had escaped from Samos and was sailing to Lacedaemon; and having come thither and caused to be brought up to the city the things which he had taken with him when he departed, he did as follows:—first, he would set out his cups of silver and of gold, and then while the servants were cleaning them, he would be engaged in conversation with Cleomenes the son of Anaxandrides, then king of Sparta, and would bring him on to his house; and when Cleomenes saw the cups he marveled and was astonished at them, and Maiandrios would bid him take away with him as many of them as he pleased. Maiandrios said this twice or three times, but Cleomenes herein showed himself the most upright of men; for he not only did not think fit to take that which was offered, but perceiving that Maiandrios would make presents to others of the citizens, and so obtain assistance for himself, he went to the Ephors and said that it was better for Sparta that the stranger of Samos should depart from Peloponnesus, lest he might persuade either himself or some other man of the Spartans to act basely. They accordingly accepted his counsel, and expelled Maiandrios by proclamation.

149. As to Samos, the Persians, after sweeping the population off it, delivered it to Syloson stripped of men. Afterwards however the commander Otanes even joined in settling people there, moved by a vision of a dream and by a disease which seized him, so that he was diseased in the genital organs.

150. After a naval force had thus gone against Samos, the Babylonians made revolt, being for this exceedingly well prepared; for during all the time of the reign of the Magian and of the insurrection of the seven, during all this time and the attendant confusion they were preparing themselves for the siege of their city: and it chanced by some means that they were not observed to be doing this. Then when they made open revolt, they did as follows:—after setting apart their mothers first, each man set apart also for himself one woman, whosoever he wished of his own household, and all the remainder they gathered together and killed by suffocation. Each man set apart the one who has been mentioned to serve as a maker of bread, and they suffocated the rest in order that they might not consume their provisions.

151. Dareios being informed of this and having gathered together all his power, made expedition against them, and when he had marched his army up to Babylon he began to besiege them; but they cared nothing about the siege, for the Babylonians used to go up to the battlements of the wall and show contempt of Dareios and of his army by gestures and by words; and one of them uttered this saying: "Why, O Persians, do ye remain sitting here, and not depart? For then only shall ye capture us, when mules shall bring forth young." This was said by one of the Babylonians, not supposing that a mule would ever bring forth young.

152. So when a year and seven months had now passed by, Dareios began to be vexed and his whole army with him, not being able to conquer the Babylonians. And yet Dareios had used against them every kind of device and every possible means, but not even so could he conquer them, though besides other devices he had attempted it by that also

with which Cyrus conquered them; but the Babylonians were terribly on their guard and he was not able to conquer them.

153. Then in the twentieth month there happened to Zopyros the son of that Megabyzos who had been of the seven men who slew the Magian, to this Zopyros, I say, son of Megabyzos there happened a prodigy,—one of the mules which served as bearers of provisions for him produced young: and when this was reported to him, and Zopyros had himself seen the foal, because he did not believe the report, he charged those who had seen it not to tell that which had happened to any one, and he considered with himself what to do. And having regard to the words spoken by the Babylonian, who had said at first that when mules should produce young, then the wall would be taken, having regard (I say) to this ominous saying, it seemed to Zopyros that Babylon could be taken: for he thought that both the man had spoken and his mule had produced young by divine dispensation.

154. Since then it seemed to him that it was now fated that Babylon should be captured, he went to Dareios and inquired of him whether he thought it a matter of very great moment to conquer Babylon; and hearing in answer that he thought it of great consequence, he considered again how he might be the man to take it and how the work might be his own: for among the Persians benefits are accounted worthy of a very high degree of honor. He considered accordingly that he was not able to make conquest of it by any other means, but only if he should maltreat himself and desert to their side. So, making light esteem of himself, he maltreated his own body in a manner which could not be cured; for he cut off his nose and his ears, and shaved his hair round in an unseemly way, and scourged himself, and so went into the presence of Dareios.

155. And Dareios was exceedingly troubled when he saw the man of most repute with him thus maltreated; and leaping from his seat he cried aloud and asked him who was the person who had maltreated him, and for what deed. He replied: "That man does not exist, excepting thee, who has so great power as to bring me into this condition; and not any stranger, O king, has done this, but I myself to myself, accounting it a very grievous thing that the Assyrians should make a mock of the Persians." He made answer: "Thou most reckless of men, thou didst set the fairest name to the foulest deed when thou saidest that on account of those who are besieged thou didst bring thyself into a condition which cannot be cured. How, O thou senseless one, will the enemy surrender to us more quickly, because thou hast maltreated thyself? Surely thou didst wander out of thy senses in thus destroying thyself." And he said, "If I had communicated to thee that which I was about to do, thou wouldst not have permitted me to do it; but as it was, I did it on my own account. Now therefore, unless something is wanting on thy part, we shall conquer Babylon: for I shall go straightway as a deserter to the wall; and I shall say to them that I suffered this treatment at thy hands: and I think that when I have convinced them that this is so, I shall obtain the command of a part of their forces. Do thou then on the tenth day from that on which I shall enter within the wall take of those troops about which thou wilt have no concern if they be destroyed,—of these, I say, get a thousand by the gate of the city which is called the gate of Semiramis; and after this again on the seventh day after the tenth set, I pray thee, two thousand by the gate which is called the gate of the Ninevites; and after this seventh day let twenty days elapse, and then lead other four thousand and place them by the gate called the gate of the Chaldeans: and let neither the former men nor these have any weapons to defend them except daggers, but this weapon let them

have. Then after the twentieth day at once bid the rest of the army make an attack on the wall all round, and set the Persians, I pray thee, by those gates which are called the gate of Belos and the gate of Kissia: for, as I think, when I have displayed great deeds of prowess, the Babylonians will entrust to me, besides their other things, also the keys which draw the bolts of the gates. Then after that it shall be the care of myself and the Persians to do that which ought to be done."

156. Having thus enjoined he proceeded to go to the gate of the city, turning to look behind him as he went, as if he were in truth a deserter; and those who were set in that part of the wall, seeing him from the towers ran down, and slightly opening one wing of the gate asked who he was, and for what purpose he had come. And he addressed them and said that he was Zopyros, and that he came as a deserter to them. The gate-keepers accordingly when they heard this led him to the public assembly of the Babylonians; and being introduced before it he began to lament his fortunes, saying that he had in fact suffered at his own hands, and that he had suffered this because he had counselled the king to withdraw his army, since in truth there seemed to be no means of taking the town: "And now," he went on to say, "I am come for very great good to you, O Babylonians, but for very great evil to Dareios and his army, and to the Persians, for he shall surely not escape with impunity for having thus maltreated me; and I know all the courses of his counsels."

157. Thus he spoke, and the Babylonians, when they saw the man of most reputation among the Persians deprived of nose and ears and smeared over with blood from scourging, supposing assuredly that he was speaking the truth and had come to be their helper, were ready to put in his power that for which he asked them, and he asked them that he might command a certain force. Then when he had obtained this from them, he did that which he had agreed with Dareios that he would do; for he led out on the tenth day the army of the Babylonians, and having surrounded the thousand men whom he had enjoined Dareios first to set there, he slew them. The Babylonians accordingly, perceiving that the deeds which he displayed were in accordance with his words, were very greatly rejoiced and were ready to serve him in all things: and after the lapse of the days which had been agreed upon, he again chose men of the Babylonians and led them out and slew the two thousand men of the troops of Dareios. Seeing this deed also, the Babylonians all had the name of Zopyros upon their tongues, and were loud in his praise. He then again, after the lapse of the days which had been agreed upon, led them out to the place appointed, and surrounded the four thousand and slew them. When this also had been done, Zopyros was everything among the Babylonians, and he was appointed both commander of their army and guardian of their walls.

158. But when Dareios made an attack according to the agreement on every side of the wall, then Zopyros discovered all his craft: for while the Babylonians, having gone up on the wall, were defending themselves against the attacks of the army of Dareios, Zopyros opened the gates called the gates of Kissia and of Belos, and let in the Persians within the wall. And of the Babylonians those who saw that which was done fled to the temple of Zeus Belos, but those who did not see remained each in his own appointed place, until at last they also learnt that they had been betrayed.

159. Thus was Babylon conquered for the second time: and Dareios when he had overcome the Babylonians, first took away the wall from round their city and pulled down all the gates; for when Cyrus took Babylon before him, he did neither of these things: and

secondly Dareios impaled the leading men to the number of about three thousand, but to the rest of the Babylonians he gave back their city to dwell in: and to provide that the Babylonians should have wives, in order that their race might be propagated, Dareios did as follows (for their own wives, as has been declared at the beginning, the Babylonians had suffocated, in provident care for their store of food):—he ordered the nations who dwelt round to bring women to Babylon, fixing a certain number for each nation, so that the sum total of fifty thousand women was brought together, and from these women the present Babylonians are descended.

160. As for Zopyros, in the judgment of Dareios no one of the Persians surpassed him in good service, either of those who came after or of those who had gone before, excepting Cyrus alone; for to Cyrus no man of the Persians ever yet ventured to compare himself: and Dareios is said to have declared often that he would rather that Zopyros were free from the injury than that he should have twenty Babylons added to his possession in addition to that one which he had. Moreover he gave him great honors; for not only did he give him every year those things which by the Persians are accounted the most honorable, but also he granted him Babylon to rule free from tribute, so long as he should live; and he added many other gifts. The son of this Zopyros was Megabyzos, who was made commander in Egypt against the Athenians and their allies; and the son of this Megabyzos was Zopyros, who went over to Athens as a deserter from the Persians.

THE FOURTH BOOK OF THE
HISTORIES, CALLED MELPOMENE

1. After Babylon had been taken, the march of Dareios himself against the Scythians took place: for now that Asia was flourishing in respect of population, and large sums were being gathered in as revenue, Dareios formed the desire to take vengeance upon the Scythians, because they had first invaded the Median land and had overcome in fight those who opposed them; and thus they had been the beginners of wrong. The Scythians in truth, as I have before said, had ruled over Upper Asia for eight-and-twenty years; for they had invaded Asia in their pursuit of the Kimmerians, and they had deposed the Medes from their rule, who had rule over Asia before the Scythians came. Now when the Scythians had been absent from their own land for eight-and-twenty years, as they were returning to it after that interval of time, they were met by a contest not less severe than that which they had had with the Medes, since they found an army of no mean size opposing them. For the wives of the Scythians, because their husbands were absent from them for a long time, had associated with the slaves.

2. Now the Scythians put out the eyes of all their slaves because of the milk which they drink; and they do as follows:—they take blow-pipes of bone just like flutes, and these they insert into the vagina of the mare and blow with their mouths, and others milk while they blow: and they say that they do this because the veins of the mare are thus filled, being blown out, and so the udder is let down. When they had drawn the milk they pour it into wooden vessels hollowed out, and they set the blind slaves in order about the vessels and agitate the milk. Then that which comes to the top they skim off, considering it the more valuable part, whereas they esteem that which settles down to be less good than the other. For this reason the Scythians put out the eyes of all whom they catch; for they are not tillers of the soil but nomads.

3. From these their slaves then, I say, and from their wives had been born and bred up a generation of young men, who having learnt the manner of their birth set themselves to oppose the Scythians as they were returning from the Medes. And first they cut off their land by digging a broad trench extending from the Tauric mountains to the Maiotian lake,

at the point where this is broadest; then afterwards when the Scythians attempted to invade the land, they took up a position against them and fought; and as they fought many times, and the Scythians were not able to get any advantage in the fighting, one of them said: "What a thing is this that we are doing, Scythians! We are fighting against our own slaves, and we are not only becoming fewer in number ourselves by being slain in battle, but also we are killing them, and so we shall have fewer to rule over in future. Now therefore to me it seems good that we leave spears and bows and that each one take his horse-whip and so go up close to them: for so long as they saw us with arms in our hands, they thought themselves equal to us and of equal birth; but when they shall see that we have whips instead of arms, they will perceive that they are our slaves, and having acknowledged this they will not await our onset."

4. When they heard this, the Scythians proceeded to do that which he said, and the others being panic-stricken by that which was done forgot their fighting and fled. Thus the Scythians had ruled over Asia; and in such manner, when they were driven out again by the Medes, they had returned to their own land. For this Dareios wished to take vengeance upon them, and was gathering together an army to go against them.

5. Now the Scythians say that their nation is the youngest of all nations, and that this came to pass as follows:—The first man who ever existed in this region, which then was desert, was one named Targitaos: and of this Targitaos they say, though I do not believe it for my part, however they say the parents were Zeus and the daughter of the river Borysthenes. Targitaos, they report, was produced from some such origin as this, and of him were begotten three sons, Lipoxaïs and Arpoxaïs and the youngest Colaxaïs. In the reign of these there came down from heaven certain things wrought of gold, a plough, a yoke, a battle-axe, and a cup, and fell in the Scythian land: and first the eldest saw and came near them, desiring to take them, but the gold blazed with fire when he approached it: then when he had gone away from it, the second approached, and again it did the same thing. These then the gold repelled by blazing with fire; but when the third and youngest came up to it, the flame was quenched, and he carried them to his own house. The elder brothers then, acknowledging the significance of this thing, delivered the whole of the kingly power to the youngest.

6. From Lixopaïs, they say, are descended those Scythians who are called the race of the Auchatai; from the middle brother Arpoxaïs those who are called Catiaroi and Traspians, and from the youngest of them the "Royal" tribe, who are called Paralatai: and the whole together are called, they say, Scolotoi, after the name of their king; but the Hellenes gave them the name of Scythians.

7. Thus the Scythians say they were produced; and from the time of their origin, that is to say from the first king Targitaos, to the passing over of Dareios against them, they say that there is a period of a thousand years and no more. Now this sacred gold is guarded by the kings with the utmost care, and they visit it every year with solemn sacrifices of propitiation: moreover if any one goes to sleep while watching in the open air over this gold during the festival, the Scythians say that he does not live out the year; and there is given him for this so much land as he shall ride round himself on his horse in one day. Now as the land was large, Colaxaïs, they say, established three kingdoms for his sons; and of these he made one larger than the rest, and in this the gold is kept. But as to the upper parts which lie on the North side of those who dwell above this land, they say one can neither see nor pass through any further by reason of feathers which are poured

down; for both the earth and the air are full of feathers, and this is that which shuts off the view.

8. Thus say the Scythians about themselves and about the region above them; but the Hellenes who dwell about the Pontus say as follows:—Heracles driving the cattle of Geryones came to this land, then desert, which the Scythians now inhabit; and Geryones, says the tale, dwelt away from the region of the Pontus, living in the island called by the Hellenes Erytheia, near Gadeira which is outside the Pillars of Heracles by the Ocean.—As to the Ocean, they say indeed that it flows round the whole earth beginning from the place of the sunrising, but they do not prove this by facts.—From thence Heracles came to the land now called Scythia; and as a storm came upon him together with icy cold, he drew over him his lion's skin and went to sleep. Meanwhile the mares harnessed in his chariot disappeared by a miraculous chance, as they were feeding.

9. Then when Heracles woke he sought for them; and having gone over the whole land, at last he came to the region which is called Hylaia; and there he found in a cave a kind of twofold creature formed by the union of a maiden and a serpent, whose upper parts from the buttocks upwards were those of a woman, but her lower parts were those of a snake. Having seen her and marveled at her, he asked her then whether she had seen any mares straying anywhere; and she said that she had them herself and would not give them up until he lay with her; and Heracles lay with her on condition of receiving them. She then tried to put off the giving back of the mares, desiring to have Heracles with her as long as possible, while he on the other hand desired to get the mares and depart; and at last she gave them back and said: "These mares when they came hither I saved for thee, and thou didst give me reward for saving them; for I have by thee three sons. Tell me then, what must I do with these when they shall be grown to manhood, whether I shall settle them here, for over this land I have power alone, or send them away to thee?" She thus asked of him, and he, they say, replied: "When thou seest that the boys are grown to men, do this and thou shalt not fail of doing right:—whichsoever of them thou seest able to stretch this bow as I do now, and to be girded with this girdle, him cause to be the settler of this land; but whosoever of them fails in the deeds which I enjoin, send him forth out of the land: and if thou shalt do thus, thou wilt both have delight thyself and perform that which has been enjoined to thee."

10. Upon this he drew one of his bows (for up to that time Heracles, they say, was wont to carry two) and showed her the girdle, and then he delivered to her both the bow and the girdle, which had at the end of its clasp a golden cup; and having given them he departed. She then, when her sons had been born and had grown to be men, gave them names first, calling one of them Agathyrsos and the next Gelonos and the youngest Skythes; then bearing in mind the charge given to her, she did that which was enjoined. And two of her sons, Agathyrsos and Gelonos, not having proved themselves able to attain to the task set before them, departed from the land, being cast out by her who bore them; but Skythes the youngest of them performed the task and remained in the land: and from Skythes the son of Heracles were descended, they say, the succeeding kings of the Scythians (Skythians): and they say moreover that it is by reason of the cup that the Scythians still even to this day wear cups attached to their girdles: and this alone his mother contrived for Skythes. Such is the story told by the Hellenes who dwell about the Pontus.

11. There is however also another story, which is as follows, and to this I am most

inclined myself. It is to the effect that the nomad Scythians dwelling in Asia, being hard pressed in war by the Massagetai, left their abode and crossing the river Araxes came towards the Kimmerian land (for the land which now is occupied by the Scythians is said to have been in former times the land of the Kimmerians); and the Kimmerians, when the Scythians were coming against them, took counsel together, seeing that a great host was coming to fight against them; and it proved that their opinions were divided, both opinions being vehemently maintained, but the better being that of their kings: for the opinion of the people was that it was necessary to depart and that they ought not to run the risk of fighting against so many, but that of the kings was to fight for their land with those who came against them: and as neither the people were willing by means to agree to the counsel of the kings nor the kings to that of the people, the people planned to depart without fighting and to deliver up the land to the invaders, while the kings resolved to die and to be laid in their own land, and not to flee with the mass of the people, considering the many goods of fortune which they had enjoyed, and the many evils which it might be supposed would come upon them, if they fled from their native land. Having resolved upon this, they parted into two bodies, and making their numbers equal they fought with one another: and when these had all been killed by one another's hands, then the people of the Kimmerians buried them by the bank of the river Tyras (where their burial-place is still to be seen), and having buried them, then they made their way out from the land, and the Scythians when they came upon it found the land deserted of its inhabitants.

12. And there are at the present time in the land of Scythia Kimmerian walls, and a Kimmerian ferry; and there is also a region which is called Kimmeria, and the so-called Kimmerian Bosphorus. It is known moreover that the Kimmerians, in their flight to Asia from the Scythians, also made a settlement on that peninsula on which now stands the Hellenic city of Sinope; and it is known too that the Scythians pursued them and invaded the land of Media, having missed their way; for while the Kimmerians kept ever along by the sea in their flight, the Scythians pursued them keeping Caucasus on their right hand, until at last they invaded Media, directing their course inland. This then which has been told is another story, and it is common both to Hellenes and Barbarians.

13. Aristeas however the son of Caÿstrobios, a man of Proconnesos, said in the verses which he composed, that he came to the land of the Issedonians being possessed by Phoebus, and that beyond the Issedonians dwelt Arimaspians, a one-eyed race, and beyond these the gold-guarding griffins, and beyond them the Hyperboreans extending as far as the sea: and all these except the Hyperboreans, beginning with the Arimaspians, were continually making war on their neighbors, and the Issedonians were gradually driven out of their country by the Arimaspians and the Scythians by the Issedonians, and so the Kimmerians, who dwelt on the Southern Sea, being pressed by the Scythians left their land. Thus neither does he agree in regard to this land with the report of the Scythians.

14. As to Aristeas who composed this, I have said already whence he was; and I will tell also the tale which I heard about him in Proconnesos and Kyzicos. They say that Aristeas, who was in birth inferior to none of the citizens, entered into a fuller's shop in Proconnesos and there died; and the fuller closed his workshop and went away to report the matter to those who were related to the dead man. And when the news had been spread abroad about the city that Aristeas was dead, a man of Kyzicos who had come from the town of Artake entered into controversy with those who said so, and declared that he had met him going towards Kyzicos and had spoken with him: and while he was

vehement in dispute, those who were related to the dead man came to the fuller's shop with the things proper in order to take up the corpse for burial; and when the house was opened, Aristeas was not found there either dead or alive. In the seventh year after this he appeared at Proconnesos and composed those verses which are now called by the Hellenes the *Arimaspeia*, and having composed them he disappeared the second time.

15. So much is told by these cities; and what follows I know happened to the people of Metapontion in Italy two hundred and forty years after the second disappearance of Aristeas, as I found by putting together the evidence at Proconnesos and Metapontion. The people of Metapontion say that Aristeas himself appeared in their land and bade them set up an altar of Apollo and place by its side a statue bearing the name of Aristeas of Proconnesos; for he told them that to their land alone of all the Italiotes Apollo had come, and he, who now was Aristeas, was accompanying him, being then a raven when he accompanied the god. Having said this he disappeared; and the Metapontines say that they sent to Delphi and asked the god what the apparition of the man meant: and the Pythian prophetess bade them obey the command of the apparition, and told them that if they obeyed, it would be the better for them. They therefore accepted this answer and performed the commands; and there stands a statue now bearing the name of Aristeas close by the side of the altar dedicated to Apollo, and round it stand laurel trees; and the altar is set up in the market-place. Let this suffice which has been said about Aristeas.

16. Now of the land about which this account has been begun, no one knows precisely what lies beyond it: for I am not able to hear of any one who alleges that he knows as an eye-witness; and even Aristeas, the man of whom I was making mention just now, even he, I say, did not allege, although he was composing verse, that he went further than the Issedonians; but that which is beyond them he spoke of by hearsay, and reported that it was the Issedonians who said these things. So far however as we were able to arrive at certainty by hearsay, carrying inquiries as far as possible, all this shall be told.

17. Beginning with the trading station of the Borysthenites,—for of the parts along the sea this is the central point of all Scythia,—beginning with this, the first regions are occupied by the Callipidai, who are Hellenic Scythians; and above these is another race, who are called Alazonians. These last and the Callipidai in all other respects have the same customs as the Scythians, but they both sow corn and use it as food, and also onions, leeks, lentils and millet. Above the Alazonians dwell Scythians who till the ground, and these sow their corn not for food but to sell.

18.Beyond them dwell the Neuroi; and beyond the Neuroi towards the North Wind is a region without inhabitants, as far as we know. These races are along the river Hypanis to the West of the Borysthenes; but after crossing the Borysthenes, first from the sea-coast is Hylaia, and beyond this as one goes up the river dwell agricultural Scythians, whom the Hellenes who live upon the river Hypanis call Borysthenites, calling themselves at the same time citizens of Olbia. These agricultural Scythians occupy the region which extends Eastwards for a distance of three days' journey, reaching to a river which is called Panticapes, and Northwards for a distance of eleven days' sail up the Borysthenes. Then immediately beyond these begins the desert and extends for a great distance; and on the other side of the desert dwell the Androphagoi, a race apart by themselves and having no connection with the Scythians. Beyond them begins a region which is really desert and has no race of men in it, as far as we know.

19. The region which lies to the East of these agricultural Scythians, after one has

crossed the river Panticapes, is occupied by nomad Scythians, who neither sow anything nor plough the earth; and this whole region is bare of trees except Hylaia. These nomads occupy a country which extends to the river Gerros, a distance of fourteen days' journey Eastwards.

20. Then on the other side of the Gerros we have those parts which are called the "Royal" lands and those Scythians who are the bravest and most numerous and who esteem the other Scythians their slaves. These reach Southwards to the Tauric land, and Eastwards to the trench which those who were begotten of the blind slaves dug, and to the trading station which is called Cremnoi upon the Maiotian lake; and some parts of their country reach to the river Tanaïs. Beyond the Royal Scythians towards the North Wind dwell the Melanchlainoi, of a different race and not Scythian. The region beyond the Melanchlainoi is marshy and not inhabited by any, so far as we know.

21. After one has crossed the river Tanaïs the country is no longer Scythia, but the first of the divisions belongs to the Sauromatai, who beginning at the corner of the Maiotian lake occupy land extending towards the North Wind fifteen days' journey, and wholly bare of trees both cultivated and wild. Above these, holding the next division of land, dwell the Budinoi, who occupy a land wholly overgrown with forest consisting of all kinds of trees.

22. Then beyond the Budinoi towards the North, first there is desert for seven days' journey; and after the desert turning aside somewhat more towards the East Wind we come to land occupied by the Thyssagetai, a numerous people and of separate race from the others. These live by hunting; and bordering upon them there are settled also in these same regions men who are called Irycai, who also live by hunting, which they practice in the following manner:—the hunter climbs up a tree and lies in wait there for his game (now trees are abundant in all this country), and each has a horse at hand, which has been taught to lie down upon its belly in order that it may make itself low, and also a dog: and when he sees the wild animal from the tree, he first shoots his arrow and then mounts upon his horse and pursues it, and the dog seizes hold of it. Above these in a direction towards the East dwell other Scythians, who have revolted from the Royal Scythians and so have come to this region.

23. As far as the country of these Scythians the whole land which has been described is level plain and has a deep soil; but after this point it is stony and rugged. Then when one has passed through a great extent of this rugged country, there dwell in the skirts of lofty mountains men who are said to be all bald-headed from their birth, male and female equally, and who have flat noses and large chins and speak a language of their own, using the Scythian manner of dress, and living on the produce of trees. The tree on the fruit of which they live is called the Pontic tree, and it is about the size of a fig-tree: this bears a fruit the size of a bean, containing a stone. When the fruit has ripened, they strain it through cloths and there flows from it a thick black juice, and this juice which flows from it is called *as-chy*. This they either lick up or drink mixed with milk, and from its lees, that is the solid part, they make cakes and use them for food; for they have not many cattle, since the pastures there are by no means good. Each man has his dwelling under a tree, in winter covering the tree all round with close white felt-cloth, and in summer without it. These are injured by no men, for they are said to be sacred, and they possess no weapon of war. These are they also who decide the disputes rising among their neighbors; and

besides this, whatever fugitive takes refuge with them is injured by no one: and they are called Argippaians.

24. Now as far as these bald-headed men there is abundantly clear information about the land and about the nations on this side of them; for not only do certain of the Scythians go to them, from whom it is not difficult to get information, but also some of the Hellenes who are at the trading-station of the Borysthenes and the other trading-places of the Pontic coast: and those of the Scythians who go to them transact their business through seven interpreters and in seven different languages.

25. So far as these, I say, the land is known; but concerning the region to the North of the bald-headed men no one can speak with certainty, for lofty and impassable mountains divide it off, and no one passes over them. However these bald-headed men say (though I do not believe it) that the mountains are inhabited by men with goats' feet; and that after one has passed beyond these, others are found who sleep through six months of the year. This I do not admit at all as true. However, the country to the East of the bald-headed men is known with certainty, being inhabited by the Issedonians, but that which lies beyond both the bald-headed men and the Issedonians towards the North Wind is unknown, except so far as we know it from the accounts given by these nations which have just been mentioned.

26. The Issedonians are said to have these customs:—when a man's father is dead, all the relations bring cattle to the house, and then having slain them and cut up the flesh, they cut up also the dead body of the father of their entertainer, and mixing all the flesh together they set forth a banquet. His skull however they strip of the flesh and clean it out and then gild it over, and after that they deal with it as a sacred thing and perform for the dead man great sacrifices every year. This each son does for his father, just as the Hellenes keep the day of memorial for the dead. In other respects however this race also is said to live righteously, and their women have equal rights with the men.

27. These then also are known; but as to the region beyond them, it is the Issedonians who report that there are there one-eyed men and gold-guarding griffins; and the Scythians report this having received it from them, and from the Scythians we, that is the rest of mankind, have got our belief; and we call them in Scythian language Arimaspians, for the Scythians call the number one *arima* and the eye *spu*.

28. This whole land which has been described is so exceedingly severe in climate, that for eight months of the year there is frost so hard as to be intolerable; and during these if you pour out water you will not be able to make mud, but only if you kindle a fire can you make it; and the sea is frozen and the whole of the Kimmerian Bosphorus, so that the Scythians who are settled within the trench make expeditions and drive their wagons over into the country of the Sindians. Thus it continues to be winter for eight months, and even for the remaining four it is cold in those parts. This winter is distinguished in its character from all the winters which come in other parts of the world; for in it there is no rain to speak of at the usual season for rain, whereas in summer it rains continually; and thunder does not come at the time when it comes in other countries, but is very frequent, in the summer; and if thunder comes in winter, it is marveled at as a prodigy: just so, if an earthquake happens, whether in summer or in winter, it is accounted a prodigy in Scythia. Horses are able to endure this winter, but neither mules nor asses can endure it at all, whereas in other countries horses if they stand in frost lose their limbs by mortification, while asses and mules endure it.

29. I think also that it is for this reason that the hornless breed of oxen in that country have no horns growing; and there is a verse of Homer in the Odyssey supporting my opinion, which runs this:—

"Also the Libyan land, where the sheep very quickly grow hornèd,"

for it is rightly said that in hot regions the horns come quickly, whereas in extreme cold the animals either have no horns growing at all, or hardly any.

30. In that land then this takes place on account of the cold; but (since my history proceeded from the first seeking occasions for digression) I feel wonder that in the whole land of Elis mules cannot be bred, though that region is not cold, nor is there any other evident cause. The Eleians themselves say that in consequence of some curse mules are not begotten in their land; but when the time approaches for the mares to conceive, they drive them out into the neighboring lands and there in the land of their neighbors they admit to them the he-asses until the mares are pregnant, and then they drive them back.

31. As to the feathers of which the Scythians say that the air is full, and that by reason of them they are not able either to see or to pass through the further parts of the continent, the opinion which I have is this:—in the parts beyond this land it snows continually, though less in summer than in winter, as might be supposed. Now whomsoever has seen close at hand snow falling thickly, knows what I mean without further explanation, for the snow is like feathers: and on account of this wintry weather, being such as I have said, the Northern parts of this continent are uninhabitable. I think therefore that by the feathers the Scythians and those who dwell near them mean symbolically the snow. This then which has been said goes to the furthest extent of the accounts given.

32. About a Hyperborean people the Scythians report nothing, nor do any of those who dwell in this region, unless it be the Issedonians: but in my opinion neither do these report anything; for if they did the Scythians also would report it, as they do about the one-eyed people. Hesiod however has spoken of Hyperboreans, and so also has Homer in the poem of the "Epigonoi," at least if Homer was really the composer of that Epic.

33. But much more about them is reported by the people of Delos than by any others. For these say that sacred offerings bound up in wheat straw are carried from the land of the Hyperboreans and come to the Scythians, and then from the Scythians the neighboring nations in succession receive them and convey them Westwards, finally as far as the Adriatic: thence they are sent forward towards the South, and the people of Dodona receive them first of all the Hellenes, and from these they come down to the Malian gulf and are passed over to Euboea, where city sends them on to city till they come to Carystos. After this Andros is left out, for the Carystians are those who bring them to Tenos, and the Tenians to Delos. Thus they say that these sacred offerings come to Delos; but at first, they say, the Hyperboreans sent two maidens bearing the sacred offerings, whose names, say the Delians, were Hyperoche and Laodike, and with them for their protection the Hyperboreans sent five men of their nation to attend them, those namely who are now called *Perphereës* and have great honors paid to them in Delos. Since however the Hyperboreans found that those who were sent away did not return back, they were troubled to think that it would always befall them to send out and not to receive back; and so they bore the offerings to the borders of their land bound up in wheat straw, and laid a charge upon their neighbors, bidding them send these forward from themselves to another nation. These things then, they say, come to Delos being thus sent forward; and I know of my own knowledge that a thing is done which has resemblance to these offerings, namely that the

women of Thrace and Paionia, when they sacrifice to Artemis "the Queen," do not make their offerings without wheat straw.

34. These I know do as I have said; and for those maidens from the Hyperboreans, who died in Delos, both the girls and the boys of the Delians cut off their hair: the former before marriage cut off a lock and having wound it round a spindle lay it upon the tomb (now the tomb is on the left hand as one goes into the temple of Artemis, and over it grows an olive-tree), and all the boys of the Delians wind some of their hair about a green shoot of some tree, and they also place it upon the tomb.

35. The maidens, I say, have this honor paid them by the dwellers in Delos: and the same people say that Arge and Opis also, being maidens, came to Delos, passing from the Hyperboreans by the same nations which have been mentioned, even before Hyperoche and Laodike. These last, they say, came bearing for Eileithuia the tribute which they had laid upon themselves for the speedy birth, but Arge and Opis came with the divinities themselves, and other honors have been assigned to them by the people of Delos: for the women, they say, collect for them, naming them by their names in the hymn which Olen a man of Lykia composed in their honor; and both the natives of the other islands and the Ionians have learnt from them to sing hymns naming Opis and Arge and collecting:—now this Olen came from Lukia and composed also the other ancient hymns which are sung in Delos:—and moreover they say that when the thighs of the victim are consumed upon the altar, the ashes of them are used to cast upon the grave of Opis and Arge. Now their grave is behind the temple of Artemis, turned towards the East, close to the banqueting hall of the Keïeans.

36. Let this suffice which has been said of the Hyperboreans; for the tale of Abaris, who is reported to have been a Hyperborean, I do not tell, namely how he carried the arrow about all over the earth, eating no food. If however there are any Hyperboreans, it follows that there are also Hypernotians; and I laugh when I see that, though many before this have drawn maps of the Earth, yet no one has set the matter forth in an intelligent way; seeing that they draw Ocean flowing round the Earth, which is circular exactly as if drawn with compasses, and they make Asia equal in size to Europe. In a few words I shall declare the size of each division and of what nature it is as regards outline.

37. The Persians inhabit Asia extending to the Southern Sea, which is called the Erythraian; and above these towards the North Wind dwell the Medes, and above the Medes the Saspeirians, and above the Saspeirians the Colchians, extending to the Northern Sea, into which the river Phasis runs. These four nations inhabit from sea to sea.

38. From them Westwards two peninsulas stretch out from Asia into the sea, and these I will describe. The first peninsula on the one of its sides, that is the Northern, stretches along beginning from the Phasis and extending to the sea, going along the Pontus and the Hellespont as far as Sigeion in the land of Troy; and on the Southern side the same peninsula stretches from the Myriandrian gulf, which lies near Phenicia, in the direction of the sea as far as the headland Triopion; and in this peninsula dwell thirty races of men.

39. This then is one of the peninsulas, and the other beginning from the land of the Persians stretches along to the Erythraian Sea, including Persia and next after it Assyria, and Arabia after Assyria: and this ends, or rather is commonly supposed to end, at the Arabian gulf, into which Dareios conducted a channel from the Nile. Now in the line stretching to Phenicia from the land of the Persians the land is broad and the space abun-

dant, but after Phenicia this peninsula goes by the shore of our Sea along Palestine, Syria, and Egypt, where it ends; and in it there are three nations only.

40. These are the parts of Asia which tend towards the West from the Persian land; but as to those which lie beyond the Persians and Medes and Saspeirians and Colchians towards the East and the sunrising, on one side the Erythraian Sea runs along by them, and on the North both the Caspian Sea and the river Araxes, which flows towards the rising sun: and Asia is inhabited as far as the Indian land; but from this onwards towards the East it becomes desert, nor can anyone say what manner of land it is.

41. Such and so large is Asia: and Libya is included in the second peninsula; for after Egypt Libya succeeds at once. Now about Egypt this peninsula is narrow, for from our Sea to the Erythraian Sea is a distance there of ten myriads of fathoms, which would amount to a thousand furlongs; but after this narrow part, the portion of the peninsula which is called Libya is, as it chances, extremely broad.

42. I wonder then at those who have parted off and divided the world into Libya, Asia, and Europe, since the difference between these is not small; for in length Europe extends along by both, while in breadth it is clear to me that it is beyond comparison larger; for Libya furnishes proofs about itself that it is surrounded by sea, except so much of it as borders upon Asia; and this fact was shown by Necos king of the Egyptians first of all those about whom we have knowledge. He when he had ceased digging the channel which goes through from the Nile to the Arabian gulf, sent Phoenicians with ships, bidding them sail and come back through the Pillars of Heracles to the Northern Sea and so to Egypt. The Phoenicians therefore set forth from the Erythraian Sea and sailed through the Southern Sea; and when autumn came, they would put to shore and sow the land, wherever in Libya they might happen to be as they sailed, and then they waited for the harvest: and having reaped the corn they would sail on, so that after two years had elapsed, in the third year they turned through the Pillars of Heracles and arrived again in Egypt. And they reported a thing which I cannot believe, but another man may, namely that in sailing round Libya they had the sun on their right hand.

43. Thus was this country first known to be what it is, and after this it is the Carthaginians who make report of it; for as to Sataspes the son of Teaspis the Achaimenid, he did not sail round Libya, though he was sent for this very purpose, but was struck with fear by the length of the voyage and the desolate nature of the land, and so returned back and did not accomplish the task which his mother laid upon him. For this man had outraged a daughter of Zopyros the son of Megabyzos, a virgin; and then when he was about to be impaled by order of king Xerxes for this offence, the mother of Sataspes, who was a sister of Dareios, entreated for his life, saying that she would herself lay upon him a greater penalty than Xerxes; for he should be compelled (she said) to sail round Libya, until in sailing round it he came to the Arabian gulf. So then Xerxes having agreed upon these terms, Sataspes went to Egypt, and obtaining a ship and sailors from the Egyptians, he sailed to the Pillars of Heracles; and having sailed through them and turned the point of Libya which is called the promontory of Soloeis, he sailed on towards the South. Then after he had passed over much sea in many months, as there was needed ever more and more voyaging, he turned about and sailed back again to Egypt: and having come from thence into the presence of king Xerxes, he reported saying that at the furthest point which he reached he was sailing by dwarfish people, who used clothing made from the palm-tree, and who, whenever they came to land with their ship, left their towns and fled away

to the mountains: and they, he said, did no injury when they entered into the towns, but took food from them only. And the cause, he said, why he had not completely sailed round Libya was that the ship could not advance any further but stuck fast. Xerxes however did not believe that he was speaking the truth, and since he had not performed the appointed task, he impaled him, inflicting upon him the penalty pronounced before. A eunuch belonging to this Sataspes ran away to Samos as soon as he heard that his master was dead, carrying with him large sums of money; and of this a man of Samos took possession, whose name I know, but I purposely pass it over without mention.

44. Of Asia the greater part was explored by Dareios, who desiring to know of the river Indus, which is a second river producing crocodiles of all the rivers in the world,—to know, I say, of this river where it runs out into the sea, sent with ships, besides others whom he trusted to speak the truth, Skylax also, a man of Caryanda. These starting from the city of Caspatyros and the land of Pactyïke, sailed down the river towards the East and the sunrising to the sea; and then sailing over the sea Westwards they came in the thirtieth month to that place from whence the king of the Egyptians had sent out the Phoenicians of whom I spoke before, to sail round Libya. After these had made their voyage round the coast, Dareios both subdued the Indians and made use of this sea. Thus Asia also, excepting the parts of it which are towards the rising sun, has been found to be similar to Libya.

45. As to Europe, however, it is clearly not known by any, either as regards the parts which are towards the rising sun or those towards the North, whether it be surrounded by sea: but in length it is known to stretch along by both the other divisions. And I am not able to understand for what reason it is that to the Earth, which is one, three different names are given derived from women, and why there were set as boundaries to divide it the river Nile of Egypt and the Phasis in Colchis (or as some say the Maiotian river Tanaïs and the Kimmerian ferry); nor can I learn who those persons were who made the boundaries, or for what reason they gave the names. Libya indeed is said by most of the Hellenes to have its name from Libya a woman of that country, and Asia from the wife of Prometheus: but this last name is claimed by the Lydians, who say that Asia has been called after Asias the son of Cotys the son of Manes, and not from Asia the wife of Prometheus; and from him too they say the Asian tribe in Sardis has its name. As to Europe however, it is neither known by any man whether it is surrounded by sea, nor does it appear whence it got this name or who he was who gave it, unless we shall say that the land received its name from Europa the Tyrian; and if so, it would appear that before this it was nameless like the rest. She however evidently belongs to Asia and did not come to this land which is now called by the Hellenes Europe, but only from Phenicia to Crete, and from Crete to Lykia. Let this suffice now which has been said about these matters; for we will adopt those which are commonly accepted of the accounts.

46. Now the region of the Euxine upon which Dareios was preparing to march has, apart from the Scythian race, the most ignorant nations within it of all lands: for we can neither put forward any nation of those who dwell within the region of Pontus as eminent in ability, nor do we know of any man of learning having arisen there, apart from the Scythian nation and Anacharsis. By the Scythian race one thing which is the most important of all human things has been found out more cleverly than by any other men of whom we know; but in other respects I have no great admiration for them: and that most important thing which they have discovered is such that none can escape again who has

come to attack them, and if they do not desire to be found, it is not possible to catch them: for they who have neither cities founded nor walls built, but all carry their houses with them and are mounted archers, living not by the plough but by cattle, and whose dwellings are upon cars, these assuredly are invincible and impossible to approach.

47. This they have found out, seeing that their land is suitable to it and at the same time the rivers are their allies: for first this land is plain land and is grassy and well-watered, and then there are rivers flowing through it not much less in number than the channels in Egypt. Of these as many as are noteworthy and also can be navigated from the sea, I will name: there is Ister with five mouths, and after this Tyras, Hypanis, Borysthenes, Panticapes, Kypakyris, Gerros and Tanaïs. These flow as I shall now describe.

48. The Ister, which is the greatest of all the rivers which we know, flows always with equal volume in summer and winter alike. It is the first towards the West of all the Scythian rivers, and it has become the greatest of all rivers because other rivers flow into it. And these are they which make it great: —five in number are those which flow through the Scythian land, namely that which the Scythians call Porata and the Hellenes Pyretos, and besides this, Tiarantos and Araros and Naparis and Ordessos. The first-mentioned of these is a great river lying towards the East, and there it joins waters with the Ister, the second Tiarantos is more to the West and smaller, and the Araros and Naparis and Ordessos flow into the Ister going between these two.

49. These are the native Scythian rivers which join to swell its stream, while from the Agathyrsians flows the Maris and joins the Ister, and from the summits of Haimos flow three other great rivers towards the North Wind and fall into it, namely Atlas and Auras and Tibisis. Through Thrace and the Thracian Crobyzians flow the rivers Athrys and Noes and Artanes, running into the Ister; and from the Paionians and Mount Rhodope the river Kios, cutting through Haimos in the midst, runs into it also. From the Illyrians the river Angros flows Northwards and runs out into the Triballian plain and into the river Brongos, and the Brongos flows into the Ister; thus the Ister receives both these, being great rivers. From the region which is above the Ombricans, the river Carpis and another river, the Alpis, flow also towards the North Wind and run into it; for the Ister flows in fact through the whole of Europe, beginning in the land of the Keltoi, who after the Kynesians dwell furthest towards the sun-setting of all the peoples of Europe; and thus flowing through all Europe it falls into the sea by the side of Scythia.

50. So then it is because these which have been named and many others join their waters together, that Ister becomes the greatest of rivers; since if we compare the single streams, the Nile is superior in volume of water; for into this no river or spring flows, to contribute to its volume. And the Ister flows at an equal level always both in summer and in winter for some such cause as this, as I suppose:—in winter it is of the natural size, or becomes only a little larger than its nature, seeing that this land receives very little rain in winter, but constantly has snow; whereas in summer the snow which fell in the winter, in quantity abundant, melts and runs from all parts into the Ister. This snow of which I speak, running into the river helps to swell its volume, and with it also many and violent showers of rain, for it rains during the summer: and thus the waters which mingle with the Ister are more copious in summer than they are in winter by about as much as the water which the Sun draws to himself in summer exceeds that which he draws in winter; and by the setting of these things against one another there is produced a balance; so that the river is seen to be of equal volume always.

51. One, I say, of the rivers which the Scythians have is the Ister; and after it the Tyras, which starts from the North and begins its course from a large lake which is the boundary between the land of the Scythians and that of the Neuroi. At its mouth are settled those Hellenes who are called Tyritai.

52. The third river is the Hypanis, which starts from Scythia and flows from a great lake round which feed white wild horses; and this lake is rightly called "Mother of Hypanis." From this then the river Hypanis takes its rise and for a distance of five days' sail it flows shallow and with sweet water still; but from this point on towards the sea for four days' sail it is very bitter, for there flows into it the water of a bitter spring, which is so exceedingly bitter that, small as it is, it changes the water of the Hypanis by mingling with it, though that is a river to which few are equal in greatness. This spring is on the border between the lands of the agricultural Scythians and of the Alazonians, and the name of the spring and of the place from which it flows is in Scythian Exampaios, and in the Hellenic tongue Hierai Hodoi. Now the Tyras and the Hypanis approach one another in their windings in the land of the Alazonians, but after this each turns off and widens the space between them as they flow.

53. Fourth is the river Borysthenes, which is both the largest of these after the Ister, and also in our opinion the most serviceable not only of the Scythian rivers but also of all the rivers of the world besides, excepting only the Nile of Egypt, for to this it is not possible to compare any other river: of the rest however the Borysthenes is the most serviceable, seeing that it provides both pastures which are the fairest and the richest for cattle, and fish which are better by far and more numerous than those of any other river, and also it is the sweetest water to drink, and flows with clear stream, though others beside it are turbid, and along its banks crops are produced better than elsewhere, while in parts where it is not sown, grass grows deeper. Moreover at its mouth salt forms of itself in abundance, and it produces also huge fish without spines, which they call *antacaioi*, to be used for salting, and many other things also worthy of wonder. Now as far as the region of the Gerrians, to which it is a voyage of forty days, the Borysthenes is known as flowing from the North Wind; but above this none can tell through what nations it flows: it is certain however that it runs through desert to the land of the agricultural Scythians; for these Scythians dwell along its banks for a distance of ten days' sail. Of this river alone and of the Nile I cannot tell where the sources are, nor, I think, can any of the Hellenes. When the Borysthenes comes near the sea in its course, the Hypanis mingles with it, running out into the same marsh; and the space between these two rivers, which is as it were a beak of land, is called the point of Hippoles, and in it is placed a temple of the Mother, and opposite the temple upon the river Hypanis are settled the Borysthenites.

54. This is that which has to do with these rivers; and after these there is a fifth river besides, called Panticapes. This also flows both from the North and from a lake, and in the space between this river and the Borysthenes dwell the agricultural Scythians: it runs out into the region of Hylaia, and having passed by this it mingles with the Borysthenes.

55. Sixth comes the river Hypakyris, which starts from a lake, and flowing through the midst of the nomad Scythians runs out into the sea by the city of Carkinitis, skirting on its right bank the region of Hylaia and the so-called racecourse of Achilles.

56. Seventh is the Gerros, which parts off from the Borysthenes near about that part of the country where the Borysthenes ceases to be known,—it parts off, I say, in this region and has the same name which this region itself has, namely Gerros; and as it flows to the

sea it borders the country of the nomad and that of the Royal Scythians, and runs out into the Hypakyris.

57. The eighth is the river Tanaïs, which starts in its flow at first from a large lake, and runs out into a still larger lake called Maiotis, which is the boundary between the Royal Scythians and the Sauromatai. Into this Tanaïs falls another river, whose name is Hyrgis.

58. So many are the rivers of note with which the Scythians are provided: and for cattle the grass which comes up in the land of Scythia is the most productive of bile of any grass which we know; and that this is so you may judge when you open the bodies of the cattle.

59. Thus abundant supply have they of that which is most important; and as for the rest their customs are as follows. The gods whom they propitiate by worship are these only:—Hestia most of all, then Zeus and the Earth, supposing that Earth is the wife of Zeus, and after these Apollo, and Aphrodite Urania, and Heracles, and Ares. Of these all the Scythians have the worship established, and the so-called Royal Scythians sacrifice also to Poseidon. Now Hestia is called in Scythian Tabiti, and Zeus, being most rightly named in my opinion, is called Papaios, and Earth Api, and Apollo Oitosyros, and Aphrodite Urania is called Argimpasa, and Poseidon Thagimasidas. It is not their custom however to make images, altars or temples to any except Ares, but to him it is their custom to make them.

60. They have all the same manner of sacrifice established for all their religious rites equally, and it is thus performed:—the victim stands with its fore-feet tied, and the sacrificing priest stands behind the victim, and by pulling the end of the cord he throws the beast down; and as the victim falls, he calls upon the god to whom he is sacrificing, and then at once throws a noose round its neck, and putting a small stick into it he turns it round and so strangles the animal, without either lighting a fire or making any first offering from the victim or pouring any libation over it: and when he has strangled it and flayed off the skin, he proceeds to boil it.

61. Now as the land of Scythia is exceedingly ill wooded, this contrivance has been invented for the boiling of the flesh:—having flayed the victims, they strip the flesh off the bones and then put it into caldrons, if they happen to have any, of native make, which very much resemble Lesbian mixing-bowls except that they are much larger,—into these they put the flesh and boil it by lighting under it the bones of the victim: if however thy have not at hand the caldron, they put all the flesh into the stomachs of the victims and adding water they light the bones under them; and these blaze up beautifully, and the stomachs easily hold the flesh when it has been stripped off the bones: thus an ox is made to boil itself, and the other kinds of victims each boil themselves also. Then when the flesh is boiled, the sacrificer takes a first offering of the flesh and of the vital organs and casts it in front of him. And they sacrifice various kinds of cattle, but especially horses.

62. To the others of the gods they sacrifice thus and these kinds of beasts, but to Ares as follows:—In each district of the several governments they have a temple of Ares set up in this way:—bundles of brushwood are heaped up for about three furlongs in length and in breadth, but less in height; and on the top of this there is a level square made, and three of the sides rise sheer but by the remaining one side the pile may be ascended. Every year they pile on a hundred and fifty wagon-loads of brushwood, for it is constantly settling down by reason of the weather. Upon this pile of which I speak each people has an ancient iron sword set up, and this is the sacred symbol of Ares. To this sword they bring yearly offerings of cattle and of horses; and they have the following sacrifice in addition, beyond

what they make to the other gods, that is to say, of all the enemies whom they take captive in war they sacrifice one man in every hundred, not in the same manner as they sacrifice cattle, but in a different manner: for they first pour wine over their heads, and after that they cut the throats of the men, so that the blood runs into a bowl; and then they carry this up to the top of the pile of brushwood and pour the blood over the sword. This, I say, they carry up; and meanwhile below by the side of the temple they are doing thus:—they cut off all the right arms of the slaughtered men with the hands and throw them up into the air, and then when they have finished offering the other victims, they go away; and the arm lies wheresoever it has chanced to fall, and the corpse apart from it.

63. Such are the sacrifices which are established among them; but of swine these make no use, nor indeed are they wont to keep them at all in their land.

64. That which relates to war is thus ordered with them:—When a Scythian has slain his first man, he drinks some of his blood: and of all those whom he slays in the battle he bears the heads to the king; for if he has brought a head he shares in the spoil which they have taken, but otherwise not. And he takes off the skin of the head by cutting it round about the ears and then taking hold of the scalp and shaking it off; afterwards he scrapes off the flesh with the rib of an ox, and works the skin about with his hands; and when he has thus tempered it, he keeps it as a napkin to wipe the hands upon, and hangs it from the bridle of the horse on which he himself rides, and takes pride in it; for whosoever has the greatest number of skins to wipe the hands upon, he is judged to be the bravest man. Many also make cloaks to wear of the skins stripped off, sewing them together like shepherds' cloaks of skins; and many take the skin together with the finger-nails off the right hands of their enemies when they are dead, and make them into covers for their quivers: now human skin it seems is both thick and glossy in appearance, more brilliantly white than any other skin. Many also take the skins off the whole bodies of men and stretch them on pieces of wood and carry them about on their horses.

65. Such are their established customs about these things; and to the skulls themselves, not of all but of their greatest enemies, they do thus:—the man saws off all below the eyebrows and clears out the inside; and if he is a poor man he only stretches ox-hide round it and then makes use of it; but if he be rich, besides stretching the ox-hide he gilds it over within, and makes use of it as a drinking-cup. They do this also if any of their own family have been at variance with them and the man gets the better of his adversary in trial before the king; and when strangers come to him whom he highly esteems, he sets these skulls before them, and adds the comment that they being of his own family had made war against him, and that he had got the better of them; and this they hold to be a proof of manly virtue.

66. Once every year each ruler of a district mixes in his own district a bowl of wine, from which those of the Scythians drink by whom enemies have been slain; but those by whom this has not been done do not taste of the wine, but sit apart dishonored; and this is the greatest of all disgraces among them: but those of them who have slain a very great number of men, drink with two cups together at the same time.

67. Diviners there are many among the Scythians, and they divine with a number of willow rods in the following manner:—they bring large bundles of rods, and having laid them on the ground they unroll them, and setting each rod by itself apart they prophesy; and while speaking thus, they roll the rods together again, and after that they place them in order a second time one by one. This manner of divination they have from their fathers:

but the Enareës or "man-women" say that Aphrodite gave them the gift of divination, and they divine accordingly with the bark of the linden-tree. Having divided the linden-bark into three strips, the man twists them together in his fingers and untwists them again, and as he does this he utters the oracle.

68. When the king of the Scythians is sick, he sends for three of the diviners, namely those who are most in repute, who divine in the manner which has been said: and these say for the most part something like this, namely that so and so has sworn falsely by the hearth of the king, and they name one of the citizens, whosoever it may happen to be: now it is the prevailing custom of the Scythians to swear by the hearth of the king at the times when they desire to swear the most solemn oath. He then who they say has sworn falsely, is brought forthwith held fast on both sides; and when he has come the diviners charge him with this, that he is shown by their divination to have sworn falsely by the hearth of the king, and that for this reason the king is suffering pain: and he denies and says that he did not swear falsely, and complains indignantly: and when he denies it, the king sends for other diviners twice as many in number, and if these also by looking into their divination pronounce him guilty of having sworn falsely, at once they cut off the man's head, and the diviners who came first part his goods among them by lot; but if the diviners who came in afterwards acquit him, other diviners come in, and again others after them. If then the greater number acquit the man, the sentence is that the first diviners shall themselves be put to death.

69. They put them to death accordingly in the following manner:—first they fill a wagon with brushwood and yoke oxen to it; then having bound the feet of the diviners and tied their hands behind them and stopped their mouths with gags, they fasten them down in the middle of the brushwood, and having set fire to it they scare the oxen and let them go: and often the oxen are burnt to death together with the diviners, and often they escape after being scorched, when the pole to which they are fastened has been burnt: and they burn the diviners in the manner described for other causes also, calling them false prophets. Now when the king puts any to death, he does not leave alive their sons either, but he puts to death all the males, not doing any hurt to the females.

70. In the following manner the Scythians make oaths to whomsoever they make them: —they pour wine into a great earthenware cup and mingle with it blood of those who are taking the oath to one another, either making a prick with an awl or cutting with a dagger a little way into their body, and then they dip into the cup a sword and arrows and a battle-axe and a javelin; and having done this, they invoke many curses on the breaker of the oath, and afterwards they drink it off, both they who are making the oath and the most honorable of their company.

71. The burial-place of the kings is in the land of the Gerrians, the place up to which the Borysthenes is navigable. In this place, when their king has died, they make a large square excavation in the earth; and when they have made this ready, they take up the corpse (the body being covered over with wax and the belly ripped up and cleansed, and then sewn together again, after it has been filled with *kyperos* cut up and spices and pars-ley-seed and anise), and they convey it in a wagon to another nation. Then those who receive the corpse thus conveyed to them do the same as the Royal Scythians, that is they cut off a part of their ear and shave their hair round about and cut themselves all over the arms and tear their forehead and nose and pass arrows through their left hand. Thence they convey in the wagon the corpse of the king to another of the nations over whom they

rule; and they to whom they came before accompany them: and when they have gone round to all conveying the corpse, then they are in the land of the Gerrians, who have their settlements furthest away of all the nations over whom they rule, and they have reached the spot where the burial place is. After that, having placed the corpse in the tomb upon a bed of leaves, they stick spears along on this side and that of the corpse and stretch pieces of wood over them, and then they cover the place in with matting. Then they strangle and bury in the remaining space of the tomb one of the king's mistresses, his cup-bearer, his cook, his horse-keeper, his attendant, and his bearer of messages, and also horses, and a first portion of all things else, and cups of gold; for silver they do not use at all, nor yet bronze. Having thus done they all join together to pile up a great mound, vying with one another and zealously endeavoring to make it as large as possible.

72. Afterwards, when the year comes round again, they do as follows:—they take the most capable of the remaining servants,—and these are native Scythians, for those serve him whom the king himself commands to do so, and his servants are not bought for money,—of these attendants then they strangle fifty and also fifty of the finest horses; and when they have taken out their bowels and cleansed the belly, they fill it with chaff and sew it together again. Then they set the half of a wheel upon two stakes with the hollow side upwards, and the other half of the wheel upon other two stakes, and in this manner they fix a number of these; and after this they run thick stakes through the length of the horses as far as the necks, and they mount them upon the wheels; and the front pieces of wheel support the shoulders of the horses, while those behind bear up their bellies, going by the side of the thighs; and both front and hind legs hang in the air. On the horses they put bridles and bits, and stretch the bridles tight in front of them and then tie them up to pegs: and of the fifty young men who have been strangled they mount each one upon his horse, having first run a straight stake through each body along by the spine up to the neck; and a part of this stake projects below, which they fasten into a socket made in the other stake that runs through the horse. Having set horsemen such as I have described in a circle round the tomb, they then ride away.

73. Thus they bury their kings; but as for the other Scythians, when they die their nearest relations carry them round laid in wagons to their friends in succession; and of them each one when he receives the body entertains those who accompany it, and before the corpse they serve up of all things about the same quantity as before the others. Thus private persons are carried about for forty days, and then they are buried: and after burying them the Scythians cleanse themselves in the following way:—they soap their heads and wash them well, and then, for their body, they set up three stakes leaning towards one another and about them they stretch woolen felt coverings, and when they have closed them as much as possible they throw stones heated red-hot into a basin placed in the middle of the stakes and the felt coverings.

74. Now they have hemp growing in their land, which is very like flax except in thickness and in height, for in these respects the hemp is much superior. This grows both of itself and with cultivation; and of it the Thracians even make garments, which are very like those made of flaxen thread, so that he who was not specially conversant with it would not be able to decide whether the garments were of flax or of hemp; and he who had not before seen stuff woven of hemp would suppose that the garment was made of flax.

75. The Scythians then take the seed of this hemp and creep under the felt coverings,

and then they throw the seed upon the stones which have been heated red-hot: and it burns like incense and produces a vapour so thick that no vapour-bath in Hellas would surpass it: and the Scythians being delighted with the vapour-bath howl like wolves. This is to them instead of washing, for in fact they do not wash their bodies at all in water. Their women however pound with a rough stone the wood of the cypress and cedar and frankincense tree, pouring in water with it, and then with this pounded stuff, which is thick, they plaster over all their body and also their face; and not only does a sweet smell attach to them by reason of this, but also when they take off the plaster on the next day, their skin is clean and shining.

76. This nation also is very averse to adopting strange customs, rejecting even those of other tribes among themselves, but especially those of the Hellenes, as the history of Anacharsis and also afterwards of Skyles proved. For as to Anacharsis first, when he was returning to the abodes of the Scythians, after having visited many lands and displayed in them much wisdom, as he sailed through the Hellespont he put in to Kyzicos: and since he found the people of Kyzicos celebrating a festival very magnificently in honor of the Mother of the gods, Anacharsis vowed to the Mother that if he should return safe and sound to his own land, he would both sacrifice to her with the same rites as he saw the men of Kyzicos do, and also hold a night festival. So when he came to Scythia he went down into the region called Hylaia (this is along by the side of the racecourse of Achilles and is quite full, as it happens, of trees of all kinds),—into this, I say, Anacharsis went down, and proceeded to perform all the ceremonies of the festival in honor of the goddess, with a kettle-drum and with images hung about himself. And one of the Scythians perceived him doing this and declared it to Saulios the king; and the king came himself also, and when he saw Anacharsis doing this, he shot him with an arrow and killed him. Accordingly at the present time if one asks about Anacharsis, the Scythians say that they do not know him, and for this reason, because he went out of his own country to Hellas and adopted foreign customs. And as I heard from Tymnes the steward of Ariapeithes, he was the uncle on the father's side of Idanthyrsos king of the Scythians, and the son of Gnuros, the son of Lycos, the son of Spargapeithes. If then Anacharsis was of this house, let him know that he died by the hand of his brother, for Idanthyrsos was the son of Saulios, and Saulios was he who killed Anacharsis.

77. However I have heard also another story, told by the Peloponnesians, that Anacharsis was sent out by the king of the Scythians, and so made himself a disciple of Hellas; and that when he returned back he said to him that had sent him forth, that the Hellenes were all busied about every kind of cleverness except the Lacedemonians; but these alone knew how to exchange speech sensibly. This story however has been invented without any ground by the Hellenes themselves; and however that may be, the man was slain in the way that was related above.

78. This man then fared thus badly by reason of foreign customs and communication with Hellenes; and very many years afterwards Skyles the son of Ariapeithes suffered nearly the same fate as he. For Ariapeithes the king of the Scythians with other sons had Skyles born to him: and he was born of a woman who was of Istria, and certainly not a native of Scythia; and this mother taught him the language and letters of Hellas. Afterwards in course of time Ariapeithes was brought to his end by treachery at the hands of Spargapeithes the king of the Agathyrsians, and Skyles succeeded to the kingdom; and he took not only that but also the wife of his father, whose name was Opoia: this Opoia was a

native Scythian and from her was born Oricos to Ariapeithes. Now when Skyles was king of the Scythians, he was by no means satisfied with the Scythian manner of life, but was much more inclined towards Hellenic ways because of the training with which he had been brought up, and he used to do somewhat as follows:—When he came with the Scythians in arms to the city of the Borysthenites (now these Borysthenites say that they are of Miletos),—when Skyles came to these, he would leave his band in the suburbs of the city and go himself within the walls and close the gates. After that he would lay aside his Scythian equipments and take Hellenic garments, and wearing them he would go about in the market-place with no guards or any other man accompanying him (and they watched the gates meanwhile, that none of the Scythians might see him wearing this dress): and while in other respects too he adopted Hellenic manners of life, he used also to perform worship to the gods according to the customs of the Hellenes. Then having stayed a month or more than that, he would put on the Scythian dress and depart. This he did many times, and he both built for himself a house in Borysthenes and also took to it a woman of the place as his wife.

79. Since however it was fated that evil should happen to him, it happened by an occasion of this kind:—he formed a desire to be initiated in the rites of Bacchus-Dionysos, and as he was just about to receive the initiation, there happened a very great portent. He had in the city of the Borysthenites a house of great size and built with large expense, of which also I made mention a little before this, and round it were placed sphinxes and griffins of white stone: on this house Zeus caused a bolt to fall; and the house was altogether burnt down, but Skyles none the less for this completed his initiation. Now the Scythians make the rites of Bacchus a reproach against the Hellenes, for they say that it is not fitting to invent a god like this, who impels men to frenzy. So when Skyles had been initiated into the rites of Bacchus, one of the Borysthenites went off to the Scythians and said: "Whereas ye laugh at us, O Scythians, because we perform the rite of Bacchus and because the god seizes us, now this divinity has seized also your king; and he is both joining in the rite of Bacchus and maddened by the influence of the god. And if ye disbelieve me, follow and I will show you." The chief men of the Scythians followed him, and the Borysthenite led them secretly into the town and set them upon a tower. So when Skyles passed by with the company of revelers, and the Scythians saw him joining in the rite of Bacchus, they were exceedingly grieved at it, and they went out and declared to the whole band that which they had seen.

80. After this when Skyles was riding out again to his own abode, the Scythians took his brother Octamasades for their leader, who was a son of the daughter of Teres, and made insurrection against Skyles. He then when he perceived that which was being done to his hurt and for what reason it was being done, fled for refuge to Thrace; and Octamasades being informed of this, proceeded to march upon Thrace. So when he had arrived at the river Ister, the Thracians met him; and as they were about to engage battle, Sitalkes sent a messenger to Octamasades and said: "Why must we make trial of one another in fight? Thou art my sister's son and thou hast in thy power my brother. Do thou give him back to me, and I will deliver to thee thy brother Skyles: and let us not either of us set our armies in peril, either thou or I." Thus Sitalkes proposed to him by a herald; for there was with Octamasades a brother of Sitalkes, who had gone into exile for fear of him. And Octamasades agreed to this, and by giving up his own mother's brother to Sitalkes he received his brother Skyles in exchange: and Sitalkes when he received his brother led

him away as a prisoner, but Octamasades cut off the head of Skyles there upon the spot. Thus do the Scythians carefully guard their own customary observances, and such are the penalties which they inflict upon those who acquire foreign customs besides their own.

81. How many the Scythians are I was not able to ascertain precisely, but I heard various reports of the number: for reports say both that they are very many in number and also that they are few, at least as regards the true Scythians. Thus far however they gave me evidence of my own eyesight:—there is between the river Borysthenes and the Hypanis a place called Exampaios, of which also I made mention somewhat before this, saying that there was in it a spring of bitter water, from which the water flows and makes the river Hypanis unfit to drink. In this place there is set a bronze bowl, in size at least six times as large as the mixing-bowl at the entrance of the Pontus, which Pausanias the son of Cleombrotos dedicated: and for him who has never seen that, I will make the matter clear by saying that the bowl in Scythia holds easily six hundred amphors, and the thickness of this Scythian bowl is six fingers. This then the natives of the place told me had been made of arrow-heads: for their king, they said, whose name was Ariantas, wishing to know how many the Scythians were, ordered all the Scythians to bring one arrow-head, each from his own arrow, and whosoever should not bring one, he threatened with death. So a great multitude of arrow-heads was brought, and he resolved to make of them a memorial and to leave it behind him: from these then, they said, he made this bronze bowl and dedicated it in this place Exampaios.

82. This is what I heard about the number of the Scythians. Now this land has no marvelous things except that it has rivers which are by far larger and more numerous than those of any other land. One thing however shall be mentioned which it has to show, and which is worthy of wonder even besides the rivers and the greatness of the plain, that is to say, they point out a footprint of Heracles in the rock by the bank of the river Tyras, which in shape is like the mark of a man's foot but in size is two cubits long. This then is such as I have said; and I will go back now to the history which I was about to tell at first.

83. While Dareios was preparing to go against the Scythians and was sending messengers to appoint to some the furnishing of a land-army, to others that of ships, and to others the bridging over of the Thracian Bosphorus, Artabanos, the son of Hystaspes and brother of Dareios, urged him by no means to make the march against the Scythians, telling him how difficult the Scythians were to deal with. Since however he did not persuade him, though he gave him good counsel, he ceased to urge; and Dareios, when all his preparations had been made, began to march his army forth from Susa.

84. Then one of the Persians, Oiobazos, made request to Dareios that as he had three sons and all were serving in the expedition, one might be left behind for him: and Dareios said that as he was a friend and made a reasonable request, he would leave behind all the sons. So Oiobazos was greatly rejoiced, supposing that his sons had been freed from service, but Dareios commanded those who had the charge of such things to put to death all the sons of Oiobazos.

85. These then were left, having been slain upon the spot where they were: and Dareios meanwhile set forth from Susa and arrived at the place on the Bosphorus where the bridge of ships had been made, in the territory of Chalcedon; and there he embarked in a ship and sailed to the so-called Kyanean rocks, which the Hellenes say formerly moved backwards and forwards; and taking his seat at the temple he gazed upon the Pontus, which is a sight well worth seeing. Of all seas indeed it is the most marvelous in its nature. The

length of it is eleven thousand one hundred furlongs, and the breadth, where it is broadest, three thousand three hundred: and of this great Sea the mouth is but four furlongs broad, and the length of the mouth, that is of the neck of water which is called Bosphorus, where, as I said, the bridge of ships had been made, is not less than a hundred and twenty furlongs. This Bosphorus extends to the Propontis; and the Propontis, being in breadth five hundred furlongs and in length one thousand four hundred, has its outlet into the Hellespont, which is but seven furlongs broad at the narrowest place, though it is four hundred furlongs in length: and the Hellespont runs out into that expanse of sea which is called the Egean.

86. These measurements I have made as follows:—a ship completes on an average in a long day a distance of seventy thousand fathoms, and in a night sixty thousand. Now we know that to the river Phasis from the mouth of the Sea (for it is here that the Pontus is longest) is a voyage of nine days and eight nights, which amounts to one hundred and eleven myriads of fathoms; and these fathoms are eleven thousand one hundred furlongs. Then from the land of the Sindians to Themiskyra on the river Thermodon (for here is the broadest part of the Pontus) it is a voyage of three days and two nights, which amounts to thirty-three myriads of fathoms or three thousand three hundred furlongs. This Pontus then and also the Bosphorus and the Hellespont have been measured by me thus, and their nature is such as has been said: and this Pontus also has a lake which has its outlet into it, which lake is not much less in size than the Pontus itself, and it is called Maiotis and "Mother of the Pontus."

87. Dareios then having gazed upon the Pontus sailed back to the bridge, of which Mandrocles a Samian had been chief constructor; and having gazed upon the Bosphorus also, he set up two pillars by it of white stone with characters cut upon them, on the one Assyrian and on the other Hellenic, being the names of all the nations which he was leading with him: and he was leading with him all over whom he was ruler. The whole number of them without the naval force was reckoned to be seventy myriads including cavalry, and ships had been gathered together to the number of six hundred. These pillars the Byzantians conveyed to their city after the events of which I speak, and used them for the altar of Artemis Orthosia, excepting one stone, which was left standing by the side of the temple of Dionysos in Byzantion, covered over with Assyrian characters. Now the place on the Bosphorus where Dareios made his bridge is, as I conclude, midway between Byzantion and the temple at the mouth of the Pontus.

88. After this Dareios being pleased with the floating bridge rewarded the chief constructor of it, Mandrocles the Samian, with gifts tenfold; and as an offering from these Mandrocles had a painting made of figures to present the whole scene of the bridge over the Bosphorus and king Dareios sitting in a prominent seat and his army crossing over; this he caused to be painted and dedicated it as an offering in the temple of Hera, with the following inscription:

> "Bosphorus having bridged over, the straits fish-abounding, to Hera
>   Mandrocleës dedicates this, of his work to record;
> A crown on himself he set, and he brought to the Samians glory,
>   And for Dareios performed everything after his mind."

89. This memorial was made of him who constructed the bridge: and Dareios, after he

had rewarded Mandrocles with gifts, passed over into Europe, having first commanded the Ionians to sail into the Pontus as far as the river Ister, and when they arrived at the Ister, there to wait for him, making a bridge meanwhile over the river; for the chief of his naval force were the Ionians, the Aiolians and the Hellespontians. So the fleet sailed through between the Kyanean rocks and made straight for the Ister; and then they sailed up the river a two days' voyage from the sea and proceeded to make a bridge across the neck, as it were, of the river, where the mouths of the Ister part off. Dareios meanwhile, having crossed the Bosphorus on the floating bridge, was advancing through Thrace, and when he came to the sources of the river Tearos he encamped for three days.

90. Now the Tearos is said by those who dwell near it to be the best of all rivers, both in other respects which tend to healing and especially for curing diseases of the skin both in men and in horses: and its springs are thirty-eight in number, flowing all from the same rock, of which some are cold and others warm. The way to them is of equal length from the city of Heraion near Perinthos and from Apollonia upon the Euxine Sea, that is to say two days' journey by each road. This Tearos runs into the river Contadesdos and the Contadesdos into the Agrianes and the Agrianes into the Hebros, which flows into the sea by the city of Ainos.

91. Dareios then, having come to this river and having encamped there, was pleased with the river and set up a pillar there also, with an inscription as follows: "The head-springs of the river Tearos give the best and fairest water of all rivers; and to them came leading an army against the Scythians the best and fairest of all men, Dareios the son of Hystaspes, of the Persians and of all the Continent king." These were the words which were there written.

92. Dareios then set out from thence and came to another river whose name is Artescos, which flows through the land of the Odrysians. Having come to this river he did as follows:—he appointed a place for his army and bade every man as he passed out by it place one stone in this appointed place: and when the army had performed this, then he marched away his army leaving behind great mounds of these stones.

93. But before he came to the Ister he conquered first the Getai, who believe in immortality: for the Thracians who occupy Salmydessos and are settled above the cities of Apollonian and Mesambria, called the Kyrmianai and the Nipsaioi, delivered themselves over to Dareios without fighting; but the Getai, who are the bravest and the most upright in their dealings of all the Thracians, having betaken themselves to obstinacy were forthwith subdued.

94. And their belief in immortality is of this kind, that is to say, they hold that they do not die, but that he who is killed goes to Salmoxis, a divinity, whom some of them call Gebeleizis; and at intervals of four years they send one of themselves, whomsoever the lot may select, as a messenger to Salmoxis, charging him with such requests as they have to make on each occasion; and they send him thus:—certain of them who are appointed for this have three javelins, and others meanwhile take hold on both sides of him who is being sent to Salmoxis, both by his hands and his feet, and first they swing him up, then throw him into the air so as to fall upon the spear-points: and if when he is pierced through he is killed, they think that the god is favorable to them; but if he is not killed, they find fault with the messenger himself, calling him a worthless man, and then having found fault with him they send another: and they give him the charge beforehand, while he is yet alive. These same Thracians also shoot arrows up towards the sky when thunder

and lightning come, and use threats to the god, not believing that there exists any other god except their own.

95. This Salmoxis I hear from the Hellenes who dwell about the Hellespont and the Pontus, was a man, and he became a slave in Samos, and was in fact a slave of Pythagoras the son of Mnesarchos. Then having become free he gained great wealth, and afterwards returned to his own land: and as the Thracians both live hardly and are rather simple-minded, this Salmoxis, being acquainted with the Ionian way of living and with manners more cultivated than the Thracians were used to see, since he had associated with Hellenes (and not only that but with Pythagoras, not the least able philosopher of the Hellenes), prepared a banqueting-hall, where he received and feasted the chief men of the tribe and instructed them meanwhile that neither he himself nor his guests nor their descendants in succession after them would die; but that they would come to a place where they would live forever and have all things good. While he was doing that which has been mentioned and was saying these things, he was making for himself meanwhile a chamber under the ground; and when his chamber was finished, he disappeared from among the Thracians and went down into the underground chamber, where he continued to live for three years: and they grieved for his loss and mourned for him as dead. Then in the fourth year he appeared to the Thracians, and in this way the things which Salmoxis said became credible to them.

96. Thus they say that he did; but as to this matter and the chamber underground, I neither disbelieve it nor do I very strongly believe, but I think that this Salmoxis lived many years before Pythagoras. However, whether there ever lived a man Salmoxis, or whether he is simply a native deity of the Getai, let us bid farewell to him now.

97. These, I say, having such manners as I have said, were subdued by the Persians and accompanied the rest of the army: and when Dareios and with him the land-army arrived at the Ister, then after all had passed over, Dareios commanded the Ionians to break up the floating bridge and to accompany him by land, as well as the rest of the troops which were in the ships: and when the Ionians were just about to break it up and to do that which he commanded, Coës the son of Erxander, who was commander of the Mytilenians, said thus to Dareios, having first inquired whether he was disposed to listen to an opinion from one who desired to declare it: "O king, seeing that thou art about to march upon a land where no cultivated ground will be seen nor any inhabited town, do thou therefore let this bridge remain where it is, leaving to guard it those same men who constructed it. Then, if we find the Scythians and fare as we desire, we have a way of return; and also even if we shall not be able to find them, at least our way of return is secured: for that we should be worsted by the Scythians in fight I never feared yet, but rather that we might not be able to find them, and might suffer some disaster in wandering about. Perhaps someone will say that in speaking thus I am speaking for my own advantage, in order that I may remain behind; but in truth I am bringing forward, O king, the opinion which I found best for thee, and I myself will accompany thee and not be left behind." With this opinion Dareios was very greatly pleased and made answer to him in these words: "Friend from Lesbos, when I have returned safe to my house, be sure that thou appear before me, in order that I may requite thee with good deeds for good counsel."

98. Having thus said and having tied sixty knots in a thong, he called the despots of the Ionians to speak with him and said as follows: "Men of Ionia, know that I have given up the opinion which I formerly declared with regard to the bridge; and do ye keep this

thong and do as I shall say:—so soon as ye shall have seen me go forward against the Scythians, from that time begin, and untie a knot on each day: and if within this time I am not here, and ye find that the days marked by the knots have passed by, then sail away to your own lands. Till then, since our resolve has thus been changed, guard the floating bridge, showing all diligence to keep it safe and to guard it. And thus acting, ye will do for me a very acceptable service." Thus said Dareios and hastened on his march forwards.

99. Now in front of Scythia in the direction towards the sea lies Thrace; and where a bay is formed in this land, there begins Scythia, into which the Ister flows out, the mouth of the river being turned towards the South-East Wind. Beginning at the Ister then I am about to describe the coast land of the true Scythia, with regard to measurement. At once from the Ister begins this original land of Scythia, and it lies towards the midday and the South Wind, extending as far as the city called Carkinitis. After this the part which lies on the coast of the same sea still, a country which is mountainous and runs out in the direction of the Pontus, is occupied by the Tauric race, as far as the peninsula which is called the "Rugged Chersonese"; and this extends to the sea which lies towards the East Wind: for two sides of the Scythian boundaries lie along by the sea, one by the sea on the South, and the other by that on the East, just as it is with Attica: and in truth the Tauroi occupy a part of Scythia which has much resemblance to Attica; it is as if in Attica another race and not the Athenians occupied the hill region of Sunion, supposing it to project more at the point into the sea, that region namely which is cut off by a line from Thoricos to Anaphlystos. Such I say, if we may be allowed to compare small things such as this with great, is the form of the Tauric land. For him however who has not sailed along this part of the coast of Attica I will make it clear by another comparison:—it is as if in Iapygia another race and not the Iapygians had cut off for themselves and were holding that extremity of the land which is bounded by a line beginning at the harbor of Brentesion and running to Taras. And in mentioning these two similar cases I am suggesting many other things also to which the Tauric land has resemblance.

100. After the Tauric land immediately come Scythians again, occupying the parts above the Tauroi and the coasts of the Eastern sea, that is to say the parts to the West of the Kimmerian Bosphorus and of the Maiotian lake, as far as the river Tanaïs, which runs into the corner of this lake. In the upper parts which tend inland Scythia is bounded (as we know) by the Agathyrsians first, beginning from the Ister, and then by the Neuroi, afterwards by the Androphagoi, and lastly by the Melanchlainoi.

101. Scythia then being looked upon as a four-sided figure with two of its sides bordered by the sea, has its border lines equal to one another in each direction, that which tends inland and that which runs along by the sea: for from Ister to the Borysthenes is ten days' journey, and from the Borysthenes to the Maiotian lake ten days' more; and the distance inland to the Melanchlainoi, who are settled above the Scythians, is a journey of twenty days. Now I have reckoned the day's journey at two hundred furlongs: and by this reckoning the cross lines of Scythia would be four thousand furlongs in length, and the perpendiculars which tend inland would be the same number of furlongs. Such is the size of this land.

102. The Scythians meanwhile having considered with themselves that they were not able to repel the army of Dareios alone by a pitched battle, proceeded to send messengers to those who dwelt near them: and already the kings of these nations had come together and were taking counsel with one another, since so great an army was marching towards

them. Now those who had come together were the kings of the Tauroi, Agathyrsians, Neuroi, Androphagoi, Melanchlainoi, Gelonians, Budinoi and Sauromatai.

103. Of these the Tauroi have the following customs:—they sacrifice to the "Maiden" both ship-wrecked persons and also those Hellenes whom they can capture by putting out to sea against them; and their manner of sacrifice is this:—when they have made the first offering from the victim they strike his head with a club: and some say that they push the body down from the top of the cliff (for it is upon a cliff that the temple is placed) and set the head up on a stake; but others, while agreeing as to the heads, say nevertheless that the body is not pushed down from the top of the cliff, but buried in the earth. This divinity to whom they sacrifice, the Tauroi themselves say is Iphigeneia the daughter of Agamemnon. Whatsoever enemies they have conquered they treat in this fashion:—each man cuts off a head and bears it away to his house; then he impales it on a long stake and sets it up above his house raised to a great height, generally above the chimney; and they say that these are suspended above as guards to preserve the whole house. This people has its living by plunder and war.

104. The Agathyrsians are the most luxurious of men and wear gold ornaments for the most part: also they have promiscuous intercourse with their women, in order that they may be brethren to one another and being all nearly related may not feel envy or malice one against another. In their other customs they have come to resemble the Thracians.

105. The Neuroi practice the Scythian customs: and one generation before the expedition of Dareios it so befell them that they were forced to quit their land altogether by reason of serpents: for their land produced serpents in vast numbers, and they fell upon them in still larger numbers from the desert country above their borders; until at last being hard pressed they left their own land and settled among the Budinoi. These men it would seem are wizards; for it is said of them by the Scythians and by the Hellenes who are settled in the Scythian land that once in every year each of the Neuroi becomes a wolf for a few days and then returns again to his original form. For my part I do not believe them when they say this, but they say it nevertheless, and swear it moreover.

106. The Androphagoi have the most savage manners of all human beings, and they neither acknowledge any rule of right nor observe any customary law. They are nomads and wear clothing like that of the Scythians, but have a language of their own; and alone of all these nations they are man-eaters.

107. The Melanchlainoi wear all of them black clothing, whence also they have their name; and they practice the customs of the Scythians.

108. The Budinoi are a very great and numerous race, and are all very blue-eyed and fair of skin: and in their land is built a city of wood, the name of which is Gelonos, and each side of the wall is thirty furlongs in length and lofty at the same time, all being of wood; and the houses are of wood also and the temples; for there are in it temples of Hellenic gods furnished after Hellenic fashion with sacred images and altars and cells, all of wood; and they keep festivals every other year to Dionysos and celebrate the rites of Bacchus: for the Gelonians are originally Hellenes, and they removed from the trading stations on the coast and settled among the Budinoi; and they use partly the Scythian language and partly the Hellenic. The Budinoi however do not use the same language as the Gelonians, nor is their manner of living the same:

109, for the Budinoi are natives of the soil and a nomad people, and alone of the nations in these parts feed on fir-cones; but the Gelonians are tillers of the ground and feed on corn and have gardens, and resemble them not at all either in appearance or in complexion of skin. However by the Hellenes the Budinoi also are called Gelonians, not being rightly so called. Their land is all thickly overgrown with forests of all kinds of trees, and in the thickest forest there is a large and deep lake, and round it marshy ground and reeds. In this are caught otters and beavers and certainly other wild animals with square-shaped faces. The fur of these is sewn as a fringe round their coats of skin, and the testicles are made use of by them for curing diseases of the womb.

110. About the Sauromatai the following tale is told:—When the Hellenes had fought with the Amazons,—now the Amazons are called by the Scythians *Oiorpata*, which name means in the Hellenic tongue "slayers of men," for "man" they call *oior*, and *pata* means "to slay,"—then, as the story goes, the Hellenes, having conquered them in the battle at the Thermodon, were sailing away and conveying with them in three ships as many Amazons as they were able to take prisoners. These in the open sea set upon the men and cast them out of the ships; but they knew nothing about ships, nor how to use rudders or sails or oars, and after they had cast out the men they were driven about by wave and wind and came to that part of the Maiotian lake where Cremnoi stands; now Cremnoi is in the land of the free Scythians. There the Amazons disembarked from their ships and made their way into the country, and having met first with a troop of horses feeding they seized them, and mounted upon these they plundered the property of the Scythians.

111. The Scythians meanwhile were not able to understand the matter, for they did not know either their speech or their dress or the race to which they belonged, but were in wonder as to whence they had come and thought that they were men, of an age corresponding to their appearance: and finally they fought a battle against them, and after the battle the Scythians got possession of the bodies of the dead, and thus they discovered that they were women. They took counsel therefore and resolved by no means to go on trying to kill them, but to send against them the youngest men from among themselves, making conjecture of the number so as to send just as many men as there were women. These were told to encamp near them, and do whatsoever they should do; if however the women should come after them, they were not to fight but to retire before them, and when the women stopped, they were to approach near and encamp. This plan was adopted by the Scythians because they desired to have children born from them.

112. The young men accordingly were sent out and did that which had been commanded them: and when the Amazons perceived that they had not come to do them any harm, they let them alone; and the two camps approached nearer to one another every day: and the young men, like the Amazons, had nothing except their arms and their horses, and got their living, as the Amazons did, by hunting and by taking booty.

113. Now the Amazons at midday used to scatter abroad either one by one or by two together, dispersing to a distance from one another to ease themselves; and the Scythians also having perceived this did the same thing: and one of the Scythians came near to one of those Amazons who were apart by themselves, and she did not repulse him but allowed him to lie with her: and she could not speak to him, for they did not understand one another's speech, but she made signs to him with her hand to come on the following day to the same place and to bring another with him, signifying to him that there should be two of them, and that she would bring another with her. The young man therefore, when he returned, reported this to the others; and on the next day he came himself to the place and also brought another, and he found the Amazon awaiting him with another in

her company. Then hearing this the rest of the young men also in their turn tamed for themselves the remainder of the Amazons;

114, and after this they joined their camps and lived together, each man having for his wife her with whom he had had dealings at first; and the men were not able to learn the speech of the women, but the women came to comprehend that of the men. So when they understood one another, the men spoke to the Amazons as follows: "We have parents and we have possessions; now therefore let us no longer lead a life of this kind, but let us go away to the main body of our people and dwell with them; and we will have you for wives and no others." They however spoke thus in reply: "We should not be able to live with your women, for we and they have not the same customs. We shoot with bows and hurl javelins and ride horses, but the works of women we never learnt; whereas your women do none of these things which we said, but stay in the wagons and work at the works of women, neither going out to the chase nor anywhither else. We therefore should not be able to live in agreement with them: but if ye desire to keep us for your wives and to be thought honest men, go to your parents and obtain from them your share of the goods, and then let us go and dwell by ourselves."

115. The young men agreed and did this; and when they had obtained the share of the goods which belonged to them and had returned back to the Amazons, the women spoke to them as follows: "We are possessed by fear and trembling to think that we must dwell in this place, having not only separated you from your fathers, but also done great damage to your land. Since then ye think it right to have us as your wives, do this together with us,—come and let us remove from this land and pass over the river Tanaïs and there dwell."

116. The young men agreed to this also, and they crossed over the Tanaïs and made their way towards the rising sun for three days' journey from Tanaïs, and also towards the North Wind for three days' journey from the Maiotian lake: and having arrived at the place where they are now settled, they took up their abode there: and from thenceforward the women of the Sauromatai practice their ancient way of living, going out regularly on horseback to the chase both in company with the men and apart from them, and going regularly to war, and wearing the same dress as the men.

117. And the Sauromatai make use of the Scythian tongue, speaking it barbarously however from the first, since the Amazons did not learn it thoroughly well. As regards marriages their rule is this, that no maiden is married until she has slain a man of their enemies; and some of them even grow old and die before they are married, because they are not able to fulfil the requirement of the law.

118. To the kings of these nations then, which have been mentioned in order, the messengers of the Scythians came, finding them gathered together, and spoke declaring to them how the Persian king, after having subdued all things to himself in the other continent, had laid a bridge over the neck of the Bosphorus and had crossed over to that continent, and having crossed over and subdued the Thracians, was making a bridge over the river Ister, desiring to bring under his power all these regions also. "Do ye therefore," they said, "by no means stand aloof and allow us to be destroyed, but let us become all of one mind and oppose him who is coming against us. If ye shall not do so, we on our part shall either be forced by necessity to leave our land, or we shall stay in it and make a treaty with the invader; for what else can we do if ye are not willing to help us? and for you after this it will be in no respect easier; for the Persian has come not at all less against you than

against us, nor will it content him to subdue us and abstain from you. And of the truth of that which we say we will mention a strong evidence: if the Persian had been making his expedition against us alone, because he desired to take vengeance for the former servitude, he ought to have abstained from all the rest and to have come at once to invade our land, and he would thus have made it clear to all that he was marching to fight against the Scythians and not against the rest. In fact however, ever since he crossed over to this continent, he has compelled all who came in his way to submit to him, and he holds under him now not only the other Thracians but also the Getai, who are our nearest neighbors."

119. When the Scythians proposed this, the kings who had come from the various nations took counsel together, and their opinions were divided. The kings of the Gelonians, of the Budinoi and of the Sauromatai agreed together and accepted the proposal that they should help the Scythians, but those of the Agathyrsians, Neuroi, Androphagoi, Melanchlainoi and Tauroi returned answer to the Scythians as follows: "If ye had not been the first to do wrong to the Persians and to begin war, then we should have surely thought that ye were speaking justly in asking for those things for which ye now ask, and we should have yielded to your request and shared your fortunes. As it is however, ye on the one hand made invasion without us into their land, and bare rule over the Persians for so long a time as God permitted you; and they in their turn, since the same God stirs them up, are repaying you with the like. As for us however, neither at that time did we do any wrong to these men nor now shall we attempt to do any wrong to them unprovoked: if however the Persians shall come against our land also, and do wrong first to us, we also shall refuse to submit : but until we shall see this, we shall remain by ourselves, for we are of opinion that the Persians have come not against us, but against those who were the authors of the wrong."

120. When the Scythians heard this answer reported, they planned not to fight a pitched battle openly, since these did not join them as allies, but to retire before the Persians and to drive away their cattle from before them, choking up with earth the wells and the springs of water by which they passed and destroying the grass from off the ground, having parted themselves for this into two bodies; and they resolved that the Sauromatai should be added to one of their divisions, namely that over which Scopasis was king, and that these should move on, if the Persians turned in that direction, straight towards the river Tanaïs, retreating before him by the shore of the Maiotian lake; and when the Persian marched back again, they should come after and pursue him. This was one division of their kingdom, appointed to go by the way which has been said; and the other two of the kingdoms, the large one over which Idanthyrsos was king, and the third of which Taxakis was king, were to join together in one, with the Gelonians and the Budinoi added to them, and they also were to retire before the Persians one day's march in front of them, going on out of their way and doing that which had been planned. First they were to move on straight for the countries which had refused to give their alliance, in order that they might involve these also in the war, and though these had not voluntarily undertaken the war with the Persians, they were to involve them in it nevertheless against their will; and after that they were to return to their own land and attack the enemy, if it should seem good to them in council so to do.

121. Having formed this plan the Scythians went to meet the army of Dareios, sending off the best of their horsemen before them as scouts; but all the wagons in which their children and their women lived they sent on, and with them all their cattle (leaving only so

much as was sufficient to supply them with food), and charged them that they should proceed continually towards the North Wind. These, I say, were being carried on before:

122, but when the scouts who went in front of the Scythians discovered the Persians distant about three days' march from Ister, then the Scythians having discovered them continued to pitch their camp one day's march in front, destroying utterly that which grew from the ground: and when the Persians saw that the horsemen of the Scythians had made their appearance, they came after them following in their track, while the Scythians continually moved on. After this, since they had directed their march towards the first of the divisions, the Persians continued to pursue towards the East and the river Tanaïs; and when the Scythians crossed over the river Tanaïs, the Persians crossed over after them and continued still to pursue, until they had passed quite through the land of the Sauromatai and had come to that of the Budinoi.

123. Now so long as the Persians were passing through Scythia and the land of the Sauromatai, they had nothing to destroy, seeing that the land was bare, but when they invaded the land of the Budinoi, then they fell in with the wooden wall, which had been deserted by the Budinoi and left wholly unoccupied, and this they destroyed by fire. Having done so they continued to follow on further in the tracks of the enemy, until they had passed through the whole of this land and had arrived at the desert. This desert region is occupied by no men, and it lies above the land of the Budinoi, extending for a seven days' journey; and above this desert dwell the Thyssagetai, and four large rivers flow from them through the land of the Maiotians and run into that which is called the Maiotian lake, their names being as follows,—Lycos, Oaros, Tanaïs, Syrgis.

124. When therefore Dareios came to the desert region, he ceased from his course and halted his army upon the river Oaros. Having so done he began to build eight large fortifications at equal distances from one another, that is to say about sixty furlongs, of which the ruins still existed down to my time; and while he was occupied in this, the Scythians whom he was pursuing came round by the upper parts and returned back to Scythia. Accordingly, since these had altogether disappeared and were no longer seen by the Persians at all, Dareios left those fortifications half finished, and turning back himself began to go towards the West, supposing that these were the whole body of the Scythians and that they were flying towards the West.

125. And marching his army as quickly as possible, when he came to Scythia he met with the two divisions of the Scythians together, and having fallen in with these he continued to pursue them, while they retired out of his way one day's journey in advance: and as Dareios did not cease to come after them, the Scythians according to the plan which they had made continued to retire before him towards the land of those who had refused to give their alliance, and first towards that of the Melanchlainoi; and when Scythians and Persians both together had invaded and disturbed these, the Scythians led the way to the country of the Androphagoi; and when these had also been disturbed, they proceeded to the land of the Neuroi; and while these too were being disturbed, the Scythians went on retiring before the enemy to the Agathyrsians. The Agathyrsians however, seeing that their next neighbors also were flying from the Scythians and had been disturbed, sent a herald before the Scythians invaded their land and proclaimed to the Scythians not to set foot upon their confines, warning them that if they should attempt to invade the country, they would first have to fight with them. The Agathyrsians then having given this warning came out in arms to their borders, meaning to drive off those

who were coming upon them; but the Melanchlainoi and Androphagoi and Neuroi, when the Persians and Scythians together invaded them, did not betake themselves to brave defense but forgot their former threat and fled in confusion ever further towards the North to the desert region. The Scythians however, when the Agathyrsians had warned them off, did not attempt any more to come to these, but led the Persians from the country of the Neuroi back to their own land.

126. Now as this went on for a long time and did not cease, Dareios sent a horseman to Idanthyrsos king of the Scythians and said as follows: "Thou most wondrous man, why dost thou fly forever, when thou mightest do of these two things one?—if thou thinkest thyself able to make opposition to my power, stand thou still and cease from wandering abroad, and fight; but if thou dost acknowledge thyself too weak, cease then in that case also from thy course, and come to speech with thy master, bringing to him gifts of earth and water."

127. To this the king of the Scythians Idanthyrsos made answer thus: "My case, O Persian, stands thus:—Never yet did I fly because I was afraid, either before this time from any other man, or now from thee; nor have I done anything different now from that which I was wont to do also in time of peace: and as to the cause why I do not fight with thee at once, this also I will declare to thee. We have neither cities nor land sown with crops, about which we should fear lest they should be captured or laid waste, and so join battle more speedily with you; but if it be necessary by all means to come to this speedily, know that we have sepulchres in which our fathers are buried; therefore come now, find out these and attempt to destroy them, and ye shall know then whether we shall fight with you for the sepulchres or whether we shall not fight. Before that however, unless the motion comes upon us, we shall not join battle with thee. About fighting let so much as has been said suffice; but as to masters, I acknowledge none over me but Zeus my ancestor and Hestia the queen of the Scythians. To thee then in place of gifts of earth and water I shall send such things as it is fitting that thou shouldest receive; and in return for thy saying that thou art my master, for that I say, woe betide thee." This is the proverbial "saying of the Scythians."

128. The herald then had departed to report this to Dareios; and the kings of the Scythians, having heard mention of subjection to a master, were filled with wrath. They sent accordingly the division which was appointed to be joined with the Sauromatai, that division of which Scopasis was in command, bidding them come to speech with the Ionians, namely those who were guarding the bridge of the Ister, and meanwhile they who were left behind resolved not to lead the Persians wandering about any more, but to attack them constantly as they were getting provisions. Therefore they observed the soldiers of Dareios as they got provisions, and did that which they had determined: and the cavalry of the Scythians always routed that of the enemy, but the Persian horsemen as they fled fell back upon the men on foot, and these would come up to their assistance; and meanwhile the Scythians when they had driven in the cavalry turned back, fearing the men on foot. Also by night the Scythians used to make similar attacks:

129, and the thing which, strange to say, most helped the Persians and hindered the Scythians in their attacks upon the camp of Dareios, I will mention, namely the voice of the asses and the appearance of the mules; for Scythia produces neither ass nor mule, as I have declared before, nor is there at all in the Scythian country either ass or mule on account of the cold. The asses accordingly by riotously braying used to throw into confusion the cavalry of the Scythians; and often, as they were in the middle of riding against the Persians, when the horses heard the voice of the asses they turned back in confusion and were possessed with wonder, pricking up their ears, because they had never heard such a voice nor seen the form of the creature before.

130. So far then the Persians had the advantage for a small part of the war. But the Scythians, whenever they saw that the Persians were disquieted, then in order that they might remain a longer time in Scythia and in remaining might suffer by being in want of everything, would leave some of their own cattle behind with the herdsmen, while they themselves rode out of the way to another place, and the Persians would come upon the cattle and take them, and having taken them they were elated at what they had done.

131. As this happened often, at length Dareios began to be in straits; and the kings of the Scythians perceiving this sent a herald bearing as gifts to Dareios a bird and a mouse and a frog and five arrows. The Persians accordingly asked the bearer of the gifts as to the meaning of the gifts which were offered; but he said that nothing more had been commanded to him but to give them and get away as speedily as possible; and he bade the Persians find out for themselves, if they had wisdom, that which the gifts were meant to express.

132. Having heard this the Persians took counsel with one another; and the opinion of Dareios was that the Scythians were giving to him both themselves and also earth and water, making his conjecture by this, namely that a mouse is produced in the earth and feeds on the same produce of the earth as man, and a frog in the water, while a bird has great resemblance to a horse; and moreover that in giving the arrows they were delivering up their own might in battle. This was the opinion expressed by Dareios; but the opinion of Gobryas, one of the seven men who killed the Magian, was at variance with it, for he conjectured that the gifts expressed this: "Unless ye become birds and fly up into the heaven, O Persians, or become mice and sink down under the earth, or become frogs and leap into the lakes, ye shall not return back home, but shall be smitten by these arrows."

133. The Persians then, I say, were making conjecture of the gifts: and meanwhile the single division of the Scythians, that which had been appointed at first to keep guard along the Maiotian lake and then to go to the Ister and come to speech with the Ionians, when they arrived at the bridge spoke as follows: "Ionians, we have come bringing you freedom, if at least ye are willing to listen to us; for we are informed that Dareios gave you command to guard the bridge for sixty days only, and then, if he had not arrived within that time, to get you away to your own land. Now therefore, if ye do as we say, ye will be without blame from his part and without blame also from ours: stay the appointed days and then after that get you away." They then, when the Ionians had engaged themselves to do this, hastened back again by the quickest way:

134, and meanwhile, after the coming of the gifts to Dareios, the Scythians who were left had arrayed themselves against the Persians with both foot and horse, meaning to engage battle. Now when the Scythians had been placed in battle-array, a hare darted through them into the space between the two armies, and each company of them, as they saw the hare, began to run after it. When the Scythians were thus thrown into disorder and were raising loud cries, Dareios asked what was this clamour arising from the enemy; and hearing that they were running after the hare, he said to those men to whom he was wont to say things at other times: "These men have very slight regard for us, and I perceive now that Gobryas spoke rightly about the Scythian gifts. Seeing then that now I myself too think that things are so, we have need of good counsel, in order that our retreat homewards may be safely made." To this replied Gobryas and said: "O king, even by report I was almost assured of the difficulty of dealing with these men; and when I came I learnt it still more thoroughly, since I saw that they were mocking us. Now therefore my opinion is, that as soon as night comes on, we kindle the camp-fires as we are wont to do at other times also, and deceive with a false tale those of our men who are weakest to endure hardships, and tie up all the asses and get us away, before either the Scythians make for the Ister to destroy the bridge or something be resolved by the Ionians which may be our ruin."

135. Thus Gobryas advised; and after this, when night came on, Dareios acted on this opinion. Those of his men who were weakened by fatigue and whose loss was of least account, these he left behind in the camp, and the asses also tied up: and for the following reasons he left behind the asses and the weaker men of his army,—the asses in order that they might make a noise which should be heard, and the men really because of their weakness, but on a pretense stated openly that he was about to attack the Scythians with the effective part of the army, and that they meanwhile were to be defenders of the camp. Having thus instructed those who were left behind, and having kindled camp-fires, Dareios hastened by the quickest way towards the Ister: and the asses, having no longer about them the usual throng, very much more for that reason caused their voice to be heard; so the Scythians, hearing the asses, supposed surely that the Persians were remaining in their former place.

136. But when it was day, those who were left behind perceived that they had been betrayed by Dareios, and they held out their hands in submission to the Scythians, telling them what their case was; and the Scythians, when they heard this, joined together as quickly as possible, that is to say the two combined divisions of the Scythians and the single division, and also the Sauromatai, Budinoi, and Gelonians, and began to pursue the Persians, making straight for the Ister: but as the Persian army for the most part consisted of men on foot, and was not acquainted with the roads (the roads not being marked with tracks), while the Scythian army consisted of horsemen and was acquainted with the shortest cuts along the way, they missed one another and the Scythians arrived at the bridge much before the Persians. Then having learnt that the Persians had not yet arrived, they said to the Ionians who were in the ships: "Ionians, the days of your number are past, and ye are not acting uprightly in that ye yet remain waiting: but as ye stayed before from fear, so now break up the passage as quickly as ye may, and depart free and unhurt, feeling thankfulness both to the gods and to the Scythians: and him who was formerly your master we will so convince, that he shall never again march with an army upon any nation."

137. Upon this the Ionians took counsel together; and Miltiades the Athenian on the one hand, who was commander and despot of the men of the Chersonese in Hellespont, was of opinion that they should follow the advice of the Scythians and set Ionia free: but Histiaios the Milesian was of the opposite opinion to this; for he said that at the present time it was by means of Dareios that each one of them was ruling as despot over a city; and if the power of Dareios should be destroyed, neither he himself would be able to bear rule over the Milesians, nor would any other of them be able to bear rule over any other city; for each of the cities would choose to have popular rather than despotic rule. When

Histiaios declared his opinion thus, forthwith all turned to this opinion, whereas at the first they were adopting that of Miltiades.

138. Now these were they who gave the vote between the two opinions, and were men of consequence in the eyes of the king, —first the despots of the Hellespontians, Daphnis of Abydos, Hippoclos of Lampsacos, Herophantos of Parion, Metrodoros of Proconnesos, Aristagoras of Kyzicos, and Ariston of Byzantion, these were those from the Hellespont; and from Ionia, Strattis of Chios, Aiakes of Samos, Laodamas of Phocaia, and Histiaios of Miletos, whose opinion had been proposed in opposition to that of Miltiades; and of the Aiolians the only man of consequence there present was Aristagoras of Kyme.

139. When these adopted the opinion of Histiaios, they resolved to add to it deeds and words as follows, namely to break up that part of the bridge which was on the side towards the Scythians, to break it up, I say, for a distance equal to the range of an arrow, both in order that they might be thought to be doing something, though in fact they were doing nothing, and for fear that the Scythians might make an attempt using force and desiring to cross the Ister by the bridge: and in breaking up that part of the bridge which was towards Scythia they resolved to say that they would do all that which the Scythians desired. This they added to the opinion proposed, and then Histiaios coming forth from among them made answer to the Scythians as follows: "Scythians, ye are come bringing good news, and it is a timely haste that ye make to bring it; and ye on your part give us good guidance, while we on ours render to you suitable service. For, as ye see, we are breaking up the passage, and we shall show all zeal in our desire to be free: and while we are breaking up the bridge, it is fitting that ye should be seeking for those of whom ye speak, and when ye have found them, that ye should take vengeance on them on behalf of us as well as of yourselves in such manner as they deserve."

140. The Scythians then, believing for the second time that the Ionians were speaking the truth, turned back to make search for the Persians, but they missed altogether their line of march through the land. Of this the Scythians themselves were the cause, since they had destroyed the pastures for horses in that region and had choked up with earth the springs of water; for if they had not done this, it would have been possible for them easily, if they desired it, to discover the Persians: but as it was, by those things wherein they thought they had taken their measures best, they failed of success. The Scythians then on their part were passing through those regions of their own land where there was grass for the horses and springs of water, and were seeking for the enemy there, thinking that they too were taking a course in their retreat through such country as this; while the Persians in fact marched keeping carefully to the track which they had made before, and so they found the passage of the river, though with difficulty: and as they arrived by night and found the bridge broken up, they were brought to the extreme of fear, lest the Ionians should have deserted them.

141. Now there was with Dareios an Egyptian who had a voice louder than that of any other man on earth, and this man Dareios ordered to take his stand upon the bank of the Ister and to call Histiaios of Miletos. He accordingly proceeded to do so; and Histiaios, hearing the first hail, produced all the ships to carry the army over and also put together the bridge.

142. Thus the Persians escaped, and the Scythians in their search missed the Persians the second time also: and their judgment of the Ionians is that on the one hand, if they be regarded as free men, they are the most worthless and cowardly of all men, but on the

other hand, if regarded as slaves, they are the most attached to their master and the least disposed to run away of all slaves. This is the reproach which is cast against the Ionians by the Scythians.

143. Dareios then marching through Thrace arrived at Sestos in the Chersonese; and from that place, he passed over himself in his ships to Asia, but to command his army in Europe he left Megabazos a Persian, to whom Dareios once gave honor by uttering in the land of Persia this saying:—Dareios was beginning to eat pomegranates, and at once when he opened the first of them, Artabanos his brother asked him of what he would desire to have as many as there were seeds in the pomegranate: and Dareios said that he would desire to have men like Megabazos as many as that in number, rather than to have Hellas subject to him. In Persia, I say, he honored him by saying these words, and at this time he left him in command with eight myriads of his army.

144. This Megabazos uttered one saying whereby he left of himself an imperishable memory with the peoples of Hellespont: for being once at Byzantion he heard that the men of Calchedon had settled in that region seventeen years before the Byzantians, and having heard it he said that those of Calchedon at that time chanced to be blind; for assuredly they would not have chosen the worse place, when they might have settled in that which was better, if they had not been blind. This Megabazos it was who was left in command at that time in the land of the Hellespontians, and he proceeded to subdue all who did not take the side of the Medes.

145. He then was doing thus; and at this very same time a great expedition was being made also against Libya, on an occasion which I shall relate when I have first related this which follows.—The children's children of those who voyaged in the Argo, having been driven forth by those Pelasgians who carried away at Brauron the women of the Athenians,—having been driven forth I say by these from Lemnos, had departed and sailed to Lacedaemon, and sitting down on Mount Taÿgetos they kindled a fire. The Lacedemonians seeing this sent a messenger to inquire who they were and from whence; and they answered the question of the messenger saying that they were Minyai and children of heroes who sailed in the Argo, for these, they said, had put in to Lemnos and propagated the race of which they sprang. The Lacedemonians having heard the story of the descent of the Minyai, sent a second time and asked for what purpose they had come into the country and were causing a fire to blaze. They said that they had been cast out by the Pelasgians, and were come now to the land of their fathers, for most just it was that this should so be done; and they said that their request was to be permitted to dwell with these, having a share of civil rights and a portion allotted to them of the land. And the Lacedemonians were content to receive the Minyai upon the terms which they themselves desired, being most of all impelled to do this by the fact that the sons of Tyndareus were voyagers in the Argo. So having received the Minyai they gave them a share of land and distributed them in the tribes; and they forthwith made marriages, and gave in marriage to others the women whom they brought with them from Lemnos.

146. However, when no very long time had passed, the Minyai forthwith broke out into insolence, asking for a share of the royal power and also doing other impious things: therefore the Lacedemonians resolved to put them to death; and having seized them they cast them into a prison. Now the Lacedemonians put to death by night all those whom they put to death, but no man by day. When therefore they were just about to kill them, the wives of the Minyai, being native Spartans and daughters of the first citizens of Sparta,

entreated to be allowed to enter the prison and come to speech every one with her own husband: and they let them pass in, not supposing that any craft would be practiced by them. They however, when they had entered, delivered to their husbands all the garments which they were wearing, and themselves received those of their husbands: thus the Minyai having put on the women's clothes went forth out of prison as women, and having escaped in this manner they went again to Taÿgetos and sat down there.

147. Now at this very same time Theras the son of Autesion, the son of Tisamenos, the son of Thersander, the son of Polyneikes, was preparing to set forth from Lacedaemon to found a settlement. This Theras, who was of the race of Cadmos, was mother's brother to the sons of Aristodemos, Eurysthenes and Procles; and while these sons were yet children, Theras as their guardian held the royal power in Sparta. When however his nephews were grown and had taken the power into their hands, then Theras, being grieved that he should be ruled by others after he had tasted of rule himself, said that he would not remain in Lacedaemon, but would sail away to his kinsmen. Now there were in the island which is now called Thera, but formerly was called Callista, descendants of Membliaros the son of Poikiles, a Phoenician: for Cadmos the son of Agenor in his search for Europa put in to land at the island which is now called Thera; and, whether it was that the country pleased him when he had put to land, or whether he chose to do so for any other reason, he left in this island, besides other Phoenicians, Membliaros also, of his own kinsmen. These occupied the island called Callista for eight generations of men, before Theras came from Lacedaemon.

148. To these then, I say, Theras was preparing to set forth, taking with him people from the tribes, and intending to settle together with those who have been mentioned, not with any design to drive them out, but on the contrary claiming them very strongly as kinfolk. And when the Minyai after having escaped from the prison went and sat down on Taÿgetos, Theras entreated of the Lacedemonians, as they were proposing to put them to death, that no slaughter might take place, and at the same time he engaged himself to take them forth out of the land. The Lacedemonians having agreed to this proposal, he sailed away with three thirty-oared galleys to the descendants of Membliaros, not taking with him by any means all the Minyai, but a few only; for the greater number of them turned towards the land of the Paroreatai and Caucones, and having driven these out of their country, they parted themselves into six divisions and founded in their territory the following towns,—Lepreon, Makistos, Phrixai, Pyrgos, Epion, Nudion; of these the Eleians sacked the greater number within my own lifetime. The island meanwhile got its name of Thera after Theras who led the settlement.

149. And since his son said that he would not sail with him, therefore he said that he would leave him behind as a sheep among wolves; and in accordance with that saying this young man got the name of Oiolycos, and it chanced that this name prevailed over his former name: then from Oiolycos was begotten Aigeus, after whom are called the Aigeidai, a powerful clan in Sparta: and the men of this tribe, since their children did not live to grow up, established by the suggestion of an oracle a temple to the Avenging Deities of Laïos and OEdipus, and after this the same thing was continued in Thera by the descendants of these men.

150. Up to this point of the story the Lacedemonians agree in their report with the men of Thera; but in what is to come it is those of Thera alone who report that it happened as follows. Grinnos the son of Aisanios, a descendant of the Theras who has been mentioned,

and king of the island of Thera, came to Delphi bringing the offering of a hecatomb from his State; and there were accompanying him, besides others of the citizens, also Battos the son of Polymnestos, who was by descent of the family of Euphemos of the race of the Minyai. Now when Grinnos the king of the Theraians was consulting the Oracle about other matters, the Pythian prophetess gave answer bidding him found a city in Libya; and he made reply saying: "Lord, I am by this time somewhat old and heavy to stir, but do thou bid some one of these younger ones do this." As he thus said he pointed towards Battos. So far at that time: but afterwards when he had come away they were in difficulty about the saying of the Oracle, neither having any knowledge of Libya, in what part of the earth it was, nor venturing to send a colony to the unknown.

151. Then after this for seven years there was no rain in Thera, and in these years all the trees in their island were withered up excepting one: and when the Theraians consulted the Oracle, the Pythian prophetess alleged this matter of colonizing Libya to be the cause. As then they had no remedy for their evil, they sent messengers to Crete, to find out whether any of the Cretans or of the sojourners in Crete had ever come to Libya. These as they wandered round about the country came also the city of Itanos, and there they met with a fisher for purple named Corobios, who said that he had been carried away by winds and had come to Libya, and in Libya to the island of Platea. This man they persuaded by payment of money and took him to Thera, and from Thera there set sail men to explore, at first not many in number; and Corobios having guided them to this same island of Platea, they left Corobios there, leaving behind with him provisions for a certain number of months, and sailed themselves as quickly as possible to make report about the island to the men of Thera.

152. Since however these stayed away longer than the time appointed, Corobios found himself destitute; and after this a ship of Samos, of which the master was Colaios, while sailing to Egypt was carried out of its course and came to this island of Platea; and the Samians hearing from Corobios the whole story left him provisions for a year. They themselves then put out to sea from the island and sailed on, endeavoring to reach Egypt but carried away continually by the East Wind; and as the wind did not cease to blow, they passed through the Pillars of Heracles and came to Tartessos, guided by divine providence. Now this trading-place was at that time untouched by any, so that when these returned back home they made profit from their cargo greater than any other Hellenes of whom we have certain knowledge, with the exception at least of Sostratos the son of Laodamas the Eginetan, for with him it is not possible for any other man to contend. And the Samians set apart six talents, the tenth part of their gains, and had a bronze vessel made like an Argolic mixing-bowl with round it heads of griffins projecting in a row; and this they dedicated as an offering in the temple of Hera, setting as supports under it three colossal statues of bronze seven cubits in height, resting upon their knees. By reason first of this deed great friendship was formed by those of Kyrene and Thera with the Samians.

153. The Theraians meanwhile, when they arrived at Thera after having left Corobios in the island, reported that they had colonized an island on the coast of Libya: and the men of Thera resolved to send one of every two brothers selected by lot and men besides taken from all the regions of the island, which are seven in number; and further that Battos should be both their leader and their king. Thus then they sent forth two fifty-oared galleys to Platea.

154. This is the report of the Theraians; and for the remainder of the account from this

point onwards the Theraians are in agreement with the men of Kyrene: from this point onwards, I say, since in what concerns Battos the Kyrenians tell by no means the same tale as those of Thera; for their account is this:—There is in Crete a city called Oäxos in which one Etearchos became king, who when he had a daughter, whose mother was dead, named Phronime, took to wife another woman notwithstanding. She having come in afterwards, thought fit to be a stepmother to Phronime in deed as well as in name, giving her evil treatment and devising everything possible to her hurt; and at last she brings against her a charge of lewdness and persuades her husband that the truth is so. He then being convinced by his wife, devised an unholy deed against the daughter: for there was in Oäxos one Themison, a merchant of Thera, whom Etearchos took to himself as a guest-friend and caused him to swear that he would surely serve him in whatsoever he should require: and when he had caused him to swear this, he brought and delivered to him his daughter and bade him take her away and cast her into the sea. Themison then was very greatly vexed at the deceit practiced in the matter of the oath, and he dissolved his guest-friendship and did as follows, that is to say, he received the girl and sailed away, and when he got out into the open sea, to free himself from blame as regards the oath which Etearchos had made him swear, he tied her on each side with ropes and let her down into the sea, and then drew her up and came to Thera.

155. After that, Polymnestos, a man of repute among the Theraians, received Phronime from him and kept her as his concubine; and in course of time there was born to him from her a son with an impediment in his voice and lisping, to whom, as both Theraians and Kyrenians say, was given the name Battos, but I think that some other name was then given, and he was named Battos instead of this after he came to Libya, taking for himself this surname from the oracle which was given to him at Delphi and from the rank which he had obtained; for the Libyans call a king *battos*: and for this reason, I think, the Pythian prophetess in her prophesying called him so, using the Libyan tongue, because she knew that he would be a king in Libya. For when he had grown to be a man, he came to Delphi to inquire about his voice; and when he asked, the prophetess thus answered him:

"For a voice thou camest, O Battos, but thee lord Phoebus Apollo
Sendeth as settler forth to the Libyan land sheep-abounding,"

just as if she should say using the Hellenic tongue, "For a voice thou camest, O king." He thus made answer: "Lord, I came to thee to inquire concerning my voice, but thou answerest me other things which are not possible, bidding me go as a settler to Libya; but with what power, or with what force of men should I go?" Thus saying he did not at all persuade her to give him any other reply; and as she was prophesying to him again the same things as before, Battos departed while she was yet speaking, and went away to Thera.

156. After this there came evil fortune both to himself and to the other men of Thera; and the Theraians, not understanding that which befell them, sent to Delphi to inquire about the evils which they were suffering: and the Pythian prophetess gave them reply that if they joined with Battos in founding Kyrene in Libya, they would fare the better. After this the Theraians sent Battos with two fifty-oared galleys; and these sailed to Libya, and then came away back to Thera, for they did not know what else to do: and the Theraians pelted them with missiles when they endeavored to land, and would not allow them

to put to shore, but bade them sail back again. They accordingly being compelled sailed away back, and they made a settlement in an island lying near the coast of Libya, called, as was said before, Platea. This island is said to be of the same size as the now existing city of Kyrene.

157. In this they continued to dwell two years; but as they had no prosperity, they left one of their number behind and all the rest sailed away to Delphi, and having come to the Oracle they consulted it, saying that they were dwelling in Libya and that, though they were dwelling there, they fared none the better: and the Pythian prophetess made answer to them thus:

"Better than I if thou knowest the Libyan land sheep-abounding,
Not having been there than I who have been, at thy wisdom I wonder."

Having heard this Battos and his companions sailed away back again; for in fact the god would not let them off from the task of settlement till they had come to Libya itself: and having arrived at the island and taken up him whom they had left, they made a settlement in Libya itself at a spot opposite the island, called Aziris, which is enclosed by most fair woods on both sides and a river flows by it on one side.

158. In this spot they dwelt for six years; and in the seventh year the Libyans persuaded them to leave it, making request and saying that they would conduct them to a better region. So the Libyans led them from that place making them start towards evening; and in order that the Hellenes might not see the fairest of all the regions as they passed through it, they led them past it by night, having calculated the time of daylight: and this region is called Irasa. Then having conducted them to the so-called spring of Apollo, they said, "Hellenes, here is a fit place for you to dwell, for here the heaven is pierced with holes."

159. Now during the lifetime of the first settler Battos, who reigned forty years, and of his son Arkesilaos, who reigned sixteen years, the Kyrenians continued to dwell there with the same number as when they first set forth to the colony; but in the time of the third king, called Battos the Prosperous, the Pythian prophetess gave an oracle wherein she urged the Hellenes in general to sail and join with the Kyrenians in colonizing Libya. For the Kyrenians invited them, giving promise of a division of land; and the oracle which she uttered was as follows:

"Who to the land much desirèd, to Libya, afterwards cometh,
After the land be divided, I say he shall some day repent it."

Then great numbers were gathered at Kyrene, and the Libyans who dwelt round had much land cut off from their possessions; therefore they with their king whose name was Adicran, as they were not only deprived of their country but also were dealt with very insolently by the Kyrenians, sent to Egypt and delivered themselves over to Apries king of Egypt. He then having gathered a great army of Egyptians, sent it against Kyrene; and the men of Kyrene marched out to the region of Irasa and to the spring Theste, and there both joined battle with the Egyptians and defeated them in the battle: for since the Egyptians had not before made trial of the Hellenes in fight and therefore despised them, they were so slaughtered that but few of them returned back to Egypt. In consequence of this and because they laid the blame of it upon Apries, the Egyptians revolted from him.

160. This Battos had a son called Arkesilaos, who first when he became king made a quarrel with his own brothers, until they finally departed to another region of Libya, and making the venture for themselves founded that city which was then and is now called Barca; and at the same time as they founded this, they induced the Libyans to revolt from the Kyrenians. After this, Arkesilaos made an expedition against those Libyans who had received them and who had also revolted from Kyrene, and the Libyans fearing him departed and fled towards the Eastern tribes of Libyans: and Arkesilaos followed after them as they fled, until he arrived in his pursuit at Leucon in Libya, and there the Libyans resolved to attack him. Accordingly they engaged battle and defeated the Kyrenians so utterly that seven thousand hoplites of the Kyrenians fell there. After this disaster Arkesilaos, being sick and having swallowed a potion, was strangled by his brother Haliarchos, and Haliarchos was killed treacherously by the wife of Arkesilaos, whose name was Eryxo.

161. Then Battos the son of Arkesilaos succeeded to the kingdom, who was lame and not sound in his feet: and the Kyrenians with a view to the misfortune which had befallen them sent men to Delphi to ask what form of rule they should adopt, in order to live in the best way possible; and the Pythian prophetess bade them take to themselves a reformer of their State from Mantineia of the Arcadians. The men of Kyrene accordingly made request, and those of Mantineia gave them the man of most repute among their citizens, whose name was Demonax. This man therefore having come to Kyrene and having ascertained all things exactly, in the first place caused them to have three tribes, distributing them thus:—one division he made of the Theraians and their dependents, another of the Peloponnesians and Cretans, and a third of all the islanders. Then secondly for the king Battos he set apart domains of land and priesthoods, but all the other powers which the kings used to possess before, he assigned as of public right to the people.

162. During the reign of this Battos things continued to be thus, but in the reign of his son Arkesilaos there arose much disturbance about the offices of the State: for Arkesilaos son of Battos the Lame and of Pheretime said that he would not suffer it to be according as the Mantineian Demonax had arranged, but asked to have back the royal rights of his forefathers. After this, stirring up strife he was worsted and went as an exile to Samos, and his mother to Salamis in Cyprus. Now at that time the ruler of Salamis was Euelthon, the same who dedicated as an offering the censer at Delphi, a work well worth seeing, which is placed in the treasury of the Corinthians. To him having come, Pheretime asked him for an army to restore herself and her son to Kyrene. Euelthon however was ready to give her anything else rather than that; and she when she received that which he gave her said that this too was a fair gift, but fairer still would be that other gift of an army for which she was asking. As she kept saying this to everything which was given, at last Euelthon sent out to her a present of a golden spindle and distaff, with wool also upon it: and when Pheretime uttered again the same saying about this present, Euelthon said that such things as this were given as gifts to women and not an army.

163. Arkesilaos meanwhile, being in Samos, was gathering everyone together by a promise of dividing land; and while a great host was being collected, Arkesilaos set out to Delphi to inquire of the Oracle about returning from exile: and the Pythian prophetess gave him this answer: "For four named Battos and four named Arkesilaos, eight genera-

tions of men, Loxias grants to you to be kings of Kyrene, but beyond this he counsels you not even to attempt it. Thou however must keep quiet when thou hast come back to thy land; and if thou findest the furnace full of jars, heat not the jars fiercely, but let them go with a fair wind: if however thou heat the furnace fiercely, enter not thou into the place flowed round by water; for if thou dost thou shalt die, both thou and the bull which is fairer than all the rest."

164. Thus the Pythian prophetess gave answer to Arkesilaos; and he, having taken to him those in Samos, made his return to Kyrene; and when he had got possession of the power, he did not remember the saying of the Oracle but endeavored to exact penalties from those of the opposite faction for having driven him out. Of these some escaped out of the country altogether, but some Arkesilaos got into his power and sent them away to Cyprus to be put to death. These were driven out of their course to Cnidos, and the men of Cnidos rescued them and sent them away to Thera. Some others however of the Kyrenians fled to a great tower belonging to Aglomachos a private citizen, and Arkesilaos burnt them by piling up brushwood round. Then after he had done the deed he perceived that the Oracle meant this, in that the Pythian prophetess forbade him, if he found the jars in the furnace, to heat them fiercely; and he voluntarily kept away from the city of the Kyrenians, fearing the death which had been prophesied by the Oracle and supposing that Kyrene was flowed round by water. Now he had to wife a kinswoman of his own, the daughter of the king of Barca whose name was Alazeir: to him he came, and men of Barca together with certain of the exiles from Kyrene, perceiving him going about in the market-place, killed him, and also besides him his father-in-law Alazeir. Arkesilaos accordingly, having missed the meaning of the oracle, whether with his will or against his will, fulfilled his own destiny.

165. His mother Pheretime meanwhile, so long as Arkesilaos having worked evil for himself dwelt at Barca, herself held the royal power of her son at Kyrene, both exercising his other rights and also sitting in council: but when she heard that her son had been slain in Barca, she departed and fled to Egypt: for she had on her side services done for Cambyses the son of Cyrus by Arkesilaos, since this was the Arkesilaos who had given over Kyrene to Cambyses and had laid a tribute upon himself. Pheretime then having come to Egypt sat down as a suppliant of Aryandes, bidding him help her, and alleging as a reason that it was on account of his inclination to the side of the Medes that her son had been slain. 166. Now this Aryandes had been appointed ruler of the province of Egypt by Cambyses; and after the time of these events he lost his life because he would measure himself with Dareios. For having heard and seen that Dareios desired to leave behind him as a memorial of himself a thing which had not been made by any other king, he imitated him, until at last he received his reward: for whereas Dareios refined gold and made it as pure as possible, and of this caused coins to be struck, Aryandes, being ruler of Egypt, did the same thing with silver; and even now the purest silver is that which is called Aryandic. Dareios then having learnt that he was doing this put him to death, bringing against him another charge of attempting rebellion.

167. Now at the time of which I speak this Aryandes had compassion on Pheretime and gave her all the troops that were in Egypt, both the land and the sea forces, appointing Amasis a Maraphian to command the land-army and Badres, of the race of the Pasargadai, to command the fleet: but before he sent away the army, Aryandes dispatched a herald to Barca and asked who it was who had killed Arkesilaos; and the men of Barca

all took it upon themselves, for they said they suffered formerly many great evils at his hands. Having heard this, Aryandes at last sent away the army together with Pheretime. This charge then was the pretext alleged; but in fact the army was being sent out (as I believe) for the purpose of subduing Libya: for of the Libyans there are many nations of nations of various kinds, and but few of them are subject to the king, while the greater number paid no regard to Dareios.

168. Now the Libyans have their dwelling as follows:—Beginning from Egypt, first of the Libyans are settled the Adyrmachidai, who practice for the most part the same customs as the Egyptians, but wear clothing similar to that of the other Libyans. Their women wear a bronze ring upon each leg, and they have long hair on their heads, and when they catch their lice, each one bites her own in retaliation and then throws them away. These are the only people of the Lybians who do this; and they alone display to the king their maidens when they are about to be married, and whosoever of them proves to be pleasing to the king is deflowered by him. These Adyrmachidai extend along the coast from Egypt as far as the port which is called Plynos.

169. Next after these come the Giligamai, occupying the country towards the West as far as the island of Aphrodisias. In the space within this limit lies off the coast the island of Platea, where the Kyrenians made their settlement; and on the coast of the mainland there is Port Menelaos, and Aziris, where the Kyrenians used to dwell. From this point begins the *silphion* and it extends along the coast from the island of Platea as far as the entrance of the Syrtis. This nation practices customs nearly resembling those of the rest.

170. Next to the Giligamai on the West are the Asbystai: these dwell above Kyrene, and the Asbystai do not reach down the sea, for the region along the sea is occupied by Kyrenians. These most of all the Libyans are drivers of four-horse chariots, and in the greater number of their customs they endeavor to imitate the Kyrenians.

171. Next after the Asbystai on the West come the Auchisai: these dwell above Barca and reach down to the sea by Euesperides: and in the middle of the country of the Auchisai dwell the Bacales, a small tribe, who reach down to the sea by the city of Taucheira in the territory of Barca: these practice the same customs as those above Kyrene.

172. Next after these Auschisai towards the West come the Nasamonians, a numerous race, who in the summer leave their flocks behind by the sea and go up to the region of Augila to gather the fruit of the date-palms, which grow in great numbers and very large and are all fruit-bearing: these hunt the wingless locusts, and they dry them in the sun and then pound them up, and after that they sprinkle them upon milk and drink them. Their custom is for each man to have many wives, and they make their intercourse with them common in nearly the same manner as the Massagetai, that is they set up a staff in front of the door and so have intercourse. When a Nasamonian man marries his first wife, the custom is for the bride on the first night to go through the whole number of the guests having intercourse with them, and each man when he has lain with her gives a gift, whatsoever he has brought with him from his house. The forms of oath and of divination which they use are as follows:—they swear by the men among themselves who are reported to have been the most righteous and brave, by these, I say, laying hands upon their tombs; and they divine by visiting the sepulchral mounds of their ancestors and lying down to sleep upon them after having prayed; and whatsoever thing the man sees in his dream, this he accepts. They practice also the exchange of pledges in the following manner, that is to say, one gives the other to drink from his hand, and drinks himself from

the hand of the other; and if they have no liquid, they take of the dust from the ground and lick it.

173. Adjoining the Nasamonians is the country of the Psylloi. These have perished utterly in the following manner:—The South Wind blowing upon them dried up all their cisterns of water, and their land was waterless, lying all within the Syrtis. They then having taken a resolve by common consent, marched in arms against the South Wind (I report that which is reported by the Libyans), and when they had arrived at the sandy tract, the South Wind blew and buried them in the sand. These then having utterly perished, the Nasamonians from that time forward possess their land.

174. Above these towards the South Wind in the region of wild beasts dwell the Garamantians, who fly from every man and avoid the company of all; and they neither possess any weapon of war, nor know how to defend themselves against enemies.

175. These dwell above the Nasamonians; and next to the Nasamonians along the sea coast towards the West come the Macai, who shave their hair so as to leave tufts, letting the middle of their hair grow long, but round this on all sides shaving it close to the skin; and for fighting they carry shields made of ostrich skins. Through their land the river Kinyps runs out into the sea, flowing from a hill called the "Hill of the Charites." This Hill of the Charites is overgrown thickly with wood, while the rest of Libya which has been spoken of before is bare of trees; and the distance from the sea to this hill is two hundred furlongs.

176. Next to these Macai are the Gindanes, whose women wear each of them a number of anklets made of the skins of animals, for the following reason, as it is said:—for every man who has commerce with her she binds on an anklet, and the woman who has most is esteemed the best, since she has been loved by the greatest number of men.

177. In a peninsula which stands out into the sea from the land of these Gindanes dwell the Lotophagoi, who live by eating the fruit of the *lotos* only. Now the fruit of the lotos is in size like that of the mastich-tree, and in flavor it resembles that of the date-palm. Of this fruit the Lotophagoi even make for themselves wine.

178. Next after the Lotophagoi along the sea-coast are the Machlyans, who also make use of the lotos, but less than those above mentioned. These extend to a great river named the river Triton, and this runs out into a great lake called Tritonis, in which there is an island named Phla. About this island they say there was an oracle given to the Lacedemonians that they should make a settlement in it.

179. The following moreover is also told, namely that Jason, when the Argo had been completed by him under Mount Pelion, put into it a hecatomb and with it also a tripod of bronze, and sailed round Pelopponese, desiring to come to Delphi; and when in sailing he got near Malea, a North Wind seized his ship and carried it off to Libya, and before he caught sight of land he had come to be in the shoals of the lake Tritonis. Then as he was at a loss how he should bring his ship forth, the story goes that Triton appeared to him and bade Jason give him the tripod, saying that he would show them the right course and let them go away without hurt: and when Jason consented to it, then Triton showed them the passage out between the shoals and set the tripod in his own temple, after having first uttered a prophecy over the tripod and having declared to Jason and his company the whole matter, namely that whensoever one of the descendants of those who sailed with him in the Argo should carry away this tripod, then it was determined by fate that a

hundred cities of Hellenes should be established about the lake Tritonis. Having heard this the native Libyans concealed the tripod.

180. Next to these Machlyans are the Auseans. These and the Machlyans dwell round the lake Tritonis, and the river Triton is the boundary between them: and while the Machlyans grow their hair long at the back of the head, the Auseans do so in front. At a yearly festival of Athene their maidens take their stand in two parties and fight against one another with stones and staves, and they say that in doing so they are fulfilling the rites handed down by their fathers for the divinity who was sprung from that land, whom we call Athene: and those of the maidens who die of the wounds received they call "false-maidens." But before they let them begin the fight they do this:—all join together and equip the maiden who is judged to be the fairest on each occasion, with a Corinthian helmet and with full Hellenic armor, and then causing her to go up into a chariot they conduct her round the lake. Now I cannot tell with what they equipped the maidens in old time, before the Hellenes were settled near them; but I suppose that they used to be equipped with Egyptian armor, for it is from Egypt that both the shield and the helmet have come to the Hellenes, as I affirm. They say moreover that Athene is the daughter of Poseidon and of the lake Tritonis, and that she had some cause of complaint against her father and therefore gave herself to Zeus, and Zeus made her his own daughter. Such is the story which these tell; and they have their intercourse with women in common, not marrying but having intercourse like cattle: and when the child of any woman has grown big, he is brought before a meeting of the men held within three months of that time, and whomsoever of the men the child resembles, his son he is accounted to be.

181. Thus then have been mentioned those nomad Libyans who live along the sea-coast: and above these inland is the region of Libya which has wild beasts; and above the wild-beast region there stretches a raised belt of sand, extending from Thebes of the Egyptians to the Pillars of Heracles. In this belt at intervals of about ten days' journey there are fragments of salt in great lumps forming hills, and at the top of each hill there shoots up from the middle of the salt a spring of water cold and sweet; and about the spring dwell men, at the furthest limit towards the desert, and above the wild-beast region. First, at a distance of ten days' journey from Thebes, are the Ammonians, whose temple is derived from that of the Theban Zeus, for the image of Zeus in Thebes also, as I have said before, has the head of a ram. These, as it chances, have also other water of a spring, which in the early morning is warm; at the time when the market fills, cooler; when midday comes, it is quite cold, and then they water their gardens; but as the day declines, it abates from its coldness, until at last, when the sun sets, the water is warm; and it continues to increase in heat still more until it reaches midnight, when it boils and throws up bubbles; and when midnight passes, it becomes cooler gradually till dawn of day. This spring is called the fountain of the Sun.

182. After the Ammonians, as you go on along the belt of sand, at an interval again of ten days' journey there is a hill of salt like that of the Ammonians, and a spring of water, with men dwelling about it; and the name of this place is Augila. To this the Nasamonians come year by year to gather the fruit of the date-palms.

183. From Augila at a distance again of ten days' journey there is another hill of salt and spring of water and a great number of fruit-bearing date-palms, as there are also in the other places: and men dwell here who are called the Garmantians, a very great nation, who carry earth to lay over the salt and then sow crops. From this point is the shortest

way to the Lotophagoi, for from these it is a journey of thirty days to the country of the Garmantians. Among them also are produced the cattle which feed backwards; and they feed backwards for this reason, because they have their horns bent down forwards, and therefore they walk backwards as they feed; for forwards they cannot go, because the horns run into the ground in front of them; but in nothing else do they differ from other cattle except in this and in the thickness and firmness to the touch of their hide. These Garamantians of whom I speak hunt the "Cave-dwelling" Ethiopians with their four-horse chariots, for the Cave-dwelling Ethiopians are the swiftest of foot of all men about whom we hear report made: and the Cave-dwellers feed upon serpents and lizards and such creeping things, and they use a language which resembles no other, for in it they squeak just like bats.

184. From the Garmantians at a distance again of ten days' journey there is another hill of salt and spring of water, and men dwell round it called Atarantians, who alone of all men about whom we know are nameless; for while all taken together have the name Atarantians, each separate man of them has no name given to him. These utter curses against the Sun when he is at his height, and moreover revile him with all manner of foul terms, because he oppresses them by his burning heat, both themselves and their land. After this at a distance of ten days' journey there is another hill of salt and spring of water, and men dwell round it. Near this salt hill is a mountain named Atlas, which is small in circuit and rounded on every side; and so exceedingly lofty is it said to be, that it is not possible to see its summits, for clouds never leave them either in the summer or in the winter. This the natives say is the pillar of the heaven. After this mountain these men got their name, for they are called Atlantians; and it is said that they neither eat anything that has life nor have any dreams.

185. As far as these Atlantians I am able to mention in order the names of those who are settled in the belt of sand; but for the parts beyond these I can do so no more. However, the belt extends as far as the Pillars of Heracles and also in the parts outside them: and there is a mine of salt in it at a distance of ten days' journey from the Atlantians, and men dwelling there; and these all have their houses built of the lumps of salt, since these parts of Libya which we have now reached are without rain; for if it rained, the walls being made of salt would not be able to last: and the salt is dug up there both white and purple in color. Above the sand-belt, in the parts which are in the direction of the South Wind and towards the interior of Libya, the country is uninhabited, without water and without wild beasts, rainless and treeless, and there is no trace of moisture in it.

186. I have said that from Egypt as far as the lake Tritonis Libyans dwell who are nomads, eating flesh and drinking milk; and these do not taste at all of the flesh of cows, for the same reason as the Egyptians also abstain from it, nor do they keep swine. Moreover the women of the Kyrenians too think it not right to eat cows' flesh, because of the Egyptian Isis, and they even keep fasts and celebrate festivals for her; and the women of Barca, in addition from cows' flesh, do not taste of swine either.

187. Thus it is with these matters: but in the region to the West of lake Tritonis the Libyans cease to be nomads, and they do not practice the same customs, nor do to their children anything like that which the nomads are wont to do; for the nomad Libyans, whether all of them I cannot say for certain, but many of them, do as follows:—when their children are four years old, they burn with a greasy piece of sheep's wool the veins in the crowns of their heads, and some of them burn the veins of the temples, so that for all their

lives to come the cold humor may not run down from their heads and do them hurt: and for this reason it is (they say) that they are so healthy; for the Libyans are in truth the most healthy of all races concerning which we have knowledge, whether for this reason or not I cannot say for certain, but the most healthy they certainly are: and if, when they burn the children, a convulsion comes on, they have found out a remedy for this; for they pour upon them the water of a he-goat and so save them. I report that which is reported by the Libyans themselves.

188. The following is the manner of sacrifice which the nomads have:—they cut off a part of the animal's ear as a first offering and throw it over the house, and having done this they twist its neck. They sacrifice only to the Sun and the Moon; that is to say, to these all the Libyans sacrifice, but those who dwell round the lake Tritonis sacrifice most of all to Athene, and next to Triton and Poseidon.

189. It would appear also that the Hellenes made the dress and the *aigis* of the images of Athene after the model of the Libyan women; for except that the dress of the Libyan women is of leather, and the tassels which hang from their *aigis* are not formed of serpents but of leather thongs, in all other respects Athene is dressed like them. Moreover the name too declares that the dress of the figures of Pallas has come from Libya, for the Libyan women wear over their other garments bare goat-skins (*aigeas*) with tasseled fringes and colored over with red madder, and from the name of these goat-skins the Hellenes formed the name *aigis*. I think also that in these regions first arose the practice of crying aloud during the performance of sacred rites, for the Libyan women do this very well. The Hellenes learnt from the Libyans also the yoking together of four horses.

190. The nomads bury those who die just in the same manner as the Hellenes, except only the Nasamonians: these bury bodies in a sitting posture, taking care at the moment when the man expires to place him sitting and not to let him die lying down on his back. They have dwellings composed of the stems of asphodel entwined with rushes, and so made that they can be carried about. Such are the customs followed by these tribes.

191. On the West of the river Triton next after the Auseans come Libyans who are tillers of the soil, and whose custom it is to possess fixed habitations; and they are called Maxyans. They grow their hair long on the right side of their heads and cut it short upon the left, and smear their bodies over with red ochre. These say that they are of the men who came from Troy.

This country and the rest of Libya which is towards the West is both much more frequented by wild beasts and much more thickly wooded than the country of the nomads: for whereas the part of Libya which is situated towards the East, where the nomads dwell, is low-lying and sandy up to the river Triton, that which succeeds it towards the West, the country of those who till the soil, is exceedingly mountainous and thickly-wooded and full of wild beasts: for in the land of these are found both the monstrous serpent and the lion and the elephant, and bears and venomous snakes and horned asses, besides the dog-headed men, and the headless men with their eyes set in their breasts (at least so say the Libyans about them), and the wild men and wild women, and a great multitude of other beasts which are not fabulous like these.

192. In the land of the nomads however there exist none of these, but other animals as follows:—white-rump antelopes, gazelles, buffaloes, asses, not the horned kind but others which go without water (for in fact these never drink), oryes, whose horns are made into the sides of the Phoenician lyre (this animal is in size about equal to an ox), small foxes,

hyenas, porcupines, wild rams, wolves, jackals, panthers, boryes, land-crocodiles about three cubits in length and very much resembling lizards, ostriches, and small snakes, each with one horn: these wild animals there are in this country, as well as those which exist elsewhere, except the stag and the wild-boar; but Libya has no stags nor wild boars at all. Also there are in this country three kinds of mice, one is called the "two-legged" mouse, another the *zegeris* (a name which is Libyan and signifies in the Hellenic tongue a "hill"), and a third the "prickly" mouse. There are also weasels produced in the *silphion*, which are very like those of Tartessos. Such are the wild animals which the land of the Libyans possesses, so far as we were able to discover by inquiries extended as much as possible.

193. Next to the Maxyan Libyans are the Zauekes, whose women drive their chariots for them to war.

194. Next to these are the Gyzantes, among whom honey is made in great quantity by bees, but in much greater quantity still it is said to be made by men, who work at it as a trade. However that may be, these all smear themselves over with red ochre and eat monkeys, which are produced in very great numbers upon their mountains.

195. Opposite these, as the Carthaginians say, there lies an island called Kyrauis, two hundred furlongs in length but narrow, to which one may walk over from the mainland; and it is full of olives and vines. In it they say there is a pool, from which the native girls with birds' feathers smeared over with pitch bring up gold-dust out of the mud. Whether this is really so I do not know, but I write that which is reported; and nothing is impossible, for even in Zakynthos I saw myself pitch brought up out of a pool of water. There are there several pools, and the largest of them measures seventy feet each way and is two fathoms in depth. Into this they plunge a pole with a myrtle-branch bound to it, and then with the branch of the myrtle they bring up pitch, which has the smell of asphalt, but in other respects it is superior to the pitch of Pieria. This they pour into a pit dug near the pool; and when they have collected a large quantity, then they pour it into the jars from the pit: and whatever thing falls into the pool goes under ground and reappears in the sea, which is distant about four furlongs from the pool. Thus then the report about the island lying near the coast of Libya is also probably enough true.

196. The Carthaginians say also this, namely that there is a place in Libya and men dwelling there, outside the Pillars of Heracles, to whom when they have come and have taken the merchandise forth from their ships, they set it in order along the beach and embark again in their ships, and after that they raise a smoke; and the natives of the country seeing the smoke come to the sea, and then they lay down gold as an equivalent for the merchandise and retire to a distance away from the merchandise. The Carthaginians upon that disembark and examine it, and if the gold is in their opinion sufficient for the value of the merchandise, they take it up and go their way; but if not, they embark again in their ships and sit there; and the others approach and straightway add more gold to the former, until they satisfy them: and they say that neither party wrongs the other; for neither do the Carthaginians lay hands on the gold until it is made equal to the value of their merchandise, nor do the others lay hands on the merchandise until the Carthaginians have taken the gold.

197. These are the Libyan tribes whom we are able to name; and of these the greater number neither now pay any regard to the king of the Medes nor did they then. Thus much also I have to say about this land, namely that it is occupied by four races and no more, so far as we know; and of these races two are natives of the soil and the other two

not so; for the Libyans and the Ethiopians are natives, the one race dwelling in the Northern parts of Libya and the other in the Southern, while the Phoenicians and the Hellenes are strangers.

198. I think moreover that (besides other things) in goodness of soil Libya does not very greatly excel as compared with Asia or Europe, except only the region of Kinyps, for the same name is given to the land as to the river. This region is equal to the best of lands in bringing forth the fruit of Demeter, nor does it at all resemble the rest of Libya; for it has black soil and is watered by springs, and neither has it fear of drought nor is it hurt by drinking too abundantly of rain; for rain there is in this part of Libya. Of the produce of the crops the same measures hold good here as for the Babylonian land. And that is good land also which the Euesperites occupy, for when it bears best it produces a hundred-fold, but the land in the region of Kinyps produces sometimes as much as three-hundred-fold.

199. Moreover the land of Kyrene, which is the highest land of the part of Libya which is occupied by nomads, has within its confines three seasons of harvest, at which we may marvel: for the parts by the sea-coasts first have their fruits ripe for reaping and for gathering the vintage; and when these have been gathered in, the parts which lie above the sea-side places, those situated in the middle, which they call the hills, are ripe for the gathering in; and as soon as this middle crop has been gathered in, that in the highest part of the land comes to perfection and is ripe; so that by the time the first crop has been eaten and drunk up, the last is just coming in. Thus the harvest for the Kyrenians lasts eight months. Let so much as has been said suffice for these things.

200. Now when the Persian helpers of Pheretime, having been sent from Egypt by Aryandes, had arrived at Barca, they laid siege to the city, proposing to the inhabitants that they should give up those who were guilty of the murder of Arkesilaos: but as all their people had taken a share in the guilt, they did not accept the proposals. Then they besieged Barca for nine months, both digging underground passages which led to the wall and making vigorous attacks upon it. Now the passages dug were discovered by a worker of bronze with a shield covered over with bronze, who had thought of a plan as follows:— carrying it round within the wall he applied it to the ground in the city, and whereas the other places to which he applied it were noiseless, at those places where digging was going on the bronze of the shield gave a sound; and the men of Barca would make a counter-mine there and slay the Persians who were digging mines. This then was discovered as I have said, and the attacks were repulsed by the men of Barca.

201. Then as they were suffering hardship for a long time and many were falling on both sides, and especially on that of the Persians, Amasis the commander of the land-army contrived as follows:—perceiving that the Barcaians were not to be conquered by force but might be conquered by guile, he dug by night a broad trench and over it he laid timber of no great strength, and brought earth and laid it above on the top of the timber, making it level with the rest of the ground: then at daybreak he invited the men of Barca to a parley; and they gladly consented, and at last they agreed to make a treaty: and the treaty they made with one another was taken over the hidden trench, namely that so long as this earth should continue to be as it was, so long the oath should remain firm, and that the men of Barca should promise to pay tribute of due amount to the king, and the Persians should do no further violence to the men of Barca. After the oath the men of Barca trusting to these engagements both went forth themselves from their city and let any who desired it of the enemy pass within their walls, having opened all the gates; but

the Persians first broke down the concealed bridge and then began to run inside the city wall. And the reason why they broke down the bridge which they had made was that they might keep their oaths, since they had sworn to the men of Barca that the oath should remain firm continually for so long time as the earth should remain as it then was, but after that they had broken it down, the oath no longer remained firm.

202. Now the most guilty of the Barcaians, when they were delivered to her by the Persians, Pheretime impaled in a ring round about the wall; and she cut off the breasts of their wives and set the wall round with these also in order: but the rest of the men of Barca she bade the Persians carry off as spoil, except so many of them as were of the house of Battos and not sharers in the guilt of the murder; and to these Pheretime gave the city in charge.

203. So the Persians having made slaves of the rest of the Barcaians departed to go back: and when they appeared at the gates of the city of Kyrene, the Kyrenians let them go through their town in order to avoid neglect of some oracle. Then as the army was going through, Badres the commander of the fleet urged that they should capture the city, but Amasis the commander of the land-army would not consent to it; for he said that they had been sent against no other city of the Hellenes except Barca. When however they had passed through and were encamping on the hill of Zeus Lycaios, they repented of not having taken possession of Kyrene; and they endeavored again to pass into it, but the men of Kyrene would not allow them. Then upon the Persians, although no one fought against them, there fell a sudden panic, and they ran away for about sixty furlongs and then encamped. And when the camp had been placed here, there came to it a messenger from Aryandes summoning them back; so the Persians asked the Kyrenians to give them provisions for their march and obtained their request; and having received these, they departed to go to Egypt. After this the Libyans took them up, and killed for the sake of their clothes and equipment those of them who at any time were left or straggled behind, until at last they came to Egypt.

204. This army of the Persians reached Euesperides, and this was their furthest point in Libya: and those of the Barcaians whom they had reduced to slavery they removed again from Egypt and brought them to the king, and king Dareios gave them a village in the land of Bactria in which to make a settlement. To this village they gave the name of Barca, and it still continued to be inhabited by them even down to my own time, in the land of Bactria.

205. Pheretime however did not bring her life happily to an end any more than they: for as soon as she had returned from Libya to Egypt after having avenged herself on the Barcaians, she died an evil death, having become suddenly full of worms while yet alive: for, as it seems, too severe punishments inflicted by men prove displeasing to the gods. Such and so great was the punishment inflicted by Pheretime the wife of Battos on the men of Barca.

ૐ 5 ૐ

THE FIFTH BOOK OF THE
HISTORIES, CALLED TERPSICHORE

1. In the meantime those of the Persians who had been left behind in Europe by Dareios, of whom Megabazos was the commander, had subdued the people of Perinthos first of the Hellespontians, since they refused to be subject to Dareios. These had in former times also been hardly dealt with by the Paionians: for the Paionians from the Strymon had been commanded by an oracle of their god to march against the Perinthians; and if the Perinthians, when encamped opposite to them, should shout aloud and call to them by their name, they were to attack them; but if they should not shout to them, they were not to attack them: and thus the Paionians proceeded to do. Now when the Perinthians were encamped opposite to them in the suburb of their city, a challenge was made and a single combat took place in three different forms; for they matched a man against a man, and a horse against a horse, and a dog against a dog. Then, as the Perinthians were getting the better in two of the three, in their exultation they raised a shout of *paion*, and the Paionians conjectured that this was the very thing which was spoken of in the oracle, and said doubtless to one another, "Now surely the oracle is being accomplished for us, now it is time for us to act." So the Paionians attacked the Perinthians when they had raised the shout of paion, and they had much the better in the fight, and left but few of them alive.

2. Thus it happened with respect to those things which had been done to them in former times by the Paionians; and at this time, although the Perinthians proved themselves brave men in defense of their freedom, the Persians and Megabazos got the better of them by numbers. Then after Perinthos had been conquered, Megabazos marched his army through the length of Thracia, forcing every city and every race of those who dwell there to submit to the king, for so it had been commanded him by Dareios, to subdue Thracia.

3. Now the Thracian race is the most numerous, except the Indians, in all the world: and if it should come to be ruled over by one man, or to agree together in one, it would be irresistible in fight and the strongest by far of all nations, in my opinion. Since however

this is impossible for them and cannot ever come to pass among them, they are in fact weak for that reason. They have many names, belonging to their various tribes in different places; but they all follow customs which are nearly the same in all respects, except the Getai and Trausians and those who dwell above the Crestonians.

4. Of these the practices of the Getai, who believe themselves to be immortal, have been spoken of by me already: and the Trausians perform everything else in the same manner as the other Thracians, but in regard to those who are born and die among them they do as follows:—when a child has been born, the nearest of kin sit round it and make lamentation for all the evils of which he must fulfil the measure, now that he is born, enumerating the whole number of human ills; but when a man is dead, they cover him up in the earth with sport and rejoicing, saying at the same time from what great evils he has escaped and is now in perfect bliss.

5. Those who dwell above the Crestonians do as follows:—each man has many wives, and when any man of them is dead, a great competition takes place among his wives, with much exertion on the part of their friends, about the question of which of them was most loved by their husband; and she who is preferred by the decision and so honored, is first praised by both men and women, then her throat is cut over the tomb by her nearest of kin, and afterwards she is buried together with her husband; and the others are exceedingly grieved at it, for this is counted as the greatest reproach to them.

6. Of the other Thracians the custom is to sell their children to be carried away out of the country; and over their maidens they do not keep watch, but allow them to have commerce with whatever men they please, but over their wives they keep very great watch; and they buy their wives for great sums of money from their parents. To be pricked with figures is accounted a mark of noble rank, and not to be so marked is a sign of low birth. Not to work is counted most honorable, and to be a worker of the soil is above all things dishonorable: to live on war and plunder is the most honorable thing.

7. These are their most remarkable customs; and of the gods they worship only Ares and Dionysos and Artemis. Their kings, however, apart from the rest of the people, worship Hermes more than all gods, and swear by him alone; and they say that they are descended from Hermes. 8. The manner of burial for the rich among them is this:—for three days they expose the corpse to view, and they slay all kinds of victims and feast, having first made lamentation. Then they perform the burial rites, either consuming the body with fire or covering it up in the earth without burning; and afterwards when they have heaped up a mound they celebrate games with every kind of contest, in which reasonably the greatest prizes are assigned for single combat. This is the manner of burial among the Thracians.

9. Of the region lying further on towards the North of this country no one can declare accurately who the men are who dwell in it; but the parts which lie immediately beyond the Ister are known to be uninhabited and vast in extent. The only men of whom I can hear who dwell beyond the Ister are those who are said to be called Sigynnai, and who use the Median fashion of dress. Their horses, it is said, have shaggy hair all over their bodies, as much as five fingers long; and these are small and flat-nosed and too weak to carry men, but when yoked in chariots they are very high-spirited; therefore the natives of the country drive chariots. The boundaries of this people extend, it is said, to the parts near the Enetoi, who live on the Adriatic; and people say that they are colonists from the

Medes. In what way however these have come to be colonists from the Medes I am not able for my part to conceive, but everything is possible in the long course of ages. However that may be, the Ligurians who dwell in the region inland above Massalia call traders *sigynnai*, and the men of Cyprus give the same name to spears.

10. Now the Thracians say that the other side of the Ister is occupied by bees, and that by reason of them it is not possible to pass through and proceed further: but to me it seems that when they so speak, they say that which is not probable; for these creatures are known to be intolerant of cold, and to me it seems that the regions which go up towards the pole are uninhabitable by reason of the cold climate. These then are the tales reported about this country; and however that may be, Megabazos was then making the coast-regions of it subject to the Persians.

11. Meanwhile Dareios, so soon as he had crossed over the Hellespont and come to Sardis, called to mind the service rendered to him by Histiaios the Milesian and also the advice of the Mytilenian Coës, and having sent for them to come to Sardis he offered them a choice of rewards. Histiaios then, being despot of Miletos, did not make request for any government in addition to that, but he asked for the district of Myrkinos which belonged to the Edonians, desiring there to found a city. Histiaios chose this for himself; but Coës, not being a despot but a man of the people, asked to be made despot of Mitylene.

12. After the desires of both had been fulfilled, they betook themselves to that which they had chosen: and at this same time it chanced that Dareios saw a certain thing which made him desire to command Megabazos to conquer the Paionians and remove them forcibly from Europe into Asia: and the thing was this:—There were certain Paionians named Pigres and Mantyas, who when Dareios had crossed over into Asia, came to Sardis, because they desired themselves to have rule over the Paionians, and with them they brought their sister, who was tall and comely. Then having watched for a time when Dareios took his seat publicly in the suburb of the Lydian city, they dressed up their sister in the best way they could, and sent her to fetch water, having a water-jar upon her head and leading a horse after her by a bridle round her arm, and at the same time spinning flax. Now when the woman passed out of the city by him, Dareios paid attention to the matter, for that which was done by the woman was not of Persian nor yet of Lydian fashion, nor indeed after the manner of any people of Asia. He sent therefore some of his spearmen, bidding them watch what the woman would do with the horse. They accordingly followed after her; and she having arrived at the river watered the horse, and having watered him and filled her jar with the water, she passed along by the same way, bearing the water upon her head, leading the horse after her by a bridle round her arm, and at the same time turning the spindle.

13. Then Dareios, marveling both at that which he heard from those who went to observe and also at that which he saw himself, bade them bring her into his presence: and when she was brought, her brothers also came, who had been watching these things at no great distance off. So then when Dareios asked of what country she was, the young men said that they were Paionians and that she was their sister; and he replied: "Who then are these Paionians, and where upon the earth do they dwell?" and he asked them also what they desired, that they had come to Sardis. They declared to him that they had come to give themselves up to him, and that Paionia was a country situated upon the river Strymon, and that the Strymon was not far from the Hellespont, and finally that they were

colonists from the Teucrians of Troy. All these things severally they told him; and he asked whether all the women of that land were as industrious as their sister; and they very readily replied to this also, saying that it was so, for it was with a view to that very thing that they had been doing this.

14. Then Dareios wrote a letter to Megabazos, whom he had left to command his army in Thrace, bidding him remove the Paionians from their place of habitation and bring them to the king, both themselves and their children and their wives. Then forthwith a horseman set forth to ride in haste bearing the message to the Hellespont, and having passed over to the other side he gave the paper to Megabazos. So he having read it and having obtained guides from Thrace, set forth to march upon Paionia:

15. and the Paionians, being informed that the Persians were coming against them, gathered all their powers together and marched out in the direction of the sea, supposing that the Persians when they invaded them would make their attack on that side. The Paionians then were prepared, as I say, to drive off the army of Megabazos when it came against them; but the Persians hearing that the Paionians had gathered their powers and were guarding the entrance which lay towards the sea, directed their course with guides along the upper road; and passing unperceived by the Paionians they fell upon their cities, which were left without men, and finding them without defenders they easily took possession of them. The Paionians when they heard that their cities were in the hands of the enemy, at once dispersed, each tribe to its own place of abode, and proceeded to deliver themselves up to the Persians. Thus then it happened that these tribes of the Paionians, namely the Siropaionians, the Paioplians and all up to the lake Prasias, were removed from their place of habitation and brought to Asia;

16, but those who dwell about mount Pangaion, and about the Doberians and Agrianians and Odomantians, and about the lake Prasias itself, were not conquered at all by Megabazos. He tried however to remove even those who lived in the lake and who had their dwellings in the following manner:—a platform fastened together and resting upon lofty piles stood in the middle of the water of the lake, with a narrow approach to it from the mainland by a single bridge. The piles which supported the platform were no doubt originally set there by all the members of the community working together, but since that time they continue to set them by observance of this rule, that is to say, every man who marries brings from the mountain called Orbelos three piles for each wife and sets them as supports; and each man takes to himself many wives. And they have their dwelling thus, that is each man has possession of a hut upon the platform in which he lives and of a trapdoor leading through the platform down to the lake: and their infant children they tie with a rope by the foot, for fear that they should roll into the water. To their horses and beasts of burden they give fish for fodder; and of fish there is so great quantity that if a man open the trap-door and let down an empty basket by a cord into the lake, after waiting quite a short time he draws it up again full of fish. Of the fish there are two kinds, and they call them *paprax* and *tilon*.

17. So then those of the Paionians who had been conquered were being brought to Asia: and Megabazos meanwhile, after he had conquered the Paionians, sent as envoys to Macedonia seven Persians, who after himself were the men of most repute in the army. These were being sent to Amyntas to demand of him earth and water for Dareios the king. Now from lake Prasias there is a very short way into Macedonia; for first, quite close to

the lake, there is the mine from which after this time there came in regularly a talent of silver every day to Alexander; and after the mine, when you have passed over the mountain called Dysoron, you are in Macedonia.

18. These Persians then, who had been sent to Amyntas, having arrived came into the presence of Amyntas and proceeded to demand earth and water for king Dareios. This he was willing to give, and also he invited them to be his guests; and he prepared a magnificent dinner and received the Persians with friendly hospitality. Then when dinner was over, the Persians while drinking pledges to one another said thus: "Macedonian guest-friend, it is the custom among us Persians, when we set forth a great dinner, then to bring in also our concubines and lawful wives to sit beside us. Do thou then, since thou didst readily receive us and dost now entertain us magnificently as thy guests, and since thou art willing to give to king Dareios earth and water, consent to follow our custom." To this Amyntas replied: "Persians, among us the custom is not so, but that men should be separate from women. Since however ye being our masters make this request in addition, this also shall be given you." Having so said Amyntas proceeded to send for the women; and when they came being summoned, they sat down in order opposite to the Persians. Then the Persians, seeing women of comely form, spoke to Amyntas and said that this which had been done was by no means well devised; for it was better that the women should not come at all, than that they should come and should not seat themselves by their side, but sit opposite and be a pain to their eyes. So Amyntas being compelled bade them sit by the side of the Persians; and when the women obeyed, forthwith the Persians, being much intoxicated, began to touch their breasts, and some no doubt also tried to kiss them.

19. Amyntas seeing this kept quiet, notwithstanding that he felt anger, because he excessively feared the Persians; but Alexander the son of Amyntas, who was present and saw this, being young and without experience of calamity was not able to endure any longer; but being impatient of it he said to Amyntas: "My father, do thou grant that which thy age demands, and go away to rest, nor persevere longer in the drinking; but I will remain here and give to our guests all that is convenient." On this Amyntas, understanding that Alexander was intending to do some violence, said: "My son, I think that I understand thy words, as the heat of anger moves thee, namely that thou desirest to send me away and then do some deed of violence: therefore I ask of thee not to do violence to these men, that it may not be our ruin, but endure to see that which is being done: as to my departure, however, in that I will do as thou sayest."

20. When Amyntas after having made of him this request had departed, Alexander said to the Persians: "With these women ye have perfect freedom, guests, to have commerce with all, if ye so desire, or with as many of them as ye will. About this matter ye shall be they who give the word; but now, since already the hour is approaching for you to go to bed and I see that ye have well drunk, let these women go away, if so it is pleasing to you, to bathe themselves; and when they have bathed, then receive them back into your company." Having so said, since the Persians readily agreed, he dismissed the women, when they had gone out, to the women's chambers; and Alexander himself equipped men equal in number to the women and smooth-faced, in the dress of the women, and giving them daggers he led them into the banqueting-room; and as he led them in, he said thus to the Persians: "Persians, it seems to me that ye have been entertained with a feast to which nothing was wanting; for other things, as many as we had,

and moreover such as we were able to find out and furnish, are all supplied to you, and there is this especially besides, which is the chief thing of all, that is, we give you freely in addition our mothers and our sisters, in order that ye may perceive fully that ye are honored by us with that treatment which ye deserve, and also in order that ye may report to the king who sent you that a man of Hellas, ruler under him of the Macedonians, entertained you well at board and bed." Having thus said Alexander caused a Macedonian man in the guise of a woman to sit by each Persian, and they, when the Persians attempted to lay hands on them, slew them.

21. So these perished by this fate, both they themselves and their company of servants; for there came with them carriages and servants and all the usual pomp of equipage, and this was all made away with at the same time as they. Afterwards in no long time a great search was made by the Persians for these men, and Alexander stopped them with cunning by giving large sums of money and his own sister, whose name was Gygaia;—by giving, I say, these things to Bubares a Persian, commander of those who were searching for the men who had been killed, Alexander stopped their search.

22. Thus the death of these Persians was kept concealed. And that these descendants of Perdiccas are Hellenes, as they themselves say, I happen to know myself, and not only so, but I will prove in the succeeding history that they are Hellenes. Moreover the Hellanodicai, who manage the games at Olympia, decided that they were so: for when Alexander wished to contend in the games and had descended for this purpose into the arena, the Hellenes who were to run against him tried to exclude him, saying that the contest was not for Barbarians to contend in but for Hellenes: since however Alexander proved that he was of Argos, he was judged to be a Hellene, and when he entered the contest of the foot-race his lot came out with that of the first.

23. Thus then it happened with regard to these things: and at the same time Megabazos had arrived at the Hellespont bringing with him the Paionians; and thence after passing over the straits he came to Sardis. Then, since Histiaios the Milesian was already engaged in fortifying with a wall the place which he had asked and obtained from Dareios as a reward for keeping safe the bridge of boats (this place being that which is called Myrkinos, lying along the bank of the river Strymon), Megabazos, having perceived that which was being done by Histiaios, as soon as he came to Sardis bringing the Paionians, said thus to Dareios: "O king, what a thing is this that thou hast done, granting permission to a Hellene who is skillful and cunning to found a city in Thracia in a place where there is forest for shipbuilding in abundance and great quantity of wood for oars and mines of silver and great numbers both of Hellenes and Barbarians living round, who when they have obtained a leader will do that which he shall command them both by day and by night. Therefore stop this man from doing so, that thou be not involved in a domestic war: and stop him by sending for him in a courteous manner; but when thou hast got him in thy hands, then cause that he shall never again return to the land of the Hellenes."

24. Thus saying Megabazos easily persuaded Dareios, who thought that he was a true prophet of that which was likely to come to pass: and upon that Dareios sent a messenger to Myrkinos and said as follows: "Histiaios, king Dareios saith these things:—By taking thought I find that there is no one more sincerely well-disposed than thou art to me and to my power; and this I know having learnt by deeds not words. Now therefore, since I have it in my mind to accomplish great matters, come hither to me by all means, that I may

communicate them to thee." Histiaios therefore, trusting to these sayings and at the same time accounting it a great thing to become a counsellor of the king, came to Sardis; and when he had come Dareios spoke to him as follows: "Histiaios, I sent for thee for this reason, namely because when I had returned from the Scythians and thou wert gone away out of the sight of my eyes, never did I desire to see anything again within so short a time as I desired then both to see thee and that thou shouldst come to speech with me; since I perceived that the most valuable of all possessions is a friend who is a man of under-standing and also sincerely well-disposed, both which qualities I know exist in thee, and I am able to bear witness of them in regard to my affairs. Now therefore (for thou didst well in that thou camest hither) this is that which I propose to thee:—leave Miletos alone and also thy newly-founded city in Thracia, and coming with me to Susa, have whatsoever things I have, eating at my table and being my counselor."

25. Thus said Dareios, and having appointed Artaphrenes his own brother and the son of his father to be governor of Sardis, he marched away to Susa taking with him Histiaios, after he had first named Otanes to be commander of those who dwelt along the sea coasts. This man's father Sisamnes, who had been made one of the Royal Judges, king Cambyses slew, because he had judged a cause unjustly for money, and flayed off all his skin: then after he had torn away the skin he cut leathern thongs out of it and stretched them across the seat where Sisamnes had been wont to sit to give judgment; and having stretched them in the seat, Cambyses appointed the son of that Sisamnes whom he had slain and flayed, to be judge instead of his father, enjoining him to remember in what seat he was sitting to give judgment.

26. This Otanes then, who was made to sit in that seat, had now become the successor of Megabazos in the command: and he conquered the Byzantians and Calchedonians, and he conquered Antandros in the land of Troas, and Lamponion; and having received ships from the Lesbians he conquered Lemnos and Imbros, which were both at that time still inhabited by Pelasgians.

27. Of these the Lemnians fought well, and defending themselves for a long time were at length brought to ruin; and over those of them who survived the Persians set as governor Lycaretos the brother of that Maiandrios who had been king of Samos. This Lycaretos ruled in Lemnos till his death. And the cause of it was this:—he continued to reduce all to slavery and subdue them, accusing some of desertion to the Scythians and others of doing damage to the army of Dareios as it was coming back from Scythia.

28. Otanes then effected so much when he was made commander: and after this for a short time there was an abatement of evils; and then again evils began a second time to fall upon the Ionians, arising from Naxos and Miletos. For Naxos was superior to all the other islands in wealth, and Miletos at the same time had just then come to the very height of its prosperity and was the ornament of Ionia; but before these events for two genera-tions of men it had been afflicted most violently by faction until the Parians reformed it; for these the Milesians chose of all the Hellenes to be reformers of their State.

29. Now the Parians thus reconciled their factions:—the best men of them came to Miletos, and seeing that the Milesians were in a grievously ruined state, they said that they desired to go over their land: and while doing this and passing through the whole territory of Miletos, whenever they saw in the desolation of the land any field that was well cultivated, they wrote down the name of the owner of that field. Then when they had passed through the whole land and had found but few of such men, as soon as they

returned to the city they called a general gathering and appointed these men to manage the State, whose fields they had found well cultivated; for they said that they thought these men would take care of the public affairs as they had taken care of their own: and the rest of the Milesians, who before had been divided by factions, they commanded to be obedient to these men.

30. The Parians then had thus reformed the Milesians; but at the time of which I speak evils began to come to Ionia from these States in the following manner:—From Naxos certain men of the wealthier class were driven into exile by the people, and having gone into exile they arrived at Miletos. Now of Miletos it happened that Aristagoras son of Molpagoras was ruler in charge, being both a son-in-law and also a cousin of Histiaios the son of Lysagoras, whom Dareios was keeping at Susa: for Histiaios was despot of Miletos, and it happened that he was at Susa at this time when the Naxians came, who had been in former times guest-friends of Histiaios. So when the Naxians arrived, they made request of Aristagoras, to see if perchance he would supply them with a force, and so they might return from exile to their own land: and he, thinking that if by his means they should return to their own State, he would be ruler of Naxos, but at the same time making a pretext of the guest-friendship of Histiaios, made proposal to them thus: "I am not able to engage that I can supply you with sufficient force to bring you back from exile against the will of those Naxians who have control of the State; for I hear that the Naxians have an army which is eight thousand shields strong and many ships of war: but I will use every endeavor to devise a means; and my plan is this:—it chances that Artaphrenes is my friend: now Artaphrenes, ye must know, is a son of Hystaspes and brother of Dareios the king; and he is ruler of all the people of the sea-coasts in Asia, with a great army and many ships. This man then I think will do whatsoever we shall request of him." Hearing this the Naxians gave over the matter to Aristagoras to manage as best he could, and they bade him promise gifts and the expenses of the expedition, saying that they would pay them; for they had full expectation that when they should appear at Naxos, the Naxians would do all their bidding, and likewise also the other islanders. For of these islands, that is the Cyclades, not one was as yet subject to Dareios.

31. Aristagoras accordingly having arrived at Sardis, said to Artaphrenes that Naxos was an island not indeed large in size, but fair nevertheless and of fertile soil, as well as near to Ionia, and that there was in it much wealth and many slaves: "Do thou therefore send an expedition against this land, and restore it to those who are now exiles from it: and if thou shalt do this, first I have ready for thee large sums of money apart from the expenses incurred for the expedition (which it is fair that we who conduct it should supply), and next thou wilt gain for the king not only Naxos itself but also the islands which are dependent upon it, Paros and Andros and the others which are called Cyclades; and setting out from these thou wilt easily attack Euboea, an island which is large and wealth, as large indeed as Cyprus, and very easy to conquer. To subdue all these a hundred ships are sufficient." He made answer in these words: "Thou makest thyself a reporter of good things to the house of the king; and in all these things thou advisest well, except as to the number of the ships: for instead of one hundred there shall be prepared for thee two hundred by the beginning of the spring. And it is right that the king himself also should join in approving this matter."

32. So Aristagoras hearing this went back to Miletos greatly rejoiced; and Artaphrenes meanwhile, when he had sent to Susa and communicated that which was said by

Aristagoras, and Dareios himself also had joined in approving it, made ready two hundred triremes and a very great multitude both of Persians and their allies, and appointed to be commander of these Megabates a Persian, one of the Achaimenidai and a cousin to himself and to Dareios, to whose daughter afterwards Pausanias the son of Cleombrotus the Lacedaemonian (at least if the story be true) betrothed himself, having formed a desire to become a despot of Hellas. Having appointed Megabates, I say, to be commander, Artaphrenes sent away the armament to Aristagoras.

33. So when Megabates had taken force together with the Naxians, he sailed with the pretense of going to the Hellespont; but when he came to Chios, he directed his ships to Caucasa, in order that he might from thence pass them over to Naxos with a North Wind. Then, since it was not fated that the Naxians should be destroyed by this expedition, there happened an event which I shall narrate. As Megabates was going round to visit the guards set in the several ships, it chanced that in a ship of Myndos there was no one on guard; and he being very angry bade his spearmen find out the commander of the ship, whose name was Skylax, and bind him in an oar-hole of his ship in such a manner that his head should be outside and his body within. When Skylax was thus bound, someone reported to Aristagoras that Megabates had bound his guest-friend of Myndos and was doing to him shameful outrage. He accordingly came and asked the Persian for his release, and as he did not obtain anything of that which he requested, he went himself and let him loose. Being informed of this Megabates was exceedingly angry and broke out in rage against Aristagoras; and he replied: "What hast thou to do with these matters? Did not Artaphrenes send thee to obey me, and to sail whithersoever I should order? Why dost thou meddle with things which concern thee not?" Thus said Aristagoras; and the other being enraged at this, when night came on sent men in a ship to Naxos to declare to the Naxians all the danger that threatened them.

34. For the Naxians were not at all expecting that this expedition would be against them: but when they were informed of it, forthwith they brought within the wall the property which was in the fields, and provided for themselves food and drink as for a siege, and strengthened their wall. These then were making preparations as for war to come upon them; and the others meanwhile having passed their ships over from Chios to Naxos, found them well defended when they made their attack, and besieged them for four months. Then when the money which the Persians had brought with them had all been consumed by them, and not only that, but Aristagoras himself had spent much in addition, and the siege demanded ever more and more, they built walls for the Naxian exiles and departed to the mainland again with ill success.

35. And so Aristagoras was not able to fulfil his promise to Artaphrenes; and at the same time he was hard pressed by the demand made to him for the expenses of the expedition, and had fears because of the ill success of the armament and because he had become an enemy of Megabates; and he supposed that he would be deprived of his rule over Miletos. Having all these various fears he began to make plans of revolt: for it happened also that just at this time the man who had been marked upon the head had come from Hisiaios who was at Susa, signifying that Aristagoras should revolt from the king. For Histiaios, desiring to signify to Aristagoras that he should revolt, was not able to do it safely in any other way, because the roads were guarded, but shaved off the hair of the most faithful of his slaves, and having marked his head by pricking it, waited till the hair had grown again; and as soon as it was grown, he sent him away to Miletos, giving

him no other charge but this, namely that when he should have arrived at Miletos he should bid Aristagoras shave his hair and look at his head: and the marks, as I have said before, signified revolt. This thing Histiaios was doing, because he was greatly vexed by being detained at Susa. He had great hopes then that if a revolt occurred he would be let go to the sea-coast; but if no change was made at Miletos he had no expectation of ever returning thither again.

36. Accordingly Hisiaios with this intention was sending the messenger; and it chanced that all these things happened to Aristagoras together at the same time. He took counsel therefore with his partisans, declaring to them both his own opinion and the message from Hisiaios; and while all the rest expressed an opinion to the same effect, urging him namely to make revolt, Hecataios the historian urged first that they should not undertake war with the king of the Persians, enumerating all the nations over whom Dareios was ruler, and his power: and when he did not succeed in persuading him, he counselled next that they should manage to make themselves masters of the sea. Now this, he continued, could not come to pass in any other way, so far as he could see, for he knew that the force of the Milesians was weak, but if the treasures should be taken which were in the temple at Branchidai, which Croesus the Lydian dedicated as offerings, he had great hopes that they might become masters of the sea; and by this means they would not only themselves have wealth at their disposal, but the enemy would not be able to carry the things off as plunder. Now these treasures were of great value, as I have shown in the first part of the history. This opinion did not prevail; but nevertheless it was resolved to make revolt, and that one of them should sail to Myus, to make the force which had returned from Naxos and was then there, and endeavor to seize the commanders who sailed in the ships.

37. So Iatragoras was sent for this purpose and seized by craft Oliatos the son of Ibanollis of Mylasa, and Histiaios the son of Tymnes of Termera, and Coës the son of Erxander, to whom Dareios had given Mytilene as a gift, and Aristagoras the son of Heracleides of Kyme, and many others; and then Aristagoras openly made revolt and devised all that he could to the hurt of Dareios. And first he pretended to resign the despotic power and give to Miletos equality, in order that the Milesians might be willing to revolt with him: then afterwards he proceeded to do this same thing in the rest of Ionia also; and some of the despots he drove out, but those whom he had taken from the ships which had sailed with him to Naxis, these he surrendered, because he desired to do a pleasure to their cities, delivering them over severally to that city from which each one came.

38. Now the men of Mitylene, so soon as they received Coës into their hands, brought him out and stoned him to death; but the men of Kyme let their despot go, and so also most of the others let them go. Thus then the despots were deposed in the various cities; and Aristagoras the Milesian, after having deposed the despots, bade each people appoint commanders in their several cities, and then himself set forth as an envoy to Lacedaemon; for in truth it was necessary that he should find out some powerful alliance.

39. Now at Sparta Anaxandrides the son of Leon was no longer surviving as king, but had brought his life to an end; and Cleomenes the son of Anaxandrides was holding the royal power, not having obtained it by merit but by right of birth. For Anaxandrides had to wife his own sister's daughter and she was by him much beloved, but no children were born to him by her. This being so, the Ephors summoned him before them and said: "If thou dost not for thyself take thought in time, yet we cannot suffer this to happen, that

the race of Eurysthenes should become extinct. Do thou therefore put away from thee the wife whom thou now hast, since, as thou knowest, she bears thee no children, and marry another: and in doing so thou wilt please the Spartans." He made answer saying that he would do neither of these two things, and that they did not give him honorable counsel, in that they advised him to send away the wife whom he had, though she had done him no wrong, and to take to his house another; and in short he would not follow their advice.

40. Upon this the Ephors and the Senators deliberated together and proposed to Anaxandrides as follows: "Since then we perceive that thou art firmly attached to the wife whom thou now hast, consent to do this, and set not thyself against it, lest the Spartans take some counsel about thee other than might be wished. We do not ask of thee the putting away of the wife whom thou hast; but do thou give to her all that thou givest now and at the same time take to thy house another wife in addition to this one, to bear thee children." When they spoke to him after this manner, Anaxandrides consented, having two wives, a thing which was not by any means after the Spartan fashion.

41. Then when no long time had elapsed, the wife who had come in afterwards bore this Cleomenes of whom we spoke; and just when she was bringing to the light an heir to the kingdom of the Spartans, the former wife, who had during the time before been child- less, then by some means conceived, chancing to do so just at that time: and though she was in truth with child, the kinsfolk of the wife who had come in afterwards, when they heard of it cried out against her and said that she was making a vain boast, and that she meant to pass off another child as her own. Since then they made a great show of indigna- tion, as the time was fast drawing near, the Ephors being incredulous sat round and watched the woman during the birth of her child: and she bore Dorieos and then straightway conceived Leonidas and after him at once Cleombrotos,—nay, some even say that Cleombrotos and Leonidas were twins. The wife however who had born Cleomenes and had come in after the first wife, being the daughter of Primetades the son of Demar- menos, did not bear a child again.

42. Now Cleomenes, it is said, was not quite in his right senses but on the verge of madness, while Dorieos was of all his equals in age the first, and felt assured that he would obtain the kingdom by merit. Seeing then that he had this opinion, when Anaxan- drides died and the Lacedemonians followed the usual custom established the eldest, namely Cleomenes, upon the throne, Dorieos being indignant and not thinking it fit that he should be a subject of Cleomenes, asked the Spartans to give him a company of followers and led them out to found a colony, without either inquiring of the Oracle at Delphi to what land he should go to make a settlement, or doing any of the things which are usually done; but being vexed he sailed away with his ships to Libya, and the Thera- ians were his guides thither. Then having come to Kinyps he made a settlement in the fairest spot of all Libya, along the banks of the river; but afterwards in the third year he was driven out from thence by the Macai and the Libyans and the Carthaginians, and returned to Peloponnesus.

43. Then Antichares a man of Eleon gave him counsel out of the oracles of Laïos to make a settlement at Heracleia in Sicily, saying that the whole land of Eryx belonged to the Heracleidai, since Heracles himself had won it: and hearing this he went forthwith to Delphi to inquire of the Oracle whether he would be able to conquer the land to which he was setting forth; and the Pythian prophetess replied to him that he would conquer it.

Dorieos therefore took with him the armament which he conducted before to Libya, and voyaged along the coast of Italy.

44. Now at this time, the men of Sybaris say that they and their king Telys were about to make an expedition against Croton, and the men of Croton being exceedingly alarmed asked Dorieos to help them and obtained their request. So Dorieos joined them in an expedition against Sybaris and helped them to conquer Sybaris. This is what the men of Sybaris say of the doings of Dorieos and his followers; but those of Croton say that no stranger helped them in the war against the Sybarites except Callias alone, a diviner of Elis and one of the descendants of Iamos, and he in the following manner:—he ran away, they say, from Telys the despot of the Sybarites, when the sacrifices did not prove favorable, as he was sacrificing for the expedition against Croton, and so he came to them.

45. Such, I say, are the tales which these tell, and they severally produce as evidence of them the following facts:—the Sybarites point to a sacred enclosure and temple by the side of the dried-up bed of the Crathis, which they say that Dorieos, after he had joined in the capture of the city, set up to Athene surnamed "of the Crathis"; and besides they consider the death of Dorieos himself to be a very strong evidence, thinking that he perished because he acted contrary to the oracle which was given to him; for if he had not done anything by the way but had continued to do that for which he was sent, he would have conquered the land of Eryx and having conquered it would have become possessor of it, and he and his army would not have perished. On the other hand the men of Croton declare that many things were granted in the territory of Croton as special gifts to Callias the Eleisan, of which the descendants of Callias were still in possession down to my time, and that nothing was granted to Dorieos or the descendants of Dorieos: but if Dorieos had in fact helped them in the way with Sybaris, many times as much, they say, would have been given to him as to Callias. These then are the evidences which the two sides produce, and we may assent to whichever of them we think credible.

46. Now there sailed with Dorieos others also of the Spartans, to be joint-founders with him of the colony, namely Thessalos and Paraibates and Keleas and Euryleon; and these when they had reached Sicily with all their armament, were slain, being defeated in battle by the Phoenicians and the men of Egesta; and Euryleon only of the joint-founders survived this disaster. This man then having collected the survivors of the expedition, took possession of Minoa the colony of Selinus, and he helped to free the men of Selinus from their despot Peithagoras. Afterwards, when he had deposed him, he laid hands himself upon the despotism in Selinus and became sole ruler there, though but for a short time; for the men of Selinus rose in revolt against him and slew him, notwithstanding that he had fled for refuge to the altar of Zeus Agoraios.

47. There had accompanied Dorieos also and died with him Philip the son of Butakides, a man of Croton, who having betrothed himself to the daughter of Telys the Sybarite, became an exile from Croton; and then being disappointed of this marriage he sailed away to Kyrene, whence he set forth and accompanied Dorieos with a trireme of his own, himself supplying the expenses of the crew. Now this man had been a victor at the Olympic games, and he was the most beautiful of the Hellenes who lived in his time; and on account of his beauty he obtained from the men of Egesta that which none else ever obtained from them, for they established a hero-temple over his tomb, and they propitiate him still with sacrifices.

48. In this manner Dorieos ended his life: but if he had endured to be a subject of

Cleomenes and had remained in Sparta, he would have been king of Lacedaemon; for Cleomenes reigned no very long time, and died leaving no son to succeed him but a daughter only, whose name was Gorgo.

49. However, Aristagoras the despot of Miletos arrived at Sparta while Cleomenes was reigning: and accordingly with him he came to speech, having, as the Lacedemonians say, a tablet of bronze, on which was engraved a map of the whole Earth, with all the sea and all the rivers. And when he came to speech with Cleomenes he said to him as follows: "Marvel not, Cleomenes, at my earnestness in coming hither, for the case is this.—That the sons of the Ionians should be slaves instead of free is a reproach and a grief most of all indeed to ourselves, but of all others most to you, inasmuch as ye are the leaders of Hellas. Now therefore I entreat you by the gods of Hellas to rescue from slavery the Ionians, who are your own kinsmen: and ye may easily achieve this, for the Barbarians are not valiant in fight, whereas ye have attained to the highest point of valor in that which relates to war: and their fighting is of this fashion, namely with bows and arrows and a short spear, and they go into battle wearing trousers and with caps on their heads. Thus they are easily conquered. Then again they who occupy that continent have good things in such quantity as not all the other nations of the world together possess; first gold, then silver and bronze and embroidered garments and beasts of burden and slaves; all which ye might have for yourselves, if ye so desired. And the nations moreover dwell in such order one after the other as I shall declare:—the Ionians here; and next to them the Lydians, who not only dwell in a fertile land, but are also exceedingly rich in gold and silver," —and as he said this he pointed to the map of the Earth, which he carried with him engraved upon the tablet,—"and here next to the Lydians," continued Aristagoras, "are the Eastern Phrygians, who have both the greatest number of sheep and cattle of any people that I know, and also the most abundant crops. Next to the Phrygians are the Cappadokians, whom we call Syrians; and bordering upon them are the Kilikians, coming down to this sea, in which lies the island of Cyprus here; and these pay five hundred talents to the king for their yearly tribute. Next to these Kilikians are the Armenians, whom thou mayest see here, and these also have great numbers of sheep and cattle. Next to the Armenians are the Matienians occupying this country here; and next to them is the land of Kissia here, in which land by the banks of this river Choaspes is situated that city of Susa where the great king has his residence, and where the money is laid up in treasuries. After ye have taken this city ye may then with good courage enter into a contest with Zeus in the matter of wealth. Nay, but can it be that ye feel yourselves bound to take upon you the risk of battles against Messenians and Arcadians and Argives, who are equally matched against you, for the sake of land which is not much in extent nor very fertile, and for confines which are but small, though these peoples have neither gold nor silver at all, for the sake of which desire incites one to fight and to die,—can this be, I say, and will ye choose some other way now, when it is possible for you easily to have the rule over all Asia?" Aristagoras spoke thus, and Cleomenes answered him saying: "Guest-friend from Miletos, I defer my answer to thee until the day after to-morrow."

50. Thus far then they advanced at that time; and when the appointed day arrived for the answer, and they had come to the place agreed upon, Cleomenes asked Aristagoras how many days' journey it was from the sea of the Ionians to the residence of the king. Now Aristagoras, who in other respects acted cleverly and imposed upon him well, in this point made a mistake: for whereas he ought not to have told him the truth, at least if he

desired to bring the Spartans out to Asia, he said in fact that it was a journey up from the sea of three months: and the other cutting short the rest of the account which Aristagoras had begun to give of the way, said: "Guest-friend from Miletos, get thee away from Sparta before the sun has set; for thou speakest a word which sounds not well in the ears of the Lacedemonians, desiring to take them a journey of three months from the sea."

51. Cleomenes accordingly having so said went away to his house: but Aristagoras took the suppliant's branch and went to the house of Cleomenes; and having entered in as a suppliant, he bade Cleomenes send away the child and listen to him; for the daughter of Cleomenes was standing by him, whose name was Gorgo, and this as it chanced was his only child, being of the age now of eight or nine years. Cleomenes however bade him say that which he desired to say, and not to stop on account of the child. Then Aristagoras proceeded to promise him money, beginning with ten talents, if he would accomplish for him that for which he was asking; and when Cleomenes refused, Aristagoras went on increasing the sums of money offered, until at last he had promised fifty talents, and at that moment the child cried out: "Father, the stranger will do thee hurt, if thou do not leave him and go." Cleomenes, then, pleased by the counsel of the child, departed into another room, and Aristagoras went away from Sparta altogether, and had no opportunity of explaining any further about the way up from the sea to the residence of the king.

52. As regards this road the truth is as follows.—Everywhere there are royal stages and excellent resting-places, and the whole road runs through country which is inhabited and safe. Through Lydia and Phrygia there extend twenty stages, amounting to ninety-four and a half leagues; and after Phrygia succeeds the river Halys, at which there is a gate which one must needs pass through in order to cross the river, and a strong guard-post is established there. Then after crossing over into Cappadokia it is twenty-eight stages, being a hundred and four leagues, by this way to the borders of Kilikia; and on the borders of the Kilikians you will pass through two several gates and go by two several guard-posts: then after passing through these it is three stages, amounting to fifteen and a half leagues, to journey through Kilikia; and the boundary of Kilikia and Armenia is a navigable river called Euphrates. In Armenia the number of stages with resting-places is fifteen, and of leagues fifty-six and a half, and there is a guard-post on the way: then from Armenia, when one enters the land of Matiene, there are thirty-four stages, amounting to a hundred and thirty-seven leagues; and through this land flow four navigable rivers, which cannot be crossed but by ferries, first the Tigris, then a second and third called both by the same name, though they are not the same river nor do they flow from the same region (for the first-mentioned of them flows from the Armenian land and the other from that of the Matienians), and the fourth of the rivers is called Gyndes, the same which once Cyrus divided into three hundred and sixty channels. Passing thence into the Kissian land, there are eleven stages, forty-two and a half leagues, to the river Choaspes, which is also a navigable stream; and upon this is built the city of Susa. The number of these stages amounts in all to one hundred and eleven.

53. This is the number of stages with resting-places, as one goes up from Sardis to Susa: and if the royal road has been rightly measured as regards leagues, and if the league is equal to thirty furlongs, (as undoubtedly it is), the number of furlongs from Sardis to that which is called the palace of Memnon is thirteen thousand five hundred, the number of leagues being four hundred and fifty. So if one travels a hundred and fifty furlongs each day, just ninety days are spent on the journey. .

54. Thus the Milesian Aristagoras, when he told Cleomenes the Lacedemonian that the journey up from the sea to the residence of the king was one of three months, spoke correctly: but if any one demands a more exact statement yet than this, I will give him that also: for we ought to reckon in addition to this the length of the road from Ephesos to Sardis; and I say accordingly that the whole number of furlongs from the sea of Hellas to Susa (for by that name the city of Memnon is known) is fourteen thousand and forty; for the number of furlongs from Ephesos to Sardis is five hundred and forty: thus the three months' journey is lengthened by three days added.

55. Aristagoras then being driven out of Sparta proceeded to Athens; which had been set free from the rule of despots in the way which I shall tell.—When Hipparchos the son of Peisistratos and brother of the despot Hippias, after seeing a vision of a dream which signified it to him plainly, had been slain by Aristogeiton and Harmodios, who were originally by descent Gephyraians, the Athenians continued for four years after this to be despotically governed no less than formerly,—nay, even more.

56. Now the vision of a dream which Hipparchos had was this:—in the night before the Panathenaia it seemed to Hipparchos that a man came and stood by him, tall and of fair form, and riddling spoke to him these verses:

"With enduring soul as a lion endure unendurable evil:
No one of men who doth wrong shall escape from the judgment appointed."

These verses, as soon as it was day, he publicly communicated to the interpreters of dreams; but afterwards he put away thought of the vision and began to take part in that procession during which he lost his life.

57. Now the Gephyraians, of whom were those who murdered Hipparchos, according to their own account were originally descended from Eretria; but as I find by carrying inquiries back, they were Phoenicians of those who came with Cadmos to the land which is now called Boeotia, and they dwelt in the district of Tanagra, which they had had allotted to them in that land. Then after the Cadmeians had first been driven out by the Argives, these Gephyraians next were driven out by the Boeotians and turned then towards Athens: and the Athenians received them on certain fixed conditions to be citizens of their State, laying down rules that they should be excluded from a number of things not worth mentioning here.

58. Now these Phoenicians who came with Cadmos, of whom were the Gephyraians, brought in among the Hellenes many arts when they settled in this land of Boeotia, and especially letters, which did not exist, as it appears to me, among the Hellenes before this time; and at first they brought in those which are used by the Phoenician race generally, but afterwards, as time went on, they changed with their speech the form of the letters also. During this time the Ionians were the race of Hellenes who dwelt near them in most of the places where they were; and these, having received letters by instruction of the Phoenicians, changed their form slightly and so made use of them, and in doing so they declared them to be called "phoenicians," as was just, seeing that the Phoenicians had introduced them into Hellas. Also the Ionians from ancient time call paper "skins," because formerly, paper being scarce, they used skins of goat and sheep; nay, even in my own time many of the Barbarians write on such skins.

59. I myself too once saw Cadmeian characters in the temple of Ismenian Apollo at

Thebes of the Boeotians, engraved on certain tripods, and in most respects resembling the Ionic letters: one of these tripods has the inscription,

"Me Amphitryon offered from land Teleboian returning:"

this inscription would be of an age contemporary with Laïos the son of Labdacos, the son of Polydoros, the son of Cadmos.

60. Another tripod says thus in hexameter rhythm:

"Me did Scaios offer to thee, far-darting Apollo,
Victor in contest of boxing, a gift most fair in thine honor:"

now Scaios would be the son of Hippocoön (at least if it were really he who offered it, and not another with the same name as the son of Hippocoön), being of an age contemporary with OEdipus the son of Laïos: 61, and the third tripod, also in hexameter rhythm, says:

"Me Laodamas offered to thee, fair-aiming Apollo,
He, of his wealth, being king, as a gift most fair in thine honor:"

now it was in the reign of this very Laodamas the son of Eteocles that the Cadmeians were driven out by the Argives and turned to go to the Enchelians; and the Gephyraians being then left behind were afterwards forced by the Boeotians to retire to Athens. Moreover they have temples established in Athens, in which the other Athenians have no part, and besides others which are different from the rest, there is especially a temple of Demeter Achaia and a celebration of her mysteries.

62. I have told now of the vision of a dream seen by Hipparchos, and also whence the Gephrynians were descended, of which race were the murderers of Hipparchos; and in addition to this I must resume and continue the story which I was about to tell at first, how the Athenians were freed from despots. When Hippias was despot and was dealing harshly with the Athenians because of the death of Hipparchos, the Alcmaionidai, who were of Athenian race and were fugitives from the sons of Peisistratos, as they did not succeed in their attempt made together with the other Athenian exiles to return by force, but met with great disaster when they attempted to return and set Athens free, after they had fortified Leipsydrion which is above Paionia,—these Alcmaionidai after that, still devising every means against the sons of Peisistratos, accepted the contract to build and complete the temple at Delphi, that namely which now exists but then did not as yet: and being wealthy and men of repute already from ancient time, they completed the temple in a manner more beautiful than the plan required, and especially in this respect, that having agreed to make the temple of common limestone, they built the front parts of it in Parian marble.

63. So then, as the Athenians say, these men being settled at Delphi persuaded the Pythian prophetess by gifts of money, that whenever men of the Spartans should come to inquire of the Oracle, either privately or publicly sent, she should propose to them to set Athens free. The Lacedemonians therefore, since the same utterance was delivered to them on all occasions, sent Anchimolios the son of Aster, who was of repute among their

citizens, with an army to drive out the sons of Peisistratos from Athens, although these were very closely connected with them by guest-friendship; for they held that the concerns of the god should be preferred to those of men: and this force they sent by sea in ships. He therefore, having put in to shore at Phaleron, disembarked his army; but the sons of Peisistratos being informed of this beforehand called in to their aid an auxiliary force from Thessaly, for they had made an alliance with the Thessalians; and the Thessalians at their request sent by public resolution a body of a thousand horse and also their king Kineas, a man of Conion. So having obtained these as allies, the sons of Peisistratos contrived as follows:—they cut down the trees in the plain of Phaleron and made this district fit for horsemen to ride over, and after that they sent the cavalry to attack the enemy's camp, who falling upon it slew (besides many others of the Lacedemonians) Anchimolios himself also: and the survivors of them they shut up in their ships. Such was the issue of the first expedition from Lacedaemon: and the burial-place of Anchimolios is at Alopecai in Attica, near the temple of Heracles which is at Kynosarges.

64. After this the Lacedemonians equipped a larger expedition and sent it forth against Athens; and they appointed to be commander of the army their king Cleomenes the son of Anaxandrides, and sent it this time not by sea but by land. With these, when they had invaded the land of Attica, first the Thessalian horse engaged battle; and in no long time they were routed and there fell of them more than forty men; so the survivors departed without more ado and went straight back to Thessaly. Then Cleomenes came to the city together with those of the Athenians who desired to be free, and began to besiege the despots shut up in the Pelasgian wall.

65. And the Lacedemonians would never have captured the sons of Peisistratos at all; for they on their side had no design to make a long blockade, and the others were well provided with food and drink; so that they would have gone away back to Sparta after besieging them for a few days only: but as it was, a thing happened just at this time which was unfortunate for those, and at the same time of assistance to these; for the children of the sons of Peisistratos were captured, while being secretly removed out of the country: and when this happened, all their matters were thereby cast into confusion, and they surrendered receiving back their children on the terms which the Athenians desired, namely that they should depart out of Attica within five days. After this they departed out of the country and went to Sigeion on the Scamander, after their family had ruled over the Athenians for six-and-thirty years. These also were originally Pylians and sons of Neleus, descended from the same ancestors as the family of Codros and Melanthos, who had formerly become kings of Athens being settlers from abroad. Hence too Hippocrates had given to his son the name of Peisistratos as a memorial, calling him after Peisistratos the son of Nestor.

Thus the Athenians were freed from despots; and the things worthy to be narrated which they did or suffered after they were liberated, up to the time when Ionia revolted from Dareios and Aristagoras the Milesian came to Athens and asked them to help him, these I will set forth first before I proceed further.

66. Athens, which even before that time was great, then, after having been freed from despots, became gradually yet greater; and in it two men exercised power, namely Cleisthenes a descendant of Alcmaion, the same who is reported to have bribed the Pythian prophetess, and Isagoras, the son of Tisander, of a family which was highly reputed, but of his original descent I am not able to declare; his kinsmen however offer sacrifices to the

Carian Zeus. These men came to party strife for power; and then Cleisthenes was being worsted in the struggle, he made common cause with the people. After this he caused the Athenians to be in ten tribes, who were formerly in four; and he changed the names by which they were called after the sons of Ion, namely Geleon, Aigicoreus, Argades, and Hoples, and invented for them names taken from other heroes, all native Athenians except Ajax, whom he added as a neighbor and ally, although he was no Athenian.

67. Now in these things it seems to me that this Cleisthenes was imitating his mother's father Cleisthenes the despot of Sikyon: for Cleisthenes when he went to war with Argos first caused to cease in Sikyon the contests of rhapsodists, which were concerned with the poems of Homer, because Argives and Argos are celebrated in them almost everywhere; then secondly, since there was (as still there is) in the market-place itself of the Sikyonians a hero-temple of Adrastos the son of Talaos, Cleisthenes had a desire to cast him forth out of the land, because he was an Argive. So having come to Delphi he consulted the Oracle as to whether he should cast out Adrastos; and the Pythian prophetess answered him saying that Adrastos was king of the Sikyonians, whereas he was a stoner of them. So since the god did not permit him to do this, he went away home and considered means by which Adrastos should be brought to depart of his own accord: and when he thought that he had discovered them, he sent to Thebes in Boeotia and said that he desired to introduce into his city Melanippos the son of Astacos, and the Thebans gave him leave. So Cleisthenes introduced Melanippos into his city, and appointed for him a sacred enclosure within the precincts of the City Hall itself, and established him there in the strongest position. Now Cleisthenes introduced Melanippos (for I must relate this also) because he was the greatest enemy of Adrastos, seeing that he had killed both his brother Mekisteus and his son-in-law Tydeus: and when he had appointed the sacred enclosure for him, he took away the sacrifices and festivals of Adrastos and gave them to Melanippos. Now the Sikyonians were accustomed to honor Adrastos with very great honors; for this land was formerly the land of Polybos, and Adrastos was daughter's son to Polybos, and Polybos dying without sons gave his kingdom to Adrastos: the Sikyonians then not only gave other honors to Adrastos, but also with reference to his sufferings they specially honored him with tragic choruses, not paying the honor to Dionysos but to Adrastos. Cleisthenes however gave back the choruses to Dionysos, and the other rites besides this he gave to Melannipos.

68. Thus he had done to Adrastos; and he also changed the names of the Dorian tribes, in order that the Sikyonians might not have the same tribes as the Argives; in which matter he showed great contempt of the Sikyonians, for the names he gave were taken from the names of a pig and an ass by changing only the endings, except in the case of his own tribe, to which he gave a name from his own rule. These last then were called Archelaoi, while of the rest those of one tribe were called Hyatai, of another Oneatai, and of the remaining tribe Choireatai. These names of tribes were used by the men of Sikyon not only in the reign of Cleisthenes, but also beyond that for sixty years after his death; then however they considered the matter and changed them into Hylleis, Pamphyloi, and Dymanatai, adding to these a fourth, to which they gave the name Aigialeis after Aigialeus the son of Adrastos.

69. Thus had the Cleisthenes of Sikyon done: and the Athenian Cleisthenes, who was his daughter's son and was called after him, despising, as I suppose, the Ionians, as he the Dorians, imitated his namesake Cleisthenes in order that the Athenians might not have

the same tribes as the Ionians: for when at the time of which we speak he added to his own party the whole body of the common people of the Athenians, which in former time he had despised, he changed the names of the tribes and made them more in number than they had been; he made in fact ten rulers of tribes instead of four, and by tens also he distributed the demes in the tribes; and having added the common people to his party he was much superior to his opponents.

70. Then Isagoras, as he was being worsted in his turn, contrived a plan in opposition to him, that is to say, he called in Cleomenes the Lacedemonian to help him, who had been a guest-friend to himself since the siege of the sons of Peisistratos; moreover Cleomenes was accused of being intimate with the wife of Isagoras. First then Cleomenes sent a herald to Athens demanding the expulsion of Cleisthenes and with him many others of the Athenians, calling them the men who were under the curse: this message he sent by instruction of Isagoras, for the Alcmaionidai and their party were accused of the murder to which reference was thus made, while he and his friends had no part in it.

71. Now the men of the Athenians who were "under the curse" got this name as follows:—there was one Kylon among the Athenians, a man who had gained the victory at the Olympic games: this man behaved with arrogance, wishing to make himself despot; and having formed for himself an association of men of his own age, he endeavored to seize the Acropolis: but not being able to get possession of it, he sat down as a suppliant before the image of the goddess. These men were taken from their place as suppliants by the presidents of the naucraries, who then administered affairs at Athens, on the condition that they should be liable to any penalty short of death; and the Alcmaionidai are accused of having put them to death. This had occurred before the time of Peisistratos.

72. Now when Cleomenes sent demanding the expulsion of Cleisthenes and of those under the curse, Cleisthenes himself retired secretly; but after that nevertheless Cleomenes appeared in Athens with no very large force, and having arrived he proceeded to expel as accursed seven hundred Athenian families, of which Isagoras had suggested to him the names. Having done this he next endeavored to dissolve the Senate, and he put the offices of the State into the hands of three hundred, who were the partisans of Isagoras. The Senate however making opposition, and not being willing to submit, Cleomenes with Isagoras and his partisans seized the Acropolis. Then the rest of the Athenians joined together by common consent and besieged them for two days; and on the third day so many of them as were Lacedemonians departed out of the country under a truce. Thus was accomplished for Cleomenes the ominous saying which was uttered to him: for when he had ascended the Acropolis with the design of taking possession of it, he was going to the sanctuary of the goddess, as to address her in prayer; but the priestess stood up from her seat before he had passed through the door, and said, "Lacedemonian stranger, go back and enter not into the temple, for it is not lawful for Dorians to pass in hither." He said: "Woman, I am not a Dorian, but an Achaian." So then, paying no attention to the ominous speech, he made his attempt and then was expelled again with the Lacedemonians; but the rest of the men the Athenians laid in bonds to be put to death, and among them Timesitheos the Delphian, with regard to whom I might mention very great deeds of strength and courage which he performed.

73. These then having been thus laid in bonds were put to death; and the Athenians after this sent for Cleisthenes to return, and also for the seven hundred families which had been driven out by Cleomenes: and then they sent envoys to Sardis, desiring to make an

alliance with the Persians; for they were well assured that the Lacedemonians and Cleomenes had been utterly made their foes. So when these envoys had arrived at Sardis and were saying that which they had been commanded to say, Artaphrenes the son of Hystaspes, the governor of Sardis, asked what men these were who requested to be allies of the Persians, and where upon the earth they dwelt; and having heard this from the envoys, he summed up his answer to them thus, saying that if the Athenians were willing to give earth and water to Dareios, he was willing to make alliance with them, but if not, he bade them begone: and the envoys taking the matter upon themselves said that they were willing to do so, because they desired to make the alliance.

74. These, when they returned to their own land, were highly censured: and Cleomenes meanwhile, conceiving that he had been outrageously dealt with by the Athenians both with words and with deeds, was gathering together an army from the whole of the Peloponnese, not declaring the purpose for which he was gathering it, but desiring to take vengeance on the people of the Athenians, and intending to make Isagoras despot; for he too had come out of the Acropolis together with Cleomenes. Cleomenes then with a large army entered Eleusis, while at the same time the Boeotians by agreement with him captured Oinoe and Hysiai, the demes which lay upon the extreme borders of Attica, and the Chalkidians on the other side invaded and began to ravage various districts of Attica. The Athenians then, though attacked on more sides than one, thought that they would remember the Boeotians and Chalkidians afterwards, and arrayed themselves against the Peloponnesians who were in Eleusis.

75. Then as the armies were just about the join battle, the Corinthians first, considering with themselves that they were not acting rightly, changed their minds and departed; and after that Demaratos the son of Ariston did the same, who was king of the Spartans as well as Cleomenes, though he had joined with him in leading the army out from Lacedaemon and had not been before this at variance with Cleomenes. In consequence of this dissension a law was laid down at Sparta that it should not be permitted, when an army went out, that both the kings should go with it, for up to this time both used to go with it, and that as one of the kings was set free from service, so one of the sons of Tyndareus also should be left behind; for before this time both of these two were called upon by them for help and went with the armies.

76. At this time then in Eleusis the rest of the allies, seeing that the kings of the Lacedemonians did not agree and also that the Corinthians had deserted their place in the ranks, themselves too departed and got them away quickly. And this was the fourth time that the Dorians had come to Attica, twice having invaded it to make war against it, and twice to help the mass of the Athenian people,—first when they at the same time colonized Megara (this expedition may rightly be designated as taking place when Codros was king of the Athenians), for the second and third times when they came making expeditions from Sparta to drive out the sons of Peisistratos, and fourthly on this occasion, when Cleomenes at the head of the Peloponnesians invaded Eleusis: thus the Dorians invaded Athens then for the fourth time.

77. This army then having been ingloriously broken up, the Athenians after that, desiring to avenge themselves, made expedition first against the Chalkidians; and the Boeotians came to the Euripos to help the Chalkidians. The Athenians, therefore, seeing those who had come to help, resolved first to attack the Boeotians before the Chalkidians. Accordingly they engaged battle with the Boeotians, and had much the better of them,

and after having slain very many they took seven hundred of them captive. On this very same day the Athenians passed over into Euboea and engaged battle with the Chalkidians as well; and having conquered these also, they left four thousand holders of allotments in the land belonging to the "Breeders of Horses": now the wealthier of the Chalkidians were called the Breeders of Horses. And as many of them as they took captive, they kept in confinement together with the Boeotians who had been captured, bound with fetters; and then after a time they let them go, having fixed their ransom at two pounds of silver apiece: but their fetters, in which they had been bound, they hung up on the Acropolis; and these were still existing even to my time hanging on walls which had been scorched with fire by the Mede, and just opposite the sanctuary which lies towards the West. The tenth part of the ransom also they dedicated for an offering, and made of it a four-horse chariot of bronze, which stands on the left hand as you enter the Propylaia in the Acropolis, and on it is the following inscription:

> "Matched in the deeds of war with the tribes of Boeotia and Chalkis
>   The sons of Athens prevailed, conquered and tamed them in fight:
> In chains of iron and darkness they quenched their insolent spirit;
>   And to Athene present these, of their ransom a tithe."

78. The Athenians accordingly increased in power; and it is evident, not by one instance only but in every way, that Equality is an excellent thing, since the Athenians while they were ruled by despots were not better in war that any of those who dwelt about them, whereas after they had got rid of despots they became far the first. This proves that when they were kept down they were willfully slack, because they were working for a master, whereas when they had been set free each one was eager to achieve something for himself.

79. These then were faring thus: and the Thebans after this sent to the god, desiring to be avenged on the Athenians; the Pythian prophetess however said that vengeance was not possible for them by their own strength alone, but bade them report the matter to the "many-voiced" and ask help of those who were "nearest" to them. So when those who were sent to consult the Oracle returned, they made a general assembly and reported the oracle; and then the Thebans heard them say that they were to ask help of those who were nearest to them, they said: "Surely those who dwell nearest to us are the men of Tanagra and Coroneia and Thespiai; and these always fight zealously on our side and endure the war with us to the end: what need is there that we ask of these? Rather perhaps that is not the meaning of the oracle."

80. While they commented upon it thus, at length one perceived "that which the oracle means to tell us. Asopos is said to have had two daughters born to him, Thebe and Egina; and as these are sisters, I think that the god gave us for answer that we should ask the men of Egina to become our helpers." Then as there seemed to be no opinion expressed which was better than this, they sent forthwith and asked the men of Egina to help them, calling upon them in accordance with the oracle; and they, when these made request, said that they sent with them the sons of Aiacos to help them.

81. After that the Thebans, having made an attempt with the alliance of the sons of Aiacos and having been roughly handled by the Athenians, sent again and gave them back the sons of Aiacos and asked them for men. So the Eginetans, exalted by great pros-

perity and calling to mind an ancient grudge against the Athenians, then on the request of the Thebans commenced a war against the Athenians without notice: for while the Athenians were intent on the Boeotians, they sailed against them to Attica with ships of war, and they devastated Phaleron and also many demes in the remainder of the coast region, and so doing they deeply stirred the resentment of the Athenians.

82. Now the grudge which was due beforehand from the Eginetans to the Athenians came about from a beginning which was as follows:—The land of the Epidaurians yielded to its inhabitants no fruit; and accordingly with reference to this calamity the Epidaurians went to inquire at Delphi, and the Pythian prophetess bade them set up images of Damia and Auxesia, and said that when they had set up these, they would meet with better fortune. The Epidaurians then asked further whether they should make images of bronze or of stone; and the prophetess bade them not use either of these, but make them of the wood of a cultivated olive-tree. The Epidaurians therefore asked the Athenians to allow them to cut for themselves an olive-tree, since they thought that their olives were the most sacred; nay some say that at that time there were no olives in any part of the earth except at Athens. The Athenians said that they would allow them on condition that they should every year bring due offerings to Athene Polias and to Erechtheus. The Epidaurians, then, having agreed to these terms, obtained that which they asked, and they made images out of these olive-trees and set them up: and their land bore fruit and they continued to fulfil towards the Athenians that which they had agreed to do.

83. Now during this time and also before this the Eginetans were subject to the Epidaurians, and besides other things they were wont to pass over to Epidauros to have their disputes with one another settled by law: but after this time they built for themselves ships and made revolt from the Epidaurians, moved thereto by willfulness. So as they were at variance with them, they continued to inflict damage on them, since in fact they had command of the sea, and especially they stole away from them these images of Damia and Auxesia, and they brought them and set them up in the inland part of their country at a place called Oia, which is about twenty furlongs distant from their city. Having set them up in this spot they worshipped them with sacrifices and choruses of women accompanied with scurrilous jesting, ten men being appointed for each of the deities to provide the choruses: and the choruses spoke evil of no man, but only of the women of the place. Now the Epidaurians also had the same rites; and they have also rites which may not be divulged.

84. These images then having been stolen, the Epidaurians no longer continued to fulfil towards the Athenians that which they had agreed. The Athenians accordingly sent and expressed displeasure to the Epidaurians; and they declared saying that they were doing no wrong; for during the time when they had the images in their country they continued to fulfil that which they had agreed upon, but since they had been deprived of them, it was not just that they should make the offerings anymore; and they bade them demand these from the men of Egina, who had the images. So the Athenians sent to Egina and demanded the images back; but the Eginetans said that they had nothing to do with the Athenians.

85. The Athenians then report that in one single trireme were dispatched those of their citizens who were sent by the State after this demand; who having come to Egina, attempted to tear up from off their pedestals the images, (alleging that they were made of wood which belonged to the Athenians), in order to carry them back with them: but not

being able to get hold of them in this manner (say the Athenians) they threw ropes round them and were pulling them, when suddenly, as they pulled, thunder came on and an earthquake at the same time with the thunder; and the crew of the trireme who were pulling were made beside themselves by these, and being brought to this condition they killed one another as if they were enemies, until at last but one of the whole number was left; and he returned alone to Phaleron.

86. Thus the Athenians report that it came to pass: but the Eginetans say that it was not with a single ship that the Athenians came; for a single ship, and even a few more than one, they could have easily repelled, even if they had not happened to have ships of their own: but they say that the Athenians sailed upon their country with a large fleet of ships, and they gave way before them and did not fight a sea-battle. They cannot however declare with certainty whether they gave way thus because they admitted that they were not strong enough to fight the battle by sea, or because they intended to do something of the kind which they actually did. The Athenians then, they say, as no one met them in fight, landed from their ships and made for the images; but not being able to tear them up from their pedestals, at last they threw ropes round them and began to pull, until the images, as they were being pulled, did both the same thing (and here they report something which I cannot believe, but some other man may), for they say that the images fell upon their knees to them and that they continue to be in that position ever since this time. The Athenians, they say, were doing thus; and meanwhile they themselves (say the Eginetans), being informed that the Athenians were about to make an expedition against them, got the Argives to help them; and just when the Athenians had disembarked upon the Eginetan land, the Argives had come to their rescue, and not having been perceived when they passed over from Epidauros to the island, they fell upon the Athenians before these had heard anything of the matter, cutting them off secretly from the way to their ships; and at this moment it was that the thunder and the earthquake came upon them.

87. This is the report which is given by the Argives and Eginetans both, and it is admitted by the Athenians also that but one alone of them survived and came back to Attica: only the Argives say that this one remained alive from destruction wrought by them upon the army of Athens, while the Athenians say that the divine power was the destroyer. However, even this one man did not remain alive, but perished, they say, in the following manner:—when he returned to Athens he reported the calamity which had happened; and the wives of the men who had gone on the expedition to Egina, hearing it and being very indignant that he alone of all had survived, came round this man and proceeded to stab him with the brooches of their mantles, each one of them asking of him where her husband was. Thus he was slain; and to the Athenians it seemed that the deed of the women was a much more terrible thing even than the calamity which had happened; and not knowing, it is said, how they should punish the women in any other way, they changed their fashion of dress to that of Ionia,—for before this the women of the Athenians wore Dorian dress, very like that of Corinth,—they changed it therefore to the linen tunic, in order that they might not have use for brooches.

88. In truth however this fashion of dress is not Ionian originally but Carian, for the old Hellenic fashion of dress for women was universally the same as that which we now call Dorian. Moreover it is said that with reference to these events the Argives and Eginetans made it a custom among themselves in both countries to have the brooches made half as large again as the size which was then established in use, and that their women should

offer brooches especially in the temple of these goddesses, and also that they should carry neither pottery of Athens nor anything else of Athenian make to the temple, but that it should be the custom for the future to drink there from pitchers made in the lands themselves.

89. The women of the Argives and Eginetans from this time onwards because of the quarrel with the Athenians continued to wear brooches larger than before, and still do so even to my time; and the origin of the enmity of the Athenians towards the Eginetans came in the manner which has been said. So at this time, when the Thebans invaded them, the Eginetans readily came to the assistance of the Boeotians, calling to mind what occurred about the images. The Eginetans then were laying waste, as I have said, the coast regions of Attica; and when the Athenians were resolved to make an expedition against the Eginetans, an oracle came to them from Delphi bidding them stay for thirty years reckoned from the time of the wrong done by the Eginetans, and in the one-and-thirtieth year to appoint a sacred enclosure for Aiacos and then to begin the war against the Eginetans, and they would succeed as they desired; but if they should make an expedition against them at once, they would suffer in the meantime very much evil and also inflict very much, but at last they would subdue them. When the Athenians heard the report of this, they appointed a sacred enclosure for Aiacos, namely that which is now established close to the market-place, but they could not endure to hear that they must stay for thirty years, when they had suffered injuries from the Eginetans.

90. While however they were preparing to take vengeance, a matter arose from the Lacedemonians which provided a hindrance to them: for the Lacedemonians, having learnt that which had been contrived by the Alcmaionidai with respect to the Pythian prophetess, and that which had been contrived by the Pythian prophetess against themselves and the sons of Peisistratos, were doubly grieved, not only because they had driven out into exile men who were their guest-friends, but also because after they had done this no gratitude was shown to them by the Athenians. Moreover in addition to this, they were urged on by the oracles which said that many injuries would be suffered by them from the Athenians; of which oracles they had not been aware of before, but they had come to know them, since Cleomenes had brought them to Sparta. In fact Cleomenes had obtained from the Acropolis of the Athenians those oracles which the sons of Peisistratos possessed before and had left in the temple when they were driven out; and Cleomenes recovered them after they had been left behind.

91. At this time, then, when the Lacedemonians had recovered the oracles and when they saw that the Athenians were increasing in power and were not at all willing to submit to them, observing that the Athenian race now that it was free was becoming a match for their own, whereas when held down by despots it was weak and ready to be ruled,—perceiving, I say, all these things, they sent for Hippias the son of Peisistratos to come from Sigeion on the Hellespont, whither the family of Peisistratos go for refuge; and when Hippias had come upon the summons, the Spartans sent also for envoys to come from their other allies and spoke to them as follows: "Allies, we are conscious within ourselves that we have not acted rightly; for incited by counterfeit oracles we drove out into exile men who were very closely united with us as guest-friends and who undertook the task of rendering Athens submissive to us, and then after having done this we delivered over the State to a thankless populace, which so soon as it had raised its head, having been freed by our means drove out us and our king with wanton outrage; and now

exalted with pride it is increasing in power, so that the neighbors of these men first of all, that is the Boeotians and Chalkidians, have already learnt, and perhaps some others also will afterwards learn, that they committed an error. As however we erred in doing those things of which we have spoken, we will try now to take vengeance on them, going thither together with you; since it was for this very purpose that we sent for Hippias, whom ye see here, and for you also, to come from your cities, in order that with common counsel and a common force we might conduct him to Athens and render back to him that which we formerly took away."

92. Thus they spoke; but the majority of the allies did not approve of their words. The rest however kept silence, but the Corinthian Socles spoke as follows: (a) "Surely now the heaven shall be below the earth, and the earth raised up on high above the heaven, and men shall have their dwelling in the sea, and fishes shall have that habitation which men had before, seeing that ye, Lacedemonians, are doing away with free governments and are preparing to bring back despotism again into our cities, than which there is no more unjust or more murderous thing among men. For if in truth this seems to you to be good, namely that the cities should be ruled by despots, do ye yourselves first set up a despot in your own State, and then endeavor to establish them also for others: but as it is, ye are acting unfairly towards your allies, seeing that ye have had no experience of despots your-selves and provide with the greatest care at Sparta that this may never come to pass. If however ye had had experience of it, as we have had, ye would be able to contribute juster opinions of it than at present. (b) For the established order of the Corinthian State was this:—the government was an oligarchy, and the oligarchs, who were called Bacchi-adai, had control over the State and made marriages among themselves. Now one of these men, named Amphion, had a daughter born to him who was lame, and her name was Labda. This daughter, since none of the Bacchiadai wished to marry her, was taken to wife by Aëtion the son of Echecrates, who was of the deme of Petra, but by original descent a Lapith and of the race of Caineus. Neither from this wife nor from another were children born to him, therefore he set out to Delphi to inquire about offspring; and as he entered, forthwith the prophetess addressed him in these lines:

"'Much to be honored art thou, yet none doth render thee honor.
Labda conceives, and a rolling rock will she bear, which shall ruin
Down on the heads of the kings, and with chastisement visit Corinthos.'

This answer given to Aëtion was by some means reported to the Bacchiadai, to whom the oracle which had come to Corinth before this was not intelligible, an oracle which had reference to the same thing as that of Aëtion and said thus:

"'An eagle conceives in the rocks and shall bear a ravening lion,
Strong and fierce to devour, who the knees of many shall loosen.
Ponder this well in your minds, I bid you, Corinthians, whose dwelling
Lies about fair Peirene's spring and in craggy Corinthos.'

(c) This oracle, I say, having come before to the Bacchiadai was obscure; but afterwards when they heard that which had come to Aëtion, forthwith they understood the former also, that it was in accord with that of Aëtion; and understanding this one also they kept quiet, desiring to destroy the offspring which should be born to Aëtion. Then, so soon as his wife bore a child, they sent ten of their own number to the deme in which Aëtion had his dwelling, to slay the child; and when these had come to Petra and had passed into the court of Aëtion's house, they asked for the child; and Labda, not knowing anything of the purpose for which they had come, and supposing them to be asking for the child on account of friendly feeling towards its father, brought it and placed it in the hands of one of them. Now they, it seems, had resolved by the way that the first of them who received the child should dash it upon the ground. However, when Labda brought and gave it, it happened by divine providence that the child smiled at the man who had received it; and when he perceived this, a feeling of compassion prevented him from killing it, and having this compassion he delivered it to the next man, and he to the third. Thus it passed through the hands of all the ten, delivered from one to another, since none of them could bring himself to destroy its life. So they gave the child back to its mother and went out; and then standing by the doors they abused and found fault with one another, laying blame especially on the one who had first received the child, because he had not done according to that which had been resolved; until at last after some time they determined again to enter and all to take a share in the murder. (d) From the offspring of Aëtion however it was destined that evils should spring up for Corinth: for Labda was listening to all this as she stood close by the door, and fearing lest they should change their mind and take the child a second time and kill it, she carried it and concealed it in the place which seemed to her the least likely to be discovered, that is to say a corn-chest, feeling sure that if they should return and come to a search, they were likely to examine every-thing: and this in fact happened. So when they had come, and searching had failed to find it, they thought it best to return and say to those who had sent them that they had done all that which they had been charged by them to do. (e) They then having departed said this; and after this the son of Aëtion grew, and because he had escaped this danger, the name of Kypselos was given him as a surname derived from the corn-chest. Then when Kypselos had grown to manhood and was seeking divination, a two-edged answer was given him at Delphi, placing trust in which he made an attempt upon Corinth and obtained posses-sion of it. Now the answer was as follows:

"'Happy is this man's lot of a truth, who enters my dwelling,
Offspring of Aëtion, he shall rule in famous Corinthos,
Kypselos, he and his sons, but his children's children no longer.'

Such was the oracle: and Kypselos when he became despot was a man of this charac-ter,—many of the Corinthians he drove into exile, many he deprived of their wealth, and very many more of their lives. (f) And when he had reigned for thirty years and had brought his life to a prosperous end, his son Periander became his successor in the despo-tism. Now Periander at first was milder than his father; but after he had had dealings through messengers with Thrasybulos the despot of Miletos, he became far more murderous even than Kypselos. For he sent a messenger to Thrasybulos and asked what settlement of affairs was the safest for him to make, in order that he might best govern his State: and Thrasybulos led forth the messenger who had come from Periander out of the city, and entered into a field of growing corn; and as he passed through the crop of corn, while inquiring and asking questions repeatedly of the messenger about the occasion of his coming from Corinth, he kept cutting off the heads of those ears of corn which he saw higher than the rest; and as he cut off their heads he cast them away, until he had destroyed in this manner the finest and richest part of the crop. So having passed through the place and having suggested no word of counsel, he dismissed the messenger. When the messenger returned to Corinth, Periander was anxious to hear the counsel which had been given; but he said that Thrasybulos had given him no counsel, and added that he wondered at the deed of Periander in sending him to such a man, for the man was out of his senses and a waster of his own goods,—relating at the same time that which he had seen Thrasybulos do. (g) So Periander, understanding that which had been done and perceiving that Thrasybulos counselled him to put to death those who were eminent among his subjects, began then to display all manner of evil treatment to the citizens of the State; for whatsoever Kypselos had left undone in killing and driving into exile, this Periander completed. And in one day he stripped all the wives of the Corinthians of their clothing on account of his own wife Melissa. For when he had sent messengers to the Thesprotians on the river Acheron to ask the Oracle of the dead about a deposit made with him by a guest-friend, Melissa appeared and said she would not tell in what place the deposit was laid, for she was cold and had no clothes, since those which he had buried with her were of no use to her, not having been burnt; and this, she said, would be an evidence to him that she was speaking the truth, namely that when the oven was cold, Periander had put his loaves into it. When the report of this was brought back to Periander, the token made him believe, because he had had commerce with Melissa after she was dead; and straightway after receiving the message he caused proclamation to be made that all the wives of the Corinthians should come out to the temple of Hera. They accordingly went as to a festival in their fairest adornment; and he having set the spearmen of his guard in ambush, stripped them all alike, both the free women and their attendant; and having gathered together all their clothes in a place dug out, he set fire to them, praying at the same time to Melissa. Then after he had done this and had sent a second time, the apparition of Melissa told him in what spot he had laid the deposit entrusted to him by his guest-friend.

"Such a thing, ye must know, Lacedemonians, is despotism, and such are its deeds: and we Corinthians marveled much at first when we saw that ye were sending for Hippias, and now we marvel even more because ye say these things; and we adjure you, calling upon the gods of Hellas, not to establish despotisms in the cities. If however ye will not cease from your design, but endeavor to restore Hippias contrary to that which is just, know that the Corinthians at least do not give their consent to that which ye do."

93. Socles being the envoy of Corinth thus spoke, and Hippias made answer to him, calling to witness the same gods as he, that assuredly the Corinthians would more than all others regret the loss of the sons of Peisistratos, when the appointed days should have come for them to be troubled by the Athenians. Thus Hippias made answer, being acquainted with the oracles more exactly than any other man: but the rest of the allies, who for a time had restrained themselves and kept silence, when they heard Socles speak freely, gave utterance every one of them to that which they felt, and adopted the opinion of the Corinthian envoy, adjuring the Lacedemonians not to do any violence to a city of Hellas.

94. Thus was this brought to an end: and Hippias being dismissed from thence had Anthemus offered to him by Amyntas king of the Macedonians and Iolcos by the Thes-

salians. He however accepted neither of these, but retired again to Sigeion; which city Peisistratos had taken by force of arms from the Mytilenians, and having got possession of it, had appointed his own natural son Hegesistratos, born of an Argive woman, to be despot of it: he however did not without a struggle keep possession of that which he received from Peisistratos; for the Mytilenians and Athenians carried on war for a long time, having their strongholds respectively at Achilleion and at Sigeion, the one side demanding that the place be restored to them, and the Athenians on the other hand not admitting this demand, but proving by argument that the Aiolians had no better claim to the territory of Ilion than they and the rest of the Hellenes, as many as joined with Menelaos in exacting vengeance for the rape of Helen.

95. Now while these carried on the war, besides many other things of various kinds which occurred in the battles, once when a fight took place and the Athenians were conquering, Alcaios the poet, taking to flight, escaped indeed himself, but the Athenians retained possession of his arms and hung them up on the walls of the temple of Athene which is at Sigeion. About this matter Alcaios composed a song and sent it to Mytilene, reporting therein his misadventure to one Melanippos, who was his friend. Finally Periander the son of Kypselos made peace between the Athenians and the Mytilenians, for to him they referred the matter as arbitrator; and he made peace between them on the condition that each should continue to occupy that territory which they then possessed.

96. Sigeion then in this matter had come under the rule of the Athenians. And when Hippias had returned to Asia from Lacedaemon, he set everything in motion, stirring up enmity between the Athenians and Artaphrenes, and using every means to secure that Athens should come under the rule of himself and of Dareios. Hippias, I say, was thus engaged; and the Athenians meanwhile hearing of these things sent envoys to Sardis, and endeavored to prevent the Persians from following the suggestions of the exiled Athenians. Artaphrenes however commanded them, if they desired to be preserved from ruin, to receive Hippias back again. This proposal the Athenians were not by any means disposed to accept when it was reported; and as they did not accept this, it became at once a commonly received opinion among them that they were enemies of the Persians.

97. While they had these thoughts and had been set at enmity with the Persians, at this very time Aristagoras the Milesian, ordered away from Sparta by Cleomenes the Lacedemonian, arrived at Athens; for this was the city which had most power of all the rest besides Sparta. And Aristagoras came forward before the assembly of the people and said the same things as he had said at Sparta about the wealth which there was in Asia, and about the Persian manner of making war, how they used neither shield nor spear and were easy to overcome. Thus I say he said, and also he added this, namely that the Milesians were colonists from the Athenians, and that it was reasonable that the Athenians should rescue them, since they had such great power; and there was nothing which he did not promise, being very urgent in his request, until at last he persuaded them: for it would seem that it is easier to deceive many than one, seeing that, though he did not prove able to deceive Cleomenes the Lacedemonian by himself, yet he did this to thirty thousand Athenians. The Athenians then, I say, being persuaded, voted a resolution to dispatch twenty ships to help the Ionians, and appointed to command them Melanthios one of their citizens, who was in all things highly reputed. These ships proved to be the beginning of evils for the Hellenes and the Barbarians.

98. Aristagoras however sailed on before and came to Miletos; and then having

devised a plan from which no advantage was likely to come for the Ionians (nor indeed was he doing what he did with a view to that, but in order to vex king Dareios), he sent a man to Phrygia to the Paionians who had been taken captive by Megabazos from the river Strymon, and who were dwelling in a district and village of Phrygia apart by themselves; and when the messenger came to the Paionians he spoke these words: "Paionians, Aristagoras the despot of Miletos sent me to offer to you salvation, if ye shall be willing to do as he says; for now all Ionia has revolted from the king and ye have an opportunity of coming safe to your own land: to reach the sea shall be your concern, and after this it shall be thenceforth ours." The Paionians hearing this received it as a most welcome proposal, and taking with them their children and their women they began a flight to the sea; some of them however were struck with fear and remained in the place where they were. Having come to the coast the Paionians crossed over thence to Chios, and when they were already in Chios there arrived in their track a large body of Persian horsemen pursuing the Paionians. These, as they did not overtake them, sent over to Chios to bid the Paionians return back: the Paionians however did not accept their proposal, but the men of Chios conveyed them from Chios to Lesbos, and the Lesbians brought them to Doriscos, and thence they proceeded by land and came to Paionia.

99. Aristagoras meanwhile, when the Athenians had arrived with twenty ships, bringing with them also five triremes of the Eretrians, joined the expedition not for the sake of the Athenians but of the Milesians themselves, to repay them a debt which they owed (for the Milesians in former times had borne with the Eretrians the burden of all that war which they had with the Chalkidians at the time when the Chalkidians on their side were helped by the Samians against the Eretrians and Milesians),—when these, I say, had arrived and the other allies were on the spot, Aristagoras proceeded to make a march upon Sardis. On this march he did not go himself, but remained at Miletos and appointed others to be in command of the Milesians, namely his brother Charopinos and of the other citizens one Hermophantos.

100. With this force then the Ionians came to Ephesos, and leaving their ships at Coresos in the land of Ephesos, went up themselves in a large body, taking Ephesians to guide them in their march. So they marched along by the river Caÿster, and then when they arrived after crossing the range of Tmolos, they took Sardis without any resistance, all except the citadel, but the citadel Artaphrenes himself saved from capture, having with him a considerable force of men.

101. From plundering this city after they had taken it they were prevented by this:— the houses in Sardis were mostly built of reeds, and even those of them which were of brick had their roofs thatched with reeds: of these houses one was set on fire by a soldier, and forthwith the fire going on from house to house began to spread over the whole town. So then as the town was on fire, the Lydians and all the Persians who were in the city being cut off from escape, since the fire was prevailing in the extremities round about them, and not having any way out of the town, flowed together to the market-place and to the river Pactolos, which brings down gold-dust for them from Tmolos, flowing through the middle of their market-place, and then runs out into the river Hermos, and this into the sea;—to this Pactolos, I say, and to the market-place the Lydians and Persians gathered themselves together, and were compelled to defend themselves. The Ionians then, seeing some of the enemy standing on their defense and others in great numbers coming on to

the attack, were struck with fear and retired to the mountain called Tmolos, and after that at nightfall departed to go to their ships.

102. Sardis was then destroyed by fire, and in it also the temple of the native goddess Hybebe; which the Persians alleged afterwards as a reason for setting on fire in return the temples in the land of the Hellenes. However at the time of which I speak the Persians who occupied districts within the river Halys, informed beforehand of this movement, were gathering together and coming to the help of the Lydians; and, as it chanced, they found when they came that the Ionians no longer were in Sardis; but they followed closely in their track and came up with them at Ephesos: and the Ionians stood indeed against them in array, but when they joined battle they had very much the worse; and besides other persons of note whom the Persians slaughtered, there fell also Eualkides commander of the Eretrians, a man who had won wreaths in contests of the games and who was much celebrated by Simonides of Keos: and those of them who survived the battle dispersed to their various cities.

103. Thus then they fought at that time; and after the battle the Athenians left the Ionians together, and when Aristagoras was urgent in calling upon them by messengers for assistance, they said that they would not help them: the Ionians, however, though deprived of the alliance of the Athenians, none the less continued to prepare for the war with the king, so great had been the offences already committed by them against Dareios. They sailed moreover to the Hellespont and brought under their power Byzantion and all the other cities which are in those parts; and then having sailed forth out of the Hellespont, they gained in addition the most part of Caria to be in alliance with them: for even Caunos, which before was not willing to be their ally, then, after they had burnt Sardis, was added to them also.

104. The Cyprians too, excepting those of Amathus, were added voluntarily to their alliance; for these also had revolted from the Medes in the following manner:—there was one Onesilos, younger brother of Gorgos king of Salamis, and son of Chersis, the son of Siromos, the son of Euelthon. This man in former times too had been wont often to advise Gorgos to make revolt from the king, and at this time, when he heard that the Ionians had revolted, he pressed him very hard and endeavored to urge him to it. Since however he could not persuade Gorgos, Onesilos watched for a time when he had gone forth out of the city of Salamis, and then together with the men of his own faction he shut him out of the gates. Gorgos accordingly being robbed of the city went for refuge to the Medes, and Onesilos was ruler of Salamis and endeavored to persuade all the men of Cyprus to join him in revolt. The others then he persuaded; but since those of Amathus were not willing to do as he desired, he sat down before their city and besieged it.

105. Onesilos then was besieging Amathus; and meanwhile, when it was reported to king Dareios that Sardis had been captured and burnt by the Athenians and the Ionians together, and that the leader of the league for being about these things was the Milesian Aristagoras, it is said that at first being informed of this he made no account of the Ionians, because he knew that they at all events would not escape unpunished for their revolt, but he inquired into who the Athenians were; and when he had been informed, he asked for his bow, and having received it and placed an arrow upon the string, he discharged it upwards towards heaven, and as he shot into the air he said: "Zeus, that it may be granted me to take vengeance upon the Athenians!" Having so said he charged one of his atten-

dants, that when dinner was set before the king he should say always three times: "Master, remember the Athenians."

106. When he had given this charge, he called into his presence Histiaios the Milesian, whom Dareios had now been keeping with him for a long time, and said: "I am informed, Histiaios, that thy deputy, to whom thou didst depute the government of Miletos, has made rebellion against me; for he brought in men against me from the other continent and persuaded the Ionians also,—who shall pay the penalty to me for that which they did,— these, I say, he persuaded to go together with them, and thus he robbed me of Sardis. Now therefore how thinkest thou that this is well? and how without thy counsels was anything of this kind done? Take heed lest thou afterwards find reason to blame thyself for this." Histiaios replied: "O king, what manner of speech is this that thou hast uttered, saying that I counselled a matter from which it was likely that any vexation would grow for thee, either great or small? What have I to seek for in addition to that which I have, that I should do these things; and of what am I in want? for I have everything that thou hast, and I am thought worthy by thee to hear all thy counsels. Nay, but if my deputy is indeed acting in any such manner as thou hast said, be assured that he has done it merely on his own account. I however, for my part, do not even admit the report to be true, that the Milesians and my deputy are acting in any rebellious fashion against thy power: but if it prove that they are indeed doing anything of that kind, and if that which thou hast heard, O king, be the truth, learn then what a thing thou didst in removing me away from the sea-coast; for it seems that the Ionians, when I had gone out of the sight of their eyes, did that which they had long had a desire to do; whereas if I had been in Ionia, not a city would have made the least movement. Now therefore as quickly as possible let me set forth to go to Ionia, that I may order all these matters for thee as they were before, and deliver into thy hands this deputy of Miletos who contrived these things: and when I have done this after thy mind, I swear by the gods of the royal house that I will not put off from me the tunic which I wear when I go down to Ionia, until I have made Sardinia tributary to thee, which is the largest of all islands."

107. Thus saying Histiaios endeavored to deceive the king, and Dareios was persuaded and let him go, charging him, when he should have accomplished that which he had promised, to return to him again at Susa.

108. In the meantime, while the news about Sardis was going up to the king, and while Dareios, after doing that which he did with the bow, came to speech with Histiaios, and Histiaios having been let go by Dareios was making his journey to the sea-coast,—during all that time the events were happening which here follow.—As Onesilos of Salamis was besieging those of Amathus, it was reported to him that Artybios a Persian, bringing with him in ships a large Persian army, was to be expected shortly to arrive in Cyprus. Being informed of this, Onesilos sent heralds to different places in Ionia to summon the Ionians to his assistance; and they took counsel together and came without delay with a large force. Now the Ionians arrived in Cyprus just at the time when the Persians having crossed over in ships from Kilikia were proceeding by land to attack Salamis, while the Phoenicians with the ships were sailing round the headland which is called the "Keys of Cyprus."

109. This being the case, the despots of Cyprus called together the commanders of the Ionians and said: "Ionians, we of Cyprus give you a choice which enemy ye will rather fight with, the Persians or the Phoenicians: for if ye will rather array yourselves on land

and make trial of the Persians in fight, it is time now for you to disembark from your ships and array yourselves on the land, and for us to embark in your ships to contend against the Phoenicians; but if on the other hand ye will rather make trial of the Phoenicians,—whichever of these two ye shall choose, ye must endeavor that, so far as it rests with you, both Ionia and Cyprus shall be free." To this the Ionians replied: "We were sent out by the common authority of the Ionians to guard the sea, and not to deliver our ships to the Cyprians and ourselves fight with the Persians on land. We therefore will endeavor to do good service in that place to which we were appointed; and ye must call to mind all the evils which ye suffered from the Medes, when ye were in slavery to them, and prove yourselves good men."

110. The Ionians made answer in these words; and afterwards, when the Persians had come to the plain of Salamis, the kings of the Cyprians set in order their array, choosing the best part of the troops of Salamis and of Soloi to be arrayed against the Persians and setting the other Cyprians against the rest of the enemy's troops; and against Artybios, the commander of the Persians, Onesilos took up his place in the array by his own free choice.

111. Now Artybios was riding a horse which had been trained to rear up against a hoplite. Onesilos accordingly being informed of this, and having a shield-bearer, by race of Caria, who was of very good repute as a soldier and full of courage besides, said to this man: "I am informed that the horse of Artybios rears upright and works both with his feet and his mouth against any whom he is brought to attack. Do thou therefore consider the matter, and tell me forthwith which of the two thou wilt rather watch for and strike, the horse or Artybios himself." To this his attendant replied: "O king, I am ready to do both or either of these two things, and in every case to do that which thou shalt appoint for me; but I will declare to thee the way in which I think it will be most suitable for thy condition. I say that it is right for one who is king and commander to fight with a king and commander; for if thou shalt slay the commander of the enemy, it turns to great glory for thee; and again, if he shall slay thee, which heaven forbid, even death when it is at the hands of a worthy foe is but half to be lamented: but for us who are under thy command it is suitable to fight with the others who are under his command and with his horse: and of the tricks of the horse have thou no fear at all, for I engage to thee that after this at least he shall never stand against any man more." Thus he spoke; and shortly afterwards the opposed forces joined battle both on land and with their ships.

112. On that day the Ionians for their part greatly distinguished themselves and overcame the Phoenicians, and of them the Samians were best: and meanwhile on land, when the armies met, they came to close quarters and fought; and as regards the two commanders, what happened was this:—when Artybios came to fight with Onesilos sitting upon his horse, Onesilos, as he had concerted with his shield-bearer, struck at Artybios himself, when he came to fight with him; and when the horse put its hoofs against the shield of Onesilos, then the Carian struck with a falchion and smote off the horse's feet.

113 So Artybios the commander of the Persians fell there on the spot together with his horse: and while the others also were fighting, Stesenor the despot of Curion deserted them, having with him a large force of men,—now these Curians are said to be settlers from Argos,—and when the Curians had deserted, forthwith also the war-chariots of the men of Salamis proceeded to do the same as the Curians. When these things took place, the Persians had the advantage over the Cyprians; and after their army had been put to rout, many others fell and among them Onesilos the son of Chersis, he who brought about

the revolt of the Cyprians, and also the king of the Solians, Aristokypros the son of Philokypros,—that Philokypros whom Solon the Athenian, when he came to Cyprus, commended in verse above all other despots.

114. So the men of Amathus cut off the head of Onesilos, because he had besieged them; and having brought it to Amathus they hung it over the gate of the city: and as the head hung there, when it had now become a hollow, a swarm of bees entered into it and filled it with honeycomb. This having so come to pass, the Amathusians consulted an Oracle about the head, and they received an answer bidding them take it down and bury it and sacrifice to Onesilos every year as a hero; and if they did this, it would go better with them.

115. The Amathusians accordingly continued to do so even to my time. But the Ionians who had fought the sea-fight in Cyprus, when they perceived that the fortunes of Onesilos were ruined and that the cities of the Cyprians were besieged, except Salamis, and that this city had been delivered over by the Salaminians to Gorgos the former king,—as soon as they perceived this, the Ionians sailed away back to Ionia. Now of the cities in Cyprus Soloi held out for the longest time under the siege; and the Persians took it in the fifth month by undermining the wall round.

116. The Cyprians then, after they had made themselves free for one year, had again been reduced to slavery afresh: and meanwhile Daurises, who was married to a daughter of Dareios, and Hymaies and Otanes, who were also Persian commanders and were married also to daughters of Dareios, after they had pursued those Ionians who had made the expedition to Sardis and defeating them in battle had driven them by force to their ships,—after this distributed the cities amongst themselves and proceeded to sack them.

117. Daurises directed his march to the cities on the Hellespont, and he took Dardanos and Abydos and Percote and Lampsacos and Paisos, of these he took on each day one; and as he was marching from Paisos against the city of Parion, the report came that the Carians had made common cause with the Ionians and were in revolt from the Persians. He turned back therefore from the Hellespont and marched his army upon Caria.

118. And, as it chanced, a report of this was brought to the Carians before Daurises arrived; and the Carians being informed of it gathered together at the place which is called the "White Pillars" and at the river Marsyas, which flows from the region of Idrias and runs out into the Maiander. When the Carians had been gathered together there, among many other counsels which were given, the best, as it seems to me, was that of Pixodaros the son of Mausolos, a man of Kindye, who was married to the daughter of the king of the Kilikians, Syennesis. The opinion of this man was to the effect that the Carians should cross over the Maiander and engage battle with the Persians having the river at their backs, in order that the Carians, not being able to fly backwards and being compelled to remain where they were, might prove themselves even better men in fight than they natu-rally would. This opinion did not prevail; but they resolved that the Persians rather than themselves should have the Maiander at their backs, evidently in order that if there should be a flight of the Persians and they should be worsted in the battle, they might never return home, but might fall into the river.

119. After this, when the Persians had come and had crossed the Maiander, the Carians engaged with the Persians on the river Marsyas and fought a battle which was obstinately contested and lasted long; but at length they were worsted by superior numbers: and of the Persians there fell as many as two thousand, but of the Carians ten thousand. Then

those of them who escaped were shut up in Labraunda within the sanctuary of Zeus Stratios, which is a large sacred grove of plane-trees; now the Carians are the only men we know who offer sacrifices to Zeus Stratios. These men then, being shut up there, were taking counsel together about their safety, whether they would fare better if they delivered themselves over to the Persians or if they left Asia altogether.

120. And while they were thus taking counsel, there came to their aid the Milesians and their allies. Then the Carians dismissed the plans which they were before considering and prepared to renew the war again from the beginning: and when the Persians came to attack them, they engaged with them and fought a battle, and they were worsted yet more completely than before; and while many were slain of all parties, the Milesians suffered most.

121. Then afterwards the Carians repaired this loss and retrieved their defeat; for being informed that the Persians had set forth to march upon their cities, they laid an ambush on the road which is by Pedasos, and the Persians falling into it by night were destroyed both they and their commanders, namely Daurises and Amorges and Sisimakes; and with them died also Myrsos the son of Gyges. Of this ambush the leader was Heracleides the son of Ibanollis, a man of Mylasa.

122. These then of the Persians were thus destroyed; and meanwhile Hymaies, who was another of those who pursued after the Ionians that had made the expedition to Sardis, directed his march to the Propontis and took Kios in Mysia; and having conquered this city, when he was informed that Daurises had left the Hellespont and was marching towards Caria, he left the Propontis and led his army to the Hellespont: and he conquered all the Aiolians who occupy the district of Ilion, and also the Gergithes, who were left behind as a remnant of the ancient Teucrians. While conquering these tribes Hymaies himself ended his life by sickness in the land of Troas.

123. He thus brought his life to an end; and Artaphrenes the governor of the province of Sardis was appointed with Otanes the third of the commanders to make the expedition against Ionia and that part of Aiolia which bordered upon it. Of Ionia these took the city of Clazomenai, and of the Aiolians Kyme.

124. While the cities were thus being taken, Aristagoras the Milesian, being, as he proved in this instance, not of very distinguished courage, since after having disturbed Ionia and made preparation of great matters he counselled running away when he saw these things, (moreover it had become clear to him that it was impossible to overcome king Dareios),—he, I say, having regard to these things, called together those of his own party and took counsel with them, saying that it was better that there should be a refuge prepared for them, in case that they should after all be driven out from Miletos, and proposing the question whether he should lead them from thence to Sardinia, to form a colony there, or to Myrkinos in the land of the Edonians, which Histiaios had been fortifying, having received it as a gift from Dareios. This was the question proposed by Aristagoras.

125. Now the opinion of Hecataios the son of Hegesander the historian was that he should not take a colony to either of these places, but build a wall of defense for himself in the island of Leros and keep still, if he should be forced to leave Miletos; and afterwards with this for his starting point he would be able to return to Miletos.

126. This was the counsel of Hecataios; but Aristagoras was most inclined to go forth to Myrkinos. He therefore entrusted the government of Miletos to Pythagoras, a man of

repute among the citizens, and he himself sailed away to Thrace, taking with him every one who desired to go; and he took possession of the region for which he had set out. But starting from this to make war, he perished by the hands of the Thracians, that is both Aristagoras himself and his army, when he was encamped about a certain city and the Thracians desired to go out from it under a truce.

6

THE SIXTH BOOK OF THE
HISTORIES, CALLED ERATO

1. Aristagoras accordingly, after having caused Ionia to revolt, thus brought his life to an end; and meanwhile Histiaios the despot of Miletos, having been let go by Dareios had arrived at Sardis: and when he came from Susa, Artaphrenes the governor of Sardis asked him for what reason he supposed the Ionians had revolted; and he said that he could not tell, and moreover he expressed wonder at that which had happened, pretending that he knew nothing of the state of affairs. Then Artaphrenes seeing that he was using dissimulation said, having knowledge of the truth about the revolt: "Thus it is with thee, Histiaios, about these matters,—this shoe was stitched by thee, and put on by Aristagoras."

2. Thus said Artaphrenes with reference to the revolt; and Histiaios fearing Artaphrenes because he understood the matter, ran away the next night at nightfall and went to the sea-coast, having deceived king Dareios, seeing that he had engaged to subdue Sardinia the largest of islands, and instead of that he was endeavoring to take upon himself leadership of the Ionians in the war against Dareios. Then having crossed over to Chios he was put in bonds by the Chians, being accused by them of working for a change of their State by suggestion of Dareios. When however the Chians learnt the whole story and heard that he was an enemy to the king, they released him.

3. Then Histiaios, being asked by the Ionians for what reason he had so urgently charged Aristagoras to revolt from the king and had wrought so great an evil for the Ionians, did not by any means declare to them that which had been in truth the cause, but reported to them that king Dareios had resolved to remove the Phoenicians from their land and to settle them in Ionia, and the Ionians in Phenicia; and for this reason, he said, he had given the charge. Thus he attempted to alarm the Ionians, although the king had never resolved to do so at all.

4. After this Histiaios acting through a messenger, namely Hermippos a man of Atarneus, sent papers to the Persians who were at Sardis, implying that he had already talked matters over with them about a revolt: and Hermippos did not deliver them to those to whom he was sent, but bore the papers and put them into the hands of

Artaphrenes. He then, perceiving all that was being done, bade Hermippos bear the papers sent by Histiaios and deliver them to those to whom he was sent to bear them, and to deliver to him the replies sent back by the Persians to Histiaios. These things having been discovered, Artaphrenes upon that put to death many of the Persians.

5. As regards Sardis therefore there was confusion of the design; and when Histiaios had been disappointed of this hope, the Chians attempted to restore him to Miletos at the request of Histiaios himself. The Milesians, however, who had been rejoiced before to be rid of Aristagoras, were by no means eager to receive another despot into their land, seeing that they had tasted of liberty: and in fact Histiaios, attempting to return to Miletos by force and under cover of night, was wounded in the thigh by one of the Milesians. He then, being repulsed from his own city, returned to Chios; and thence, as he could not persuade the Chians to give him ships, he crossed over to Mytilene and endeavored to persuade the Lesbians to give him ships. So they manned eight triremes and sailed with Histiaios to Byzantion, and stationing themselves there they captured the ships which sailed out of the Pontus, excepting where the crews of them said that they were ready to do the bidding of Histiaios.

6. While Histiaios and the men of Mytilene were acting thus, a large army both of sea and land forces was threatening to attack Miletos itself; for the commanders of the Persians had joined together to form one single army and were marching upon Miletos, considering the other towns of less account. Of their naval force the most zealous were the Phoenicians, and with them also served the Cyprians, who had just been subdued, and the Kilikians and Egyptians.

7. These, I say, were advancing upon Miletos and the rest of Ionia; and meanwhile the Ionians being informed of this were sending deputies chosen from themselves to the Panionion. When these had arrived at that place and took counsel together, they resolved not to gather a land-army to oppose the Persians, but that the Milesians should defend their walls by themselves, and that the Ionians should man their fleet, leaving out not one of their ships, and having done so should assemble as soon as possible at Lade, to fight a sea-battle in defense of Miletos. Now Lade is a small island lying opposite the city of the Milesians.

8. Then the Ionians manned their ships and came thither, and with them also those Aiolians who inhabit Lesbos; and they were drawn up in order thus:—the extremity of the line towards the East was held by the Milesians themselves, who furnished eighty ships; next to them were the Prienians with twelve ships and the men of Myus with three; next to those of Myus were the Teians with seventeen ships, and after the Teians the Chians with a hundred; after these were stationed the men of Erythrai and of Phocaia, the former furnishing eight ships and the latter three; next to the Phocaians were the Lesbians with seventy ships, and last, holding the extremity of the line towards the West, were stationed the Samians with sixty ships. Of all these the total number proved to be three hundred and fifty-three triremes.

9. These were the ships of the Ionians; and of the Barbarians the number of ships was six hundred. When these too were come to the Milesian coast and their whole land-army was also there, then the commanders of the Persians, being informed of the number of the Ionian ships, were struck with fear lest they should be unable to overcome them, and thus on the one hand should not be able to conquer Miletos from not having command of the sea, and at the same time should run a risk of being punished by Dareios. Reflecting upon

these things they gathered together the despots of the Ionians who were exiles with the Medes, having been deposed from their governments by Aristagoras the Milesian, and who chanced to be then joining in the expedition against Miletos,—of these men they called together those who were present and spoke to them as follows: "Ionians, now let each one of you show himself a benefactor of the king's house, that is to say, let each one of you endeavor to detach his own countrymen from the body of the alliance: and make your proposals promising at the same time that they shall suffer nothing unpleasant on account of the revolt, and neither their temples nor their private houses shall be burnt, nor shall they have any worse treatment than they had before this; but if they will not do so, but will by all means enter into a contest with us, threaten them and tell them this, which in truth shall happen to them, namely that if they are worsted in the fight they shall be reduced to slavery, and we shall make their sons eunuchs, and their maidens we shall remove to Bactria, and deliver their land to others."

10. They thus spoke; and the despots of Ionia sent each one by night to his own people announcing to them this. The Ionians however, that is those to whom these messages came, continued obstinate and would not accept the thought of treason to their cause; and each people thought that to them alone the Persians were sending this message.

11. This happened as soon as the Persians came to Miletos; and after this the Ionians being gathered together at Lade held meetings; and others no doubt also made speeches to them, but especially the Phocaian commander Dionysios, who said as follows: "Seeing that our affairs are set upon the razor's edge, Ionians, whether we shall be free or slaves, and slaves too to be dealt with as runaways, now therefore if ye shall be willing to take upon yourselves hardships, ye will have labor for the time being, but ye will be able to overcome the enemy and be free; whereas if ye continue to be self-indulgent and without discipline, I have no hope for you that ye will not pay the penalty to the king for your revolt. Nay, but do as I say, and deliver yourselves over to me; and I engage, if the gods grant equal conditions, that either the enemy will not fight with us, or that fighting he shall be greatly discomfited."

12. Hearing this the Ionians delivered themselves to Dionysios; and he used to bring the ships out every day in single file, that he might practice the rowers by making the ships break through one another's line, and that he might get the fighting-men in the ships under arms; an then for the rest of the day he would keep the ships at anchor; and thus he gave the Ionians work to do during the whole day. For seven days then they submitted and did that which he commanded; but on the day after these the Ionians, being unaccustomed to such toils and being exhausted with hard work and hot sun, spoke to one another thus: "Against which of the deities have we offended, that we thus fill up the measure of evil? for surely we have delivered ourselves to a Phocaian, an impostor, who furnishes but three ships: and he has taken us into his hands and maltreats us with evil dealing from which we can never recover; and many of us in fact have fallen into sicknesses, and many others, it may be expected, will suffer the same thing shortly; and for us it is better to endure anything else in the world rather than these ills, and to undergo the slavery which will come upon us, whatever that shall be, rather than to be oppressed by that which we have now. Come, let us not obey him after this anymore." So they said, and forthwith after this every one refused to obey him, and they pitched their tents in the island like an army, and kept in the shade, and would not go on board their ships or practice any exercises.

13. Perceiving this which was being done by the Ionians, the commanders of the Samians then at length accepted from Aiakes the son of Syloson those proposals which Aiakes sent before at the bidding of the Persians, asking them to leave the alliance of the Ionians; the Samians, I say, accepted these proposals, perceiving that there was great want of discipline on the part of the Ionians, while at the same time it was clear to them that it was impossible to overcome the power of the king; and they well knew also that even if they should overcome the present naval force of Dareios, another would be upon them five times as large. Having found an occasion then, so soon as they saw that the Ionians refused to be serviceable, they counted it gain for themselves to save their temples and their private property. Now Aiakes, from whom the Samians accepted the proposals, was the son of Syloson, the son of Aiakes, and being despot of Samos he had been deprived of his rule by Aristagoras the Milesian, like the other despots of Ionia.

14. So when the Phoenicians sailed to the attack, the Ionians also put out their ships from shore against them, sailing in single file: and when they came near and engaged battle with one another, as regards what followed I am not able exactly to record which of the Ionians showed themselves cowards or good men in this sea-fight, for they throw blame upon one another. The Samians however, it is said, according to their agreement with Aiakes put up their sails then and set forth from their place in the line to sail back to Samos, excepting only eleven ships: of these the captains stayed in their places and took part in the sea-fight, refusing to obey the commanders of their division; and the public authority of the Samians granted them on account of this to have their names written up on a pillar with their fathers' names also, as having proved themselves good men; and this pillar exists still in the market-place. Then the Lesbians also, when they saw that those next them in order were taking to flight, did the same things as the Samians had done, and so also most of the Ionians did the very same thing.

15. Of those which remained in their places in the sea-fight the Chians suffered very severely, since they displayed brilliant deeds of valor and refused to play the coward. These furnished, as was before said, a hundred ships and in each of them forty picked men of their citizens served as fighting-men; and when they saw the greater number of their allies deserting them, they did not think fit to behave like the cowards among them, but left along with a few only of their allies they continued to fight and kept breaking through the enemy's line; until at last, after they had conquered many ships of the enemy, they lost the greater number of their own.

16. The Chians then with the remainder of their ships fled away to their own land; but those of the Chians whose ships were disabled by the damage which they had received, being pursued fled for refuge to Mycale; and their ships they ran ashore there and left them behind, while the men proceeded over the mainland on foot: and when the Chians had entered the Ephesian territory on their way, then since they came into it by night and at a time when a festival of Thesmophoria was being celebrated by the women of the place, the Ephesians, not having heard beforehand how it was with the Chians and seeing that an armed body had entered their land, supposed certainly that they were robbers and had a design upon the women; so they came out to the rescue in a body and slew the Chians.

17. Such was the fortune which befell these men: but Dionysios the Phocaian, when he perceived that the cause of the Ionians was ruined, after having taken three ships of the enemy sailed away, not to Pocaia any more, for he knew well that it would be reduced to

slavery together with the rest of Ionia, and he sailed forthwith straight to Phenicia; and having there sunk merchant ships and taken a great quantity of goods, he sailed thence to Sicily. Then with that for his starting-point he became a freebooter, not plundering any Hellenes, but Carthaginians and Tyrsenians only.

18. The Persians, then, being conquerors of the Ionians in the sea-fight, besieged Miletos by land and sea, undermining the walls and bringing against it all manner of engines; and they took it completely in the sixth year from the revolt of Aristagoras, and reduced the people to slavery; so that the disaster agreed with the oracle which had been uttered with reference to Miletos.

19. For when the Argives were inquiring at Delphi about the safety of their city, there was given to them an oracle which applied to both, that is to say, part of it had reference to the Argives themselves, while that which was added afterwards referred to the Milesians. The part of it which had reference to the Argives I will record when I reach that place in the history, but that which the Oracle uttered with reference to the Milesians, who were not there present, is as follows:

"And at that time, O Miletos, of evil deeds the contriver,
Thou shalt be made for many a glorious gift and a banquet:
Then shall thy wives be compelled to wash the feet of the long-haired,
And in Didyma then my shrine shall be tended by others."

At the time of which I speak these things came upon the Milesians, since most of the men were killed by the Persians, who are long-haired, and the women and children were dealt with as slaves; and the temple at Didyma, with the sacred building and the sanctuary of the Oracle, was first plundered and then burnt. Of the things in this temple I have made mention frequently in other parts of the history. .

20. After this the Milesians who had been taken prisoner were conducted to Susa; and king Dareios did to them no other evil, but settled them upon the Sea called Erythraian, in the city of Ampe, by which the Tigris flows when it runs out into the sea. Of the Milesian land the Persians themselves kept the surroundings of the city and the plain, but the heights they gave to the Carians of Pedasa for a possession.

21. When the Milesians suffered this treatment from the Persians, the men of Sybaris, who were dwelling in Laos and Skidros, being deprived of their own city, did not repay like with like: for when Sybaris was taken by the men of Croton, the Milesians all from youth upwards shaved their heads and put on great mourning: for these cities were more than all others of which we know bound together by ties of friendship. Not like the Sybarites were the Athenians; for these made it clear that they were grieved at the capture of Miletos, both in many other ways and also by this, that when Phrynichos had composed a drama called the "Capture of Miletos" and had put it on the stage, the body of spectators fell to weeping, and the Athenians moreover fined the poet a thousand drachmas on the ground that he had reminded them of their own calamities; and they ordered also that no one in future should represent this drama.

22. Miletos then had been stripped bare of its former inhabitants: but of the Samians they who had substance were by no means satisfied with that which had been concerted by the commanders of their fleet with the Medes; and taking counsel forthwith after the sea-fight it seemed good to them, before their despot Aiakes arrived in the country, to sail

away and make a colony, and not to stay behind and be slaves of the Medes and of Aiakes: for just at this time the people of Zancle in Sicily were sending messengers to Ionia and inviting the Ionians to come to the "Fair Strand," desiring there to found a city of Ionians. Now this which is called the Fair Strand is in the land of the Sikelians and on that side of Sicily which lies towards Tyrsenia. So when these gave the invitation, the Samians alone of all the Ionians set forth, having with them those of the Milesians who had escaped: and in the course of this matter it happened as follows:—

23. The Samians as they made their way towards Sicily reached Locroi Epizephyroi, and at the same time the people of Zancle, both themselves and their king, whose name was Skythes, were encamped about a city of the Sikelians, desiring to conquer it. Perceiving these things, Anaxilaos the despot of Rhegion, being then at variance with those of Zancle, communicated with the Samians and persuaded them that they ought to leave the Fair Strand alone, to which they were sailing, and take possession of Zancle instead, since it was left now without men to defend it. The Samians accordingly did as he said and took possession of Zancle; and upon this the men of Zancle, being informed that their city was possessed by an enemy, set out to rescue it, and invited Hippocrates the despot of Gela to help them, for he was their ally. When however Hippocrates also with his army had come up to their rescue, first he put Skythes the ruler of the Zanclaians in fetters, on the ground that he had been the cause of the city being lost, and together with him his brother Pythogenes, and sent them away to the town of Incyos; then he betrayed the cause of the remaining Zanclaians by coming to terms with the Samians and exchanging oaths with them; and in return for this it had been promised by the Samians that Hippocrates should receive as his share the half of all the movable goods in the city and of the slaves, and the whole of the property in the fields round. So the greater number of the Zanclaians he put in bonds and kept himself as slaves, but the chief men of them, three hundred in number, he gave to the Samians to put to death; which however the Samians did not do.

24. Now Skythes the ruler of the Zanclaians escaped from Incyos to Himera, and thence he came to Asia and went up to the court of Dareios: and Dareios accounted him the most righteous of all the men who had come up to him from Hellas; for he obtained leave of the king and went away to Sicily, and again came back from Sicily to the king; and at last he brought his life to an end among the Persians in old age and possessing great wealth. The Samians then, having got rid of the rule of the Medes, had gained for themselves without labor the fair city of Zancle.

25. After the sea-battle which was fought for Miletos, the Phoenicians by the command of the Persians restored to Samos Aiakes the son of Syloson, since he had been to them of much service and had done for them great things; and the Samians alone of all who revolted from Dareios, because of the desertion of their ships which were in the sea-fight, had neither their city nor their temples burnt. Then after the capture of Miletos the Persians forthwith got possession of Caria, some of the cities having submitted to their power voluntarily, while others of them they brought over by force.

26. Thus it came to pass as regards these matters: and meanwhile Histiaios the Milesian, who was at Byzantion and was seizing the merchant vessels of the Ionians as they sailed forth out of the Pontus, received the report of that which had happened about Miletos. Upon that he entrusted the matters which had to do with the Hellespont to Bisaltes the son of Apollophanes, a man of Abydos, while he himself with the Lesbians sailed to

Chios; and when a body of the Chians who were on guard did not allow him to approach, he fought with them at that spot in the Chian land which is called the "Hollows." Histiaios then not only slew many of these, but also, taking Polichne of the Chians as his base, he conquered with the help of the Lesbians the remainder of the Chians as well, since they had suffered great loss by the sea-fight.

27. And heaven is wont perhaps to give signs beforehand whenever great evils are about to happen to a city or a race of men; for to the Chians also before these events remarkable signs had come. In the first place when they had sent to Delphi a chorus of a hundred youths, two only returned home, the remaining ninety-eight of them having been seized by a plague and carried off; and then secondly in their city about the same time, that is shortly before the sea-fight, as some children were being taught in school the roof fell in upon them, so that of a hundred and twenty children only one escaped. These signs God showed to them beforehand; and after this the sea-fight came upon them and brought their State down upon its knees; and as the Chians had suffered great loss, he without difficulty effected the conquest of them.

28. Thence Histiaios made an expedition against Thasos, taking with him a large force of Ionians and Aiolians; and while he was encamped about the town of Thasos, a report came to him that the Phoenicians were sailing up from Miletos to conquer the rest of Ionia. Being informed of this he left Thasos unconquered and himself hastened to Lesbos, taking with him his whole army. Then, as his army was in want of food, he crossed over from Lesbos to reap the corn in Atarneus and also that in the plain of the Caïcos, which belonged to the Mysians. In these parts there chanced to be a Persian named Harpagos commanding a considerable force; and this man fought a battle with him after he had landed, and he took Histiaios himself prisoner and destroyed the greater part of his army.

29. And Histiaios was taken prisoner in the following manner:—As the Hellenes were fighting with the Persians at Malene in the district of Atarneus, after they had been engaged in close combat for a long time, the cavalry at length charged and fell upon the Hellenes; and the cavalry in fact decided the battle. So when the Hellenes had been turned to flight, Histiaios trusting that he would not be put to death by the king on account of his present fault, conceived a love of life, so that when he was being caught in his flight by a Persian and was about to be run through by him in the moment of his capture, he spoke in Persian and made himself known, saying that he was Histiaios the Milesian.

30. If then upon being taken prisoner he had been brought to king Dareios, he would not, as I think, have suffered any harm, but Dareios would have forgiven the crime with which he was charged; as it was, however, for this very reason and in order that he might not escape from punishment and again become powerful with the king, Artaphrenes the governor of Sardis and Harpagos who had captured him, when he had reached Sardis on his way to the king, put him to death there and then, and his body they impaled, but embalmed his head and brought it up to Dareios at Susa. Dareios having been informed of this, found fault with those who had done so, because they had not brought him up to his presence alive; and he bade wash the head of Histiaios and bestow upon it proper care, and then bury it, as that of one who had been greatly a benefactor both of the king himself and of the Persians.

31. Thus it happened about Histiaios; and meanwhile the Persian fleet, after wintering near Miletos, when it put to sea again in the following year conquered without difficulty the islands lying near the mainland, Chios, Lesbos, and Tenedos; and whenever they took

one of the islands, the Barbarians, as each was conquered, swept the inhabitants off it; and this they do in the following manner:—they extend themselves from the sea on the North to the sea on the South, each man having hold of the hand of the next, and then they pass through the whole island hunting the people out of it. They took also the Ionian cities on the mainland in the same manner, except that they did not sweep off the inhabitants thus, for it was not possible.

32. Then the commanders of the Persians proved not false to the threats with which they had threatened the Ionians when these were encamped opposite to them: for in fact when they conquered the cities, they chose out the most comely of the boys and castrated them, making eunuchs of them, and the fairest of the maidens they carried off by force to the king; and not only this, but they also burnt the cities together with the temples. Thus for the third time had the Ionians been reduced to slavery, first by the Lydians and then twice in succession by the Persians.

33. Departing from Ionia the fleet proceeded to conquer all the places of the Hellespont on the left as one sails in, for those on the right had been subdued already by the Persians themselves, approaching them by land. Now the cities of the Hellespont in Europe are these:—first comes the Chersonese, in which there are many cities, then Perinthos, the strongholds of the Thracian border, Selymbria, and Byzantion. The people of Byzantion and those of Calchedon opposite did not even wait for the coming of the Persian ships, but had left their own land first and departed, going within the Euxine; and there they settled in the city of Mesambria. So the Phoenicians, having burnt these places which have been mentioned, directed their course next to Proconnesos and Artake; and when they had delivered these also to the flames, they sailed back to the Chersonese to destroy the remaining cities which they had not sacked when they touched there before: but against Kyzicos they did not sail at all; for the men of Kyzicos even before the time when the Phoenicians sailed in had submitted to the king of their own accord, and had made terms with Oibares the son of Megabazos, the Persian governor at Daskyleion. .

34. In the Chersonese then the Phoenicians made themselves masters of all the other cities except the city of Cardia. Of these cities up to that time Miltiades the son of Kimon, the son of Stesagoras, had been despot, Miltiades the son of Kypselos having obtained this government in the manner which here follows:—The inhabitants of this Chersonese were Dolonkian Thracians; and these Dolonkians, being hard pressed in war by the Apsinthians, sent their kings to Delphi to consult the Oracle about the war. And the Pythian prophetess answered them that they must bring into their land as founder of a settlement the man who should first offer them hospitality as they returned from the temple. The Dolonkians then passed along the Sacred Road through the land of the Phokians and of the Boeotians, and as no man invited them, they turned aside and came to Athens.

35. Now at that time in Athens the government was held by Peisistratos, but Miltiades also the son of Kypselos had some power, who belonged to a family which kept four-horse chariot teams, and who was descended originally from Aiacos and Egina, though in more recent times his family was Athenian, Philaios the son of Ajax having been the first of his house who became an Athenian. This Miltiades was sitting in the entrance of his own dwelling, and seeing the Dolonkians going by with dress that was not of the native Athenian fashion and with spears, he shouted to them; and when they approached, he offered them lodging and hospitality. They then having accepted and having been entertained by him, proceeded to declare all the utterances of the Oracle; and having declared it

they asked him to do as the god had said: and Miltiades when he heard it was at once disposed to agree, because he was vexed by the rule of Peisistratos and desired to be removed out of the way. He set out therefore forthwith to Delphi to inquire of the Oracle whether he should do that which the Dolonkians asked of him:.

36, and as the Pythian prophetess also bade him do so, Miltiades the son of Kypselos, who had before this been victor at Olympia with a four-horse chariot, now taking with him of the Athenians everyone who desired to share in the expedition, sailed with the Dolonkians and took possession of the land: and they who had invited him to come to them made him despot over them. First then he made a wall across the isthmus of the Chersonese from the city of Cardia to Pactye, in order that the Apsinthians might not be able to invade the land and do them damage. Now the number of furlongs across the isthmus at this place is six-and-thirty, and from this isthmus the Chersonese within is altogether four hundred and twenty furlongs in length.

37. Having made a wall then across the neck of the Chersonese and having in this manner repelled the Apsinthians, Miltiades made war upon the people of Lampsacos first of all others; and the people of Lampsacos laid an ambush and took him prisoner. Now Miltiades had come to be a friend of Croesus the Lydian; and Croesus accordingly, being informed of this event, sent and commanded the people of Lampsacos to let Miltiades go; otherwise he threatened to destroy them utterly like a pine-tree. Then when the people of Lampsacos were perplexed in their counsels as to what that saying should mean with which Croesus had threatened them, namely that he would destroy them utterly like a pine-tree, at length one of the elder men with difficulty perceived the truth, and said that a pine alone of all trees when it has been cut down does not put forth any further growth but perishes, being utterly destroyed. The people of Lampsacos therefore fearing Croesus loosed Miltiades and let him go.

38. He then escaped by means of Croesus, but afterwards he brought his life to an end leaving no son to succeed him, but passing over his rule and his possessions to Stesagoras, who was the son of Kimon, his brother on the mother's side: and the people of the Chersonese still offer sacrifices to him after his death as it is usual to do to a founder, and hold in his honor a contest of horse-races and athletic exercises, in which none of the men of Lampsacos are allowed to contend. After this there was war with those of Lampsacos; and it happened to Stesagoras also that he died without leaving a son, having been struck on the head with an axe in the City Hall by a man who pretended to be a deserter, but who proved himself to be in fact an enemy and a rather hot one moreover.

39. Then after Stesagoras also had ended his life in this manner, Miltiades son of Kimon and brother of that Stesagoras who was dead, was sent in a trireme to the Chersonese to take possession of the government by the sons of Peisistratos, who had dealt well with him at Athens also, pretending that they had had no share in the death of his father Kimon, of which in another part of the history I will set forth how it came to pass. Now Miltiades, when he came to the Chersonese, kept himself within his house, paying honors in all appearance to the memory of his brother Stesagoras; and the chief men of the inhabitants of the Chersonese in every place, being informed of this, gathered themselves together from all the cities and came in a body to condole with him, and when they had come they were laid in bonds by him. Miltiades then was in possession of the Chersonese, supporting a body of five hundred mercenary troops; and he married the daughter of Oloros the king of the Thracians, who was named Hegesipyle.

40. Now this Miltiades son of Kimon had at the time of which we speak but lately returned to the Chersonese; and after he had returned, there befell him other misfortunes worse than those which had befallen him already; for two years before this he had been a fugitive out of the land from the Scythians, since the nomad Scythians provoked by king Dareios had joined all in a body and marched as far as this Chersonese, and Miltiades had not awaited their attack but had become a fugitive from the Chersonese, until at last the Scythians departed and the Dolonkians brought him back again. These things happened two years before the calamities which now oppressed him:.

41, and now, being informed that the Phoenicians were at Tenedos, he filled five triremes with the property which he had at hand and sailed away for Athens. And having set out from the city of Cardia he was sailing through the gulf of Melas; and as he passed along by the shore of the Chersonese, the Phoenicians fell in with his ships, and while Miltiades himself with four of his ships escaped to Imbros, the fifth of his ships was captured in the pursuit by the Phoenicians. Of this ship it chanced that Metiochos the eldest of the sons of Miltiades was in command, not born of the daughter of Oloros the Thracian, but of another woman. Him the Phoenicians captured together with his ship; and being informed about him, that he was the son of Miltiades, they brought him up to the king, supposing that they would lay up for themselves a great obligation; because it was Miltiades who had declared as his opinion to the Ionians that they should do as the Scythians said, at that time when the Scythians requested them to break up the bridge of boats and sail away to their own land. Dareios however, when the Phoenicians brought up to him Metiochos the son of Miltiades, did Metiochos no harm but on the contrary very much good; for he gave him a house and possessions and a Persian wife, by whom he had children born who have been ranked as Persians. Miltiades meanwhile came from Imbros to Athens.

42. In the course of this year there was done by the Persians nothing more which tended to strife with the Ionians, but these things which follow were done in this year very much to their advantage.—Artaphrenes the governor of Sardis sent for envoys from all the cities and compelled the Ionians to make agreements among themselves, so that they might give satisfaction for wrongs and not plunder one another's land. This he compelled them to do, and also he measured their territories by parasangs,—that is the name which the Persians give to the length of thirty furlongs, —he measured, I say, by these, and appointed a certain amount of tribute for each people, which continues still unaltered from that time even to my own days, as it was appointed by Artaphrenes; and the tribute was appointed to be nearly of the same amount for each as it had been before.

43. These were things which tended to peace for the Ionians; but at the beginning of the spring, the other commanders having all been removed by the king, Mardonios the son of Gobryas came down to the sea, bringing with him a very large land-army and a very large naval force, being a young man and lately married to Artozostra daughter of king Dareios. When Mardonios leading this army came to Kilikia, he embarked on board a ship himself and proceeded together with the other ships, while other leaders led the land-army to the Hellespont. Mardonios however sailing along the coast of Asia came to Ionia: and here I shall relate a thing which will be a great marvel to those of the Hellenes who do not believe that to the seven men of the Persians Otanes declared as his opinion that the Persians ought to have popular rule; for Mardonios deposed all the despots of the Ionians and established popular governments in the cities. Having so done he hastened on

to the Hellespont; and when there was collected a vast number of ships and a large land-army, they crossed over the Hellespont in the ships and began to make their way through Europe, and their way was directed against Eretria and Athens.

44. These, I say, furnished them the pretense for the expedition, but they had it in their minds to subdue as many as they could of the Hellenic cities; and in the first place they subdued with their ships the Thasians, who did not even raise a hand to defend themselves: then with the land-army they gained the Macedonians to be their servants in addition to those whom they had already; for all the nations on the East of the Macedonians had become subject to them already before this. Crossing over then from Thasos to the opposite coast, they proceeded on their way near the land as far as Acanthos, and then starting from Acanthos they attempted to get round Mount Athos; but as they sailed round, there fell upon them a violent North Wind, against which they could do nothing, and handled them very roughly, casting away very many of their ships on Mount Athos. It is said indeed that the number of the ships destroyed was three hundred, and more than twenty thousand men; for as this sea which is about Athos is very full of sea monsters, some were seized by these and so perished, while others were dashed against the rocks; and some of them did not know how to swim and perished for that cause, others again by reason of cold.

45. Thus fared the fleet; and meanwhile Mardonios and the land-army while encamping in Macedonia were attacked in the night by the Brygian Thracians, and many of them were slain by the Brygians and Mardonios himself was wounded. However not even these escaped being enslaved by the Persians, for Mardonios did not depart from that region until he had made them subject. But when he had subdued these, he proceeded to lead his army back, since he had suffered great loss with his land-army in fighting against the Brygians and with his fleet in going round Athos. So this expedition departed back to Asia having gained no honor by its contests.

46. In the next year after this Dareios first sent a messenger to the men of Thasos, who had been accused by their neighbors of planning revolt, and bade them take away the wall around their town and bring their ships to Abdera. The Thasians in fact, as they had been besieged by Histiaios the Milesian and at the same time had large revenues coming in, were using their money in building ships of war and in surrounding their city with a stronger wall. Now the revenues came to them from the mainland and from the mines: from the gold-mines in Scapte Hyle there came in generally eighty talents a year, and from those in Thasos itself a smaller amount than this but so much that in general the Thasians, without taxes upon the produce of their soil, had a revenue from the mainland and from the mines amounting yearly to two hundred talents, and when the amount was highest, to three hundred.

47. I myself saw these mines, and by much the most marvelous of them were those which the Phoenicians discovered, who made the first settlement in this island in company with Thasos; and the island had the name which it now has from this Thasos the Phoenician. These Phoenician mines are in that part of Thasos which is between the places called Ainyra and Koinyra and opposite Samothrake, where there is a great mountain which has been all turned up in the search for metal. Thus it is with this matter: and the Thasians on the command of the king both razed their walls and brought all their ships to Abdera.

48. After this Dareios began to make trial of the Hellenes, what they meant to do,

whether to make war with him or to deliver themselves up. He sent abroad heralds there-fore, and appointed them to go some to one place and others to another throughout Hellas, bidding them demand earth and water for the king. These, I say, he sent to Hellas; and meanwhile he was sending abroad other heralds to his own tributary cities which lay upon the sea-coast, and he bade them have ships of war built and also vessels to carry horses.

49. They then were engaged in preparing these things; and meanwhile when the heralds had come to Hellas, many of those who dwelt upon the mainland gave that for which the Persian made demand, and all those who dwelt in the islands did so, to whom-soever they came to make their demand. The islanders, I say, gave earth and water to Dareios, and among them also those of Egina, and when these had done so, the Athenians went forthwith urgent against them, supposing that the Eginetans had given with hostile purpose against themselves, in order to make an expedition against them in combination with the Persians; and also they were glad to get hold of an occasion against them. Accordingly they went backward and forwards to Sparta and accused the Eginetans of that which they had done, as having proved themselves traitors to Hellas.

50. In consequence of this accusation Cleomenes the son of Anaxandrides, king of the Spartans, crossed over to Egina meaning to seize those of the Eginetans who were the most guilty; but as he was attempting to seize them, certain of the Eginetans opposed him, and among them especially Crios the son of Polycritos, who said that he should not with impunity carry off a single Eginetan, for he was doing this (said he) without authority from the Spartan State, having been persuaded to it by the Athenians with money; other-wise he would have come and seized them in company with the other king: and this he said by reason of a message received from Demaratos. Cleomenes then as he departed from Egina, asked Crios what was his name, and he told him the truth; and Cleomenes said to him: "Surely now, O Ram, thou must cover over thy horns with bronze for thou wilt shortly have a great trouble to contend with."

51. Meanwhile Demaratos the son of Ariston was staying behind in Sparta and bringing charges against Cleomenes, he also being king of the Spartans but of the inferior house; which however is inferior in no other way (for it is descended from the same ances-tor), but the house of Eurysthenes has always been honored more, apparently because he was the elder brother.

52. For the Lacedemonians, who herein agree with none of the poets, say that Aris-todemos the son of Aristomachos, the son of Cleodaios, the son of Hyllos, being their king, led them himself (and not the sons of Aristodemos) to this land which they now possess. Then after no long time the wife of Aristodemos, whose name was Argeia,—she was the daughter, they say, of Autesion, the son of Tisamenes, the son of Thersander, the son of Polyneikes,—she, it is said, brought forth twins; and Aristodemos lived but to see his children and then ended his life by sickness. So the Lacedemonians of that time resolved according to established custom to make the elder of the children their king; but they did not know which of them they should take, because they were like one another and of equal size; and when they were not able to make out, or even before this, they inquired of their mother; and she said that even she herself did not know one from the other. She said this, although she knew in truth very well, because she desired that by some means both might be made kings. The Lacedemonians then were in a strait; and being in a strait they sent to Delphi to inquire what they should do in the matter. And the

Pythian prophetess bade them regard both children as their kings, but honor most the first in age. The prophetess, they say, thus gave answer to them; and when the Lacedemonians were at a loss none the less how to find out the elder of them, a Messenian whose name was Panites made a suggestion to them: this Panites, I say, suggested to the Lacedemonians that they should watch the mother and see which of the children she washed and fed before the other; and if she was seen to do this always in the same order, then they would have all that they were seeking and desiring to find out, but if she too was uncertain and did it in a different order at different times, it would be plain to them that even she had no more knowledge than any other, and they must turn to some other way. Then the Spartans following the suggestion of the Messenian watched the mother of the sons of Aristodemos and found that she gave honor thus to the first-born both in feeding and in washing; for she did not know with that design she was being watched. They took therefore the child which was honored by its mother and brought it up as the first-born in the public hall, and to it was given the name of Eurysthenes, while the other was called Procles. These, when they had grown up, both themselves were at variance, they say, with one another, though they were brothers, throughout the whole time of their lives, and their descendants also continued after the same manner.

53. This is the report given by the Lacedemonians alone of all the Hellenes; but this which follows I write in accordance with that which is reported by the Hellenes generally, —I mean that the names of these kings of the Dorians are rightly enumerated by the Hellenes up to Perseus the son of Danae (leaving the god out of account), and proved to be of Hellenic race; for even from that time they were reckoned as Hellenes. I said "up to Perseus" and did not take the descent from a yet higher point, because there is no name mentioned of a mortal father for Perseus, as Amphitryon is for Heracles. Therefore with reason, as is evident, I have said "rightly up to Perseus"; but if one enumerates their ancestors in succession going back from Danae the daughter of Acrisios, the rulers of the Dorians will prove to be Egyptians by direct descent.

54. Thus I have traced the descent according to the account given by the Hellenes; but as the story is reported which the Persians tell, Perseus himself was an Assyrian and became a Hellene, whereas the ancestors of Perseus were not Hellenes; and as for the ancestors of Acrisios, who (according to this account) belonged not to Perseus in any way by kinship, they say that these were, as the Hellenes report, Egyptians.

55. Let it suffice to have said so much about these matters; and as to the question how and by what exploits being Egyptians they received the scepters of royalty over the Dorians, we will omit these things, since others have told about them; but the things with which other narrators have not dealt, of these I will make mention.

56. These are the royal rights which have been given by the Spartans to their kings, namely, two priesthoods, of Zeus Lakedaimon and Zeus Uranios; and the right of making war against whatsoever land they please, and that no man of the Spartans shall hinder this right, or if he do, he shall be subject to the curse; and that when they go on expeditions the kings shall go out first and return last; that a hundred picked men shall be their guard upon expeditions; and that they shall use in their goings forth to war as many cattle as they desire, and take both the hides and the backs of all that are sacrificed.

57. These are their privileges in war; and in peace moreover things have been assigned to them as follows:—if any sacrifice is performed at the public charge, it is the privilege of the kings to sit down at the feast before all others, and that the attendants shall begin with

them first, and serve to each of them a portion of everything double of that which is given to the other guests, and that they shall have the first pouring of libations and the hides of the animals slain in sacrifice; that on every new moon and seventh day of the month there shall be delivered at the public charge to each one of these a full-grown victim in the temple of Apollo, and a measure of barley-groats and a Laconian "quarter" of wine; and that at all the games they shall have seats of honor specially set apart for them: moreover it is their privilege to appoint as protectors of strangers whomsoever they will of the citizens, and to choose each two "Pythians:" now the Pythians are men sent to consult the god at Delphi, and they eat with the kings at the public charge. And if the kings do not come to the dinner, it is the rule that there shall be sent out for them to their houses two quarts of barley-groats for each one and half a pint of wine; but if they are present, double shares of everything shall be given them, and moreover they shall be honored in this same manner when they have been invited to dinner by private persons. The kings also, it is ordained, shall have charge of the oracles which are given, but the Pythians also shall have knowledge of them. It is the rule moreover that the kings alone give decision on the following cases only, that is to say, about the maiden who inherits her father's property, namely who ought to have her, if her father have not betrothed her to any one, and about public ways; also if any man desires to adopt a son, he must do it in presence of the kings: and it is ordained that they shall sit in council with the Senators, who are in number eight-and-twenty, and if they do not come, those of the Senators who are most closely related to them shall have the privileges of the kings and give two votes besides their own, making three in all. .

58. These rights have been assigned to the kings for their lifetime by the Spartan State; and after they are dead these which follow:—horsemen go round and announce that which has happened throughout the whole of the Laconian land, and in the city women go about and strike upon a copper kettle. Whenever this happens so, two free persons of each household must go into mourning, a man and a woman, and for those who fail to do this great penalties are appointed. Now the custom of the Lacedemonians about the deaths of their kings is the same as that of the Barbarians who dwell in Asia, for most of the Barbarians practice the same customs as regards the death of their kings. Whensoever a king of the Lacedemonians is dead, then from the whole territory of Lacedaemon, not reckoning the Spartans, a certain fixed number of the "dwellers round" are compelled to go to the funeral ceremony:

59. and when there have been gathered together of these and of the Helots and of the Spartans themselves many thousands in the same place, with their women intermingled, they beat their foreheads with a good will and make lamentation without stint, saying that this one who has died last of their kings was the best of all: and whenever any of their kings has been killed in war, they prepare an image to represent him, laid upon a couch with fair coverings, and carry it out to be buried. Then after they have buried him, no assembly is held among them for ten days, nor is there any meeting for choice of magistrates, but they have mourning during these days. In another respect too these resemble the Persians; that is to say, when the king is dead and another is appointed king, this king who is newly coming in sets free any man of the Spartans who was a debtor to the king or to the State; while among the Persians the king who comes to the throne remits to all the cities the arrears of tribute which are due.

60. In the following point also the Lacedemonians resemble the Egyptians; that is to

say, their heralds and fluteplayers and cooks inherit the crafts of their fathers, and a fluteplayer is the son of a fluteplayer, a cook of a cook, and a herald of a herald; other men do not lay hands upon the office because they have loud and clear voices, and so shut them out of it, but they practice their craft by inheritance from their fathers.

61. Thus are these things done: and at this time of which we speak, while Cleomenes was in Egina doing deeds which were for the common service of Hellas, Demaratos brought charges against him, not so much because he cared for the Eginetans as because he felt envy and jealousy of him. Then Cleomenes, after he returned from Egina, planned to depose Demaratos from being king, making an attempt upon him on account of this matter which follows:—Ariston being king in Sparta and having married two wives, yet had no children born to him; and since he did not acknowledge that he himself was the cause of this, he married a third wife; and he married her thus:—he had a friend, a man of the Spartans, to whom of all the citizens Ariston was most inclined; and it chanced that this man had a wife who was of all the women in Sparta the fairest by far, and one too who had become the fairest from having been the foulest. For as she was mean in her aspect, her nurse, considering that she was the daughter of wealthy persons and was of uncomely aspect, and seeing moreover that her parents were troubled by it,—perceiving I say these things, her nurse devised as follows:—every day she bore her to the temple of Helen, which is in the place called Therapne, lying above the temple of Phoebus; and whenever the nurse bore her thither, she placed her before the image and prayed the goddess to deliver the child from her unshapeliness. And once as the nurse was going away out of the temple, it is said that a woman appeared to her, and having appeared asked her what she was bearing in her arms; and she told her that she was bearing a child; upon which the other bade her show the child to her, but she refused, for it had been forbidden to her by the parents to show it to any one: but the woman continued to urge her by all means to show it to her. So then perceiving that the woman earnestly desired to see it, the nurse showed her the child. Then the woman stroking the head of the child said that she should be the fairest of all the women in Sparta; and from that day her aspect was changed. Afterwards when she came to the age for marriage, she was married to Agetos the son of Alkeides, this friend of Ariston of whom we spoke.

62. Now Ariston it seems was ever stung by the desire of this woman, and accordingly he contrived as follows:—he made an engagement himself with his comrade, whose wife this woman was, that he would give him as a gift one thing of his own possessions, whatsoever he should choose, and he bade his comrade make return to him in similar fashion. He therefore, fearing nothing for his wife, because he saw that Ariston also had a wife, agreed to this; and on these terms they imposed oaths on one another. After this Ariston on his part gave that which Agetos had chosen from the treasures of Ariston, whatever the thing was; and he himself, seeking to obtain from him the like return, endeavored then to take away the wife of his comrade from him: and he said that he consented to give anything else except this one thing only, but at length being compelled by the oath and by the treacherous deception, he allowed her to be taken away from him.

63. Thus had Ariston brought into his house the third wife, having dismissed the second: and this wife, not having fulfilled the ten months but in a shorter period of time, bore him that Demaratos of whom we were speaking; and one of his servants reported to him as he was sitting in council with the Ephors, that a son had been born to him. He then, knowing the time when he took to him his wife, and reckoning the months upon his

fingers, said, denying with an oath, "The child would not be mine." This the Ephors heard, but they thought it a matter of no importance at the moment; and the child grew up and Ariston repented of that which he had said, for he thought Demaratos was certainly his own son; and he gave him the name "Demaratos" for this reason, namely because before these things took place the Spartan people all in a body had made a vow praying that a son might be born to Ariston, as one who was pre-eminent in renown over all the kings who had ever arisen in Sparta.

64. For this reason the name Demaratos was given to him. And as time went on Ariston died, and Demaratos obtained the kingdom: but it was fated apparently that these things should become known and should cause Demaratos to be deposed from the king- dom; and therefore Demaratos came to be at variance greatly with Cleomenes both at the former time when he withdrew his army from Eleusis, and also now especially, when Cleomenes had crossed over to take those of the Eginetans who had gone over to the Medes.

65. Cleomenes then, being anxious to take vengeance on him, concerted matters with Leotychides the son of Menares, the son of Agis, who was of the same house as Demaratos, under condition that if he should set him up as king instead of Demaratos, he would go with him against the Eginetans. Now Leotychides had become a bitter foe of Demaratos on account of this matter which follows:—Leotychides had betrothed himself to Percalos the daughter of Chilon son of Demarmenos; and Demaratos plotted against him and deprived Leotychides of his marriage, carrying off Percalos himself beforehand, and getting her for his wife. Thus had arisen the enmity of Leotychides against Demaratos; and now by the instigation of Cleomenes Leotychides deposed against Demaratos, saying that he was not rightfully reigning over the Spartans, not being a son of Ariston: and after this deposition he prosecuted a suit against him, recalling the old saying which Ariston uttered at the time when his servant reported to him that a son was born to him, and he reckoning up the months denied with an oath, saying that it was not his. Taking his stand upon this utterance, Leotychides proceeded to prove that Demaratos was not born of Ariston nor was rightfully reigning over Sparta; and he produced as witnesses those Ephors who chanced then to have been sitting with Ariston in council and to have heard him say this.

66. At last, as there was contention about those matters, the Spartans resolved to ask the Oracle at Delphi whether Demaratos was the son of Ariston. The question then having been referred by the arrangement of Cleomenes to the Pythian prophetess, thereupon Cleomenes gained over to his side Cobon the son of Aristophantos, who had most power among the Delphians, and Cobon persuaded Perialla the prophetess of the Oracle to say that which Cleomenes desired to have said. Thus the Pythian prophetess, when those who were sent to consult the god asked her their question, gave decision that Demaratos was not the son of Ariston. Afterwards however these things became known, and both Cobon went into exile from Delphi and Perialla the prophetess of the Oracle was removed from her office.

67. With regard to the deposing of Demaratos from the kingdom it happened thus: but Demaratos became an exile from Sparta to the Medes on account of a reproach which here follows:—After he had been deposed from the kingdom Demaratos was holding a public office to which he had been elected. Now it was the time of the Gymnopaidiai; and as Demaratos was a spectator of them, Leotychides, who had now become king himself

instead of Demaratos, sent his attendant and asked Demaratos in mockery and insult what kind of a thing it was to be a magistrate after having been king; and he vexed at the question made answer and said that he himself had now had experience of both, but Leotychides had not; this question however, he said, would be the beginning either of countless evil or countless good fortune for the Lacedemonians. Having thus said, he veiled his head and went forth out of the theatre to his own house; and forthwith he made preparations and sacrificed an ox to Zeus, and after having sacrificed he called his mother.

68. Then when his mother had come, he put into her hands some of the inner parts of the victim, and besought her, saying as follows: "Mother, I beseech thee, appealing to the other gods and above all to this Zeus the guardian of the household, to tell me the truth, who is really and truly my father. For Leotychides spoke in his contention with me, saying that thou didst come to Ariston with child by thy former husband; and others besides, reporting that which is doubtless an idle tale, say that thou didst go in to one of the servants, namely the keeper of the asses, and that I am his son. I therefore entreat thee by the gods to tell me the truth; for if thou hast done any of these things which are reported, thou hast not done them alone, but with many other women; and the report is commonly believed in Sparta that there was not in Ariston seed which should beget children; for if so, then his former wives also would have borne children."

69. Thus he spoke, and she made answer as follows: "My son, since thou dost beseech me with entreaties to speak the truth, the whole truth shall be told to thee. When Ariston had brought me into his house, on the third night there came to me an apparition in the likeness of Ariston, and having lain with me it put upon me the garlands which it had on; and the apparition straightway departed, and after this Ariston came; and when he saw me with garlands, he asked who it was who had given me them; and I said that he had given them, but he did not admit it; and I began to take oath of it, saying that he did not well to deny it, for he had come (I said) a short time before and had lain with me and given me the garlands. Then Ariston, seeing that I made oath of it, perceived that the matter was of the gods; and first the garlands were found to be from the hero-temple which stands by the outer door of the house, which they call the temple of Astrabacos, and secondly the diviners gave answer that it was this same hero. Thus, my son, thou hast all, as much as thou desirest to learn; for either thou art begotten of this hero and the hero Astrabacos is thy father, or Ariston is thy father, for on that night I conceived thee: but as to that wherein thy foes most take hold of thee, saying that Ariston himself, when thy birth was announced to him, in the hearing of many declared that thou wert not his son, because the time, the ten months namely, had not yet been fulfilled, in ignorance of such matters he cast forth that saying; for women bring forth children both at the ninth month and also at the seventh, and not all after they have completed ten months; and I bore thee, my son, at the seventh month: and Ariston himself also perceived after no long time that he had uttered this saying in folly. Do not thou then accept any other reports about thy begetting, for thou hast heard in all the full truth; but to Leotychides and to those who report these things may their wives bear children by keepers of asses!"

70. Thus she spoke; and he, having learnt that which he desired to learn, took supplies for travelling and set forth to go to Elis, pretending that he was going to Delphi to consult the Oracle: but the Lacedemonians, suspecting that he was attempting to escape, pursued after him; and it chanced that before they came Demaratos had passed over to Zakynthos from Elis; and the Lacedemonians crossing over after him laid hands on his person and

carried away his attendants from him. Afterwards however, since those of Zakynthos refused to give him up, he passed over from thence to Asia, to the presence of king Dareios; and Dareios both received him with great honor as a guest, and also gave him land and cities. Thus Demaratos had come to Asia, and such was the fortune which he had had, having been distinguished in the estimation of the Lacedemonians in many other ways both by deeds and by counsels, and especially having gained for them an Olympic victory with the four-horse chariot, being the only one who achieved this of all the kings who ever arose in Sparta.

71. Demaratos being deposed, Leotychides the son of Menares succeeded to the kingdom; and he had born to him a son Zeuxidemos, whom some of the Spartans called Kyniscos. This Zeuxidemos did not become king of Sparta, for he died before Leotychides, leaving a son Archidemos: and Leotychides having lost Zeuxidemos married a second wife Eurydame, the sister of Menios and daughter of Diactorides, by whom he had no male issue, but a daughter Lampito, whom Archidemos the son of Zeuxidemos took in marriage, she being given to him by Leotychides.

72. Leotychides however did not himself live to old age in Sparta, but paid a retribution for Demaratos as follows:—he went as commander of the Lacedemonians to invade Thessaly, and when he might have reduced all to subjection, he accepted gifts of money amounting to a large sum; and being taken in the act there in the camp, as he was sitting upon a glove full of money, he was brought to trial and banished from Sparta, and his house was razed to the ground. So he went into exile to Tegea and ended his life there.

73. These things happened later; but at this time, when Cleomenes had brought to a successful issue the affair which concerned Demaratos, forthwith he took with him Leotychides and went against the Eginetans, being very greatly enraged with them because of their insults towards him. So the Eginetans on their part, since both the kings had come against them, thought fit no longer to resist; and the Spartans selected ten men who were the most considerable among the Eginetans both by wealth and by birth, and took them away as prisoners, and among others also Crios the son of Polycritos and Casambos the son of Aristocrates, who had the greatest power among them; and having taken these away to the land of Attica, they deposited them as a charge with the Athenians, who were the bitterest enemies of the Eginetans.

74. After this Cleomenes, since it had become known that he had devised evil against Demaratos, was seized by fear of the Spartans and retired to Thessaly. Thence he came to Arcadia, and began to make mischief and to combine the Arcadians against Sparta; and besides other oaths with which he caused them to swear that they would assuredly follow him whithersoever he should lead them, he was very desirous also to bring the chiefs of the Arcadians to the city of Nonacris and cause them to swear by the water of Styx; for near this city it is said by the Arcadians that there is the water of Styx, and there is in fact something of this kind: a small stream of water is seen to trickle down from a rock into a hollow ravine, and round the ravine runs a wall of rough stones. Now Nonacris, where it happens that this spring is situated, is a city of Arcadia near Pheneos.

75. The Lacedemonians, hearing that Cleomenes was acting thus, were afraid, and proceeded to bring him back to Sparta to rule on the same terms as before: but when he had come back, forthwith a disease of madness seized him (who had been even before this somewhat insane), and whenever he met any of the Spartans, he dashed his staff against the man's face. And as he continued to do this and had gone quite out of his senses, his

kinsmen bound him in stocks. Then being so bound, and seeing his warder left alone by the rest, he asked him for a knife; and the warder not being at first willing to give it, he threatened him with that which he would do to him afterwards if he did not; until at last the warder fearing the threats, for he was one of the Helots, gave him a knife. Then Cleomenes, when he had received the steel, began to maltreat himself from the legs upwards: for he went on cutting his flesh lengthways from the legs to the thighs and from the thighs to the loins and flanks, until at last he came to the belly; and cutting this into strips he died in that manner. And this happened, as most of the Hellenes report, because he persuaded the Pythian prophetess to advise that which was done about Demaratos; but as the Athenians alone report, it was because when he invaded Eleusis he laid waste the sacred enclosure of the goddesses; and according to the report of the Argives, because from their sanctuary dedicated to Argos he caused to come down those of the Argives who had fled for refuge from the battle and slew them, and also set fire to the grove itself, holding it in no regard.

76. For when Cleomenes was consulting the Oracle at Delphi, the answer was given him that he should conquer Argos; so he led the Spartans and came to the river Erasinos, which is said to flow from the Stymphalian lake; for this lake, they say, running out into a viewless chasm, appears again above ground in the land of Argos; and from thence onwards this water is called by the Argives Erasinos: having come, I say, to this river, Cleomenes did sacrifice to it; and since the sacrifices were not at all favorable for him to cross over, he said that he admired the Erasinos for not betraying the men of its country, but the Argives should not even so escape. After this he retired back from thence and led his army down to Thyrea; and having done sacrifice to the Sea by slaying a bull, he brought them in ships to the land of Tiryns and Nauplia.

77. Being informed of this, the Argives came to the rescue towards the sea; and when they had got near Tiryns and were at the place which is called Hesipeia, they encamped opposite to the Lacedemonians leaving no very wide space between the armies. There the Argives were not afraid of the open fighting, but only lest they should be conquered by craft; for to this they thought referred the oracle which the Pythian prophetess gave in common to these and to the Milesians, saying as follows:

> "But when the female at length shall conquer the male in the battle,
> Conquer and drive him forth, and glory shall gain among Argives,
> Then many wives of the Argives shall tear both cheeks in their mourning;
> So that a man shall say some time, of the men that came after,
> 'Quelled by the spear it perished, the three-coiled terrible serpent,'

The conjunction of all these things caused fear to the Argives, and with a view to this they resolved to make use of the enemy's herald; and having so resolved they proceeded to do as follows:—whenever the Spartan herald proclaimed anything to the Lacedemonians, the Argives also did that same thing.

78. So Cleomenes, perceiving that the Argives were doing whatever the herald of the Lacedemonians proclaimed, passed the word to the Lacedemonians that when the herald should proclaim that they were to get breakfast, then they should take up their arms and go to attack the Argives. This was carried out even so by the Lacedemonians; for as the Argives were getting breakfast according to the herald's proclamation, they attacked

them; and many of them they slew, but many more yet took refuge in the sacred grove of Argos, and upon these they kept watch, sitting round about the place. Then Cleomenes did this which follows:—

79. He had with him deserters, and getting information by inquiring of these, he sent a herald and summoned forth those of the Argives who were shut up in the sanctuary, mentioning each by name; and he summoned them forth saying that he had received their ransom. Now among the Peloponnesians ransom is two pounds weight of silver appointed to be paid for each prisoner. So Cleomenes summoned forth about fifty of the Argives one by one and slew them; and it chanced that the rest who were in the enclosure did not perceive that this was being done; for since the grove was thick, those within did not see how it fared with those who were without, at least until one of them climbed up a tree and saw from above that which was being done. Accordingly they then no longer came forth when they were called.

80. So Cleomenes thereupon ordered all the Helots to pile up brushwood round the sacred grove; and they obeying, he set fire to the grove. And when it was now burning, he asked one of the deserters to what god the grove was sacred, and the man replied that it was sacred to Argos. When he heard that, he groaned aloud and said, "Apollo who utterest oracles, surely thou hast greatly deceived me, saying that I should conquer Argos: I conjecture that the oracle has had its fulfilment for me already."

81. After this Cleomenes sent away the greater part of his army to go back to Sparta, but he himself took a thousand of the best men and went to the temple of Hera to sacrifice: and when he wished to sacrifice upon the altar, the priest forbade him, saying that it was not permitted by religious rule for a stranger to sacrifice in that place. Cleomenes however bade the Helots take away the priest from the altar and scourge him, and he himself offered the sacrifice. Having so done he returned back to Sparta;.

82, and after his return his opponents brought him up before the Ephors, saying that he had received gifts and therefore had not conquered Argos, when he might easily have conquered it. He said to them,—but whether he was speaking falsely or whether truly I am not able with certainty to say,—however that may be, he spoke and said that when he had conquered the sanctuary of Argos, it seemed to him that the oracle of the god had had its fulfilment for him; therefore he did not think it right to make an attempt on the city, at least until he should have had recourse to sacrifice, and should have learnt whether the deity permitted him or whether she stood opposed to him: and as he was sacrificing for augury in the temple of Hera, a flame of fire blazed forth from the breasts of the image; and thus he knew the certainty of the matter, namely that he would not conquer Argos: for if fire had blazed forth from the head of the image, he would have been conqueror of the city from top to bottom, but since it blazed from the breasts, everything had been accomplished for him which the god desired should come to pass. Thus speaking he seemed to the Spartans to speak credibly and reasonably, and he easily escaped his pursuers.

83. Argos however was so bereft of men that their slaves took possession of all the State, ruling and managing it until the sons of those who had perished grew to be men. Then these, endeavoring to gain Argos back to themselves, cast them out; and the slaves being driven forth gained possession of Tiryns by fighting. Now for a time these two parties had friendly relations with one another; but afterwards there came to the slaves a prophet named Cleander, by race a Phigalian from Arcadia: this man persuaded the slaves

to attack their masters, and in consequence of this there was war between them for a long time, until at last with difficulty the Argives overcame them.

84. The Argives then say that this was the reason why Cleomenes went mad and had an evil end: but the Spartans themselves say that Cleomenes was not driven mad by any divine power, but that he had become a drinker of unmixed wine from having associated with Scythians, and that he went mad in consequence of this: for the nomad Scythians, they say, when Dareios had made invasion of their land, desired eagerly after this to take vengeance upon him; and they sent to Sparta and tried to make an alliance, and to arrange that while the Scythians themselves attempted an invasion of Media by the way of the river Phasis, the Spartans should set forth from Ephesos and go up inland, and then that they should meet in one place: and they say that Cleomenes when the Scythians had come for this purpose, associated with them largely, and that thus associating more than was fit, he learnt the practice of drinking wine unmixed with water; and for this cause (as the Spartans think) he went mad. Thenceforth, as they say themselves, when they desire to drink stronger wine, they say "Fill up in Scythian fashion." Thus the Spartans report about Cleomenes; but to me it seems that this was a retribution which Cleomenes paid for Demaratos.

85. Now when the Eginetans heard that Cleomenes had met his end, they sent messengers to Sparta to denounce Leotychides for the matter of the hostages which were being kept at Athens: and the Lacedemonians caused a court to assemble and judged that the Eginetans had been dealt with outrageously by Leotychides; and they condemned him to be taken to Egina and delivered up in place of the men who were being kept at Athens. Then when the Eginetans were about to take Leotychides, Theasides the son of Leoprepes, a man of repute in Sparta, said to them: "What are ye proposing to do, men of Egina? Do ye mean to take away the king of the Spartans, thus delivered up to you by his fellow-citizens? If the Spartans now being in anger have decided so, beware lest at some future time, if ye do this, they bring an evil upon your land which may destroy it." Hearing this the Eginetans abstained from taking him; but they came to an agreement that Leotychides should accompany them to Athens and restore the men to the Eginetans.

86. When however Leotychides came to Athens and asked for the deposit back, the Athenians, not being willing to give up the hostages, produced pretexts for refusing, and alleged that two kings had deposited them and they did not think it right to give them back to the one without the other: so since the Athenians said that they would not give them back, Leotychides spoke to them as follows:

(a) "Athenians, do whichever thing ye yourselves desire; for ye know that if ye give them up, ye do that which religion commands, and if ye refuse to give them up, ye do the opposite of this: but I desire to tell you what kind of a thing came to pass once in Sparta about a deposit. We Spartans report that there was in Lacedaemon about two generations before my time one Glaucos the son of Epikydes. This man we say attained the highest merit in all things besides, and especially he was well reported of by all who at that time dwelt in Lacedaemon for his uprightness: and we relate that in due time it happened to him thus:—a man of Miletos came to Sparta and desired to have speech with him, alleging the reasons which follow: 'I am a Milesian,' he said, 'and I am come hither desiring to have benefit from thy uprightness, Glaucos; for as there was much report of thy uprightness throughout all the rest of Hellas and also in Ionia, I considered with myself that Ionia is ever in danger, whereas Peloponnesus is safely established, and also that we never see wealth continue in the possession of the same persons long;—reflecting, I say, on these things and taking counsel with myself, I resolved to turn into money the half of my possessions, and to place it with thee, being well assured that if it were placed with thee I should have it safe. Do thou therefore, I pray thee, receive the money, and take and keep these tallies; and whosoever shall ask for the money back having the tokens answering to these, to him do thou restore it.' (b) The stranger who had come from Miletos said so much; and Glaucos accepted the deposit on the terms proposed. Then after a long time had gone by, there came to Sparta the sons of him who had deposited the money with Glaucos; and they came to speech with Glaucos, and producing the tokens asked for the money to be given back: but he repulsed them answering them again thus: 'I do not remember the matter, nor does my mind bring back to me any knowledge of those things whereof ye speak; but I desire to recollect and do all that is just; for if I received it, I desire to restore it honestly; and if on the other hand I did not receive it at all, I will act towards you in accordance with the customs of the Hellenes: therefore I defer the settling of the matter with you for three months from now.' (c) The Milesians accordingly went away grieved, for they supposed that they had been robbed of the money; but Glaucos set forth to Delphi to consult the Oracle: and when he inquired of the Oracle whether he should rob them of the money by an oath, the Pythian prophetess rebuked him with these lines:

"'Glaucos, thou, Epikydes' son, yea, this for the moment,
This, to conquer their word by an oath and to rob, is more gainful.
Swear, since the lot of death waits also for him who swears truly.
But know thou that Oath has a son, one nameless and handless and
footless, Yet without feet he pursues, without hands he seizes, and
wholly He shall destroy the race and the house of the man who offendeth.
But for the man who swears truly his race is the better hereafter.'

Having heard this Glaucos entreated that the god would pardon him for that which he had said, but the prophetess said that to make trial of the god and to do the deed were things equivalent. (d) Glaucos then, having sent for the Milesians, gave back to them the money: but the reason for which, O Athenians, I set forth to relate to you this story, shall now be told. At the present time there is no descendant of Glaucos existing, nor any hearth which is esteemed to be that of Glaucos, but he has been utterly destroyed and rooted up out of Sparta. Thus it is good not even to entertain a thought about a deposit other than that of restoring it, when they who made it ask for it again."

87. When Leotychides had thus spoken, since not even so were the Athenians willing to listen to him, he departed back; and the Eginetans, before paying the penalty for their former wrongs wherein they did outrage to the Athenians to please the Thebans, acted as follows:—complaining of the conduct of the Athenians and thinking that they were being wronged, they made preparations to avenge themselves upon the Athenians; and since the Athenians were celebrating a four-yearly festival at Sunion, they lay in wait for the sacred ship which was sent to it and took it, the vessel being full of men who were the first among the Athenians; and having taken it they laid the men in bonds.

88. The Athenians after they had suffered this wrong from the Eginetans no longer delayed to contrive all things possible to their hurt. And there was in Egina a man of repute, one Nicodromos the son of Cnithos: this man had cause of complaint against the

Eginetans for having before this driven him forth out of the island; and hearing now that the Athenians had resolved to do mischief to the Eginetans, he agreed with the Athenians to deliver up Egina to them, telling them on what day he would make his attempt and by what day it would be necessary for them to come to his assistance.

89. After this Nicodromos, according as he had agreed with the Athenians, seized that which is called the old city, but the Athenians did not come to his support at the proper time; for, as it chanced, they had not ships sufficient to fight with the Eginetans; so while they were asking the Corinthians to lend them ships, during this time their cause went to ruin. The Corinthians however, being at this time exceedingly friendly with them, gave the Athenians twenty ships at their request; and these they gave by selling them at five drachmas apiece, for by the law it was not permitted to give them as a free gift. Having taken these ships of which I speak and also their own, the Athenians with seventy ships manned in all sailed to Egina, and they were later by one day than the time agreed.

90. Nicodromos meanwhile, as the Athenians did not come to his support at the proper time, embarked in a ship and escaped from Egina, and with him also went others of the Eginetans; and the Athenians gave them Sunion to dwell in, starting from whence these men continued to plunder the Eginetans who were in the island.

91. This happened afterwards: but at the time of which we speak the well-to-do class among the Eginetans prevailed over the men of the people, who had risen against them in combination with Nicodromos, and then having got them into their power they were bringing their prisoners forth to execution. From this there came upon them a curse which they were not able to expiate by sacrifice, though they devised against it all they could; but they were driven forth from the island before the goddess became propitious to them. For they had taken as prisoners seven hundred of the men of the people and were bringing them forth to execution, when one of them escaped from his bonds and fled for refuge to the entrance of the temple of Demeter the Giver of Laws, and he took hold of the latch of the door and clung to it; and when they found that they could not drag him from it by pulling him away, they cut off his hands and so carried him off, and those hands remained clinging to the latch of the door.

92. Thus did the Eginetans to one another: and when the Athenians came, they fought against them with seventy ships, and being worsted in the sea-fight they called to their assistance the same whom they had summoned before, namely the Argives. These would no longer come to their help, having cause of complaint because the ships of Egina compelled by Cleomenes had put in to the land of Argos and their crews had landed with the Lacedemonians; with whom also had landed men from ships of Sikyon in this same invasion: and as a penalty for this there was laid upon them by the Argives a fine of a thousand talents, five hundred for each State. The Sikyonians accordingly, acknowledging that they had committed a wrong, had made an agreement to pay a hundred talents and be free from the penalty; the Eginetans however did not acknowledge their wrong, but were more stubborn. For this reason then, when they made request, none of the Argives now came to their help at the charge of the State, but volunteers came to the number of a thousand; and their leader was a commander named Eurybates, a man who had practiced the five contests. Of these men the greater number never returned back, but were slain by the Athenians in Egina; and the commander himself, Eurybates, fighting in single combat killed in this manner three men and was himself slain by the fourth, Sophanes namely of Dekeleia.

93. The Eginetans however engaged in contest with the Athenians in ships, when these were in disorder, and defeated them; and they took of them four ships together with their crews.

94. So the Athenians were at war with the Eginetans; and meanwhile the Persian was carrying forward his design, since he was put in mind ever by his servant to remember the Athenians, and also because of the sons of Peisistratos were near at hand and brought charges continually against the Athenians, while at the same time Dareios himself wished to take hold of this pretext and subdue those nations of Hellas which had not given him earth and water. Mardonios then, since he had fared miserably in his expedition, he removed from his command; and appointing other generals to command he dispatched them against Eretria and Athens, namely Datis, who was a Mede by race, and Artaphrenes the son of Artaphrenes, a nephew of the king: and he sent them forth with the charge to reduce Athens and Eretria to slavery and to bring the slaves back into his presence.

95. When these who had been appointed to command came in their march from the king to the Aleïan plain in Kilikia, taking with them a large and well-equipped land-army, then while they were encamping there, the whole naval armament came up, which had been appointed for several nations to furnish; and there came to them also the ships for carrying horses, which in the year before Dareios had ordered his tributaries to make ready. In these they placed their horses, and having embarked the land-army in the ships they sailed for Ionia with six hundred triremes. After this they did not keep their ships coasting along the mainland towards the Hellespont and Thrace, but they started from Samos and made their voyage by the Icarian Sea and between the islands; because, as I think, they feared more than all else the voyage round Athos, seeing that in the former year while making the passage by this way they had come to great disaster. Moreover also Naxos compelled them, since it had not been conquered at the former time. .

96. And when they had arrived at Naxos, coming against it from the Icarian Sea (for it was against Naxos first that the Persians intended to make expedition, remembering the former events), the Naxians departed forthwith fleeing to the mountains, and did not await their attack; but the Persians made slaves of those of them whom they caught and set fire to both the temples and the town. Having so done they put out to sea to attack the other islands.

97. While these were doing thus, the Delians also had left Delos and fled away to Tenos; and when the armament was sailing in thither, Datis sailed on before and did not allow the ships to anchor at the island of Delos, but at Rhenaia on the other side of the channel; and he himself, having found out by inquiry where the men of Delos were, sent a herald and addressed them thus: "Holy men, why are ye fled away and departed, having judged of me that which is not convenient? for even I of myself have wisdom at least so far, and moreover it has been thus commanded me by the king, not to harm at all that land in which the two divinities were born, neither the land itself nor the inhabitants of it. Now therefore return to your own possessions and dwell in your island." Thus he proclaimed by a herald to the Delians; and after this he piled up and burned upon the altar three hundred talents' weight of frankincense.

98. Datis having done these things sailed away with his army to fight against Eretria first, taking with him both Ionians and Aiolians; and after he had put out to sea from thence, Delos was moved, not having been shaken (as the Delians reported to me) either

before that time or since that down to my own time; and this no doubt the god manifested as a portent to men of the evils that were about to be; for in the time of Dareios the son of Hystaspes and Xerxes the son of Dareios and Artoxerxes the son of Xerxes, three generations following upon one another, there happened more evils to Hellas than during the twenty other generations which came before Dareios, some of the evils coming to it from the Persians, and others from the leaders themselves of Hellas warring together for supremacy. Thus it was not unreasonable that Delos should be moved, which was before unmoved. [And in an oracle it was thus written about it:

"Delos too will I move, unmoved though it hath been aforetime."

Now in the Hellenic tongue the names which have been mentioned have this meaning —Dareios means "compeller," Xerxes "warrior," Artoxerxes "great warrior." Thus then might the Hellenes rightly call these kings in their own tongue.

99. The Barbarians then, when they had departed from Delos, touched at the islands as they went, and from them received additional forces and took sons of the islanders as hostages: and when in sailing round about the islands they put in also to Carystos, seeing that the Carystians would neither give them hostages nor consent to join in an expedition against cities that were their neighbors, meaning Eretria and Athens, they began to besiege them and to ravage their land; until at last the Carystians also came over to the will of the Persians.

100. The Eretrians meanwhile being informed that the armament of the Persians was sailing to attack them, requested the Athenians to help them; and the Athenians did not refuse their support, but gave as helpers those four thousand to whom had been allotted the land of the wealthy Chalkidians. The Eretrians however, as it turned out, had no sound plan of action, for while they sent for the Athenians, they had in their minds two different designs: some of them, that is, proposed to leave the city and go to the heights of Euboea; while others of them, expecting to win gain for themselves from the Persian, were preparing to surrender the place. Having got knowledge of how things were as regards both these plans, Aischines the son of Nothon, one of the leaders of the Eretrians, told the whole condition of their affairs to those of the Athenians who had come, and entreated them to depart and go to their own land, that they might not also perish. So the Athenians did according to this counsel given to them by Aischines.

101. And while these passed over to Oropos and saved themselves, the Persians sailed on and brought their ships to land about Temenos and Chioreai and Aigilea in the Eretrian territory; and having taken possession of these places, forthwith they began to disembark their horses and prepared to advance against the enemy. The Eretrians however did not intend to come forth against them and fight; but their endeavor was if possible to hold out by defending their walls, since the counsel prevailed not to leave the city. Then a violent assault was made upon the wall, and for six days there fell many on both sides; but on the seventh day Euphorbos the son of Alkimachos and Philagros the son of Kyneos, men of repute among the citizens, gave up the city to the Persians. These having entered the city plundered and set fire to the temples in retribution for the temples which were burned at Sardis, and also reduced the people to slavery according to the commands of Dareios.

102. Having got Eretria into their power, they stayed a few days and then sailed for the land of Attica, pressing on hard and supposing that the Athenians would do the same as

the Eretrians had done. And since Marathon was the most convenient place in Attica for horsemen to act and was also very near to Eretria, therefore Hippias the son of Peisistratos was guiding them thither.

103. When the Athenians had information of this, they too went to Marathon to the rescue of their land; and they were led by ten generals, of whom the tenth was Miltiades, whose father Kimon of Stesagoras had been compelled to go into exile from Athens because of Peisistratos the son of Hippocrates: and while he was in exile it was his fortune to win a victory at the Olympic games with a four-horse chariot, wherein, as it happened, he did the same thing as his half-brother Miltiades had done, who had the same mother as he. Then afterwards in the next succeeding Olympic games he gained a victory with the same mares and allowed Peisistratos to be proclaimed as victor; and having resigned to him the victory he returned to his own native land under an agreement for peace. Then after he had won with the same mares at another Olympic festival, it was his hap to be slain by the sons of Peisistratos, Peisistratos himself being no longer alive. These killed him near the City Hall, having set men to lie in wait for him by night; and the burial-place of Kimon is in the outskirts of the city, on the other side of the road which is called the way through Coile, and just opposite him those mares are buried which won in three Olympic games. This same thing was done also by the mares belonging to Euagoras the Laconian, but besides these by none others. Now the elder of the sons of Kimon, Stesagoras, was at that time being brought up in the house of his father's brother Miltiades in the Chersonese, while the younger son was being brought up at Athens with Kimon himself, having been named Miltiades after Miltiades the settler of the Chersonese.

104. This Miltiades then at the time of which we speak had come from the Chersonese and was a general of the Athenians, after escaping death in two forms; for not only did the Phoenicians, who had pursued after him as far as Imbros, endeavor earnestly to take him and bring him up to the presence of the king, but also after this, when he had escaped from these and had come to his own native land and seemed to be in safety from that time forth, his opponents, who had laid wait for him there, brought him up before a court and prosecuted him for his despotism in the Chersonese. Having escaped these also, he had then been appointed a general of the Athenians, being elected by the people.

105. First of all, while they were still in the city, the generals sent off to Sparta a herald, namely Pheidippides an Athenian and for the rest a runner of long day-courses and one who practiced this as his profession. With this man, as Pheidippides himself said and as he made report to the Athenians, Pan chanced to meet by mount Parthenion, which is above Tegea; and calling aloud the name of Pheidippides, Pan bade him report to the Athenians and ask for what reason they had no care of him, though he was well disposed to the Athenians and had been serviceable to them on many occasions before that time, and would be so also yet again. Believing that this tale was true, the Athenians, when their affairs had been now prosperously settled, established under the Acropolis a temple of Pan; and in consequence of this message they propitiate him with sacrifice offered every year and with a torch-race.

106. However at that time, the time namely when he said that Pan appeared to him, this Pheidippides having been sent by the generals was in Sparta on the next day after that on which he left the city of the Athenians; and when he had come to the magistrates he said: "Lacedemonians, the Athenians make request of you to come to their help and not to allow a city most anciently established among the Hellenes to fall into slavery by

the means of Barbarians; for even now Eretria has been enslaved, and Hellas has become the weaker by a city of renown." He, as I say, reported to them that with which he had been charged, and it pleased them well to come to help the Athenians; but it was impossible for them to do so at once, since they did not desire to break their law; for it was the ninth day of the month, and on the ninth day they said they would not go forth, nor until the circle of the moon should be full.

107. These men were waiting for the full moon: and meanwhile Hippias the son of Peisistratos was guiding the Barbarians in to Marathon, after having seen on the night that was just past a vision in his sleep of this kind,—it seemed to Hippias that he lay with his own mother. He conjectured then from the dream that he should return to Athens and recover his rule, and then bring his life to an end in old age in his own land. From the dream, I say, he conjectured this; and after this, as he guided them in, first he disembarked the slaves from Eretria on the island belonging to the Styrians, called Aigleia; and then, as the ships came in to shore at Marathon, he moored them there, and after the Barbarians had come from their ships to land, he was engaged in disposing them in their places. While he was ordering these things, it came upon him to sneeze and cough more violently than was his wont. Then since he was advanced in years, most of his teeth were shaken thereby, and one of these teeth he cast forth by the violence of the cough: and the tooth having fallen from him upon the sand, he was very desirous to find it; since however the tooth was not to be found when he searched, he groaned aloud and said to those who were by him: "This land is not ours, nor shall we be able to make it subject to us; but so much part in it as belonged to me the tooth possesses."

108. Hippias then conjectured that his vision had been thus fulfilled: and meanwhile, after the Athenians had been drawn up in the sacred enclosure of Heracles, there joined them the Plataians coming to their help in a body: for the Plataians had given themselves to the Athenians, and the Athenians before this time undertook many toils on behalf of them; and this was the manner in which they gave themselves:—Being oppressed by the Thebans, the Plataians at first desired to give themselves to Cleomenes the son of Anaxandrides and to the Lacedemonians, who chanced to come thither; but these did not accept them, and said to them as follows: "We dwell too far off, and such support as ours would be to you but cold comfort; for ye might many times be reduced to slavery before any of us had information of it: but we counsel you rather to give yourselves to the Athenians, who are both neighbors and also not bad helpers." Thus the Lacedemonians counselled, not so much on account of their goodwill to the Plataians as because they desired that the Athenians should have trouble by being involved in a conflict with the Boeotians. The Lacedemonians, I say, thus counselled the men of Plataia; and they did not fail to follow their counsel, but when the Athenians were doing sacrifice to the twelve gods, they sat down as suppliants at the altar and so gave themselves. Then the Thebans having been informed of these things marched against the Plataians, and the Athenians came to their assistance: and as they were about to join battle, the Corinthians did not permit them to do so, but being by chance there, they reconciled their strife; and both parties having put the matter into their hands, they laid down boundaries for the land, with the condition that the Thebans should leave those of the Boeotians alone who did not desire to be reckoned with the other Boeotians. The Corinthians having given this decision departed; but as the Athenians were going back, the Boeotians attacked them, and having attacked them they were worsted in the fight. Upon that the Athenians passed beyond the boundaries

which the Corinthians had set to be for the Plataians, and they made the river Asopos itself to be the boundary of the Thebans towards the land of Plataia and towards the district of Hysiai. The Plataians then had given themselves to the Athenians in the manner which has been said, and at this time they came to Marathon to bring them help.

109. Now the opinions of the generals of the Athenians were divided, and the one party urged that they should not fight a battle, seeing that they were too few to fight with the army of the Medes, while the others, and among them Miltiades, advised that they should do so: and when they were divided and the worse opinion was like to prevail, then, since he who had been chosen by lot to be polemarch of the Athenians had a vote in addition to the ten (for in old times the Athenians gave the polemarch an equal vote with the generals) and at that time the polemarch was Callimachos of the deme of Aphidnai, to him came Miltiades and said as follows: "With thee now it rests, Callimachos, either to bring Athens under slavery, or by making her free to leave behind thee for all the time that men shall live a memorial such as not even Harmodios and Aristogeiton have left. For now the Athenians have come to a danger the greatest to which they have ever come since they were a people; and on the one hand, if they submit to the Medes, it is determined what they shall suffer, being delivered over to Hippias, while on the other hand, if this city shall gain the victory, it may become the first of the cities of Hellas. How this may happen and how it comes to thee of all men to have the decision of these matters, I am now about to tell. Of us the generals, who are ten in number, the opinions are divided, the one party urging that we fight a battle and the others that we do not fight. Now if we do not, I expect that some great spirit of discord will fall upon the minds of the Athenians and so shake them that they shall go over to the Medes; but if we fight a battle before any unsoundness appear in any part of the Athenian people, then we are able to gain the victory in the fight, if the gods grant equal conditions. These things then all belong to thee and depend on thee; for if thou attach thyself to my opinions, thou hast both a fatherland which is free and a native city which shall be the first among the cities of Hellas; but if thou choose the opinion of those who are earnest against fighting, thou shalt have the opposite of those good things of which I told thee."

110. Thus speaking Miltiades gained Callimachos to his side; and the opinion of the polemarch being added, it was thus determined to fight a battle. After this, those generals whose opinion was in favor of fighting, as the turn of each one of them to command for the day came round, gave over their command to Miltiades; and he, accepting it, would not however yet bring about a battle, until his own turn to command had come.

111. And when it came round to him, then the Athenians were drawn up for battle in the order which here follows:—On the right wing the polemarch Callimachos was leader (for the custom of the Athenians then was this, that the polemarch should have the right wing); and he leading, next after him came the tribes in order as they were numbered one after another, and last were drawn up the Plataians occupying the left wing: for ever since this battle, when the Athenians offer sacrifices in the solemn assemblies which are made at the four-yearly festivals, the herald of the Athenians prays thus, "that blessings may come to the Athenians and to the Plataians both." On this occasion however, when the Athenians were being drawn up at Marathon something of this kind was done:—their army being made equal in length of front to that of the Medes, came to drawn up in the middle with a depth of but few ranks, and here their army was weakest, while each wing was strengthened with numbers.

112. And when they had been arranged in their places and the sacrifices proved favorable, then the Athenians were let go, and they set forth at a run to attack the Barbarians. Now the space between the armies was not less than eight furlongs: and the Persians seeing them advancing to the attack at a run, made preparations to receive them; and in their minds they charged the Athenians with madness which must be fatal, seeing that they were few and yet were pressing forwards at a run, having neither cavalry nor archers. Such was the thought of the Barbarians; but the Athenians when all in a body they had joined in combat with the Barbarians, fought in a memorable fashion: for they were the first of all the Hellenes about whom we know who went to attack the enemy at a run, and they were the first also who endured to face the Median garments and the men who wore them, whereas up to this time the very name of the Medes was to the Hellenes a terror to hear.

113. Now while they fought in Marathon, much time passed by; and in the center of the army, where the Persians themselves and the Sacans were drawn up, the Barbarians were winning,—here, I say, the Barbarians had broken the ranks of their opponents and were pursuing them inland, but on both wings the Athenians and the Plataians severally were winning the victory; and being victorious they left that part of the Barbarians which had been routed to fly without molestation, and bringing together the two wings they fought with those who had broken their center, and the Athenians were victorious. So they followed after the Persians as they fled, slaughtering them, until they came to the sea; and then they called for fire and began to take hold of the ships.

114. In this part of the work was slain the polemarch Callimachos after having proved himself a good man, and also one of the generals, Stesilaos the son of Thrasylaos, was killed; and besides this Kynegeiros the son of Euphorion while taking hold there of the ornament at the stern of a ship had his hand cut off with an axe and fell; and many others also of the Athenians who were men of note were killed.

115. Seven of the ships the Athenians got possession of in this manner, but with the rest the Barbarians pushed off from land, and after taking the captives from Eretria off the island where they had left them, they sailed round Sunion, purposing to arrive at the city before the Athenians. And an accusation became current among the Athenians to the effect that they formed this design by contrivance of the Alcmaionidai; for these, it was said, having concerted matters with the Persians, displayed to them a shield when they had now embarked in their ships.

116. These then, I say, were sailing round Sunion; and meanwhile the Athenians came to the rescue back to the city as speedily as they could, and they arrived there before the Barbarians came; and having arrived from the temple of Heracles at Marathon they encamped at another temple of Heracles, namely that which is in Kynosarges. The Barbarians however came and lay with their ships in the sea which is off Phaleron, (for this was then the seaport of the Athenians), they anchored their ships, I say, off this place, and then proceeded to sail back to Asia.

117. In this fight at Marathon there were slain of the Barbarians about six thousand four hundred men, and of the Athenians a hundred and ninety and two. Such was the number which fell on both sides; and it happened also that a marvel occurred there of this kind:—an Athenian, Epizelos the son of Cuphagoras, while fighting in the close combat and proving himself a good man, was deprived of the sight of his eyes, neither having received a blow in any part of his body nor having been hit with a missile, and for the rest

of his life from this time he continued to be blind: and I was informed that he used to tell about that which had happened to him a tale of this kind, namely that it seemed to him that a tall man in full armor stood against him, whose beard overshadowed his whole shield; and this apparition passed him by, but killed his comrade who stood next to him. Thus, as I was informed, Epizelos told the tale.

118. Datis, however, as he was going with his army to Asia, when he had come to Myconos saw a vision in his sleep; and of what nature the vision was it is not reported, but as soon as day dawned he caused a search to be made of the ships, and finding in a Phoenician ship an image of Apollo overlaid with gold, he inquired from whence it had been carried off. Then having been informed from what temple it came, he sailed in his own ship to Delos: and finding that the Delians had returned then to the island, he deposited the image in the temple and charged the men of Delos to convey it back to Delion in the territory of the Thebans, which is situated by the sea-coast just opposite Chalkis. Datis having given this charge sailed away: the Delians however did not convey the statue back, but after an interval of twenty years the Thebans themselves brought it to Delion by reason of an oracle.

119. Now as to those Eretrians who had been reduced to slavery, Datis and Artaphrenes, when they reached Asia in their voyage, brought them up to Susa; and king Dareios, though he had great anger against the Eretrians before they were made captive, because the Eretrians had done wrong to him unprovoked, yet when he saw that they had been brought up to him and were in his power, he did them no more evil, but established them as settlers in the Kissian land upon one of his own domains, of which the name is Ardericca: and this is distant two hundred and ten furlongs from Susa and forty from the well which produces things of three different kinds; for they draw from it asphalt, salt and oil, in the manner which here follows:—the liquid is drawn with a swipe, to which there is fastened half a skin instead of a bucket, and a man strikes this down into it and draws up, and then pours it into a cistern, from which it runs through into another vessel, taking three separate ways. The asphalt and the salt become solid at once, and the oil which is called by the Persians *rhadinake*, is black and gives out a disagreeable smell. Here king Dareios established the Eretrians as settlers; and even to my time they continued to occupy this land, keeping still their former language. Thus it happened with regard to the Eretrians.

120. Of the Lacedemonians there came to Athens two thousand after the full moon, making great haste to be in time, so that they arrived in Attica on the third day after leaving Sparta: and though they had come too late for the battle, yet they desired to behold the Medes; and accordingly they went out to Marathon and looked at the bodies of the slain: then afterwards they departed home, commending the Athenians and the work which they had done.

121. Now it is a cause of wonder to me, and I do not accept the report, that the Alcmaionidai could ever have displayed to the Persians a shield by a previous under-standing, with the desire that the Athenians should be under the Barbarians and under Hippias; seeing that they are evidently proved to have been haters of despots as much or more than Callias the son of Phainippos and father of Hipponicos, while Callias for his part was the only man of all the Athenians who dared, when Peisistratos was driven out of Athens, to buy his goods offered for sale by the State, and in other ways also he contrived against him everything that was most hostile:

122. Of this Callias it is fitting that everyone should have remembrance for many reasons: first because of that which has been before said, namely that he was a man of excellence in freeing his country; and then also for that which he did at the Olympic games, wherein he gained a victory in the horse-race and was second in the chariot-race, and he had before this been a victor at the Pythian games, so that he was distinguished in the sight of all Hellenes by the sums which he expended; and finally because he showed himself a man of such liberality towards his daughters, who were three in number; for when they came to be of ripe age for marriage, he gave them a most magnificent dowry and also indulged their inclinations; for whomsoever of all the Athenians each one of them desired to choose as a husband for herself, to that man he gave her.] .

123, and similarly, the Alcmaionidai were haters of despots equally or more than he. Therefore this is a cause of wonder to me, and I do not admit the accusation that these they were who displayed the shield; seeing that they were in exile from the despots during their whole time, and that by their contrivance the sons of Peisistratos gave up their rule. Thus it follows that they were the men who set Athens free much more than Harmodios and Aristogeiton, as I judge: for these my slaying Hipparchos exasperated the rest of the family of Peisistratos, and did not at all cause the others to cease from their despotism; but the Alcmaionidai did evidently set Athens free, at least if these were in truth the men who persuaded the Pythian prophetess to signify to the Lacedemonians that they should set Athens free, as I have set forth before.

124. It may be said however that they had some cause of complaint against the people of the Athenians, and therefore endeavored to betray their native city. But on the contrary there were no men in greater repute than they, among the Athenians at least, nor who had been more highly honored. Thus it is not reasonable to suppose that by them a shield should have been displayed for any such purpose. A shield was displayed, however; that cannot be denied, for it was done: but as to who it was who displayed it, I am not able to say more than this.

125. Now the family of Alcmaionidai was distinguished in Athens in the earliest times also, and from the time of Alcmaion and of Megacles after him they became very greatly distinguished. For first Alcmaion the son of Megacles showed himself a helper of the Lydians from Sardis who came from Croesus to the Oracle at Delphi, and assisted them with zeal; and Croesus having heard from the Lydians who went to the Oracle that this man did him service, sent for him to Sardis; and when he came, he offered to give him a gift of as much gold as he could carry away at once upon his own person. With a view to this gift, its nature being such, Alcmaion made preparations and used appliances as follows:—he put on a large tunic leaving a deep fold in the tunic to hang down in front, and he draw on his feet the widest boots which he could find, and so went to the treasury to which they conducted him. Then he fell upon a heap of gold-dust, and first he packed in by the side of his legs so much of the gold as his boots would contain, and then he filled the whole fold of the tunic with the gold and sprinkled some of the gold dust on the hair of his head and took some into his mouth, and having so done he came forth out of the treasury, with difficulty dragging along his boots and resembling anything in the world rather than a man; for his mouth was stuffed full, and every part of him was swelled out: and upon Croesus came laughter when he saw him, and he not only gave him all that, but also presented him in addition with more not inferior in value to that. Thus this house became exceedingly wealthy,

and thus the Alcmaion of whom I speak became a breeder of chariot-horses and won a victory at Olympia.

126. Then in the next generation after this, Cleisthenes the despot of Sikyon exalted the family, so that it became of much more note among the Hellenes than it had been formerly. For Cleisthenes the son of Arisonymos, the son of Myron, the son of Andreas, had a daughter whose name was Agariste; and as to her he formed a desire to find out the best man of all the Hellenes and to assign her to him in marriage. So when the Olympic games were being held and Cleisthenes was victor in them with a four-horse chariot, he caused a proclamation to be made, that whosoever of the Hellenes thought himself worthy to be the son-in-law of Cleisthenes should come on the sixtieth day, or before that if he would, to Sikyon; for Cleisthenes intended to conclude the marriage within a year, reckoning from the sixtieth day. Then all those of the Hellenes who had pride either in themselves or in their high descent, came as wooers, and for them Cleisthenes had a running-course and a wrestling-place made and kept them expressly for their use.

127. From Italy came Smindyrides the son of Hippocrates of Sybaris, who of all men on earth reached the highest point of luxury (now Sybaris at this time was in the height of its prosperity), and Damasos of Siris, the son of that Amyris who was called the Wise; these came from Italy: from the Ionian gulf came Amphimnestos the son of Epistrophos of Epidamnos, this man from the Ionian gulf: from Aitolia came Males, the brother of that Titormos who surpassed all the Hellenes in strength and who fled from the presence of men to the furthest extremities of the Aitolian land: from Peloponnesus, Leokedes the son of Pheidon the despot of the Argives, that Pheidon who established for the Pelopon- nesians the measures which they use, and who went beyond all other Hellenes in wanton insolence, since he removed from their place the presidents of the games appointed by the Eleians and himself presided over the games at Olympia,—his son, I say, and Amiantos the son of Lycurgos an Arcadian from Trapezus, and Laphanes an Azanian from the city of Paios, son of that Euphorion who (according to the story told in Arcadia) received the Dioscuroi as guests in his house and from thenceforth was wont to entertain all men who came, and Onomastos the son of Agaios of Elis; these, I say, came from Peloponnesus itself: from Athens came Megacles the son of that Alcmaion who went to Croesus, and besides him Hippocleides the son of Tisander, one who surpassed the other Athenians in wealth and in comeliness of form: from Eretria, which at that time was flourishing, came Lysanias, he alone from Euboea: from Thessalia came Diactorides of Crannon, one of the family of the Scopadai: and from the Molossians, Alcon.

128. So many in number did the wooers prove to be: and when these had come by the appointed day, Cleisthenes first inquired of their native countries and of the descent of each one, and then keeping them for a year he made trial continually both of their manly virtue and of their disposition, training and temper, associating both with each one sepa- rately and with the whole number together: and he made trial of them both by bringing out to bodily exercises those of them who were younger, and also especially in the common feast: for during all the time that he kept them he did everything that could be done, and at the same time he entertained them magnificently. Now it chanced that those of the wooers pleased him most who had come from Athens, and of these Hippocleides the son of Tisander was rather preferred, both by reason of manly virtues and also because he was connected by descent with the family of Kypselos at Corinth.

129. Then when the appointed day came for the marriage banquet and for Cleisthenes

himself to declare whom he selected from the whole number, Cleisthenes sacrificed a hundred oxen and feasted both the wooers themselves and all the people of Sikyon; and when the dinner was over, the wooers began to vie with one another both in music and in speeches for the entertainment of the company; and as the drinking went forward and Hippocleides was very much holding the attention of the others, he bade the flute-player play for him a dance-measure; and when the flute-player did so, he danced: and it so befell that he pleased himself in his dancing, but Cleisthenes looked on at the whole matter with suspicion. Then Hippocleides after a certain time bade one bring in a table; and when the table came in, first he danced upon it Laconian figures, and then also Attic, and thirdly he planted his head upon the table and gesticulated with his legs. Cleisthenes meanwhile, when he was dancing the first and the second time, though he abhorred the thought that Hippocleides should now become his son-in-law, because of his dancing and his shamelessness, yet restrained himself, not desiring to break out in anger against him; but when he saw that he thus gesticulated with his legs, he was no longer able to restrain himself, but said: "Thou hast danced away thy marriage however, son of Tisander!" and Hippocleides answered and said: "Hippocleides cares not!"

130. and hence comes this saying. Then Cleisthenes caused silence to be made, and spoke to the company as follows: "Men who are wooers of my daughter, I commend you all, and if it were possible I would gratify you all, neither selecting one of you to be preferred, nor rejecting the remainder. Since however it is not possible, as I am deliberating about one maiden only, to act so as to please all, therefore to those of you who are rejected from this marriage I give as a gift a talent of silver to each one for the worthy estimation ye had of me, in that ye desired to marry from my house, and for the time of absence from your homes; and to the son of Alcmaion, Megacles, I offer my daughter Agariste in betrothal according to the customs of the Athenians." Thereupon Megacles said that he accepted the betrothal, and so the marriage was determined by Cleisthenes.

131. Thus it happened as regards the judgment of the wooers, and thus the Alcmaionidai got renown over all Hellas. And these having been married, there was born to them that Cleisthenes who established the tribes and the democracy for the Athenians, he being called after the Sikyonian Cleisthenes, his mother's father; this son, I say, was born to Megacles, and also Hippocrates: and of Hippocrates came another Megacles and another Agariste, called after Agariste, the daughter of Cleisthenes, who having been married to Xanthippos the son of Ariphron and being with child, saw a vision in her sleep, and it seemed to her that she had brought forth a lion: then after a few days she bore to Xanthippos Pericles.

132. After the defeat at Marathon, Miltiades, who even before was well reputed with the Athenians, came then to be in much higher estimation: and when he asked the Athenians for seventy ships and an army with supplies of money, not declaring to them against what land he was intending to make an expedition, but saying that he would enrich them greatly if they would go with him, for he would lead them to a land of such a kind that they would easily get from it gold in abundance,—thus saying he asked for the ships; and the Athenians, elated by these words, delivered them over to him.

133. Then Miltiades, when he had received the army, proceeded to sail to Paris with the pretense that the Parians had first attacked Athens by making expedition with triremes to Marathon in company with the Persian: this was the pretext which he put forward, but he had also a grudge against the Parians on account of Lysagoras the son of Tisias, who was

by race of Paros, for having accused him to Hydarnes the Persian. So when Miltiades had arrived at the place to which he was sailing, he began to besiege the Parians with his army, first having shut them up within their wall; and sending in to them a herald he asked for a hundred talents, saying that if they refused to give them, his army should not return back until it had conquered them completely. The Parians however had no design of giving any money to Miltiades, but contrived only how they might defend their city, devising various things besides and also this,—wherever at any time the wall proved to be open to attack, that point was raised when night came on to double its former height.

134. So much of the story is reported by all the Hellenes, but as to what followed the Parians alone report, and they say that it happened thus:—When Miltiades was at a loss, it is said, there came a woman to speech with him, who had been taken prisoner, a Parian by race whose name was Timo, an under-priestess of the Earth goddesses; she, they say, came into the presence of Miltiades and counselled him that if he considered it a matter of much moment to conquer Paros, he could do that which she should suggest to him; and upon that she told him her meaning. He accordingly passed through to the hill which is before the city and leapt over the fence of the temple of Demeter Giver of Laws, not being able to open the door; and then having leapt over he went on towards the sanctuary with the design of doing something within, whether it were that he meant to lay hands on some of the things which should not be touched, or whatever else he intended to do; and when he had reached the door, forthwith a shuddering fear came over him and he set off to go back the same way as he came, and as he leapt down from the wall of rough stones his thigh was dislocated, or, as others say, he struck his knee against the wall.

135. Miltiades accordingly, being in a wretched case, set forth to sail homewards, neither bringing wealth to the Athenians nor having added to them the possession of Paros, but having besieged the city for six-and-twenty days and laid waste the island: and the Parians being informed that Timo the under-priestess of the goddesses had acted as a guide to Miltiades, desired to take vengeance upon her for this, and they sent messengers to Delphi to consult the god, so soon as they had leisure from the siege; and these messengers they sent to ask whether they should put to death the under-priestess of the goddesses, who had been a guide to their enemies for the capture of her native city and had revealed to Miltiades the mysteries which might not be uttered to a male person. The Pythian prophetess however forbade them, saying that Timo was not the true author of these things, but since it was destined that Miltiades should end his life not well, she had appeared to guide him to his evil fate.

136. Thus the Pythian prophetess replied to the Parians: and the Athenians, when Miltiades had returned back from Paros, began to talk of him, and among the rest especially Xanthippos the son of Ariphron, who brought Miltiades up before the people claiming the penalty of death and prosecuted him for his deception of the Athenians: and Miltiades did not himself make his own defense, although he was present, for he was unable to do so because his thigh was mortifying; but he lay in public view upon a bed, while his friends made a defense for him, making mention much both of the battle which had been fought at Marathon and of the conquest of Lemnos, namely how he had conquered Lemnos and taken vengeance on the Pelasgians, and had delivered it over to the Athenians: and the people came over to his part as regards the acquittal from the penalty of death, but they imposed a fine of fifty talents for the wrong committed: and

after this Miltiades died, his thigh having gangrened and mortified, and the fifty talents were paid by his son Kimon.

137. Now Miltiades son of Kimon had thus taken possession of the Lemnos:—After the Pelasgians had been cast out of Attica by the Athenians, whether justly or unjustly,—for about this I cannot tell except the things reported, which are these:—Hecataois on the one hand, the son of Hegesander, said in his history that it was done unjustly; for he said that when the Athenians saw the land which extends below Hymettos, which they had themselves given them to dwell in, as payment for the wall built round the Acropolis in former times, when the Athenians, I say, saw that this land was made good by cultivation, which before was bad and worthless, they were seized with jealousy and with longing to possess the land, and so drove them out, not alleging any other pretext: but according to the report of the Athenians themselves they drove them out justly; for the Pelasgians being settled under Hymettos made this a starting-point and committed wrong against them as follows: —the daughters and sons of the Athenians were wont ever to go for water to the spring of Enneacrunos; for at that time neither they nor the other Hellenes as yet had household servants; and when these girls came, the Pelasgians in wantonness and contempt of the Athenians would offer them violence; and it was not enough for them even to do this, but at last they were found in the act of plotting an attack upon the city: and the narrators say that they herein proved themselves better men than the Pelasgians, inasmuch as when they might have slain the Pelasgians, who had been caught plotting against them, they did not choose to do so, but ordered them merely to depart out of the land: and thus having departed out of the land, the Pelasgians took possession of several older places and especially of Lemnos. The former story is that which was reported by Hecataios, while the latter is that which is told by the Athenians.

138. These Pelasgians then, dwelling after that in Lemnos, desired to take vengeance on the Athenians; and having full knowledge also of the festivals of the Athenians, they got fifty-oared galleys and laid wait for the women of the Athenians when they were keeping festival to Artemis in Brauron; and having carried off a number of them from thence, they departed and sailed away home, and taking the women to Lemnos they kept them as concubines. Now when these women had children gradually more and more, they made it their practice to teach their sons both the Attic tongue and the manners of the Athenians. And these were not willing to associate with the sons of the Pelasgian women, and moreover if any of them were struck by any one of those, they all in a body came to the rescue and helped one another. Moreover the boys claimed to have authority over the other boys and got the better of them easily. Perceiving these things the Pelasgians considered the matter; and when they took counsel together, a fear came over them and they thought, if the boys were indeed resolved now to help one another against the sons of the legitimate wives, and were endeavoring already from the first to have authority over them, what would they do when they were grown up to be men? Then they determined to put to death the sons of the Athenian women, and this they actually did; and in addition to them they slew their mothers also. From this deed and from that which was done before this, which the women did when they killed Thoas and the rest, who were their own husbands, it has become a custom in Hellas that all deeds of great cruelty should be called "Lemnian deeds."

139. After the Pelasgians had killed their own sons and wives, the earth did not bear fruit for them, nor did their women or their cattle bring forth young as they did before;

and being hard pressed by famine and by childlessness, they sent to Delphi to ask for a release from the evils which were upon them; and the Pythian prophetess bade them pay such penalty to the Athenians as the Athenians themselves should appoint. The Pelasgians came accordingly to Athens and professed that they were willing to pay the penalty for all the wrong which they had done: and the Athenians laid a couch in the fairest possible manner in the City Hall, and having set by it a table covered with all good things, they bade the Pelasgians deliver up to them their land in that condition. Then the Pelasgians answered and said: "When with a North Wind in one single day a ship shall accomplish the voyage from your land to ours, then we will deliver it up," feeling assured that it was impossible for this to happen, since Attica lies far away to the South of Lemnos.

140. Such were the events which happened then: and very many years later, after the Chersonese which is by the Hellespont had come to be under the Athenians, Miltiades the son of Kimon, when the Etesian Winds blew steadily, accomplished the voyage in a ship from Elaius in the Chersonese to Lemnos, and proclaimed to the Pelasgians that they should depart out of the island, reminding them of the oracle, which the Pelasgians had never expected would be accomplished for them. The men of Hephaistia accordingly obeyed; but those of Myrina, not admitting that the Chersonese was Attica, suffered a siege, until at last these also submitted. Thus it was that the Athenians and Miltiades took possession of Lemnos.

7

THE SEVENTH BOOK OF THE
HISTORIES, CALLED POLYMNIA

1. Now when the report came to Dareios the son of Hystaspes of the battle which was fought at Marathon, the king, who even before this had been greatly exasperated with the Athenians on account of the attack made upon Sardis, then far more than before displayed indignation, and was far more desirous of making a march against Hellas. Accordingly at once he sent messengers to the various cities and ordered that they should get ready a force, appointing to each people to supply much more than at the former time, and not only ships of war, but also horses and provisions and transport vessels; and when these commands were carried round, all Asia was moved for three years, for all the best men were being enlisted for the expedition against Hellas, and were making preparations. In the fourth year however the Egyptians, who had been reduced to subjection by Cambyses, revolted from the Persians; and then he was even more desirous of marching against both these nations.

2. While Dareios was thus preparing to set out against Egypt and against Athens, there arose a great strife among his sons about the supreme power; and they said that he must not make his expeditions until he had designated one of them to be king, according to the custom of the Persians. For to Dareios already before he became king three sons had been born of his former wife the daughter of Gobryas, and after he became king four other sons of Atossa the daughter of Cyrus: of the first the eldest was Artobazanes, and of those who had been born later, Xerxes. These being not of the same mother were at strife with one another, Artobazanes contending that he was the eldest of all the sons, and that it was a custom maintained by all men that the eldest should have the rule, and Xerxes arguing that he was the son of Atossa the daughter of Cyrus, and that Cyrus was he who had won for the Persians their freedom.

3. Now while Dareios did not as yet declare his judgment, it chanced that Demaratos also, the son of Ariston, had come up to Susa at this very same time, having been deprived of the kingdom in Sparta and having laid upon himself a sentence of exile from Lacedaemon. This man, hearing of the difference between the sons of Dareios, came (as it

is reported of him) and counselled Xerxes to say in addition to those things which he was wont to say, that he had been born to Dareios at the time when he was already reigning as king and was holding the supreme power over the Persians, while Artobazanes had been born while Dareios was still in a private station: it was not fitting therefore nor just that another should have the honor before him; for even in Sparta, suggested Demaratos, this was the custom, that is to say, if some of the sons had been born first, before their father began to reign, and another came after, born later while he was reigning, the succession of the kingdom belonged to him who had been born later. Xerxes accordingly made use of the suggestion of Demaratos; and Dareios perceiving that he spoke that which was just, designated him to be king. It is my opinion however that even without this suggestion Xerxes would have become king, for Atossa was all-powerful.

4. Then having designated Xerxes to the Persians as their king, Dareios wished to go on his expeditions. However in the next year after this and after the revolt of Egypt, it came to pass that Dareios himself died, having been king in all six-and-thirty years; and thus he did not succeed in taking vengeance either upon the revolted Egyptians or upon the Athenians.

5. Dareios being dead the kingdom passed to his son Xerxes. Now Xerxes at the first was by no means anxious to make a march against Hellas, but against Egypt he continued to gather a force. Mardonios however, the son of Gobryas, who was a cousin of Xerxes, being sister's son to Dareios, was ever at his side, and having power with him more than any other of the Persians, he kept continually to such discourse as this which follows, saying: "Master, it is not fitting that the Athenians, after having done to the Persians very great evil, should not pay the penalty for that which they have done. What if thou shouldest at this present time do that which thou hast in thy hands to do; and when thou hast tamed the land of Egypt, which has broken out insolently against us, then do thou march an army against Athens, that a good report may be made of thee by men, and that in future every one may beware of making expeditions against thy land." Thus far his speech had to do with vengeance, and to this he would make addition as follows, saying that Europe was a very fair land and bore all kinds of trees that are cultivated for fruit, and was of excellent fertility, and such that the king alone of all mortals was worthy to possess it.

6. These things he was wont to say, since he was one who had a desire for perilous enterprise and wished to be himself the governor of Hellas under the king. So in time he prevailed upon Xerxes and persuaded him to do this; for other things also assisted him and proved helpful to him in persuading Xerxes. In the first place there had come from Thessaly messengers sent by the Aleuadai, who were inviting the king to come against Hellas and were showing great zeal in his cause, (now these Aleuadai were kings of Thessaly): and then secondly those of the sons of Peisistratos who had come up to Susa were inviting him also, holding to the same arguments as the Aleuadai; and moreover they offered him yet more inducement in addition to these; for there was one Onomacritos an Athenian, who both uttered oracles and also had collected and arranged the oracles of Musaios; and with this man they had come up, after they had first reconciled the enmity between them. For Onomacritos had been driven forth from Athens by Hipparchos the son of Peisistratos, having been caught by Lasos of Hermion interpolating in the works of Musaios an oracle to the effect that the islands which lie off Lemnos should disappear under the sea. For this reason Hipparchos drove him forth, having before this time been

very much wont to consult him. Now however he had gone up with them; and when he had come into the presence of the king, the sons of Peisistratos spoke of him in magnificent terms, and he repeated some of the oracles; and if there was in them anything which imported disaster to the Barbarians, of this he said nothing; but choosing out of them the most fortunate things he told how it was destined that the Hellespont should be yoked with a bridge by a Persian, and he set forth the manner of the march. He then thus urged Xerxes with oracles, while the sons of Peisistratos and the Aleuadai pressed him with their advice.

7. So when Xerxes had been persuaded to make an expedition against Hellas, then in the next year after the death of Dareios he made a march first against those who had revolted. Having subdued these and having reduced all Egypt to slavery much greater than it had suffered in the reign of Dareios, he entrusted the government of it to Achaimenes his own brother, a son of Dareios. Now this Achaimenes being a governor of Egypt was slain afterwards by Inaros the son of Psammetichos, a Libyan.

8. Xerxes then after the conquest of Egypt, being about to take in hand the expedition against Athens, summoned a chosen assembly of the best men among the Persians, that he might both learn their opinions and himself in the presence of all declare that which he intended to do; and when they were assembled, Xerxes spoke to them as follows: (a) "Persians, I shall not be the first to establish this custom in your nation, but having received it from others I shall follow it: for as I am informed by those who are older than myself, we never yet have kept quiet since we received this supremacy in succession to the Medes, when Cyrus overthrew Astyages; but God thus leads us, and for ourselves tends to good that we are busied about many things. Now about the nations which Cyrus and Cambyses and my father Dareios subdued and added to their possessions there is no need for me to speak, since ye know well: and as for me, from the day when I received by inheritance this throne upon which I sit I carefully considered always how in this honorable place I might not fall short of those who have been before me, nor add less power to the dominion of the Persians: and thus carefully considering I find a way by which not only glory may be won by us, together with a land not less in extent nor worse than that which we now possess, (and indeed more varied in its productions), but also vengeance and retribution may be brought about. Wherefore I have assembled you together now, in order that I may communicate to you that which I have it in my mind to do. (b) I design to yoke the Hellespont with a bridge, and to march an army through Europe against Hellas, in order that I may take vengeance on the Athenians for all the things which they have done both to the Persians and to my father. Ye saw how my father Dareios also was purposing to make an expedition against these men; but he has ended his life and did not succeed in taking vengeance upon them. I however, on behalf of him and also of the other Persians, will not cease until I have conquered Athens and burnt it with fire; seeing that they did wrong unprovoked to me and to my father. First they went to Sardis, having come with Aristagoras the Milesian our slave, and they set fire to the sacred groves and the temples; and then secondly, what things they did to us when we disembarked in their land, at the time when Datis and Artaphrenes were commanders of our army, ye all know well, as I think. (c) For these reasons I have resolved to make an expedition against them, and reckoning I find in the matter so many good things as ye shall hear:—if we shall subdue these and the neighbors of these, who dwell in the land of Pelops the Phrygian, we shall cause the Persian land to have the same boundaries as the heaven of Zeus; since in truth upon

no land will the sun look down which borders ours, but I with your help shall make all the lands into one land, having passed through the whole extent of Europe. For I am informed that things are so, namely that there is no city of men nor any race of human beings remaining, which will be able to come to a contest with us, when those whom I just now mentioned have been removed out of the way. Thus both those who have committed wrong against us will have the yoke of slavery, and also those who have not committed wrong. (d) And ye will please me best if ye do this: whensoever I shall signify to you the time at which ye ought to come, ye must appear every one of you with zeal for the service; and whosoever shall come with a force best equipped, to him I will give gifts such as are accounted in our land to be the most honorable. Thus must these things be done: but that I may not seem to you to be following my own counsel alone, I propose the matter for discussion, bidding any one of you who desires it, declare his opinion."

9. Having thus spoken he ceased; and after him Mardonios said: "Master, thou dost surpass not only all the Persians who were before thee, but also those who shall come after, since thou didst not only attain in thy words to that which is best and truest as regards other matters, but also thou wilt not permit the Ionians who dwell in Europe to make a mock of us, having no just right to do so: for a strange thing it would be if, when we have subdued and kept as our servants Sacans, Indians, Ethiopians, Assyrians, and other nations many in number and great, who have done no wrong to the Persians, because we desired to add to our dominions, we should not take vengeance on the Hellenes who committed wrong against us unprovoked. (a) Of what should we be afraid? —what gathering of numbers, or what resources of money? for their manner of fight we know, and as for their resources, we know that they are feeble; and we have moreover subdued already their sons, those I mean who are settled in our land and are called Ionians, Aiolians, and Dorians. Moreover I myself formerly made trial of marching against these men, being commanded thereto by thy father; and although I marched as far as Macedonia, and fell but little short of coming to Athens itself, no man came to oppose me in fight. (b) And yet it is true that the Hellenes make wars, but (as I am informed) very much without wise consideration, by reason of obstinacy and want of skill: for when they have proclaimed war upon one another, they find out first the fairest and smoothest place, and to this they come down and fight; so that even the victors depart from the fight with great loss, and as to the vanquished, of them I make no mention at all, for they are utterly destroyed. They ought however, being men who speak the same language, to make use of heralds and messengers and so to take up their differences and settle them in any way rather than by battles; but if they must absolutely war with one another, they ought to find out each of them that place in which they themselves are hardest to overcome, and here to make their trial. Therefore the Hellenes, since they use no good way, when I had marched as far as the land of Macedonia, did not come to the resolution of fighting with me. (c) Who then is likely to set himself against thee, O king, offering war, when thou art leading both all the multitudes of Asia and the whole number of the ships? I for my part am of opinion that the power of the Hellenes has not attained to such a pitch of boldness: but if after all I should prove to be deceived in my judgment, and they stirred up by inconsiderate folly should come to battle with us, they would learn that we are the best of all men in the matters of war. However that may be, let not anything be left untried; for nothing comes of itself, but from trial all things are wont to come to men."

10. Mardonios having thus smoothed over the resolution expressed by Xerxes had

ceased speaking: and when the other Persians were silent and did not venture to declare an opinion contrary to that which had been proposed, then Artabanos the son of Hystaspes, being father's brother to Xerxes and having reliance upon that, spoke as follows: (a) "O king, if opinions opposed to one another be not spoken, it is not possible to select the better in making the choice, but one must accept that which has been spoken; if however opposite opinions be uttered, this is possible; just as we do not distinguish the gold which is free from alloy when it is alone by itself, but when we rub it on the touch-stone in comparison with other gold, then we distinguish that which is the better. Now I gave advice to thy father Dareios also, who was my brother, not to march against the Scythians, men who occupied no abiding city in any part of the earth. He however, expecting that he would subdue the Scythians who were nomads, did not listen to me; but he made a march and came back from it with the loss of many good men of his army. But thou, O king, art intending to march against men who are much better than the Scythians, men who are reported to be excellent both by sea and on land: and the thing which is to be feared in this matter it is right that I should declare to thee. (b) Thou sayest that thou wilt yoke the Hellespont with a bridge and march an army through Europe to Hellas. Now supposing it chance that we are worsted either by land or by sea, or even both, for the men are reported to be valiant in fight, (and we may judge for ourselves that it is so, since the Athenians by themselves destroyed that great army which came with Datis and Artaphrenes to the Attic land),—suppose however that they do not succeed in both, yet if they shall attack with their ships and conquer in a sea-fight, and then sail to the Helle-spont and break up the bridge, this of itself, O king, will prove to be a great peril. (c) Not however by any native wisdom of my own do I conjecture that this might happen: I am conjecturing only such a misfortune as all but came upon us at the former time, when thy father, having yoked the Bosphorus of Thracia and made a bridge over the river Ister, had crossed over to go against the Scythians. At that time the Scythians used every means of entreaty to persuade the Ionians to break up the passage, to whom it had been entrusted to guard the bridges of the Ister. At that time, if Histiaios the despot of Miletos had followed the opinion of the other despots and had not made opposition to them, the power of the Persians would have been brought to an end. Yet it is a fearful thing even to hear it reported that the whole power of the king had come to depend upon one human creature. (d) Do not thou therefore propose to go into any such danger when there is no need, but do as I say:—at the present time dissolve this assembly; and afterwards at what-ever time it shall seem good to thee, when thou hast considered prudently with thyself, proclaim that which seems to thee best: for good counsel I hold to be a very great gain; since even if anything shall prove adverse, the counsel which has been taken is no less good, though it has been defeated by fortune; while he who took counsel badly at first, if good fortune should go with him has lighted on a prize by chance, but none the less for that his counsel was bad. (e) Thou seest how God strikes with thunderbolts the creatures which stand above the rest and suffers them not to make a proud show; while those which are small do not provoke him to jealousy: thou seest also how he hurls his darts ever at those buildings which are the highest and those trees likewise; for God is wont to cut short all those things which stand out above the rest. Thus also a numerous army is destroyed by one of few men in some such manner as this, namely when God having become jealous of them casts upon them panic or thundering from heaven, then they are destroyed utterly and not as their worth deserves; for God suffers not any other to have high thoughts save only himself. (f) Moreover the hastening of any matter breeds disasters, whence great losses are wont to be produced; but in waiting there are many good things contained, as to which, if they do not appear to be good at first, yet one will find them to be so in course of time. (g) To thee, O king, I give this counsel: but thou son of Gobryas, Mardonios, cease speaking foolish words about the Hellenes, since they in no way deserve to be spoken of with slight; for by uttering slander against the Hellenes thou art stirring the king himself to make an expedition, and it is to this very end that I think thou art straining all thy endeavor. Let not this be so; for slander is a most grievous thing: in it the wrongdoers are two, and the person who suffers wrong is one. The slanderer does a wrong in that he speaks against one who is not present, the other in that he is persuaded of the thing before he gets certain knowledge of it, and he who is not present when the words are spoken suffers wrong in the matter thus,—both because he has been slandered by the one and because he has been believed to be bad by the other. (h) However, if it be absolutely needful to make an expedition against these men, come, let the king himself remain behind in the abodes of the Persians, and let us both set to the wager our sons; and then do thou lead an army by thyself, choosing for thyself the men whom thou desirest, and taking an army as large as thou thinkest good: and if matters turn out for the king as thou sayest, let my sons be slain and let me also be slain in addition to them; but if in the way which I predict, let thy sons suffer this, and with them thyself also, if thou shalt return back. But if thou art not willing to undergo this proof, but wilt by all means lead an army against Hellas, then I say that those who are left behind in this land will hear that Mardonios, after having done a great mischief to the Persians, is torn by dogs and birds, either in the land of the Athenians, or else perchance thou wilt be in the land of the Lacedemonians (unless indeed this should have come to pass even before that upon the way), and that thou hast at length been made aware against what kind of men thou art persuading the king to march."

11. Artabanos thus spoke; and Xerxes enraged by it made answer as follows: "Artabanos, thou art my father's brother, and this shall save thee from receiving any recompense such as thy foolish words deserve. Yet I attach to thee this dishonor, seeing that thou art a coward and spiritless, namely that thou do not march with me against Hellas, but remain here together with the women; and I, even without thy help, will accomplish all the things which I said: for I would I might not be descended from Dareios, the son of Hystaspes, the son of Arsames, the son of Ariaramnes, the son of Teïspes, or from Cyrus, the son of Cambyses, the son of Teïspes, the son of Achaimenes, if I take not vengeance on the Athenians; since I know well that if we shall keep quiet, yet they will not do so, but will again march against our land, if we may judge by the deeds which have been done by them to begin with, since they both set fire to Sardis and marched upon Asia. It is not possible therefore that either side should retire from the quarrel, but the question before us is whether we shall do or whether we shall suffer; whether all these regions shall come to be under the Hellenes or all those under the Persians: for in our hostility there is no middle course. It follows then now that it is well for us, having suffered wrong first, to take revenge, that I may find out also what is this terrible thing which I shall suffer if I lead an army against these men,—men whom Pelops the Phrygian, who was the slave of my forefathers, so subdued that even to the present day both the men themselves and their land are called after the name of him who subdued them."

12. Thus far was it spoken then; but afterwards when darkness came on, the opinion of

Artabanos tormented Xerxes continually; and making night his counsellor he found that it was by no means to his advantage to make the march against Hellas. So when he had thus made a new resolve, he fell asleep, and in the night he saw, as is reported by the Persians, a vision as follows:—Xerxes thought that a man tall and comely of shape came and stood by him and said: "Art thou indeed changing thy counsel, O Persian, of leading an expedition against Hellas, now that thou hast made proclamation that the Persians shall collect an army? Thou dost not well in changing thy counsel, nor will he who is here present with thee excuse thee from it; but as thou didst take counsel in the day to do, by that way go."

13. After he had said this, Xerxes thought that he who had spoken flew away; and when day had dawned he made no account of this dream, but gathered together the Persians whom he had assembled also the former time and said to them these words: "Persians, pardon me that I make quick changes in my counsel; for in judgment not yet am I come to my prime, and they who advise me to do the things which I said, do not for any long time leave me to myself. However, although at first when I heard the opinion of Artabanos my youthful impulses burst out, so that I cast out unseemly words against a man older than myself; yet now I acknowledge that he is right, and I shall follow his opinion. Consider then I have changed my resolve to march against Hellas, and do ye remain still."

14. The Persians accordingly when they heard this were rejoiced and made obeisance: but when night had come on, the same dream again came and stood by Xerxes as he lay asleep and said: "Son of Dareios, it is manifest then that thou hast resigned this expedition before the assembly of the Persians, and that thou hast made no account of my words, as if thou hadst heard them from no one at all. Now therefore be well assured of this:—if thou do not make thy march forthwith, there shall thence spring up for thee this result, namely that, as thou didst in short time become great and mighty, so also thou shalt speedily be again brought low."

15. Xerxes then, being very greatly disturbed by fear of the vision, started up from his bed and sent a messenger to summon Artabanos; to whom when he came Xerxes spoke thus: "Artabanos, at the first I was not discreet, when I spoke to thee foolish words on account of thy good counsel; but after no long time I changed my mind and perceived that I ought to do these things which thou didst suggest to me. I am not able however to do them, although I desire it; for indeed, now that I have turned about and changed my mind, a dream appears haunting me and by no means approving that I should do so; and just now it has left me even with a threat. If therefore it is God who sends it to me, and it is his absolute will and pleasure that an army should go against Hellas, this same dream will fly to thee also, laying upon thee a charge such as it has laid upon me; and it occurs to my mind that this might happen thus, namely if thou shouldst take all my attire and put it on, and then seat thyself on my throne, and after that lie down to sleep in my bed."

16. Xerxes spoke to him thus; and Artabanos was not willing to obey the command at first, since he did not think himself worthy to sit upon the royal throne; but at last being urged further he did that which was commanded, first having spoken these words: (a) "It is equally good in my judgment, O king, whether a man has wisdom himself or is willing to follow the counsel of him who speaks well: and thou, who hast attained to both these good things, art caused to err by the communications of evil men; just as they say that the Sea, which is of all things the most useful to men, is by blasts of winds falling upon it prevented from doing according to its own nature. I however, when I was evil spoken of

by thee, was not so much stung with pain for this, as because, when two opinions were laid before the Persians, the one tending to increase wanton insolence and the other tending to check it and saying that it was a bad thing to teach the soul to endeavor always to have something more than the present possession,—because, I say, when such opinions as these were laid before us, thou didst choose that one which was the more dangerous both for thyself and for the Persians. (b) And now that thou hast turned to the better counsel, thou sayest that when thou art disposed to let go the expedition against the Hellenes, a dream haunts thee sent by some god, which forbids thee to abandon thy enterprise. Nay, but here too thou dost err, my son, since this is not of the Deity; for the dreams of sleep which come roaming about to men, are of such nature as I shall inform thee, being by many years older than thou. The visions of dreams are wont to hover above us in such form for the most part as the things of which we were thinking during the day; and we in the days preceding were very much occupied with this campaign. (c) If however after all this is not such a thing as I interpret it to be, but is something which is concerned with God, thou hast summed the matter up in that which thou hast said: let it appear, as thou sayest, to me also, as to thee, and give commands. But supposing that it desires to appear to me at all, it is not bound to appear to me any the more if I have thy garments on me than if I have my own, nor any more if I take my rest in thy bed than if I am in thy own; for assuredly this thing, whatever it may be, which appears to thee in thy sleep, is not so foolish as to suppose, when it sees me, that it is thou, judging so because the garments are thine. That however which we must find out now is this, namely if it will hold me in no account, and not think fit to appear to me, whether I have my own garments or whether I have thine, but continue still to haunt thee; for if it shall indeed haunt thee perpetually, I shall myself also be disposed to say that it is of the Deity. But if thou hast resolved that it shall be so, and it is not possible to turn aside this thy resolution, but I must go to sleep in thy bed, then let it appear to me also, when I perform these things: but until then I shall hold to the opinion which I now have."

17. Having thus said Artabanos, expecting that he would prove that Xerxes was speaking folly, did that which was commanded him; and having put on the garments of Xerxes and seated himself in the royal throne, he afterwards went to bed: and when he had fallen asleep, the same dream came to him which used to come to Xerxes, and standing over Artabanos spoke these words: "Art thou indeed he who endeavors to dissuade Xerxes from making a march against Hellas, pretending to have a care of him? However, neither in the future nor now at the present shalt thou escape unpunished for trying to turn away that which is destined to come to pass: and as for Xerxes, that which he must suffer if he disobeys, hath been shown already to the man himself."

18. Thus it seemed to Artabanos that the dream threatened him, and at the same time was just about to burn out his eyes with hot irons; and with a loud cry he started up from his bed, and sitting down beside Xerxes he related to him throughout the vision of the dream, and then said to him as follows: "I, O king, as one who has seen before now many great things brought to their fall by things less, urged thee not to yield in all things to the inclination of thy youth, since I knew that it was evil to have desire after many things; remembering on the one hand the march of Cyrus against the Massagetai, what fortune it had, and also that of Cambyses against the Ethiopians; and being myself one who took part with Dareios in the campaign against the Scythians. Knowing these things I had the opinion that thou wert to be envied of all men, so long as thou shouldest keep still. Since

however there comes a divine impulse, and, as it seems, a destruction sent by heaven is taking hold of the Hellenes, I for my part am both changed in myself and also I reverse my opinions; and do thou signify to the Persians the message which is sent to thee from God, bidding them follow the commands which were given by thee at first with regard to the preparations to be made; and endeavor that on thy side nothing may be wanting, since God delivers the matter into thy hands." These things having been said, both were excited to confidence by the vision, and so soon as it became day, Xerxes communicated the matter to the Persians, and Artabanos, who before was the only man who came forward to dissuade him, now came forward to urge on the design.

19. Xerxes being thus desirous to make the expedition, there came to him after this a third vision in his sleep, which the Magians, when they heard it, explained to have reference to the dominion of the whole Earth and to mean that all men should be subject to him; and the vision was this:—Xerxes thought that he had been crowned with a wreath of an olive-branch and that the shoots growing from the olive-tree covered the whole Earth; and after that, the wreath, placed as it was about his head, disappeared. When the Magians had thus interpreted the vision, forthwith every man of the Persians who had been assembled together departed to his own province and was zealous by all means to perform the commands, desiring each one to receive for himself the gifts which had been proposed: and thus Xerxes was gathering his army together, searching every region of the continent.

20. During four full years from the conquest of Egypt he was preparing the army and the things that were of service for the army, and in the course of the fifth year he began his campaign with a host of great multitude. For of all the armies of which we have knowledge this proved to be by far the greatest; so that neither that led by Dareios against the Scythians appears anything as compared with it, nor the Scythian host, when the Scythians pursuing the Kimmerians made invasion of the Median land and subdued and occupied nearly all the upper parts of Asia, for which invasion afterwards Dareios attempted to take vengeance, nor that led by the sons of Atreus to Ilion, to judge by that which is reported of their expedition, nor that of the Mysians and Teucrians, before the Trojan war, who passed over into Europe by the Bosphorus and not only subdued all the Thracians, but came down also as far as the Ionian Sea and marched southwards to the river Peneios.

21. All these expeditions put together, with others, if there be any, added to them, are not equal to this one alone. For what nation did Xerxes not lead out of Asia against Hellas? and what water was not exhausted, being drunk by his host, except only the great rivers? For some supplied ships, and others were appointed to serve in the land-army; to some it was appointed to furnish cavalry, and to others vessels to carry horses, while they served in the expedition themselves also; others were ordered to furnish ships of war for the bridges, and others again ships with provisions.

22. Then in the first place, since the former fleet had suffered disaster in sailing round Athos, preparations had been going on for about three years past with regard to Athos: for triremes lay at anchor at Elaius in the Chersonese, and with this for their starting point men of all nations belonging to the army worked at digging, compelled by the lash; and the men went to the work regularly in succession: moreover those who dwelt round about Athos worked also at the digging: and Bubares the son of Megabazos and Artachaies the son of Artaios, Persians both, were set over the work. Now Athos is a mountain great and

famous, running down to the sea and inhabited by men: and where the mountain ends on the side of the mainland the place is like a peninsula with an isthmus about twelve furlongs across. Here it is plain land or hills of no great size, extending from the sea of the Acanthians to that which lies off Torone; and on this isthmus, where Athos ends, is situated a Hellenic city called Sane: moreover there are others beyond Sane and within the peninsula of Athos, all which at this time the Persian had resolved to make into cities of an island and no longer of the mainland; these are, Dion, Olophyxos, Acrothoon, Thyssos, Cleonai.

23. These are the cities which occupy Athos: and they dug as follows, the country being divided among the Barbarians by nations for the work:—at the city of Sane they drew a straight line across the isthmus, and when the channel became deep, those who stood lowest dug, while others delivered the earth as it was dug out to other men who stood above, as upon steps, and they again to others when it was received, until they came to those that were highest; and these bore it away and cast it forth. Now the others except the Phoenicians had double toil by the breaking down of the steep edges of their excavation; for since they endeavored to make the opening at the top and that at the bottom both of the same measure, some such thing was likely to result, as they worked: but the Phoenicians, who are apt to show ability in their works generally, did so in this work also; for when they had had assigned to them by lot so much as fell to their share, they proceeded to dig, making the opening of the excavation at the top twice as wide as the channel itself was to be; and as the work went forward, they kept contracting the width; so that, when they came to the bottom, their work was made of equal width with that of the others. Now there is a meadow there, in which there was made for them a market and a place for buying and selling; and great quantities of corn came for them regularly from Asia, ready ground.

24. It seems to me, making conjecture of this work, that Xerxes when he ordered this to be dug was moved by a love of magnificence and by a desire to make a display of his power and to leave a memorial behind him; for though they might have drawn the ships across the isthmus with no great labor, he bade them dig a channel for the sea of such breadth that two triremes might sail through, propelled side by side. To these same men to whom the digging had been appointed, it was appointed also to make a bridge over the river Strymon, yoking together the banks.

25. These things were being done by Xerxes thus; and meanwhile he caused ropes also to be prepared for the bridges, made of papyrus and of white flax, appointing this to the Phoenicians and Egyptians; and also he was making preparations to store provisions for his army on the way, that neither the army itself nor the baggage animals might suffer from scarcity, as they made their march against Hellas. Accordingly, when he had learnt by inquiry of the various places, he bade them make stores where it was most convenient, carrying supplies to different parts by merchant ships and ferry-boats from all the countries of Asia. So they conveyed the greater part of the corn to the place which is called Leuke Acte in Thrace, while others conveyed stores to Tyrodiza of the Perinthians, others to Doriscos, others to Eïon on the Strymon, and others to Macedonia, the work being distributed between them.

26. During the time that these were working at the task which had been proposed to them, the whole land-army had been assembled together and was marching with Xerxes to Sardis, setting forth from Critalla in Cappadokia; for there it had been ordered that the

whole army should assemble, which was to go with Xerxes himself by the land: but which of the governors of provinces brought the best equipped force and received from the king the gifts proposed, I am not able to say, for I do not know that they even came to a competition in this matter. Then after they had crossed the river Halys and had entered Phrygia, marching through this land they came to Kelainai, where the springs of the river Maiander come up, and also those of another river not less than the Maiander, whose name is Catarractes; this rises in the market-place itself of Kelainai and runs into the Maiander: and here also is hanging up in the city the skin of Marsyas the Silenos, which is said by the Phrygians to have been flayed off and hung up by Apollo.

27. In this city Pythios the son of Atys, a Lydian, was waiting for the king and entertained his whole army, as well as Xerxes himself, with the most magnificent hospitality: moreover he professed himself ready to supply money for the war. So when Pythios offered money, Xerxes asked those of the Persians who were present, who Pythios was and how much money he possessed, that he made this offer. They said: "O king, this is he who presented thy father Dareios with the golden plane-tree and the golden vine; and even now he is in wealth the first of all men of whom we know, excepting thee only."

28. Marveling at the conclusion of these words Xerxes himself asked of Pythios then, how much money he had; and he said: "O king, I will not conceal the truth from thee, nor will I allege as an excuse that I do not know my own substance, but I will enumerate it to thee exactly, since I know the truth: for as soon as I heard that thou wert coming down to the Sea of Hellas, desiring to give thee money for the war I ascertained the truth, and calculating I found that I had of silver two thousand talents, and of gold four hundred myriads of daric staters all but seven thousand: and with this money I present thee. For myself I have sufficient livelihood from my slaves and from my estates of land."

29. Thus he said; and Xerxes was pleased by the things which he had spoken, and replied: "Lydian host, ever since I went forth from the Persian land I have encountered no man up to this time who was desirous to entertain my army, or who came into my presence and made offer of his own free will to contribute money to me for the war, except only thee: and thou not only didst entertain my army magnificently, but also now dost make offer of great sums of money. To thee therefore in return I give these rewards,—I make thee my guest-friend, and I will complete for thee the four hundred myriads of staters by giving from myself the seven thousand, in order that thy four hundred myriads may not fall short by seven thousand, but thou mayest have a full sum in thy reckoning, completed thus by me. Keep possession of that which thou hast got for thyself, and be sure to act always thus; for if thou doest so, thou wilt have no cause to repent either at the time or afterwards."

30. Having thus said and having accomplished his promise, he continued his march onwards; and passing by a city of the Phrygians called Anaua and a lake whence salt is obtained, he came to Colossai, a great city of Phrygia, where the river Lycos falls into an opening of the earth and disappears from view, and then after an interval of about five furlongs it comes up to view again, and this river also flows into the Maiander. Setting forth from Colossai towards the boundaries of the Phrygians and Lydians, the army arrived at the city of Kydrara, where a pillar is fixed, set up by Croesus, which declares by an inscription that the boundaries are there.

31. From Phrygia then he entered Lydia; and here the road parts into two, and that which goes to the left leads towards Caria, while that which goes to the right leads to

Sardis; and travelling by this latter road one must needs cross the river Maiander and pass by the city of Callatebos, where men live whose trade it is to make honey of the tamarisk-tree and of wheat-flour. By this road went Xerxes and found a plane-tree, to which for its beauty he gave an adornment of gold, and appointed that someone should have charge of it always in undying succession; and on the next day he came to the city of the Lydians.

32. Having come to Sardis he proceeded first to send heralds to Hellas, to ask for earth and water, and also to give notice beforehand to prepare meals for the king; except that he sent neither to Athens nor Lacedaemon to ask for earth, but to all the other States: and the reason why he sent the second time to ask for earth and water was this,—as many as had not given at the former time to Dareios when he sent, these he thought would certainly give now by reason of their fear: this matter it was about which he desired to have certain knowledge, and he sent accordingly.

33. After this he made his preparations intending to march to Abydos: and meanwhile they were bridging over the Hellespont from Asia to Europe. Now there is in the Chersonese of the Hellespont between the city of Sestos and Madytos, a broad foreland running down into the sea right opposite Abydos; this is the place where no long time afterwards the Athenians under the command of Xanthippos the son of Ariphron, having taken Artaÿctes a Persian, who was the governor of Sestos, nailed him alive to a board with hands and feet extended (he was the man who was wont to take women with him to the temple of Protesilaos at Elaius and to do things there which are not lawful).

34. To this foreland they on whom this work was laid were making their bridges, starting from Abydos, the Phoenicians constructing the one with ropes of white flax, and the Egyptians the other, which was made with papyrus rope. Now from Abydos to the opposite shore is a distance of seven furlongs. But when the strait had been bridged over, a great storm came on and dashed together all the work that had been made and broke it up. Then when Xerxes heard it he was exceedingly enraged, and bade them scourge the Hellespont with three hundred strokes of the lash and let down into the sea a pair of fetters. Nay, I have heard further that he sent branders also with them to brand the Hellespont. However this may be, he enjoined them, as they were beating, to say Barbarian and presumptuous words as follows: "Thou bitter water, thy master lays upon thee this penalty, because thou didst wrong him not having suffered any wrong from him: and Xerxes the king will pass over thee whether thou be willing or no; but with right, as it seems, no man doeth sacrifice to thee, seeing that thou art a treacherous and briny stream." The sea he enjoined them to chastise thus, and also he bade them cut off the heads of those who were appointed to have charge over the bridging of the Hellespont.

36. Thus then the men did, to whom this ungracious office belonged; and meanwhile other chief-constructors proceeded to make the bridges; and thus they made them:—They put together fifty-oared galleys and triremes, three hundred and sixty to be under the bridge towards the Euxine Sea, and three hundred and fourteen to be under the other, the vessels lying in the direction of the stream of the Hellespont (though crosswise in respect to the Pontus), to support the tension of the ropes. They placed them together thus, and let down very large anchors, those on the one side towards the Pontus because of the winds which blow from within outwards, and on the other side, towards the West and the Egean, because of the South-East and South Winds. They left also an opening for a passage through, so that any who wished might be able to sail into the Pontus with small vessels, and also from the Pontus outwards. Having thus done, they proceeded to stretch

tight the ropes, straining them with wooden windlasses, not now appointing the two kinds of rope to be used apart from one another, but assigning to each bridge two ropes of white flax and four of the papyrus ropes. The thickness and beauty of make was the same for both, but the flaxen ropes were heavier in proportion, and of this rope a cubit weighed one talent. When the passage was bridged over, they sawed up logs of wood, and making them equal in length to the breadth of the bridge they laid them above the stretched ropes, and having set them thus in order they again fastened them above. When this was done, they carried on brushwood, and having set the brushwood also in place, they carried on to it earth; and when they had stamped down the earth firmly, they built a barrier along on each side, so that the baggage-animals and horses might not be frightened by looking out over the sea.

37. When the construction of the bridges had been finished, and the works about Athos, both the embankments about the mouths of the channel, which were made because of the breaking of the sea upon the beach, that the mouths of it might not be filled up, and the channel itself, were reported to be fully completed, then, after they had passed the winter at Sardis, the army set forth from thence fully equipped, at the beginning of spring, to march to Abydos; and when it had just set forth, the Sun left his place in the heaven and was invisible, though there was no gathering of clouds and the sky was perfectly clear; and instead of day it became night. When Xerxes saw and perceived this, it became a matter of concern to him; and he asked the Magians what the appearance meant to portend. These declared that the god was foreshowing to the Hellenes a leaving of their cities, saying that the Sun was the foreshower of events for the Hellenes, but the Moon for the Persians. Having been thus informed, Xerxes proceeded on the march with very great joy.

38. Then as he was leading forth his army on its march, Pythios the Lydian, being alarmed by the appearance in the heavens and elated by the gifts which he had received, came to Xerxes, and said as follows: "Master, I would desire to receive from thee a certain thing at my request, which, as it chances, is for thee an easy thing to grant, but a great thing for me, if I obtain it." Then Xerxes, thinking that his request would be for anything rather than that which he actually asked, said that he would grant it, and bade him speak and say what he desired. He then, when he heard this, was encouraged, and spoke these words: "Master, I have, as it chances, five sons, and it is their fortune to be all going together with thee on the march against Hellas. Do thou, therefore, O king, have compassion upon me, who have come to so great an age, and release from serving in the expedition one of my sons, the eldest, in order that he may be caretaker both of myself and of my wealth: but the other four take with thyself, and after thou hast accomplished that which thou hast in thy mind, mayest thou have a safe return home."

38. Then Xerxes was exceedingly angry and made answer with these words: "Thou wretched man, dost thou dare, when I am going on a march myself against Hellas, and am taking my sons and my brothers and my relations and friends, dost thou dare to make any mention of a son of thine, seeing that thou art my slave, who ought to have been accompanying me thyself with thy whole household and thy wife as well? Now therefore be assured of this, that the passionate spirit of man dwells within the ears; and when it has heard good things, it fills the body with delight, but when it has heard the opposite things to this, it swells up with anger. As then thou canst not boast of having surpassed the king in conferring benefits formerly, when thou didst to us good deeds and madest offer to do

more of the same kind, so now that thou hast turned to shamelessness, thou shalt receive not thy desert but less than thou deservest: for thy gifts of hospitality shall rescue from death thyself and the four others of thy sons, but thou shalt pay the penalty with the life of the one to whom thou dost cling most." Having answered thus, he forthwith commanded those to whom it was appointed to do these things, to find out the eldest of the sons of Pythios and to cut him in two in the middle; and having cut him in two, to dispose the halves, one on the right hand of the road and the other on the left, and that the army should pass between them by this way.

40. When these had so done, the army proceeded to pass between; and first the baggage-bearers led the way together with their horses, and after these the host composed of all kinds of nations mingled together without distinction: and when more than the half had gone by, an interval was left and these were separated from the king. For before him went first a thousand horsemen, chosen out of all the Persians; and after them a thousand spearmen chosen also from all the Persians, having the points of their spears turned down to the ground; and then ten sacred horses, called "Nesaian," with the fairest possible trappings. Now the horses are called Nesaian for this reason:—there is a wide plain in the land of Media which is called the Nesaian plain, and this plain produces the great horses of which I speak. Behind these ten horses the sacred chariot of Zeus was appointed to go, which was drawn by eight white horses; and behind the horses again followed on foot a charioteer holding the reins, for no human creature mounts upon the seat of that chariot. Then behind this came Xerxes himself in a chariot drawn by Nesaian horses, and by the side of him rode a charioteer, whose name was Patiramphes, son of Otanes a Persian.

41. Thus did Xerxes march forth out of Sardis; and he used to change, whenever he was so disposed, from the chariot to a carriage. And behind him went spearmen, the best and most noble of the Persians, a thousand in number, holding their spear-points in the customary way; and after them another thousand horsemen chosen out from the Persians; and after the horsemen ten thousand men chosen out from the remainder of the Persians. This body went on foot; and of these a thousand had upon their spears pomegranates of gold instead of the spikes at the butt-end, and these enclosed the others round, while the remaining nine thousand were within these and had silver pomegranates. And those also had golden pomegranates who had their spear-points turned towards the earth, while those who followed next after Xerxes had golden apples. Then to follow the ten thousand there was appointed a body of ten thousand Persian cavalry; and after the cavalry there was an interval of as much as two furlongs. Then the rest of the host came marching without distinction.

42. So the army proceeded on its march from Lydia to the river Caïcos and the land of Mysia; and then setting forth from the Caïcos and keeping the mountain of Cane on the left hand, it marched through the region of Atarneus to the city of Carene. From this it went through the plain of Thebe, passing by the cities of Adramytteion and Antandros of the Pelasgians; and taking mount Ida on the left hand, it came on to the land of Ilion. And first, when it had stopped for the night close under mount Ida, thunder and bolts of lightning fell upon it, and destroyed here in this place a very large number of men.

43. Then when the army had come to the river Scamander,—which of all rivers to which they had come, since they set forth from Sardis and undertook their march, was the first of which the stream failed and was not sufficient for the drinking of the army and of the animals with it,—when, I say, Xerxes had come to this river, he went up to the Citadel

of Priam, having a desire to see it; and having seen it and learnt by inquiry of all those matters severally, he sacrificed a thousand heifers to Athene of Ilion, and the Magians poured libations in honor of the heroes: and after they had done this, a fear fell upon the army in the night. Then at break of day he set forth from thence, keeping on his left hand the cities of Rhoition and Ophryneion and Dardanos, which last borders upon Abydos, and having on the right hand the Gergith Teucrians.

44. When Xerxes had come into the midst of Abydos, he had a desire to see all the army; and there had been made purposely for him beforehand upon a hill in this place a raised seat of white stone, which the people of Abydos had built at the command of the king given beforehand. There he took his seat, and looking down upon the shore he gazed both upon the land-army and the ships; and gazing upon them he had a longing to see a contest take place between the ships; and when it had taken place and the Phoenicians of Sidon were victorious, he was delighted both with the contest and with the whole armament.

45. And seeing all the Hellespont covered over with the ships, and all the shores and the plains of Abydos full of men, then Xerxes pronounced himself a happy man, and after that he fell to weeping.

46. Artabanos his uncle therefore perceiving him,—the same who at first boldly declared his opinion advising Xerxes not to march against Hellas,—this man, I say, having observed that Xerxes wept, asked as follows: "O king, how far different from one another are the things which thou hast done now and a short while before now! for having pronounced thyself a happy man, thou art now shedding tears." He said: "Yea, for after I had reckoned up, it came into my mind to feel pity at the thought how brief was the whole life of man, seeing that of these multitudes not one will be alive when a hundred years have gone by." He then made answer and said: "To another evil more pitiful than this we are made subject in the course of our life; for in the period of life, short as it is, no man, either of these here or of others, is made by nature so happy, that there will not come to him many times, and not once only, the desire to be dead rather than to live; for misfortunes falling upon us and diseases disturbing our happiness make the time of life, though short indeed, seem long: thus, since life is full of trouble, death has become the most acceptable refuge for man; and God, having given him to taste of the sweetness of life, is discovered in this matter to be full of jealousy."

47. Xerxes made answer saying: "Artabanos, of human life, which is such as thou dost define it to be, let us cease to speak, and do not remember evils when we have good things in hand: but do thou declare to me this:—If the vision of the dream had not appeared with so much evidence, wouldest thou still be holding thy former opinion, endeavoring to prevent me from marching against Hellas, or wouldest thou have changed from it? Come, tell me this exactly." He answered saying: "O king, may the vision of the dream which appeared have such fulfilment as we both desire! but I am even to this moment full of apprehension and cannot contain myself, taking into account many things besides, and also seeing that two things, which are the greatest things of all, are utterly hostile to thee."

48. To this Xerxes made answer in these words: "Thou strangest of men, of what nature are these two things which thou sayest are utterly hostile to me? Is it that the land-army is to be found fault with in the matter of numbers, and that the army of the Hellenes appears to thee likely to be many times as large as ours? or dost thou think that our fleet will fall short of theirs? or even that both of these things together will prove true? For if thou

thinkest that in these respects our power is deficient, one might make gathering at once of another force."

49. Then he made answer and said: "O king, neither with this army would anyone who has understanding find fault, nor with the number of the ships; and indeed if thou shalt assemble more, the two things of which I speak will be made thereby yet more hostile: and these two things are—the land and the sea. For neither in the sea is there, as I suppose, a harbor anywhere large enough to receive this fleet of thine, if a storm should arise, and to ensure the safety of the ships till it be over; and yet not one alone ought this harbor to be, but there should be such harbors along the whole coast of the continent by which thou sailest; and if there are not harbors to receive thy ships, know that accidents will rule men and not men the accidents. Now having told thee of one of the two things, I am about to tell thee of the other. The land, I say, becomes hostile to thee in this way:—if nothing shall come to oppose thee, the land is hostile to thee by so much the more in proportion as thou shalt advance more, ever stealing on further and further, for there is no satiety of good fortune felt by men: and this I say, that with no one to stand against thee the country traversed, growing more and more as time goes on, will produce for thee famine. Man, however, will be in the best condition, if when he is taking counsel he feels fear, reckoning to suffer everything that can possibly come, but in doing the deed he is bold."

50. Xerxes made answer in these words: "Artabanos, reasonably dost thou set forth these matters; but do not thou fear everything nor reckon equally for everything: for if thou shouldest set thyself with regard to all matters which come on at any time, to reckon for everything equally, thou wouldest never perform any deed. It is better to have good courage about everything and to suffer half the evils which threaten, than to have fear beforehand about everything and not to suffer any evil at all: and if, while contending against everything which is said, thou omit to declare the course which is safe, thou dost incur in these matters the reproach of failure equally with him who says the opposite to this. This then, I say, is evenly balanced: but how should one who is but man know the course which is safe? I think, in no way. To those then who choose to act, for the most part gain is wont to come; but to those who reckon for everything and shrink back, it is not much wont to come. Thou seest the power of the Persians, to what great might it has advanced: if then those who came to be kings before me had had opinions like to thine, or, though not having such opinions, had had such counsellors as thou, thou wouldest never have seen it brought forward to this point. As it is however, by running risks they conducted it on to this: for great power is in general gained by running great risks. We therefore, following their example, are making our march now during the fairest season of the year; and after we have subdued all Europe we shall return back home, neither having met with famine anywhere nor having suffered any other thing which is unpleasant. For first we march bearing with us ourselves great store of food, and secondly we shall possess the corn-crops of all the peoples to whose land and nation we come; and we are making a march now against men who plough the soil, and not against nomad tribes."

51. After this Artabanos said: "O king, since thou dost urge us not to have fear of anything, do thou I pray thee accept a counsel from me; for when speaking of many things it is necessary to extend speech to a greater length. Cyrus the son of Cambyses subdued all Ionia except the Athenians, so that it was tributary to the Persians. These men therefore I counsel thee by no means to lead against their parent stock, seeing that even

without these we are able to get the advantage over our enemies. For supposing that they go with us, either they must prove themselves doers of great wrong, if they join in reducing their mother city to slavery, or doers of great right, if they join in freeing her: now if they show themselves doers of great wrong, they bring us no very large gain in addition; but if they show themselves doers of great right, they are able then to cause much damage to thy army. Therefore lay to heart also the ancient saying, how well it has been said that at the first beginning of things the end does not completely appear."

52. To this Xerxes made answer: "Artabanos, of all the opinions which thou hast uttered, thou art mistaken most of all in this; seeing that thou fearest lest the Ionians should change side, about whom we have a most sure proof, of which thou art a witness thyself and also the rest are witnesses who went with Dareios on his march against the Scythians,—namely this, that the whole Persian army then came to be dependent upon these men, whether they would destroy or whether they would save it, and they displayed righteous dealing and trustworthiness, and naught at all that was unfriendly. Besides this, seeing that they have left children and wives and wealth in our land, we must not even imagine that they will make any rebellion. Fear not then this thing either, but have a good heart and keep safe my house and my government; for to thee of all men I entrust my scepter of rule."

53. Having thus spoken and having sent Artabanos back to Susa, next Xerxes summoned to his presence the men of most repute among the Persians, and when they were come before him, he spoke to them as follows: "Persians, I assembled you together desiring this of you, that ye should show yourselves good men and should not disgrace the deeds done in former times by the Persians, which are great and glorious; but let us each one of us by himself, and all together also, be zealous in our enterprise; for this which we labor for is a common good for all. And I exhort you that ye preserve in the war without relaxing your efforts, because, as I am informed, we are marching against good men, and if we shall overcome them, there will not be any other army of men which will ever stand against us. Now therefore let us begin the crossing, after having made prayer to those gods who have the Persians for their allotted charge."

54. During this day then they were making preparation to cross over; and on the next day they waited for the Sun, desiring to see him rise, and in the meantime they offered all kinds of incense upon the bridges and strewed the way with branches of myrtle. Then, as the Sun was rising, Xerxes made libation from a golden cup into the sea, and prayed to the Sun, that no accident might befall him such as should cause him to cease from subduing Europe, until he had come to its furthest limits. After having thus prayed he threw the cup into the Hellespont and with it a golden mixing-bowl and a Persian sword, which they call *akinakes*: but whether he cast them into the sea as an offering dedicated to the Sun, or whether he had repented of his scourging of the Hellespont and desired to present a gift to the sea as amends for this, I cannot for certain say.

55. When Xerxes had done this, they proceeded to cross over, the whole army both the footmen and the horsemen going by one bridge, namely that which was on the side of the Pontus, while the baggage-animals and the attendants went over the other, which was towards the Egean. First the ten thousand Persians led the way, all with wreaths, and after them came the mixed body of the army made up of all kinds of nations: these on that day; and on the next day, first the horsemen and those who had their spear-points turned downwards, these also wearing wreaths; and after them the sacred horses and the sacred

chariot, and then Xerxes himself and the spear-bearers and the thousand horsemen; and after them the rest of the army. In the meantime the ships also put out from shore and went over to the opposite side. I have heard however another account which says that the king crossed over the very last of all.

56. When Xerxes had crossed over into Europe, he gazed upon the army crossing under the lash; and his army crossed over in seven days and seven nights, going on continuously without any pause. Then, it is said, after Xerxes had now crossed over the Hellespont, a man of that coast exclaimed: "Why, O Zeus, in the likeness of a Persian man and taking for thyself the name of Xerxes instead of Zeus, art thou proposing to lay waste Hellas, taking with thee all the nations of men? for it was possible for thee to do so even without the help of these."

57. When all had crossed over, after they had set forth on their way a great portent appeared to them, of which Xerxes made no account, although it was easy to conjecture its meaning,—a mare gave birth to a hare. Now the meaning of this was easy to conjecture in this way, namely that Xerxes was about to march an army against Hellas very proudly and magnificently, but would come back again to the place whence he came, running for his life. There happened also a portent of another kind while he was still at Sardis,—a mule brought forth young and gave birth to a mule which had organs of generation of two kinds, both those of the male and those of the female, and those of the male were above. Xerxes however made no account of either of these portents, but proceeded on his way, and with him the land-army.

58. The fleet meanwhile was sailing out of the Hellespont and coasting along, going in the opposite direction to the land-army; for the fleet was sailing towards the West, making for the promontory of Sarpedon, to which it had been ordered beforehand to go, and there wait for the army; but the land-army meanwhile was making its march towards the East and the sunrising, through the Chersonese, keeping on its right the tomb of Helle the daughter of Athamas, and on its left the city of Cardia, and marching through the midst of a town the name of which is Agora. Thence bending round the gulf called Melas and having crossed over the river Melas, the stream of which did not suffice at this time for the army but failed,—having crossed, I say, this river, from which the gulf also has its name, it went on Westwards, passing by Ainos a city of the Aiolians, and by the lake Stentoris, until at last it came to Doriscos.

59. Now Doriscos is a sea-beach and plain of great extent in Thrace, and through it flows the great river Hebros: here a royal fortress had been built, the same which is now called Doriscos, and a garrison of Persians had been established in it by Dareios, ever since the time when he went on his march against the Scythians. It seemed then to Xerxes that the place was convenient to order his army and to number it throughout, and so he proceeded to do. The commanders of the ships at the bidding of Xerxes had brought all their ships, when they arrived at Doriscos, up to the sea-beach which adjoins Doriscos, on which there is situated both Sale a city of the Samothrakians, and also Zone, and of which the extreme point is the promontory of Serreion, which is well known; and the region belonged in ancient time to the Kikonians. To this beach then they had brought in their ships, and having drawn them up on land they were letting them get dry: and during this time he proceeded to number the army at Doriscos.

60. Now of the number which each separate nation supplied I am not able to give certain information, for this is not reported by any persons; but of the whole land-army

taken together the number proved to be one hundred and seventy myriads: and they numbered them throughout in the following manner:—they gathered together in one place a body of ten thousand men, and packing them together as closely as they could, they drew a circle round outside: and thus having drawn a circle round and having let the ten thousand men go from it, they built a wall of rough stones round the circumference of the circle, rising to the height of a man's navel. Having made this, they caused others to go into the space which had been built round, until they had in this manner numbered them all throughout: and after they had numbered them, they ordered them separately by nations.

61. Now those who served were as follows:—The Persians with this equipment:—about their heads they had soft felt caps called *tiaras*, and about their body tunics of various colors with sleeves, presenting the appearance of iron scales like those of a fish, and about the legs trousers; and instead of the ordinary shields they had shields of wicker-work, under which hung quivers; and they had short spears and large bows and arrows of reed, and moreover daggers hanging by the right thigh from the girdle: and they acknowledged as their commander Otanes the father of Amestris the wife of Xerxes. Now these were called by the Hellenes in ancient time Kephenes; by themselves however and by their neighbors they were called Artaians: but when Perseus, the son of Danae and Zeus, came to Kepheus the son of Belos and took to wife his daughter Andromeda, there was born to them a son to whom he gave the name Perses, and this son he left behind there, for it chanced that Kepheus had no male offspring: after him therefore this race was named.

62. The Medes served in the expedition equipped in precisely the same manner; for this equipment is in fact Median and not Persian: and the Medes acknowledged as their commander Tigranes an Achaimenid. These in ancient time used to be generally called Arians; but when Medea the Colchian came from Athens to these Arians, they also changed their name. Thus the Medes themselves report about themselves. The Kissians served with equipment in other respects like that of the Persians, but instead of the felt caps they wore fillets: and of the Kissians Anaphes the son of Otanes was commander. The Hyrcanians were armed like the Persians, acknowledging as their leader Megapanos, the same who after these events became governor of Babylon.

63. The Assyrians served with helmets about their heads made of bronze or plaited in a Barbarian style which it is not easy to describe; and they had shields and spears, and daggers like the Egyptian knives, and moreover they had wooden clubs with knobs of iron, and corslets of linen. These are by the Hellenes called Syrians, but by the Barbarians they have been called always Assyrians: [among these were the Chaldeans]: and the commander of them was Otaspes the son of Artachaies.

64. The Bactrians served wearing about their heads nearly the same covering as the Medes, and having native bows of reed and short spears. The Scaran Scythians had about their heads caps which were carried up to a point and set upright and stiff; and they wore trousers, and carried native bows and daggers, and besides this axes of the kind called *sagaris*. These were called Amyrgian Sacans, being in fact Scythians; for the Persians call all the Scythians Sacans: and of the Bactrians and Sacans the commander was Hystaspes, the son of Dareios and of Atossa the daughter of Cyrus.

65. The Indians wore garments made of tree-wool, and they had bows of reed and

arrows of reed with iron points. Thus were the Indians equipped; and serving with the rest they had been assigned to Pharnazathres the son of Artabates.

66. The Arians were equipped with Median bows, and in other respects like the Bactrians: and of the Arians Sisamnes the son of Hydarnes was in command. The Parthians and Chorasmians and Sogdians and Gandarians and Dadicans served with the same equipment as the Bactrians. Of these the commanders were, Artabazos the son of Pharnakes of the Parthians and Chorasmians, Azanes the son of Artaios of the Sogdians, and Artyphios the son of Artabanos of the Gandarians and Dadicans. The Caspians served wearing coats of skin and having native bows of reed and short swords: thus were these equipped; and they acknowledged as their leader Ariomardos the brother of Artyphios. The Sarangians were conspicuous among the rest by wearing dyed garments; and they had boots reaching up to the knee, and Median bows and spears: of these the commander was Pherendates the son of Megabazos. The Pactyans were wearers of skin coats and had native bows and daggers: these acknowledged as their commander Artaÿntes the son of Ithamitres.

68. The Utians and Mycans and Paricanians were equipped like the Pactyans: of these the commanders were, Arsamenes the son of Dareios of the Utians and Mycans, and of the Paricanians Siromitres the son of Oiobazos.

69. The Arabians wore loose mantles girt up, and they carried at their right side bows that bent backward of great length. The Ethiopians had skins of leopards and lions tied upon them, and bows made of a slip of palm-wood, which were of great length, not less than four cubits, and for them small arrows of reed with a sharpened stone at the head instead of iron, the same stone with which they engrave seals: in addition to this they had spears, and on them was the sharpened horn of a gazelle by way of a spear-head, and they had also clubs with knobs upon them. Of their body they used to smear over half with white, when they went into battle, and the other half with red. Of the Arabians and the Ethiopians who dwelt above Egypt the commander was Arsames, the son of Dareios and of Artystone, the daughter of Cyrus, whom Dareios loved most of all his wives, and had an image made of her of beaten gold.

70. Of the Ethiopians above Egypt and of the Arabians the commander, I say, was Arsames; but the Ethiopians from the direction of the sunrising (for the Ethiopians were in two bodies) had been appointed to serve with the Indians, being in no way different from the other Ethiopians, but in their language and in the nature of their hair only; for the Ethiopians from the East are straight-haired, but those of Libya have hair more thick and woolly than that of any other men. These Ethiopians from Asia were armed for the most part like the Indians, but they had upon their heads the skin of a horse's forehead flayed off with the ears and the mane, and the mane served instead of a crest, while they had the ears of the horse set up straight and stiff: and instead of shields they used to make defenses to hold before themselves of the skins of cranes.

71. The Libyans went with equipments of leather, and they used javelins burnt at the point. These acknowledged as their commander Massages the son of Oarizos.

72. The Paphlagonians served with plaited helmets upon their heads, small shields, and spears of no great size, and also javelins and daggers; and about their feet native boots reaching up to the middle of the shin. The Ligyans and Matienians and Mariandynoi and Syrians served with the same equipment as the Paphlagonians: these Syrians are called by the Persians Cappadokians. Of the Paphlagonians and Matienians the

commander was Dotos the son of Megasidros, and of the Mariandynoi and Lygians and Syrians, Gobryas, who was the son of Dareios and Artystone.

73. The Phrygians had an equipment very like that of the Paphlagonians with some slight difference. Now the Phrygians, as the Macedonians say, used to be called Brigians during the time that they were natives of Europe and dwelt with the Macedonians; but after they had changed into Asia, with their country they changed also their name and were called Phrygians. The Armenians were armed just like the Phrygians, being settlers from the Phrygians. Of these two together the commander was Artochmes, who was married to a daughter of Dareios.

74. The Lydians had arms very closely resembling those of the Hellenes. Now the Lydians were in old time called Medonians, and they were named again after Lydos the son of Atys, changing their former name. The Mysians had upon their heads native helmets, and they bore small shields and used javelins burnt at the point. These are settlers from the Lydians, and from mount Olympos they are called Olympienoi. Of the Lydians and Mysians the commander was Artaphrenes the son of Artaphrenes, he who invaded Marathon together with Datis.

75. The Thracians served having fox-skins upon their heads and tunics about their body, with loose mantles of various colors thrown round over them; and about their feet and lower part of the leg they wore boots of deer-skin; and besides this they had javelins and round bucklers and small daggers. These when they had crossed over into Asia came to be called Bithynians, but formerly they were called, as they themselves report, Strymonians, since they dwelt upon the river Strymon; and they say that they were driven out of their abode by the Teucrians and Mysians. Of the Thracians who lived in Asia the commander was Bassakes the son of Artabanos.

76. and they had small shields of raw ox-hide, and each man carried two hunting-spears of Lykian workmanship. On their heads they wore helmets of bronze, and to the helmets the ears and horns of an ox were attached, in bronze, and upon them also there were crests; and the lower part of their legs was wrapped round with red-colored strips of cloth. Among these men there is an Oracle of Ares.

77. The Meonian Cabelians, who are called Lasonians, had the same equipment as the Kilikians, and what this was I shall explain when in the course of the catalogue I come to the array of the Kilikians. The Milyans had short spears, and their garments were fastened on with buckles; some of them had Lykian bows, and about their heads they had caps made of leather. Of all these Badres the son of Hystanes was in command.

78. The Moschoi had wooden caps upon their heads, and shields and small spears, on which long points were set. The Tibarenians and Macronians and Mossynoicoi served with equipment like that of the Moschoi, and these were arrayed together under the following commanders,—the Moschoi and Tibarenians under Ariomardos, who was the son of Dareios and of Parmys, the daughter of Smerdis son of Cyrus; the Macronians and Mossynoicoi under Artayctes the son of Cherasmis, who was governor of Sestos on the Hellespont.

79. The Mares wore on their heads native helmets of plaited work, and had small shields of hide and javelins; and the Colchians wore wooden helmets about their heads, and had small shields of raw ox-hide and short spears, and also knives. Of the Mares and Colchians the commander was Pharandates the son of Teaspis. The Alarodians and

Saspeirians served armed like the Colchians; and of these the commander was Masistios the son of Siromitres.

80. The island tribes which came with the army from the Erythraian Sea, belonging to the islands in which the king settles those who are called the "Removed," had clothing and arms very like those of the Medes. Of these islanders the commander was Mardontes the son of Bagaios, who in the year after these events was a commander of the army at Mykale and lost his life in the battle.

81. These were the nations which served in the campaign by land and had been appointed to be among the foot-soldiers. Of this army those who have been mentioned were commanders; and they were the men who set it in order by divisions and numbered it and appointed commanders of thousands and commanders of tens of thousands, but the commanders of hundreds and of tens were appointed by the commanders of ten thousands; and there were others who were leaders of divisions and nations.

82. These, I say, who have been mentioned were commanders of the army; and over these and over the whole army together that went on foot there were in command Mardonios the son of Gobryas, Tritantaichmes the son of that Artabanos who gave the opinion that they should not make the march against Hellas, Smerdomenes the son of Otanes (both these being sons of brothers of Dareios and so cousins of Xerxes), Masistes the son of Dareios and Atossa, Gergis the son of Ariazos, and Megabyzos the son of Zopyros.

83. These were generals of the whole together that went on foot, excepting the ten thousand; and of these ten thousand chosen Persians the general was Hydarnes the son of Hydarnes; and these Persians were called "Immortals," because, if any one of them made the number incomplete, being overcome either by death or disease, another man was chosen to his place, and they were never either more or fewer than ten thousand. Now of all the nations, the Persians showed the greatest splendor of ornament and were themselves the best men. They had equipment such as has been mentioned, and besides this they were conspicuous among the rest for great quantity of gold freely used; and they took with them carriages, and in them concubines and a multitude of attendants well furnished; and provisions for them apart from the soldiers were borne by camels and beasts of burden.

84. The nations who serve as cavalry are these; not all however supplied cavalry, but only as many as here follow:—the Persians equipped in the same manner as their foot-soldiers, except that upon their heads some of them had beaten-work of metal, either bronze or iron.

85. There are also certain nomads called Sagartians, Persian in race and in language and having a dress which is midway between that of the Persians and that of the Pactyans. These furnished eight thousand horse, and they are not accustomed to have any arms either of bronze or of iron excepting daggers, but they use ropes twisted of thongs, and trust to these when they go into war: and the manner of fighting of these men is as follows:—when they come to conflict with the enemy, they throw the ropes with nooses at the end of them, and whatsoever the man catches by the throw, whether horse or man, he draws to himself, and they being entangled in toils are thus destroyed.

86. This is the manner of fighting of these men, and they were arrayed next to the Persians. The Medes had the same equipment as their men on foot, and the Kissians likewise. The Indians were armed in the same manner as those of them who served on foot, and they both rode horses and drove chariots, in which were harnessed horses or wild

asses. The Bactrians were equipped in the same way as those who served on foot, and the Caspians likewise. The Libyans too were equipped like those who served on foot, and these also all drove chariots. So too the Caspians and Paricanians were equipped like those who served on foot, and they all rode on camels, which in swiftness were not inferior to horses.

87. These nations alone served as cavalry, and the number of the cavalry proved to be eight myriads, apart from the camels and the chariots. Now the rest of the cavalry was arrayed in squadrons, but the Arabians were placed after them and last of all, for the horses could not endure the camels, and therefore they were placed last, in order that the horses might not be frightened.

88. The commanders of the cavalry were Harmamithras and Tithaios sons of Datis, but the third, Pharnuches, who was in command of the horse with them, had been left behind at Sardis sick: for as they were setting forth from Sardis, an accident befell him of an unwished-for kind,—as he was riding, a dog ran up under his horse's feet, and the horse not having seen it beforehand was frightened, and rearing up he threw Pharnuches off his back, who falling vomited blood, and his sickness turned to a consumption. To the horse however they forthwith at the first did as he commanded, that is to say, the servants led him away to the place where he had thrown his master and cut off his legs at the knees. Thus was Pharnuches removed from his command.

89. Of the triremes the number proved to be one thousand two hundred and seven, and these were they who furnished them:—the Phoenicians, together with the Syrians who dwell in Palestine furnished three hundred; and they were equipped thus, that is to say, they had about their heads leathern caps made very nearly in the Hellenic fashion, and they wore corslets of linen, and had shields without rims and javelins. These Phoenicians dwelt in ancient time, as they themselves report, upon the Erythraian Sea, and thence they passed over and dwell in the country along the sea coast of Syria; and this part of Syria and all as far as Egypt is called Palestine. The Egyptians furnished two hundred ships: these men had about their heads helmets of plaited work, and they had hollow shields with the rims large, and spears for sea-fighting, and large axes: the greater number of them wore corslets, and they had large knives.

90. These men were thus equipped; and the Cyprians furnished a hundred and fifty ships, being themselves equipped as follows,—their kings had their heads wound round with fillets, and the rest had tunics, but in other respects they were like the Hellenes. Among these there are various races as follows,—some of them are from Salamis and Athens, others from Arcadia, others from Kythnos, others again from Phenicia and others from Ethiopia, as the Cyprians themselves report.

91. The Kilikians furnished a hundred ships; and these again had about their heads native helmets, and for shields they carried targets made of raw ox-hide: they wore tunics of wool and each man had two javelins and a sword, this last being made very like the Egyptian knives. These in old time were called Hypachaians, and they got their later name from Kilix the son of Agenor, a Phoenician. The Pamphylians furnished thirty ships and were equipped in Hellenic arms. These Pamphylians are of those who were dispersed from Troy together with Amphilochos and Calchas.

92. The Lykians furnished fifty ships; and they were wearers of corslets and greaves, and had bows of cornel-wood and arrows of reeds without feathers and javelins and a goat-skin hanging over their shoulders, and about their heads felt caps wreathed round

with feathers; also they had daggers and falchions. The Lykians were formerly called Termilai, being originally of Crete, and they got their later name from Lycos the son of Pandion, an Athenian.

93. The Dorians of Asia furnished thirty ships; and these had Hellenic arms and were originally from the Peloponnese. The Carians supplied seventy ships; and they were equipped in other respects like Hellenes but they had also falchions and daggers. What was the former name of these has been told in the first part of the history.

94. The Ionians furnished a hundred ships, and were equipped like Hellenes. Now the Ionians, so long time as they dwelt in the Peloponnese, in the land which is now called Achaia, and before the time when Danaos and Xuthos came to the Peloponnese, were called, as the Hellenes report, Pelasgians of the Coast-land, and then Ionians after Ion the son of Xuthos.

95. The islanders furnished seventeen ships, and were armed like Hellenes, this also being a Pelasgian race, though afterwards it came to be called Ionian by the same rule as the Ionians of the twelve cities, who came from Athens. The Aiolians supplied sixty ships; and these were equipped like Hellenes and used to be called Pelasgians in the old time, as the Hellenes report. The Hellespontians, excepting those of Abydos (for the men of Abydos had been appointed by the king to stay in their place and be guards of the bridges), the rest, I say, of those who served in the expedition from the Pontus furnished a hundred ships, and were equipped like Hellenes: these are colonists of the Ionians and Dorians.

96. In all the ships there served as fighting-men Persians, Medes, or Sacans;: and of the ships, those which sailed best were furnished by the Phoenicians, and of the Phoenicians the best by the men of Sidon. Over all these men and also over those of them who were appointed to serve in the land-army, there were for each tribe native chieftains, of whom, since I am not compelled by the course of the inquiry, I make no mention by the way; for in the first place the chieftains of each separate nation were not persons worthy of mention, and then moreover within each nation there were as many chieftains as there were cities. These went with the expedition too not as commanders, but like the others serving as slaves; for the generals who had the absolute power and commanded the various nations, that is to say those who were Persians, having already been mentioned by me.

97. Of the naval force the following were commanders,—Ariabignes the son of Dareios, Prexaspes the son of Aspathines, Megabazos the son of Megabates, and Achaimenes the son of Dareios; that is to say, of the Ionian and Carian force Ariabignes, who was the son of Dareios and of the daughter of Gobryas; of the Egyptians Achaimenes was commander, being brother of Xerxes by both parents; and of the rest of the armament the other two were in command: and galleys of thirty oars and of fifty oars, and light vessels, and long ships to carry horses had been assembled together, as it proved, to the number of three thousand.

98. Of those who sailed in the ships the men of most note after the commanders were these,—of Sidon, Tetramnestos son of Anysos; of Tyre, Matten son of Siromos; or Arados, Merbalos son of Agbalos; of Kilikia, Syennesis son of Oromedon; of Lykia, Kyberniscos son of Sicas; of Cyprus, Gorgos son of Chersis and Timonax son of Timagoras; of Caria, Histiaios son of Tymnes, Pigres son of Hysseldomos, and Damasithymos son of Candaules.

99. Of the rest of the officers I make no mention by the way (since I am not bound to do so), but only of Artemisia, at whom I marvel most that she joined the expedition against Hellas, being a woman; for after her husband died, she holding the power herself, although she had a son who was a young man, went on the expedition impelled by high spirit and manly courage, no necessity being laid upon her. Now her name, as I said, was Artemisia and she was the daughter of Lygdamis, and by descent she was of Halicarnassos on the side of her father, but of Crete by her mother. She was ruler of the men of Halicarnassos and Cos and Nisyros and Calydna, furnishing five ships; and she furnished ships which were of all the fleet reputed the best after those of the Sidonians, and of all his allies she set forth the best counsels to the king. Of the States of which I said that she was leader I declare the people to be all of Dorian race, those of Halicarnassos being Troizenians, and the rest Epidaurians. So far then I have spoken of the naval force.

100. Then when Xerxes had numbered the army, and it had been arranged in divisions, he had a mind to drive through it himself and inspect it: and afterwards he proceeded so to do; and driving through in a chariot by each nation, he inquired about them and his scribes wrote down the names, until he had gone from end to end both of the horse and of the foot. When he had done this, the ships were drawn down into the sea, and Xerxes changing from his chariot to a ship of Sidon sat down under a golden canopy and sailed along by the prows of the ships, asking of all just as he had done with the land-army, and having the answers written down. And the captains had taken their ships out to a distance of about four hundred feet from the beach and were staying them there, all having turned the prows of the ships towards the shore in an even line and having armed all the fighting-men as for war; and he inspected them sailing within, between the prows of the ships and the beach.

101. Now when he had sailed through these and had disembarked from his ship, he sent for Demaratos the son of Ariston, who was marching with him against Hellas; and having called him he asked as follows: "Demaratos, now it is my pleasure to ask thee somewhat which I desire to know. Thou art not only a Hellene, but also, as I am informed both by thee and by the other Hellenes who come to speech with me, of a city which is neither the least nor the feeblest of Hellas. Now therefore declare to me this, namely whether the Hellenes will endure to raise hands against me: for, as I suppose, even if all the Hellenes and the remaining nations who dwell towards the West should be gathered together, they are not strong enough in fight to endure my attack, supposing them to be my enemies. I desire however to be informed also of thy opinion, what thou sayest about these matters." He inquired thus, and the other made answer and said: "O king, shall I utter the truth in speaking to thee, or that which will give pleasure?" and he bade him utter the truth, saying that he should suffer nothing unpleasant in consequence of this, any more than he suffered before.

102. When Demaratos heard this, he spoke as follows: "O king, since thou biddest me by all means utter the truth, and so speak as one who shall not be afterwards convicted by thee of having spoken falsely, I say this:—with Hellas poverty is ever an inbred growth, while valor is one that has been brought in, being acquired by intelligence and the force of law; and of it Hellas makes use ever to avert from herself not only poverty but also servitude to a master. Now I commend all the Hellenes who are settled in those Dorian lands, but this which I am about to say has regard not to all, but to the Lacedemonians alone: of these I say, first that it is not possible that they will ever accept thy terms, which carry with

them servitude for Hellas; and next I say that they will stand against thee in fight, even if all the other Hellenes shall be of thy party: and as for numbers, ask now how many they are, that they are able to do this; for whether it chances that a thousand of them have come out into the field, these will fight with thee, or if there be less than this, or again if there be more."

103. Xerxes hearing this laughed, and said: "Demaratos, what a speech is this which thou hast uttered, saying that a thousand men will fight with this vast army! Come tell me this:—thou sayest that thou wert thyself king of these men; wilt thou therefore consent forthwith to fight with ten men? and yet if your State is such throughout as thou dost describe it, thou their king ought by your laws to stand in array against double as many as another man; that is to say, if each of them is a match for ten men of my army, I expect of thee that thou shouldest be a match for twenty. Thus would be confirmed the report which is made by thee: but if ye, who boast thus greatly are such men and in size so great only as the Hellenes who come commonly to speech with me, thyself included, then beware lest this which has been spoken prove but an empty vaunt. For come, let me examine it by all that is probable: how could a thousand or ten thousand or even fifty thousand, at least if they were all equally free and were not ruled by one man, stand against so great an army? since, as thou knowest, we shall be more than a thousand coming about each one of them, supposing them to be in number five thousand. If indeed they were ruled by one man after our fashion, they might perhaps from fear of him become braver than it was their nature to be, or they might go compelled by the lash to fight with greater numbers, being themselves fewer in number; but if left at liberty, they would do neither of these things: and I for my part suppose that, even if equally matched in numbers, the Hellenes would hardly dare to fight with the Persians taken alone. With us however this of which thou speakest is found in single men, not indeed often, but rarely; for there are Persians of my spearmen who will consent to fight with three men of the Hellenes at once: but thou hast had no experience of these things and therefore thou speakest very much at random."

104. To this Demaratos replied: "O king, from the first I was sure that if I uttered the truth I should not speak that which was pleasing to thee; since however thou didst compel me to speak the very truth, I told thee of the matters which concern the Spartans. And yet how I am at this present time attached to them by affection thou knowest better than any; seeing that first they took away from me the rank and privileges which came to me from my fathers, and then also they have caused me to be without native land and an exile; but thy father took me up and gave me livelihood and a house to dwell in. Surely it is not to be supposed likely that the prudent man will thrust aside friendliness which is offered to him, but rather that he will accept it with full contentment. And I do not profess that I am able to fight either with ten men or with two, nay, if I had my will, I would not even fight with one; but if there were necessity or if the cause which urged me to the combat were a great one, I would fight most willingly with one of these men who says that he is a match for three of the Hellenes. So also the Lacedemonians are not inferior to any men when fighting one by one, and they are the best of all men when fighting in a body: for though free, yet they are not free in all things, for over them is set Law as a master, whom they fear much more even than thy people fear thee. It is certain at least that they do whatsoever that master commands; and he commands ever the same thing, that is to say, he bids them not flee out of battle from any multitude of men, but stay in their post and win the

victory or lose their life. But if when I say these things I seem to thee to be speaking at random, of other things for the future I prefer to be silent; and at this time I spake only because I was compelled. May it come to pass however according to thy mind, O king."

105. He thus made answer, and Xerxes turned the matter to laughter and felt no anger, but dismissed him with kindness. Then after he had conversed with him, and had appointed Mascames son of Megadostes to be governor at this place Doriscos, removing the governor who had been appointed by Dareios, Xerxes marched forth his army through Thrace to invade Hellas.

106. And Mascames, whom he left behind here, proved to be a man of such qualities that to him alone Xerxes used to send gifts, considering him the best of all the men whom either he himself or Dareios had appointed to be governors,—he used to send him gifts, I say, every year, and so also did Artaxerxes the son of Xerxes to the descendants of Mascames. For even before this march governors had been appointed in Thrace and everywhere about the Hellespont; and these all, both those in Thrace and in the Hellespont, were conquered by the Hellenes after this expedition, except only the one who was at Doriscos; but Mascames at Doriscos none were ever able to conquer, though many tried. For this reason the gifts are sent continually for him from the king who reigns over the Persians.

107. Of those however who were conquered by the Hellenes Xerxes did not consider any to be a good man except only Boges, who was at Eïon: him he never ceased commending, and he honored very highly his children who survived him in the land of Persia. For in truth Boges proved himself worthy of great commendation, seeing that when he was besieged by the Athenians under Kimon the son of Miltiades, though he might have gone forth under a truce and so returned home to Asia, he preferred not to do this, for fear that the king should that it was by cowardice that he survived; and he continued to hold out till the last. Then when there was no longer any supply of provisions within the wall, he heaped together a great pyre, and he cut the throats of his children, his wife, his concubines and his servants, and threw them into the fire; and after this he scattered all the gold and silver in the city from the wall into the river Strymon, and having so done he threw himself into the fire. Thus he is justly commended even to this present time by the Persians.

108. Xerxes from Doriscos was proceeding onwards to invade Hellas; and as he went he compelled those who successively came in his way, to join his march: for the whole country as far as Thessaly had been reduced to subjection, as has been set forth by me before, and was tributary under the king, having been subdued by Megabazos and afterwards by Mardonios. And he passed in his march from Doriscos first by the Samothrakian strongholds, of which that which is situated furthest towards the West is a city called Mesambria. Next to this follows Stryme, a city of the Thasians, and midway between them flows the river Lisos, which at this time did not suffice when supplying its water to the army of Xerxes, but the stream failed. This country was in old time called Gallaïke, but now Briantike; however by strict justice this also belongs to the Kikonians.

109. Having crossed over the bed of the river Lisos after it had been dried up, he passed by these Hellenic cities, namely Maroneia, Dicaia and Abdera. These I say he passed by, and also the following lakes of note lying near them,—the Ismarian lake, lying between Maroneia and Stryme; the Bistonian lake near Dicaia, into which two rivers pour their waters, the Trauos and the Compsantos; and at Abdera no lake indeed of any note

was passed by Xerxes, but the river Nestos, which flows there into the sea. Then after passing these places he went by the cities of the mainland, near one of which there is, as it chances, a lake of somewhere about thirty furlongs in circumference, abounding in fish and very brackish; this the baggage-animals alone dried up, being watered at it: and the name of this city is Pistyros.

110. These cities, I say, lying by the sea coast and belonging to Hellenes, he passed by, leaving them on the left hand; and the tribes of Thracians through whose country he marched were as follows, namely the Paitians, Kikonians, Bistonians, Sapaians, Dersaians, Edonians, Satrians. Of these they who were settled along the sea coast accompanied him with their ships, and those of them who dwelt inland and have been enumerated by me, were compelled to accompany him on land, except the Satrians:

111, the Satrians however never yet became obedient to any man, so far as we know, but they remain up to my time still free, alone of all the Thracians; for they dwell in lofty mountains, which are covered with forest of all kinds and with snow, and also they are very skillful in war. These are they who possess the Oracle of Dionysos; which Oracle is on their most lofty mountains. Of the Satrians those who act as prophets of the temple are the Bessians; it is a prophetess who utters the oracles, as at Delphi; and beyond this there is nothing further of a remarkable character.

112. Xerxes having passed over the land which has been spoken of, next after this passed the strongholds of the Pierians, of which the name of the one is Phagres and of the other Pergamos. By this way, I say, he made his march, going close by the walls of these, and keeping Mount Pangaion on the right hand, which is both great and lofty and in which are mines both of gold and of silver possessed by the Pierians and Odomantians, and especially by the Satrians.

113. Thus passing by the Paionians, Doberians and Paioplians, who dwell beyond Pangaion towards the North Wind, he went on Westwards, until at last he came to the river Strymon and the city of Eïon, of which, so long as he lived, Boges was commander, the same about whom I was speaking a short time back. This country about Mount Pangaion is called Phyllis, and it extends Westwards to the river Angites, which flows into the Strymon, and Southwards it stretches to the Strymon itself; and at this river the Magians sacrificed for good omens, slaying white horses.

114. Having done this and many other things in addition to this, as charms for the river, at the Nine Ways in the land of the Edonians, they proceeded by the bridges, for they had found the Strymon already yoked with bridges; and being informed that this place was called the Nine Ways, they buried alive in it that number of boys and maidens, children of the natives of the place. Now burying alive is a Persian custom; for I am informed that Amestris also, the wife of Xerxes, when she had grown old, made return for her own life to the god who is said to be beneath the earth by burying twice seven children of Persians who were men of renown.

115. As the army proceeded on its march from the Strymon, it found after this a sea-beach stretching towards the setting of the sun, and passed by the Hellenic city, Argilos, which was there placed. This region and that which lies above it is called Bisaltia. Thence, keeping on the left hand the gulf which lies of Posideion, he went through the plain which is called the plain of Syleus, passing by Stageiros a Hellenic city, and so came to Acanthos, taking with him as he went each one of these tribes and also of those who dwell about Mount Pangaion, just as he did those whom I enumerated before, having the men who

dwelt along the sea coast to serve in the ships and those who dwelt inland to accompany him on foot. This road by which Xerxes the king marched his army, the Thracians do not disturb nor sow crops over, but pay very great reverence to it down to my own time.

116. Then when he had come to Acanthos, Xerxes proclaimed a guest-friendship with the people of Acanthos and also presented them with the Median dress and commended them, perceiving that they were zealous to serve him in the war and hearing of that which had been dug.

117. And while Xerxes was in Acanthos, it happened that he who had been set over the making of the channel, Artachaies by name, died of sickness, a man who was highly esteemed by Xerxes and belonged to the Achaimenid family; also he was in stature the tallest of all the Persians, falling short by only four fingers of being five royal cubits in height, and he had a voice the loudest of all men; so that Xerxes was greatly grieved at the loss of him, and carried him forth and buried him with great honor, and the whole army joined in throwing up a mound for him. To this Artachaies the Acanthians by the bidding of an oracle do sacrifice as a hero, calling upon his name in worship.

118. King Xerxes, I say, was greatly grieved at the loss of Artachaies: and meanwhile the Hellenes who were entertaining his army and providing Xerxes with dinners had been brought to utter ruin, so that they were being driven from house and home; seeing that when the Thasians, for example, entertained the army of Xerxes and provided him with a dinner on behalf of their towns upon the mainland, Antipater the son of Orgeus, who had been appointed for this purpose, a man of repute among the citizens equal to the best, reported that four hundred talents of silver had been spent upon the dinner.

119. Just so or nearly so in the other cities also those who were set over the business reported the reckoning to be: for the dinner was given as follows, having been ordered a long time beforehand, and being counted by them a matter of great importance:—In the first place, so soon as they heard of it from the heralds who carried round the proclamation, the citizens in the various cities distributed corn among their several households, and all continued to make wheat and barley meal for many months; then they fed cattle, finding out and obtaining the finest animals for a high price; and they kept birds both of the land and of the water, in cages or in pools, all for the entertainment of the army. Then again they had drinking-cups and mixing-bowls made of gold and of silver, and all the other things which are placed upon the table: these were made for the king himself and for those who ate at his table; but for the rest of the army only the things appointed for food were provided. Then whenever the army came to any place, there was a tent pitched ready wherein Xerxes himself made his stay, while the rest of the army remained out in the open air; and when it came to be time for dinner, then the entertainers had labor; but the others, after they had been satiated with food and had spent the night there, on the next day tore up the tent and taking with them all the movable furniture proceeded on their march, leaving nothing, but carrying all away with them.

120. Then was uttered a word well-spoken by Megacreon, a man of Abdera, who advised those of Abdera to go in a body, both themselves and their wives, to their temples, and to sit down as suppliants of the gods, entreating them that for the future also they would ward off from them the half of the evils which threatened; and he bade them feel great thankfulness to the gods for the past events, because king Xerxes had not thought good to take food twice in each day; for if it had been ordered to them beforehand to prepare breakfast also in like manner as the dinner, it would have remained for the men

of Abdera either not to await the coming of Xerxes, or if they stayed, to be crushed by misfortune more than any other men upon the Earth.

121. They then, I say, though hard put to it, yet were performing that which was appointed to them; and from Acanthos Xerxes, after having commanded the generals to wait for the fleet at Therma, let the ships take their course apart from himself, (now this Therma is that which is situated on the Thermaic gulf, from which also this gulf has its name); and thus he did because he was informed that this was the shortest way: for from Doriscos as far as Acanthos the army had been making its march thus:—Xerxes had divided the whole land-army into three divisions, and one of them he had set to go along the sea accompanying the fleet, of which division Mardonios and Masistes were commanders; another third of the army had been appointed to go by the inland way, and of this the generals in command were Tritantaichmes and Gergis; and meanwhile the third of the subdivisions, with which Xerxes himself went, marched in the middle between them, and acknowledged as its commanders Smerdomenes and Megabyzos.

122. The fleet, when it was let go by Xerxes and had sailed right through the channel made in Athos (which went across to the gulf on which are situated the cities of Assa, Piloros, Singos and Sarte), having taken up a contingent from these cities also, sailed thence with a free course to the Thermaïc gulf, and turning round Ampelos the headland of Torone, it left on one side the following Hellenic cities, from which it took up contingents of ships and men, namely Torone, Galepsos, Sermyle, Mekyberna, Olynthos: this region is called Sithonia.

123. And the fleet of Xerxes, cutting across from the headland of Ampelos to that of Canastron, which runs out furthest to sea of all Pallene, took up there contingents of ships and men from Potidaia, Aphytis, Neapolis, Aige, Therambo, Skione, Mende and Sane, for these are the cities which occupy the region which now is called Pallene, but was formerly called Phlegra. Then sailing along the coast of this country also the fleet continued its course towards the place which has been mentioned before, taking up contingents also from the cities which come next after Pallene and border upon the Thermaïc gulf; and the names of them are these,—Lipaxos, Combreia, Lisai, Gigonos, Campsa, Smila, Aineia; and the region in which these cities are is called even to the present day Crossaia. Then sailing from Aineia, with which name I brought to an end the list of the cities, at once the fleet came into the Thermaïc gulf and to the region of Mygdonia, and so it arrived at the aforesaid Therma and at the cities of Sindos and Chalestra upon the river Axios. This river is the boundary between the land of Mygdonia and Bottiaia, of which district the narrow region which lies on the sea coast is occupied by the cities of Ichnai and Pella.

124. Now while his naval force was encamped about the river Axios and the city of Therma and the cities which lie between these two, waiting for the coming of the king, Xerxes and the land-army were proceeding from Acanthos, cutting through the middle by the shortest way with a view to reaching Therma: and he was proceeding through Paionia and Crestonia to the river Cheidoros, which beginning from the land of the Crestonians, runs through the region of Mygdonia and comes out alongside of the marsh which is by the river Axios.

125. As he was proceeding by this way, lions attacked the camels which carried his provisions; for the lions used to come down regularly by night, leaving their own haunts, but they touched nothing else, neither beast of burden nor man, but killed the camels only: and I marvel what was the cause, and what was it that impelled the lions to abstain

from all else and to attack the camels only, creatures which they had never seen before, and of which they had had no experience.

126. Now there are in these parts both many lions and also wild oxen, those that have the very large horns which are often brought into Hellas: and the limit within which these lions are found is on the one side the river Nestos, which flows through Abdera, and on the other the Achelos, which flows through Acarnania; for neither do the East of the Nestos, in any part of Europe before you come to this, would you see a lion, nor again in the remaining part of the continent to the West of the Acheloos, but they are produced in the middle space between these rivers.

127. When Xerxes had reached Therma he established the army there; and his army encamping there occupied of the land along by the sea no less than this,—beginning from the city of Therma and from Mygdonia it extended as far as the river Lydias and the Haliacmon, which form the boundary between the lands of Bottiaia and Macedonia, mingling their waters together in one and the same stream. The Barbarians, I say, were encamped in these regions; and of the rivers which have been enumerated, only the river Cheidoros flowing from the Crestonian land was insufficient for the drinking of the army and failed in its stream.

128. Then Xerxes seeing from Therma the mountains of Thessaly, Olympos and Ossa, that they were of very great height, and being informed that in the midst between them there was a narrow channel, through which flows the Peneios, and hearing also that by this way there was a good road leading to Thessaly, formed a desire to sail thither and look at the outlet of the Peneios, because he was meaning to march by the upper road, through the land of the Macedonians who dwell inland, until he came to the Perraibians, passing by the city of Gonnos; for by this way he was informed that it was safest to go. And having formed this desire, so also he proceeded to do; that is, he embarked in a Sidonian ship, the same in which he used always to embark when he wished to do anything of this kind, and he displayed a signal for the others to put out to sea also, leaving there the land-army. Then when Xerxes had looked at the outlet of the Peneios, he was possessed by great wonder, and summoning his guides he asked them whether it was possible to turn the river aside and bring it out to the sea by another way.

129. Now it is said that Thessaly was in old time a lake, being enclosed on all sides by very lofty mountains: for the parts of it which lie towards the East are shut in by the ranges of Pelion and Ossa, which join one another in their lower slopes, the parts towards the North Wind by Olympos, those towards the West by Pindos and those towards the mid-day and the South Wind by Othrys; and the region in the midst, between these mountains which have been named, is Thessaly, forming as it were a hollow. Whereas then many rivers flow into it and among them these five of most note, namely Peneios, Apidanos, Onochonos, Enipeus and Pamisos, these, which collect their waters from the mountains that enclose Thessaly round, and flow into this plain, with names separate each one, having their outflow into the sea by one channel and that a narrow one, first mingling their waters all together in one and the same stream; and so soon as they are mingled together, from that point onwards the Peneios prevails with its name over the rest and causes the others to lose their separate names. And it is said that in ancient time, there not being yet this channel and outflow between the mountains, these rivers, and besides these rivers the lake Boibeïs also, had no names as they have now, but by their waters they made Thessaly to be all sea. The Thessalians themselves say that Poseidon made the

channel through which the Peneios flows; and reasonably they report it thus, because whosoever believes that it is Poseidon who shakes the Earth and that the partings asunder produced by earthquake are the work of this god, would say, if he saw this, that it was made by Poseidon; for the parting asunder of the mountains is the work of an earthquake, as is evident to me.

130. So the guides, when Xerxes asked whether there was any other possible outlet to the sea for the Peneios, said with exact knowledge of the truth: "O king, for this river there is no other outgoing which extends to the sea, but this alone; for all Thessaly is circled about with mountains as with a crown." To this Xerxes is said to have replied: "The Thessalians then are prudent men. This it appears was that which they desired to guard against in good time when they changed their counsel, reflecting on this especially besides other things, namely that they had a country which, it appears, is easy to conquer and may quickly be taken: for it would have been necessary only to let the river flow over their land by making an embankment to keep it from going through the narrow channel and so diverting the course by which now it flows, in order to put all Thessaly under water except the mountains." This he said in reference to the sons of Aleuas, because they, being Thessalians, were the first of the Hellenes who gave themselves over to the king; for Xerxes thought that they offered him friendship on behalf of their whole nation. Having said thus and having looked at the place, he sailed back to Therma.

131. He then was staying in the region of Pieria many days, for the road over the mountains of Macedonia was being cut meanwhile by a third part of his army, that all the host might pass over by this way into the land of the Perraibians: and now the heralds returned who had been sent to Hellas to demand the gift of earth, some empty-handed and others bearing earth and water.

132. And among those who gave that which was demanded were the following, namely the Thessalians, Dolopians, Enianians, Perraibians, Locrians, Megnesians, Malians, Achaians of Phthiotis, and Thebans, with the rest of the Boeotians also excepting the Thespians and Plataians. Against these the Hellenes who took up war with the Barbarian made an oath; and the oath was this,—that whosoever being Hellenes had given themselves over to the Persian, not being compelled, these, if their own affairs should come to a good conclusion, they would dedicate as an offering to the god at Delphi.

133. Thus ran the oath which was taken by the Hellenes: Xerxes however had not sent to Athens or to Sparta heralds to demand the gift of earth, and for this reason, namely because at the former time when Dareios had sent for this very purpose, the one people threw the men who made the demand into the pit and the others into a well, and bade them take from thence earth and water and bear them to the king. For this reason Xerxes did not send men to make this demand. And what evil thing came upon the Athenians for having done this to the heralds, I am not able to say, except indeed that their land and city were laid waste; but I do not think that this happened for that cause:

134, on the Lacedemonians however the wrath fell of Talthybios, the herald of Agamemnon; for in Sparta there is a temple of Talthybios, and there are also descendants of Talthybios called Talthybiads, to whom have been given as a right all the missions of heralds which go from Sparta; and after this event it was not possible for the Spartans when they sacrificed to obtain favorable omens. This was the case with them for a long time; and as the Lacedemonians were grieved and regarded it as a great misfortune, and general assemblies were repeatedly gathered together and proclamation made, asking if any one of the Lacedemonians was willing to die for Sparta, at length Sperthias the son of Aneristos and Bulis the son of Nicolaos, Spartans of noble birth and in wealth attaining to the first rank, voluntarily submitted to pay the penalty to Xerxes for the heralds of Dareios which had perished at Sparta. Thus the Spartans sent these to the Medes to be put to death.

135. And not only the courage then shown by these men is worthy of admiration, but also the following sayings in addition: for as they were on their way to Susa they came to Hydarnes (now Hydarnes was a Persian by race and commander of those who dwelt on the sea coasts of Asia), and he offered them hospitality and entertained them; and while they were his guests he asked them as follows: "Lacedemonians, why is it that ye flee from becoming friends to the king? for ye may see that the king knows how to honor good men, when ye look at me and at my fortunes. So also ye, Lacedemonians, if ye gave yourselves to the king, since ye have the reputation with him already of being good men, would have rule each one of you over Hellenic land by the gift of the king." To this they made answer thus: "Hydarnes, thy counsel with regard to us is not equally balanced, for thou givest counsel having made trial indeed of the one thing, but being without experience of the other: thou knowest well what it is to be a slave, but thou hast never yet made trial of freedom, whether it is pleasant to the taste or no; for if thou shouldest make trial of it, thou wouldest then counsel us to fight for it not with spears only but also with axes."

136. Thus they answered Hydarnes; and then, after they had gone up to Susa and had come into the presence of the king, first when the spearmen of the guard commanded them and endeavored to compel them by force to do obeisance to the king by falling down before him, they said that they would not do any such deed, though they should be pushed down by them head foremost; for it was not their custom to do obeisance to a man, and it was not for this that they had come. Then when they had resisted this, next they spoke these words or words to this effect: "O king of the Medes, the Lacedemonians sent us in place of the heralds who were slain in Sparta, to pay the penalty for their lives." When they said this, Xerxes moved by a spirit of magnanimity replied that he would not be like the Lacedemonians; for they had violated the rules which prevailed among all men by slaying heralds, but he would not do that himself which he blamed them for having done, nor would he free the Lacedemonians from their guilt by slaying these in return.

137. Thus the wrath of Talthybios ceased for the time being, even though the Spartans had done no more than this and although Sperthias and Bulis returned back to Sparta; but a long time after this it was roused again during the war between the Peloponnesians and Athenians, as the Lacedemonians report. This I perceive to have been most evidently the act of the Deity: for in that the wrath of Talthybios fell upon messengers and did not cease until it had been fully satisfied, so much was but in accordance with justice; but that it happened to come upon the sons of these men who went up to the king on account of the wrath, namely upon Nicolaos the son of Bulis and Aneristos the son of Sperthias (the same who conquered the men of Halieis, who came from Tiryns, by sailing into their harbor with a merchant ship filled with fighting men),—by this it is evident to me that the matter came to pass by the act of the Deity caused by this wrath. For these men, sent by the Lacedemonians as envoys to Asia, having been betrayed by Sitalkes the son of Teres king of the Thracians and by Nymphodoros the son of Pythes a man of Abdera, were captured at Bisanthe on the Hellespont; and then having been carried away to Attica they

were put to death by the Athenians, and with them also Aristeas the son of Adeimantos the Corinthian. These things happened many years after the expedition of the king; and I return now to the former narrative.

138. Now the march of the king's army was in name against Athens, but in fact it was going against all Hellas: and the Hellenes being informed of this long before were not all equally affected by it; for some of them having given earth and water to the Persian had confidence, supposing that they would suffer no hurt from the Barbarian; while others not having given were in great terror, seeing that there were not ships existing in Hellas which were capable as regards number of receiving the invader in fight, and seeing that the greater part of the States were not willing to take up the war, but adopted readily the side of the Medes.

139. And here I am compelled by necessity to declare an opinion which in the eyes of most men would seem to be invidious, but nevertheless I will not abstain from saying that which I see evidently to be the truth. If the Athenians had been seized with fear of the danger which threatened them and had left their land, or again, without leaving their land, had stayed and given themselves up to Xerxes, none would have made any attempt by sea to oppose the king. If then none had opposed Xerxes by sea, it would have happened on the land somewhat thus:—even if many tunics of walls had been thrown across the Isthmus by the Peloponnesians, the Lacedemonians would have been deserted by their allies, not voluntarily but of necessity, since these would have been conquered city after city by the naval force of the Barbarian, and so they would have been left alone: and having been left alone and having displayed great deeds of valor, they would have met their death nobly. Either they would have suffered this fate, or before this, seeing the other Hellenes also taking the side of the Medes, they would have made an agreement with Xerxes; and thus in either case Hellas would have come to be under the rule of the Persians: for as to the good to be got from the walls thrown across the Isthmus, I am unable to discover what it would have been, when the king had command of the sea. As it is however, if a man should say that the Athenians proved to be the saviors of Hellas, he would not fail to hit the truth; for to whichever side these turned, to that the balance was likely to incline: and these were they who, preferring that Hellas should continue to exist in freedom, roused up all of Hellas which remained, so much, that is, as had not gone over to the Medes, and (after the gods at least) these were they who repelled the king. Nor did fearful oracles, which came from Delphi and cast them into dread, induce them to leave Hellas, but they stayed behind and endured to receive the invader of their land.

140. For the Athenians had sent men to Delphi to inquire and were preparing to consult the Oracle; and after these had performed the usual rites in the sacred precincts, when they had entered the sanctuary and were sitting down there, the Pythian prophetess, whose name was Aristonike, uttered to them this oracle:

"Why do ye sit, O ye wretched? Flee thou to the uttermost
limits, Leaving thy home and the heights of the wheel-round city
behind thee! Lo, there remaineth now nor the head nor the body in
safety, — Neither the feet below nor the hands nor the middle are
left thee, — All are destroyed together; for fire and the
passionate War-god, Urging the Syrian car to speed, doth
hurl them to ruin. Not thine alone, he shall cause many more

great strongholds to perish, Yes, many temples of gods to the
ravening fire shall deliver, — Temples which stand now surely with
sweat of their terror down-streaming, Quaking with dread; and lo!
from the topmost roof to the pavement Dark blood trickles,
forecasting the dire unavoidable evil. Forth with you, forth from
the shrine, and steep your soul in the sorrow!"

141. Hearing this the men who had been sent by the Athenians to consult the Oracle were very greatly distressed; and as they were despairing by reason of the evil which had been prophesied to them, Timon the son of Androbulos, a man of the Delphians in reputation equal to the first, counselled them to take a suppliant's bough and to approach the second time and consult the Oracle as suppliants. The Athenians did as he advised and said: "Lord, we pray thee utter to us some better oracle about our native land, having respect to these suppliant boughs which we have come to thee bearing; otherwise surely we will not depart away from the sanctuary, but will remain here where we are now, even until we bring our lives to an end." When they spoke these words, the prophetess gave them a second oracle as follows:

"Pallas cannot prevail to appease great Zeus in Olympos, Though she
with words very many and wiles close-woven entreat him. But I will
tell thee this more, and will clench it with steel adamantine: Then
when all else shall be taken, whatever the boundary of Kecrops
Holdeth within, and the dark ravines of divinest Kithairon, A
bulwark of wood at the last Zeus grants to the Trito-born goddess
Sole to remain unwasted, which thee and thy children shall profit.
Stay thou not there for the horsemen to come and the footmen
unnumbered; Stay thou not still for the host from the mainland to
come, but retire thee, Turning thy back to the foe, for yet thou
shalt face him hereafter. Salamis, thou the divine, thou shalt cause
sons of women to perish, Or when the grain is scattered or
when it is gathered together."

142. This seemed to them to be (as in truth it was) a milder utterance than the former one; therefore they had it written down and departed with it to Athens: and when the messengers after their return made report to the people, many various opinions were expressed by persons inquiring into the meaning of the oracle, and among them these, standing most in opposition to one another:—some of the elder men said they thought that the god had prophesied to them that the Acropolis should survive; for the Acropolis of the Athenians was in old time fenced with a thorn hedge; and they conjectured accordingly that this saying about the "bulwark of wood" referred to the fence: others on the contrary said that the god meant by this their ships, and they advised to leave all else and get ready these. Now they who said that the ships were the bulwark of wood were shaken in their interpretation by the two last verses which the prophetess uttered:

"Salamis, thou the divine, thou shalt cause sons of women to perish,
Or when the grain is scattered or when it is gathered together."

In reference to these verses the opinions of those who said that the ships were the bulwark of wood were disturbed; for the interpreters of oracles took these to mean that it was fated for them, having got ready for a sea-fight, to suffer defeat round about Salamis.

143. Now there was one man of the Athenians who had lately been coming forward to take a place among the first, whose name was Themistocles, called son of Neocles. This man said that the interpreters of oracles did not make right conjecture of the whole, and he spoke as follows, saying that if these words that had been uttered referred really to the Athenians, he did not think it would have been so mildly expressed in the oracle, but rather thus, "Salamis, thou the merciless," instead of "Salamis, thou the divine," at least if its settlers were destined to perish round about it: but in truth the oracle had been spoken by the god with reference to the enemy, if one understood it rightly, and not to the Athenians: therefore he counselled them to get ready to fight a battle by sea, for in this was their bulwark of wood. When Themistocles declared his opinion thus, the Athenians judged that this was to be preferred by them rather than the advice of the interpreters of oracles, who bade them not make ready for a sea-fight, nor in short raise their hands at all in opposition, but leave the land of Attica and settle in some other.

144. Another opinion too of Themistocles before this one proved the best at the right moment, when the Athenians, having got large sums of money in the public treasury, which had come in to them from the mines which are at Laureion, were intending to share it among themselves, taking each in turn the sum of ten drachmas. Then Themistocles persuaded the Athenians to give up this plan of division and to make for themselves with this money two hundred ships for the war, meaning by that the war with the Eginetans: for this war having arisen proved in fact the salvation of Hellas at that time, by compelling the Athenians to become a naval power. And the ships, not having been used for the purpose for which they had been made, thus proved of service at need to Hellas. These ships then, I say, the Athenians had already, having built them beforehand, and it was necessary in addition to these to construct others. They resolved then, when they took counsel after the oracle was given, to receive the Barbarian invading Hellas with their ships in full force, following the commands of the god, in combination with those of the Hellenes who were willing to join them.

145. These oracles had been given before to the Athenians: and when those Hellenes who had the better mind about Hellas came together to one place, and considered their affairs and interchanged assurances with one another, then deliberating together they thought it well first of all things to reconcile the enmities and bring to an end the wars which they had with one another. Now there were wars engaged between others also, and especially between the Athenians and the Eginetans. After this, being informed that Xerxes was with his army at Sardis, they determined to send spies to Asia to make observation of the power of the king; and moreover they resolved to send envoys to Argos to form an alliance against the Persian, and to send others to Sicily to Gelon the son of Deinomenes and also to Corcyra, to urge them to come to the assistance of Hellas, and others again to Crete; for they made it their aim that if possible the Hellenic race might unite in one, and that they might join all together and act towards the same end, since dangers were threatening all the Hellenes equally. Now the power of Gelon was said to be great, far greater than any other Hellenic power.

146. When they had thus resolved, they reconciled their enmities and then sent first three men as spies to Asia. These having come to Sardis and having got knowledge about

the king's army, were discovered, and after having been examined by the generals of the land-army were being led off to die. For these men, I say, death had been determined; but Xerxes, being informed of this, found fault with the decision of the generals and sent some of the spearmen of his guard, enjoining them, if they should find the spies yet alive, to bring them to his presence. So having found them yet surviving they brought them into the presence of the king; and upon that Xerxes, being informed for what purpose they had come, commanded the spearmen to lead them round and to show them the whole army both foot and horse, and when they should have had their fill of looking at these things, to let them go unhurt to whatsoever land they desired.

147. Such was the command which he gave, adding at the same time this saying, namely that if the spies had been put to death, the Hellenes would not have been informed beforehand of his power, how far beyond description it was; while on the other hand by putting to death three men they would not very greatly have damaged the enemy; but when these returned back to Hellas, he thought it likely that the Hellenes, hearing of his power, would deliver up their freedom to him themselves, before the expedition took place which was being set in motion; and thus there would be no need for them to have the labor of marching an army against them. This opinion of his is like his manner of thinking at other times; for when Xerxes was in Abydos, he saw vessels which carried corn from the Pontus sailing out through the Hellespont on their way to Egina and the Peloponnese. Those then who sat by his side, being informed that the ships belonged to the enemy, were prepared to capture them, and were looking to the king to see when he would give the word; but Xerxes asked about them whither the men were sailing, and they replied: "Master, to thy foes, conveying to them corn": he then made answer and said: "Are we not also sailing to the same place as these men, furnished with corn as well as with other things necessary? How then do these wrong us, since they are conveying provisions for our use?"

148. The spies then, having thus looked at everything and after that having been dismissed, returned back to Europe: and meanwhile those of the Hellenes who had sworn alliance against the Persian, after the sending forth of the spies proceeded to send envoys next to Argos. Now the Argives report that the matters concerning themselves took place as follows:—They were informed, they say, at the very first of the movement which was being set on foot by the Barbarian against Hellas; and having been informed of this and perceiving that the Hellenes would endeavor to get their alliance against the Persians, they had sent messengers to inquire of the god at Delphi, and to ask how they should act in order that it might be best for themselves: because lately there had been slain of them six thousand men by the Lacedemonians and by Cleomenes the son of Anaxandrides, and this in fact was the reason that they were sending to inquire: and when they inquired, the Pythian prophetess made answer to them as follows:

"Thou to thy neighbors a foe, by the gods immortal beloved,
Keep thou thy spear within bounds, and sit well-guarded behind it:
Guard well the head, and the head shall preserve the limbs and the body."

Thus, they say, the Pythian prophetess had replied to them before this; and afterwards when the messengers of the Hellenes came, as I said, to Argos, they entered the Council-chamber and spoke that which had been enjoined to them; and to that which was said the

Council replied that the Argives were ready to do as they were requested, on condition that they got peace made with the Lacedemonians for thirty years and that they had half the leadership of the whole confederacy: and yet by strict right (they said) the whole leadership fell to their share, but nevertheless it was sufficient for them to have half.

149. Thus they report that the Council made answer, although the oracle forbade them to make the alliance with the Hellenes; and they were anxious, they say, that a truce from hostilities for thirty years should be made, although they feared the oracle, in order, as they allege, that their sons might grow to manhood in these years; whereas if a truce did not exist, they had fear that, supposing another disaster should come upon them in fighting against the Persian in addition to that which had befallen them already, they might be for all future time subject to the Lacedemonians. To that which was spoken by the Council those of the envoys who were of Sparta replied, that as to the truce they would refer the matter to their public assembly, but as to the leadership they had themselves been commissioned to make reply, and did in fact say this, namely that they had two kings, while the Argives had one; and it was not possible to remove either of the two who were of Sparta from the leadership, but there was nothing to prevent the Argive king from having an equal vote with each of their two. Then, say the Argives, they could not endure the grasping selfishness of the Spartans, but chose to be ruled by the Barbarians rather than to yield at all to the Lacedemonians; and they gave notice to the envoys to depart out of the territory of the Argives before sunset, or, if not, they would be dealt with as enemies.

150. The Argives themselves report so much about these matters: but there is another story reported in Hellas to the effect that Xerxes sent a herald to Argos before he set forth to make an expedition against Hellas, and this herald, they say, when he had come, spoke as follows: "Men of Argos, king Xerxes says to you these things:—We hold that Perses, from whom we are descended, was the son of Perseus, the son of Danae, and was born of the daughter of Kepheus, Andromeda; and according to this it would seem that we are descended from you. It is not fitting then that we should go forth on an expedition against those from whom we trace our descent, nor that ye should set yourselves in opposition to us by rendering assistance to others; but it is fitting that ye keep still and remain by yourselves: for if things happen according to my mind, I shall not esteem any people to be of greater consequence than you." Having heard this the Argives, it is said, considered it a great matter; and therefore at first they made no offer of help nor did they ask for any share; but afterwards, when the Hellenes tried to get them on their side, then, since they knew well that the Lacedemonians would not give them a share in the command, they asked for this merely in order that they might have a pretext for remaining still.

151. Also some of the Hellenes report that the following event, in agreement with this account, came to pass many years after these things:—there happened, they say, to be in Susa the city of Memnon envoys of the Athenians come about some other matter, namely Callias the son of Hipponicos and the others who went up with him; and the Argives at that very time had also sent envoys to Susa, and these asked Artoxerxes the son of Xerxes, whether the friendship which they had formed with Xerxes still remained unbroken, if they themselves desired to maintain it, or whether they were esteemed by him to be enemies; and king Artoxerxes said that it most certainly remained unbroken, and that there was no city which he considered to be more his friend than Argos.

152. Now whether Xerxes did indeed send a herald to Argos saying that which has

been reported, and whether envoys of the Argives who had gone up to Susa inquired of Artoxerxes concerning friendship, I am not able to say for certain; nor do I declare any opinion about the matters in question other than that which the Argives themselves report: but I know this much, that if all the nations of men should bring together into one place the evils which they have suffered themselves, desiring to make exchange with their neighbors, each people of them, when they had examined closely the evils suffered by their fellows, would gladly carry away back with them those which they had brought. Thus it is not the Argives who have acted most basely of all. I however am bound to report that which is reported, though I am not bound altogether to believe it; and let this saying be considered to hold good as regards every narrative in the history: for I must add that this also is reported, namely that the Argives were actually those who invited the Persian to invade Hellas, because their war with the Lacedemonians had had an evil issue, being willing to suffer anything whatever rather than the trouble which was then upon them.

153. That which concerns the Argives has now been said: and meanwhile envoys had come to Sicily from the allies, to confer with Gelon, among whom was also Syagros from the Lacedemonians. Now the ancestor of this Gelon, he who was at Gela as a settler, was a native of the island of Telos, which lies off Triopion; and when Gela was founded by the Lindians of Rhodes and by Antiphemos, he was not left behind. Then in course of time his descendants became and continued to be priests of the mysteries of the Earth goddesses, an office which was acquired by Telines one of their ancestors in the following manner:— certain of the men of Gela, being worsted in a party struggle, had fled to Mactorion, the city which stands above Gela: these men Telines brought back to Gela from exile with no force of men but only with the sacred rites of these goddesses; but from whom he received them, or whether he obtained them for himself, this I am not able to say; trusting in these however, he brought the men back from exile, on the condition that his descendants should be priests of the mysteries of the goddesses. To me it has caused wonder also that Telines should have been able to perform so great a deed, considering that which I am told; for such deeds, I think, are not apt to proceed from every man, but from one who has a brave spirit and manly vigor, whereas Telines is said by the dwellers in Sicily to have been on the contrary a man of effeminate character and rather poor spirit.

154. He then had thus obtained the privilege of which I speak: and when Cleander the son of Pantares brought his life to an end, having been despot of Gela for seven years and being killed at last by Sabyllos a man of Gela, then Hippocrates succeeded to the monarchy, who was brother of Cleander. And while Hippocrates was despot, Gelon, who was a descendant of Telines the priest of the mysteries, was spearman of the guard to Hippocrates with many others and among them Ainesidemos the son of Pataicos. Then after no long time he was appointed by reason of valor to be commander of the whole cavalry; for when Hippocrates besieged successively the cities of Callipolis, Naxos, Zancle, Leontini, and also Syracuse and many towns of the Barbarians, in these wars Gelon showed himself a most brilliant warrior; and of the cities which I just now mentioned, not one except Syracuse escaped being reduced to subjection by Hippocrates: the Syracusans however, after they had been defeated in battle at the river Eloros, were rescued by the Corinthians and Corcyreans; these rescued them and brought the quarrel to a settlement on this condition, namely that the Syracusans should deliver up Camarina to Hippocrates. Now Camarina used in ancient time to belong to the men of Syracuse.

155. Then when it was the fate of Hippocrates also, after having been despot for the same number of years as his brother Cleander, to be killed at the city of Hybla, whither he had gone on an expedition against the Sikelians, then Gelon made a pretense of helping the sons of Hippocrates, Eucleides and Cleander, when the citizens were no longer willing to submit; but actually, when he had been victorious in a battle over the men of Gela, he robbed the sons of Hippocrates of the power and was ruler himself. After this stroke of fortune Gelon restored those of the Syracusans who were called "land-holders," after they had been driven into exile by the common people and by their own slaves, who were called Kyllyrians, these, I say, he restored from the city of Casmene to Syracuse, and so got possession of this last city also, for the common people of Syracuse, when Gelon came against them, delivered up to him their city and themselves.

156. So after he had received Syracuse into his power, he made less account of Gela, of which he was ruler also in addition, and he gave it in charge to Hieron his brother, while he proceeded to strengthen Syracuse. So forthwith that city rose and shot up to prosperity; for in the first place he brought all those of Camarina to Syracuse and made them citizens, and razed to the ground the city of Camarina; then secondly he did the same to more than half of the men of Gela, as he had done to those of Camarina: and as regards the Megarians of Sicily, when they were besieged and had surrendered by capitulation, the well-to-do men of them, though they had stirred up war with him and expected to be put to death for this reason, he brought to Syracuse and made them citizens, but the common people of the Megarians, who had no share in the guilt of this war and did not expect that they would suffer any evil, these also he brought to Syracuse and sold them as slaves to be carried away from Sicily: and the same thing he did moreover to the men of Euboia in Sicily, making a distinction between them: and he dealt thus with these two cities because he thought that a body of commons was a most unpleasant element in the State.

157. In the manner then which has been described Gelon had become a powerful despot; and at this time when the envoys of the Hellenes had arrived at Syracuse, they came to speech with him and said as follows: "The Lacedemonians and their allies sent us to get thee to be on our side against the Barbarian; for we suppose that thou art certainly informed of him who is about to invade Hellas, namely that a Persian is designing to bridge over the Hellespont, and to make an expedition against Hellas, leading against us out of Asia all the armies of the East, under color of marching upon Athens, but in fact meaning to bring all Hellas to subjection under him. Do thou therefore, seeing that thou hast attained to a great power and hast no small portion of Hellas for thy share, being the ruler of Sicily, come to the assistance of those who are endeavoring to free Hellas, and join in making her free; for if all Hellas be gathered together in one, it forms a great body, and we are made a match in fight for those who are coming against us; but if some of us go over to the enemy and others are not willing to help, and the sound portion of Hellas is consequently small, there is at once in this a danger that all Hellas may fall to ruin. For do not thou hope that if the Persian shall overcome us in battle he will not come to thee, but guard thyself against this beforehand; for in coming to our assistance thou art helping thyself; and the matter which is wisely planned has for the most part a good issue afterwards."

158. The envoys spoke thus; and Gelon was very vehement with them, speaking to them as follows: "Hellenes, a selfish speech is this, with which ye have ventured to come and invite me to be your ally against the Barbarian; whereas ye yourselves, when I in

former time requested of you to join with me in fighting against an army of Barbarians, contention having arisen between me and the Carthaginians, and when I charged you to exact vengeance of the men of Egesta for the death of Dorieos the son of Anaxandrides, while at the same time I offered to help in setting free the trading-places, from which great advantages and gains have been reaped by you,—ye, I say, then neither for my own sake came to my assistance, nor in order to exact vengeance for the death of Dorieos; and, so far as ye are concerned, all these parts are even now under the rule of Barbarians. But since it turned out well for us and came to a better issue, now that the war has come round and reached you, there has at last arisen in your minds a recollection of Gelon. However, though I have met with contempt at your hands, I will not act like you; but I am prepared to come to your assistance, supplying two hundred triremes and twenty thousand hoplites, with two thousand horsemen, two thousand bowmen, two thousand slingers and two thousand light-armed men to run beside the horsemen; and moreover I will undertake to supply corn for the whole army of the Hellenes, until we have finished the war. These things I engage to supply on this condition, namely that I shall be commander and leader of the Hellenes against the Barbarian; but on any other condition I will neither come myself nor will I send others."

159. Hearing this Syagros could not contain himself but spoke these words: "Deeply, I trow, would Agamemnon son of Pelops lament, if he heard that the Spartans had had the leadership taken away from them by Gelon and by the Syracusans. Nay, but make thou no further mention of this condition, namely that we should deliver the leadership to thee; but if thou art desirous to come to the assistance of Hellas, know that thou wilt be under the command of the Lacedemonians; and if thou dost indeed claim not to be under command, come not thou to our help at all."

160. To this Gelon, seeing that the speech of Syagros was adverse, set forth to them his last proposal thus: "Stranger from Sparta, reproaches sinking into the heart of a man are wont to rouse his spirit in anger against them; thou however, though thou hast uttered insults against me in thy speech, wilt not bring me to show myself unseemly in my reply. But whereas ye so strongly lay claim to the leadership, it were fitting that I should lay claim to it more than ye, seeing that I am the leader of an army many times as large and of ships many more. Since however this condition is so distasteful to you, we will recede somewhat from our former proposal. Suppose that ye should be leaders of the land-army and I of the fleet; or if it pleases you to lead the sea-forces, I am willing to be leader of those on land; and either ye must be contented with these terms or go away without the alliance which I have to give."

161. Gelon, I say, made these offers, and the envoy of the Athenians, answering before that of the Lacedemonians, replied to him as follows: "O king of the Syracusans, it was not of a leader that Hellas was in want when it sent us to thee, but of an army. Thou however dost not set before us the hope that thou wilt send an army, except thou have the leadership of Hellas; and thou art striving how thou mayest become commander of the armies of Hellas. So long then as it was thy demand to be leader of the whole army of the Hellenes, it was sufficient for us Athenians to keep silence, knowing that the Lacedemonian would be able to make defense even for us both; but now, since being repulsed from the demand for the whole thou art requesting to be commander of the naval force, we tell that thus it is:—not even if the Lacedemonian shall permit thee to be commander of it, will we permit thee; for this at least is our own, if the Lacedemonians do not them-

selves desire to have it. With these, if they desire to be the leaders, we do not contend; but none others beside ourselves shall we permit to be in command of the ships: for then to no purpose should we be possessors of a sea-force larger than any other which belongs to the Hellenes, if, being Athenians, we should yield the leadership to Syracusans, we who boast of a race which is the most ancient of all and who are of all the Hellenes the only people who have not changed from one land to another; to whom also belonged a man whom Homer the Epic poet said was the best of all who came to Ilion in drawing up an army and setting it in array. Thus we are not justly to be reproached if we say these things."

162. To this Gelon made answer thus: "Stranger of Athens, it would seem that ye have the commanders, but that ye will not have the men to be commanded. Since then ye will not at all give way, but desire to have the whole, it were well that ye should depart home as quickly as possible and report to the Hellenes that the spring has been taken out of their year." Now this is the meaning of the saying:—evidently the spring is the noblest part of the year; and so he meant to say that his army was the noblest part of the army of the Hellenes: for Hellas therefore, deprived of his alliance, it was, he said, as if the spring had been taken out of the year.

163. The envoys of the Hellenes, having thus had conference with Gelon, sailed away; and Gelon upon this, fearing on the one hand about the Hellenes, lest they should not be able to overcome the Barbarian, and on the other hand considering it monstrous and not to be endured that he should come to Peloponnesus and be under the command of the Lacedemonians, seeing that he was despot of Sicily, gave up the thought of this way and followed another: for so soon as he was informed that the Persian had crossed over the Hellespont, he sent Cadmos the son of Skythes, a man of Cos, with three fifty-oared galleys to Delphi, bearing large sums of money and friendly proposals, to wait there and see how the battle would fall out: and if the Barbarian should be victorious, he was to give him the money and also to offer him earth and water from those over whom Gelon had rule; but if the Hellenes should be victorious, he was bidden to bring it back.

164. Now this Cadmos before these events, having received from his father in a prosperous state the government of the people of Cos, had voluntarily and with no danger threatening, but moved merely by uprightness of nature, placed the government in the hands of the people of Cos and had departed to Sicily, where he took from the Samians and newly colonized the city of Zancle, which had changed its name to Messene. This same Cadmos, having come thither in such manner as I have said, Gelon was now sending, having selected him on account of the integrity which in other matters he had himself found to be in him; and this man, in addition to the other upright acts which had been done by him, left also this to be remembered, which was not the least of them: for having got into his hands that great sum of money which Gelon entrusted to his charge, though he might have taken possession of it himself he did not choose to do so; but when the Hellenes had got the better in the sea-fight and Xerxes had marched away and departed, he also returned to Sicily bringing back with him the whole sum of money.

165. The story which here follows is also reported by those who dwell in Sicily, namely that, even though he was to be under the command of the Lacedemonians, Gelon would have come to the assistance of the Hellenes, but that Terillos, the son of Crinippos and despot of Himera, having been driven out of Himera by Theron the son of Ainesidemos the ruler of the Agrigentines, was just at this very time bringing in an army of Phoenicians, Libyans, Iberians, Ligurians, Elisycans, Sardinians and Corsicans, to the number of

thirty myriads, with Amilcas the son of Annon king of the Carthaginians as their commander, whom Terillos had persuaded partly by reason of his own guest-friendship, and especially by the zealous assistance of Anaxilaos the son of Cretines, who was despot of Rhegion, and who to help his father-in-law endeavored to bring in Amilcas to Sicily, and had given him his sons as hostages; for Anaxilaos was married to the daughter of Terillos, whose name was Kydippe. Thus it was, they say, that Gelon was not able to come to the assistance of the Hellenes, and sent therefore the money to Delphi.

166. In addition to this they report also that, as it happened, Gelon and Theron were victorious over Amilcas the Carthaginian on the very same day when the Hellenes were victorious at Salamis over the Persian. And this Amilcas, who was a Carthaginian on the father's side but on the mother's Syracusan, and who had become king of the Carthaginians by merit, when the engagement took place and he was being worsted in the battle, disappeared, as I am informed; for neither alive nor dead did he appear again anywhere upon the earth, though Gelon used all diligence in the search for him.

167. Moreover there is also this story reported by the Carthaginians themselves, who therein relate that which is probable in itself, namely that while the Barbarians fought with the Hellenes in Sicily from the early morning till late in the afternoon (for to such a length the combat is said to have been protracted), during this time Amilcas was remaining in the camp and was making sacrifices to get good omens of success, offering whole bodies of victims upon a great pyre: and when he saw that there was a rout of his own army, he being then, as it chanced, in the act of pouring a libation over the victims, threw himself into the fire, and thus he was burnt up and disappeared. Amilcas then having disappeared, whether it was in such a manner as this, as it is reported by the Phoenicians, or in some other way, the Carthaginians both offer sacrifices to him now, and also they made memorials of him then in all the cities of their colonies, and the greatest in Carthage itself.

168. So far of the affairs of Sicily: and as for the Corcyreans, they made answer to the envoys as follows, afterwards acting as I shall tell: for the same men who had gone to Sicily endeavored also to obtain the help of these, saying the same things which they said to Gelon; and the Corcyreans at the time engaged to send a force and to help in the defense, declaring that they must not permit Hellas to be ruined without an effort on their part, for if it should suffer disaster, they would be reduced to subjection from the very first day; but they must give assistance so far as lay in their power. Thus speciously they made reply; but when the time came to send help, they manned sixty ships, having other intentions in their minds, and after making much difficulty they put out to sea and reached Peloponnese; and then near Pylos and Tainaron in the land of the Lacedemonians they kept their ships at anchor, waiting, as Gelon did, to see how the war would turn out: for they did not expect that the Hellenes would overcome, but thought that the Persian would gain the victory over them with ease and be ruler of all Hellas. Accordingly they were acting of set purpose, in order that they might be able to say to the Persian some such words as these: "O king, when the Hellenes endeavored to obtain our help for this war, we, who have a power which is not the smallest of all, and could have supplied a contingent of ships in number not the smallest, but after the Athenians the largest, did not choose to oppose thee or to do anything which was not to thy mind." By speaking thus they hoped that they would obtain some advantage over the rest, and so it would have happened, as I am of opinion: while they had for the Hellenes an excuse ready-made, that

namely of which they actually made use: for when the Hellenes reproached them because they did not come to help, they said that they had manned sixty triremes, but had not been able to get past Malea owing to the Etesian Winds; therefore it was that they had not come to Salamis, nor was it by any want of courage on their part that they had been left of the sea-fight.

169. These then evaded the request of the Hellenes thus: but the Cretans, when those of the Hellenes who had been appointed to deal with these endeavored to obtain their help, did thus, that is to say, they joined together and sent men to inquire of the god at Delphi whether it would be better for them if they gave assistance to Hellas: and the Pythian prophetess answered: "Ye fools, do ye think those woes too few, which Minos sent upon you in his wrath, because of the assistance that ye gave to Menelaos? seeing that, whereas they did not join with you in taking vengeance for his death in Camicos, ye nevertheless joined with them in taking vengeance for the woman who by a Barbarian was carried off from Sparta." When the Cretans heard this answer reported, they abstained from the giving of assistance.

170. For the story goes that Minos, having come to Sicania, which is now called Sicily, in search of Daidalos, died there by a violent death; and after a time the Cretans, urged thereto by a god, all except the men of Polichne and Praisos, came with a great armament to Sicania and besieged for seven years the city of Camicos, which in my time was occupied by the Agrigentines; and at last not being able either to capture it or to remain before it, because they were hard pressed by famine, they departed and went away. And when, as they sailed, they came to be off the coast of Iapygia, a great storm seized them and cast them away upon the coast; and their vessels being dashed to pieces, they, since they saw no longer any way of coming to Crete, founded there the city of Hyria; and there they stayed and were changed so that they became instead of Cretans, Messapians of Iapygia, and instead of islanders, dwellers on the mainland: then from the city of Hyria they founded those other settlements which the Tarentines long afterwards endeavored to destroy and suffer great disaster in that enterprise, so that this in fact proved to be the greatest slaughter of Hellenes that is known to us, and not only of the Tarentines themselves but of those citizens of Rhegion who were compelled by Mikythos the son of Choiros to go to the assistance of the Tarentines, and of whom there were slain in this manner three thousand men: of the Tarentines themselves however, who were slain there, there was no numbering made. This Mikythos, who was a servant of Anaxilaos, had been left by him in charge of Rhegion; and he it was who after being driven out of Rhegion took up his abode at Tegea of the Arcadians and dedicated those many statues at Olympia.

171. This of the men of Rhegion and of the Tarentines has been an episode in my narrative: in Crete however, as the men of Praisos report, after it had been thus stripped of inhabitants, settlements were made by various nations, but especially by Hellenes; and in the next generation but one after the death of Minos came the Trojan war, in which the Cretans proved not the most contemptible of those who came to assist Menelaos. Then after this, when they had returned home from Troy, famine and pestilence came upon both the men and their cattle, until at last Crete was stripped of its inhabitants for the second time, and a third population of Cretans now occupy it together with those which were left of the former inhabitants. The Pythian prophetess, I say, by calling these things to their minds stopped them from giving assistance to the Hellenes, though they desired to do so.

172. As for the Thessalians, they at first had taken the side of the Persians against their

will, and they gave proof that they were not pleased by that which the Aleuadai were designing; for so soon as they heard that the Persian was about to cross over into Europe, they sent envoys to the Isthmus: now at the Isthmus were assembled representatives of Hellas chosen by the cities which had the better mind about Hellas: having come then to these, the envoys of the Thessalians said: "Hellenes, ye must guard the pass by Olympos, in order that both Thessaly and the whole of Hellas may be sheltered from the war. We are prepared to join with you in guarding it, but ye must send a large force as well as we; for if ye shall not send, be assured that we shall make agreement with the Persian; since it is not right that we, standing as outposts so far in advance of the rest of Hellas, should perish alone in your defense: and not being willing to come to our help, ye cannot apply to us any force to compel inability; but we shall endeavor to devise some means of safety for ourselves."

173. Thus spoke the Thessalians; and the Hellenes upon this resolved to send to Thessaly by sea an army of men on foot to guard the pass: and when the army was assembled it set sail through Euripos, and having come to Alos in the Achaian land, it disembarked there and marched into Thessaly leaving the ships behind at Alos, and arrived at Tempe, the pass which leads from lower Macedonia into Thessaly by the river Peneios, going between the mountains of Olympos and Ossa. There the Hellenes encamped, being assembled to the number of about ten thousand hoplites, and to them was added the cavalry of the Thessalians; and the commander of the Lacedemonians was Euainetos the son of Carenos, who had been chosen from the polemarchs, not being of the royal house, and of the Athenians Themistocles the son of Neocles. They remained however but few days here, for envoys came from Alexander the son of Amyntas the Macedonian, who advised them to depart thence and not to remain in the pass and be trodden under foot by the invading host, signifying to them at the same time both the great numbers of the army and the ships which they had. When these gave them this counsel, they followed the advice, for they thought that the counsel was good, and the Macedonian was evidently well-disposed towards them. Also, as I think, it was fear that persuaded them to it, when they were informed that there was another pass besides this to the Thessalian land by upper Macedonia through the Perraibians and by the city of Gonnos, the way by which the army of Xerxes did in fact make its entrance. So the Hellenes went down to their ships again and made their way back to the Isthmus.

174. Such was the expedition to Thessaly, which took place when the king was about to cross over from Asia to Europe and was already at Abydos. So the Thessalians, being stripped of allies, upon this took the side of the Medes with a good will and no longer half-heartedly, so that in the course of events they proved very serviceable to the king.

175. When the Hellenes had returned to the Isthmus, they deliberated, having regard to that which had been said by Alexander, where and in what regions they should set the war on foot: and the opinion which prevailed was to guard the pass at Thermopylai; for it was seen to be narrower than that leading into Thessaly, and at the same time it was single, and nearer also to their own land; and as for the path by means of which were taken those of the Hellenes who were taken by the enemy at Thermopylai, they did not even know of its existence until they were informed by the people of Trachis after they had come to Thermopylai. This pass then they resolved to guard, and not permit the Barbarian to go by into Hellas; and they resolved that the fleet should sail to Artemision in the territory of Histiaia: for these points are near to one another, so that each division of

their forces could have information of what was happening to the other. And the places are so situated as I shall describe.

176. As to Artemision first, coming out of the Thracian Sea the space is contracted from great width to that narrow channel which lies between the island of Skiathos and the mainland of Magnesia; and after the strait there follows at once in Euboea the sea-beach called Artemision, upon which there is a temple of Artemis. Then secondly the passage into Hellas by Trechis is, where it is narrowest, but fifty feet wide: it is not here however that the narrowest part of this whole region lies, but in front of Thermopylai and also behind it, consisting of a single wheel-track only both by Alpenoi, which lies behind Thermopylai and again by the river Phoinix near the town of Anthela there is no space but a single wheel-track only: and on the West of Thermopylai there is a mountain which is impassable and precipitous, rising up to a great height and extending towards the range of Oite, while on the East of the road the sea with swampy pools succeeds at once. In this passage there are hot springs, which the natives of the place call the "Pots," and an altar of Heracles is set up near them. Moreover a wall had once been built at this pass, and in old times there was a gate set in it; which wall was built by the Phokians, who were struck with fear because the Thessalians had come from the land of the Thesprotians to settle in the Aiolian land, the same which they now possess. Since then the Thessalians, as they supposed, were attempting to subdue them, the Phokians guarded themselves against this beforehand; and at that time they let the water of the hot springs run over the passage, that the place might be converted into a ravine, and devised every means that the Thessalians might not make invasion of their land. Now the ancient wall had been built long before, and the greater part of it was by that time in ruins from lapse of time; the Hellenes however resolved to set it up again, and at this spot to repel the Barbarian from Hellas: and very near the road there is a village called Alpenoi, from which the Hellenes counted on getting supplies.

177. These places then the Hellenes perceived to be such as their purpose required; for they considered everything beforehand and calculated that the Barbarians would not be able to take advantage either of superior numbers or of cavalry, and therefore they resolved here to receive the invader of Hellas: and when they were informed that the Persian was in Pieria, they broke up from the Isthmus and set forth for the campaign, some going to Thermopylai by land, and others making for Artemision by sea.

178. The Hellenes, I say, were coming to the rescue with speed, having been appointed to their several places: and meanwhile the men of Delphi consulted the Oracle of the god on behalf of themselves and on behalf of Hellas, being struck with dread; and a reply was given them that they should pray to the Winds, for these would be powerful helpers of Hellas in fight. So the Delphians, having accepted the oracle, first reported the answer which had been given them to those of the Hellenes who desired to be free; and having reported this to them at a time when they were in great dread of the Barbarian, they laid up for themselves an immortal store of gratitude: then after this the men of Delphi established an altar for the Winds in Thuia, where is the sacred enclosure of Thuia the daughter of Kephisos, after whom moreover this place has its name; and also they approached them with sacrifices.

179. The Delphians then according to the oracle even to this day make propitiary offerings to the Winds: and meanwhile the fleet of Xerxes setting forth from the city of Therma had passed over with ten of its ships, which were those that sailed best, straight towards

Skiathos, where three Hellenic ships, a Troizenian, an Eginetan and an Athenian, were keeping watch in advance. When the crews of these caught sight of the ships of the Barbarians, they set off to make their escape:

180, and the ship of Troizen, of which Prexinos was in command, was pursued and captured at once by the Barbarians; who upon that took the man who was most distinguished by beauty among the fighting-men on board of her, and cut his throat at the prow of the ship, making a good omen for themselves of the first of the Hellenes whom they had captured who was pre-eminent for beauty. The name of this man who was sacrificed was Leon, and perhaps he had also his name to thank in some degree for what befell him.

181. The ship of Egina however, of which Asonides was master, even gave them some trouble to capture it, seeing that Pytheas the son of Ischenoös served as a fighting-man on board of her, who proved himself a most valiant man on this day; for when the ship was being taken, he held out fighting until he was hacked all to pieces: and as when he had fallen he did not die, but had still breath in him, the Persians who served as fighting-men on board the ships, because of his valor used all diligence to save his life, both applying unguents of myrrh to heal his wounds and also wrapping him up in bands of the finest linen; and when they came back to their own main body, they showed him to all the army, making a marvel of him and giving him good treatment; but the rest whom they had taken in this ship they treated as slaves.

182. Two of the three ships, I say, were captured thus; but the third, of which Phormos an Athenian was master, ran ashore in its flight at the mouth of the river Peneios; and the Barbarians got possession of the vessel but not of the crew; for so soon as the Athenians had run the ship ashore, they leapt out of her, and passing through Thessaly made their way to Athens.

183. Of these things the Hellenes who were stationed at Artemision were informed by fire-signals from Skiathos; and being informed of them and being struck with fear, they removed their place of anchorage from Atermision to Chalkis, intending to guard the Euripos, but leaving at the same time watchers by day on the heights of Euboea. Of the ten ships of the Barbarians three sailed up to the reef called Myrmex, which lies between Skiathos and Magnesia; and when the Barbarians had there erected a stone pillar, which for that purpose they brought to the reef, they set forth with their main body from Therma, the difficulties of the passage having now been cleared away, and sailed thither with all their ships, having let eleven days go by since the king set forth on his march from Therma. Now of this reef lying exactly in the middle of the fairway they were informed by Pammon of Skyros. Sailing then throughout the day the Barbarians accomplished the voyage to Sepias in Magnesia and to the sea-beach which is between the city of Casthanaia and the headland of Sepias.

184. So far as this place and so far as Thermopylai the army was exempt from calamity; and the number was then still, as I find by computation, this:—Of the ships which came from Asia, which were one thousand two hundred and seven, the original number of the crews supplied by the several nations I find to have been twenty-four myriads and also in addition to them one thousand four hundred, if one reckons at the rate of two hundred men to each ship: and on board of each of these ships there served as fighting-men, besides the fighting-men belonging to its own nation in each case, thirty men who were Persians, Medes, or Sacans; and this amounts to three myriads six thousand two hundred and ten in addition to the others. I will add also to this and to the former number the

crews of the fifty-oared galleys, assuming that there were eighty men, more or less, in each one. Of these vessels there were gathered together, as was before said, three thousand: it would follow therefore that there were in them four-and-twenty myriads of men. This was the naval force which came from Asia, amounting in all to fifty-one myriads and also seven thousand six hundred and ten in addition. Then of the footmen there had been found to be a hundred and seventy myriads, and of the horsemen eight myriads: and I will add also to these the Arabian camel-drivers and the Libyan drivers of chariots, assuming them to amount to twenty thousand men. The result is then that the number of the ships' crews combined with that of the land-army amounts to two hundred and thirty-one myriads and also in addition seven thousand six hundred and ten. This is the statement of the Army which was brought up out of Asia itself, without counting the attendants which accompanied it or the corn-transports and the men who sailed in these.

185. There is still to be reckoned, in addition to all this which has been summed up, the force which was being led from Europe; and of this we must give a probable estimate. The Hellenes of Thrace and of the islands which lie off the coast of Thrace supplied a hundred and twenty ships; from which ships there results a sum of twenty-four thousand men: and as regards the land-force which was supplied by the Thracians, Paionians, Eordians, Bottiaians, the race which inhabits Chalkidike, the Brygians, Pierians, Macedonians, Perraibians, Enianians, Dolopians, Magnesians, Achaians, and all those who dwell in the coast-region of Thrace, of these various nations I estimate that there were thirty myriads. These myriads then added to those from Asia make a total sum of two hundred and sixty-four myriads of fighting men and in addition to these sixteen hundred and ten.

186. Such being the number of this body of fighting-men, the attendants who went with these and the men who were in the small vessels which carried corn, and again in the other vessels which sailed with the army, these I suppose were not less in number but more than the fighting men. I assume them to be equal in number with these, and neither at all more nor less; and so, being supposed equal in number with the fighting body, they make up the same number of myriads as they. Thus five hundred and twenty-eight myriads three thousand two hundred and twenty was the number of men whom Xerxes son of Dareios led as far as Sepias and Thermopylai.

187. This is the number of the whole army of Xerxes; but of the women who made bread for it, and of the concubines and eunuchs no man can state any exact number, nor again of the draught-animals and other beasts of burden or of the Indian hounds, which accompanied it, could anyone state the number by reason of their multitude: so that it does not occur to me to wonder that the streams of some rivers should have failed them, but I wonder rather how the provisions were sufficient to feed so many myriads; for I find on computation that if each man received a quart of wheat every day and nothing more, there would be expended every day eleven myriads of *medimnoi* and three hundred and forty *medimnoi* besides: and here I am not reckoning anything for the women, eunuchs, baggage-animals, or dogs. Of all these men, amounting to so many myriads, not one was for beauty and stature more worthy than Xerxes himself to possess this power.

188. The fleet, I say, set forth and sailed: and when it had put in to land in the region of Magnesia at the beach which is between the city of Casthanaia and the headland of Sepias, the first of the ships which came lay moored by the land and the others rode at anchor behind them; for, as the beach was not large in extent, they lay at anchor with prows projecting towards the sea in an order which was eight ships deep. For that night they lay

thus; but at early dawn, after clear sky and windless calm, the sea began to be violently agitated and a great storm fell upon them with a strong East Wind, that wind which they who dwell about those parts call Hellespontias. Now as many of them as perceived that the wind was rising and who were so moored that it was possible for them to do so, drew up their ships on land before the storm came, and both they and their ships escaped; but as for those of the ships which it caught out at sea, some it cast away at the place called Ipnoi in Pelion and others on the beach, while some were wrecked on the headland of Sepias itself, others at the city of Meliboia, and others were thrown up on shore at Casthanaia: and the violence of the storm could not be resisted.

189. There is a story reported that the Athenians had called upon Boreas to aid them, by suggestion of an oracle, because there had come to them another utterance of the god bidding them call upon their brother by marriage to be their helper. Now according to the story of the Hellenes Boreas has a wife who is of Attica, Oreithuia the daughter of Erechththeus. By reason of this affinity, I say, the Athenians, according to the tale which has gone abroad, conjectured that their "brother by marriage" was Boreas, and when they perceived the wind rising, as they lay with their ships at Chalkis in Euboea, or even before that, they offered sacrifices and called upon Boreas and Oreithuia to assist them and to destroy the ships of the Barbarians, as they had done before round about mount Athos. Whether it was for this reason that the wind Boreas fell upon the Barbarians while they lay at anchor, I am not able to say; but however that may be, the Athenians report that Boreas had come to their help in former times, and that at this time he accomplished those things for them of which I speak; and when they had returned home they set up a temple dedicated to Boreas by the river Ilissos.

190. In this disaster the number of the ships which were lost was not less than four hundred, according to the report of those who state the number which is lowest, with men innumerable and an immense quantity of valuable things; insomuch that to Ameinocles the son of Cretines, a Magnesian who held lands about Sepias, this shipwreck proved very gainful; for he picked up many cups of gold which were thrown up afterwards on the shore, and many also of silver, and found treasure-chests which had belonged to the Persians, and made acquisition of other things of gold more than can be described. This man however, though he became very wealthy by the things which he found, yet in other respects was not fortunate; for he too suffered misfortune, being troubled by the slaying of a child.

191. Of the corn-transports and other vessels which perished there was no numbering made; and so great was the loss that the commanders of the fleet, being struck with fear lest the Thessalians should attack them now that they had been brought into an evil plight, threw round their camp a lofty palisade built of the fragments of wreck. For the storm continued during three days; but at last the Magians, making sacrifice of victims and singing incantations to appease the Wind by enchantments, and in addition to this, offering to Thetis and the Nereïds, caused it to cease on the fourth day, or else for some other reason it abated of its own will. Now they offered sacrifice to Thetis, being informed by the Ionians of the story that she was carried off from the place by Peleus, and that the whole headland of Sepias belonged to her and to the other Nereïds.

192. The storm then had ceased on the fourth day; and meanwhile the day-watchers had run down from the heights of Euboea on the day after the first storm began, and were keeping the Hellenes informed of all that had happened as regards the shipwreck. They

then, being informed of it, prayed first to Poseidon the Savior and poured libations, and then they hastened to go back to Artemision, expecting that there would be but a very few ships of the enemy left to come against them.

193. They, I say, came for the second time and lay with their ships about Artemision: and from that time even to this they preserve the use of the surname "Savior" for Poseidon. Meanwhile the Barbarians, when the wind had ceased and the swell of the sea had calmed down, drew their ships into the sea and sailed on along the shore of the mainland, and having rounded the extremity of Magnesia they sailed straight into the gulf which leads towards Pagasai. In this gulf of Magnesia there is a place where it is said that Heracles was left behind by Jason and his comrades, having been sent from the Argo to fetch water, at the time when they were sailing for the fleece to Aia in the land of Colchis: for from that place they designed, when they had taken in water, to loose their ship into the open sea; and from this the place has come to have the name Aphetai. Here then the fleet of Xerxes took up its moorings.

194. Now it chanced that fifteen of these ships put out to sea a good deal later than the rest, and they happened to catch sight of the ships of the Hellenes at Artemision. These ships the Barbarians supposed to be their own, and they sailed thither accordingly and fell among the enemy. Of these the commander was Sandokes the son of Thamasios, the governor of Kyme in Aiolia, whom before this time king Dareios had taken and crucified (he being one of the Royal Judges) for this reason, namely that Sandokes had pronounced judgment unjustly for money. So then after he was hung up, Dareios reckoned and found that more good services had been done by him to the royal house than were equal to his offences; and having found this, and perceived that he had himself acted with more haste than wisdom, he let him go. Thus he escaped from king Dareios, and did not perish but survived; now, however, when he sailed in toward the Hellenes, he was destined not to escape the second time; for when the Hellenes saw them sailing up, perceiving the mistake which was being made they put out against them and captured them without difficulty.

195. Sailing in one of these ships Aridolis was captured, the despot of Alabanda in Caria, and in another the Paphian commander Penthylos son of Demonoös, who brought twelve ships from Paphos, but had lost eleven of them in the storm which had come on by Sepias, and now was captured sailing in towards Artemision with the one which had escaped. These men the Hellenes sent away in bonds to the Isthmus of the Corinthians, after having inquired of them that which they desired to learn of the army of Xerxes.

196. The fleet of the Barbarians then, except the fifteen ships of which I said that Sandokes was in command, had arrived at Aphetai; and Xerxes meanwhile with the land-army, having marched through Thessalia and Achaia, had already entered the land of the Malians two days before, after having held in Thessaly a contest for his own horses, making trial also of the Thessalian cavalry, because he was informed that it was the best of all among the Hellenes; and in this trial the horses of Hellas were far surpassed by the others. Now of the rivers in Thessalia the Onochonos alone failed to suffice by its stream for the drinking of the army; but of the rivers which flow in Achaia even that which is the largest of them, namely Epidanos, even this, I say, held out but barely.

197. When Xerxes had reached Alos of Achaia, the guides who gave him information of the way, wishing to inform him fully of everything, reported to him a legend of the place, the things, namely, which have to do with the temple of Zeus Laphystios; how

Athamas the son of Aiolos contrived death for Phrixos, having taken counsel with Ino, and after this how by command of an oracle the Achaians propose to his descendants the following tasks to be performed:—whosoever is the eldest of this race, on him they lay an injunction that he is forbidden to enter the City Hall, and they themselves keep watch; now the City Hall is called by the Achaians the "Hall of the People"; and if he enter it, it may not be that he shall come forth until he is about to be sacrificed. They related moreover in addition to this, that many of these who were about to be sacrificed had before now run away and departed to another land, because they were afraid; and if afterwards in course of time they returned to their own land and were caught, they were placed in the City Hall: and they told how the man is sacrificed all thickly covered with wreaths, and with what form of procession he is brought forth to the sacrifice. This is done to the descendants of Kytissoros the son of Phrixos, because, when the Achaians were making of Athamas the son of Aiolos a victim to purge the sins of the land according to the command of an oracle, and were just about to sacrifice him, this Kytissoros coming from Aia of the Colchians rescued him; and having done so he brought the wrath of the gods upon his own descendants. Having heard these things, Xerxes, when he came to the sacred grove, both abstained from entering it himself, and gave the command to his whole army to so likewise; and he paid reverence both to the house and to the sacred enclosure of the descendants of Athamas.

198. These then are the things which happened in Thessalia and in Achaia; and from these regions he proceeded to the Malian land, going along by a gulf of the sea, in which there is an ebb and flow of the tide every day. Round about this gulf there is a level space, which in parts is broad but in other parts very narrow; and mountains lofty and inaccessible surrounding this place enclose the whole land of Malis and are called the rocks of Trachis. The first city upon this gulf as one goes from Achaia is Antikyra, by which the river Spercheios flowing from the land of the Enianians runs out into the sea. At a distance of twenty furlongs or thereabouts from this river there is another, of which the name is Dyras; this is said to have appeared that it might bring assistance to Heracles when he was burning: then again at a distance of twenty furlongs from this there is another river called Melas.

199. From this river Melas the city of Trachis is distant five furlongs; and here, in the parts where Trachis is situated, is even the widest portion of all this district, as regards the space from the mountains to the sea; for the plain has an extent of twenty-two thousand *plethra*. In the mountain-range which encloses the land of Trachis there is a cleft to the South of Trachis itself; and through this cleft the river Asopos flows, and runs along by the foot of the mountain.

200. There is also another river called Phoinix, to the South of the Asopos, of no great size, which flowing from these mountains runs out into the Asopos; and at the river Phoinix is the narrowest place, for here has been constructed a road with a single wheel-track only. Then from the river Phoinix it is a distance of fifteen furlongs to Thermopylai; and in the space between the river Phoinix and Thermopylai there is a village called Anthela, by which the river Asopos flows, and so runs out into the sea; and about this village there is a wide space in which is set up a temple dedicated to Demeter of the Amphictyons, and there are seats for the Amphictyonic councilors and a temple dedicated to Amphictyon himself.

201. King Xerxes, I say, was encamped within the region of Trachis in the land of the

Malians, and the Hellenes within the pass. This place is called by the Hellenes in general Thermopylai, but by the natives of the place and those who dwell in the country round it is called Pylai. Both sides then were encamped hereabout, and the one had command of all that lies beyond Trachis in the direction of the North Wind, and the others of that which tends towards the South Wind and the mid-day on this side of the continent.

202. These were the Hellenes who awaited the attack of the Persian in this place:—of the Spartans three hundred hoplites; of the men of Tegea and Mantineia a thousand, half from each place, from Orchomenos in Arcadia a hundred and twenty, and from the rest of Arcadia a thousand,—of the Arcadians so many; from Corinth four hundred, from Phlius two hundred, and of the men of Mykene eighty: these were they who came from the Peloponnese; and from the Boeotians seven hundred of the Thespians, and of the Thebans four hundred.

203. In addition to these the Locrians of Opus had been summoned to come in their full force, and of the Phokians a thousand: for the Hellenes had of themselves sent a summons to them, saying by messengers that they had come as forerunners of the others, that the rest of the allies were to be expected every day, that their sea was safely guarded, being watched by the Athenians and the Eginetans and by those who had been appointed to serve in the fleet, and that they need fear nothing: for he was not a god, they said, who was coming to attack Hellas, but a man; and there was no mortal, nor would be any, with those fortunes evil had not been mingled at his very birth, and the greatest evils for the greatest men; therefore he also who was marching against them, being mortal, would be destined to fail of his expectation. They accordingly, hearing this, came to the assistance of the others at Trachis.

204. Of these troops, although there were other commanders also according to the State to which each belonged, yet he who was most held in regard and who was leader of the whole army was the Lacedemonian Leonidas son of Anaxandrides, son of Leon, son of Eurycratides, son of Anaxander, son of Eurycrates, son of Polydoros, son of Alcamenes, son of Teleclos, son of Archelaos, son of Hegesilaos, son of Doryssos, son of Leobotes, son of Echestratos, son of Agis, son of Eurysthenes, son of Aristodemos, son of Aristomachos, son of Cleodaios, son of Hyllos, son of Heracles; who had obtained the kingdom of Sparta contrary to expectation.

205. For as he had two brothers each older than himself, namely Cleomenes and Dorieos, he had been far removed from the thought of becoming king. Since however Cleomenes had died without male child, and Dorieos was then no longer alive, but he also had brought his life to an end in Sicily, thus the kingdom came to Leonidas, both because was of elder birth than Cleombrotos (for Cleombrotos was the youngest of the sons of Anaxandrides) and also because he had in marriage the daughter of Cleomenes. He then at this time went to Thermopylai, having chosen the three hundred who were appointed by law and men who chanced to have sons; and he took with him besides, before he arrived, those Thebans whom I mentioned when I reckoned them in the number of the troops, of whom the commander was Leontiades the son of Eurymachos: and for this reason Leonidas was anxious to take up these with him of all the Hellenes, namely because accusations had been strongly brought against them that they were taking the side of the Medes; therefore he summoned them to the war, desiring to know whether they would send troops with them or whether they would openly renounce the alliance of the Hellenes; and they sent men, having other thoughts in their mind the while.

206. These with Leonidas the Spartans had sent out first, in order that seeing them the other allies might join in the campaign, and for fear that they also might take the side of the Medes, if they heard that the Spartans were putting off their action. Afterwards, however, when they had kept the festival, (for the festival of the Carneia stood in their way), they intended then to leave a garrison in Sparta and to come to help in full force with speed: and just so also the rest of the allies had thought of doing themselves; for it chanced that the Olympic festival fell at the same time as these events. Accordingly, since they did not suppose that the fighting in Thermopylai would so soon be decided, they sent only the forerunners of their force.

207. These, I say, had intended to do thus: and meanwhile the Hellenes at Thermopylai, when the Persian had come near to the pass, were in dread, and deliberated about making retreat from their position. To the rest of the Peloponnesians then it seemed best that they should go to the Peloponnese and hold the Isthmus in guard; but Leonidas, when the Phokians and Locrians were indignant at this opinion, gave his vote for remaining there, and for sending at the same time messengers to the several States bidding them to come up to help them, since they were but few to repel the army of the Medes.

208. As they were thus deliberating, Xerxes sent a scout on horseback to see how many they were in number and what they were doing; for he had heard while he was yet in Thessaly that there had been assembled in this place a small force, and that the leaders of it were Lacedemonians together with Leonidas, who was of the race of Heracles. And when the horseman had ridden up towards their camp, he looked upon them and had a view not indeed of the whole of their army, for of those which were posted within the wall, which they had repaired and were keeping a guard, it was not possible to have a view, but he observed those who were outside, whose station was in front of the wall; and it chanced at that time that the Lacedemonians were they who were posted outside. So then he saw some of the men practicing athletic exercises and some combing their long hair: and as he looked upon these things he marveled, and at the same time he observed their number: and when he had observed all exactly, he rode back unmolested, for no one attempted to pursue him and he found himself treated with much indifference. And when he returned he reported to Xerxes all that which he had seen.

209. Hearing this Xerxes was not able to conjecture the truth about the matter, namely that they were preparing themselves to die and to deal death to the enemy so far as they might; but it seemed to him that they were acting in a manner merely ridiculous; and therefore he sent for Demaratos the son of Ariston, who was in his camp, and when he came, Xerxes asked him of these things severally, desiring to discover what this was which the Lacedemonians were doing: and he said: "Thou didst hear from my mouth at a former time, when we were setting forth to go against Hellas, the things concerning these men; and having heard them thou madest me an object of laughter, because I told thee of these things which I perceived would come to pass; for to me it is the greatest of all ends to speak the truth continually before thee, O king. Hear then now also: these men have come to fight with us for the passage, and this is it that they are preparing to do; for they have a custom which is as follows;—whenever they are about to put their lives in peril, then they attend to the arrangement of their hair. Be assured however, that if thou shalt subdue these and the rest of them which remain behind in Sparta, there is no other race of men which will await thy onset, O king, or will raise hands against thee: for now thou art

about to fight against the noblest kingdom and city of those which are among the Hellenes, and the best men." To Xerxes that which was said seemed to be utterly incredible, and he asked again a second time in what manner being so few they would fight with his host. He said; "O king, deal with me as with a liar, if thou find not that these things come to pass as I say."

210. Thus saying he did not convince Xerxes, who let four days go by, expecting always that they would take to flight; but on the fifth day, when they did not depart but remained, being obstinate, as he thought, in impudence and folly, he was enraged and sent against them the Medes and the Kissians, charging them to take the men alive and bring them into his presence. Then when the Medes moved forward and attacked the Hellenes, there fell many of them, and others kept coming up continually, and they were not driven back, though suffering great loss: and they made it evident to every man, and to the king himself not least of all, that human beings are many but men are few. This combat went on throughout the day:

211, and when the Medes were being roughly handled, then these retired from the battle, and the Persians, those namely whom the king called "Immortals," of whom Hydarnes was commander, took their place and came to the attack, supposing that they at least would easily overcome the enemy. When however these also engaged in combat with the Hellenes, they gained no more success than the Median troops but the same as they, seeing that they were fighting in a place with a narrow passage, using shorter spears than the Hellenes, and not being able to take advantage of their superior numbers. The Lacedemonians meanwhile were fighting in a memorable fashion, and besides other things of which they made display, being men perfectly skilled in fighting opposed to men who were unskilled, they would turn their backs to the enemy and make a pretense of taking to flight; and the Barbarians, seeing them thus taking a flight, would follow after them with shouting and clashing of arms: then the Lacedemonians, when they were being caught up, turned and faced the Barbarians; and thus turning round they would slay innumerable multitudes of the Persians; and there fell also at these times a few of the Spartans themselves. So, as the Persians were not able to obtain any success by making trial of the entrance and attacking it by divisions and every way, they retired back.

212. And during these onsets it is said that the king, looking on, three times leapt up from his seat, struck with fear for his army. Thus they contended then: and on the following day the Barbarians strove with no better success; for because the men opposed to them were few in number, they engaged in battle with the expectation that they would be found to be disabled and would not be capable any longer of raising their hands against them in fight. The Hellenes however were ordered by companies as well as by nations, and they fought successively each in turn, excepting the Phokians, for these were posted upon the mountain to guard the path. So the Persians, finding nothing different from that which they had seen on the former day, retired back from the fight.

213. Then when the king was in a strait as to what he should do in the matter before him, Epialtes the son of Eurydemos, a Malian, came to speech with him, supposing that he would win a very great reward from the king; and this man told him of the path which leads over the mountain to Thermopylai, and brought about the destruction of those Hellenes who remained in that place. Afterwards from fear of the Lacedemonians he fled to Thessaly, and when he had fled, a price was proclaimed for his life by the Deputies, when the Amphictyons met for their assembly at Pylai. Then some time afterwards

having returned to Antikyra he was slain by Athenades a man of Trachis. Now this Athenades killed Epialtes for another cause, which I shall set forth in the following part of the history, but he was honored for it none the less by the Lacedemonians.

214. Thus Epialtes after these events was slain: there is however another tale told, that Onetes the son of Phanagoras, a man of Carystos, and Corydallos of Antikyra were those who showed the Persians the way round the mountain; but this I can by no means accept: for first we must judge by this fact, namely that the Deputies of the Hellenes did not proclaim a price for the lives of Onetes and Corydallos, but for that of Epialtes the Trachinian, having surely obtained the most exact information of the matter; and secondly we know that Epialtes was an exile from his country to avoid this charge. True it is indeed that Onetes might know of this path, even though he were not a Malian, if he had had much intercourse with the country; but Epialtes it was who led them round the mountain by the path, and him therefore I write down as the guilty man.

215. Xerxes accordingly, being pleased by that which Epialtes engaged to accomplish, at once with great joy proceeded to send Hydarnes and the men of whom Hydarnes was commander; and they set forth from the camp about the time when the lamps are lit. This path of which we speak had been discovered by the Malians who dwell in that land, and having discovered it they led the Thessalians by it against the Phokians, at the time when the Phokians had fenced the pass with a wall and thus were sheltered from the attacks upon them: so long ago as this had the pass been proved by the Malians to be of no value. And this path lies as follows:—it begins from the river Asopos, which flows through the cleft, and the name of this mountain and of the path is the same, namely Anopaia; and this Anopaia stretches over the ridge of the mountain and ends by the town of Alpenos, which is the first town of the Locrians towards Malis, and by the stone called Black Buttocks and the seats of the Kercopes, where is the very narrowest part.

217. By this path thus situated the Persians after crossing over the Asopos proceeded all through the night, having on their right hand the mountains of the Oitaians and on the left those of the Trachinians: and when dawn appeared, they had reached the summit of the mountain. In this part of the mountain there were, as I have before shown, a thousand hoplites of the Phokians keeping guard, to protect their own country and to keep the path: for while the pass below was guarded by those whom I have mentioned, the path over the mountain was guarded by the Phokians, who had undertaken the business for Leonidas by their own offer.

218. While the Persians were ascending they were concealed from these, since all the mountain was covered with oak-trees; and the Phokians became aware of them after they had made the ascent as follows:—the day was calm, and not a little noise was made by the Persians, as was likely when leaves were lying spread upon the ground under their feet; upon which the Phokians started up and began to put on their arms, and by this time the Barbarians were close upon them. These, when they saw men arming themselves, fell into wonder, for they were expecting that no one would appear to oppose them, and instead of that they had met with an armed force. Then Hydarnes, seized with fear lest the Phokians should be Lacedemonians, asked Epialtes of what people the force was; and being accurately informed he set the Persians in order for battle. The Phokians however, when they were hit by the arrows of the enemy, which flew thickly, fled and got away at once to the topmost peak of the mountain, fully assured that it was against them that the enemy had designed to come, and here they were ready to meet death. These, I say, were in this mind;

but the Persians meanwhile with Epialtes and Hydarnes made no account of the Phokians, but descended the mountain with all speed.

219. To the Hellenes who were in Thermopylai first the soothsayer Megistias, after looking into the victims which were sacrificed, declared the death which was to come to them at dawn of day; and afterwards deserters brought the report of the Persians having gone round. These signified it to them while it was yet night, and thirdly came the day-watchers, who had run down from the heights when day was already dawning. Then the Hellenes deliberated, and their opinions were divided; for some urged that they should not desert their post, while others opposed this counsel. After this they departed from their assembly, and some went away and dispersed each to their several cities, while others of them were ready to remain there together with Leonidas.

220. However it is reported also that Leonidas himself sent them away, having a care that they might not perish, but thinking that it was not seemly for himself and for the Spartans who were present to leave the post to which they had come at first to keep guard there. I am inclined rather to be of this latter opinion, namely that because Leonidas perceived that the allies were out of heart and did not desire to face the danger with him to the end, he ordered them to depart, but held that for himself to go away was not honorable, whereas if he remained, a great fame of him would be left behind, and the prosperity of Sparta would not be blotted out: for an oracle had been given by the Pythian prophetess to the Spartans, when they consulted about this war at the time when it was being first set on foot, to the effect that either Lacedaemon must be destroyed by the Barbarians, or their king must lose his life. This reply the prophetess gave them in hexameter verses, and it ran thus:

> "But as for you, ye men who in wide-spaced Sparta inhabit,
> Either your glorious city is sacked by the children of Perses,
> Or, if it be not so, then a king of the stock Heracleian
> Dead shall be mourned for by all in the boundaries of broad Lacedaemon.
> Him nor the might of bulls nor the raging of lions shall hinder;
> For he hath might as of Zeus; and I say he shall not be restrained,
> Till one of the other of these he have utterly torn and divided."

I am of opinion that Leonidas considering these things and desiring to lay up for himself glory above all the other Spartans, dismissed the allies, rather than that those who departed did so in such disorderly fashion, because they were divided in opinion.

221. Of this the following has been to my mind a proof as convincing as any other, namely that Leonidas is known to have endeavored to dismiss the soothsayer also who accompanied this army, Megistias the Acarnanian, who was said to be descended from Melampus, that he might not perish with them after he had declared from the victims that which was about to come to pass for them. He however when he was bidden to go would not himself depart, but sent away his son who was with him in the army, besides whom he had no other child.

222. The allies then who were dismissed departed and went away, obeying the word of Leonidas, and only the Thespians and the Thebans remained behind with the Lacedemonians. Of these the Thebans stayed against their will and not because they desired it, for Leonidas kept them, counting them as hostages; but the Thespians very willingly, for they

said that they would not depart and leave Leonidas and those with him, but they stayed behind and died with them. The commander of these was Demophilos the son of Diadromes.

223. Xerxes meanwhile, having made libations at sunrise, stayed for some time, until about the hour when the market fills, and then made an advance upon them; for thus it had been enjoined by Epialtes, seeing that the descent of the mountain is shorter and the space to be passed over much less than the going round and the ascent. The Barbarians accordingly with Xerxes were advancing to the attack; and the Hellenes with Leonidas, feeling that they were going forth to death, now advanced out much further than at first into the broader part of the defile; for when the fence of the wall was being guarded, they on the former days fought retiring before the enemy into the narrow part of the pass; but now they engaged with them outside the narrows, and very many of the Barbarians fell: for behind them the leaders of the divisions with scourges in their hands were striking each man, ever urging them on to the front. Many of them then were driven into the sea and perished, and many more still were trodden down while yet alive by one another, and there was no reckoning of the number that perished: for knowing the death which was about to come upon them by reason of those who were going round the mountain, they displayed upon the Barbarians all the strength which they had, to its greatest extent, disregarding danger and acting as if possessed by a spirit of recklessness.

224. Now by this time the spears of the greater number of them were broken, so it chanced, in this combat, and they were slaying the Persians with their swords; and in this fighting fell Leonidas, having proved himself a very good man, and others also of the Spartans with him, men of note, of whose names I was informed as of men who had proved themselves worthy, and indeed I was told also the names of all the three hundred. Moreover of the Persians there fell here, besides many others of note, especially two sons of Dareios, Abrocomes and Hyperanthes, born to Dareios of Phratagune the daughter of Artanes: now Artanes was the brother of king Dareios and the son of Hystaspes, the son of Arsames; and he in giving his daughter in marriage to Dareios gave also with her all his substance, because she was his only child.

225. Two brothers of Xerxes, I say, fell here fighting; and meanwhile over the body of Leonidas there arose a great struggle between the Persians and the Lacedemonians, until the Hellenes by valor dragged this away from the enemy and turned their opponents to flight four times. This conflict continued until those who had gone with Epialtes came up; and when the Hellenes learnt that these had come, from that moment the nature of the combat was changed; for they retired backwards to the narrow part of the way, and having passed by the wall they went and placed themselves upon the hillock, all in a body together except only the Thebans: now this hillock is in the entrance, where now the stone lion is placed for Leonidas. On this spot while defending themselves with daggers, that is those who still had them left, and also with hands and with teeth, they were overwhelmed by the missiles of the Barbarians, some of these having followed directly after them and destroyed the fence of the wall, while others had come round and stood about them on all sides.

226. Such were the proofs of valor given by the Lacedemonians and Thespians; yet the Spartan Dienekes is said to have proved himself the best man of all, the same who, as they report, uttered this saying before they engaged battle with the Medes:—being informed by one of the men of Trachis that when the Barbarians discharged their arrows they obscured

the light of the sun by the multitude of the arrows, so great was the number of their host, he was not dismayed by this, but making small account of the number of the Medes, he said that their guest from Trachis brought them very good news, for if the Medes obscured the light of the sun, the battle against them would be in the shade and not in the sun.

227. This and other sayings of this kind they report that Dienekes the Lacedemonian left as memorials of himself; and after him the bravest they say of the Lacedemonians were two brothers Alpheos and Maron, sons of Orsiphantos. Of the Thespians the man who gained most honor was named Dithyrambos son of Harmatides.

228. The men were buried were they fell; and for these, as well as for those who were slain before being sent away by Leonidas, there is an inscription which runs thus:

"Here once, facing in fight three hundred myriads of foemen,
Thousands four did contend, men of the Peloponnese."

This is the inscription for the whole body; and for the Spartans separately there is this:

"Stranger, report this word, we pray, to the Spartans, that lying
Here in this spot we remain, faithfully keeping their laws."

This, I say, for the Lacedemonians; and for the soothsayer as follows:

"This is the tomb of Megistias renowned, whom the Median foemen,
Where Sperchios doth flow, slew when they forded the stream;
Soothsayer he, who then knowing clearly the fates that were coming,
Did not endure in the fray Sparta's good leaders to leave."

The Amphictyons it was who honored them with inscriptions and memorial pillars, excepting only in the case of the inscription to the soothsayer; but that of the soothsayer Megistias was inscribed by Simonides the son of Leoprepes on account of guest-friendship.

229. Two of these three hundred, it is said, namely Eurystos and Aristodemos, who, if they had made agreement with one another, might either have come safe home to Sparta together (seeing that they had been dismissed from the camp by Leonidas and were lying at Alpenoi with disease of the eyes, suffering extremely), or again, if they had not wished to return home, they might have been slain together with the rest,—when they might, I say, have done either one of these two things, would not agree together; but the two being divided in opinion, Eurystos, it is said, when he was informed that the Persians had gone round, asked for his arms and having put them on ordered his Helot to lead him to those who were fighting; and after he had led him thither, the man who had led him ran away and departed, but Eurystos plunged into the thick of the fighting, and so lost his life: but Aristodemos was left behind fainting. Now if either Aristodemos had been ill alone, and so had returned home to Sparta, or the men had both of them come back together, I do not suppose that the Spartans would have displayed any anger against them; but in this case, as the one of them had lost his life and the other, clinging to an excuse which the first also might have used, had not been willing to die, it necessarily happened that the Spartans had great indignation against Aristodemos.

230. Some say that Aristodemos came safe to Sparta in this manner, and on a pretext such as I have said; but others, that he had been sent as a messenger from the camp, and when he might have come up in time to find the battle going on, was not willing to do so, but stayed upon the road and so saved his life, while his fellow-messenger reached the battle and was slain.

231. When Aristodemos, I say, had returned home to Lacedaemon, he had reproach and dishonor; and that which he suffered by way of dishonor was this,—no one of the Spartans would either give him light for a fire or speak with him, and he had reproach in that he was called Aristodemos the coward.

232. He however in the battle at Plataia repaired all the guilt that was charged against him: but it is reported that another man also survived of these three hundred, whose name was Pantites, having been sent as a messenger to Thessaly, and this man, when he returned back to Sparta and found himself dishonored, is said to have strangled himself.

233. The Thebans however, of whom the commander was Leontiades, being with the Hellenes had continued for some time to fight against the king's army, constrained by necessity; but when they saw that the fortunes of the Persians were prevailing, then and not before, while the Hellenes with Leonidas were making their way with speed to the hillock, they separated from these and holding out their hands came near to the Barbarians, saying at the same time that which was most true, namely that they were on the side of the Medes and that they had been among the first to give earth and water to the king; and moreover that they had come to Thermopylai constrained by necessity, and were blameless for the loss which had been inflicted upon the king: so that thus saying they preserved their lives, for they had also the Thessalians to bear witness to these words. However, they did not altogether meet with good fortune, for some had even been slain as they had been approaching, and when they had come and the Barbarians had them in their power, the greater number of them were branded by command of Xerxes with the royal marks, beginning with their leader Leontiades, the same whose son Eurymachos was afterwards slain by the Plataians, when he had been made commander of four hundred Thebans and had seized the city of the Plataians.

234. Thus did the Hellenes at Thermopylai contend in fight; and Xerxes summoned Demaratos and inquired of him, having first said this: "Demaratos, thou art a good man; and this I conclude by the truth of thy words, for all that thou saidest turned out so as thou didst say. Now, however, tell me how many in number are the remaining Lacedemonians, and of them how many are like these in matters of war; or are they so even all of them?" He said: "O king, the number of all the Lacedemonians is great and their cities are many, but that which thou desirest to learn, thou shalt know. There is in Lacedaemon the city of Sparta, having about eight thousand men; and these are all equal to those who fought here: the other Lacedemonians are not equal to these, but they are good men too." To this Xerxes said: "Demaratos, in what manner shall we with least labor get the better of these men? Come set forth to us this; for thou knowest the courses of their counsels, seeing that thou wert once their king."

235. He made answer: "O king, if thou dost in very earnest take counsel with me, it is right that I declare to thee the best thing. What if thou shouldest send three hundred ships from thy fleet to attack the Laconian land? Now there is lying near it an island named Kythera, about which Chilon, who was a very wise man among us, said that it would be a greater gain for the Spartans that it should be sunk under the sea than that it should

remain above it; for he always anticipated that something would happen from it of such a kind as I am now setting forth to thee: not that he knew of thy armament beforehand, but that he feared equally every armament of men. Let thy forces then set forth from this island and keep the Lacedemonians in fear; and while they have a war of their own close at their doors, there will be no fear for thee from them that when the remainder of Hellas is being conquered by the land-army, they will come to the rescue there. Then after the remainder of Hellas has been reduced to subjection, from that moment the Lacedemonian power will be left alone and therefore feeble. If however thou shalt not do this, I will tell thee what thou must look for. There is a narrow isthmus leading to the Peloponnese, and in this place thou must look that other battles will be fought more severe than those which have taken place, seeing that all the Peloponnesians have sworn to a league against thee: but if thou shalt do the other thing of which I spoke, this isthmus and the cities within it will come over to thy side without a battle."

236. After him spoke Achaimenes, brother of Xerxes and also commander of the fleet, who chanced to have been present at this discourse and was afraid lest Xerxes should be persuaded to do this: "O king," he said, "I see that thou art admitting the speech of a man who envies thy good fortune, or is even a traitor to thy cause: for in truth the Hellenes delight in such a temper as this; they envy a man for his good luck, and they hate that which is stronger than themselves. And if, besides other misfortunes which we have upon us, seeing that four hundred of our ships have suffered wreck, thou shalt send away another three hundred from the station of the fleet to sail round Peloponnese, then thy antagonists become a match for thee in fight; whereas while it is all assembled together our fleet is hard for them to deal with, and they will not be at all a match for thee: and moreover the whole sea-force will support the land-force and be supported by it, if they proceed onwards together; but if thou shalt divide them, neither wilt thou be of service to them nor they to thee. My determination is rather to set thy affairs in good order and not to consider the affairs of the enemy, either where they will set on foot the war or what they will do or how many in number they are; for it is sufficient that they should themselves take thought for themselves, and we for ourselves likewise: and if the Lacedemonians come to stand against the Persians in fight, they will assuredly not heal the wound from which they are now suffering."

237. To him Xerxes made answer as follows: "Achaimenes, I think that thou speakest well, and so will I do; but Demaratos speaks that which he believes to be best for me, though his opinion is defeated by thine: for I will not certainly admit that which thou saidest, namely that he is not well-disposed to my cause, judging both by what was said by him before this, and also by that which is the truth, namely that though one citizen envies another for his good fortune and shows enmity to him by his silence, nor would a citizen when a fellow-citizen consulted him suggest that which seemed to him the best, unless he had attained to a great height of virtue, and such men doubtless are few; yet guest-friend to guest-friend in prosperity is well-disposed as nothing else on earth, and if his friend should consult him, he would give him the best counsel. Thus then as regards the evil-speaking against Demaratos, that is to say about one who is my guest-friend, I bid every one abstain from it in the future."

238. Having thus said Xerxes passed in review the bodies of the dead; and as for Leonidas, hearing that he had been the king and commander of the Lacedemonians he bade them cut off his head and crucify him. And it has been made plain to me by many

proofs besides, but by none more strongly than by this, that king Xerxes was enraged with Leonidas while alive more than with any other man on earth; for otherwise he would never have done this outrage to his corpse; since of all the men whom I know, the Persians are accustomed most to honor those who are good men in war. They then to whom it was appointed to do these things, proceeded to do so.

239. I will return now to that point of my narrative where it remained unfinished. The Lacedemonians had been informed before all others that the king was preparing an expedition against Hellas; and thus it happened that they sent to the Oracle at Delphi, where that reply was given them which I reported shortly before this. And they got this information in a strange manner; for Demaratos the son of Ariston after he had fled for refuge to the Medes was not friendly to the Lacedemonians, as I am of opinion and as likelihood suggests supporting my opinion; but it is open to any man to make conjecture whether he did this thing which follows in a friendly spirit or in malicious triumph over them. When Xerxes had resolved to make a campaign against Hellas, Demaratos, being in Susa and having been informed of this, had a desire to report it to the Lacedemonians. Now in no other way was he able to signify it, for there was danger that he should be discovered, but he contrived thus, that is to say, he took a folding tablet and scraped off the wax which was upon it, and then he wrote the design of the king upon the wood of the tablet, and having done so he melted the wax and poured it over the writing, so that the tablet (being carried without writing upon it) might not cause any trouble to be given by the keepers of the road. Then when it had arrived at Lacedaemon, the Lacedemonians were not able to make conjecture of the matter; until at last, as I am informed, Gorgo, the daughter of Cleomenes and wife of Leonidas, suggested a plan of which she had herself thought, bidding them scrape the wax and they would find writing upon the wood; and doing as she said they found the writing and read it, and after that they sent notice to the other Hellenes. These things are said to have come to pass in this manner.

❧ 8 ❧

THE EIGHTH BOOK OF THE
HISTORIES, CALLED URANIA

1. Those of the Hellenes who had been appointed to serve in the fleet were these:—the Athenians furnished a hundred and twenty-seven ships, and the Plataians moved by valor and zeal for the service, although they had had no practice in seamanship, yet joined with the Athenians in manning their ships. The Corinthians furnished forty ships, the Megarians twenty; the Chalkidians manned twenty ships with which the Athenians furnished them; the Eginetans furnished eighteen ships, the Sikyonians twelve, the Lacedemonians ten, the Epidaurians eight, the Eretrians seven, the Troizenians five, the Styrians two, the Keïans two ships and two fifty-oared galleys, while the Locrians of Opus came also to the assistance of the rest with seven fifty-oared galleys.

2. These were those who joined in the expedition to Artemision, and I have mentioned them according to the number of the ships which they severally supplied: so the number of the ships which were assembled at Artemision was (apart from the fifty-oared galleys) two hundred and seventy-one: and the commander who had the supreme power was furnished by the Spartans, namely Eurybiades son of Eurycleides, since the allies said that they would not follow the lead of the Athenians, but unless a Lacedemonian were leader they would break up the expedition which was to be made:

3, for it had come to be said at first, even before they sent to Sicily to obtain allies, that the fleet ought to be placed in the charge of the Athenians. So as the allies opposed this, the Athenians yielded, having it much at heart that Hellas should be saved, and perceiving that if they should have disagreement with one another about the leadership, Hellas would perish: and herein they judged rightly, for disagreement between those of the same race is worse than war undertaken with one consent by as much as war is worse than peace. Being assured then of this truth, they did not contend, but gave way for so long time as they were urgently in need of the allies; and that this was so their conduct proved; for when, after repelling the Persian from themselves, they were now contending for his land and no longer for their own, they alleged the insolence of Pausanias as a pretext and took away the leadership from the Lacedemonians. This however took place afterwards.

4. But at this time these Hellenes also who had come to Artemision, when they saw that a great number of ships had put in to Aphetai and that everything was filled with their armament, were struck with fear, because the fortunes of the Barbarians had different issue from that which they expected, and they deliberated about retreating from Artemision to the inner parts of Hellas. And the Euboeans perceiving that they were so deliberating, asked Eurybiades to stay there by them for a short time, until they should have removed out of their land their children, and their households; and as they did not persuade him, they went elsewhere and persuaded Themistocles the commander of the Athenians by a payment of thirty talents, the condition being that the fleet should stay and fight the sea-battle in front of Euboea.

5. Themistocles then caused the Hellenes to stay in the following manner:—to Eurybiades he imparted five talents of the sum with the pretense that he was giving it from himself; and when Eurybiades had been persuaded by him to change his resolution, Adeimantos son of Okytos, the Corinthian commander, was the only one of all the others who still made a struggle, saying that he would sail away from Artemision and would not stay with the others: to him therefore Themistocles said with an oath: "Thou at least shalt not leave us, for I will give thee greater gifts than the king of the Medes would send to thee, if thou shouldest desert thy allies." Thus he spoke, and at the same time he sent to the ship of Adeimantos three talents of silver. So these all had been persuaded by gifts to change their resolution, and at the same time the request of the Euboeans had been gratified and Themistocles himself gained money; and it was not known that he had the rest of the money, but those who received a share of this money were fully persuaded that it had come from the Athenian State for this purpose.

6. Thus they remained in Euboea and fought a sea-battle; and it came to pass as follows:—when the Barbarians had arrived at Aphetai about the beginning of the afternoon, having been informed even before they came that a few ships of the Hellenes were stationed about Artemision and now seeing them for themselves, they were eager to attack them, to see if they could capture them. Now they did not think it good yet to sail against them directly for this reason,—for fear namely that the Hellenes, when they saw them sailing against them, should set forth to take flight and darkness should come upon them in their flight; and so they were likely (thought the Persians) to get away; whereas it was right, according to their calculation, that not even the fire-bearer should escape and save his life.

7. With a view to this then they contrived as follows:—of the whole number of their ships they parted off two hundred and sent them round to sail by Caphereus and round Geriastos to the Euripos, going outside Skiathos so that they might not be sighted by the enemy as they sailed round Euboea: and their purpose was that with these coming up by that way, and blocking the enemies' retreat, and themselves advancing against them directly, they might surround them on all sides. Having formed this plan they proceeded to send off the ships which were appointed for this, and they themselves had no design of attacking the Hellenes on that day nor until the signal agreed upon should be displayed to them by those who were sailing round, to show that they had arrived. These ships, I say, they were sending round, and meanwhile they were numbering the rest at Aphetai.

8. During this time, while these were numbering their ships, it happened thus:—there was in that camp a man of Skione named Skyllias, as a diver the best of all the men of that time, who also in the shipwreck which took place by Pelion had saved for the Persians many of their goods and many of them also he had acquired for himself: this Skyllias it appears had had an intention even before this of deserting to the side of the Hellenes, but it had not been possible for him to do so then. In what manner after this attempt he did actually come to the Hellenes, I am not able to say with certainty, but I marvel if the tale is true which is reported; for it is said that he dived into the sea at Aphetai and did not come up till he reached Artemision, having traversed here somewhere about eighty furlongs through the sea. Now there are told about this man several other tales which seem likely to be false, but some also which are true: about this matter however let it be stated as my opinion that he came to Artemision in a boat. Then when he had come, he forthwith informed the commanders about the shipwreck, how it had come to pass, and of the ships which had been sent away to go round Euboea.

9. Hearing this the Hellenes considered the matter with one another; and after many things had been spoken, the prevailing opinion was that they should remain there that day and encamp on shore, and then, when midnight was past, they should set forth and go to meet those ships which were sailing round. After this however, as no one sailed out to attack them, they waited for the coming of the late hours of the afternoon and sailed out themselves to attack the Barbarians, desiring to make a trial both of their manner of fighting and of the trick of breaking their line.

10. And seeing them sailing thus against them with few ships, not only the others in the army of Xerxes but also their commanders judged them to be moved by mere madness, and they themselves also put out their ships to sea, supposing that they would easily capture them: and their expectation was reasonable enough, since they saw that the ships of the Hellenes were few, while theirs were many times as numerous and sailed better. Setting their mind then on this, they came round and enclosed them in the middle. Then so many of the Ionians as were kindly disposed to the Hellenes and were serving in the expedition against their will, counted it a matter of great grief to themselves when they saw them being surrounded and felt assured that not one of them would return home, so feeble did they think the power of the Hellenes to be; while those to whom that which was happening was a source of pleasure, were vying with one another, each one endeavoring to be the first to take an Athenian ship and receive gifts from the king: for in their camps there was more report of the Athenians than of any others.

11. The Hellenes meanwhile, when the signal was given, first set themselves with prows facing the Barbarians and drew the sterns of their ships together in the middle; and when the signal was given a second time, although shut off in a small space and prow against prow, they set to work vigorously; and they captured thirty ships of the Barbarians and also Philaon the son of Chersis, the brother of Gorgos kind of the Salaminians, who was a man of great repute in the army. Now the first of the Hellenes who captured a ship of the enemy was an Athenian, Lycomedes the son of Aischraios, and he received the prize for valor. So these, as they were contending in this sea-fight with doubtful result, were parted from one another by the coming on of night. The Hellenes accordingly sailed away to Artemision and the Barbarians to Aphetai, the contest having been widely different from their expectation. In this sea-fight Antidoros of Lemnos alone of the

Hellenes who were with the king deserted to the side of the Hellenes, and the Athenians on account of this deed gave him a piece of land in Salamis.

12. When the darkness had come on, although the season was the middle of summer, yet there came on very abundant rain, which lasted through the whole of the night, with crashing thunder from Mount Pelion; and the dead bodies and pieces of wreck were cast up at Aphetai and became entangled round the prows of the ships and struck against the blades of the oars: and the men of the army who were there, hearing these things became afraid, expecting that they would certainly perish, to such troubles had they come; for before they had had even breathing space after the shipwreck and the storm which had arisen off Mount Pelion, there had come upon them a hard sea-fight, and after the sea-fight a violent storm of rain and strong streams rushing to the sea and crashing thunder.

13. These then had such a night as I have said; and meanwhile those of them who had been appointed to sail round Euboea experienced the very same night, but against them it raged much more fiercely, inasmuch as it fell upon them while they were making their course in the open sea. And the end of it proved distressful to them; for when the storm and the rain together came upon them as they sailed, being then off the "Hollows" of Euboea, they were borne by the wind not knowing by what way they were carried, and were cast away upon the rocks. And all this was being brought about by God in order that the Persian force might be made more equal to that of the Hellenes and might not be by very much the larger.

14. These then, I say, were perishing about the Hollows of Euboea, and meanwhile the Barbarians at Aphetai, when day had dawned upon them, of which they were glad, were keeping their ships quiet, and were satisfied in their evil plight to remain still for the present time; but to the Hellenes there came as a reinforcement three-and-fifty Athenian ships. The coming of these gave them more courage, and at the same time they were encouraged also by a report that those of the Barbarians who had been sailing round Euboea had all been destroyed by the storm that had taken place. They waited then for the same time of day as before, and then they sailed and fell upon some Kilikian ships; and having destroyed these, they sailed away when the darkness came on, and returned to Artemision.

15. On the third day the commanders of the Barbarians, being exceedingly indignant that so small a number of ships should thus do them damage, and fearing what Xerxes might do, did not wait this time for the Hellenes to begin the fight, but passed the word of command and put out their ships to sea about the middle of the day. Now it so happened that these battles at sea and the battles on land at Thermopylai took place on the same days; and for those who fought by sea the whole aim of the fighting was concerned with the channel of Euripos, just as the aim of Leonidas and of his band was to guard the pass: the Hellenes accordingly exhorted one another not to let the Barbarians go by into Hellas; while these cheered one another on to destroy the fleet of the Hellenes and to get possession of the straits.

16. Now while the forces of Xerxes were sailing in order towards them, the Hellenes kept quiet at Artemision; and the Barbarians, having made a crescent of their ships that they might enclose them, were endeavoring to surround them. Then the Hellenes put out to sea and engaged with them; and in this battle the two sides were nearly equal to one another; for the fleet of Xerxes by reason of its great size and numbers suffered damage

from itself, since the ships were thrown into confusion and ran into one another: nevertheless it stood out and did not give way, for they disdained to be turned to flight by so few ships. Many ships therefore of the Hellenes were destroyed and many men perished, but many more ships and men of the Barbarians. Thus contending they parted and went each to their own place.

17. In this sea-fight the Egyptians did best of the men who fought for Xerxes; and these, besides other great deeds which they displayed, captured five ships of the Hellenes together with their crews: while of the Hellenes those who did best on this day were the Athenians, and of the Athenians Cleinias the son of Alkibiades, who was serving with two hundred man and a ship of his own, furnishing the expense at his own proper cost.

18. Having parted, both sides gladly hastened to their moorings; and after they had separated and got away out of the sea-fight, although the Hellenes had possession of the bodies of the dead and of the wrecks of the ships, yet having suffered severely (and especially the Athenians, of whose ships half had been disabled), they were deliberating now about retreating to the inner parts of Hellas.

19. Themistocles however had conceived that if there should be detached from the force of the Barbarians the Ionian and Carian nations, they would be able to overcome the rest; and when the people of Euboea were driving their flocks down to that sea, he assembled the generals and said to them that he thought he had a device by which he hoped to cause the best of the king's allies to leave him. This matter he revealed to that extent only; and with regard to their present circumstances, he said that they must do as follows:— everyone must slaughter of the flocks of the Euboeans as many as he wanted, for it was better that their army should have them than the enemy; moreover he advised that each one should command his own men to kindle a fire: and as for the time of their departure he would see to it in such wise that they should come safe to Hellas. This they were content to do, and forthwith when they had kindled a fire they turned their attention to the flocks.

20. For in fact the Euboeans, neglecting the oracle of Bakis as if it had no meaning at all, had neither carried away anything from their land nor laid in any store of provisions with a view to war coming upon them, and by their conduct moreover they had brought trouble upon themselves. For the oracle uttered by Bakis about these matters runs as follows:

"Mark, when a man, a Barbarian, shall yoke the Sea with papyrus,
Then do thou plan to remove the loud-bleating goats from Euboea."

In the evils which at this time were either upon them or soon to be expected they might feel not a little sorry that they had paid no attention to these lines.

21. While these were thus engaged, there came to them the scout from Trachis: for there was at Artemision a scout named Polyas, by birth of Antikyra, to whom it had been appointed, if the fleet should be disabled, to signify this to those at Thermopylai, and he had a vessel equipped and ready for this purpose; and similarly there was with Leonidas Abronichos son of Lysicles, an Athenian, ready to carry news to those at Artemision with a thirty-oared galley, if any disaster should happen to the land-army. This Abronichos then had arrived, and he proceeded to signify to them that which had come to pass about

Leonidas and his army; and then when they were informed of it no longer put off their retreat, but set forth in the order in which they were severally posted, the Corinthians first and the Athenians last.

22. Themistocles however selected those ships of the Athenians which sailed best, and went round to the springs of drinking-water, cutting inscriptions on the stones there, which the Ionians read when they came to Artemision on the following day. These inscriptions ran thus: "Ionians, ye act not rightly in making expedition against the fathers of your race and endeavoring to enslave Hellas. Best of all were it that ye should come and be on our side; but if that may not be done by you, stand aside even now from the combat against us and ask the Carians to do the same as ye. If however neither of these two things is possible to be done, and ye are bound down by too strong compulsion to be able to make revolt, then in the action, when we engage battle, be purposely slack, remember that ye are descended from us and that our quarrel with the Barbarian took its rise at the first from you." Themistocles wrote thus, having, as I suppose, two things together in his mind, namely that either the inscriptions might elude the notice of the king and cause the Ionians to change and come over to the side on which he was, or that having been reported and denounced to Xerxes they might cause the Ionians to be distrusted by him, and so he might keep them apart from the sea-fights.

23. Themistocles then had set these inscriptions: and to the Barbarians there came immediately after these things a man of Histaia in a boat bringing word of the retreat of the Hellenes from Artemision. They however, not believing it, kept the messenger under guard and sent swift-sailing ships to look on before. Then these having reported the facts, at last as daylight was spreading over the sky, the whole armament sailed in a body to Artemision; and having stayed at this place till mid-day, after this they sailed to Histaia, and there arrived they took possession of the city of Histaia and overran all the villages which lie along the coast in the region of Ellopia, which is the land of Histaia.

24. While they were there, Xerxes, after he had made his dispositions with regard to the bodies of the dead, sent a herald to the fleet: and the dispositions which he made beforehand were as follows:—for all those of his army who were lying dead at Thermopylai, (and there were as many as twenty thousand in all), with the exception of about a thousand whom he left, he dug trenches and buried them, laying over them leaves and heaping earth upon them, that they might not be seen by the men of the fleet. Then when the herald had gone over to Histaia, he gathered an assembly of the whole force and spoke these words: "Allies, king Xerxes grants permission to any one of you who desires it, to leave his post and to come and see how he fights against those most senseless men who looked to overcome the power of the king."

25. When the herald had proclaimed this, then boats were of all things most in request, so many were they who desired to see this sight; and when they had passed over they went through the dead bodies and looked at them: and every one supposed that those who were lying there were all Lacedemonians or Thespians, though the Helots also were among those that they saw: however, they who had passed over did not fail to perceive that Xerxes had done that which I mentioned about the bodies of his own dead; for in truth it was a thing to cause laughter even: on the one side there were seen a thousand dead bodies lying, while the others lay all gathered together in the same place, four thousand of them. During this day then they busied themselves with looking, and on the day

after this they sailed back to the ships at Histaia, while Xerxes and his army set forth upon their march.

26. There had come also to them a few deserters from Arcadia, men in want of livelihood and desiring to be employed. These the Persians brought into the king's presence and inquired about the Hellenes, what they were doing; and one man it was who asked them this for all the rest. They told them that the Hellenes were keeping the Olympic festival and were looking on at a contest of athletics and horsemanship. He then inquired again, what was the prize proposed to them, for the sake of which they contended; and they told them of the wreath of olive which is given. Then Tigranes the son of Artabanos uttered a thought which was most noble, though thereby he incurred from the king the reproach of cowardice: for hearing that the prize was a wreath and not money, he could not endure to keep silence, but in the presence of all he spoke these words: "Ah! Mardonios, what kind of men are these against whom thou hast brought us to fight, who make their contest not for money but for honor!" Thus was it spoken by this man.

27. In the meantime, so soon as the disaster at Thermopylai had come about, the Thessalians sent a herald forthwith to the Phokians, against whom they had a grudge always, but especially because of the latest disaster which they had suffered: for when both the Thessalians themselves and their allies had invaded the Phokian land not many years before this expedition of the king, they had been defeated by the Phokians and handled by them roughly. For the Phokians had been shut up in Mount Parnassos having with them a soothsayer, Tellias the Eleian; and this Tellias contrived for them a device of the following kind:—he took six hundred men, the best of the Phokians, and whitened them over with chalk, both themselves and their armor, and then he attacked the Thessalians by night, telling the Phokians beforehand to slay every man whom they should see not colored over with white. So not only the sentinels of the Thessalians, who saw these first, were terrified by them, supposing it to be something portentous and other than it was, but also after the sentinels the main body of their army; so that the Phokians remained in possession of four thousand bodies of slain men and shields; of which last they dedicated half at Abai and half at Delphi; and from the tithe of booty got by this battle were made the large statues which are contending for the tripod in front of the temple at Delphi, and others similar to these are dedicated as an offering at Abai.

28. Thus had the Phokians done to the Thessalian footmen, when they were besieged by them; and they had done irreparable hurt to their cavalry also, when this had invaded their land: for in the pass which is by Hyampolis they had dug a great trench and laid down in it empty wine-jars; and then having carried earth and laid it on the top and made it like the rest of the ground, they waited for the Thessalians to invade their land. These supposing that they would make short work with the Phokians, riding in full course fell upon the wine-jars; and there the legs of their horses were utterly crippled.

29. Bearing then a grudge for both of these things, the Thessalians sent a herald and addressed them thus: "Phokians, we advise you to be more disposed now to change your minds and to admit that ye are not on a level with us: for in former times among the Hellenes, so long as it pleased us to be on that side, we always had the preference over you, and now we have such great power with the Barbarian that it rests with us to cause you to be deprived of your land and to be sold into slavery also. We however, though we have all the power in our hands, do not bear malice, but let there be paid to us fifty talents

of silver in return for this, and we will engage to avert the dangers which threaten to come upon your land."

30. Thus the Thessalians proposed to them; for the Phokians alone of all the people in those parts were not taking the side of the Medes, and this for no other reason, as I conjecture, but only because of their enmity with the Thessalians; and if the Thessalians had supported the cause of the Hellenes, I am of opinion that the Phokians would have been on the side of the Medes. When the Thessalians proposed this, they said that they would not give the money, and that it was open to them to take the Median side just as much as the Thessalians, if they desired it for other reasons; but they would not with their own will be traitors to Hellas.

31. When these words were reported, then the Thessalians, moved with anger against the Phokians, became guides to the Barbarian to show him the way: and from the land of Trachis they entered Doris; for a narrow strip of the Dorian territory extends this way, about thirty furlongs in breadth, lying between Malis and Phokis, the region which was in ancient time called Dryopis; this land is the mother-country of the Dorians in Peloponnese. Now the Barbarians did not lay waste this land of Doris when they entered it, for the people of it were taking the side of the Medes, and also the Thessalians did not desire it.

32. When however from Doris they entered Phokis, they did not indeed capture the Phokians themselves; for some of them had gone up to the heights of Parnassos,—and that summit of Parnassos is very convenient to receive a large number, which lies by itself near the city of Neon, the name of it being Tithorea,—to this, I say, some of them had carried up their goods and gone up themselves; but most of them had conveyed their goods out to the Ozolian Locrians, to the city of Amphissa, which is situated above the Crissaian plain. The Barbarians however overran the whole land of Phokis, for so the Thessalians led their army, and all that they came to as they marched they burned or cut down, and delivered to the flames both the cities and the temples:

33, for they laid everything waste, proceeding this way by the river Kephisos, and they destroyed the city of Drymos by fire, and also the following, namely Charadra, Erochos, Tethronion, Amphikaia, Neon, Pedieis, Triteis, Elateia, Hyampolis, Parapotamioi and Abai, at which last-named place there was a temple of Apollo, wealthy and furnished with treasuries and votive offerings in abundance; and there was then, as there is even now, the seat of an Oracle there: this temple they plundered and burnt. Some also of the Phokians they pursued and captured upon the mountains, and some women they did to death by repeated outrage.

34. Passing by Parapotamioi the Barbarians came to Panopeus, and from this point onwards their army was separated and went different ways. The largest and strongest part of the army, proceeding with Xerxes himself against Athens, entered the land of the Boeotians, coming into the territory of Orchomenos. Now the general body of the Boeotians was taking the side of the Medes, and their cities were being kept by Macedonians appointed for each, who had been sent by Alexander; and they were keeping them this aim, namely in order to make it plain to Xerxes that the Boeotians were disposed to be on the side of the Medes.

35. These, I say, of the Barbarians took their way in this direction; but others of them with guides had set forth to go to the temple at Delphi, keeping Parnassos on their right hand: and all the parts of Phokis over which these marched they ravaged; for they set fire to the towns of Panopeus and Daulis and Aiolis. And for this reason they marched in that

direction, parted off from the rest of the army, namely in order that they might plunder the temple at Delphi and deliver over the treasures there to king Xerxes: and Xerxes was well acquainted with all that there was in it of any account, better, I am told, than with the things which he had left in his own house at home, seeing that many constantly reported of them, and especially of the votive offerings of Croesus the son of Alyattes.

36. Meanwhile the Delphians, having been informed of this, had been brought to extreme fear; and being in great terror they consulted the Oracle about the sacred things, whether they should bury them in the earth or carry them forth to another land; but the god forbade them to meddle with these, saying that he was able by himself to take care of his own. Hearing this they began to take thought for themselves, and they sent their children and women over to Achaia on the other side of the sea, while most of the men themselves ascended up towards the summits of Parnassos and carried their property to the Corykian cave, while others departed for refuge to Amphissa of the Locrians. In short the Delphians had all left the town excepting sixty men and the prophet of the Oracle.

37. When the Barbarians had come near and could see the temple, then the prophet, whose name was Akeratos, saw before the cell arms lying laid out, having been brought forth out of the sanctuary, which were sacred and on which it was not permitted to any man to lay hands. He then was going to announce the portent to those of the Delphians who were still there, but when the Barbarians pressing onwards came opposite the temple of Athene Pronaia, there happened to them in addition portents yet greater than that which had come to pass before: for though that too was a marvel, that arms of war should appear of themselves laid forth outside the cell, yet this, which happened straightway after that, is worthy of marvel even beyond all other prodigies. When the Barbarians in their approach were opposite the temple of Athene Pronaia, at this point of time from the heaven there fell thunderbolts upon them, and from Parnassos two crags were broken away and rushed down upon them with a great crashing noise falling upon many of them, while from the temple of Pronaia there was heard a shout, and a battle-cry was raised.

38. All these things having come together, there fell fear upon the Barbarians; and the Delphians having perceived that they were flying, came down after them and slew a great number of them; and those who survived fled straight to Boeotia. These who returned of the Barbarians reported, as I am informed, that in addition to this which we have said they saw also other miraculous things; for two men (they said) in full armor and of stature more than human followed them slaying and pursuing.

39. These two the Delphians say were the native heroes Phylacos and Autonoös, whose sacred enclosures are about the temple, that of Phylacos being close by the side of the road above the temple of Pronaia and that of Autonoös near Castalia under the peak called Hyampeia. Moreover the rocks which fell from Parnassos were still preserved even to my time, lying in the sacred enclosure of Athene Pronaia, into which they fell when they rushed through the ranks of the Barbarians. Such departure had these men from the temple.

40. Meanwhile the fleet of the Hellenes after leaving Artemision put in to land at Salamis at the request of the Athenians: and for this reason the Athenians requested them to put in to Salamis, namely in order that they might remove out of Attica to a place of safety their children and their wives, and also deliberate what they would have to do; for in their present case they meant to take counsel afresh, because they had been deceived in

their expectation. For they had thought to find the Peloponnesians in full force waiting for the Barbarians in Boeotia; they found however nothing of this, but they were informed on the contrary that the Peloponnesians were fortifying the Isthmus with a wall, valuing above all things the safety of the Peloponnese and keeping this in guard; and that they were disposed to let all else go. Being informed of this, the Athenians therefore made request of them to put in to Salamis.

41. The others then put in their ships to land at Salamis, but the Athenians went over to their own land; and after their coming they made a proclamation that every one of the Athenians should endeavor to save his children and household as best he could. So the greater number sent them to Troizen, but others to Egina, and others to Salamis, and they were urgent to put these out of danger, both because they desired to obey the oracle and also especially for another reason, which was this:—the Athenians say that a great serpent lives in the temple and guards the Acropolis; and they not only say this, but also they set forth for it monthly offerings, as if it were really there; and the offering consists of a honey-cake. This honey-cake, which before used always to be consumed, was at this time left untouched. When the priestess had signified this, the Athenians left the city much more and with greater eagerness than before, seeing that the goddess also had (as they supposed) left the Acropolis. Then when all their belongings had been removed out of danger, they sailed to the encampment of the fleet.

42. When those who came from Artemision had put their ships in to land at Salamis, the remainder of the naval force of the Hellenes, being informed of this, came over gradually to join them from Troizen: for they had been ordered beforehand to assemble at Pogon, which is the harbor of the Troizenians. There were assembled accordingly now many more ships than those which were in the sea-fight at Artemision, and from more cities. Over the whole was set as admiral the same man as at Artemision, namely Eurybiades the son of Eurycleides, a Spartan but not of the royal house; the Athenians however supplied by far the greatest number of ships and those which sailed the best.

43. The following were those who joined the muster:—From Peloponnese the Lacedemonians furnishing sixteen ships, the Corinthians furnishing the same complement as at Artemision, the Sikyonians furnishing fifteen ships, the Epidaurians ten, the Troizenians five, the men of Hermion three, these all, except the Hermionians, being of Doric and Makednian race and having made their last migration from Erineos and Pindos and the land of Dryopis; but the people of Hermion are Dryopians, driven out by Heracles and the Malians from the land which is now called Doris.

44. These were the Peloponnesians who joined the fleet, and those of the mainland outside the Peloponnese were as follows:—the Athenians, furnishing a number larger than all the rest, namely one hundred and eighty ships, and serving alone, since the Plataians did not take part with the Athenians in the sea-fight at Salamis, because when the Hellenes were departing from Artemision and come near Chalkis, the Plataians disembarked on the opposite shore of Boeotia and proceeded to the removal of their households. So being engaged in saving these, they had been left behind. As for the Athenians, in the time when the Pelasgians occupied that which is now called Hellas, they were Pelasgians, being named Cranaoi, and in the time of king Kecrops they came to be called Kecropidai; then when Erechtheus had succeeded to his power, they had their name changed to Athenians; and after Ion the son of Xuthos became commander of the Athenians, they got the name from him of Ionians.

45. The Megarians furnished the same complement as at Artermision; the Amprakiots came to the assistance of the rest with seven ships, and the Leucadians with three, these being by race Dorians from Corinth.

46. Of the islanders the Eginetans furnished thirty; these had also other ships manned, but with them they were guarding their own land, while with the thirty which sailed best they joined in the sea-fight at Salamis. Now the Eginetans are Dorians from Epidauros, and their island had formerly the name of Oinone. After the Eginetans came the Chalkidians with the twenty ships which were at Artemision, and the Eretrians with their seven: these are Ionians. Next the Keïans, furnishing the same as before and being by race Ionians from Athens. The Naxians furnished four ships, they having been sent out by the citizens of their State to join the Persians, like the other islanders; but neglecting these commands they had come to the Hellenes, urged thereto by Democritos, a man of repute among the citizens and at that time commander of a trireme. Now the Naxians are Ionians coming originally from Athens. The Styrians furnished the same ships as at Artemision, and the men of Kythnos one ship and one fifty-oared galley, these both being Dryopians. Also the Seriphians, the Siphnians and the Melians served with the rest; for they alone of the islanders had not given earth and water to the Barbarian.

47. These all who have been named dwelt inside the land of the Thesprotians and the river Acheron; for the Thesprotians border upon the land of the Amprakiots and Leucadians, and these were they who came from the greatest distance to serve: but of those who dwell outside these limits the men of Croton were the only people who came to the assistance of Hellas in her danger; and these sent one ship, of whom the commander was Phaÿlos, a man who had three times won victories at the Pythian games. Now the men of Croton are by descent Achaians.

48. All the rest who served in the fleet furnished triremes, but the Melians, Siphnian and Seriphians fifty-oared galleys: the Melians, who are by descent from Lacedaemon, furnished two, the Siphnians and Seriphians, who are Ionians from Athens, each one. And the whole number of the ships, apart from the fifty-oared galleys, was three hundred and seventy-eight.

49. When the commanders had assembled at Salamis from the States which have been mentioned, they began to deliberate, Eurybiades having proposed that anyone who desired it should declare his opinion as to where he thought it most convenient to fight a sea-battle in those regions of which they had command; for Attica had already been let go, and he was now proposing the question about the other regions. And the opinions of the speakers for the most part agreed that they should sail to the Isthmus and there fight a sea-battle in defense of the Peloponnese, arguing that if they should be defeated in the sea-battle, supposing them to be at Salamis they would be blockaded in an island, where no help would come to them, but at the Isthmus they would be able to land where their own men were.

50. While the commanders from the Peloponnese argued thus, an Athenian had come in reporting that the Barbarians were arrived in Attica and that all the land was being laid waste with fire. For the army which directed its march through Boeotia in company with Xerxes, after it had burnt the city of the Thespians (the inhabitants having left it and gone to the Peloponnese) and that of the Plataians likewise, had now come to Athens and was laying waste everything in those regions. Now he had burnt Thespiai and Plataia because he was informed by the Thebans that these were not taking the side of the Medes.

51. So in three months from the crossing of the Hellespont, whence the Barbarians began their march, after having stayed there one month while they crossed over into Europe, they had reached Attica, in the year when Calliades was archon of the Athenians. And they took the lower city, which was deserted, and then they found that there were still a few Athenians left in the temple, either stewards of the temple or needy persons, who had barred the entrance to the Acropolis with doors and with a palisade of timber and endeavored to defend themselves against the attacks of the enemy, being men who had not gone out to Salamis partly because of their poverty, and also because they thought that they alone had discovered the meaning of the oracle which the Pythian prophetess had uttered to them, namely that the "bulwark of wood" should be impregnable, and supposed that this was in fact the safe refuge according to the oracle, and not the ships.

52. So the Persians taking their post upon the rising ground opposite the Acropolis, which the Athenians call the Hill of Ares, proceeded to besiege them in this fashion, that is they put tow round about their arrows and lighted it, and then shot them against the palisade. The Athenians who were besieged continued to defend themselves nevertheless, although they had come to the extremity of distress and their palisade had played them false; nor would they accept proposals for surrender, when the sons of Peisistratos brought them forward: but endeavoring to defend themselves they contrived several contrivances against the enemy, and among the rest they rolled down large stones when the Barbarians approached the gates; so that for a long time Xerxes was in a difficulty, not being able to capture them.

53. In time however there appeared for the Barbarians a way of approach after their difficulties, since by the oracle it was destined that all of Attica which is on the mainland should come to be under the Persians. Thus then it happened that on the front side of the Acropolis behind the gates and the way up to the entrance, in a place where no one was keeping guard, nor would one have supposed that any man could ascend by this way, here men ascended by the temple of Aglauros the daughter of Kecrops, although indeed the place is precipitous: and when the Athenians saw that they had ascended up to the Acropolis, some of them threw themselves down from the wall and perished, while others took refuge in the sanctuary of the temple. Then those of the Persians who had ascended went first to the gates, and after opening these they proceeded to kill the suppliants; and when all had been slain by them, they plundered the temple and set fire to the whole of the Acropolis.

54. Then Xerxes, having fully taken possession of Athens, sent to Susa a mounted messenger to report to Artabanos the good success which they had. And on the next day after sending the herald he called together the exiles of the Athenians who were accompanying him, and bade them go up to the Acropolis and sacrifice the victims after their own manner; whether it was that he had seen some vision of a dream which caused him to give this command, or whether perchance he had a scruple in his mind because he had set fire to the temple. The Athenian exiles did accordingly that which was commanded them:

55, and the reason why I made mention of this I will here declare:—there is in this Acropolis a temple of Erechtheus, who is said to have been born of the Earth, and in this there is an olive-tree and a sea, which (according to the story told by the Athenians) Poseidon and Athene, when they contended for the land, set as witnesses of themselves. Now it happened to this olive-tree to be set on fire with the rest of the temple by the Barbarians; and on the next day after the conflagration those of the Athenians who were commanded by the king to offer sacrifice, saw when they had gone up to the temple that a shoot had run up from the stock of the tree about a cubit in length. These then made report of this.

56. The Hellenes meanwhile at Salamis, when it was announced to them how it had been as regards the Acropolis of the Athenians, were disturbed so greatly that some of the commanders did not even wait for the question to be decided which had been proposed, but began to go hastily to their ships and to put up their sails, meaning to make off with speed; and by those of them who remained behind it was finally decided to fight at sea in defense of the Isthmus. So night came on, and they having been dismissed from the council were going to their ships:

57, and when Themistocles had come to his ship, Mnesiphilos an Athenian asked him what they had resolved; and being informed by him that it had been determined to take out the ships to the Isthmus and fight a battle by sea in defense of the Peloponnese, he said: "Then, if they set sail with the ships from Salamis, thou wilt not fight any more sea-battles at all for the fatherland, for they will all take their way to their several cities and neither Eurybiades nor any other man will be able to detain them or to prevent the fleet from being dispersed: and Hellas will perish by reason of evil counsels. But if there by any means, go thou and try to unsettle that which has been resolved, if perchance thou mayest persuade Eurybiades to change his plans, so as to stay here."

58. This advice very much commended itself to Themistocles; and without making any answer he went to the ship of Eurybiades. Having come thither he said that he desired to communicate to him a matter which concerned the common good; and Eurybiades bade him come into his ship and speak, if he desired to say anything. Then Themistocles sitting down beside him repeated to him all those things which he had heard Mnesiphilos say, making as if they were his own thoughts, and adding to them many others; until at last by urgent request he persuaded him to come out of his ship and gather the commanders to the council.

59. So when they were gathered together, before Eurybiades proposed the discussion of the things for which he had assembled the commanders, Themistocles spoke with much vehemence being very eager to gain his end; and as he was speaking, the Corinthian commander, Adeimantos the son of Okytos, said: "Themistocles, at the games those who stand forth for the contest before the due time are beaten with rods." He justifying himself said: "Yes, but those who remain behind are not crowned."

60. At that time he made answer mildly to the Corinthian; and to Eurybiades he said not now any of those things which he had said before, to the effect that if they should set sail from Salamis they would disperse in different directions; for it was not seemly for him to bring charges against the allies in their presence: but he held to another way of reasoning, saying: "Now it is in thy power to save Hellas, if thou wilt follow my advice, which is to stay here and here to fight a sea-battle, and if thou wilt not follow the advice of those among these men who bid thee remove the ships to the Isthmus. For hear both ways, and then set them in comparison. If thou engage battle at the Isthmus, thou wilt fight in an open sea, into which it is by no means convenient for us that we go to fight, seeing that we have ships which are heavier and fewer in number than those of the enemy. Then secondly thou wilt give up to destruction Salamis and Megara and Egina, even if we have success in all else; for with their fleet will come also the land-army, and thus thou wilt thyself lead them to the Peloponnese and wilt risk the safety of all Hellas. If however thou

shalt do as I say, thou wilt find therein all the advantages which I shall tell thee of:—in the first place by engaging in a narrow place with few ships against many, if the fighting has that issue which it is reasonable to expect, we shall have very much the better; for to fight a sea-fight in a narrow space is for our advantage, but to fight in a wide open space is for theirs. Then again Salamis will be preserved, whither our children and our wives have been removed for safety; and moreover there is this also secured thereby, to which ye are most of all attached, namely that by remaining here thou wilt fight in defense of the Peloponnese as much as if the fight were at the Isthmus; and thou wilt not lead the enemy to Peloponnese, if thou art wise. Then if that which I expect come to pass and we gain a victory with our ships, the Barbarians will not come to you at the Isthmus nor will they advance further than Attica, but they will retire in disorder; and we shall be the gainers by the preservation of Megara and Egina and Salamis, at which place too an oracle tells us that we shall get the victory over our enemies. Now when men take counsel reasonably for themselves, reasonable issues are wont as a rule to come, but if they do not take counsel reasonably, then God is not wont generally to attach himself to the judgment of men."

61. When Themistocles thus spoke, the Corinthian Adeimantos inveighed against him for the second time, bidding him to be silent because he had no native land, and urging Eurybiades not to put to the vote the proposal of one who was a citizen of no city; for he said that Themistocles might bring opinions before the council if he could show a city belonging to him, but otherwise not. This objection he made against him because Athens had been taken and was held by the enemy. Then Themistocles said many evil things of him and of the Corinthians both, and declared also that he himself and his countrymen had in truth a city and a land larger than that of the Corinthians, so long as they had two hundred ships fully manned; for none of the Hellenes would be able to repel the Athenians if they came to fight against them.

62. Signifying this he turned then to Eurybiades and spoke yet more urgently: "If thou wilt remain here, and remaining here wilt show thyself a good man, well; but if not, thou wilt bring about the overthrow of Hellas, for upon the ships depends all our power in the war. Nay, but do as I advise. If, however, thou shalt not do so, we shall forthwith take up our households and voyage to Siris in Italy, which is ours already of old and the oracles say that it is destined to be colonized by us; and ye, when ye are left alone and deprived of allies such as we are, will remember my words."

63. When Themistocles thus spoke, Eurybiades was persuaded to change his mind; and, as I think, he changed his mind chiefly from fear lest the Athenians should depart and leave them, if he should take the ships to the Isthmus; for if the Athenians left them and departed, the rest would be no longer able to fight with the enemy. He chose then this counsel, to stay in that place and decide matters there by a sea-fight.

64. Thus those at Salamis, after having skirmished with one another in speech, were making preparations for a sea-fight there, since Eurybiades had so determined: and as day was coming on, at the same time when the sun rose there was an earthquake felt both on the land and on the sea: and they determined to pray to the gods and to call upon the sons of Aiacos to be their helpers. And as they had determined, so also they did; for when they had prayed to all the gods, they called Ajax and Telamon to their help from Salamis, where the fleet was, and sent a ship to Egina to bring Aiacos himself and the rest of the sons of Aiacos.

65. Moreover Dicaios the son of Theokydes, an Athenian, who was an exile and had become of great repute among the Medes at this time, declared that when the Attic land was being ravaged by the land-army of Xerxes, having been deserted by the Athenians, he happened then to be in company with Demaratos the Lacedemonian in the Thriasian plain; and he saw a cloud of dust going up from Eleusis, as if made by a company of about thirty thousand men, and they wondered at the cloud of dust, by what men it was caused. Then forthwith they heard a sound of voices, and Dicaios perceived that the sound was the mystic cry *Iacchos*; but Demaratos, having no knowledge of the sacred rites which are done at Eleusis, asked him what this was that uttered the sound, and he said: "Demaratos, it cannot be but that some great destruction is about to come to the army of the king: for as to this, it is very manifest, seeing that Attica is deserted, that this which utters the sound is of the gods, and that it is going from Eleusis to help the Athenians and their allies: if then it shall come down in the Peloponnese, there is danger for the king himself and for the army which is upon the mainland, but if it shall direct its course towards the ships which are at Salamis, the king will be in danger of losing his fleet. This feast the Athenians celebrate every year to the Mother and the Daughter; and he that desires it, both of them and of the other Hellenes, is initiated in the mysteries; and the sound of voices which thou hearest is the cry *Iacchos* which they utter at this feast." To this Demaratos said: "Keep silence and tell not this tale to any other man; for if these words of thine be reported to the king, thou wilt surely lose thy head, and neither I nor any other man upon earth will be able to save thee: but keep thou quiet, and about this expedition the gods will provide." He then thus advised, and after the cloud of dust and the sound of voices there came a mist which was borne aloft and carried towards Salamis to the camp of the Hellenes: and thus they learnt (said he) that the fleet of Xerxes was destined to be destroyed. Such was the report made by Dicaios the son of Theodykes, appealing to Demaratos and others also as witnesses.

66. Meanwhile those who were appointed to serve in the fleet of Xerxes, having gazed in Trachis upon the disaster of the Lacedemonians and having passed over from thence to Histiaia, after staying three days sailed through Euripos, and in other three days they had reached Phaleron. And, as I suppose, they made their attack upon Athens not fewer in number both by land and sea than when they had arrived at Sepias and at Thermopylai: for against those of them who perished by reason of the storm and those who were slain at Thermopylai and in the sea-fights at Artemision, I will set those who at that time were not yet accompanying the king, the Malians, Dorians, Locrians, and Boeotians (who accompanied him in a body, except the Thespians and Plataians), and moreover those of Carystos, Andros, and Tenos, with all the other islanders except the five cities of which I mentioned the names before; for the more the Persian advanced towards the center of Hellas, the more nations accompanied him.

67. So then, when all these had come to Athens except the Parians (now the Parians had remained behind at Kythnos waiting to see how the war would turn out),—when all the rest, I say, had come to Phaleron, then Xerxes himself came down to the ships desiring to visit them and to learn the opinions of those who sailed in them: and when he had come and was set in a conspicuous place, then those who were despots of their own nations or commanders of divisions being sent for came before him from their ships, and took their seats as the king had assigned rank to each one, first the king of Sidon, then he of Tyre, and after them the rest: and when they were seated in due order, Xerxes sent

Mardonios and inquired, making trial of each one, whether he should fight a battle by sea.

68. So when Mardonios went round asking them, beginning with the king of Sidon, the others gave their opinions all to the same effect, advising him to fight a battle by sea, but Artemisia spoke these words:—(a) "Tell the king I pray thee, Mardonios, that I, who have proved myself not to be the worst in the sea-fights which have been fought near Euboea, and have displayed deeds not inferior to those of others, speak to him thus: Master, it is right that I set forth the opinion which I really have, and say that which I happen to think best for thy cause: and this I say,—spare thy ships and do not make a sea-fight; for the men are as much stronger than thy men by sea, as men are stronger than women. And why must thou needs run the risk of sea-battles? Hast thou not Athens in thy possession, for the sake of which thou didst set forth on thy march, and also the rest of Hellas? and no man stands in thy way to resist, but those who did stand against thee came off as it was fitting that they should. (b) Now the manner in which I think the affairs of thy adversaries will have their issue, I will declare. If thou do not hasten to make a sea-fight, but keep thy ships here by the land, either remaining here thyself or even advancing on to the Peloponnese, that which thou hast come to do, O master, will easily be effected; for the Hellenes are not able to hold out against thee for any long time, but thou wilt soon disperse them and they will take flight to their several cities: since neither have they provisions with them in this island, as I am informed, nor is it probable that if thou shalt march thy land-army against the Peloponnese, they who have come from thence will remain still; for these will have no care to fight a battle in defense of Athens. (c) If however thou hasten to fight forthwith, I fear that damage done to the fleet may ruin the land-army also. Moreover, O king, consider also this, that the servants of good men are apt to grow bad, but those of bad men good; and thou, who art of all men the best, hast bad servants, namely those who are reckoned as allies, Egyptians and Cyprians and Kilikians and Pamphylians, in whom there is no profit."

69. When she thus spoke to Mardonios, those who were friendly to Artemisia were grieved at her words, supposing that she would suffer some evil from the king because she urged him not to fight at sea; while those who had envy and jealousy of her, because she had been honored above all the allies, were rejoiced at the opposition, supposing that she would now be ruined. When however the opinions were reported to Xerxes, he was greatly pleased with the opinion of Artemisia; and whereas even before this he thought her excellent, he commended her now yet more. Nevertheless he gave orders to follow the advice of the greater number, thinking that when they fought by Euboea they were purposely slack, because he was not himself present with them, whereas now he had made himself ready to look on while they fought a sea-battle.

70. So when they passed the word to put out to sea, they brought their ships out to Salamis and quietly ranged themselves along the shore in their several positions. At that time the daylight was not sufficient for them to engage battle, for night had come on; but they made their preparations to fight on the following day. Meanwhile the Hellenes were possessed by fear and dismay, especially those who were from Peloponnese: and these were dismayed because remaining in Salamis they were to fight a battle on behalf of the land of the Athenians, and being defeated they would be cut off from escape and blockaded in an island, leaving their own land unguarded. And indeed the land-army of the Barbarians was marching forward during that very night towards the Peloponnese.

THE HISTORIES OF HERODOTUS 359

71. Yet every means had been taken that the Barbarians might not be able to enter Pelo-ponnesus by land: for as soon as the Peloponnesians heard that Leonidas and his company had perished at Thermopylai, they came together quickly from the cities and took post at the Isthmus, and over them was set as commander Cleombrotos, the son of Anaxandrides and brother of Leonidas. These being posted at the Isthmus had destroyed the Skironian way, and after this (having so determined in counsel with one another) they began to build a wall across the Isthmus; and as they were many myriads and every man joined in the work, the work proceeded fast; for stones and bricks and pieces of timber and baskets full of sand were carried to it continually, and they who had thus come to help paused not at all in their work either by night or by day.

72. Now those of the Hellenes who came in full force to the Isthmus to help their country were these,—the Lacedemonians, the Arcadians of every division, the Eleians, Corinthians, Sikyonians, Epidaurians, Phliasians, Troizenians and Hermionians. These were they who came to the help of Hellas in her danger and who had apprehension for her, while the rest of the Peloponnesians showed no care: and the Olympic and Carneian festivals had by this time gone by.

73. Now Peloponnesus is inhabited by seven races; and of these, two are natives of the soil and are settled now in the place where they dwelt of old, namely the Arcadians and the Kynurians; and one race, that of the Achaians, though it did not remove from the Pelo-ponnese, yet removed in former time from its own land and dwells now in that which was not its own. The remaining races, four in number, have come in from without, namely the Dorians, Aitolians, Dryopians and Lemnians. Of the Dorians there are many cities and of great renown; of the Aitolians, Elis alone; of the Dryopians, Hermion and Asine, which latter is opposite Cardamyle in the Laconian land; and of the Lemnians, all the Paroreatai. The Kynurians, who are natives of the soil, seem alone to be Ionians, but they have become Dorians completely because they are subject to the Argives and by lapse of time, being originally citizens of Orneai or the dwellers in the country round Orneai. Of these seven nations the remaining cities, except those which I enumerated just now, stood aside and did nothing; and if one may be allowed to speak freely, in thus standing aside they were in fact taking the side of the Medes.

74. Those at the Isthmus were struggling with the labor which I have said, since now they were running a course in which their very being was at stake, and they did not look to have any brilliant success with their ships: while those who were at Salamis, though informed of this work, were yet dismayed, not fearing so much for themselves as for Pelo-ponnesus. For some time then they spoke of it in private, one man standing by another, and they marveled at the ill-counsel of Eurybiades; but at last it broke out publicly. A meeting accordingly was held, and much was spoken about the same points as before, some saying that they ought to sail away to Peloponnesus and run the risk in defense of that, and not stay and fight for a land which had been captured by the enemy, while the Athenians, Eginetans and Megarians urged that they should stay there and defend themselves.

75. Then Themistocles, when his opinion was like to be defeated by the Pelopon-nesians, secretly went forth from the assembly, and having gone out he sent a man to the encampment of the Medes in a boat, charging him with that which he must say: this man's name was Sikinnos, and he was a servant of Themistocles and tutor to his children; and after these events Themistocles entered him as a Thespian citizen, when the Thespians

were admitting new citizens, and made him a wealthy man. He at this time came with a boat and said to the commanders of the Barbarians these words: "The commander of the Athenians sent me privately without the knowledge of the other Hellenes (for, as it chances, he is disposed to the cause of the king, and desires rather that your side should gain the victory than that of the Hellenes), to inform you that the Hellenes are planning to take flight, having been struck with dismay; and now it is possible for you to execute a most noble work, if ye do not permit them to flee away: for they are not of one mind with one another and they will not stand against you in fight, but ye shall see them fighting a battle by sea with one another, those who are disposed to your side against those who are not."

76. He then having signified to them this, departed out of the way; and they, thinking that the message deserved credit, landed first a large number of Persians in the small island of Psyttaleia, which lies between Salamis and the mainland; and then, as midnight came on, they put out the Western wing of their fleet to sea, circling round towards Salamis, and also those stationed about Keos and Kynosura put out their ships to sea; and they occupied all the passage with their ships as far as Munychia. And for this reason they put out their ships, namely in order that the Hellenes might not even be permitted to get away, but being cut off in Salamis might pay the penalty for the contests at Artemision: and they disembarked men of the Persians on the small island called Psyttaleia for this reason, namely that when the fight should take place, these might save the men of one side and destroy those of the other, since there especially it was likely that the men and the wrecks of ships would be cast up on shore, for the island lay in the way of the sea-fight which was to be. These things they did in silence, that the enemy might not have information of them.

77. They then were making their preparations thus in the night without having taken any sleep at all: and with regard to oracles, I am not able to make objections against them that they are not true, for I do not desire to attempt to overthrow the credit of them when they speak clearly, looking at such matters as these which here follow:

"But when with ships they shall join the sacred strand of the goddess,
Artemis golden-sword-girded, and thee, wave-washed Kynosura,
Urged by a maddening hope, having given rich Athens to plunder,
Then shall Justice divine quell Riot, of Insolence first-born,
Longing to overthrow all things and terribly panting for bloodshed:
Brass shall encounter with brass, and Ares the sea shall empurple,
Tinging its waves with the blood: then a day of freedom for Hellas
Cometh from wide-seeing Zeus and from Victory, lady and mother."

Looking to such things as this, and when Bakis speaks so clearly, I do not venture myself to make any objections about oracles, nor can I admit them from others.

78. Now between the commanders that were at Salamis there came to be great contention of speech and they did not yet know that the Barbarians were surrounding them with their ships, but they thought that they were still in their place as they saw them disposed in the day.

79. Then while the commanders were engaged in strife, there came over from Egina Aristeides the son of Lysimachos, an Athenian who had been ostracized by the people, a

man whom I hold (according to that which I hear of his character) to have been the best and most upright of all Athenians. This man came into the council and called forth Themistocles, who was to him not a friend, but an enemy to the last degree; but because of the greatness of the present troubles he let those matters be forgotten and called him forth, desiring to communicate with him. Now he had heard beforehand that the Peloponnesians were pressing to take the ships away to the Isthmus. So when Themistocles came forth to him, Aristeides spoke these words: "Both at other times when occasion arises, and also especially at this time we ought to carry on rivalry as to which of us shall do more service to our country. And I tell thee now that it is indifferent whether the Peloponnesians say many words or few about sailing away from hence; for having been myself an eye-witness I tell thee that now not even if the Corinthians and Eurybiades himself desire to sail out, will they be able; for we are encompassed round by the enemy. Go thou in then, and signify this to them."

80. He made answer as follows: "Thou advisest very well, and also the news which thou hast brought is good, since thou art come having witnessed with thine own eyes that which I desired might come to pass: for know that this which is being done by the Medes is of my suggestion; because, when the Hellenes would not come to a battle of their own will, it was necessary to bring them over to us against their will. Do thou however, since thou art come bearing good news, thyself report it to them; for if I say these things, I shall be thought to speak that which I have myself invented, and I shall not persuade them, but they will think that the Barbarians are not doing so. Do thou thyself however come forward to speak, and declare to them how things are; and when thou hast declared this, if they are persuaded, that will be the best thing, but if this is not credible to them, it will be the same thing so far as concerns us, for they will no longer be able to take to flight, if we are encompassed on all sides, as thou sayest."

81. Aristeides accordingly came forward and told them this, saying that he had come from Egina and had with difficulty escaped without being perceived by those who were blockading them; for the whole encampment of the Hellenes was encompassed by the ships of Xerxes; and he counselled them to get ready to defend themselves. He then having thus spoken retired, and among them again there arose dispute, for the greater number of the commanders did not believe that which was reported to them:

82. and while these were doubting, there came a trireme manned by Tenians, deserting from the enemy, of which the commander was Panaitios the son of Sosimenes, which brought them the whole truth. For this deed the Tenians were inscribed at Delphi on the tripod among those who had conquered the Barbarians. With the ship which deserted at Salamis and the Lemnian ship which deserted before and came to Artemision, the naval force of the Hellenes was completed to the number of three hundred and eighty ships, for before this two ships were yet wanting to make up this number.

83. The Hellenes then, since they believed that which was said by the Tenians, were preparing for a sea-fight: and as the dawn appeared, they made an assembly of those who fought on board the ships and addressed them, Themistocles making a speech which was eloquent beyond the rest; and the substance of it was to set forth all that is better as opposed to that which is worse, of the several things which arise in the nature and constitution of man; and having exhorted them to choose the better, and thus having wound up his speech, he bade them embark in their ships. These then proceeded to embark, and

there came in meanwhile the trireme from Egina which had gone away to bring the sons of Aiacos.

84. Then the Hellenes put out all their ships, and while they were putting out from shore, the Barbarians attacked them forthwith. Now the other Hellenes began backing their ships and were about to run them aground, but Ameinias of Pallene, an Athenian, put forth with his ship and charged one of the enemy; and his ship being entangled in combat and the men not being able to get away, the others joined in the fight to assist Ameinias. The Athenians say that the beginning of the battle was made thus, but the Eginetans say that the ship which went away to Egina to bring the sons of Aiacos was that which began the fight. It is also reported that an apparition of a woman was seen by them, and that having appeared she encouraged them to the fight so that the whole of the army of the Hellenes heard it, first having reproached them in these words: "Madmen, how far will ye yet back your ships?"

85. Opposite the Athenians had been ranged the Phoenicians, for these occupied the wing towards Eleusis and the West, and opposite the Lacedemonians were the Ionians, who occupied the wing which extended to the East and to Piræus. Of them however a few were purposely slack in the fight according to the injunctions of Themistocles, but the greater number were not so. I might mention now the names of many captains of ships who destroyed ships of the Hellenes, but I will make no use of their names except in the case of Theomestor, the son of Androdamas and Phylacos the son of Histiaios, of Samos both: and for this reason I make mention of these and not of the rest, because Theomestor on account of this deed became despot of Samos, appointed by the Persians, and Phylacos was recorded as a benefactor of the king and received much land as a reward. Now the benefactors of the king are called in the Persian tongue *orosangai*.

86. Thus it was with these; but the greater number of their ships were disabled at Salamis, being destroyed some by the Athenians and others by the Eginetans: for since the Hellenes fought in order and ranged in their places, while the Barbarians were no longer ranged in order nor did anything with design, it was likely that there would be some such result as in fact followed. Yet on this day they surpassed themselves much more than when they fought by Euboea, every one being eager and fearing Xerxes, and each man thinking that the king was looking especially at him.

87. As regards the rest I cannot speak of them separately, or say precisely how the Barbarians or the Hellenes individually contended in the fight; but with regard to Artemisia that which happened was this, whence she gained yet more esteem than before from the king.—When the affairs of the king had come to great confusion, at this crisis a ship of Artemisia was being pursued by an Athenian ship; and as she was not able to escape, for in front of her were other ships of her own side, while her ship, as it chanced, was furthest advanced towards the enemy, she resolved what she would do, and it proved also much to her advantage to have done so. While she was being pursued by the Athenian ship she charged with full career against a ship of her own side manned by Calyndians and in which the king of the Calyndians Damasithymos was embarked. Now even though it be true that she had had some strife with him before, while they were still about the Hellespont, yet I am not able to say whether she did this by intention, or whether the Calyndian ship happened by chance to fall in her way. Having charged against it however and sunk it, she enjoyed good fortune and got for herself good in two ways; for first the captain of the Athenian ship, when he saw her charge against a ship

manned by Barbarians, turned away and went after others, supposing that the ship of Artemisia was either a Hellenic ship or was deserting from the Barbarians and fighting for the Hellenes,

88,—first, I say, it was her fortune to have this, namely to escape and not suffer destruction; and then secondly it happened that though she had done mischief, she yet gained great reputation by this thing with Xerxes. For it is said that the king looking on at the fight perceived that her ship had charged the other; and one of those present said: "Master, dost thou see Artemisia, how well she is fighting, and how she sank even now a ship of the enemy?" He asked whether this was in truth the deed of Artemisia, and they said that it was; for (they declared) they knew very well the sign of her ship: and that which was destroyed they thought surely was one of the enemy; for besides other things which happened fortunately for her, as I have said, there was this also, namely that not one of the crew of the Calyndian ship survived to become her accuser. And Xerxes in answer to that which was said to him is reported to have uttered these words: "My men have become women, and my women men." Thus it is said that Xerxes spoke.

89. And meanwhile in this struggle there was slain the commander Ariabignes, son of Dareios and brother of Xerxes, and there were slain too many others of note of the Persians and Medes and also of the allies; and of the Hellenes on their part a few; for since they knew how to swim, those whose ships were destroyed and who were not slain in hand-to-hand conflict swam over to Salamis; but of the Barbarians the greater number perished in the sea, not being able to swim. And when the first ships turned to flight, then it was that the largest number perished, for those who were stationed behind, while endeavoring to pass with their ships to the front in order that they also might display some deed of valor for the king to see, ran into the ships of their own side as they fled.

90. It happened also in the course of this confusion that some of the Phoenicians, whose ships had been destroyed, came to the king and accused the Ionians, saying that by means of them their ships had been lost, and that they had been traitors to the cause. Now it so came about that not only the commanders of the Ionians did not lose their lives, but the Phoenicians who accused them received a reward such as I shall tell. While these men were yet speaking thus, a Samothrakian ship charged against an Athenian ship: and as the Athenian ship was being sunk by it, an Eginetan ship came up against the Samothrakian vessel and ran it down. Then the Samothrakians, being skillful javelin-throwers, by hurling cleared off the fighting-men from the ship which had wrecked theirs and then embarked upon it and took possession of it. This event saved the Ionians from punishment; for when Xerxes saw that they had performed a great exploit, he turned to the Phoenicians (for he was exceedingly vexed and disposed to find fault with all) and bade cut off their heads, in order that they might not, after having been cowards themselves, accuse others who were better men than they. For whensoever Xerxes (sitting just under the mountain opposite Salamis, which is called Aigaleos) saw any one of his own side display a deed of valor in the sea-fight, he inquired about him who had done it, and the scribes recorded the name of the ship's captain with that of his father and the city from whence he came. Moreover also Ariaramnes, a Persian who was present, shared the fate of the Phoenicians, being their friend. They then proceeded to deal with the Phoenicians.

91. In the meantime, as the Barbarians turned to flight and were sailing out towards Phaleron, the Eginetans waited for them in the passage and displayed memorable actions: for while the Athenians in the confused tumult were disabling both those ships which

resisted and those which were fleeing, the Eginetans were destroying those which attempted to sail away; and whenever any escaped the Athenians, they went in full course and fell among the Eginetans.

92. Then there met one another the ship of Themistocles, which was pursuing a ship of the enemy, and that of Polycritos the son of Crios the Eginetan. This last had charged against a ship of Sidon, the same that had taken the Eginetan vessel which was keeping watch in advance at Skiathos, and in which sailed Pytheas the son of Ischenoös, whom the Persians kept in their ship, all cut to pieces as he was, making a marvel of his valor. The Sidonian ship then was captured bearing with it this man as well as the Persians of whom I spoke, so that Pytheas thus came safe to Egina. Now when Polycritos looked at the Athenian vessel he recognized when he saw it the sign of the admiral's ship, and shouting out he addressed Themistocles with mockery about the accusation brought against the Eginetans of taking the side of the Medes, and reproached him. This taunt Polycritos threw out against Themistocles after he had charged against the ship of Sidon. And meanwhile those Barbarians whose ships had escaped destruction fled and came to Phaleron to be under cover of the land-army.

93. In this sea-fight the Eginetans were of all the Hellenes the best reported of, and next to them the Athenians; and of the individual men the Eginetan Polycritos and the Athenians Eumenes of Anagyrus and Ameinias of Pallene, the man who had pursued after Artemisia. Now if he had known that Artemisia was sailing in this ship, he would not have ceased until either he had taken her or had been taken himself; for orders had been given to the Athenian captains, and moreover a prize was offered of ten thousand drachmas for the man who should take her alive; since they thought it intolerable that a woman should make an expedition against Athens. She then, as has been said before, had made her escape; and the others also, whose ships had escaped destruction, were at Phaleron.

94. As regards Adeimantos the commander of the Corinthians, the Athenians say that forthwith at the beginning when the ships were engaging in the fight, being struck with panic and terror he put up his sails and fled away; and the Corinthians, when they saw the admiral's ship fleeing, departed likewise: and after this, as the story goes, when they came in their flight opposite to the temple of Athene Skiras in the land of Salamis, there fell in with them by divine guidance a light vessel, which no one was ever found to have sent, and which approached the Corinthians at a time when they knew nothing of that which was happening with the fleet. And by this it is conjectured that the matter was of the Deity; for when they came near to the ships, the men in the light vessel said these words: "Adeimantos, thou hast turned thy ships away and hast set forth to flee, deserting the cause of the Hellenes, while they are in truth gaining a victory and getting the better of their foes as much as they desired." When they said this, since Adeimantos doubted of it, they spoke a second time and said that they might be taken as hostages and slain, if the Hellenes should prove not to be gaining the victory. Then he turned his ship back, he and the others with him, and they reached the camp when the work was finished. Such is the report spread by the Athenians against these: the Corinthians however do not allow this to be so, but hold that they were among the first in the sea-fight; and the rest of Hellas also bears witness on their side.

95. Aristeides moreover the son of Lysimachos, the Athenian, of whom I made mention also shortly before this as a very good man, he in this tumult which had arisen

about Salamis did as follows:—taking with him a number of the hoplites of Athenian race who had been ranged along the shore of the land of Salamis, with them he disembarked on the island of Psyttaleia; and these slew all the Persians who were in this islet.

96. When the sea-fight had been broken off, the Hellenes towed in to Salamis so many of the wrecks as chanced to be still about there, and held themselves ready for another sea-fight, expecting that the king would yet make use of the ships which remained unhurt; but many of the wrecks were taken by the West Wind and borne to that strand in Attica which is called Colias; so as to fulfil not only all that other oracle which was spoken about this sea-fight by Bakis and Musaios, but also especially, with reference to the wrecks cast up here, that which had been spoken in an oracle many years before these events by Lysistratos, an Athenian who uttered oracles, and which had not been observed by any of the Hellenes:

"Then shall the Colian women with firewood of oars roast barley."

This was destined to come to pass after the king had marched away.

97. When Xerxes perceived the disaster which had come upon him, he feared lest some one of the Ionians should suggest to the Hellenes, or they should themselves form the idea, to sail to the Hellespont and break up the bridges; and so he might be cut off in Europe and run the risk of perishing utterly: therefore he began to consider about taking flight. He desired however that his intention should not be perceived either by the Hellenes or by those of his own side; therefore he attempted to construct a mole going across to Salamis, and he bound together Phoenician merchant vessels in order that they might serve him both for a bridge and a wall, and made preparations for fighting as if he were going to have another battle by sea. Seeing him do so, all the rest made sure that he had got himself ready in earnest and intended to stay and fight; but Mardonios did not fail to perceive the true meaning of all these things, being by experience very well versed in his way of thinking.

98. While Xerxes was doing thus, he sent a messenger to the Persians, to announce the calamity which had come upon them. Now there is nothing mortal which accomplishes a journey with more speed than these messengers, so skillfully has this been invented by the Persians: for they say that according to the number of days of which the entire journey consists, so many horses and men are set at intervals, each man and horse appointed for a day's journey. These neither snow nor rain nor heat nor darkness of night prevents from accomplishing each one the task proposed to him, with the very utmost speed. The first then rides and delivers the message with which he is charged to the second, and the second to the third; and after that it goes through them handed from one to the other, as in the torch-race among the Hellenes, which they perform for Hephaistos. This kind of running of their horses the Persians call *angareion*.

99. The first message then which came to Susa, announcing that Xerxes had Athens in his possession, so greatly rejoiced the Persians who had been left behind, that they strewed all the ways with myrtle boughs and offered incense perpetually, and themselves continued in sacrifices and feasting. The second message however, which came to them after this, so greatly disturbed them that they all tore their garments and gave themselves up to crying and lamentation without stint, laying the blame upon Mardonios: and this

the Persians did not so much because they were grieved about the ships, as because they feared for Xerxes himself.

100. As regards the Persians this went on for all the time which intervened, until the coming of Xerxes himself caused them to cease: and Mardonios seeing that Xerxes was greatly troubled by reason of the sea-fight, and suspecting that he was meaning to take flight from Athens, considered with regard to himself that he would have to suffer punishment for having persuaded the king to make an expedition against Hellas, and that it was better for him to run the risk of either subduing Hellas or ending his own life honorably, placing his safety in suspense for a great end, though his opinion was rather that he would subdue Hellas;—he reckoned up these things, I say, and addressed his speech to the king as follows: "Master, be not thou grieved, nor feel great trouble on account of this thing which has come to pass; for it is not upon a contest of timbers that all our fortunes depend, but of men and of horses: and none of these who suppose now that all has been achieved by them will attempt to disembark from the ships and stand against thee, nor will any in this mainland do so; but those who did stand against us paid the penalty. If therefore thou thinkest this good to do, let us forthwith attempt the Peloponnese, or if thou thinkest good to hold back, we may do that. Do not despond however, for there is no way of escape for the Hellenes to avoid being thy slaves, after they have first given an account of that which they did to thee both now and at former times. Thus it were best to do; but if thou hast indeed resolved to retire thyself and to withdraw thy army, I have another counsel to offer for that case too. Do not thou, O king, let the Persians be an object of laughter to the Hellenes; for none of thy affairs have suffered by means of the Persians, nor wilt thou be able to mention any place where we proved ourselves cowards: but if Phoenicians or Egyptians or Cyprians or Kilikians proved themselves cowards, the calamity which followed does not belong to the Persians in any way. Now therefore, since it is not the Persians who are guilty towards thee, follow my counsel. If thou hast determined not to remain here, retire thou to thine own abode, taking with thee the main body of the army, and it must then be for me to deliver over to thee Hellas reduced to subjection, choosing for this purpose thirty myriads from the army."

101. Hearing this Xerxes was rejoiced and delighted so far as he might be after his misfortunes, and to Mardonios he said that when he had taken counsel he would reply and say which of these two things he would do. So when he was taking counsel with those of the Persians who were called to be his advisers, it seemed good to him to send for Artemisia also to give him counsel, because at the former time she alone had showed herself to have perception of that which ought to be done. So when Artemisia had come, Xerxes removed from him all the rest, both the Persian councilors and also the spearmen of the guard and spoke to her thus: "Mardonios bids me stay here and make an attempt on the Peloponnese, saying that the Persians and the land-army are not guilty of any share in my calamity, and that they would gladly give me proof of this. He bids me therefore either do this or, if not, he desires himself to choose thirty myriads from the army and to deliver over to me Hellas reduced to subjection; and he bids me withdraw with the rest of the army to my own abode. Do thou therefore, as thou didst well advise about the sea-fight which was fought, urging that we should not bring it on, so also now advise me which of these things I shall do, that I may succeed in determining well."

102. He thus consulted her, and she spoke these words: "O king, it is hard for me to succeed in saying the best things when one asks me for counsel; yet it seems good to me at

the present that thou shouldest retire back and leave Mardonios here, if he desires it and undertakes to do this, together with those whom he desires to have: for on the one hand if he subdue those whom he says that he desires to subdue, and if those matters succeed well which he has in mind when he thus speaks, the deed will after all be thine, master, seeing that thy slaves achieved it: and on the other hand if the opposite shall come to pass of that which Mardonios intends, it will be no great misfortune, seeing that thou wilt thyself remain safe, and also the power in those parts which concerns thy house: for if thou shalt remain safe with thy house, many contests many times over repeated will the Hellenes have to pass through for their own existence. Of Mardonios however, if he suffer any disaster, no account will be made; and if the Hellenes conquer they gain a victory which is no victory, having destroyed one who is but thy slave. Thou however wilt retire having done that for which thou didst make thy march, that is to say, having delivered Athens to the fire."

103. With this advice Xerxes was greatly delighted, since she succeeded in saying that very thing which he himself was meaning to do: for not even if all the men and all the women in the world had been counselling him to remain, would he have done so, as I think, so much had he been struck with terror. He commended Artemisia therefore and sent her away to conduct his sons to Ephesos, for there were certain bastard sons of his which accompanied him.

104. With these sons he sent Hermotimos to have charge of them, who was by race of Pedasa and was in the estimation of the king second to none of the eunuchs. [Now the Pedasians dwell above Halicarnassos, and at this Pedasa a thing happens as follows:— whenever to the whole number of those who dwell about this city some trouble is about to come within a certain time, then the priestess of Athene in that place gets a long beard; and this has happened to them twice before now.

105. Of these Pedasians was Hermotimos.] And this man of all persons whom we know up to this time obtained the greatest revenge for a wrong done to him. For he had been captured by enemies and was being sold, and Panionios a man of Chios bought him, one who had set himself to gain his livelihood by the most impious practices; for when-ever he obtained boys who possessed some beauty, he would make eunuchs of them, and then taking them to Sardis or Ephesos sold them for large sums of money, since with the Barbarians eunuchs are held to be of more value for all matters of trust than those who are not eunuchs. Panionios then, I say, made eunuchs of many others, since by this he got his livelihood, and also of this man about whom I speak: and Hermotimos, being not in everything unfortunate, was sent from Sardis to the king with other gifts, and as time went on he came to be honored more than all the other eunuchs in the sight of Xerxes.

106. And when the king, being at that time in Sardis, was setting the Persian army in motion to march against Athens, then Hermotimos, having gone down for some business to that part of Mysia which the Chians occupy and which is called Atarneus, found there Panionios: and having recognized him he spoke to him many friendly words, first recounting to him all the good things which he had by his means, and next making promises in return for this, and saying how many good things he would do for him, if he would bring his household and dwell in that land; so that Panionios gladly accepting his proposals brought his children and his wife. Then, when he had caught him together with his whole house, Hermotimos spoke as follows: "O thou, who of all men that ever lived up to this time didst gain thy substance by the most impious deeds, what evil did either I

myself or any of my forefathers do either to thee or to any of thine, that thou didst make me to be that which is naught instead of a man? Didst thou suppose that thou wouldest escape the notice of the gods for such things as then thou didst devise? They however following the rule of justice delivered thee into my hands, since thou hadst done impious deeds; so that thou shalt not have reason to find fault with the penalty which shall be inflicted upon thee by me." When he had thus reproached him, the man's sons were brought into his presence and Panionios was compelled to make eunuchs of his own sons, who were four in number, and being compelled he did so; and then when he had so done, the sons were compelled to do the same thing to him. Thus vengeance by the hands of Hermotimos overtook Panionios.

107. When Xerxes had entrusted his sons to Artemisia to carry them back to Ephesos, he called Mardonios and bade him choose of the army whom he would, and make his deeds, if possible, correspond to his words. During this day then things went so far; and in the night on the command of the king the leaders of the fleet began to withdraw their ships from Phaleron to the Hellespont, as quickly as they might each one, to guard the bridges for the king to pass over. And when the Barbarians were near Zoster as they sailed, then seeing the small points of rock which stretch out to sea from this part of the mainland, they thought that these were ships and fled for a good distance. In time however, perceiving that they were not ships but points of rock, they assembled together again and continued on their voyage.

108. When day dawned, the Hellenes, seeing that the land-army was staying still in its place, supposed that the ships also were about Phaleron; and thinking that they would fight another sea-battle, they made preparations to repel them. When however they were informed that the ships had departed, forthwith upon this they thought it good to pursue after them. They pursued therefore as far as Andros, but did not get a sight of the fleet of Xerxes; and when they had come to Andros, they deliberated what they should do. Themistocles then declared as his opinion that they should take their course through the islands and pursue after the ships, and afterwards sail straight to the Hellespont to break up the bridges; but Eurybiades expressed the opposite opinion to this, saying that if they should break up the floating-bridges, they would therein do the greatest possible evil to Hellas: for if the Persian should be cut off and compelled to remain in Europe, he would endeavor not to remain still, since if he remained still, neither could any of his affairs go forward, nor would any way of returning home appear; but his army would perish of hunger: whereas if he made the attempt and persevered in it, all Europe might be brought over to him, city by city and nation by nation, the inhabitants being either conquered or surrendering on terms before they were conquered: moreover they would have for food the crops of the Hellenes which grew year by year. He thought however that conquered in the sea-fight the Persian would not stay in Europe, and therefore he might be allowed to flee until in his flight he came to his own land. Then after that they might begin the contest for the land which belonged to the Persian. To this opinion the commanders of the other Peloponnesians adhered also.

109. When Themistocles perceived that he would not be able to persuade them, or at least the greater number of them, to sail to the Hellespont, he changed his counsel and turning to the Athenians (for these were grieved most at the escape of the enemy and were anxious to sail to the Hellespont even by themselves alone, if the others were not willing) to them he spoke as follows: "I myself also have been present before now on

many occasions, and have heard of many more, on which something of this kind came to pass, namely that men who were forced into great straits, after they had been defeated fought again and repaired their former disaster: and as for us, since we have won as a prize from fortune the existence of ourselves and of Hellas by repelling from our land so great a cloud of men, let us not pursue enemies who flee from us: for of these things not we were the doors, but the gods and heroes, who grudged that one man should become king of both Asia and of Europe, and he a man unholy and presumptuous, one who made no difference between things sacred and things profane, burning and casting down the images of the gods, and who also scourged the Sea and let down into it fetters. But as things are at present, it is well that we should now remain in Hellas and look after ourselves and our households; and let each man repair his house, and have a care for sowing his land, after he has completely driven away the Barbarian: and then at the beginning of the spring let us sail down towards the Hellespont and Ionia." Thus he spoke, intending to lay up for himself a store of gratitude with the Persian, in order that if after all any evil should come upon him at the hands of the Athenians, he might have a place of refuge: and this was in fact that which came to pass.

110. Themistocles then speaking thus endeavored to deceive them, and the Athenians followed his advice: for he had had the reputation even in former times of being a man of ability and he had now proved himself to be in truth both able and of good judgment; therefore they were ready in every way to follow his advice when he spoke. So when these had been persuaded by him, forthwith after this Themistocles sent men with a vessel, whom he trusted to keep silence, to whatever test they might be brought, of that which he himself charged them to tell the king; and of them Sikinnos his servant again was one. When these came to Attica, the rest stayed behind in the ship, while Sikinnos went up to Xerxes and spoke these words: "Themistocles the son of Neocles sent me, who is commander of the Athenians, and of all the allies the best and ablest man, to tell thee that Themistocles the Athenian, desiring to be of service to thee, held back the Hellenes when they were desirous to pursue after thy ships and to destroy the bridges on the Hellespont. Now therefore thou mayest make thy way home quite undisturbed." They having signified this sailed away again.

111. The Hellenes meanwhile, having resolved not to pursue after the ships of the Barbarians further, nor to sail to the Hellespont to break up the passage, were investing Andros intending to take it: for the Andrians were the first of the islanders who, being asked by Themistocles for money, refused to give it: and when Themistocles made proposals to them and said that the Athenians had come having on their side two great deities, Persuasion and Compulsion, and therefore they must by all means give them money, they replied to this that not without reason, as it now appeared, was Athens great and prosperous, since the Athenians were well supplied with serviceable deities; but as for the Andrians, they were poor, having in this respect attained to the greatest eminence, and there were two unprofitable deities which never left their island but always remained attached to the place, Poverty, namely, and Helplessness: and the Andrians being possessed of these deities would not give money; for never could the power of the Athenians get the better of their inability.

112. These, I say, having thus made answer and having refused to give the money, were being besieged: and Themistocles not ceasing in his desire for gain sent threatening messages to the other islands and asked them for money by the same envoys, employing

those whom he had before sent to the king; and he said that if they did not give that which was demanded of them, he would bring the fleet of the Hellenes against them to besiege and take them. Thus saying he collected great sums of money from the Carystians and the Parians, who being informed how Andros was being besieged, because it had taken the side of the Medes, and how Themistocles was held in more regard than any of the other commanders, sent money for fear of this. Whether any others of the islanders also gave money I am not able to say, but I think that some others gave and not these alone. Yet to the Carystians at least there was no respite from the evil on this account, but the Parians escaped the attack, because they propitiated Themistocles with money. Thus Themistocles with Andros as his starting-point was acquiring sums of money for himself from the men of the islands without the knowledge of the other commanders.

113. Xerxes meanwhile with his army stayed for a few days after the sea-fight, and then they all began to march forth towards Boeotia by the same way by which they had come: for Mardonios thought both that it was well for him to escort the king on his way, and also that it was now too late in the year to carry on the war; it was better, he thought, to winter in Thessaly and then at the beginning of spring to attempt the Peloponnese. When he came to Thessaly, then Mardonios chose out for himself first all those Persians who are called "Immortals," except only their commander Hydarnes (for Hydarnes said that he would not be left behind by the king), and after them of the other Persians those who wore cuirasses, and the body of a thousand horse: also the Medes, Sacans, Bactrians and Indians, foot and horsemen both. These nations he chose in the mass, but from the other allies he selected by few at a time, choosing whose who had fine appearance of those of whom he knew that they had done good service. From the Persians he chose more than from any other single nation, and these wore collars of twisted metal and bracelets; and after them came the Medes, who in fact were not inferior in number to the Persians, but only in bodily strength. The result was that there were thirty myriads in all, including cavalry.

114. During this time, while Mardonios was selecting his army and Xerxes was in Thessaly, there had come an oracle from Delphi to the Lacedemonians, bidding them ask satisfaction from Xerxes for the murder of Leonidas and accept that which should be given by him. The Spartans therefore sent a herald as quickly as possible, who having found the whole army still in Thessaly came into the presence of Xerxes and spoke these words: "O king of the Medes, the Lacedemonians and the sons of Heracles of Sparta demand of thee satisfaction for murder, because thou didst kill their king, fighting in defense of Hellas." He laughed and then kept silence some time, and after that pointing to Mardonios, who happened to be standing by him, he said: "Then Mardonios here shall give them satisfaction, such as is fitting for them to have."

115. The herald accordingly accepted the utterance and departed; and Xerxes leaving Mardonios in Thessaly went on himself in haste to the Hellespont and arrived at the passage where the crossing was in five-and-thirty days, bringing back next to nothing, as one may say, of his army: and whithersoever they came on the march and to whatever nation, they seized the crops of that people and used them for provisions; and if they found no crops, then they took the grass which was growing up from the earth, and stripped off the bark from the trees and plucked down the leaves and devoured them, alike of the cultivated trees and of those growing wild; and they left nothing behind them: thus they did by reason of famine. Then plague too seized upon the army and dysentery

which destroyed them by the way, and some of them also who were sick the king left behind, laying charge upon the cities where at the time he chanced to be in his march, to take care of them and support them: of these he left some in Thessaly, and some at Siris in Paionia, and some in Macedonia. In these parts too he had left behind him the sacred chariot of Zeus, when he was marching against Hellas; but on his return he did not receive it back: for the Paionians had given it to the Thracians, and when Xerxes asked for it again, they said that the mares while at pasture had been carried off by the Thracians of the upper country, who dwelt about the source of the Strymon.

116. Here also a Thracian, the king of the Bisaltians and of the Crestonian land, did a deed of surpassing horror; for he had said that he would not himself be subject to Xerxes with his own will and had gone away up to Mount Rhodope, and also he had forbidden his sons to go on the march against Hellas. They however, either because they cared not for his command, or else because a desire came upon them to see the war, went on the march with the Persian: and when they returned all unhurt, being six in number, their father plucked out their eyes for this cause.

117. They then received this reward: and as to the Persians, when passing on from Thrace they came to the passage, they crossed over the Hellespont in haste to Abydos by means of the ships, for they did not find the floating-bridges still stretched across but broken up by a storm. While staying there for a time they had distributed to them an allowance of food more abundant than they had had by the way, and from satisfying their hunger without restraint and also from the changes of water there died many of those in the army who had remained safe till then. The rest arrived with Xerxes at Sardis.

118. There is also another story reported as follows, namely that when Xerxes on his march away from Athens came to Eïon on the Strymon, from that point he did not continue further to make marches by road, but delivered his army to Hydarnes to lead back to the Hellespont, while he himself embarked in a Phoenician ship and set forth for Asia; and as he sailed he was seized by a wind from the Strymon, violent and raising great waves; and since he was tossed by the storm more and more, the ship being heavily laden (for there were upon the deck great numbers of Persians, those namely who went with Xerxes), the king upon that falling into fear shouted aloud and asked the pilot whether there were for them any means of safety. He said: "Master, there are none, unless some way be found of freeing ourselves of the excessive number of passengers." Then it is said that Xerxes, when he heard this, spoke thus: "Persians, now let each one of you show that he has care for the king; for my safety, as it seems, depends upon you." He, they say, thus spoke, and they made obeisance to him and leapt out into the sea; and so the ship being lightened came safe to Asia. As soon as they had landed Xerxes, they say, first presented the pilot with a wreath of gold, because he had saved the life of the king, and then cut off his head, because he had caused the death of many of the Persians.

119. This other story, I say, is reported about the return of Xerxes, but I for my part can by no means believe it, either in other respects or as regards this which is said to have happened to the Persians; for if this which I have related had in truth been said by the pilot to Xerxes, not one person's opinion in ten thousand will differ from mine that the king would have done some such thing as this, that is to say, he would have caused those who were upon the deck to go down below into the hold, seeing that they were Persians of the highest rank among the Persians; and of the rowers, who were Phoenicians, he would have thrown out into the sea a number equal to the number of those. In fact

however, as I have said before, he made his return to Asia together with the rest of the army by road.

120. And this also which follows is a strong witness that it was so; for Xerxes is known to have come to Abdera on his way back, and to have made with them a guest-friendship and presented them with a Persian sword of gold and a gold-spangled tiara: and as the men of Abdera themselves say (though I for my part can by no means believe it), he loosed his girdle for the first time during his flight back from Athens, considering himself to be in security. Now Abdera is situated further towards the Hellespont than the river Strymon and Eïon, from which place the story says that he embarked in the ship.

121. The Hellenes meanwhile, when it proved that they were not able to conquer Andros, turned towards Carystos, and having laid waste the land of that people they departed and went to Salamis. First then for the gods they chose out first-fruits of the spoil, and among them three Persian triremes, one to be dedicated as an offering at the Isthmus, which remained there still up to my time, another at Sunion, and the third to Ajax in Salamis where they were. After this they divided the spoil among themselves and sent the first-fruits to Delphi, of which was made a statue holding in its hand the beak of a ship and in height measuring twelve cubits. This statue stood in the same place with the golden statue of Alexander the Macedonian.

122. Then when the Hellenes had sent first-fruits to Delphi, they asked the god on behalf of all whether the first-fruits which he had received were fully sufficient and acceptable to him. He said that from the Hellenes he had received enough, but not from the Eginetans, and from them he demanded the offering of their prize of valor for the sea-fight at Salamis. Hearing this the Eginetans dedicated golden stars, three in number, upon a ship's mast of bronze, which are placed in the corner close to the mixing-bowl of Croesus.

123. After the division of the spoil the Hellenes sailed to the Isthmus, to give the prize of valor to him who of all the Hellenes had proved himself the most worthy during this war: and when they had come thither and the commanders distributed their votes at the altar of Poseidon, selecting from the whole number the first and the second in merit, then every one of them gave in his vote for himself, each man thinking that he himself had been the best; but for the second place the greater number of votes came out in agreement, assigning that to Themistocles. They then were left alone in their votes, while Themistocles in regard to the second place surpassed the rest by far:

124, and although the Hellenes would not give decision of this by reason of envy, but sailed away each to their own city without deciding, yet Themistocles was loudly reported of and was esteemed throughout Hellas to be the man who was the ablest by far of the Hellenes: and since he had not received honor from those who had fought at Salamis, although he was the first in the voting, he went forthwith after this to Lacedaemon, desiring to receive honor there; and the Lacedemonians received him well and gave him great honors. As a prize of valor they gave to Eurybiades a wreath of olive; and for ability and skill they gave to Themistocles also a wreath of olive, and presented him besides with the chariot which was judged to be the best in Sparta. So having much commended him, they escorted him on his departure with three hundred picked men of the Spartans, the same who are called the "horsemen," as far as the boundaries of Tegea: and he is the only man of all we know to whom the Spartans ever gave escort on his way.

125. When however he had come to Athens from Lacedaemon, Timodemos of Aphid-

nai, one of the opponents of Themistocles, but in other respects not among the men of distinction, maddened by envy attacked him, bringing forward against him his going to Lacedaemon, and saying that it was on account of Athens that he had those marks of honor which he had from the Lacedemonians, and not on his own account. Then, as Timodemos continued ceaselessly to repeat this, Themistocles said: "I tell thee thus it is:—if I had been a native of Belbina I should never have been thus honored by the Spartans; but neither wouldest thou, my friend, for all that thou art an Athenian." So far then went these matters.

126. Artabazos meanwhile the son of Pharnakes, a man who was held in esteem among the Persians even before this and came to be so yet more after the events about Plataia, was escorting the king as far as the passage with six myriads of that army which Mardonios had selected for himself; and when the king was in Asia and Artabazos on his march back came near to Pallene, finding that Mardonios was wintering in Thessaly and Macedonia and was not at present urgent with him to come and join the rest of the army, he thought it not good to pass by without reducing the Potidaians to slavery, whom he had found in revolt: for the men of Potidaia, when the king had marched by them and when the fleet of the Persians had departed in flight from Salamis, had openly made revolt from the Barbarians; and so also had the others done who occupy Pallene.

127. So upon this Artabazos began to besiege Potidaia, and suspecting that the men of Olynthos also were intending revolt from the king, he began to besiege this city too, which was occupied by Bottiaians who had been driven away from the Thermaian gulf by the Macedonians. So when he had taken these men by siege, he brought them forth to a lake and slew them there; and the city he delivered to Critobulos of Torone to have in charge, and to the natives of Chalkidike; and thus it was that the Chalkidians got possession of Olynthos.

128. Having taken this city Artabazos set himself to attack Potidaia with vigor, and as he was setting himself earnestly to this work, Timoxeinos the commander of the troops from Skione concerted with him to give up the town by treachery. Now in what manner he did this at the first, I for my part am not able to say, for this is not reported; at last however it happened as follows. Whenever either Timoxeinos wrote a paper wishing to send it to Artabazos, or Artabazos wishing to send one to Timoxeinos, they wound it round by the finger-notches of an arrow, and then, putting feathers over the paper, they shot it to a place agreed upon between them. It came however to be found out that Timoxeinos was attempting by treachery to give up Potidaia; for Artabazos, shooting an arrow at the place agreed upon, missed this spot and struck a man of Potidaia in the shoulder; and when he was struck, a crowd came about him, as is apt to happen when there is fighting, and they forthwith took the arrow and having discovered the paper carried it to the commanders. Now there was present an allied force of the other men of Pallene also. Then when the commanders had read the paper and discovered who was guilty of the treachery, they resolved not openly to convict Timoxeinos of treachery, for the sake of the city of Skione, lest the men of Skione should be esteemed traitors for all time to come.

129. He then in such a manner as this had been discovered; and when three months had gone by while Artabazos was besieging the town, there came to be a great ebb of the sea backwards, which lasted for a long time; and the Barbarians, seeing that shallow water had been produced, endeavored to get by into the peninsula of Pallene, but when they had passed through two fifth-parts of the distance, and yet three-fifths remained, which

they must pass through before they were within Pallene, then there came upon them a great flood-tide of the sea, higher than ever before, as the natives of the place say, though high tides come often. So those of them who could not swim perished, and those who could were slain by the men of Potidaia who put out to them in boats. The cause of the high tide and flood and of that which befell the Persians was this, as the Potidaians say, namely that these same Persians who perished by means of the sea had committed impiety towards the temple of Poseidon and his image in the suburb of their town; and in saying that this was the cause, in my opinion they say well. The survivors of his army Artabazos led away to Thessaly to join Mardonios. Thus it fared with these who escorted the king on his way.

130. The fleet of Xerxes, so much of it as remained, when it had touched Asia in its flight from Salamis, and had conveyed the king and his army over from the Chersonese to Abydos, passed the winter at Kyme: and when spring dawned upon it, it assembled early at Samos, where some of the ships had even passed the winter; and most of the Persians and Medes still served as fighting-men on board of them. To be commanders of them there came Mardontes the son of Bagaios, and Artaÿntes the son of Artachaies, and with them also Ithamitres was in joint command, who was brother's son to Artaÿntes and had been added by the choice of Artaÿntes himself. They then, since they had suffered a heavy blow, did not advance further up towards the West, nor did any one compel them to do so; but they remained still in Samos and kept watch over Ionia, lest it should revolt, having three hundred ships including those of the Ionians; and they did not expect that the Hellenes on their part would come to Ionia, but thought that it would satisfy them to guard their own land, judging from the fact that they had not pursued after them in their flight from Salamis but were well contented then to depart homewards. As regards the sea then their spirit was broken, but on land they thought that Mardonios would get much the advantage. So they being at Samos were taking counsel to do some damage if they could to their enemies, and at the same time they were listening for news how the affairs of Mardonios would fall out.

131. The Hellenes on their part were roused both by the coming on of spring and by the presence of Mardonios in Thessaly. Their land-army had not yet begun to assemble, when the fleet arrived at Egina, in number one hundred and ten ships, and the commander and admiral was Leotychides, who was the son of Menares, the son of Hegesilaos, the son of Hippocratides, the son of Leotychides, the son of Anaxilaos, the son of Archidemos, the son of Anaxandriddes, the son of Theopompos, the son of Nicander, the son of Charilaos, the son of Eunomos, the son of Polydectes, the son of Prytanis, the son of Euryphon, the son of Procles, the son of Aristodemos, the son of Aristomachos, the son of Cleodaios, the son of Hyllos, the son of Heracles, being of the other royal house. These all, except the two enumerated first after Leotychides, had been kings of Sparta. And of the Athenians the commander was Xanthippos the son of Ariphon.

132. When all the ships had arrived at Egina, there came Ionian envoys to the camp of the Hellenes, who also came a short time before this to Sparta and asked the Lacedemonians to set Ionia free; and of them one was Herodotus the son of Basileides. These had banded themselves together and had plotted to put to death Strattis the despot of Chios, being originally seven in number; but when one of those who took part with them gave information of it and they were discovered to be plotting against him, then the remaining six escaped from Chios and came both to Sparta and also at this time to Egina, asking the

Hellenes to sail over to Ionia: but they with difficulty brought them forward as far as Delos; for the parts beyond this were all fearful to the Hellenes, since they were without experience of those regions and everything seemed to them to be filled with armed force, while their persuasion was that it was as long a voyage to Samos as to the Pillars of Heracles. Thus at the same time it so chanced that the Barbarians dared sail no further up towards the West than Samos, being smitten with fear, and the Hellenes no further down towards the East than Delos, when the Chians made request of them. So fear was guard of the space which lay between them.

133. The Hellenes, I say, sailed to Delos; and Mardonios meanwhile had been wintering in Thessaly. From thence he sent round a man, a native of Europos, whose name was Mys, to the various Oracles, charging him to go everywhere to consult, wherever they were permitted to make trial of the Oracles. What he desired to find out from the Oracles when he gave this charge, I am not able to say, for that is not reported; but I conceive for my part that he sent to consult about his present affairs and not about other things.

134. This Mys is known to have come to Lebadeia and to have persuaded by payment of money one of the natives of the place to go down to Trophonios, and also he came to the Oracle at Abai of the Phokians; and moreover when he came for the first time to Thebes, he not only consulted the Ismenian Apollo,—there one may consult just as at Olympia with victims,—but also by payment he persuaded a stranger who was not a Theban, and induced him to lie down to sleep in the temple of Amphiaraos. In this temple no one of the Thebans is permitted to seek divination, and that for the following reason:— Amphiaraos dealing by oracles bade them choose which they would of these two things, either to have him as a diviner or else as an ally in war, abstaining from the other use; and they chose that he should be their ally in war: for this reason it is not permitted to any of the Thebans to lie down to sleep in that temple.

135. After this a thing which to me is a very great marvel is said by the Thebans to have come to pass:—it seems that this man Mys of Europos, as he journeyed round to all the Oracles, came also to the sacred enclosure of the Ptoan Apollo. This temple is called "Ptoön," and belongs to the Thebans, and it lies above the lake Copaïs at the foot of the mountains, close to the town of Acraiphia. When the man called Mys came to this temple with three men chosen from the citizens in his company, who were sent by the public authority to write down that which the god should utter in his divination, forthwith it is said the prophet of the god began to give the oracle in a Barbarian tongue; and while those of the Thebans who accompanied him were full of wonder, hearing a Barbarian instead of the Hellenic tongue, and did not know what to make of the matter before them, it is said that the man of Europos, Mys, snatched from them the tablet which they bore and wrote upon it that which was being spoken by the prophet; and he said that the prophet was giving his answer in the Carian tongue: and then when he had written it, he went away and departed to Thessaly.

136. Mardonios having read that which the Oracles uttered, whatever that was, after this sent as an envoy to Athens Alexander the son of Amyntas, the Macedonian, both because the Persians were connected with him by marriage, (for Gygaia the sister of Alexander and daughter of Amyntas had been married to a Persian Bubares, and from her had been born to him that Amyntas who lived in Asia, having the name of his mother's father, to whom the king gave Alabanda, a great city of Phrygia, to possess), and also Mardonios was sending him because he was informed that Alexander was a public guest-

friend and benefactor of the Athenians; for by this means he thought that he would be most likely to gain over the Athenians to his side, about whom he heard that they were a numerous people and brave in war, and of whom he knew moreover that these were they who more than any others had brought about the disasters which had befallen the Persians by sea. Therefore if these should be added to him, he thought that he should easily have command of the sea (and this in fact would have been the case), while on land he supposed himself to be already much superior in force. Thus he reckoned that his power would be much greater than that of the Hellenes. Perhaps also the Oracles told him this beforehand, counselling him to make the Athenian his ally, and so he was sending in obedience to their advice.

137. Now of this Alexander the seventh ancestor was that Perdiccas who first became despot of the Macedonians, and that in the manner which here follows:—From Argos there fled to the Illyrians three brothers of the descendants of Temenos, Gauanes, Aëropos, and Perdiccas; and passing over from the Illyrians into the upper parts of Macedonia they came to the city of Lebaia. There they became farm-servants for pay in the household of the king, one pasturing horses, the second oxen, and the youngest of them, namely Perdiccas, the smaller kinds of cattle; for in ancient times even those who were rulers over men were poor in money, and not the common people only; and the wife of the king cooked for them their food herself. And whenever she baked, the loaf of the boy their servant, namely Perdiccas, became double as large as by nature it should be. When this happened constantly in the same manner, she told it to her husband, and he when he heard it conceived forthwith that this was a portent and tended to something great. He summoned the farm-servants therefore, and gave notice to them to depart out of his land; and they said that it was right that before they went forth they should receive the wages which were due. Now it chanced that the sun was shining into the house down through the opening which received the smoke, and the king when he heard about the wages said, being infatuated by a divine power: "I pay you then this for wages, and it is such as ye deserve," pointing to the sunlight. So then Gauanes and Aëropos the elder brothers stood struck with amazement when they heard this, but the boy, who happened to have in his hand a knife, said these words: "We accept, O king, that which thou dost give;" and he traced a line with his knife round the sunlight on the floor of the house, and having traced the line round he thrice drew of the sunlight into his bosom, and after that he departed both himself and his fellows.

138. They then were going away, and to the king one of those who sat by him at table told what manner of thing the boy had done, and how the youngest of them had taken that which was given with some design: and he hearing this and being moved with anger, sent after them horsemen to slay them. Now there is a river in this land to which the descendents of these men from Argos sacrifice as a savior. This river, so soon as the sons of Temenos had passed over it, began to flow with such great volume of water that the horsemen became unable to pass over. So the brothers, having come to another region of Macedonia, took up their dwelling near the so-called gardens of Midas the son of Gordias, where roses grow wild which have each one sixty petals and excel all others in perfume. In these gardens too Silenos was captured, as is reported by the Macedonians: and above the gardens is situated a mountain called Bermion, which is inaccessible by reason of the cold. Having taken possession of that region, they made this their starting-point, and proceeded to subdue also the rest of Macedonia.

139. From this Perdiccas the descent of Alexander was as follows:—Alexander was the son of Amyntas, Amyntas was the son of Alketes, the father of Alketes was Aëropos, of him Philip, of Philip Argaios, and of this last the father was Perdiccas, who first obtained the kingdom.

140. Thus then, I say, Alexander the son of Amyntas was descended; and when he came to Athens sent from Mardonios, he spoke as follows: (a) "Athenians, Mardonios speaks these words:—There has come to me a message from the king which speaks in this manner:—To the Athenians I remit all the offences which were committed against me: and now, Mardonios, thus do,—first give them back their own land; then let them choose for themselves another in addition to this, whichsoever they desire, remaining independent; and set up for them again all their temples, which I set on fire, provided that they consent to make a treaty with me. This message having come to me, it is necessary for me to do so, unless by your means I am prevented: and thus I speak to you now:—Why are ye so mad as to raise up war against the king? since neither will ye overcome him, nor are ye able to hold out against him forever: for ye saw the multitude of the host of Xerxes and their deeds, and ye are informed also of the power which is with me at the present time; so that even if ye overcome and conquer us (of which ye can have no hope if ye are rightly minded), another power will come many times as large. Do not ye then desire to match yourselves with the king, and so to be both deprived of your land and forever running a course for your own lives; but make peace with him: and ye have a most honorable occasion to make peace, since the king has himself set out upon this road: agree to a league with us then without fraud or deceit, and remain free. (b) These things Mardonios charged me to say to you, O Athenians; and as for me, I will say nothing of the goodwill towards you on my part, for ye would not learn that now for the first time; but I ask of you to do as Mardonios says, since I perceive that ye will not be able to war with Xerxes forever,—if I perceived in you ability to do this, I should never have come to you speaking these words, —for the power of the king is above that of a man and his arm is very long. If therefore ye do not make an agreement forthwith, when they offer you great things as the terms on which they are willing to make a treaty, I have fear on your behalf, seeing that ye dwell more upon the highway than any of your allies, and are exposed ever to destruction alone, the land which ye possess being parted off from the rest and lying between the armies which are contending together. Nay, but be persuaded, for this is a matter of great consequence to you, that to you alone of the Hellenes the great king remits the offences committed and desires to become a friend."

141. Thus spoke Alexander; and the Lacedemonians having been informed that Alexander had come to Athens to bring the Athenians to make a treaty with the Barbarians, and remembering the oracles, who it was destined that they together with the other Dorians should be driven forth out of the Peloponnese by the Medes and the Athenians combined, had been very greatly afraid lest the Athenians should make a treaty with the Persians; and forthwith they had resolved to send envoys. It happened moreover that they were introduced at the same time with Alexander; for the Athenians had waited for them, protracting the time, because they were well assured that the Lacedemonians would hear that an envoy had come from the Barbarians to make a treaty, and that having heard it they would themselves send envoys with all speed. They acted therefore of set purpose, so as to let the Lacedemonians see their inclination.

142. So when Alexander had ceased speaking, the envoys from Sparta followed him

forthwith and said: "As for us, the Lacedemonians sent us to ask of you not to make any change in that which concerns Hellas, nor to accept proposals from the Barbarian; since this is not just in any way nor honorable for any of the Hellenes to do, but least of all for you, and that for many reasons. Ye were they who stirred up this war, when we by no means willed it; and the contest came about for your dominion, but now it extends even to the whole of Hellas. Besides this it is by no means to be endured that ye Athenians, who are the authors of all this, should prove to be the cause of slavery to the Hellenes, seeing that ye ever from ancient time also have been known as the liberators of many. We feel sympathy however with you for your sufferings and because ye were deprived of your crops twice and have had your substance ruined now for a long time. In compensation for this the Lacedemonians and their allies make offer to support your wives and all those of your households who are unfitted for war, so long as this war shall last: but let not Alexander the Macedonian persuade you, making smooth the speech of Mardonios; for these things are fitting for him to do, since being himself a despot he is working in league with a despot: for you however they are not fitting to do, if ye chance to be rightly minded; for ye know that in Barbarians there is neither faith nor truth at all."

Thus spoke the envoys:

143, and to Alexander the Athenians made answer thus: "Even of ourselves we know so much, that the Mede has a power many times as numerous as ours; so that there is no need for thee to cast this up against us. Nevertheless because we long for liberty we shall defend ourselves as we may be able: and do not thou endeavor to persuade us to make a treaty with the Barbarian, for we on our part shall not be persuaded. And now report to Mardonios that the Athenians say thus:—So long as the Sun goes on the same course by which he goes now, we will never make an agreement with Xerxes; but we will go forth to defend ourselves against him, trusting in the gods and the heroes as allies, for whom he had no respect when he set fire to their houses and to their sacred images. And in the future do not thou appear before the Athenians with any such proposals as these, nor think that thou art rendering them good service in advising them to do that which is not lawful; for we do not desire that thou shouldest suffer anything unpleasant at the hands of the Athenians, who art their public guest and friend."

144. To Alexander they thus made answer, but to the envoys from Sparta as follows: "That the Lacedemonians should be afraid lest we should make a treaty with the Barbarian was natural no doubt; but it seems to be an unworthy fear for men who know so well the spirit of the Athenians, namely that there is neither so great quantity of gold anywhere upon the earth, nor any land so much excelling in beauty and goodness, that we should be willing to accept it and enslave Hellas by taking the side of the Medes. For many and great are the reasons which hinder us from doing this, even though we should desire it; first and greatest the images and houses of the gods set on fire or reduced to ruin, which we must necessarily avenge to the very utmost rather than make an agreement with him who did these deeds; then secondly there is the bond of Hellenic race, by which we are of one blood and of one speech, the common temples of the gods and the common sacrifices, the manners of life which are the same for all; to these it would not be well that the Athenians should become traitors. And be assured of this, if by any chance ye were not assured of it before, that so long as one of the Athenians remains alive, we will never make an agreement with Xerxes. We admire however the forethought which ye had with regard to us, in that ye took thought for us who have had our substance destroyed, and

are willing to support the members of our households; and so far as ye are concerned, the kindness has been fully performed: but we shall continue to endure as we may, and not be a trouble in any way to you. Now therefore, with full conviction this is so, send out an army as speedily as ye may: for, as we conjecture, the Barbarian will be here invading our land at no far distant time but so soon as he shall be informed of the message sent, namely that we shall do none of those things which he desired of us. Therefore before he arrives here in Attica, it is fitting that ye come to our rescue quickly in Boeotia." Thus the Athenians made answer, and upon that the envoys went away back to Sparta.

THE NINTH BOOK OF THE
HISTORIES, CALLED CALLIOPE

1. Mardonios, when Alexander had returned back and had signified to him that which was said by the Athenians, set forth from Thessaly and began to lead his army with all diligence towards Athens: and to whatever land he came, he took up with him the people of that land. The leaders of Thessaly meanwhile did not repent of all that which had been done already, but on the contrary they urged on the Persian yet much more; and Thorax of Larissa had joined in escorting Xerxes in his flight and at this time he openly offered Mardonios passage to invade Hellas.

2. Then when the army in its march came to Boeotia, the Thebans endeavored to detain Mardonios, and counselled him saying that there was no region more convenient for him to have his encampment than that; and they urged him not to advance further, but to sit down there and endeavor to subdue to himself the whole of Hellas without fighting: for to overcome the Hellenes by open force when they were united, as at the former time they were of one accord together, was a difficult task even for the whole world combined, "but," they proceeded, "if thou wilt do that which we advise, with little labor thou wilt have in thy power all their plans of resistance. Send money to the men who have power in their cities, and thus sending thou wilt divide Hellas into two parties: after that thou wilt with ease subdue by the help of thy party those who are not inclined to thy side."

3. Thus they advised, but he did not follow their counsel; for there had instilled itself into him a great desire to take Athens for the second time, partly from obstinacy and partly because he meant to signify to the king in Sardis that he was in possession of Athens by beacon-fires through the islands. However he did not even at this time find the Athenians there when he came to Attica; but he was informed that the greater number were either in Salamis or in the ships, and he captured the city finding it deserted. Now the capture of the city by the king had taken place ten months before the later expedition of Mardonios against it.

4. When Mardonios had come to Athens, he sent to Salamis Morychides a man of the Hellespont, bearing the same proposals as Alexander the Macedonian had brought over to

the Athenians. These he sent for the second time, being aware beforehand that the dispositions of the Athenians were not friendly, but hoping that they would give way and leave
their obstinacy, since the Attic land had been captured by the enemy and was in his
power.

5. For this reason he sent Morychides to Salamis; and he came before the Council and
reported the words of Mardonios. Then one of the Councilors, Lykidas, expressed the
opinion that it was better to receive the proposal which Morychides brought before them
and refer it to the assembly of the people. He, I say, uttered this opinion, whether because
he had received money from Mardonios, or because this was his own inclination: however
the Athenians forthwith, both those of the Council and those outside, when they heard of
it, were very indignant, and they came about Lykidas and stoned him to death; but the
Hellespontian Morychides they dismissed unhurt. Then when there had arisen much
uproar in Salamis about Lykidas, the women of the Athenians heard of that which was
being done, and one woman passing the word to another and one taking another with her,
they went of their own accord to the house of Lykidas and stoned his wife and his children to death.

6. The Athenians had passed over to Salamis as follows:—So long as they were looking
that an army should come from the Peloponnese to help them, they remained in Attica;
but as those in Peloponnesus acted very slowly and with much delay, while the invader
was said to be already in Boeotia, they accordingly removed everything out of danger, and
themselves passed over to Salamis; and at the same time they sent envoys to Lacedaemon
to reproach the Lacedemonians for having permitted the Barbarian to invade Attica and
for not having gone to Boeotia to meet him in company with them, and also to remind
them how many things the Persian had promised to give the Athenians if they changed
sides; bidding the envoys warn them that if they did not help the Athenians, the Athenians would find some shelter for themselves.

7. For the Lacedemonians in fact were keeping a feast during this time, and celebrating
the Hyakinthia; and they held it of the greatest consequence to provide for the things
which concerned the god, while at the same time their wall which they had been building
at the Isthmus was just at this moment being completed with battlements. And when the
envoys from the Athenians came to Lacedaemon, bringing with them also envoys from
Megara and Plataia, they came in before the Ephors and said as follows: "The Athenians
sent us saying that the king of the Medes not only offers to give us back our land, but also
desires to make us his allies on fair and equal terms without deceit or treachery, and is
desirous moreover to give us another land in addition to our own, whichsoever we shall
ourselves choose. We however, having respect for Zeus of the Hellenes and disdaining to
be traitors to Hellas, did not agree but refused, although we were unjustly dealt with by
the other Hellenes and left to destruction, and although we knew that it was more profitable to make a treaty with the Persian than to carry on war: nor shall we make a treaty at
any future time, if we have our own will. Thus sincerely is our duty done towards the
Hellenes: but as for you, after having come then to great dread lest we should make a
treaty with the Persian, so soon as ye learnt certainly what our spirit was, namely that we
should never betray Hellas, and because your wall across the Isthmus is all but finished,
now ye make no account of the Athenians, but having agreed with us to come to Boeotia
to oppose the Persian, ye have now deserted us, and ye permitted the Barbarian moreover
to make invasion of Attica. For the present then the Athenians have anger against you, for

ye did not do as was fitting to be done: and now they bid you with all speed send out an army together with us, in order that we may receive the Barbarian in the land of Attica; for since we failed of Boeotia, the most suitable place to fight in our land is the Thriasian plain."

8. When the Ephors heard this they deferred their reply to the next day, and then on the next day to the succeeding one; and this they did even for ten days, deferring the matter from day to day, while during this time the whole body of the Peloponnesians were building the wall over the Isthmus with great diligence and were just about to complete it. Now I am not able to say why, when Alexander the Macedonian had come to Athens, they were so very anxious lest the Athenians should take the side of the Medes, whereas now they had no care about it, except indeed that their wall over the Isthmus had now been built, and they thought they had no need of the Athenians anymore; whereas when Alexander came to Attica the wall had not yet been completed, but they were working at it in great dread of the Persians.

9. At last however the answer was given and the going forth of the Spartans took place in the following manner:—on the day before that which was appointed for the last hearing of the envoys, Chileos a man of Tegea, who of all strangers had most influence in Lacedaemon, heard from the Ephors all that which the Athenians were saying; and he, it seems, said to them these words: "Thus the matter stands, Ephors:—if the Athenians are not friendly with us but are allies of the Barbarian, then though a strong wall may have been built across the Isthmus, yet a wide door has been opened for the Persian into Peloponnesus. Listen to their request, however, before the Athenians resolve upon something else tending to the fall of Hellas."

10. Thus he counselled them, and they forthwith took his words to heart; and saying nothing to the envoys who had come from the cities, while yet it was night they sent out five thousand Spartans, with no less than seven of the Helots set to attend upon each man of them, appointing Pausanias the son of Cleombrotos to lead them forth. Now the leadership belonged to Pleistarchos the son of Leonidas; but he was yet a boy, and the other was his guardian and cousin: for Cleombrotos, the father of Pausanias and son of Anaxandrides, was no longer alive, but when he had led home from the Isthmus the army which had built the wall, no long time after this he died. Now the reason why Cleombrotos led home the army from the Isthmus was this:—as he was offering sacrifice for fighting against the Persian, the sun was darkened in the heaven. And Pausanias chose as commander in addition to himself Euryanax the son of Dorieos, a man of the same house.

11. So Pausanias with his army had gone forth out of Sparta; and the envoys, when day had come, not knowing anything of this going forth, came in before the Ephors meaning to depart also, each to his own State: and when they had come in before them they said these words: "Ye, O Lacedemonians, are remaining here and celebrating this Hyakinthia and disporting yourselves, having left your allies to destruction; and the Athenians being wronged by you and for want of allies will make peace with the Persians on such terms as they can: and having made peace, evidently we become allies of the king, and therefore we shall join with him in expeditions against any land to which the Persians may lead us; and ye will learn then what shall be the issue for you of this matter." When the envoys spoke these words, the Ephors said and confirmed it with an oath, that they supposed by this time the men were at Orestheion on their way against the strangers: for they used to call the Barbarians "strangers." So they, not knowing of the matter, asked the meaning of

these words, and asking they learnt all the truth; so that they were struck with amazement and set forth as quickly as possible in pursuit; and together with them five thousand chosen hoplites of the Lacedemonian "dwellers in the country round" did the same thing also.

12. They then, I say, were hastening towards the Isthmus; and the Argives so soon as they heard that Pausanias with his army had gone forth from Sparta, sent as a herald to Attica the best whom they could find of the long-distance runners, because they had before of their own motion engaged for Mardonios that they would stop the Spartans from going forth: and the herald when he came to Athens spoke as follows: "Mardonios, the Argives sent me to tell thee that the young men have gone forth from Lacedaemon, and that the Argives are not able to stop them from going forth: with regard to this therefore may it be thy fortune to take measures well." .

13. He having spoken thus departed and went back; and Mardonios was by no means anxious any more to remain in Attica when he heard this message. Before he was informed of this he had been waiting, because he desired to know the news from the Athenians as to what they were about to do; and he had not been injuring or laying waste the land of Attica, because he hoped always that they would make a treaty with him; but as he did not persuade them, being now informed of everything he began to retire out of the country before the force of Pausanias arrived at the Isthmus, having first set fire to Athens and cast down and destroyed whatever was left standing of the walls, houses or temples. Now he marched away for this cause, namely first because Attica was not a land where horsemen could act freely, and also because, if he should be defeated in a battle in Attica, there was no way of retreat except by a narrow pass, so that a few men could stop them. He intended therefore to retreat to Thebes, and engage battle near to a friendly city and to a country where horsemen could act freely.

14. Mardonios then was retiring out of the way, and when he was already upon a road a message came to him saying that another body of troops in advance of the rest had come to Megara, consisting of a thousand Lacedemonians. Being thus informed he took counsel with himself, desiring if possible first to capture these. Therefore he turned back and proceeded to lead his army towards Megara, and the cavalry going in advance of the rest overran the Megaran land: this was the furthest land in Europe towards the sun-setting to which this Persian army came.

15. After this a message came to Mardonios that the Hellenes were assembled at the Isthmus; therefore he marched back by Dekeleia, for the chiefs of Boeotia had sent for those of the Asopians who dwelt near the line of march, and these were his guides along the road to Sphendaleis and thence to Tanagra. So having encamped for the night at Tanagra and on the next day having directed his march to Scolos, he was within the land of the Thebans. Then he proceeded to cut down the trees in the lands of the Thebans, although they were on the side of the Medes, moved not at all by enmity to them, but pressed by urgent necessity both to make a defense for his camp, and also he was making it for a refuge, in case that when he engaged battle things should not turn out for him as he desired. Now the encampment of his army extended from Erythrai along by Hysiai and reached the river Asopos: he was not however making the wall to extend so far as this, but with each face measuring somewhere about ten furlongs.

16. While the Barbarians were engaged upon this work, Attaginos the son of Phyrnon, a Theban, having made magnificent preparations invited to an entertainment Mardonios

himself and fifty of the Persians who were of most account; and these being invited came; and the dinner was given at Thebes. Now this which follows I heard from Thersander, an Orchomenian and a man of very high repute in Orchomenos. This Thersander said that he too was invited by Attaginos to this dinner, and there were invited also fifty men of the Thebans, and their host did not place them to recline separately each nation by themselves, but a Persian and a Theban upon every couch. Then when dinner was over, as they were drinking pledges to one another, the Persian who shared a couch with him speaking in the Hellenic tongue asked him of what place he was, and he answered that he was of Orchomenos. The other said: "Since now thou hast become my table-companion and the sharer of my libation, I desire to leave behind with thee a memorial of my opinion, in order that thou thyself also mayest know beforehand and be able to take such counsels for thyself as may be profitable. Dost thou see these Persians who are feasting here, and the army which we left behind encamped upon the river? Of all these, when a little time has gone by, thou shalt see but very few surviving." While the Persian said these words he shed many tears, as Thersander reported; and he marveling at his speech said to him: "Surely then it is right to tell Mardonios and to those of the Persians who after him are held in regard." He upon this said: "Friend, that which is destined to come from God, it is impossible for a man to avert; for no man is willing to follow counsel, even when one speaks that which is reasonable. And these things which I say many of us Persians know well; yet we go with the rest being bound in the bonds of necessity: and the most hateful grief of all human griefs is this, to have knowledge of the truth but no power over the event." These things I heard from Thersander of Orchomenos, and in addition to them this also, namely that he told them to various persons forthwith, before the battle took place at Plataia.

17. Mardonios then being encamped in Boeotia, the rest of the Hellenes who lived in these parts and took the side of the Medes were all supplying troops and had joined in the invasion of Attica, but the Phokians alone had not joined in the invasion,—the Phokians, I say, for these too were now actively taking the side of the Medes, not of their own will however, but by compulsion. Not many days however after the arrival of Mardonios at Thebes, there came of them a thousand hoplites, and their leader was Harmokydes, the man who was of most repute among their citizens. When these too came to Thebes, Mardonios sent horsemen and bade the Phokians take up their position by themselves in the plain. After they had so done, forthwith the whole cavalry appeared; and upon this there went a rumor through the army of Hellenes which was with the Medes that the cavalry was about to shoot them down with javelins, and this same report went through the Phokians themselves also. Then their commander Harmokydes exhorted them, speaking as follows: "Phokians, it is manifest that these men are meaning to deliver us to a death which we may plainly foresee, because we have been falsely accused by the Thessalians, as I conjecture: now therefore it is right that every one of you prove himself a good man; for it is better to bring our lives to an end doing deeds of valor and defending ourselves, than to be destroyed by a dishonorable death offering ourselves for the slaughter. Let each man of them learn that they are Barbarians and that we, against whom they contrived murder, are Hellenes."

18. While he was thus exhorting them, the horsemen having encompassed them round were riding towards them as if to destroy them; and they were already aiming their missiles as if about to discharge them, nay some perhaps did discharge them: and mean-

while the Phokians stood facing them gathered together and with their ranks closed as much as possible every way. Then the horsemen turned and rode away back. Now I am not able to say for certain whether they came to destroy the Phokians at the request of the Thessalians, and then when they saw them turn to defense they feared lest they also might suffer some loss, and therefore rode away back, for so Mardonios had commanded them; or whether on the other hand he desired to make trial of them and to see if they had in them any warlike spirit. Then, when the horsemen had ridden away back, Mardonios sent a herald and spoke to them as follows: "Be of good courage, Phokians, for ye proved yourselves good men, and not as I was informed. Now therefore carry on this way with zeal, for ye will not surpass in benefits either myself or the king." Thus far it happened as regards the Phokians.

19. When the Lacedemonians came to the Isthmus they encamped upon it, and hearing this the rest of the Peloponnesians who favored the better cause, and some also because they saw the Spartans going out, did not think it right to be behind the Lacedemonians in their going forth. So from the Isthmus, when the sacrifices had proved favorable, they marched all together and came to Eleusis; and having performed sacrifices there also, when the signs were favorable they marched onwards, and the Athenians together with them, who had passed over from Salamis and had joined them at Eleusis. And then they had come to Erythrai in Boeotia, then they learnt that the Barbarians were encamping on the Asopos, and having perceived this they ranged themselves over against them on the lower slopes of Kithairon.

20. Then Mardonios, as the Hellenes did not descend into the plain, sent towards them all his cavalry, of which the commander was Masistios (by the Hellenes called Makistios), a man of reputation among the Persians, who had a Nesaian horse with a bridle of gold and in other respects finely caparisoned. So when the horsemen had ridden up to the Hellenes they attacked them by squadrons, and attacking they did them much mischief, and moreover in contempt they called them women.

21. Now it happened by chance that the Megarians were posted in the place which was the most assailable of the whole position and to which the cavalry could best approach: so as the cavalry were making their attacks, the Megarians being hard pressed sent a herald to the commanders of the Hellenes, and the herald having come spoke these words: "The Megarians say:—we, O allies, are not able by ourselves to sustain the attacks of the Persian cavalry, keeping this position where we took post at the first; nay, even hitherto by endurance and valor alone have we held out against them, hard pressed as we are: and now unless ye shall send some others to take up our position in succession to us, know that we shall leave the position in which we now are." The herald brought report to them thus; and upon this Pausanias made trial of the Hellenes, whether any others would voluntarily offer to go to this place and post themselves there in succession to the Megarians: and when the rest were not desirous to go, the Athenians undertook the task, and of the Athenians those three hundred picked men of whom Olympidoros the son of Lampon was captain.

22. These they were who undertook the task and were posted at Erythrai in advance of the other Hellenes who were there present, having chosen to go with them the bow-men also. For some time then they fought, and at last an end was set to the fighting in the following manner:—while the cavalry was attacking by squadrons, the horse of Masistios, going in advance of the rest, was struck in the side by an arrow, and feeling pain he reared

upright and threw Masistios off; and when he had fallen, the Athenians forthwith pressed upon him; and his horse they took and himself, as he made resistance, they slew, though at first they could not, for his equipment was of this kind,—he wore a cuirass of gold scales underneath, and over the cuirass he had put on a crimson tunic. So as they struck upon the cuirass they could affect nothing, until someone, perceiving what the matter was, thrust into his eye. Then at length he fell and died; and by some means the other men of the cavalry had not observed this take place, for they neither saw him when he had fallen from his horse nor when he was being slain, and while the retreat and the turn were being made, they did not perceive that which was happening; but when they had stopped their horses, then at once they missed him, since there was no one to command them; and when they perceived what had happened, they passed the word to one another and all rode together, that they might if possible recover the body.

23. The Athenians upon that, seeing that the cavalry were riding to attack them no longer by squadrons but all together, shouted to the rest of the army to help them. Then while the whole number of those on foot were coming to their help, there arose a sharp fight for the body; and so long as the three hundred were alone they had much the worse and were about to abandon the body, but when the mass of the army came to their help, then the horsemen no longer sustained the fight, nor did they succeed in recovering the body; and besides him they lost others of their number also. Then they drew off about two furlongs away and deliberated what they should do; and it seemed good to them, as they had no commander, to ride back to Mardonios.

24. When the cavalry arrived at the camp, the whole army and also Mardonios made great mourning for Masistios, cutting off their own hair and that of their horses and baggage-animals and giving way to lamentation without stint; for all Boeotia was filled with the sound of it, because one had perished who after Mardonios was of the most account with the Persians and with the king.

25. The Barbarians then were paying honors in their own manner to Masistios slain: but the Hellenes, when they had sustained the attack of the cavalry and having sustained it had driven them back, were much more encouraged; and first they put the dead body in a cart and conveyed it along their ranks; and the body was a sight worth seeing for its size and beauty, wherefore also the men left their places in the ranks and went one after the other to gaze upon Masistios. After this they resolved to come down further towards Plataia; for the region of Plataia was seen to be much more convenient for them to encamp in than that of Erythrai, both for other reasons and because it is better watered. To this region then and to the spring Gargaphia, which is in this region, they resolved that they must come, and encamp in their several posts. So they took up their arms and went by the lower slopes of Kithairon past Hysiai to the Plataian land; and having there arrived they posted themselves according to their several nations near the spring Gargaphia and the sacred enclosure of Androcrates the hero, over low hills or level ground.

26. Then in the arranging of the several posts there arose a contention of much argu-ment between the Tegeans and the Athenians; for they each claimed to occupy the other wing of the army themselves, alleging deeds both new and old. The Tegeans on the one hand said as follows: "We have been always judged worthy of this post by the whole body of allies in all the common expeditions which the Peloponnesians have made before this whether in old times or but lately, ever since that time when the sons of Heracles endeav-ored after the death of Eurystheus to return to the Peloponnese. This honor we gained a

that time by reason of the following event:—When with the Achaians and the Ionians who were then in Peloponnesus we had come out to the Isthmus to give assistance and were encamped opposite those who desired to return, then it is said that Hyllos made a speech saying that it was not right that the one army should risk its safety by engaging battle with the other, and urging that that man of the army of the Peloponnesians whom they should judge to be the best of them should fight in single combat with himself on terms concerted between them. The Peloponnesians then resolved that this should be done; and they made oath with one another on this condition,—that if Hyllos should conquer the leader of the Peloponnesians, then the sons of Heracles should return to their father's heritage; but he should be conquered, then on the other hand the sons of Heracles should depart and lead away their army, and not within a hundred years attempt to return to the Peloponnese. There was selected then of all the allies, he himself making a voluntary offer, Echemos the son of Aëropos, the son of Phegeus, who was our commander and king: and he fought a single combat and slew Hyllos. By reason of this deed we obtained among the Peloponnesians of that time, besides many other great privileges which we still possess, this also of always leading the other wing of the army, when a common expedition is made. To you, Lacedemonians, we make no opposition, but we give you freedom of choice, and allow you to command whichever wing ye desire; but of the other we say that it belongs to us to be the leaders as in former time: and apart from this deed which has been related, we are more worthy than the Athenians to have this post; for in many glorious contests have we contended against you, O Spartans, and in many also against others. Therefore it is just that we have the other wing rather than the Athenians; for they have not achieved deeds such as ours, either new or old."

27. Thus they spoke, and the Athenians replied as follows: "Though we know that this gathering was assembled for battle with the Barbarian and not for speech, yet since the Tegean has proposed to us as a task to speak of things both old and new, the deeds of merit namely which by each of our two nations have been achieved in all time, it is necessary for us to point out to you whence it comes that to us, who have been brave men always, it belongs as a heritage rather than to the Arcadians to have the chief place. First as to the sons of Heracles, whose leader they say that they slew at the Isthmus, these in the former time, when they were driven away by all the Hellenes to whom they came flying from slavery under those of Mykene, we alone received; and joining with them we subdued the insolence of Eurystheus, having conquered in fight those who then dwelt in Peloponnesus. Again when the Argives who with Polyneikes marched against Thebes, had been slain and were lying unburied, we declare that we marched an army against the Cadmeians and recovered the dead bodies and gave them burial in our own land at Eleusis. We have moreover another glorious deed performed against the Amazons who invaded once the Attic land, coming from the river Thermodon: and in the toils of Troy we were not inferior to any. But it is of no profit to make mention of these things; for on the one hand, though we were brave men in those times, we might now have become worthless, and on the other hand even though we were then worthless, yet now we might be better. Let it suffice therefore about ancient deeds; but if by us no other deed has been displayed (as many there have been and glorious, not less than by any other people of the Hellenes), yet even by reason of the deed wrought at Marathon alone we are worthy to have this privilege and others besides this, seeing that we alone of all the Hellenes fought in single combat with the Persian, and having undertaken so great a deed we overcame

and conquered six-and-forty nations. Are we not worthy then to have this post by reason of that deed alone? However, since at such a time as this it is not fitting to contend for post, we are ready to follow your saying, O Lacedemonians, as to where ye think it most convenient that we should stand and opposite to whom; for wheresoever we are posted, we shall endeavor to be brave men. Prescribe to us therefore and we shall obey." They made answer thus; and the whole body of the Lacedemonians shouted aloud that the Athenians were more worthy to occupy the wing than the Arcadians. Thus the Athenians obtained the wing, and overcame the Tegeans.

28. After this the Hellenes were ranged as follows, both those of them who came in continually afterwards and those who had come at the first. The right wing was held by ten thousand Lacedemonians; and of these the five thousand who were Spartans were attended by thirty-five thousand Helots serving as light-armed troops, seven of them appointed for each man. To stand next to themselves the Spartans chose the Tegeans, both to do them honor and also because of their valor; and of these there were one thousand five hundred hoplites. After these were stationed five thousand Corinthians, and they had obtained permission from Pausanias that the three hundred who were present of the men of Potidaia in Pallene should stand by their side. Next to these were stationed six hundred Arcadians of Orchomenos; and to these three thousand Sikyonians. Next after these were eight hundred Epidaurians: by the side of these were ranged a thousand Troizenians: next to the Troizenians two hundred Lepreates: next to these four hundred of the men of Mikene and Tiryns; and then a thousand Phliasians. By the side of these stood three hundred Hermionians; and next to the Hermionians were stationed six hundred Eretrians and Styrians; next to these four hundred Chalkidians; and to these five hundred men of Amprakia. After these stood eight hundred Leucadians and Anactorians; and next to them two hundred from Pale in Kephallenia. After these were ranged five hundred Eginetans; by their side three thousand Megarians; and next to these six hundred Plataians. Last, or if you will first, were ranged the Athenians, occupying the left wing, eight thousand in number, and the commander of them was Aristeides the son of Lysimachos.

29. These all, excepting those who were appointed to attend the Spartans, seven for each man, were hoplites, being in number altogether three myriads eight thousand and seven hundred. This was the whole number of hoplites who were assembled against the Barbarian; and the number of the light-armed was as follows:—of the Spartan division thirty-five thousand men, reckoning at the rate of seven for each man, and of these everyone was equipped for fighting; and the light-armed troops of the rest of the Lacedemonians and of the other Hellenes, being about one for each man, amounted to thirty-four thousand five hundred.

30. Of the light-armed fighting men the whole number then was six myriads nine thousand and five hundred; and of the whole Hellenic force which assembled at Plataia the number (including both the hoplites and the light-armed fighting men) was eleven myriads all but one thousand eight hundred men; and with the Thespians who were present the number of eleven myriads was fully made up; for there were present also in the army those of the Thespians who survived, being in number about one thousand eight hundred, and these too were without heavy arms. These then having been ranged in order were encamped on the river Asopos.

31. Meanwhile the Barbarians with Mardonios, when they had sufficiently mourned for Masistios, being informed that the Hellenes were at Plataia came themselves also to

that part of the Asopos which flows there; and having arrived there, they were ranged against the enemy by Mardonios thus:—against the Lacedemonians he stationed the Persians; and since the Persians were much superior in numbers, they were arrayed in deeper ranks than those, and notwithstanding this they extended in front of the Tegeans also: and he ranged them in this manner,—all the strongest part of that body he selected from the rest and stationed it opposite to the Lacedemonians, but the weaker part he ranged by their side opposite to the Tegeans. This he did on the information and suggestion of the Thebans. Then next to the Persians he ranged the Medes; and these extended in front of the Corinthians, Potidaians, Orchomenians and Sikyonians. Next to the Medes he ranged the Bactrians; and these extended in front of the Epidaurians, Troizenians, Lepreates, Tirynthians, Mykenians and Phliasians. After the Bactrians he stationed the Indians; and these extended in front of the Hermionians, Eretrians, Styrians and Chalkidians. Next to the Indians he ranged the Sacans, who extended in front of the men of Amprakia, the Anactorians, Leucadians, Palians and Eginetans. Next to the Sacans and opposite to the Athenians, Plataians and Megarians, he ranged the Boeotians, Locrians, Malians, Thessalians, and the thousand men of the Phokians: for not all the Phokians had taken the side of the Medes, but some of them were even supporting the cause of the Hellenes, being shut up in Parnassos; and setting out from thence they plundered from the army of Mardonios and from those of the Hellenes who were with him. He ranged the Macedonians also and those who dwell about the borders of Thessaly opposite to the Athenians.

32. These which have been named were the greatest of the nations who were arrayed in order by Mardonios, those, I mean, which were the most renowned and of greatest consideration: but there were in his army also men of several other nations mingled together, of the Phrygians, Thracians, Mysians, Paionians, and the rest; and among them also some Ethiopians, and of the Egyptians those called Hermotybians and Calasirians, carrying knives, who of all the Egyptians are the only warriors. These men, while he was yet at Phaleron, he had caused to disembark from the ships in which they served as fighting-men; for the Egyptians had not been appointed to serve in the land-army which came with Xerxes to Athens. Of the Barbarians then there were thirty myriads, as has been declared before; but of the Hellenes who were allies of Mardonios no man knows what the number was, for they were not numbered; but by conjecture I judge that these were assembled to the number of five myriads. These who were placed in array side by side were on foot; and the cavalry was ranged apart from them in a separate body.

33. When all had been drawn up by nations and by divisions, then on the next day they offered sacrifice on both sides. For the Hellenes Tisamenos the son of Antiochos was he who offered sacrifice, for he it was who accompanied this army as diviner. This man the Lacedemonians had made to be one of their own people, being an Eleian and of the race of the Iamidai: for when Tisamenos was seeking divination at Delphi concerning issue, the Pythian prophetess made answer to him that he should win five of the greatest contests. He accordingly, missing the meaning of the oracle, began to attend to athletic games, supposing that he should win contests of athletics; and he practiced for the "five contests" and came within one fall of winning a victory at the Olympic games, being set to contend with Hieronymos of Andros. The Lacedemonians however perceived that the oracle given to Tisamenos had reference not to athletic but to martial contests, and they endeavored to persuade Tisamenos by payment of money, and to make him a leader in

their wars together with the kings of the race of Heracles. He then, seeing that the Spartans set much store on gaining him over as a friend, having perceived this, I say, he raised his price and signified to them that he would do as they desired, if they would make him a citizen of their State and give him full rights, but for no other payment. The Spartans at first when they heard this displayed indignation and altogether gave up their request, but at last, when great terror was hanging over them of this Persian armament, they gave way and consented. He then perceiving that they had changed their minds, said that he could not now be satisfied even so, nor with these terms alone; but it was necessary that his brother Hegias also should be made a Spartan citizen on the same terms as he himself became one.

34. By saying this he followed the example of Melampus in his request, if one may compare royal power with mere citizenship; for Melampus on his part, when the women in Argos had been seized by madness, and the Argives endeavored to hire him to come from Pylos and to cause their women to cease from the malady, proposed as payment for himself the half of the royal power; and the Argives did not suffer this, but departed: and afterwards, when more of their women became mad, at length they accepted that which Melampus had proposed, and went to offer him this: but he then seeing that they had changed their minds, increased his demand, and said that he would not do that which they desired unless they gave to his brother Bias also the third share in the royal power. And the Argives, being driven into straits, consented to this also. 35. Just so the Spartans also, being very much in need of Tisamenos, agreed with him on any terms which he desired: and when the Spartans had agreed to this demand also, then Tisamenos the Eleian, having become a Spartan, had part with them in winning five of the greatest contests as their diviner: and these were the only men who ever were made fellow-citizens of the Spartans. Now the five contests were these: one and the first of them was this at Plataia; and after this the contest at Tegea, which took place with the Tegeans and the Argives; then that at Dipaieis against all the Arcadians except the Mantineians; after that the contest with the Messenians at Ithome; and last of all that which took place at Tanagra against the Athenians and Argives. This, I say, was accomplished last of the five contests.

36. This Tisamenos was acting now as diviner for the Hellenes in the Plataian land, being brought by the Spartans. Now to the Hellenes the sacrifices were of good omen if they defended themselves only, but not if they crossed the Asopos and began a battle;.

37, and Mardonios too, who was eager to begin a battle, found the sacrifices not favorable to this design, but they were of good omen to him also if he defended himself only; for he too used the Hellenic manner of sacrifice, having as diviner Hegesistratos an Eleian and the most famous of the Telliadai, whom before these events the Spartans had taken and bound, in order to put him to death, because they had suffered much mischief from him. He then being in this evil case, seeing that he was running a course for his life and was likely moreover to suffer much torment before his death, had done a deed such as may hardly be believed. Being made fast on a block bound with iron, he obtained an iron tool, which in some way had been brought in, and contrived forthwith a deed the most courageous of any that we know: for having first calculated how the remaining portion of his foot might be got out of the block, he cut away the flat of his own foot, and after that, since he was guarded still by warders, he broke through the wall and so ran away to Tegea, travelling during the nights and in the daytime entering a wood and resting there; so that, though the Lacedemonians searched for him in full force, he arrived at Tegea on the third night; and the Lacedemonians were possessed by great wonder both at his courage, when they saw the piece of the foot that was cut off lying there, and also because they were not able to find him. So he at that time having thus escaped them took refuge at Tegea, which then was not friendly with the Lacedemonians; and when he was healed and had procured for himself a wooden foot, he became an open enemy of the Lacedemonians. However in the end the enmity into which he had fallen with the Lacedemonians was not to his advantage; for he was caught by them while practicing divination in Zakynthos, and was put to death.

38. However the death of Hegesistratos took place later than the events at Plataia, and he was now at the Asopos, having been hired by Mardonios for no mean sum, sacrificing and displaying zeal for his cause both on account of his enmity with the Lacedemonians and on account of the gain which he got: but as the sacrifices were not favorable for a battle either for the Persians themselves or for those Hellenes who were with them (for these also had a diviner for themselves, Hippomachos a Leucadian), and as the Hellenes had men constantly flowing in and were becoming more in number, Timagenides the son of Herpys, a Theban, counselled Mardonios to set a guard on the pass of Kithairon, saying that the Hellenes were constantly flowing in every day and that he would thus cut off large numbers.

39. Eight days had now passed while they had been sitting opposite to one another, when he gave this counsel to Mardonios; and Mardonios, perceiving that the advice was good, sent the cavalry when night came on to the pass of Kithairon leading towards Plataia, which the Boeotians call the "Three Heads" and the Athenians the "Oak Heads." Having been thus sent, the cavalry did not come without effect, for they caught five hundred baggage-animals coming out into the plain, which were bearing provisions from Peloponnesus to the army, and also the men who accompanied the carts: and having taken this prize the Persians proceeded to slaughter them without sparing either beast or man; and when they were satiated with killing they surrounded the rest and drove them into the camp to Mardonios.

40. After this deed they spent two days more, neither side wishing to begin a battle; for the Barbarians advanced as far as the Asopos to make trial of the Hellenes, but neither side would cross the river. However the cavalry of Mardonios made attacks continually and did damage to the Hellenes; for the Thebans, being very strong on the side of the Medes, carried on the war with vigor, and always directed them up to the moment of fighting; and after this the Persians and Medes took up the work and were they who displayed valor in their turn.

41. For ten days then nothing more was done than this; but when the eleventh day had come, while they still sat opposite to one another at Plataia, the Hellenes having by this time grown much more numerous and Mardonios being greatly vexed at the delay of action, then Mardonios the son of Gobryas and Artabazos the son of Pharnakes, who was esteemed by Xerxes as few of the Persians were besides, came to speech with one another; and as they conferred, the opinions they expressed were these,—that of Artabazos, that they must put the whole army in motion as soon as possible and go to the walls of the Thebans, whither great stores of corn had been brought in for them and fodder for their beasts; and that they should settle there quietly and get their business done as follows:— they had, he said, great quantities of gold, both coined and uncoined, and also of silver and of drinking-cups; and these he advised they should send about to the Hellenes

without stint, more especially to those of the Hellenes who were leaders in their several cities; and these, he said, would speedily deliver up their freedom: and he advised that they should not run the risk of a battle. His opinion then was the same as that of the Thebans, for he as well as they had some true foresight: but the opinion of Mardonios was more vehement and more obstinate, and he was by no means disposed to yield; for he said that he thought their army far superior to that of the Hellenes, and he gave as his opinion that they should engage battle as quickly as possible and not allow them to assemble in still greater numbers than were already assembled; and as for the sacrifices of Hegesistratos, they should leave them alone and not endeavor to force a good sign, but follow the custom of the Persians and engage battle.

42. When he so expressed his judgment, none opposed him, and thus his opinion prevailed; for he and not Artabazos had the command of the army given him by the king. He summoned therefore the commanders of the divisions and the generals of those Hellenes who were with him, and asked whether they knew of any oracle regarding the Persians, which said that they should be destroyed in Hellas; and when those summoned to council were silent, some not knowing the oracles and others knowing them but not esteeming it safe to speak, Mardonios himself said: "Since then ye either know nothing or do not venture to speak, I will tell you, since I know very well. There is an oracle saying that the Persians are destined when they come to Hellas to plunder the temple at Delphi, and having plundered it to perish every one of them. We therefore, just because we know this, will not go to that temple nor will we attempt to plunder it; and for this cause we shall not perish. So many of you therefore as chance to wish well to the Persians, have joy so far as regards this matter, and be assured that we shall overcome the Hellenes." Having spoken to them thus, he next commanded to prepare everything and to set all in order, since at dawn of the next day a battle would be fought.

43. Now this oracle, which Mardonios said referred to the Persians, I know for my part was composed with reference with the Illyrians and the army of the Enchelians, and not with reference to the Persians at all. However, the oracle which was composed by Bakis with reference to this battle,

"The gathering of Hellenes together and cry of Barbarian voices,
Where the Thermodon flows, by the banks of grassy Asopos;
Here very many shall fall ere destiny gave them to perish,
Medes bow-bearing in fight, when the fatal day shall approach them," —

these sayings, and others like them composed by Musaios, I know had reference to the Persians. Now the river Thermodon flows between Tanagra and Glisas.

44. After the inquiry about the oracles and the exhortation given by Mardonios nigh came on and the guards were set: and when night was far advanced, and it seemed that there was quiet everywhere in the camps, and that the men were in their deepest sleep, then Alexander the son of Amyntas, commander and king of the Macedonians, rode his horse up to the guard-posts of the Athenians and requested that he might have speech with their generals. So while the greater number of the guards stayed at their posts, some ran to the generals, and when they reached them they said that a man had come riding on a horse out of the camp of the Medes, who discovered nothing further, but only named the generals and said that he desired to have speech with them.

45. Having heard this, forthwith they accompanied the men to the guard-posts, and when they had arrived there, Alexander thus spoke to them: "Athenians, I lay up these words of mine as a trust to you, charging you to keep them secret and tell them to no one except only to Pausanias, lest ye bring me to ruin: for I should not utter them if I did not care greatly for the general safety of Hellas, seeing that I am a Hellene myself by original descent and I should not wish to see Hellas enslaved instead of free. I say then that Mardonios and his army cannot get the offerings to be according to their mind, for otherwise ye would long ago have fought. Now however he has resolved to let the offerings alone and to bring on a battle at dawn of day; for, as I conjecture, he fears lest ye should assemble in greater numbers. Therefore prepare yourselves; and if after all Mardonios should put off the battle and not bring it on, stay where ye are and hold out patiently; for they have provisions only for a few days remaining. And if this way shall have its issue according to your mind, then each one of you ought to remember me also concerning liberation, since I have done for the sake of the Hellenes so hazardous a deed by reason of my zeal for you, desiring to show you the design of Mardonios, in order that the Barbarians may not fall upon you when ye are not as yet expecting them: and I am Alexander the Macedonian." Thus having spoken he rode away back to the camp and to his own position.

46. Then the generals of the Athenians came to the right wing and told Pausanias that which they had heard from Alexander. Upon this saying he being struck with fear of the Persians spoke as follows: "Since then at dawn the battle comes on, it is right that ye, Athenians, should take your stand opposite to the Persians, and we opposite to the Boeotians and those Hellenes who are now posted against you; and for this reason, namely because ye are acquainted with the Medes and with their manner of fighting, having fought with them at Marathon, whereas we have had no experience of these men and are without knowledge of them; for not one of the Spartans has made trial of the Medes in fight, but of the Boeotians and Thessalians we have had experience. It is right therefore that ye should take up your arms and come to this wing of the army, and that we should go to the left wing." In answer to this the Athenians spoke as follows: "To ourselves also long ago at the very first, when we saw that the Persians were being ranged opposite to you, it occurred to us to say these very things, which ye now bring forward before we have uttered them; but we feared lest these words might not be pleasing to you. Since however ye yourselves have made mention of this, know that your words have caused us pleasure, and that we are ready to do this which ye say."

47. Both then were content to do this, and as dawn appeared they began to change their positions with one another: and the Boeotians perceiving that which was being done reported it to Mardonios, who, when he heard it, forthwith himself also endeavored to change positions, bringing the Persians along so as to be against the Lacedemonians: and when Pausanias learnt that this was being done, he perceived that he was not unobserved, and he led the Spartans back again to the right wing; and just so also did Mardonios upon his left.

48. When they had been thus brought to their former positions, Mardonios sent a herald to the Spartans and said as follows: "Lacedemonians, ye are said forsooth by those who are here to be very good men, and they have admiration for you because ye do not flee in war nor leave your post, but stay there and either destroy your enemies or perish yourselves. In this however, as it now appears, there is no truth; for before we engaged

battle and came to hand-to-hand conflict we saw you already flee and leave your station, desiring to make the trial with the Athenians first, while ye ranged yourselves opposite to our slaves. These are not at all the deeds of good men in war, but we were deceived in you very greatly; for we expected by reason of your renown that ye would send a herald to us, challenging us and desiring to fight with the Persians alone; but though we on our part were ready to do this, we did not find that ye said anything of this kind, but rather that ye cowered with fear. Now therefore since ye were not the first to say this, we are the first. Why do we not forthwith fight, ye on behalf of the Hellenes, since ye have the reputation of being the best, and we on behalf of the Barbarians, with equal numbers on both sides? and if we think it good that the others should fight also, then let them fight afterwards; and if on the other hand we should not think it good, but think it sufficient that we alone should fight, then let us fight it out to the end, and whichsoever of us shall be the victors, let these be counted as victorious with their whole army."

49. The herald having thus spoken waited for some time, and then, as no one made him any answer, he departed and went back; and having returned he signified to Mardonios that which had happened to him. Mardonios then being greatly rejoiced and elated by his empty victory, sent the cavalry to attack the Hellenes: and when the horsemen had ridden to attack them, they did damage to the whole army of the Hellenes by hurling javelins against them and shooting with bows, being mounted archers and hard therefore to fight against: and they disturbed and choked up the spring Gargaphia, from which the whole army of the Hellenes was drawing its water. Now the Lacedemonians alone were posted near this spring, and it was at some distance from the rest of the Hellenes, according as they chanced to be posted, while the Asopos was near at hand; but when they were kept away from the Asopos, then they used to go backwards and forwards to this spring; for they were not permitted by the horsemen and archers to fetch water from the river.

50. Such then being the condition of things, the generals of the Hellenes, since the army had been cut off from its water and was being harassed by the cavalry, assembled to consult about these and other things, coming to Pausanias upon the right wing: for other things too troubled them yet more than these of which we have spoken, since they no longer had provisions, and their attendants who had been sent to Peloponnese for the purpose of getting them had been cut off by the cavalry and were not able to reach the camp.

51. It was resolved then by the generals in council with one another, that if the Persians put off the battle for that day, they would go to the Island. This is distant ten furlongs from the Asopos and the spring Gargaphia, where they were then encamped, and is in front of the city of the Plataians: and if it be asked how there can be an island on the mainland, thus it is :—the river parts in two above, as it flows from Kithairon down to the plain, keeping a distance of about three furlongs between its streams, and after that it joins again in one stream; and the name of it is Oëroe, said by the natives of the country to be the daughter of Asopos. To this place of which I speak they determined to remove, in order that they might be able to get an abundant supply of water and that the cavalry might not do them damage, as now when they were right opposite. And they proposed to remove when the second watch of the night should have come, so that the Persians might not see them set forth and harass them with the cavalry pursuing. They proposed also, after they had arrived at this place, round which, as I say, Oëroe the daughter of Asopos

flows, parting into two streams as she runs from Kithairon, to send half the army to Kithairon during this same night, in order to take up their attendants who had gone to get the supplies of provisions; for these were cut off from them in Kithairon.

52. Having thus resolved, during the whole of that day they had trouble unceasingly, while the cavalry pressed upon them; but when the day drew to a close and the attacks of the cavalry had ceased, then as it was becoming night and the time had arrived at which it had been agreed that they should retire from their place, the greater number of them set forth and began to retire, not however keeping it in mind to go to the place which had been agreed upon; but on the contrary, when they had begun to move, they readily took occasion to flee from the cavalry towards the city of the Plataians, and in their flight they came as far as the temple of Hera, which temple is in front of the city of the Plataians at a distance of twenty furlongs from the spring Gargaphia; and when they had there arrived they halted in front of the temple.

53. These then were encamping about the temple of Hera; and Pausanias, seeing that they were retiring from the camp, gave the word to the Lacedemonians also to take up their arms and go after the others who were preceding them, supposing that these were going to the place to which they had agreed to go. Then, when all the other commanders were ready to obey Pausanias, Amompharetos the son of Poliades, the commander of the Pitanate division, said that he would not flee from the strangers, nor with his own will would he disgrace Sparta; and he expressed wonder at seeing that which was being done, not having been present at the former discussion. And Pausanias and Euryanax were greatly disturbed that he did not obey them and still more that they should be compelled to leave the Pitanate division behind, since he thus refused; for they feared that if they should leave it in order to do that which they had agreed with the other Hellenes, both Amompharetos himself would perish being left behind and also the men with him. With this thought they kept the Lacedemonian force from moving, and meanwhile they endeavored to persuade him that it was not right for him to do so.

54. They then were exhorting Amompharetos, who had been left behind alone of the Lacedemonians and Tegeans; and meanwhile the Athenians were keeping themselves quiet in the place where they had been posted, knowing the spirit of the Lacedemonians, that they were apt to say otherwise than they really meant; and when the army began to move, they sent a horseman from their own body to see whether the Spartans were attempting to set forth, or whether they had in truth no design at all to retire; and they bade him ask Pausanias what they ought to do. 55. So when the herald came to the Lacedemonians, he saw that they were still in their place and that the chiefs of them had come to strife with one another: for when Euryanax and Pausanias both exhorted Amompharetos not to run the risk of remaining behind with his men, alone of all the Lacedemonians, they did not at all persuade him, and at last they had come to downright strife; and meanwhile the herald of the Athenians had arrived and was standing by them. And Amompharetos in his contention took a piece of rock in both his hands and placed it at the feet of Pausanias, saying that with this pebble he gave his vote not to fly from the strangers, meaning the Barbarians. Pausanias then, calling him a madman and one who was not in his right senses, bade tell the state of their affairs to the Athenian herald, who was asking that which he had been charged to ask; and at the same time he requested the Athenians to come towards the Lacedemonians and to do in regard to the retreat the same as they did.

56. He then went away back to the Athenians; and as the dawn of day found them yet disputing with one another, Pausanias, who had remained still throughout all this time, gave the signal, and led away all the rest over the low hills, supposing that Amonpharetos would not stay behind when the other Lacedemonians departed (in which he was in fact right); and with them also went the Tegeans. Meanwhile the Athenians, following the commands which were given them, were going in the direction opposite to that of the Lacedemonians; for these were clinging to the hills and the lower slope of Kithairon from fear of the cavalry, while the Athenians were marching below in the direction of the plain.

57. As for Amonpharetos, he did not at first believe that Pausanias would ever venture to leave him and his men behind, and he stuck to it that they should stay there and not leave their post; but when Pausanias and his troops were well in front, then he perceived that they had actually left him behind, and he made his division take up their arms and led them slowly towards the main body. This, when it had got away about ten furlongs, stayed for the division of Amompharetos, halting at the river Moloeis and the place called Argiopion, where also there stands a temple of the Eleusinian Demeter: and it stayed there for this reason, namely in order that of Amonpharetos and his division should not leave the place where they had been posted, but should remain there, it might be able to come back to their assistance. So Amompharetos and his men were coming up to join them, and the cavalry also of the Barbarians was at the same time beginning to attack them in full force: for the horsemen did on this day as they had been wont to do every day; and seeing the place vacant in which the Hellenes had been posted on the former days, they rode their horses on continually further, and as soon as they came up with them they began to attack them.

58. Then Mardonios, when he was informed that the Hellenes had departed during the night, and when he saw their place deserted, called Thorax of Larissa and his brothers Eurypylos and Thrasydeios, and said: "Sons of Aleuas, will ye yet say anything, now that ye see these places deserted? For ye who dwell near them were wont to say that the Lacedemonians did not fly from a battle, but were men unsurpassed in war; and these men ye not only saw before this changing from their post, but now we all of us see that they have run away during the past night; and by this they showed clearly, when the time came for them to contend in battle with those who were in truth the best of all men, that after all they were men of no worth, who had been making a display of valor among Hellenes, a worthless race. As for you, since ye had had no experience of the Persians, I for my part was very ready to excuse you when ye praised these, of whom after all ye knew something good; but much more I marveled at Artabazos that *he* should have been afraid of the Lacedemonians, and that having been afraid he should have uttered that most cowardly opinion, namely that we ought to move our army away and go to the city of the Thebans to be besieged there,—an opinion about which the king shall yet be informed by me. Of these things we will speak in another place; now however we must not allow them to act thus, but we must pursue them until they are caught and pay the penalty to us for all that they did to the Persians in time past."

59. Thus having spoken he led on the Persians at a run, after they had crossed the Asopos, on the track of the Hellenes, supposing that these were running away from him; and he directed his attack upon the Lacedemonians and Tegeans only, for the Athenians, whose march was towards the plain, he did not see by reason of the hills. Then the rest of the commanders of the Barbarian divisions, seeing that the Persians had started to pursue

the Hellenes, forthwith all raised the signals for battle and began to pursue, each as fast as they could, not arranged in any order or succession of post.

60. These then were coming on with shouting and confused numbers, thinking to make short work of the Hellenes; and Pausanias, when the cavalry began to attack, sent to the Athenians a horseman and said thus: "Athenians, now that the greatest contest is set before us, namely that which has for its issue the freedom or the slavery of Hellas, we have been deserted by our allies, we Lacedemonians and ye Athenians, seeing that they have run away during the night that is past. Now therefore it is determined what we must do upon this, namely that we must defend ourselves and protect one another as best we may. If then the cavalry had set forth to attack you at the first, we and the Tegeans, who with us refuse to betray the cause of Hellas, should have been bound to go to your help; but as it is, since the whole body has come against us, it is right that ye should come to that portion of the army which is hardest pressed, to give aid. If however anything has happened to you which makes it impossible for you to come to our help, then do us a kindness by sending to us the archers; and we know that ye have been in the course of this present war by far the most zealous of all, so that ye will listen to our request in this matter also."

61. When the Athenians heard this they were desirous to come to their help and to assist them as much as possible; and as they were already going, they were attacked by those of the Hellenes on the side of the king who had been ranged opposite to them, so that they were no longer able to come to the help of the Lacedemonians, for the force that was attacking them gave them much trouble. Thus the Lacedemonians and Tegeans were left alone, being in number, together with light-armed men, the former fifty thousand and the Tegeans three thousand; for these were not parted at all from the Lacedemonians: and they began to offer sacrifice, meaning to engage battle with Mardonios and the force which had come against them. Then since their offerings did not prove favorable, and many of them were being slain during this time and many more wounded,—for the Persians had made a palisade of their wicker-work shields and were discharging their arrows in great multitude and without sparing,—Pausanias, seeing that the Spartans were hard pressed and that the offerings did not prove favorable, fixed his gaze upon the temple of Hera of the Plataians and called upon the goddess to help, praying that they might by no means be cheated of their hope:.

62, and while he was yet calling upon her thus, the Tegeans started forward before them and advanced against the Barbarians, and forthwith after the prayer of Pausanias the offerings proved favorable for the Lacedemonians as they sacrificed. So when this at length came to pass, then they also advanced against the Persians; and the Persians put away their bows and came against them. Then first there was fighting about the wicker-work shields, and when these had been overturned, after that the fighting was fierce by the side of the temple of Demeter, and so continued for a long time, until at last they came to justling; for the Barbarians would take hold of the spears and break them off. Now in courage and in strength the Persians were not inferior to the others, but they were without defensive armor, and moreover they were unversed in war and unequal to their opponents in skill; and they would dart out one at a time or in groups of about ten together, some more and some less, and fall upon the Spartans and perish.

63. In the place where Mardonios himself was, riding on a white horse and having about him the thousand best men of the Persians chosen out from the rest, here, I say, they

pressed upon their opponents most of all: and so long as Mardonios survived, they held out against them, and defending themselves they cast down many of the Lacedemonians; but when Mardonios was slain and the men who were ranged about his person, which was the strongest portion of the whole army, had fallen, then the others too turned and gave way before the Lacedemonians; for their manner of dress, without defensive armor, was a very great cause of destruction to them, since in truth they were contending light-armed against hoplites.

64. Then the satisfaction for the murder of Leonidas was paid by Mardonios according to the oracle given to the Spartans, and the most famous victory of all those about which we have knowledge was gained by Pausanias the son of Cleombrotos, the son of Anaxandrides; of his ancestors above this the names have been given for Leonidas, since, as it happens, they are the same for both. Now Mardonios was slain by Arimnestos, a man of consideration in Sparta, who afterwards, when the Median wars were over, with three hundred men fought a battle against the whole army of the Messenians, then at war with the Lacedemonians, at Stenycleros, and both he was slain and also the three hundred.

65. When the Persians were turned to flight at Plataia by the Lacedemonians, they fled in disorder to their own camp and to the palisade which they had made in the Theban territory: and it is a marvel to me that, whereas they fought by the side of the sacred grove of Demeter, not one of the Persians was found to have entered the enclosure or to have been slain within it, but round about the temple in the unconsecrated ground fell the greater number of the slain. I suppose (if one ought to suppose anything about divine things) that the goddess herself refused to receive them, because they had set fire to the temple, that is to say the "palace" at Eleusis.

66. Thus far then had this battle proceeded: but Artabazos the son of Pharnakes had been displeased at the very first because Mardonios remained behind after the king was gone; and afterwards he had been bringing forward objections continually and doing nothing, but had urged them always not to fight a battle: and for himself he acted as follows, not being pleased with the things which were being done by Mardonios.—The men of whom Artabazos was commander (and he had with him no small force but one which was in number as much as four myriads of men), these, when the fighting began, being well aware what the issue of the battle would be, he led carefully, having first given orders that all should go by the way which he should lead them and at the same pace at which they should see him go. Having given these orders he led his troops on pretense of taking them into battle; and when he was well on his way, he saw the Persians already taking flight. Then he no longer led his men in the same order as before, but set off at a run, taking flight by the quickest way not to the palisade nor yet to the wall of the Thebans, but towards Phokis, desiring as quickly as possible to reach the Hellespont.

67. These, I say, were thus directing their march: and in the meantime, while the other Hellenes who were on the side of the king were purposely slack in the fight, the Boeotians fought with the Athenians for a long space; for those of the Thebans who took the side of the Medes had no small zeal for the cause, and they fought and were not slack, so that three hundred of them, the first and best of all, fell there by the hands of the Athenians and when these also turned to flight, they fled to Thebes, not to the same place as the Persians: and the main body of the other allies fled without having fought constantly with any one or displayed any deeds of valor.

68. And this is an additional proof to me that all the fortunes of the Barbarian

depended upon the Persians, namely that at that time these men fled before they had even engaged with the enemy, because they saw the Persians doing so. Thus all were in flight except only the cavalry, including also that of the Boeotians; and this rendered service to the fugitives by constantly keeping close to the enemy and separating the fugitives of their own side from the Hellenes.

69. The victors then were coming after the troops of Xerxes, both pursuing them and slaughtering them; and during the time when this panic arose, the report was brought to the other Hellenes who had posted themselves about the temple of Hera and had been absent from the battle, that a battle had taken place and that the troops of Pausanias were gaining the victory. When they heard this, then without ranging themselves in any order the Corinthians and those near them turned to go by the skirts of the mountain and by the low hills along the way which led straight up to the temple of Demeter, while the Megarians and Phliasians and those near them went by the plain along the smoothest way. When however the Megarians and Phliasians came near to the enemy, the cavalry of the Thebans caught sight of them from a distance hurrying along without any order, and rode up to attack them, the commander of the cavalry being Asopodoros the son of Timander; and having fallen upon them they slew six hundred of them, and the rest they pursued and drove to Kithairon.

70. These then perished thus ingloriously; and meanwhile the Persians and the rest of the throng, having fled for refuge to the palisade, succeeded in getting up to the towers before the Lacedemonians came; and having got up they strengthened the wall of defense as best they could. Then when the Lacedemonians came up to attack it, there began between them a vigorous fight for the wall: for so long as the Athenians were away, they defended themselves and had much the advantage over the Lacedemonians, since these did not understand the art of fighting against walls; but when the Athenians came up to help them, then there was a fierce fight for the wall, lasting for a long time, and at length by valor and endurance the Athenians mounted up on the wall and made a breach in it, through which the Hellenes poured in. Now the Tegeans were the first who entered the wall, and these were they who plundered the tent of Mardonios, taking, besides the other things which were in it, also the manger of his horse, which was all of bronze and a sight worth seeing. This manger of Mardonios was dedicated by the Tegeans as an offering in the temple of Athene Alea, but all the other things which they took, they brought to the common stock of the Hellenes. The Barbarians however, after the wall had been captured, no longer formed themselves into any close body, nor did any of them think of making resistance, but they were utterly at a loss, as you might expect from men who were in a panic with many myriads of them shut up together in a small space: and the Hellenes were able to slaughter them so that out of an army of thirty myriads, if those four be subtracted which Artabazos took with him in his flight, of the remainder not three thousand men survived. Of the Lacedemonians from Sparta there were slain in the battle ninety-one in all, of the Tegeans sixteen, and of the Athenians two-and-fifty.

71. Among the Barbarians those who proved themselves the best men were, of those on foot the Persians, and of the cavalry the Sacans, and for a single man Mardonios it is said was the best. Of the Hellenes, though both the Tegeans and the Athenians proved themselves good men, yet the Lacedemonians surpassed them in valor. Of this I have no other proof (for all these were victorious over their opposites), but only this, that they fought against the strongest part of the enemy's force and overcame it. And the man who

proved himself in my opinion by much the best was that Aristodemos who, having come back safe from Thermopylai alone of the three hundred, had reproach and dishonor attached to him. After him the best were Poseidonios and Philokyon and Amompharetos the Spartan. However, when there came to be conversation as to which of them had proved himself the best, the Spartans who were present gave it as their opinion that Aristodemos had evidently wished to be slain in consequence of the charge which lay against him, and so, being as it were in a frenzy and leaving his place in the ranks, he had displayed great deeds, whereas Poseidonios had proved himself a good man although he did not desire to be slain; and so far he was the better man of the two. This however they perhaps said from ill-will; and all these whose names I mentioned among the men who were killed in this battle, were specially honored, except Aristodemos; but Aristodemos, since he desired to be slain on account of the before-mentioned charge, was not honored.

72. These obtained the most renown of those who fought at Plataia, for as for Callicrates, the most beautiful who came to the camp, not of the Lacedemonians alone, but also of all the Hellenes of his time, he was not killed in the battle itself; but when Pausanias was offering sacrifice, he was wounded by an arrow in the side, as he was sitting down in his place in the ranks; and while the others were fighting, he having been carried out of the ranks was dying a lingering death: and he said to Arimnestos a Plataian that it did not grieve him to die for Hellas, but it grieved him only that he had not proved his strength of hand, and that no deed of valor had been displayed by him worthy of the spirit which he had in him to perform great deeds.

73. Of the Athenians the man who gained most glory is said to have been Sophanes the son of Eutychides of the deme of Dekeleia,—a deme of which the inhabitants formerly did a deed that was of service to them for all time, as the Athenians themselves report. For when of old the sons of Tyndareus invaded the Attic land with a great host, in order to bring home Helen, and were laying waste the demes, not knowing to what place of hiding Helen had been removed, then they say that the men of Dekeleia, or as some say Dekelos himself, being aggrieved by the insolence of Theseus and fearing for all the land of the Athenians, told them the whole matter and led them to Aphidnai, which Titakos who was sprung from the soil delivered up by treachery to the sons of Tyndareus. In consequence of this deed the Dekeleians have had continually freedom from dues in Sparta and front seats at the games, privileges which exist still to this day; insomuch that even in the war which many years after these events arose between the Athenians and the Peloponnesians, when the Lacedemonians laid waste all the rest of Attica, they abstained from injury to Dekeleia.

74. To this deme belonged Sophanes, who showed himself the best of all the Athenians in this battle; and of him there are two different stories told: one that he carried an anchor of iron bound by chains of bronze to the belt of his corslet; and this he threw whensoever he came up with the enemy, in order, they say, that the enemy when they came forth out of their ranks might not be able to move him from his place; and when a flight of his opponents took place, his plan was to take up the anchor first and then pursue after them. This story is reported thus; but the other of the stories, disputing the truth of that which has been told above, is reported as follows, namely that upon his shield, which was ever moving about and never remaining still, he bore an anchor as a device, and not one of iron bound to his corslet.

75. There was another illustrious deed done too by Sophanes; for when the Athenians

besieged Egina he challenged to a fight and slew Eurybates the Argive, one who had been victor in the five contests at the games. To Sophanes himself it happened after these events that when he was general of the Athenians together with Leagros the son of Glaucon, he was slain after proving himself a good man by the Edonians at Daton, fighting for the gold mines.

76. When the Barbarians had been laid low by the Hellenes at Plataia, there approached to these a woman, the concubine of Pharandates the son of Teaspis a Persian, coming over of her own free will from the enemy, who when she perceived that the Persians had been destroyed and that the Hellenes were the victors, descended from her carriage and came up to the Lacedemonians while they were yet engaged in the slaughter. This woman had adorned herself with many ornaments of gold, and her attendants likewise, and she had put on the fairest robe of those which she had; and when she saw that Pausanias was directing everything there, being well acquainted before with his name and with his lineage, because she had heard it often, she recognized Pausanias and taking hold of his knees she said these words: "O king of Sparta, deliver me thy suppliant from the slavery of the captive: for thou hast also done me service hitherto in destroying these, who have regard neither for demigods nor yet for gods. I am by race of Cos, the daughter of Hegetorides the son of Antagoras; and the Persian took me by force in Cos and kept me a prisoner." He made answer in these words: "Woman, be of good courage, both because thou art a suppliant, and also if in addition to this it chances that thou art speaking the truth and art the daughter of Hegetorides the Coan, who is bound to me as a guest-friend more than any other of the men who dwell in those parts." Having thus spoken, for that time her gave her in charge to those Ephors who were present, and afterwards he sent her away to Egina, whither she herself desired to go.

77. After the arrival of the woman, forthwith upon this arrived the Mantineians, when all was over; and having learnt that they had come too late for the battle, they were greatly grieved, and said that they deserved to be punished: and being informed that the Medes with Artabazos were in flight, they pursued after them as far as Thessaly, though the Lacedemonians endeavored to prevent them from pursuing after fugitives. Then returning back to their own country they sent the leaders of their army into exile from the land. After the Mantineians came the Eleians; and they, like the Mantineians, were greatly grieved by it and so departed home; and these also when they had returned sent their leaders into exile. So much of the Mantineians and Eleians.

78. At Plataia among the troops of the Eginetans was Lampon the son of Pytheas, one of the leading men of the Eginetans, who was moved to go to Pausanias with a most impious proposal, and when he had come with haste, he said as follows: "Son of Cleombrotos, a deed has been done by thee which is of marvelous greatness and glory, and to thee God has permitted by rescuing Hellas to lay up for thyself the greatest renown of all the Hellenes about whom we have any knowledge. Do thou then perform also that which remains to do after these things, in order that yet greater reputation may attach to thee, and also that in future every one of the Barbarians may beware of being the beginner of presumptuous deeds towards the Hellenes. For when Leonidas was slain at Thermopylai, Mardonios and Xerxes cut off his head and crucified him: to him therefore do thou repay like with like, and thou shalt have praise first from all the Spartans and then secondly from the other Hellenes also; for if thou impale the body of Mardonios, thou wilt then have taken vengeance for Leonidas thy father's brother."

79. He said this thinking to give pleasure; but the other made him answer in these words: "Stranger of Egina, I admire thy friendly spirit and thy forethought for me, but thou hast failed of a good opinion nevertheless: for having exalted me on high and my family and my deed, thou didst then cast me down to naught by advising me to do outrage to a dead body, and by saying that if I do this I shall be better reported of. These things it is more fitting for Barbarians to do than for Hellenes; and even with them we find fault for doing so. However that may be, I do not desire in any such manner as this to please either Eginetans or others who like such things; but it is enough for me that I should keep from unholy deeds, yea and from unholy speech also, and so please the Spartans. As for Leonidas, whom thou biddest me avenge, I declare that he has been greatly avenged already, and by the unnumbered lives which have been taken of these men he has been honored, and not he only but also the rest who brought their lives to an end at Thermopylai. As for thee however, come not again to me with such a proposal, nor give me such advice; and be thankful moreover that thou hast no punishment for it now."

80. He having heard this went his way; and Pausanias made a proclamation that none should lay hands upon the spoil, and he ordered the Helots to collect the things together. They accordingly dispersed themselves about the camp and found tents furnished with gold and silver, and beds overlaid with gold and overlaid with silver, and mixing-bowls of gold, and cups and other drinking vessels. They found also sacks laid upon wagons, in which there proved to be caldrons both of gold and of silver; and from the dead bodies which lay there they stripped bracelets and collars, and also their swords if they were of gold, for as to embroidered raiment, there was no account made of it. Then the Helots stole many of the things and sold them to the Eginetans, but many things also they delivered up, as many of them as they could not conceal; so that the great wealth of the Eginetans first came from this, that they bought the gold from the Helots making pretense that it was brass.

81. Then having brought the things together, and having set apart a tithe for the god of Delphi, with which the offering was dedicated of the golden tripod which rests upon the three-headed serpent of bronze and stands close by the altar, and also for the god at Olympia, with which they dedicated the offering of a bronze statue of Zeus ten cubits high, and finally for the god at the Isthmus, with which was made a bronze statue of Poseidon seven cubits high,—having set apart these things, they divided the rest, and each took that which they ought to have, including the concubines of the Persians and the gold and the silver and the other things, and also the beasts of burden. How much was set apart and given to those of them who had proved themselves the best men at Plataia is not reported by any, though for my part I suppose that gifts were made to these also; Pausanias however had ten of each thing set apart and given to him, that is women, horses, talents, camels, and so also of the other things.

82. It is said moreover that this was done which here follows, namely that Xerxes in his flight from Hellas had left to Mardonios the furniture of his own tent, and Pausanias accordingly seeing the furniture of Mardonios furnished with gold and silver and hangings of different colors ordered the bakers and the cooks to prepare a meal as they were used to do for Mardonios. Then when they did this as they had been commanded, it is said that Pausanias seeing the couches of gold and of silver with luxurious coverings, and the tables of gold and silver, and the magnificent apparatus of the feast, was astonished at the good things set before him, and for sport he ordered his own servants to prepare a

Laconian meal; and as, when the banquet was served, the difference between the two was great, Pausanias laughed and sent for the commanders of the Hellenes; and when these had come together, Pausanias said, pointing to the preparation of the two meals severally: "Hellenes, for this reason I assembled you together, because I desired to show you the senselessness of this leader of the Medes, who having such fare as this, came to us who have such sorry fare as ye see here, in order to take it away from us." Thus it is said that Pausanias spoke to the commanders of the Hellenes.

83. However, in later time after these events many of the Plataians also found chests of gold and of silver and of other treasures; and moreover afterwards this which follows was seen in the case of the dead bodies here, after the flesh had been stripped off from the bones; for the Plataians brought together the bones all to one place:—there was found, I say, a skull with no suture but all of one bone, and there was seen also a jaw-bone, that is to say the upper part of the jaw, which had teeth joined together and all of one bone, both the teeth that bite and those that grind; and the bones were seen also of a man five cubits high.

84. The body of Mardonios however had disappeared on the day after the battle, taken by whom I am not able with certainty to say, but I have heard the names of many men of various cities who are said to have buried Mardonios, and I know that many received gifts from Artontes the son of Mardonios for having done this: who he was however who took up and buried the body of Mardonios I am not able for certain to discover, but Dionyso-phanes an Ephesian is reported with some show of reason to have been he who buried Mardonios.

85. He then was buried in some such manner as this: and the Hellenes when they had divided the spoil at Plataia proceeded to bury their dead, each nation apart by themselves. The Spartans made for themselves three several burial-places, one in which they buried the younger Spartans, of whom also were Poseidonios, Amompharetos, Philokyon and Callicrates,—in one of the graves, I say, were laid the younger men, in the second the rest of the Spartans, and in the third the Helots. These then thus buried their dead; but the Tegeans buried theirs all together in a place apart from these, and the Athenians theirs together; and the Megarians and Phliasians those who had been slain by the cavalry. Of all these the burial-places had bodies laid in them, but as to the burial-places of other States which are to be seen at Plataia, these, as I am informed, are all mere mounds of earth without any bodies in them, raised by the several peoples on account of posterity, because they were ashamed of their absence from the fight; for among others there is one there called the burial-place of the Eginetans, which I hear was raised at the request of the Eginetans by Cleades the son of Autodicos, a man of Plataia who was their public guest-friend, no less than ten years after these events.

86. When the Hellenes had buried their dead at Plataia, forthwith they determined in common council to march upon Thebes and to ask the Thebans to surrender those who had taken the side of the Medes, and among the first of them Timagenides and Attaginos, who were leaders equal to the first; and if the Thebans did not give them up, they deter-mined not to retire from the city until they had taken it. Having thus resolved, they came accordingly on the eleventh day after the battle and began to besiege the Thebans, bidding them give the men up: and as the Thebans refused to give them up, they began to lay waste their land and also to attack their wall.

87. So then, as they did not cease their ravages, on the twentieth day Timagenides

spoke as follows to the Thebans: "Thebans, since it has been resolved by the Hellenes not to retire from the siege until either they have taken Thebes or ye have delivered us up to them, now therefore let not the land of Boeotia suffer any more for our sakes, but if they desire to have money and are demanding our surrender as a color for this, let us give them money taken out of the treasury of the State; for we took the side of the Medes together with the State and not by ourselves alone: but if they are making the siege truly in order to get us into their hands, then we will give ourselves up for trial." In this it was thought that he spoke very well and seasonably, and the Thebans forthwith sent a herald to Pausanias offering to deliver up the men.

88. After they had made an agreement on these terms, Attaginos escaped out of the city; and when his sons were delivered up to Pausanias, he released them from the charge, saying that the sons had no share in the guilt of taking the side of the Medes. As to the other men whom the Thebans delivered up, they supposed that they would get a trial, and they trusted moreover to be able to repel the danger by payment of money; but Pausanias, when he had received them, suspecting this very thing, first dismissed the whole army of allies, and then took the men to Corinth and put them to death there. These were the things which happened at Plataia and at Thebes.

89. Artabazos meanwhile, the son of Pharnakes, in his flight from Plataia was by this time getting forward on his way: and the Thessalians, when he came to them, offered him hospitality and inquired concerning the rest of the army, not knowing anything of that which had happened at Plataia; and Artabazos knowing that if he should tell them the whole truth about the fighting, he would run the risk of being destroyed, both himself and the whole army which was with him, (for he thought that they would all set upon him if they were informed of that which had happened),—reflecting, I say, upon this he had told nothing of it to the Phokians, and now to the Thessalians he spoke as follows: "I, as you see, Thessalians, am earnest to march by the shortest way to Thracia; and I am in great haste, having been sent with these men for a certain business from the army; moreover Mardonios himself and his army are shortly to be looked for here, marching close after me. To him give entertainment and show yourselves serviceable, for ye will not in the end repent of so doing." Having thus said he continued to march his army with haste through Thessaly and Macedonia straight for Thracia, being in truth earnest to proceed and going through the land by the shortest possible way: and so he came to Byzantion, having left behind him great numbers of his army, who had either been cut down by the Thracians on the way or had been overcome by hunger and fatigue; and from Byzantion he passed over in ships. He himself then thus made his return back to Asia.

90. Now on the same day on which the defeat took place at Plataia, another took place also, as fortune would have it, at Mycale in Ionia. For when the Hellenes who had come in the ships with Leotychides the Lacedemonian, were lying at Delos, there came to them as envoys from Samos Lampon the son of Thrasycles and Athenagoras the son of Arches tratides and Hegesistratos the son of Aristagoras, who had been sent by the people of Samos without the knowledge either of the Persians or of the despot Theomestor the son of Androdamas, whom the Persians had set up to be despot of Samos. When these had been introduced before the commanders, Hegesistratos spoke at great length using argu ments of all kinds, and saying that so soon as the Ionians should see them they would at once revolt from the Persians, and that the Barbarians would not wait for their attack; and if after all they did so, then the Hellenes would take a prize such as they would never take

again hereafter; and appealing to the gods worshipped in common he endeavored to persuade them to rescue from slavery men who were Hellenes and to drive away the Barbarian: and this he said was easy for them to do, for the ships of the enemy sailed badly and were no match for them in fight. Moreover if the Hellenes suspected that they were endeavoring to bring them on by fraud, they were ready to be taken as hostages in their ships.

91. Then as the stranger of Samos was urgent in his prayer, Leotychides inquired thus, either desiring to hear for the sake of the omen or perhaps by a chance which Providence brought about: "Stranger of Samos, what is thy name?" He said "Hegesistratos." The other cut short the rest of the speech, stopping all that Hegesistratos had intended to say further, and said: "I accept the augury given in Hegesistratos, stranger of Samos. Do thou on thy part see that thou give us assurance, thou and the men who are with thee, that the Samians will without fail be our zealous allies, and after that sail away home."

92. Thus he spoke and to the words he added the deed; for forthwith the Samians gave assurance and made oaths of alliance with the Hellenes, and having so done the others sailed away home, but Hegesistratos he bade sail with the Hellenes, considering the name to be an augury of good success. Then the Hellenes after staying still that day made sacrifices for success on the next day, their diviner being Deïphonos the son of Euenios an Apolloniate, of that Apollonia which lies in the Ionian gulf. .

93. To this man's father Euenios it happened as follows:—There are at this place Apollonia sheep sacred to the Sun, which during the day feed by a river running from Mount Lacmon through the land of Apollonia to the sea by the haven of Oricos; and by night they are watched by men chosen for this purpose, who are the most highly considered of the citizens for wealth and noble birth, each man having charge of them for a year; for the people of Apollonia set great store on these sheep by reason of an oracle: and they are folded in a cave at some distance from the city. Here at the time of which I speak this man Euenios was keeping watch over them, having been chosen for that purpose; and it happened one night that he fell asleep during his watch, and wolves came by into the cave and killed about sixty of the sheep. When he perceived this, he kept it secret and told no one, meaning to buy others and substitute them in the place of those that were killed. It was discovered however by the people of Apollonia that this had happened; and when they were informed of it, they brought him up before a court and condemned him to be deprived of his eyesight for having fallen asleep during his watch. But when they had blinded Euenios, forthwith after this their flocks ceased to bring forth young and their land to bear crops as before. Then prophesyings were uttered to them both at Dodona and also at Delphi, when they asked the prophets the cause of the evil which they were suffering, and they told them that they had done unjustly in depriving of his sight Euenios the watcher of the sacred sheep; for the gods of whom they inquired had themselves sent the wolves to attack the sheep; and they would not cease to take vengeance for him till the men of Apollonia should have paid to Euenios such satisfaction as he himself should choose and deem sufficient; and this being fulfilled, the gods would give to Euenios a gift of such a kind that many men would think him happy in that he possessed it.

94. These oracles then were uttered to them, and the people of Apollonia, making a secret of it, proposed to certain men of the citizens to manage the affair; and they managed it for them thus:—when Euenios was sitting on a seat in public, they came and sat by him, and conversed about other matters, and at last they came to sympathizing with him in his

misfortune; and thus leading him on they asked what satisfaction he should choose, if the people of Apollonia should undertake to give him satisfaction for that which they had done. He then, not having heard the oracle, made choice and said that if there should be given him the lands belonging to certain citizens, naming those whom he knew to possess the two best lots of land in Apollonia, and a dwelling-house also with these, which he knew to be the best house in the city,—if he became the possessor of these, he said, he would have no anger against them for the future, and this satisfaction would be sufficient for him if it should be given. Then as he was thus speaking, the men who sat by him said interrupting him: "Euenios, this satisfaction the Apolloniates pay to thee for thy blinding in accordance with the oracles which have been given to them." Upon this he was angry, being thus informed of the whole matter and considering that he had been deceived; and they bought the property from those who possessed it and gave him that which he had chosen. And forthwith after this he had a natural gift of divination, so that he became very famous.

95. Of this Euenios, I say, Deïphonos was the son, and he was acting as diviner for the army, being brought by the Corinthians. I have heard however also that Deïphonos wrongly made use of the name of Euenios, and undertook work of this kind about Hellas, not being really the son of Euenios.

96. Now when the sacrifices were favorable to the Hellenes, they put their ships to sea from Delos to go to Samos; and having arrived off Calamisa in Samos, they moored their ships there opposite the temple of Hera which is at this place, and made preparations for a sea-fight; but the Persians, being informed that they were sailing thither, put out to sea also and went over to the mainland with their remaining ships, (those of the Phoenicians having been already sent away to sail home): for deliberating of the matter they thought it good not to fight a battle by sea, since they did not think that they were a match for the enemy. And they sailed away to the mainland in order that they might be under the protection of their land-army which was in Mycale, a body which had stayed behind the rest of the army by command of Xerxes and was keeping watch over Ionia: of this the number was six myriads and the commander of it was Tigranes, who in beauty and stature excelled the other Persians. The commanders of the fleet then had determined to take refuge under the protection of this army, and to draw up their ships on shore and put an enclosure round as a protection for the ships and a refuge for themselves.

97. Having thus determined they began to put out to sea; and they came along by the temple of the "Revered goddesses" to the Gaison and to Scolopoeis in Mycale, where there is a temple of the Eleusinian Demeter, which Philistos the son of Pasicles erected when he had accompanied Neileus the son of Codros for the founding of Miletos; and there they drew up their ships on shore and put an enclosure round them of stones and timber, cutting down fruit-trees for this purpose, and they fixed stakes round the enclosure and made their preparations either for being besieged or for gaining a victory, for in making their preparations they reckoned for both chances.

98. The Hellenes however, when they were informed that the Barbarians had gone away to the mainland, were vexed because they thought that they had escaped; and they were in a difficulty what they should do, whether they should go back home, or sail down towards the Hellespont. At last they resolved to do neither of these two things, but to sail on to the mainland. Therefore when they had prepared as for a sea-fight both boarding-bridges and all other things that were required, they sailed towards Mycale; and when

they came near to the camp and no one was seen to put out against them, but they perceived ships drawn up within the wall and a large land-army ranged along the shore, then first Leotychides, sailing along in his ship and coming as near to the shore as he could, made proclamation by a herald to the Ionians, saying: "Ionians, those of you who chance to be within hearing of me, attend to this which I say: for the Persians will not understand anything at all of that which I enjoin to you. When we join battle, each one of you must remember first the freedom of all, and then the watchword 'Hebe'; and this let him also who has not heard know from him who has heard." The design in this act was the same as that of Themistocles at Artemision; for it was meant that either the words uttered should escape the knowledge of the Barbarians and persuade the Ionians, or that they should be reported to the Barbarians and make them distrustful of the Hellenes.

99. After Leotychides had thus suggested, then next the Hellenes proceeded to bring their ships up to land, and they disembarked upon the shore. These then were ranging themselves for fight; and the Persians, when they saw the Hellenes preparing for battle and also that they had given exhortation to the Ionians, in the first place deprived the Samians of their arms, suspecting that they were inclined to the side of the Hellenes; for when the Athenian prisoners, the men whom the army of Xerxes had found left behind in Attica, had come in the ships of the Barbarians, the Samians had ransomed these and sent them back to Athens, supplying them with means for their journey; and for this reason especially they were suspected, since they had ransomed five hundred persons of the enemies of Xerxes. Then secondly the Persians appointed the Milesians to guard the passes which lead to the summits of Mycale, on the pretext that they knew the country best, but their true reason for doing this was that they might be out of the camp. Against these of the Ionians, who, as they suspected, would make some hostile move if they found the occasion, the Persians sought to secure themselves in the manner mentioned; and they themselves then brought together their wicker-work shields to serve them as a fence.

100. Then when the Hellenes had made all their preparations, they proceeded to the attack of the Barbarians; and as they went, a rumor came suddenly to their whole army, and at the same time a herald's staff was found lying upon the beach; and the rumor went through their army to this effect, namely that the Hellenes were fighting in Boeotia and conquering the army of Mardonios. Now by many signs is the divine power seen in earthly things, and by this among others, namely that now, when the day of the defeat at Plataia and of that which was about to take place at Mycale happened to be the same, a rumor came to the Hellenes here, so that the army was encouraged much more and was more eagerly desirous to face the danger.

101. Moreover this other thing by coincidence happened besides, namely that there was a sacred enclosure of the Eleusinian Demeter close by the side of both the battle-fields; for not only in the Plataian land did the fight take place close by the side of the temple of Demeter, as I have before said, but also in Mycale it was to be so likewise. And whereas the rumor which came to them said that a victory had been already gained by the Hellenes with Pausanias, this proved to be a true report; for that which was done at Plataia came about while it was yet early morning, but the fighting at Mycale took place in the afternoon; and that it happened on the same day of the same month as the other became evident to them not long afterwards, when they inquired into the matter. Now they had been afraid before the rumor arrived, not for themselves so much as for the Hellenes generally, lest Hellas should stumble and fall over Mardonios; but when this

report had come suddenly to them, they advanced on the enemy much more vigorously and swiftly than before. The Hellenes then and the Barbarians were going with eagerness into the battle, since both the islands and the Hellespont were placed before them as prizes of the contest.

102. Now for the Athenians and those who were ranged next to them, to the number perhaps of half the whole army, the road lay along the sea-beach and over level ground, while the Lacedemonians and those ranged in order by these were compelled to go by a ravine and along the mountain side: so while the Lacedemonians were yet going round, those upon the other wing were already beginning the fight; and as long as the wicker-work shields of the Persians still remained upright, they continued to defend themselves and had rather the advantage in the fight; but when the troops of the Athenians and of those ranged next to them, desiring that the achievement should belong to them and not to the Lacedemonians, with exhortations to one another set themselves more vigorously to the work, then from that time forth the fortune of the fight was changed; for these pushed aside the wicker-work shields and fell upon the Persians with a rush all in one body, and the Persians sustained their first attack and continued to defend themselves for a long time, but at last they fled to the wall; and the Athenians, Corinthians, Sikyonians and Troizenians, for that was the order in which they were ranged, followed close after them and rushed in together with them to the space within the wall: and when the wall too had been captured, then the Barbarians no longer betook themselves to resistance, but began at once to take flight, excepting only the Persians, who formed into small groups and continued to fight with the Hellenes as they rushed in within the wall. Of the commanders of the Persians two made their escape and two were slain; Artaÿntes and Ithamitres commanders of the fleet escaped, while Mardontes and the commander of the land-army, Tigranes, were slain.

103. Now while the Persians were still fighting, the Lacedemonians and those with them arrived, and joined in carrying through the rest of the work; and of the Hellenes themselves many fell there and especially many of the Sikyonians, together with their commander Perilaos. And those of the Samians who were serving in the army, being in the camp of the Medes and having been deprived of their arms, when they saw that from the very first the battle began to be doubtful, did as much as they could, endeavoring to give assistance to the Hellenes; and the other Ionians seeing that the Samians had set the example, themselves also upon that made revolt from the Persians and attacked the Barbarians.

104. The Milesians too had been appointed to watch the passes of the Persians in order to secure their safety, so that if that should after all come upon them which actually came, they might have guides and so get safe away to the summits of Mycale,—the Milesians, I say, had been appointed to do this, not only for that end but also for fear that, if they were present in the camp, they might make some hostile move: but they did in fact the opposite of that which they were appointed to do; for they not only directed them in the flight by other than the right paths, by paths indeed which led towards the enemy, but also at last they themselves became their worst foes and began to slay them. Thus then for the second time Ionia revolted from the Persians.

105. In this battle, of the Hellenes the Athenians were the best men, and of the Athenians Hermolycos the son of Euthoinos, a man who had trained for the *pancration*. This Hermolycos after these events, when there was war between the Athenians and the Carys-

tians, was killed in battle at Kyrnos in the Carystian land near Geraistos, and there was buried. After the Athenians the Corinthians, Troizenians and Sikyonians were the best.

106. When the Hellenes had slain the greater number of the Barbarians, some in the battle and others in their flight, they set fire to the ships and to the whole of the wall, having first brought out the spoil to the sea-shore; and among the rest they found some stores of money. So having set fire to the wall and to the ships they sailed away; and when they came to Samos, the Hellenes deliberated about removing the inhabitants of Ionia, and considered where they ought to settle them in those parts of Hellas of which they had command, leaving Ionia to the Barbarians: for it was evident to them that it was impossible on the one hand for them to be always stationed as guards to protect the Ionians, and on the other hand, if they were not stationed to protect them, they had no hope that the Ionians would escape with impunity from the Persians. Therefore it seemed good to those of the Peloponnesians that were in authority that they should remove the inhabitants of the trading ports which belonged to those peoples of Hellas who had taken the side of the Medes, and give that land to the Ionians to dwell in; but the Athenians did not think it good that the inhabitants of Ionia should be removed at all, nor that the Peloponnesians should consult about Athenian colonies; and as these vehemently resisted the proposal, the Peloponnesians gave way. So the end was that they joined as allies to their league the Samians, Chians, Lesbians, and the other islanders who chanced to be serving with the Hellenes, binding them by assurance and by oaths to remain faithful and not withdraw from the league: and having bound these by oaths they sailed to break up the bridges, for they supposed they would find them still stretched over the straits.

These then were sailing towards the Hellespont;.

107, and meanwhile those Barbarians who had escaped and had been driven to the heights of Mycale, being not many in number, were making their way to Sardis: and as they went by the way, Masistes the son of Dareios, who had been present at the disaster which had befallen them, was saying many evil things of the commander Artaÿntes, and among other things he said that in respect of the generalship which he had shown he was worse than a woman, and that he deserved every kind of evil for having brought evil on the house of the king. Now with the Persians to be called worse than a woman is the greatest possible reproach. So he, after he had been much reviled, at length became angry and drew his sword upon Masistes, meaning to kill him; and as he was running upon him, Xeinagoras the son of Prexilaos, a man of Halicarnassos, perceived it, who was standing just behind Artaÿntes; and this man seized him by the middle and lifting him up dashed him upon the ground; and meanwhile the spearmen of Masistes came in front to protect him. Thus did Xeinagoras, and thus he laid up thanks for himself both with Masistes and also with Xerxes for saving the life of his brother; and for this deed Xeinagoras became ruler of all Kilikia by the gift of the king. Nothing further happened than this as they went on their way, but they arrived at Sardis.

Now at Sardis, as it chanced, king Xerxes had been staying ever since that time when he came thither in flight from Athens, after suffering defeat in the sea-fight.

108. At that time, while he was in Sardis, he had a passionate desire, as it seems, for the wife of Masistes, who was also there: and as she could not be bent to his will by his messages to her, and he did not wish to employ force because he had regard for his brother Masistes and the same consideration withheld the woman also, for she well knew that force would not be used towards her, then Xerxes abstained from all else, and endeav-

ored to bring about the marriage of his own son Dareios with the daughter of this woman and of Masistes, supposing that if he should do so he would obtain her more easily. Then having made the betrothal and done all the customary rites, he went away to Susa; and when he had arrived there and had brought the woman into his own house for Dareios, then he ceased from attempting the wife of Masistes and changing his inclination he conceived a desire for the wife of Dareios, who was daughter of Masistes, and obtained her: now the name of this woman was Artaÿnte.

109. However as time went on, this became known in the following manner:— Amestris the wife of Xerxes had woven a mantle, large and of various work and a sight worthy to be seen, and this she gave to Xerxes. He then being greatly pleased put it on and went to Artaÿnte; and being greatly pleased with her too, he bade her ask what she would to be given to her in return for the favors which she had granted to him, for she should obtain, he said, whatsoever she asked: and she, since it was destined that she should perish miserably with her whole house, said to Xerxes upon this: "Wilt thou give me whatsoever I ask thee for?" and he, supposing that she would ask anything rather than that which she did, promised this and swore to it. Then when he had sworn, she boldly asked for the mantle; and Xerxes tried every means of persuasion, not being willing to give it to her, and that for no other reason but only because he feared Amestris, lest by her, who even before this had some inkling of the truth, he should thus be discovered in the act; and he offered her cities and gold in any quantity, and an army which no one else should command except herself. Now this of an army is a thoroughly Persian gift. Since however he did not persuade her, he gave her the mantle; and she being overjoyed by the gift wore it and prided herself upon it.

110. And Amestris was informed that she had it; and having learnt that which was being done, she was not angry with the woman, but supposing that her mother was the cause and that she was bringing this about, she planned destruction for the wife of Masistes. She waited then until her husband Xerxes had a royal feast set before him:—this feast is served up once in the year on the day on which the king was born, and the name of this feast is in Persian *tycta*, which in the tongue of the Hellenes means "complete"; also on this occasion alone the king washes his head, and he makes gifts then to the Persians:— Amestris, I say, waited for this day and then asked of Xerxes that the wife of Masistes might be given to her. And he considered it a strange and untoward thing to deliver over to her his brother's wife, especially since she was innocent of this matter; for he understood why she was making the request.

111. At last however as she continued to entreat urgently and he was compelled by the rule, namely that it is impossible among them that he who makes request when a royal feast is laid before the king should fail to obtain it, at last very much against his will consented; and in delivering her up he bade Amestris do as she desired, and meanwhile he sent for his brother and said these words: "Masistes, thou art the son of Dareios and my brother, and moreover in addition to this thou art a man of worth. I say to thee, live no longer with this wife with whom thou now livest, but I give thee instead of her my daughter; with her live as thy wife, but the wife whom thou now hast, do not keep; for it does not seem good to me that thou shouldest keep her." Masistes then, marveling at that which was spoken, said these words: "Master, how unprofitable a speech is this which thou utterest to me, in that thou biddest me send away a wife by whom I have sons who are grown up to be young men, and daughters one of whom even thou thyself didst take

as a wife for thy son, and who is herself, as it chances, very much to my mind,—that thou biddest me, I say, send away her and take to wife thy daughter! I, O king, think it a very great matter that I am judged worthy of thy daughter, but nevertheless I will do neither of these things: and do not thou urge me by force to do such a thing as this: but for thy daughter another husband will be found not in any wise inferior to me, and let me, I pray thee, live still with my own wife." He returned answer in some such words as these; and Xerxes being stirred with anger said as follows: "This then, Masistes, is thy case,—I will not give thee my daughter for thy wife, nor yet shalt thou live any longer with that one, in order that thou mayest learn to accept that which is offered thee." He then when he heard this went out, having first said these words: "Master, thou hast not surely brought ruin upon me?" .

112. During this interval of time, while Xerxes was conversing with his brother, Amestris had sent the spearmen of Xerxes to bring the wife of Masistes, and she was doing to her shameful outrage; for she cut away her breasts and threw them to dogs, and she cut off her nose and ears and lips and tongue, and sent her back home thus outraged.

113. Then Masistes, not yet having heard any of these things, but supposing that some evil had fallen upon him, came running to his house; and seeing his wife thus mutilated, forthwith upon this he took counsel with his sons and set forth to go to Bactria together with his sons and doubtless some others also, meaning to make the province of Bactria revolt and to do the greatest possible injury to the king: and this in fact would have come to pass, as I imagine, if he had got up to the land of the Bactrians and Sacans before he was overtaken, for they were much attached to him, and also he was the governor of the Bactrians: but Xerxes being informed that he was doing this, sent after him an army as he was on his way, and slew both him and his sons and his army. So far of that which happened about the passion of Xerxes and the death of Masistes.

114. Now the Hellenes who had set forth from Mycale to the Hellespont first moored their ships about Lecton, being stopped from their voyage by winds; and thence they came to Abydos and found that the bridges had been broken up, which they thought to find still stretched across, and on account of which especially they had come to the Hellespont. So the Peloponnesians which Leotychides resolved to sail back to Hellas, while the Athenians and Xanthippos their commander determined to stay behind there and to make an attempt upon the Chersonese. Those then sailed away, and the Athenians passed over from Abydos to the Chersonese and began to besiege Sestos.

115. To this town of Sestos, since it was the greatest stronghold of those in that region, men had come together from the cities which lay round it, when they heard that the Hellenes had arrived at the Hellespont, and especially there had come from the city of Cardia Oiobazos a Persian, who had brought to Sestos the ropes of the bridges. The inhabitants of the city were Aiolians, natives of the country, but there were living with them a great number of Persians and also of their allies.

116. And of the province Artaÿctes was despot, as governor under Xerxes, a Persian, but a man of desperate and reckless character, who also had practiced deception upon the king on his march against Athens, in taking away from Elaius the things belonging to Protesilaos the son of Iphiclos. For at Elaius in the Chersonese there is the tomb of Protesilaos with a sacred enclosure about it, where there were many treasures, with gold and silver cups and bronze and raiment and other offerings, which things Artaÿctes carried off as plunder, the king having granted them to him. And he deceived Xerxes by saying to

him some such words as these: "Master, there is here the house of a man, a Hellene, who made an expedition against thy land and met with his deserts and was slain: this man's house I ask thee to give to me, that every one may learn not to make expeditions against thy land." By saying this it was likely that he would easily enough persuade Xerxes to give him a man's house, not suspecting what was in his mind: and when he said that Protesilaos had made expedition against the land of the king, it must be understood that the Persians consider all Asia to be theirs and to belong to their reigning king. So when the things had been given him, he brought them from Elaius to Sestos, and he sowed the sacred enclosure for crops and occupied it as his own; and he himself, whenever he came to Elaius, had commerce with women in the inner cell of the temple. And now he was being besieged by the Athenians, when he had not made any preparation for a siege nor had been expecting that the Hellenes would come; for they fell upon him, as one may say, inevitably. .

117. When however autumn came and the siege still went on, the Athenians began to be vexed at being absent from their own land and at the same time not able to conquer the fortress, and they requested their commanders to lead them away home; but these said that they would not do so, until either they had taken the town or the public authority of the Athenians sent for them home: and so they endured their present state. .

118. Those however who were within the walls had now come to the greatest misery, so that they boiled down the girths of their beds and used them for food; and when they no longer had even these, then the Persians and with them Artaÿctes and Oiobazos ran away and departed in the night, climbing down by the back part of the wall, where the place was left most unguarded by the enemy; and when day came, the men of the Chersonese signified to the Athenians from the towers concerning that which had happened, and opened the gates to them. So the greater number of them went in pursuit, and the rest occupied the city.

119. Now Oiobazos, as he was escaping into Thrace, was caught by the Apsinthian Thracians and sacrificed to their native god Pleistoros with their rites, and the rest who were with him they slaughtered in another manner: but Artaÿctes with his companions, who started on their flight later and were overtaken at a little distance above Aigospota-moi, defended themselves for a considerable time and were some of them killed and others taken alive: and the Hellenes had bound these and were bringing them to Sestos, and among them Artaÿctes also in bonds together with his son.

120. Then, it is said by the men of the Chersonese, as one of those who guarded them was frying dried fish, a portent occurred as follows,—the dried fish when laid upon the fire began to leap and struggle just as if they were fish newly caught: and the others gathered round and were marveling at the portent, but Artaÿctes seeing it called to the man who was frying the fish and said: "Stranger of Athens, be not at all afraid of this portent, seeing that it has not appeared for thee but for me. Protesilaos who dwells at Elaius signifies thereby that though he is dead and his body is dried like those fish, yet he has power given him by the gods to exact vengeance from the man who does him wrong. Now therefore I desire to impose this penalty for him, —that in place of the things which I took from the temple I should pay down a hundred talents to the god, and moreover as ransom for myself and my son I will pay two hundred talents to the Athenians, if my life be spared." Thus he engaged to do, but he did not prevail upon the commander Xanthippos; for the people of Elaius desiring to take vengeance for Protesilaos asked that he might be put to

death, and the inclination of the commander himself tended to the same conclusion. They brought him therefore to that headland to which Xerxes made the passage across, or as some say to the hill which is over the town of Madytos, and there they nailed him to boards and hung him up; and they stoned his son to death before the eyes of Artaÿctes himself.

121. Having so done, they sailed away to Hellas, taking with them, besides other things, the ropes also of the bridges, in order to dedicate them as offerings in the temples: and for that year nothing happened further than this.

122. Now a forefather of this Artaÿctes who was hung up, was that Artembares who set forth to the Persians a proposal which they took up and brought before Cyrus, being to this effect: "Seeing that Zeus grants to the Persians leadership, and of all men to thee, O Cyrus, by destroying Astyages, come, since the land we possess is small and also rugged, let us change from it and inhabit another which is better: and there are many near at hand, and many also at a greater distance, of which if we take one, we shall have greater reverence and from more men. It is reasonable too that men who are rulers should do such things; for when will there ever be a fairer occasion than now, when we are rulers of many nations and of the whole of Asia?" Cyrus, hearing this and not being surprised at the proposal, bade them do so if they would; but he exhorted them and bade them prepare in that case to be no longer rulers but subjects; "For," said he, "from lands which are not rugged men who are not rugged are apt to come forth, since it does not belong to the same land to bring forth fruits of the earth which are admirable and also men who are good in war." So the Persians acknowledged that he was right and departed from his presence, having their opinion defeated by that of Cyrus; and they chose rather to dwell on poor land and be rulers, than to sow crops in a level plain and be slaves to others.

Made in the USA
Las Vegas, NV
27 December 2024

15408861R00246